T0364787

Mitsubishi Shogun & Pick-ups Owners Workshop Manual

Larry Warren, Curt Choate and A K Legg LAE MIMI

Models covered

Mitsubishi Shogun (3-door and 5-door models), July 1983 to 1994; 2555 cc & 2972 cc petrol engines
Mitsubishi L200 & 4WD Pick-ups, October 1986 to 1994; 1997 cc petrol engine

Also covers 2.4 litre petrol engine
Does not cover Diesel or 3.5 litre V6 engines

THE BOOK ®

Haynes Group Limited
Haynes Publications, Inc

www.haynes.com

Acknowledgements

We are grateful to the Champion Spark Plug Company for supplying the illustrations of various spark plug conditions. Technical writers who contributed to this project include Robert Maddox, Mike Stubblefield and Doug Nelson.

© **Haynes Group Limited 1994**

A book in the **Haynes Owners Workshop Manual Series**

All rights reserved. No part of this book may be reproduced or transmitted in any form or by any means, electronic or mechanical, including photocopying, recording or by any information storage or retrieval system, without permission in writing from the copyright holder.

ISBN 978 0 85733 652 1

British Library Cataloguing in Publication Data
A catalogue record for this book is available from the British Library.

Disclaimer

There are risks associated with automotive repairs. The ability to make repairs depends on the individual's skill, experience and proper tools. Individuals should act with due care and acknowledge and assume the risk of performing automotive repairs.

The purpose of this manual is to provide comprehensive, useful and accessible automotive repair information, to help you get the best value from your vehicle. However, this manual is not a substitute for a professional certified technician or mechanic.

This repair manual is produced by a third party and is not associated with an individual vehicle manufacturer. If there is any doubt or discrepancy between this manual and the owner's manual or the factory service manual, please refer to the factory service manual or seek assistance from a professional certified technician or mechanic.

Even though we have prepared this manual with extreme care and every attempt is made to ensure that the information in this manual is correct, neither the publisher nor the author can accept responsibility for loss, damage or injury caused by any errors in, or omissions from, the information given.

94-266

Contents

Mitsubishi Shogun 5-door 2.6 litre petrol model

Mitsubishi L200 Pick-up (US model shown)

About this manual

Its aim

The aim of this manual is to help you get the best value from your vehicle. It can do so in several ways. It can help you decide what work must be done (even should you choose to get it done by a garage), provide information on routine maintenance and servicing, and give a logical course of action and diagnosis when random faults occur. However, it is hoped that you will use the manual by tackling the work yourself. On simpler jobs, it may even be quicker than booking the vehicle into a garage and going there twice, to leave and collect it. Perhaps most important, a lot of money can be saved, by avoiding the costs a garage must charge to cover its labour and overheads.

The manual has drawings and descriptions to show the function of the various components, so that their layout can be understood. Then the tasks are described and photographed in a clear step-by-step sequence.

Its arrangement

Note: *UK readers should also refer to the "Notes for UK readers" Section.*

The manual is divided into Chapters, each covering a logical sub-division of the vehicle. The Chapters are each divided into numbered Sections, which are headed in bold type between horizontal lines. Where required for ease of reference, some Sections are divided into sub-Sections, and in some cases into sub-sub-Sections; all such sub-divisions are indicated by appropriately-sized sub-headings. Each Section contains individual paragraphs which (except in the case of purely-descriptive "General description" Sections) are consecutively numbered; this numbering sequence is applied throughout the Section, regardless of any subdivision.

The manual is freely illustrated, especially in those parts where there is a detailed sequence of operations to be carried out. The reference numbers used in illustration captions indicate the Section, followed by the number of the paragraph within that Section, to which the illustration refers; where more than one illustration applies to a particular paragraph, letters are added in alphabetical order to each illustration caption's reference number - for example, illustration "6.7C" is the third illustration referring to paragraph 7 of Section 6 of that Chapter.

Procedures, once described in the appropriate place in the text, are not normally repeated. When it is necessary to refer to another Chapter, the reference will be given as Chapter and Section number. Cross-references given without use of the word "Chapter" apply to other Sections in the same Chapter. For example, a cross-reference such as "see Section 8" means Section 8 in that Chapter.

There is an alphabetical index at the back of the manual, as well as a contents list at the front. Each Chapter is also preceded by its own individual contents list.

References to the "left" or "right" of the vehicle are in the sense of a person in the driver's seat facing forward, however as this manual was originated in the US, *reference to the driver's side means the left-hand side.*

Unless otherwise stated, nuts and bolts are removed by turning anti-clockwise, and tightened by turning clockwise.

We take great pride in the accuracy of information given in this manual, but vehicle manufacturers make alterations and design changes during the production run of a particular vehicle of which they do not inform us. No liability can be accepted by the authors or publishers for loss, damage or injury caused by any errors in, or omissions from, the information given.

Notes for UK readers

General

Because this manual was originally written in the US, its layout differs from our UK-originated manuals. The preliminary sections (ie up to Chapter 1) have therefore been re-written specifically for the UK market; however, it will be noticed that references to components remain in the US style, so that the reader can identify these with the components described in the main Chapters of the manual. The UK equivalent of US components and various other US words is given in the Section headed "Use of English". It should be remembered that the project vehicle used in the main Chapters of this manual was a left-hand drive model; therefore, the position of the steering wheel, steering column, clutch and brake pedals, etc. will be on the opposite side of the vehicle on UK models. References to "right" and "left" will need to be considered carefully to decide which applies to UK models (eg the headlight dipped beams should be adjusted to dip to the left of the headlight vertical line described in Chapter 12, instead of to the right on US models. However, the fusebox on UK models, for instance, remains under the left-hand side of the instrument panel as on US models). In other instances, no reference is made to the location of a particular item, but that item will be located on the opposite side of the vehicle on UK models (eg the windscreen wiper motor is on the right-hand side of the bulkhead on UK models, not the left).

The following information should be considered before referring to the main Chapters of this manual.

Model differences

The US equivalent of the Shogun is the Montero. Any reference to the Montero in the main part of the manual should be taken as referring to the Shogun. Year references (ie 1987) apply to US models, but these should be approximately the same for UK models. The 2.4 litre fuel-injected engine referred to in the manual was not fitted to UK models. Not all UK models have power-assisted steering.

Specifications

Where capacities or volumes appear in the Specifications Sections of each Chapter, note that reference to quarts means US quarts, and the correct conversion factor should be used accordingly (see "Conversion factors"). All specifications in the main Chapters of the manual appear in imperial form; the equivalent metric values can be calculated using the Conversion factors page.

General specifications for UK models are given in the introductory section headed "UK Specifications".

A multi-purpose grease should be used where NLGI no. 2 chassis grease is specified.

Maintenance intervals

The *main* maintenance interval for UK models manufactured up to late 1991 is every 12 000 miles or 12 months. From early 1992, the interval was increased to 18 000 miles or 12 months. When using the maintenance schedule given in Chapter 1, it is recommended that the intervals be altered according to the following comparison chart. The 50 000 mile/24 month and 80 000 mile/24 month services are not applicable to the UK market.

US schedule	UK schedule (to late 1991)	UK schedule (from early 1992)
Every 250 miles or weekly	Every 250 miles or weekly	Every 250 miles or weekly
Every 5000 miles or 4 months	Every 6000 miles or 6 months	Every 9000 miles or 6 months
Every 15 000 miles or 12 months	Every 12 000 miles or 12 months	Every 18 000 miles or 12 months
Every 30 000 miles or 24 months	Every 24 000 miles or 24 months	Every 36 000 miles or 24 months
Every 50 000 miles or 24 months	Not applicable	Not applicable
Every 60 000 miles or 24 months	Every 60 000 miles	Every 60 000 miles
Every 80 000 miles or 24 months	Not applicable	Not applicable

Oil cooler

UK models fitted with the V6 engine are equipped with an oil cooler located behind the radiator grille next to the radiator.

Air conditioning system

The latter Sections of Chapter 3 describe work on the air conditioning system, and the Specifications section includes the refrigerant capacity, etc. Although air conditioning equipment is becoming more common in the UK, you are strongly advised to have a specialist carry out repairs to any part of it. The refrigerant used in the air conditioning system is potentially hazardous to health, so the evacuating and recharging of the air conditioning system must be performed by a specialist in any case. It therefore makes sense to have any other repairs carried out by that specialist at the same time.

Emission control information

US emission control laws call for an information label to be attached in a prominent position in the engine compartment. At the present time, there is no requirement for this in the UK. US laws also call for the renewal of emission control components (such as the oxygen sensor and EGR valve) at specific intervals. Although renewal of these items could very well be beneficial in terms of engine efficiency, there are no equivalent laws in the UK at the time of writing.

Where reference is made to California, Federal and Canadian systems (particularly in Chapters 4 and 6), the UK system is in most cases equivalent to that of Canadian type.

Fuel injection system and fault codes

Because of the different emission control laws in the US, the instrument panel on US models includes a malfunction warning light, to warn the driver of a fault in the engine management system. This system is not normally fitted to UK models, and therefore some of the information given in Chapter 6 will not apply. In particular, the method for extracting fault codes from the ECU using an analog voltmeter is not applicable to UK models.

Ignition system

A conventional contact breaker ignition system is fitted to UK Shogun models with the 2555 cc four-cylinder engine up to 1989. Adjustment information data for this type of ignition system is given in the introductory section headed "UK Specifications". Contact breaker points should be renewed every 12 000 miles (20 000 km). Always check and if necessary adjust the ignition timing after adjusting or renewing the contact breaker points.

Rear disc brakes

Note that rear disc brakes were introduced in the UK from 1992 model year (ie from August 1991). The rear discs are of solid type, and thickness information will be found in the introductory section headed "UK Specifications". Section 13 in Chapter 9 makes reference to rear disc brakes, and pad renewal is similar to that for the front disc brakes described in the same Chapter.

Chassis electrical system

The main circuit fusible links are located on the left-hand rear corner of the engine compartment. The fusible link for the electrically-operated windows is located in the right-hand front corner of the engine compartment. The wiring diagrams shown in Chapter 12 were originated in the US. They are, however, applicable for UK models, with the exception of the fuel injection diagrams for the 2.4 litre engine.

Notes, cautions and warnings

A **Note** provides information necessary to properly complete a procedure, or information which will make the procedure easier to understand.

A **Caution** provides a special procedure or special steps which must be taken while completing the procedure where the **Caution** is found. Not heeding a **Caution** can result in damage to the assembly being worked on.

A **Warning** provides a special procedure or special steps which must be taken while completing the procedure where the **Warning** is found. Not heeding a **Warning** can result in personal injury.

Introduction to the Mitsubishi Shogun and L200 Pick-ups

Shogun models are available in three- or five-door body styles. Pick-up models are available in standard- and extended-cab body styles, with short or long wheelbase, and two- or four-wheel-drive.

Most four-cylinder engines are equipped with carburetors. Later four-cylinder and all V6 engines are equipped with port fuel injection.

The engine drives the rear wheels through either a four- or five-speed manual, or three- or four-speed automatic, transmission, via a driveshaft and solid rear axle. A transfer case and driveshaft are used to drive the front differential and driveaxles on 4WD models.

The front suspension features upper and lower control arms, shock absorbers, coil springs (2WD models) or torsion bars (4WD models). The solid rear axle is suspended by leaf springs and shock absorbers on most models. Some later models use coil spring rear suspension, with the axle located by trailing arms and a track rod.

The steering box is mounted to the right of the engine, and is connected to the steering arms by a series of rods. Power assistance is standard on most later models.

The brakes are discs at the front and drums at the rear on models up to August 1991; later models have discs all round. The brakes are servo-assisted on most models.

Jacking, towing and wheel changing

Jacking and wheel changing

The jack supplied with the vehicle should be used only for raising the vehicle when changing a tire or placing jackstands under the frame. **Warning**: *Never crawl under the vehicle or start the engine when this jack is being used as the only means of support.*

The vehicle should be on level ground with the wheels blocked, the parking brake applied and the transmission in Park (automatic) or Reverse (manual). If a tire is being changed, loosen the lug nuts one-half turn, and leave them in place until the wheel is raised off the ground. Place the jack under the vehicle suspension in the indicated position **(see illustration)**. Operate the jack with a slow, smooth motion until the wheel is raised off the ground. Remove the lug nuts, pull off the wheel, and install the spare. Thread the lug nuts back on, with the bevelled sides facing in. Tighten them snugly, but wait until the vehicle is lowered to tighten them completely. Lower the vehicle, remove the jack and tighten the nuts (if loosened or removed) in a criss-cross pattern.

Towing

As a general rule, vehicles may be towed with all four wheels on the ground. If necessary, the front or rear wheels may be raised for towing. On vehicles with an automatic transmission, do not exceed 19 MPH or tow the vehicle farther than 19 miles (there are no speed or distance limitations on vehicles with a manual transmission).

Equipment specifically designed for towing should be used, and should be attached to the main structural members of the vehicle, not the bumper or brackets. Tow hooks are attached to the frame at both ends of the vehicle. However, they are for emergency use only, and should not be used for highway towing. Stand clear of vehicles when using the tow hooks - tow straps and chains may break, causing serious injury.

While towing, the parking brake must be released, the transmission must be in Neutral, and the transfer case (if equipped) must be in 2H. The steering must be unlocked (ignition switch in the Off position). If you're towing a 4WD model with the front wheels on the ground, the front hubs must be unlocked. Remember that power steering and the brake servo will not work with the engine off, resulting in higher-than-usual levels of effort to operate them.

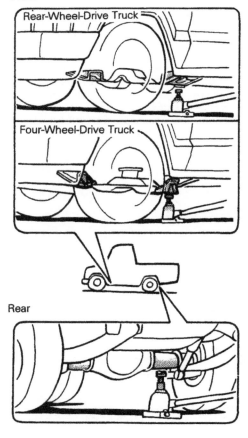

Front

Rear-Wheel-Drive Truck

Four-Wheel-Drive Truck

Rear

Jacking points

Buying spare parts and vehicle identification numbers

Buying spare parts

Spare parts are available from many sources; for example, Mitsubishi garages, other garages and accessory shops, and motor factors. Our advice regarding spare part sources is as follows.

Officially-appointed Mitsubishi garages - This is the best source for parts which are peculiar to your vehicle, and which are not generally available (eg complete cylinder heads, internal transmission components, badges, interior trim etc). It is also the only place at which you should buy parts if the vehicle is still under warranty. To be sure of obtaining the correct parts, it will be necessary to give the storeman the full Vehicle Identification Number, and if possible, to take the old parts along for positive identification. Many parts are available under a factory exchange scheme - any parts returned should always be clean. It

obviously makes good sense to go straight to the specialists on your vehicle for this type of part, as they are best equipped to supply you.

Other garages and accessory shops - These are often very good places to buy materials and components needed for the maintenance of your vehicle (eg oil filters, spark plugs, bulbs, drivebelts, oils and greases, touch-up paint, filler paste, etc). They also sell general accessories, usually have convenient opening hours, charge lower prices, and can often be found not far from home.

Motor factors - Good factors will stock all the more important components which wear out comparatively quickly (eg exhaust systems, brake pads, seals and hydraulic parts, clutch components, bearing shells, pistons, valves etc). Motor factors will often provide new or reconditioned components on a part-exchange basis - this can save a considerable amount of money.

The vehicle identification number (VIN) is stamped on a plate attached to the underside of the hood on some models

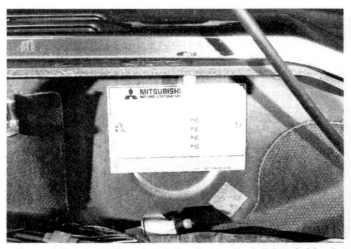

The weight information plate is located on the left-hand side of the bulkhead

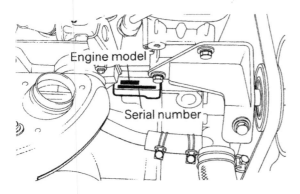

On 2.6L four-cylinder engines, the engine identification number is located on a machined surface at the right front corner of the block, just below the cylinder head

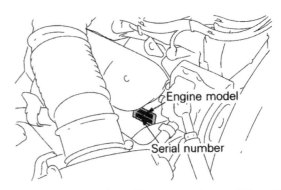

Location of the engine identification number on 2.0L and 2.4L four-cylinder engines

Vehicle identification numbers

Modifications are a continuing and unpublicised process in vehicle manufacture, quite apart from major model changes. Spare parts manuals and lists are compiled upon a numerical basis, the appropriate identification number or code being essential to correct identification of the component concerned.

When ordering spare parts, always give as much information as possible. Quote the vehicle model, year of manufacture, Vehicle Identification Number and engine numbers, as appropriate.

The *vehicle identification number (VIN)* is stamped on a plate attached to the cross panel at the front of the engine compartment. On some models, the plate is attached to the underside of the hood **(see illustration)**. Weight information is stamped on a plate attached to the left-hand side of the bulkhead **(see illustration)**.

The *chassis number* is stamped on the frame under the vehicle, near the right rear shock absorber.

The *engine identification number (ID)* consists of two parts: a model number and a serial number. On four-cylinder engines, it is located on the right side of the engine, in one of two places: 1) on a machined surface at the front corner of the block, just below the number one spark plug (2.6L engine) or 2) at the lower right front corner of block (2.0L and 2.4L engine) **(see illustrations)**. On V6 engines, the ID number is located on a pad at the right side of the block **(see illustration)**.

The *paint code identification plate* is located in the engine compartment, usually on the radiator support but also on the firewall **(see illustration)**. It tells what color and type of paint was originally applied to the vehicle.

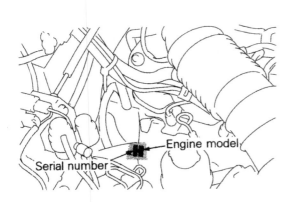

V6 engine identification number location

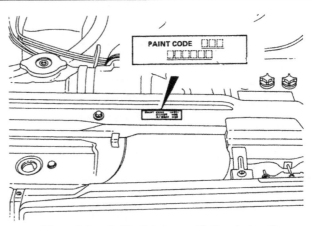

The paint code ID plate is usually located on the radiator support

Safety first!

However enthusiastic you may be about getting on with the job in hand, do take the time to ensure that your safety is not put at risk. A moment's lack of attention can result in an accident, as can failure to observe certain elementary precautions. There will always be new ways of having accidents, and the following points do not pretend to be a comprehensive list of all dangers; they are intended rather to make you aware of the risks, and to encourage a safety-conscious approach to all work you carry out on your vehicle.

Essential DOs and DON'Ts

DON'T rely on a single jack when working underneath the vehicle. Always use reliable additional means of support, such as axle stands, securely placed under a structural part of the vehicle that you know will not give way.

DON'T attempt to loosen or tighten high-torque nuts (eg wheel hub nuts) while the vehicle is on a jack; it may be pulled off.

DON'T start the engine without first ascertaining that the transmission is in neutral (or "Park" where applicable) and the handbrake applied.

DON'T suddenly remove the filler cap from a hot cooling system - cover it with a cloth, and release the pressure gradually first, or you may get scalded by escaping coolant.

DON'T attempt to drain oil, automatic transmission fluid, or coolant until you are sure it has cooled sufficiently to avoid scalding you.

DON'T grasp any part of the engine, exhaust or catalytic converter without first ascertaining that it is sufficiently cool to avoid burning you.

DON'T allow brake fluid or antifreeze to contact vehicle paintwork.

DON'T siphon toxic liquids such as fuel, brake fluid or antifreeze by mouth, or allow them to remain on your skin.

DON'T inhale dust - it may be injurious to health (see *Asbestos* below).

DON'T allow any spilt oil or grease to remain on the floor - wipe it up straight away, before someone slips on it.

DON'T use ill-fitting spanners or other tools which may slip and cause injury.

DON'T attempt to lift a heavy component which may be beyond your capability - get assistance.

DON'T rush to finish a job, or take unverified short cuts.

DON'T allow children or animals in or around an unattended vehicle.

DON'T park vehicles with catalytic converters over combustible materials such as dry grass, oily rags, etc if the engine has recently been run. As catalytic converters reach extremely high temperatures, any such materials in close proximity may ignite.

DON'T run vehicles equipped with catalytic converters without the exhaust system heat shields fitted.

DO wear eye protection when using power tools such as an electric drill, sander, bench grinder etc, and when working under the vehicle.

DO use a barrier cream on your hands prior to undertaking dirty jobs - it will protect your skin from infection, as well as making the dirt easier to remove afterwards; but make sure your hands aren't left slippery. Note that long-term contact with used engine oil can be a health hazard.

DO keep loose clothing (cuffs, tie etc) and long hair well out of the way of moving mechanical parts.

DO remove rings, wristwatch etc, before working on the vehicle - especially the electrical system.

DO ensure that any lifting tackle or jacking equipment used has a safe working load rating adequate for the job, and is used precisely as recommended by the equipment manufacturer.

DO keep your work area tidy - it is only too easy to fall over articles left lying around.

DO get someone to check periodically that all is well when working alone on the vehicle.

DO carry out work in a logical sequence, and check that everything is correctly assembled and tightened afterwards.

DO remember that your vehicle's safety affects that of yourself and others. If in doubt on any point, get specialist advice.

IF, in spite of following these precautions, you are unfortunate enough to injure yourself, seek medical attention as soon as possible.

Asbestos

Certain friction, insulating, sealing, and other products - such as brake linings, brake bands, clutch linings, gaskets, etc - contain asbestos. *Extreme care must be taken to avoid inhalation of dust from such products, since it is hazardous to health.* If in doubt, assume that they *do* contain asbestos.

Fire

Remember at all times that petrol is highly flammable. Never smoke, or have any kind of naked flame around, when working on the vehicle. But the risk does not end there - a spark caused by an electrical short-circuit, by two metal surfaces contacting each other, by careless use of tools, or even by static electricity built up in your body under certain conditions, can ignite petrol vapor, which in a confined space is highly explosive.

Whenever possible, disconnect the battery earth terminal before working on any part of the fuel or electrical system, and never risk spilling fuel onto a hot engine or exhaust. Catalytic converters run at extremely high temperatures, and consequently can be an additional fire hazard. Observe the precautions outlined elsewhere in this section.

It is recommended that a fire extinguisher of a type suitable for fuel and electrical fires is kept handy in the garage or workplace at all times. Never try to extinguish a fuel or electrical fire with water.

Note: *Any reference to a "torch" appearing in this manual should always be taken to mean a hand-held battery-operated electric lamp or flashlight. It does NOT mean a welding/gas torch or blowlamp.*

Hydrofluoric acid

Hydrofluoric acid is extremely corrosive. It is formed when certain types of synthetic rubber, which may be found in O-rings, oil seals, brake hydraulic system seals, fuel hoses etc, are exposed to temperatures above 400°C. The obvious circumstance in which this could happen on a vehicle is in the case of a fire. The rubber does not burn, but changes into a charred or sticky substance which contains the acid. *Once formed, the acid remains dangerous for years. If it gets onto the skin it may be necessary to amputate the limb concerned.*

When dealing with a vehicle which has suffered a fire, or with components salvaged from such a vehicle, always wear protective gloves and discard them carefully after use. Bear this in mind if obtaining components from a car breaker.

Fumes

Certain fumes are highly toxic, and can quickly cause unconsciousness and even death if inhaled to any extent, especially if inhalation takes place through a lighted cigarette or pipe. Petrol vapor comes into this category, as do the vapors from certain solvents such as trichloroethylene. Any draining or pouring of such volatile fluids should be done in a well-ventilated area.

When using cleaning fluids and solvents, read the instructions carefully. Never use materials from unmarked containers - they may give off poisonous vapors.

Never run the engine of a motor vehicle in an enclosed space such as a garage. Exhaust fumes contain carbon monoxide, which is extremely poisonous; if you need to run the engine, always do so in the open air, or at least have the rear of the vehicle outside the workplace. Although vehicles fitted with catalytic converters have greatly-reduced toxic exhaust emissions, the above precautions should still be observed.

If you are fortunate enough to have the use of an inspection pit, never drain or pour petrol, and never run the engine, while the vehicle is standing over it; the fumes, being heavier than air, will concentrate in the pit, with possibly lethal results.

The battery

Batteries which are sealed for life require special precautions, which are normally outlined on a label attached to the battery. Such precautions are primarily related to situations involving battery charging and jump starting from another vehicle.

With a conventional battery, never cause a spark, or allow a naked light, in close proximity to it. It will normally be giving off a certain amount of hydrogen gas, which is highly explosive.

Whenever possible, disconnect the battery earth terminal before working on the fuel or electrical systems.

If possible, loosen the battery filler plugs or battery cover when charging the battery from an external source. Do not charge at an excessive rate, or the battery may burst. Special care should be taken with the use of high-charge-rate boost chargers to prevent the battery from overheating.

Take care when topping-up and when carrying the battery. The acid electrolyte, even when diluted, is very corrosive, and should not be allowed to contact clothing, eyes or skin.

Always wear eye protection when cleaning the battery, to prevent the caustic deposits from entering your eyes.

The vehicle electrical system

Take care when making alterations or repairs to the vehicle wiring. Electrical faults are the commonest cause of vehicle fires. Make sure that any accessories are wired correctly, using an appropriately-rated fuse and wire of adequate current-carrying capacity. When possible, avoid the use of "piggy-back" or self-splicing connectors to power additional electrical equipment from existing feeds; make up a new feed with its own fuse instead.

When considering the current which a new circuit will have to handle, do not overlook the switch, especially when planning to use an existing switch to control additional components - for instance, if spotlights are to be fed via the main lighting switch. For preference, a relay should be used to switch heavy currents. If in doubt, consult an auto electrical specialist.

Any wire which passes through a body panel or bulkhead must be protected from chafing with a grommet or similar device. A wire which is allowed to chafe bare against the bodywork will cause a short-circuit and possibly a fire.

Mains electricity and electrical equipment

When using an electric power tool, inspection light, diagnostic equipment etc, which works from the mains, always ensure that the appliance is correctly connected to its plug, and that, where necessary, it is properly earthed. Do not use such appliances in damp conditions and, again, beware of creating a spark or applying excessive heat in the vicinity of fuel or fuel vapor. Also ensure that the appliances meet the relevant national safety standards.

Ignition HT voltage

A severe electric shock can result from touching certain parts of the ignition system, such as the HT leads, when the engine is running or being cranked, particularly if components are damp or the insulation is defective. Where an electronic ignition system is fitted, the HT voltage is much higher and could prove fatal, especially to wearers of cardiac pacemakers.

Jacking and vehicle support

The jack provided with the vehicle is designed primarily for emergency wheel changing, and its use for servicing and overhaul work on the vehicle is best avoided. Instead, a more substantial workshop jack (trolley jack or similar) should be used. Whichever type is employed, it is essential that additional safety support is provided by means of axle stands designed for this purpose. Never use makeshift means such as wooden blocks or piles of house bricks, as these can easily topple or, in the case of bricks, disintegrate under the weight of the vehicle. Further information on the correct positioning of the jack and axle stands is provided in the *"Jacking, towing and wheel changing"* section.

If removal of the wheels is not required, the use of drive-on ramps is recommended. Caution should be exercised to ensure that they are correctly aligned with the wheels, and that the vehicle is not driven too far along them, so that it promptly falls off the other ends, or tips the ramps.

General repair procedures

Whenever servicing, repair or overhaul work is carried out on the vehicle or its components, it is necessary to observe the following procedures and instructions. This will assist in carrying out the operation efficiently, and to a professional standard of workmanship.

Joint mating faces and gaskets

When separating components at their mating faces, never insert screwdrivers or similar implements into the joint between the faces in order to prise them apart. This can cause severe damage, which results in oil leaks, coolant leaks, etc upon reassembly. Separation is usually achieved by tapping along the joint with a soft-faced hammer in order to break the seal. However, note that this method may not be suitable where dowels are used for component location.

Where a gasket is used between the mating faces of two components, ensure that it is renewed on reassembly, and fit it dry, unless otherwise stated in the repair procedure. Make sure that the mating faces are clean and dry, with all traces of old gasket removed. When cleaning a joint face, use a tool which is not likely to score or damage the face, and remove any burrs or nicks with an oilstone or fine file.

Make sure that tapped holes are cleaned with a pipe cleaner, and keep them free of jointing compound, if this is being used, unless specifically instructed otherwise.

Ensure that all orifices, channels or pipes are clear, and blow through them, preferably using compressed air. *Wear eye protection when using compressed air!*

Oil seals

Oil seals can be removed by levering them out with a wide flat-bladed screwdriver or similar implement. Alternatively, a number of self-tapping screws may be screwed into the seal, and these used as a purchase for pliers or some similar device in order to pull the seal free.

Whenever an oil seal is removed from its working location, either individually or as part of an assembly, it should be renewed.

The very fine sealing lip of the seal is easily damaged, and will not seal if the surface it contacts is not completely clean and free from scratches, nicks or grooves. If the original sealing surface of the component cannot be restored, and the manufacturer has not made provision for slight relocation of the seal relative to the sealing surface, the component should be renewed.

Protect the lips of the seal from any surface which may damage them in the course of fitting. Use tape or a conical sleeve where possible. Lubricate the seal lips with oil before fitting and, on dual-lipped seals, fill the space between the lips with grease.

Unless otherwise stated, oil seals must be fitted with their sealing lips toward the lubricant to be sealed.

Use a tubular drift or block of wood of the appropriate size to install the seal and, if the seal housing is shouldered, drive the seal down to the shoulder. If the seal housing is unshouldered, the seal should be fitted with its face flush with the housing top face (unless otherwise instructed).

Screw threads and fastenings

Seized nuts, bolts and screws are quite a common occurrence where corrosion has set in, and the use of penetrating oil or releasing fluid will often overcome this problem if the offending item is soaked for a while before attempting to release it. The use of an impact driver may also provide a means of releasing such stubborn fastening devices, when used in conjunction with the appropriate screwdriver bit or socket. If none of these methods works, it may be necessary to resort to the careful application of heat, or the use of a hacksaw or nut splitter device.

Studs are usually removed by locking two nuts together on the threaded part, and then using a spanner on the lower nut to unscrew the stud. Studs or bolts which have broken off below the surface of the component in which they are mounted can sometimes be removed using a proprietary stud extractor (sometimes called "easy-outs"). Always ensure that a blind tapped hole is completely free from oil, grease, water or other fluid before installing the bolt or stud. Failure to do this could cause the housing to crack, due to the hydraulic action of the bolt or stud as it is screwed in.

When tightening a castellated nut to accept a split pin, tighten the nut to the specified torque, where applicable, and then tighten further to the next split pin hole. Never slacken the nut to align the split pin hole, unless stated in the repair procedure.

When checking or retightening a nut or bolt to a specified torque setting, slacken the nut or bolt by a quarter of a turn, and then retighten to the specified setting. However, this should not be attempted where angular tightening has been used.

For some screw fastenings, notably cylinder head bolts or nuts, torque wrench settings are no longer specified for the latter stages of tightening, "angular tightening" being called up instead. Typically, a fairly low torque wrench setting will be applied to the bolts/nuts in the correct sequence, followed by one or more stages of tightening through specified angles.

Locknuts, locktabs and washers

Any fastening which will rotate against a component or housing in the course of tightening should always have a washer between it and the relevant component or housing.

Spring or split washers should always be renewed when they are used to lock a critical component such as a big-end bearing retaining bolt or nut. Locktabs which are folded over to retain a nut or bolt should always be renewed.

Self-locking nuts can be re-used in non-critical areas, providing resistance can be felt when the locking portion passes over the bolt or stud thread. However, it should be noted that self-locking nuts tend to lose their effectiveness after long periods of use, and in such cases should be renewed as a matter of course.

Split pins must always be replaced with new ones of the correct size for the hole.

When thread-locking compound is found on the threads of a fastener which is to be re-used, it should be cleaned off with a wire brush and solvent, and fresh compound applied on reassembly.

Special tools

Some repair procedures in this manual entail the use of special tools such as a press, two- or three-legged pullers, spring compressors etc. Wherever possible, suitable readily-available alternatives to the manufacturer's special tools are described, and are shown in use. In some instances, where no alternative is possible, it has been necessary to resort to the use of a manufacturer's tool, and this has been done for reasons of safety, as well as the efficient completion of the repair operation. Unless you are highly skilled and have a thorough understanding of the procedures described, never attempt to bypass the use of any special tool when the procedure described specifies its use. Not only is there a very great risk of personal injury, but expensive damage could be caused to the components involved.

Environmental considerations

When disposing of used engine oil, brake fluid, antifreeze etc, give due consideration to any detrimental environmental effects. Do not, for instance, pour any of the above liquids down drains into the general sewage system, or onto the ground to soak away. Many local council refuse tips provide a facility for waste oil disposal, as do some garages. If none of these facilities are available, consult your local Environmental Health Department for further advice.

With the universal tightening-up of legislation regarding the emission of environmentally-harmful substances from motor vehicles, most current vehicles have tamperproof devices fitted to the main adjustment points of the fuel system. These devices are primarily designed to prevent unqualified persons from adjusting the fuel/air mixture with the chance of a consequent increase in toxic emissions. If such devices are encountered during servicing or overhaul, they should, wherever possible, be renewed or refitted in accordance with the vehicle manufacturer's requirements or current legislation. Owners taking their vehicles abroad should note that some countries have strict legislation relating to vehicles driven without these tamperproofing measures in place!

Tools and working facilities

Introduction

A selection of good tools is a fundamental requirement for anyone contemplating the maintenance and repair of a motor vehicle. For the owner who does not possess any, their purchase will prove a considerable expense, offsetting some of the savings made by doing-it-yourself. However, provided that the tools purchased meet the relevant national safety standards and are of good quality, they will last for many years and prove an extremely worthwhile investment.

To help the average owner to decide which tools are needed to carry out the various tasks detailed in this manual, we have compiled three lists of tools under the following headings: *Maintenance and minor repair, Repair and overhaul,* and *Special.* Newcomers to practical mechanics should start off with the *Maintenance and minor repair* tool kit, and confine themselves to the simpler jobs around the vehicle. Then, as confidence and experience grow, more difficult tasks can be undertaken, with extra tools being purchased as, and when, they are needed. In this way, a *Maintenance and minor repair* tool kit can be built up into a *Repair and overhaul* tool kit over a considerable period of time, without any major cash outlays. The experienced do-it-yourselfer will have a tool kit good enough for most repair and overhaul procedures, and will add tools from the Special category when it is felt that the expense is justified by the amount of use to which these tools will be put.

Maintenance and minor repair tool kit

The tools given in this list should be considered as a minimum requirement if routine maintenance, servicing and minor repair operations are to be undertaken. We recommend the purchase of combination spanners (ring one end, open-ended the other); although more expensive than open-ended ones, they do give the advantages of both types of spanner.

Combination spanners:
Metric - 8, 9, 10, 11, 12, 13, 14, 15, 17 & 19 mm
Adjustable spanner - 35 mm jaw (approx)
Transmission drain plug key (Allen type)

Spark plug spanner (with rubber insert)
Spark plug gap adjustment tool
Set of feeler gauges
Brake bleed nipple spanner
Screwdrivers:
Flat-bladed - approx 100 mm long x 6 mm dia
Cross-bladed - approx 100 mm long x 6 mm dia
Combination pliers
Hacksaw (junior)
Tyre pump
Tyre pressure gauge
Oil can
Oil filter removal tool
Fine emery cloth
Wire brush (small)
Funnel (medium size)

Repair and overhaul tool kit

These tools are virtually essential for anyone undertaking any major repairs to a motor vehicle, and are additional to those given in the *Maintenance and minor repair* list. Included in this list is a comprehensive set of sockets. Although these are expensive, they will be found invaluable as they are so versatile - particularly if various drives are included in the set. We recommend the 1/2 in square-drive type, as this can be used with most proprietary torque wrenches. If you cannot afford a socket set, even bought piecemeal, then inexpensive tubular box spanners are a useful alternative.

The tools in this list will occasionally need to be supplemented by tools from the *Special* list.

Sockets (or box spanners) to cover range in previous list
Reversible ratchet drive (for use with sockets) **(see illustration)**
Extension piece, 250 mm (for use with sockets)
Universal joint (for use with sockets)
Torque wrench (for use with sockets)
Self-locking grips
Ball pein hammer

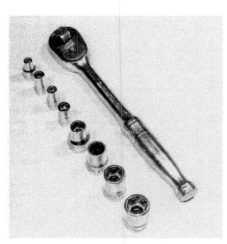

Sockets and reversible ratchet drive

Spline bit set

Spline key set

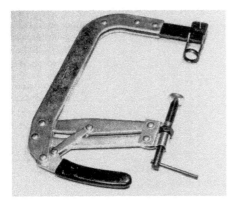

Valve spring compressor

Piston ring compressor

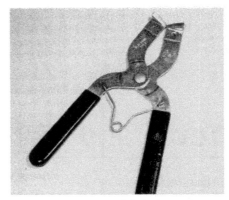

Piston ring removal/installation tool

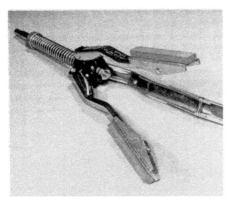

Cylinder bore hone

Three-legged hub and bearing puller

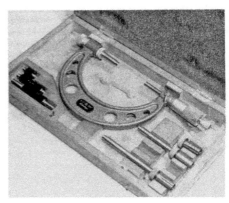

Micrometer set

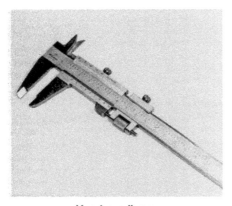

Vernier calipers

Dial test indicator and magnetic stand

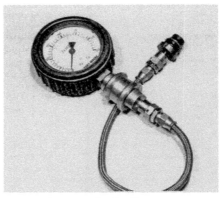

Compression testing gauge

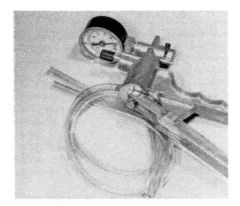

Vacuum pump and gauge

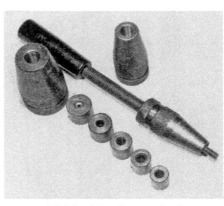

Clutch plate alignment set

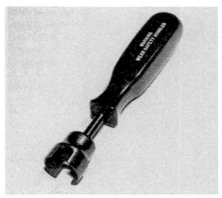

Brake shoe steady spring cup removal tool

Soft-faced mallet (plastic/aluminium or rubber)
Screwdrivers:
Flat-bladed - long & sturdy, short (chubby), and narrow
    (electrician's) types
Cross-bladed - Long & sturdy, and short (chubby) types
Pliers:
    Long-nosed
    Side cutters (electrician's)
    Circlip (internal and external)
Cold chisel - 25 mm
Scriber
Scraper
Centre-punch
Pin punch
Hacksaw
Brake hose clamp
Brake/clutch bleeding kit
Selection of twist drills
Steel rule/straight-edge
Allen keys (inc. splined/Torx type) **(see illustrations)**
Selection of files
Wire brush
Axle stands
Jack (strong trolley or hydraulic type)
Light with extension lead

Special tools

The tools in this list are those which are not used regularly, are expensive to buy, or which need to be used in accordance with their manufacturers' instructions. Unless relatively difficult mechanical jobs are undertaken frequently, it will not be economic to buy many of these tools. Where this is the case, you could consider clubbing together with friends (or joining a motorists' club) to make a joint purchase, or borrowing the tools against a deposit from a local garage or tool hire specialist. It is worth noting that many of the larger d-i-y superstores now carry a large range of special tools for hire at modest rates.

The following list contains only those tools and instruments freely available to the public, and not those special tools produced by the vehicle manufacturer specifically for its dealer network. You will find occasional references to these manufacturer's special tools in the text of this manual. Generally, an alternative method of doing the job without the vehicle manufacturer's special tool is given. However, sometimes there is no alternative to using them. Where this is the case and the relevant tool cannot be bought or borrowed, you will have to entrust the work to a franchised garage.

Valve spring compressor **(see illustration)**
Valve grinding tool
Piston ring compressor **(see illustration)**
Piston ring removal/installation tool **(see illustration)**
Cylinder bore hone **(see illustration)**

Balljoint separator
Coil spring compressors (where applicable)
Two-/three-legged hub and bearing puller **(see illustration)**
Impact screwdriver
Micrometer and/or vernier calipers **(see illustrations)**
Dial gauge/dial test indicator **(see illustration)**
Universal electrical multi-meter
Cylinder compression gauge **(see illustration)**
Hand-operated vacuum pump and gauge **(see illustration)**
Clutch plate alignment set **(see illustration)**
Brake shoe steady spring cup removal tool **(see illustration)**
Bush and bearing removal/installation set **(see illustration)**
Stud extractors **(see illustration)**
Tap and die set **(see illustration)**
Lifting tackle
Trolley jack

Buying tools

For practically all tools, a tool factor is the best source, since he will have a very comprehensive range compared with the average garage or accessory shop. Having said that, accessory shops often offer excellent quality tools at discount prices, so it pays to shop around.

Remember, you don't have to buy the most expensive items on the shelf, but it is always advisable to steer clear of the very cheap tools. There are plenty of good tools around at reasonable prices, but always aim to purchase items which meet the relevant national safety standards. If in doubt, ask the proprietor or manager of the shop for advice before making a purchase.

Care and maintenance of tools

Having purchased a reasonable tool kit, it is necessary to keep the tools in a clean and serviceable condition. After use, always wipe off any dirt, grease and metal particles using a clean, dry cloth, before putting the tools away. Never leave them lying around after they have been used. A simple tool rack on the garage or workshop wall, for items such as screwdrivers and pliers, is a good idea. Store all normal spanners and sockets in a metal box. Any measuring instruments, gauges, meters, etc, must be carefully stored, somewhere they cannot be damaged or become rusty.

Take a little care when tools are used. Hammer heads inevitably become marked, and screwdrivers lose the keen edge on their blades from time to time. A little timely attention with emery cloth or a file will soon restore items like this to a good serviceable finish.

Working facilities

Not to be forgotten when discussing tools is the workshop itself. If anything more than routine maintenance is to be carried out, some form of suitable working area becomes essential.

It is appreciated that many an owner-mechanic is forced by circumstances to remove an engine or similar item without the benefit of

Bush and bearing removal/installation set

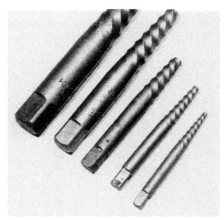
Stud extractor set

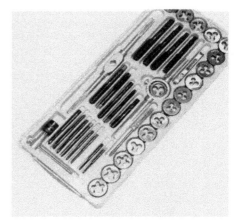
Tap and die set

a garage or workshop. Having done this, however, any repairs should always be done under the cover of a roof.

Wherever possible, any dismantling should be done on a clean, flat workbench or table at a suitable working height.

Any workbench needs a vice; one with a jaw opening of 100 mm (4 in) is suitable for most jobs. As mentioned previously, some clean dry storage space is also required for tools, as well as for any lubricants, cleaning fluids, touch-up paints and so on, which become necessary.

Another item which may be required, and which has a much more general usage, is an electric drill with a chuck capacity of at least 8 mm (5/16 in). This, together with a good range of twist drills, is virtually essential for fitting accessories.

Last, but not least, always keep a supply of old newspapers and clean, lint-free rags available, and try to keep any working area as clean as possible.

Spanner jaw gap and bolt size comparison table

Jaw gap – in (mm)	Spanner size	Bolt size
0.197 (5.00)	5 mm	M 2.5
0.216 (5.50)	5.5 mm	M 3
0.218 (5.53)	$\frac{7}{32}$ in AF	
0.236 (6.00)	6 mm	M 3.5
0.250 (6.35)	$\frac{1}{4}$ in AF	
0.275 (7.00)	7 mm	M 4
0.281 (7.14)	$\frac{9}{32}$ in AF	
0.312 (7.92)	$\frac{5}{16}$ in AF	
0.315 (8.00)	8 mm	M 5
0.343 (8.71)	$\frac{11}{32}$ in AF	
0.375 (9.52)	$\frac{3}{8}$ in AF	
0.394 (10.00)	10 mm	M 6
0.406 (10.32)	$\frac{13}{32}$ in AF	
0.433 (11.00)	11 mm	M 7
0.437 (11.09)	$\frac{7}{16}$ in AF	$\frac{1}{4}$ in SAE
0.468 (11.88)	$\frac{15}{32}$ in AF	
0.500 (12.70)	$\frac{1}{2}$ in AF	$\frac{5}{16}$ in SAE
0.512 (13.00)	13 mm	M8
0.562 (14.27)	$\frac{9}{16}$ in AF	$\frac{3}{8}$ in SAE
0.593 (15.06)	$\frac{19}{32}$ in AF	
0.625 (15.87)	$\frac{5}{8}$ in AF	$\frac{7}{16}$ in SAE
0.669 (17.00)	17 mm	M 10
0.687 (17.44)	$\frac{11}{16}$ in AF	
0.709 (19.00)	19 mm	M 12
0.750 (19.05)	$\frac{3}{4}$ in AF	$\frac{1}{2}$ in SAE
0.781 (19.83)	$\frac{25}{32}$ in AF	
0.812 (20.62)	$\frac{13}{16}$ in AF	
0.866 (22.00)	22 mm	M 14
0.875 (22.25)	$\frac{7}{8}$ in AF	$\frac{9}{16}$ in SAE
0.937 (23.79)	$\frac{15}{16}$ in AF	$\frac{5}{8}$ in SAE
0.945 (24.00)	24 mm	M 16
0.968 (24.58)	$\frac{31}{32}$ in AF	
1.000 (25.40)	1 in AF	$\frac{11}{16}$ in SAE
1.062 (26.97)	1 $\frac{1}{16}$ in AF	$\frac{3}{4}$ in SAE
1.063 (27.00)	27 mm	M 18
1.125 (28.57)	1 $\frac{1}{8}$ in AF	
1.182 (30.00)	30 mm	M 20
1.187 (30.14)	1 $\frac{3}{16}$ in AF	
1.250 (31.75)	1 $\frac{1}{4}$ in AF	$\frac{7}{8}$ in SAE
1.260 (32.00)	32 mm	M 22
1.312 (33.32)	1 $\frac{5}{16}$ in AF	
1.375 (34.92)	1 $\frac{3}{8}$ in AF	
1.418 (36.00)	36 mm	M 24
1.437 (36.49)	1 $\frac{7}{16}$ in AF	1 in SAE
1.500 (38.10)	1 $\frac{1}{2}$ in AF	
1.615 (41.00)	41 mm	M 27

Booster battery (jump) starting

When jump starting a vehicle using a booster battery, observe the following precautions:

(a) *Before connecting the booster battery, make sure that the ignition is switched off.*

(b) *Ensure that all electrical equipment (lights, heater, wipers etc) is switched off.*

(c) *Make sure that the booster battery is the same voltage as the discharged one in the vehicle.*

(d) *If the battery is being jump-started from the battery in another vehicle, the two vehicles MUST NOT TOUCH each other.*

(e) *Make sure that the transmission is in Neutral (manual transmission) or Park (automatic transmission).*

Connect one jump lead between the positive (+) terminals of the two batteries. Connect the other jump lead first to the negative (-) terminal of the booster battery, and then to a good earthing point on the vehicle to be started, such as a bolt or bracket on the engine block, at least 45 cm (18 in) from the battery if possible **(see illustration)**. Make sure that the jump leads will not come into contact with the fan, drive-belts or other moving parts of the engine.

Start the engine using the booster battery, then with the engine running at idle speed, switch on the heater blower motor (to maximum speed) or heated rear window, to reduce voltage peaks when the jump leads are disconnected. (Do not switch on the headlights instead - a high peak could blow the bulbs.) Disconnect the jump leads in the reverse order of connection.

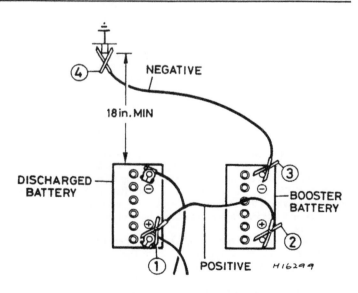

Jump start lead connections for negative-earth vehicles - connect leads in order shown

Automotive chemicals and lubricants

A number of automotive chemicals and lubricants are available for use during vehicle maintenance and repair. They include a wide variety of products ranging from cleaning solvents and degreasers to lubricants and protective sprays for rubber, plastic and vinyl.

Cleaners

Carburetor cleaner and choke cleaner is a strong solvent for gum, varnish and carbon. Most carburetor cleaners leave a dry-type lubricant film which will not harden or gum up. Because of this film it is not recommended for use on electrical components

Brake system cleaner is used to remove grease and brake fluid from the brake system, where clean surfaces are absolutely necessary. It leaves no residue and often eliminates brake squeal caused by contaminants.

Electrical cleaner removes oxidation, corrosion and carbon deposits from electrical contacts, restoring full current flow. It can also be used to clean spark plugs, carburetor jets, voltage regulators and other parts where an oil-free surface is desired.

Demoisturants remove water and moisture from electrical components such as alternators, voltage regulators, electrical connectors and fuse blocks. They are non-conductive, non-corrosive and non-flammable.

Degreasers are heavy-duty solvents used to remove grease from the outside of the engine and from chassis components. They can be sprayed or brushed on and, depending on the type, are rinsed off either with water or solvent.

Lubricants

Motor oil is the lubricant formulated for use in engines. It normally contains a wide variety of additives to prevent corrosion and reduce foaming and wear. Motor oil comes in various weights (viscosity ratings) from 5 to 80. The recommended weight of the oil depends on the season, temperature and the demands on the engine. Light oil is used in cold climates and under light load conditions. Heavy oil is used in hot climates and where high loads are encountered. Multi-viscosity oils are designed to have characteristics of both light and heavy oils and are available in a number of weights from 5W-20 to 20W-50.

Gear oil is designed to be used in differentials, manual transmissions and other areas where high-temperature lubrication is required.

Chassis and wheel bearing grease is a heavy grease used where increased loads and friction are encountered, such as for wheel bearings, balljoints, tie-rod ends and universal joints.

High-temperature wheel bearing grease is designed to withstand the extreme temperatures encountered by wheel bearings in disc brake equipped vehicles. It usually contains molybdenum disulphide (moly), which is a dry-type lubricant.

White grease is a heavy grease for metal-to-metal applications where water is a problem. White grease stays soft under both low and high temperatures, and will not wash off or dilute in the presence of water.

Assembly lube is a special extreme pressure lubricant, usually containing moly, used to lubricate high-load parts (such as main and rod bearings and cam lobes) for initial start-up of a new engine. The assembly lube lubricates the parts without being squeezed out or washed away until the engine oiling system begins to function.

Silicone lubricants are used to protect rubber, plastic, vinyl and nylon parts.

Graphite lubricants are used where oils cannot be used due to contamination problems, such as in locks. The dry graphite will lubricate metal parts while remaining uncontaminated by dirt, water, oil or acids. It is electrically conductive and will not foul electrical contacts in locks such as the ignition switch.

Moly penetrants loosen and lubricate frozen, rusted and corroded fasteners and prevent future rusting or freezing.

Heat-sink grease is a special electrically non-conductive grease that is used for mounting electronic ignition modules where it is essential that heat is transferred away from the module.

Sealants

RTV sealant is one of the most widely used gasket compounds. Made from silicone, RTV is air curing, it seals, bonds, waterproofs, fills surface irregularities, remains flexible, doesn't shrink, is relatively easy to remove, and is used as a supplementary sealer with almost all low and medium temperature gaskets.

Anaerobic sealant is much like RTV in that it can be used either to seal gaskets or to form gaskets by itself. It remains flexible, is solvent resistant and fills surface imperfections. The difference between an anaerobic sealant and an RTV-type sealant is in the curing. RTV cures when exposed to air, while an anaerobic sealant cures only in the absence of air. This means that an anaerobic sealant cures only after the assembly of parts, sealing them together.

Thread and pipe sealant is used for sealing hydraulic and pneumatic fittings and vacuum lines. It is usually made from a Teflon compound, and comes in a spray, a paint-on liquid and as a wrap-around tape.

Chemicals

Anti-seize compound prevents seizing, galling, cold welding, rust and corrosion in fasteners. High-temperature ant-seize, usually made with copper and graphite lubricants, is used for exhaust system and exhaust manifold bolts.

Anaerobic locking compounds are used to keep fasteners from vibrating or working loose and cure only after installation, in the absence of air. Medium strength locking compound is used for small nuts, bolts and screws that may be removed later. High-strength locking compound is for large nuts, bolts and studs which aren't removed on a regular basis.

Oil additives range from viscosity index improvers to chemical treatments that claim to reduce internal engine friction. It should be noted that most oil manufacturers caution against using additives with their oils.

Gas additives perform several functions, depending on their chemical makeup. They usually contain solvents that help dissolve gum and varnish that build up on carburetor, fuel injection and intake parts. They also serve to break down carbon deposits that form on the inside surfaces of the combustion chambers. Some additives contain upper cylinder lubricants for valves and piston rings, and others contain chemicals to remove condensation from the gas tank.

Miscellaneous

Brake fluid is specially formulated hydraulic fluid that can withstand the heat and pressure encountered in brake systems. Care must be taken so this fluid does not come in contact with painted surfaces or plastics. An opened container should always be resealed to prevent contamination by water or dirt.

Weatherstrip adhesive is used to bond weatherstripping around doors, windows and trunk lids. It is sometimes used to attach trim pieces.

Underseal is a petroleum-based, tar-like substance that is designed to protect metal surfaces on the underside of the vehicle from corrosion. It also acts as a sound-deadening agent by insulating the bottom of the vehicle.

Waxes and polishes are used to help protect painted and plated surfaces from the weather. Different types of paint may require the use of different types of wax and polish. Some polishes utilise a chemical or abrasive cleaner to help remove the top layer of oxidised (dull) paint on older vehicles. In recent years many non-wax polishes that contain a wide variety of chemicals such as polymers and silicones have been introduced. These non-wax polishes are usually easier to apply and last longer than conventional waxes and polishes.

Use of English

As the main part of this book has been written in the US, it uses the appropriate US component names, phrases, and spelling. Some of these differ from those used in the UK. Normally, these cause no difficulty, but to make sure, a glossary is printed below. When ordering spare parts, remember the parts list may use some of these words:

AMERICAN	ENGLISH	AMERICAN	ENGLISH
Aluminum	Aluminium	Muffler	Silencer
Antenna	Aerial	Odor	Odour
Authorized	Authorised	Oil pan	Sump
Auto parts stores	Motor factors	Open flame	Naked flame
Axleshaft	Halfshaft	Panel wagon/van	Van
Back-up	Reverse	Parking brake	Handbrake
Barrel	Choke/venturi	Parking light	Sidelight
Block	Chock	Pinging	Pinking
Box-end wrench	Ring spanner	Piston pin or wrist pin	Gudgeon pin
Bushing	Bush	Piston pin or wrist pin	Small end, little end
Carburetor	Carburettor	Pitman arm	Drop arm
Center	Centre	Power brake booster	Servo unit
Coast	Freewheel	Primary shoe (of brake)	Leading shoe (of brake)
Color	Colour	Prussian blue	Engineer's blue
Convertible	Drop head coupe	Pry	Prise (force apart)
Cotter pin	Split pin	Prybar	Lever
Counterclockwise	Anti-clockwise	Prying	Levering
Countershaft (of gearbox)	Layshaft	Quarter window	Quarterlight
Dashboard	Facia	Recap	Retread
Denatured alcohol	Methylated spirit	Release cylinder	Slave cylinder
Dome lamp	Interior light	Repair shop	Garage
Driveaxle	Driveshaft	Replacement	Renewal
Driveshaft	Propeller shaft	Ring gear (of differential)	Crownwheel
Fender	Wing/mudguard	Rocker panel (beneath doors)	Sill panel (beneath doors)
Firewall	Bulkhead	Rod bearing	Big-end bearing
Flashlight	Torch	Rotor/disk	Disc (brake)
Float bowl	Float chamber	Secondary shoe (of brake)	Trailing shoe (of brake)
Floor jack	Trolley jack	Sedan	Saloon
Freeway, turnpike etc	Motorway	Setscrew, Allen screw	Grub screw
Freeze plug	Core plug	Shock absorber, shock	Damper
Frozen	Seized	Snap-ring	Circlip
Gas tank	Petrol tank	Soft top	Hood
Gasoline (gas)	Petrol	Spacer	Distance piece
Gearshift	Gearchange	Spare tire	Spare wheel
Generator (DC)	Dynamo	Spark plug wires	HT leads
Ground (electrical)	Earth	Spindle arm	Steering arm
Header	Exhaust manifold	Stabilizer or sway bar	Anti-roll bar
Heat riser	Hot spot	Station wagon	Estate car
High	Top gear	Stumbles	Hesitates
Hood (engine cover)	Bonnet	Tang or lock	Tab washer
Installation	Refitting	Throw-out bearing	Thrust bearing
Intake	Inlet	Tie-rod or connecting rod (of steering)	Trackrod
Jackstands	Axle stands	Tire	Tyre
Jumper cable	Jump lead	Transmission	Gearbox
Keeper	Collet	Troubleshooting	Fault finding/diagnosis
Kerosene	Paraffin	Trunk	Boot (luggage compartment)
Knock pin	Roll pin	Turn signal	Indicator
Lash	Clearance	TV (throttle valve) cable	Kickdown cable
Lash	Free-play	Unpublicized	Unpublicised
Latch	Catch	Valve cover	Rocker cover
Latches	Locks	Valve lifter	Tappet
License plate	Number plate	Valve lifter or tappet	Cam follower or tappet
Light	Lamp	Vapor	Vapour
Lock (for valve spring retainer)	Split cotter (for valve spring cap)	Vise	Vice
Lopes	Hunts	Wheel cover	Roadwheel trim
Lug nut/bolt	Wheel nut/bolt	Whole drive line	Transmission
Metal chips or debris	Swarf	Windshield	Windscreen
Misses	Misfires	Wrench	Spanner

Conversion factors

Length (distance)

Inches (in)	25.4	= Millimetres (mm)	X 0.0394	= Inches (in)
Feet (ft)	0.305	= Metres (m)	X 3.281	= Feet (ft)
Miles	1.609	= Kilometres (km)	X 0.621	= Miles

Volume (capacity)

Cubic inches (cu in; in3)	X 16.387	= Cubic centimetres (cc; cm3)	X 0.061	= Cubic inches (cu in; in3)
Imperial pints (Imp pt)	X 0.568	= Litres (l)	X 1.76	= Imperial pints (Imp pt)
Imperial quarts (Imp qt)	X 1.137	= Litres (l)	X 0.88	= Imperial quarts (Imp qt)
Imperial quarts (Imp qt)	X 1.201	= US quarts (US qt)	X 0.833	= Imperial quarts (Imp qt)
US quarts (US qt)	X 0.946	= Litres (l)	X 1.057	= US quarts (US qt)
Imperial gallons (Imp gal)	X 4.546	= Litres (l)	X 0.22	= Imperial gallons (Imp gal)
Imperial gallons (Imp gal)	X 1.201	= US gallons (US gal)	X 0.833	= Imperial gallons (Imp gal)
US gallons (US gal)	X 3.785	= Litres (l)	X 0.264	= US gallons (US gal)

Mass (weight)

Ounces (oz)	X 28.35	= Grams (g)	X 0.035	= Ounces (oz)
Pounds (lb)	X 0.454	= Kilograms (kg)	X 2.205	= Pounds (lb)

Force

Ounces-force (ozf; oz)	X 0.278	= Newtons (N)	X 3.6	= Ounces-force (ozf; oz)
Pounds-force (lbf; lb)	X 4.448	= Newtons (N)	X 0.225	= Pounds-force (lbf; lb)
Newtons (N)	X 0.1	= Kilograms-force (kgf; kg)	X 9.81	= Newtons (N)

Pressure

Pounds-force per square inch (psi; lbf/in2; lb/in2)	X 0.070	= Kilograms-force per square centimetre (kgf/cm2; kg/cm2)	X 14.223	= Pounds-force per square inch (psi; lbf/in2; lb/in2)
Pounds-force per square inch (psi; lbf/in2; lb/in2)	X 0.068	= Atmospheres (atm)	X 14.696	= Pounds-force per square inch (psi; lbf/in2; lb/in2)
Pounds-force per square inch (psi; lbf/in2; lb/in2)	X 0.069	= Bars	X 14.5	= Pounds-force per square inch (psi; lbf/in2; lb/in2)
Pounds-force per square inch (psi; lbf/in2; lb/in2)	X 6.895	= Kilopascals (kPa)	X 0.145	= Pounds-force per square inch (psi; lbf/in2; lb/in2)
Kilopascals (kPa)	X 0.01	= Kilograms-force per square centimetre (kgf/cm2; kg/cm2)	X 98.1	= Kilopascals (kPa)
Millibar (mbar)	X 100	= Pascals (Pa)	X 0.01	= Millibar (mbar)
Millibar (mbar)	X 0.0145	= Pounds-force per square inch (psi; lbf/in2; lb/in2)	X 68.947	= Millibar (mbar)
Millibar (mbar)	X 0.75	= Millimetres of mercury (mmHg)	X 1.333	= Millibar (mbar)
Millibar (mbar)	X 0.401	= Inches of water (inH$_2$O)	X 2.491	= Millibar (mbar)
Millimetres of mercury (mmHg)	X 0.535	= Inches of water (inH$_2$O)	X 1.868	= Millimetres of mercury (mmHg)
Inches of water (inH$_2$O)	X 0.036	= Pounds-force per square inch (psi; lbf/in2; lb/in2)	X 27.68	= Inches of water (inH$_2$O)

Torque (moment of force)

Pounds-force inches (lbf in; lb in)	X 1.152	= Kilograms-force centimetre (kgf cm; kg cm)	X 0.868	= Pounds-force inches (lbf in; lb in)
Pounds-force inches (lbf in; lb in)	X 0.113	= Newton metres (Nm)	X 8.85	= Pounds-force inches (lbf in; lb in)
Pounds-force inches (lbf in; lb in)	X 0.083	= Pounds-force feet (lbf ft; lb ft)	X 12	= Pounds-force inches (lbf in; lb in)
Pounds-force feet (lbf ft; lb ft)	X 0.138	= Kilograms-force metres (kgf m; kg m)	X 7.233	= Pounds-force feet (lbf ft; lb ft)
Pounds-force feet (lbf ft; lb ft)	X 1.356	= Newton metres (Nm)	X 0.738	= Pounds-force feet (lbf ft; lb ft)
Newton metres (Nm)	X 0.102	= Kilograms-force metres (kgf m; kg m)	X 9.804	= Newton metres (Nm)

Power

Horsepower (hp)	X 745.7	= Watts (W)	X 0.0013	= Horsepower (hp)

Velocity (speed)

Miles per hour (miles/hr; mph)	X 1.609	= Kilometres per hour (km/hr; kph)	X 0.621	= Miles per hour (miles/hr; mph)

Fuel consumption*

Miles per gallon, Imperial (mpg)	X 0.354	= Kilometres per litre (km/l)	X 2.825	= Miles per gallon, Imperial (mpg)
Miles per gallon, US (mpg)	X 0.425	= Kilometres per litre (km/l)	X 2.352	= Miles per gallon, US (mpg)

Temperature

Degrees Fahrenheit = (°C x 1.8) + 32   Degrees Celsius (Degrees Centigrade; °C) = (°F - 32) x 0.56

It is common practice to convert from miles per gallon (mpg) to litres/100 kilometres (l/100km), where mpg (Imperial) x l/100 km = 282 and mpg (US) x l/100 km = 235

Fault diagnosis

Contents

This Section provides an easy reference guide to the more common problems which may occur during the operation of your vehicle. These problems and their possible causes are grouped under headings denoting various components or systems, such as Engine, Cooling system, etc. They also refer you to the Chapter and/or Section which deals with the problem.

Remember that successful fault diagnosis is not a mysterious black art practised only by professional mechanics. It is simply the result of the right knowledge combined with an intelligent, systematic approach to the problem. Always work by a process of elimination, starting with the simplest solution and working through to the most complex - and never overlook the obvious. Anyone can run the gas tank dry or leave the lights on overnight, so don't assume that you are exempt from such oversights.

Finally, always establish a clear idea of why a problem has occurred and take steps to ensure that it doesn't happen again. If the electrical system fails because of a poor connection, check all other connections in the system to make sure that they don't fail as well. If a particular fuse continues to blow, find out why - don't just renew one fuse after another. Remember, failure of a small component can often be indicative of potential failure or incorrect functioning of a more important component or system.

Engine and performance

1   Engine will not rotate when attempting to start

1   Battery terminal connections loose or corroded. Check the cable terminals at the battery; tighten cable clamp and/or clean off corrosion as necessary (see Chapter 1).
2   Battery discharged or faulty. If the cable ends are clean and tight on the battery posts, turn the key to the On position and switch on the headlights or windshield wipers. If they won't run, the battery is discharged.
3   Automatic transmission not engaged in park (P) or Neutral (N).
4   Broken, loose or disconnected wires in the starting circuit. Inspect all wires and connectors at the battery, starter solenoid and ignition switch (on steering column).
5   Starter motor pinion jammed in flywheel ring gear. If manual transmission, place transmission in gear and rock the vehicle to manually turn the engine. Remove starter (Chapter 5) and inspect pinion and flywheel (Chapter 2) at earliest convenience.
6   Starter solenoid faulty (Chapter 5).
7   Starter motor faulty (Chapter 5).
8   Ignition switch faulty (Chapter 12).
9   Engine seized. Try to turn the crankshaft with a large socket and breaker bar on the pulley bolt.

2   Engine rotates but will not start

1   Fuel tank empty.
2   Battery discharged (engine rotates slowly). Check the operation of electrical components as described in previous Section.
3   Battery terminal connections loose or corroded. See previous Section.
4   Fuel not reaching carburetor or fuel injector. Check for clogged fuel filter or lines and defective fuel pump. Also make sure the tank vent lines aren't clogged (Chapter 4).
5   Choke not operating properly (Chapter 1).
6   Faulty distributor components. Check the cap and rotor (Chapter 1). Where applicable, check the contact breaker points.
7   Low cylinder compression. Check as described in Chapter 2.
8   Valve clearances not properly adjusted - Chapter 1 (four-cylinder engines).
9   Water in fuel. Drain tank and fill with new fuel.
10   Defective ignition coil (Chapter 5).
11   Dirty or clogged carburetor jets or fuel injector. Carburetor out of

adjustment. Check the float level (Chapter 4).
12   Wet or damaged ignition components (Chapters 1 and 5).
13   Worn, faulty or incorrectly gapped spark plugs (Chapter 1).
14   Broken, loose or disconnected wires in the starting circuit (see previous Section).
15   Loose distributor (changing ignition timing). Turn the distributor body as necessary to start the engine, then adjust the ignition timing as soon as possible (Chapter 1).
16   Broken, loose or disconnected wires at the ignition coil or faulty coil (Chapter 5).
17   Timing chain or belt failure or wear affecting valve timing (Chapter 2).

3   Starter motor operates without turning engine

1   Starter pinion sticking. Remove the starter (Chapter 5) and inspect.
2   Starter pinion or flywheel/driveplate teeth worn or broken. Remove the inspection cover and inspect.

4   Engine hard to start when cold

1   Battery discharged or low. Check as described in Chapter 1.
2   Fuel not reaching the carburetor or fuel injectors. Check the fuel filter, lines and fuel pump (Chapters 1 and 4).
3   Choke inoperative (Chapters 1 and 4).
4   Defective spark plugs (Chapter 1).

5   Engine hard to start when hot

1   Air filter dirty (Chapter 1).
2   Fuel not reaching carburetor or fuel injectors (see Section 4). Check for a vapor lock situation, brought about by clogged fuel tank vent lines.
3   Bad engine ground connection.
4   Choke sticking (Chapter 1).
5   Defective pick-up coil in distributor (Chapter 5). Where applicable, check contact breaker points.
6   Float level too high (Chapter 4).

6   Starter motor noisy or engages roughly

1   Pinion or flywheel/driveplate teeth worn or broken. Remove the inspection cover on the left side of the engine and inspect.
2   Starter motor mounting bolts loose or missing.

7   Engine starts but stops immediately

1   Loose or damaged wire harness connections at distributor, coil or alternator.
2   Intake manifold vacuum leaks. Make sure all mounting bolts/nuts are tight and all vacuum hoses connected to the manifold are attached properly and in good condition.
3   Insufficient fuel flow (see Chapter 4).

8   Engine 'lopes' while idling, or idles erratically

1   Vacuum leaks. Check mounting bolts at the intake manifold for tightness. Make sure that all vacuum hoses are connected and in good condition. Use a stethoscope or a length of fuel hose held against your ear to listen for vacuum leaks while the engine is running. A hissing sound will be heard. A soapy water solution will also detect leaks. Check the intake manifold gasket surfaces.

2   Leaking EGR valve or plugged PCV valve (see Chapters 1 and 6).
3   Air filter clogged (Chapter 1).
4   Fuel pump not delivering sufficient fuel (Chapter 4).
5   Leaking head gasket. Perform a cylinder compression check (Chapter 2).
6   Timing chain or belt worn (Chapter 2).
7   Camshaft lobes worn (Chapter 2).
8   Valve clearance out of adjustment - Chapter 1 (four-cylinder engine).
9   Valves burned or otherwise leaking (Chapter 2).
10   Ignition timing out of adjustment (Chapter 1).
11   Ignition system not operating properly (Chapters 1 and 5). Where applicable, check the contact breaker points.
12   Thermostatic air cleaner not operating properly (Chapter 1).
13   Choke not operating properly (Chapters 1 and 4).
14   Dirty or clogged injector(s). Carburetor dirty, clogged or out of adjustment. Check the float level (Chapter 4).
15   Idle speed out of adjustment (Chapter 1).

9 Engine misses at idle speed

1   Spark plugs faulty or not gapped properly (Chapter 1).
2   Faulty spark plug wires (Chapter 1).
3   Wet or damaged distributor components (Chapter 1).
4   Short circuits in ignition, coil or spark plug wires.
5   Sticking or faulty emissions systems (see Chapter 6).
6   Clogged fuel filter and/or foreign matter in fuel. Remove the fuel filter (Chapter 1) and inspect.
7   Vacuum leaks at intake manifold or hose connections. Check as described in Section 8.
8   Incorrect idle speed (Chapter 1) or idle mixture (Chapter 4).
9   Incorrect ignition timing (Chapter 1).
10   Low or uneven cylinder compression. Check as described in Chapter 2.
11   Choke not operating properly (Chapter 1).
12   Clogged or dirty fuel injectors (Chapter 4).

10 Excessively-high idle speed

1   Sticking throttle linkage (Chapter 4).
2   Choke opened excessively at idle (Chapter 4).
3   Idle speed incorrectly adjusted (Chapter 1).
4   Valve clearances incorrectly adjusted - Chapter 1 (four cylinder engines).

11 Battery will not hold a charge

1   Alternator drivebelt defective or not adjusted properly (Chapter 1).
2   Battery cables loose or corroded (Chapter 1).
3   Alternator not charging properly (Chapter 5).
4   Loose, broken or faulty wires in the charging circuit (Chapter 5).
5   Short circuit causing a continuous drain on the battery.
6   Battery defective internally.

12 Alternator light stays on

1   Fault in alternator or charging circuit (Chapter 5).
2   Alternator drivebelt defective or not properly adjusted (Chapter 1).

13 Alternator light fails to come on when key is turned on

1   Faulty bulb (Chapter 12).
2   Defective alternator (Chapter 5).
3   Fault in the printed circuit, wiring or bulb holder (Chapter 12).

14 Engine misses throughout driving speed range

1   Fuel filter clogged and/or impurities in the fuel system. Check fuel filter (Chapter 1) or clean system (Chapter 4).
2   Faulty or incorrectly gapped spark plugs (Chapter 1).
3   Incorrect ignition timing (Chapter 1).
4   Cracked distributor cap, disconnected distributor wires or damaged distributor components (Chapter 1). Where applicable, check the contact breaker points.
5   Defective spark plug wires (Chapter 1).
6   Emissions system components faulty (Chapter 6).
7   Low or uneven cylinder compression pressures. Check as described in Chapter 2.
8   Weak or faulty ignition coil (Chapter 5).
9   Weak or faulty ignition system (Chapter 5).
10   Vacuum leaks at intake manifold or vacuum hoses (see Section 8).
11   Dirty or clogged carburetor or fuel injector (Chapter 4).
12   Leaky EGR valve (Chapter 6).
13   Carburetor out of adjustment (Chapter 4).
14   Idle speed out of adjustment (Chapter 1).

15 Hesitation or stumble during acceleration

1   Ignition timing incorrect (Chapter 1).
2   Ignition system not operating properly (Chapter 5). Where applicable, check the contact breaker points.
3   Dirty or clogged carburetor or fuel injector (Chapter 4).
4   Low fuel pressure. Check for proper operation of the fuel pump and for restrictions in the fuel filter and lines (Chapter 4).
5   Carburetor out of adjustment (Chapter 4).

16 Engine stalls

1   Idle speed incorrect (Chapter 1).
2   Fuel filter clogged and/or water and impurities in the fuel system (Chapter 1).
3   Choke not operating properly (Chapter 1).
4   Damaged or wet distributor cap and HT leads.
5   Emissions system components faulty (Chapter 6).
6   Faulty or incorrectly gapped spark plugs (Chapter 1). Also check the spark plug wires (Chapter 1).
7   Vacuum leak at the carburetor, intake manifold or vacuum hoses. Check as described in Section 8.
8   Valve clearances incorrect - Chapter 1 (four-cylinder engine).

17 Engine lacks power

1   Incorrect ignition timing (Chapter 1).
2   Excessive play in distributor shaft. At the same time check for faulty distributor cap, wires, etc. (Chapter 1).
3   Faulty or incorrectly gapped spark plugs (Chapter 1).
4   Air filter dirty (Chapter 1).
5   Faulty ignition coil (Chapter 5).
6   Brakes binding (Chapters 1 and 9).
7   Automatic transmission fluid level incorrect, causing slippage (Chapter 1).
8   Clutch slipping (Chapter 8).
9   Fuel filter clogged and/or impurities in the fuel system (Chapters 1 and 4).
10   EGR system not functioning properly (Chapter 6).
11   Use of sub-standard fuel. Fill tank with proper octane fuel.
12   Low or uneven cylinder compression pressures. Check as described in Chapter 2.
13   Air leak at carburetor or intake manifold (check as described in Section 8).

14   Dirty or clogged carburetor jets or malfunctioning choke (Chapters 1 and 4).

18 Engine backfires

1   EGR system not functioning properly (Chapter 6).
2   Ignition timing incorrect (Chapter 1).
3   Thermostatic air cleaner system not operating properly (Chapter 6).
4   Vacuum leak (refer to Section 8).
5   Valve clearances incorrect - Chapter 1 (four-cylinder engine).
6   Damaged valve springs or sticking valves (Chapter 2).
7   Intake air leak (see Section 8).
8   Carburetor float level out of adjustment (Chapter 4).

19 Engine surges while holding accelerator steady

1   Intake air leak (see Section 8).
2   Fuel pump not working properly (Chapter 4).

20 Pinging or knocking engine sounds when engine is under load

1   Incorrect grade of fuel. Fill tank with fuel of the proper octane rating.
2   Ignition timing incorrect (Chapter 1).
3   Carbon build-up in combustion chambers. Remove cylinder head(s) and clean combustion chambers (Chapter 2).
4   Incorrect spark plugs (Chapter 1).

21 Engine diesels (continues to run) after being turned off

1   Idle speed too high (Chapter 1).
2   Ignition timing incorrect (Chapter 1).
3   Incorrect spark plug heat range (Chapter 1).
4   Intake air leak (see Section 8).
5   Carbon build-up in combustion chambers. Remove the cylinder head(s) and clean the combustion chambers (Chapter 2).
6   Valves sticking (Chapter 2).
7   Valve clearances incorrect - Chapter 1 (four-cylinder engine).
8   EGR system not operating properly (Chapter 6).
9   Fuel shut-off system not operating properly (Chapter 6).
10   Check for causes of overheating (Section 27).

22 Low oil pressure

1   Improper grade of oil.
2   Oil pump worn or damaged (Chapter 2).
3   Engine overheating (refer to Section 27).
4   Clogged oil filter (Chapter 1).
5   Clogged oil strainer (Chapter 2).
6   Oil pressure gauge not working properly (Chapter 2).

23 Excessive oil consumption

1   Loose oil drain plug.
2   Loose bolts or damaged oil pan gasket (Chapter 2).
3   Loose bolts or damaged front cover gasket (Chapter 2).
4   Front or rear crankshaft oil seal leaking (Chapter 2).
5   Loose bolts or damaged rocker arm cover gasket (Chapter 2).
6   Loose oil filter (Chapter 1).
7   Loose or damaged oil pressure switch (Chapter 2).

8   Pistons and cylinders excessively worn (Chapter 2).
9   Piston rings not installed correctly on pistons (Chapter 2).
10   Worn or damaged piston rings (Chapter 2).
11   Intake and/or exhaust valve oil seals worn or damaged (Chapter 2).
12   Worn valve stems.
13   Worn or damaged valves/guides (Chapter 2).

24 Excessive fuel consumption

1   Dirty or clogged air filter element (Chapter 1).
2   Incorrect ignition timing (Chapter 1).
3   Incorrect idle speed (Chapter 1).
4   Low tire pressure or incorrect tire size (Chapter 11).
5   Fuel leakage. Check all connections, lines and components in the fuel system (Chapter 4).
6   Choke not operating properly (Chapter 1).
7   Dirty or clogged carburetor jets or fuel injectors (Chapter 4).

25 Fuel odor

1   Fuel leakage. Check all connections, lines and components in the fuel system (Chapter 4).
2   Fuel tank overfilled. Fill only to automatic shut-off.
3   Charcoal canister filter in Evaporative Emissions Control system clogged (Chapter 1).
4   Vapor leaks from Evaporative Emissions Control system lines (Chapter 6).

26 Miscellaneous engine noises

1   A strong dull noise that becomes more rapid as the engine accelerates indicates worn or damaged crankshaft bearings or an unevenly worn crankshaft. To pinpoint the trouble spot, remove the spark plug wire from one plug at a time and crank the engine over. If the noise stops, the cylinder with the removed plug wire indicates the problem area. Replace the bearing and/or service or replace the crankshaft (Chapter 2).
2   A similar (yet slightly higher pitched) noise to the crankshaft knocking described in the previous paragraph, that becomes more rapid as the engine accelerates, indicates worn or damaged connecting rod bearings (Chapter 2). The procedure for locating the problem cylinder is the same as described in Paragraph 1.
3   An overlapping metallic noise that increases in intensity as the engine speed increases, yet diminishes as the engine warms up indicates abnormal piston and cylinder wear (Chapter 2). To locate the problem cylinder, use the procedure described in Paragraph 1.
4   A rapid clicking noise that becomes faster as the engine accelerates indicates a worn piston pin or piston pin hole. This sound will happen each time the piston hits the highest and lowest points in the stroke (Chapter 2). The procedure for locating the problem piston is described in Paragraph 1.
5   A metallic clicking noise coming from the water pump indicates worn or damaged water pump bearings or pump. Replace the water pump with a new one (Chapter 3).
6   A rapid tapping sound or clicking sound that becomes faster as the engine speed increases indicates "valve tapping" or improperly adjusted valve clearances. This can be identified by holding one end of a section of hose to your ear and placing the other end at different spots along the rocker arm cover. The point where the sound is loudest indicates the problem valve. Adjust the valve clearance (Chapter 1). If the problem persists, you likely have a collapsed valve lifter or other damaged valve train component. Changing the engine oil and adding a high-viscosity oil treatment will sometimes cure a stuck lifter problem. If the problem still persists, the lifters and rocker arms must be removed for inspection (see Chapter 2).

7   A steady metallic rattling or rapping sound coming from the area of the timing chain cover indicates a worn, damaged or out-of-adjustment timing chain. Service or replace the chain and related components (Chapter 2).

Cooling system

27   Overheating

1   Insufficient coolant in system (Chapter 1).
2   Drivebelt defective or not adjusted properly (Chapter 1).
3   Radiator core blocked or radiator grille dirty or restricted (Chapter 3).
4   Thermostat faulty (Chapter 3).
5   Fan not functioning properly (Chapter 3).
6   Radiator cap not maintaining proper pressure. Have cap pressure tested by gas station or repair shop.
7   Ignition timing incorrect (Chapter 1).
8   Defective water pump (Chapter 3).
9   Improper grade of engine oil.
10   Inaccurate temperature gauge (Chapter 12).

28   Overcooling

1   Thermostat faulty (Chapter 3).
2   Inaccurate temperature gauge (Chapter 12).

29   External coolant leakage

1   Deteriorated or damaged hoses. Loose clamps at hose connections (Chapter 1).
2   Water pump seals defective. If this is the case, water will drip from the weep hole in the water pump body (Chapter 3).
3   Leakage from radiator core or header tank. This will require the radiator to be professionally repaired (see Chapter 3 for removal procedures).
4   Engine drain plugs or water jacket freeze plugs leaking (see Chapters 1 and 2).
5   Leak from coolant temperature switch (Chapter 3).
6   Leak from damaged gaskets or small cracks (Chapter 2).
7   Damaged head gasket. This can be verified by checking the condition of the engine oil as noted in Section 30.

30   Internal coolant leakage

Note: *Internal coolant leaks can usually be detected by examining the oil. Check the dipstick and inside the rocker arm cover for water deposits and an oil consistency like that of a milkshake.*
1   Leaking cylinder head gasket. Have the system pressure tested or remove the cylinder head (Chapter 2) and inspect.
2   Cracked cylinder bore or cylinder head. Dismantle engine and inspect (Chapter 2).
3   Loose cylinder head bolts (tighten as described in Chapter 2).

31   Abnormal coolant loss

1   Overfilling system (Chapter 1).
2   Coolant boiling away due to overheating (see causes in Section 27).
3   Internal or external leakage (see Sections 29 and 30).
4   Faulty radiator cap. Have the cap pressure-tested.
5   Cooling system being pressurised by engine compression. This could be due to a cracked head or block or leaking head gasket(s).

32   Poor coolant circulation

1   Inoperative water pump. A quick test is to pinch the top radiator hose closed with your hand while the engine is idling, then release it. You should feel a surge of coolant if the pump is working properly (Chapter 3).
2   Restriction in cooling system. Drain, flush and refill the system (Chapter 1). If necessary, remove the radiator (Chapter 3) and have it reverse-flushed or professionally cleaned.
3   Loose water pump drivebelt (Chapter 1).
4   Thermostat sticking (Chapter 3).
5   Insufficient coolant (Chapter 1).

33   Corrosion

1   Excessive impurities in the water. Soft, clean water is recommended. Distilled or rainwater is satisfactory.
2   Insufficient antifreeze solution (refer to Chapter 1 for the proper ratio of water to antifreeze).
3   Infrequent flushing and draining of system. Regular flushing of the cooling system should be carried out at the specified intervals as described in (Chapter 1).

Clutch

Note: *All clutch-related service information is located in Chapter 8, unless otherwise noted.*

34   Fails to release (pedal pressed to the floor - shift lever does not move freely in and out of Reverse)

1   Freeplay incorrectly adjusted (see Chapter 1).
2   Clutch contaminated with oil. Remove clutch plate and inspect.
3   Clutch plate warped, distorted or otherwise damaged.
4   Diaphragm spring fatigued. Remove clutch cover/pressure plate assembly and inspect.
5   Broken, binding or damaged release cable or linkage (models with a cable-operated release system).
6   Leakage of fluid from clutch hydraulic system. Inspect master cylinder, operating cylinder and connecting lines.
7   Air in clutch hydraulic system. Bleed the system.
8   Insufficient pedal height. Check and adjust as necessary.
9   Piston seal in operating cylinder deformed or damaged.
10   Lack of grease on pilot bearing.

35   Clutch slips (engine speed increases, with no increase in vehicle speed)

1   Worn or oil-soaked clutch plate.
2   Clutch plate not broken in. It may take 30 or 40 normal starts for a new clutch to seat.
3   Diaphragm spring weak or damaged. Remove clutch cover/pressure plate assembly and inspect.
4   Flywheel warped (Chapter 2).
5   Debris in master cylinder preventing the piston from returning to its normal position.
6   Clutch hydraulic line damaged.
7   Binding in the release mechanism.

36   Grabbing (chattering) as clutch is engaged

1   Oil on clutch plate. Remove and inspect. Repair any leaks.
2   Worn or loose engine or transmission mounts. They may move slightly when clutch is released. Inspect mounts and bolts.

3   Worn splines on transmission input shaft. Remove clutch components and inspect.
4   Warped pressure plate or flywheel. Remove clutch components and inspect.
5   Diaphragm spring fatigued. Remove clutch cover/pressure plate assembly and inspect.
6   Clutch linings hardened or warped.
7   Clutch lining rivets loose.

37   Squeal or rumble with clutch engaged (pedal released)

1   Improper pedal adjustment. Adjust pedal freeplay (Chapter 1).
2   Release bearing binding on transmission shaft. Remove clutch components and check bearing. Remove any burrs or nicks, clean and re-lubricate before reinstallation.
3   Pilot bushing worn or damaged.
4   Clutch rivets loose.
5   Clutch plate cracked.
6   Fatigued clutch plate torsion springs. Replace clutch plate.

38   Squeal or rumble with clutch disengaged (pedal depressed)

1   Worn or damaged release bearing.
2   Worn or broken pressure plate diaphragm fingers.

39   Clutch pedal stays on floor when disengaged

Binding linkage or release bearing. Inspect linkage or remove clutch components as necessary.

Manual transmission

Note: All *manual transmission service information is located in Chapter 7, unless otherwise noted.*

40   Noisy in Neutral with engine running

1   Input shaft bearing worn.
2   Damaged main drive gear bearing.
3   Insufficient transmission oil (Chapter 1).
4   Transmission oil in poor condition. Drain and fill with proper grade oil. Check old oil for water and debris (Chapter 1).
5   Noise can be caused by variations in engine torque. Change the idle speed and see if noise disappears.

41   Noisy in all gears

1   Any of the above causes, and/or:
2   Worn or damaged output gear bearings or shaft.

42   Noisy in one particular gear

1   Worn, damaged or chipped gear teeth.
2   Worn or damaged synchroniser.

43   Slips out of gear

1   Transmission loose on clutch housing.
2   Stiff shift lever seal.
3   Shift linkage binding.
4   Broken or loose input gear bearing retainer.

5   Dirt between clutch lever and engine housing.
6   Worn linkage.
7   Damaged or worn check balls, fork rod ball grooves or check springs.
8   Worn mainshaft or countershaft bearings.
9   Loose engine mounts (Chapter 2).
10   Excessive gear end play.
11   Worn synchronisers.

44   Oil leaks

1   Excessive amount of lubricant in transmission (see Chapter 1 for correct checking procedures). Drain lubricant as required.
2   Rear oil seal or speedometer oil seal damaged.
3   To pinpoint a leak, first remove all built-up dirt and grime from the transmission. Degreasing agents and/or steam-cleaning will achieve this. With the underside clean, drive the vehicle at low speeds so the airflow will not blow the leak far from its source. Raise the vehicle and determine where the leak is located.

45   Difficulty engaging gears

1   Clutch not releasing completely.
2   Loose or damaged shift linkage. Make a thorough inspection, replacing parts as necessary.
3   Insufficient transmission oil (Chapter 1).
4   Transmission oil in poor condition. Drain and fill with proper grade oil. Check oil for water and debris (Chapter 1).
5   Worn or damaged striking rod.
6   Sticking or jamming gears.

46   Noise occurs while shifting gears

1   Check for proper operation of the clutch (Chapter 8).
2   Faulty synchroniser assemblies.

Automatic transmission

Note: *Due to the complexity of the automatic transmission, it's difficult for the home mechanic to properly diagnose and service. For problems other than the following, the vehicle should be taken to a reputable mechanic.*

47   Fluid leakage

1   Automatic transmission fluid is a deep red color, and fluid leaks should not be confused with engine oil which can easily be blown by air flow to the transmission.
2   To pinpoint a leak, first remove all built-up dirt and grime from the transmission. Degreasing agents and/or steam-cleaning will achieve this. With the underside clean, drive the vehicle at low speeds so the airflow will not blow the leak far from its source. Raise the vehicle and determine where the leak is located. Common areas of leakage are:

(a) **Fluid pan:** tighten mounting bolts and/or replace pan gasket as necessary (Chapter 1). Some models have a drain plug; make sure it's tight.
(b) **Rear extension:** tighten bolts and/or replace oil seal as necessary.
(c) **Filler pipe:** replace the rubber oil seal where pipe enters transmission case.
(d) **Transmission oil lines:** tighten fittings where lines enter transmission case and/or replace lines.
(e) **Vent pipe:** transmission overfilled and/or water in fluid (see checking procedures, Chapter 1).
(f) **Speedometer connector:** replace the O-ring where speedometer cable enters transmission case.

48 General shift mechanism problems

Chapter 7 deals with checking and adjusting the shift linkage on automatic transmissions. Common problems which may be caused by out of adjustment linkage are:

(a) Engine starting in gears other than P (park) or N (Neutral).
(b) Indicator pointing to a gear other than the one actually engaged.
(c) Vehicle moves with transmission in P (Park) position.

49 Transmission will not downshift with the accelerator pedal pressed to the floor

Chapter 7 deals with adjusting the TV (kickdown) linkage to enable the transmission to downshift properly.

50 Engine will start in gears other than Park or Neutral

Chapter 7 deals with adjusting the Neutral start switch installed on automatic transmissions.

51 Transmission slips, shifts rough, is noisy, or has no drive in forward or Reverse gears

1 There are many probable causes for the above problems, but the home mechanic should concern himself only with one possibility; fluid level.
2 Before taking the vehicle to a shop, check the fluid level and condition as described in Chapter 1. Add fluid, if necessary, or change the fluid and filter if needed. If problems persist, have a professional diagnose the transmission.

Driveshaft

Note: *Refer to Chapter 8, unless otherwise specified, for service information.*

52 Leaks at front of driveshaft

Defective transmission rear seal. See Chapter 7 for replacement procedure. As this is done, check the splined yoke for burrs or roughness that could damage the new seal. Remove burrs with a fine file or whetstone.

53 Knock or clunk when transmission is under initial load (just after transmission is put into gear)

1 Loose or disconnected rear suspension components. Check all mounting bolts and bushings (Chapters 7 and 10).
2 Loose driveshaft bolts. Inspect all bolts and nuts and tighten them securely.
3 Worn or damaged universal joint bearings. Inspect the universal joints (Chapter 8).
4 Worn sleeve yoke and mainshaft spline.

54 Metallic grating sound consistent with vehicle speed

Pronounced wear in the universal joint bearings. Replace U-joints or driveshafts, as necessary.

55 Vibration

Note: *Before blaming the dnveshaft, make sure the tires are perfectly balanced and perform the following test.*

1 Install a tachometer inside the vehicle to monitor engine speed as the vehicle is driven. Drive the vehicle and note the engine speed at which the vibration (roughness) is most pronounced. Now shift the transmission to a different gear and bring the engine speed to the same point.
2 If the vibration occurs at the same engine speed (rpm) regardless of which gear the transmission is in, the driveshaft is NOT at fault since the driveshaft speed varies.
3 If the vibration decreases or is eliminated when the transmission is in a different gear at the same engine speed, refer to the following probable causes.
4 Bent or dented driveshaft. Inspect and replace as necessary.
5 Undercoating or built-up dirt, etc. on the driveshaft. Clean the shaft thoroughly.
6 Worn universal joint bearings. Replace the U-joints or driveshaft as necessary.
7 Driveshaft and/or companion flange out of balance. Check for missing weights on the shaft. Remove driveshaft and reinstall 180-degrees from original position, then recheck. Have the driveshaft balanced if problem persists.
8 Loose driveshaft mounting bolts/nuts.
9 Defective center bearing, if so equipped.
10 Worn transmission rear bushing (Chapter 7).

56 Scraping noise

Make sure the dust cover on the sleeve yoke isn't rubbing on the transmission extension housing.

57 Whining or whistling noise

Defective center bearing, if so equipped.

Rear axle and differential

Note: *For differential servicing information, refer to Chapter 8, unless otherwise specified.*

58 Noise - same when in drive as when vehicle is coasting

1 Road noise. No corrective action available.
2 Tire noise. Inspect tires and check tire pressures (Chapter 1).
3 Front wheel bearings loose, worn or damaged (Chapter 1).
4 Insufficient differential oil (Chapter 1).
5 Defective differential.

59 Knocking sound when starting or shifting gears

Defective or incorrectly adjusted differential.

60 Noise when turning

Defective differential.

61 Vibration

See probable causes under Driveshaft. Proceed under the guidelines listed for the driveshaft. If the problem persists, check the rear wheel bearings by raising the rear of the vehicle and spinning the wheels by hand. Listen for evidence of rough (noisy) bearings. Remove and inspect (Chapter 8).

62 Oil leaks

1   Pinion oil seal damaged (Chapter 8).
2   Axleshaft oil seals damaged (Chapter 8).
3   Differential cover leaking. Tighten mounting bolts or replace the gasket as required.
4   Loose filler or drain plug on differential (Chapter 1).
5   Clogged or damaged breather on differential.

Transfer case (4WD models)

Note: *Unless otherwise specified, refer to Chapter 7C for service and repair information.*

63 Gear jumping out of mesh

1   Incorrect control lever freeplay.
2   Interference between the control lever and the console.
3   Play or fatigue in the transfer case mounts.
4   Internal wear or incorrect adjustments.

64 Difficult shifting

1   Lack of oil.
2   Internal wear, damage or incorrect adjustment.

65 Noise

1   Lack of oil in transfer case.
2   Noise in 4H and 4L, but not in 2H indicates cause is in the front differential or front axle.
3   Noise in 2H, 4H and 4L indicates cause is in rear differential or rear axle.
4   Noise in 2H and 4H but not in 4L, or in 4L only, indicates internal wear or damage in transfer case.

Brakes

Note: *Before assuming a brake problem exists, make sure the tires are in good condition and inflated properly, the front end alignment is correct and the vehicle is not loaded with weight in an unequal manner. All service procedures for the brakes are included in Chapter 9, unless otherwise noted.*

66 Vehicle pulls to one side during braking

1   Defective, damaged or oil contaminated brake pad on one side. Inspect as described in Chapter 1. Refer to Chapter 10 if replacement is required.
2   Excessive wear of brake pad material or disc on one side. Inspect and repair as necessary.
3   Loose or disconnected front suspension components. Inspect and tighten all bolts securely (Chapters 1 and 9).
4   Defective caliper assembly. Remove caliper and inspect for stuck piston or damage.
5   Scored or out-of-round rotor.
6   Loose caliper mounting bolts.
7   Incorrect wheel bearing adjustment.

67 Noise (high-pitched squeal)

1   Brake pads worn out. This noise comes from the wear sensor rubbing against the disc. Replace pads with new ones immediately!
2   Glazed or contaminated pads.
3   Dirty or scored rotor.
4   Bent support plate.

68 Excessive brake pedal travel

1   Partial brake system failure. Inspect entire system (Chapter 1) and correct as required.
2   Insufficient fluid in master cylinder. Check (Chapter 1) and add fluid bleed system if necessary.
3   Air in system. Bleed system.
4   Excessive lateral rotor play.
5   Brakes out of adjustment. Check the operation of the automatic adjusters.
6   Defective proportioning valve. Replace valve and bleed system.

69 Brake pedal feels spongy when depressed

1   Air in brake lines. Bleed the brake system.
2   Deteriorated rubber brake hoses. Inspect all system hoses and lines. Replace parts as necessary.
3   Master cylinder mounting nuts loose. Inspect master cylinder bolts (nuts) and tighten them securely.
4   Master cylinder faulty.
5   Incorrect shoe or pad clearance.
6   Defective check valve. Replace valve and bleed system.
7   Clogged reservoir cap vent hole.
8   Deformed rubber brake lines.
9   Soft or swollen caliper seals.
10   Poor-quality brake fluid. Bleed entire system and fill with new approved fluid.

70 Excessive effort required to stop vehicle

1   Power brake booster not operating properly.
2   Excessively worn linings or pads. Check and replace if necessary.
3   One or more caliper pistons seized or sticking. Inspect and rebuild as required.
4   Brake pads or linings contaminated with oil or grease. Inspect and replace as required.
5   New pads or linings installed and not yet seated. It'll take a while for the new material to seat against the rotor or drum.
6   Worn or damaged master cylinder or caliper assemblies. Check particularly for frozen pistons.
7   Also see causes listed under Section 69.

71 Pedal travels to the floor with little resistance

Little or no fluid in the master cylinder reservoir caused by leaking caliper piston(s) or loose, damaged or disconnected brake lines. Inspect entire system and repair as necessary.

72 Brake pedal pulsates during brake application

1   Wheel bearings damaged, worn or out of adjustment (Chapter 1).
2   Caliper not sliding properly due to improper installation or obstructions. Remove and inspect.
3   Rotor not within specifications. Remove the rotor and check for excessive lateral runout and parallelism. Have the rotors resurfaced or

replace them with new ones. Also make sure that all rotors are the same thickness.

4   Out-of-round rear brake drums. Remove the drums and have them turned or replace them with new ones.

73   Brakes drag (indicated by sluggish engine performance or wheels being very hot after driving)

1   Output rod adjustment incorrect at the brake pedal.
2   Obstructed master cylinder compensator. Disassemble master cylinder and clean.
3   Master cylinder piston seized in bore. Overhaul master cylinder.
4   Caliper assembly in need of overhaul.
5   Brake pads or shoes worn out.
6   Piston cups in master cylinder or caliper assembly deformed. Overhaul master cylinder.
7   Rotor not within specifications (Section 72).
8   Parking brake assembly will not release.
9   Clogged brake lines.
10   Wheel bearings out of adjustment (Chapter 1).
11   Brake pedal height improperly adjusted.
12   Wheel cylinder needs overhaul.
13   Improper shoe-to-drum clearance. Adjust as necessary.

74   Rear brakes lock up under light brake application

1   Tire pressures too high.
2   Tires excessively worn (Chapter 1).

75   Rear brakes lock up under heavy brake application

1   Tire pressures too high.
2   Tires excessively worn (Chapter 1).
3   Front brake pads contaminated with oil, mud or water. Clean or replace the pads.
4   Front brake pads excessively worn.
5   Defective master cylinder or caliper assembly.

Suspension and steering

Note: *All service procedures for the suspension and steering systems are included in Chapter 10, unless otherwise noted.*

76   Vehicle pulls to one side

1   Tire pressures uneven (Chapter 1).
2   Defective tire (Chapter 1).
3   Excessive wear in suspension or steering components (Chapter 1).
4   Wheel alignment incorrect.
5   Front brakes dragging. Inspect as described in Section 73.
6   Wheel bearings improperly adjusted (Chapter 1 or 8).
7   Wheel lug nuts loose.

77   Shimmy, shake or vibration

1   Tire or wheel out of balance or out of round. Have them balanced on the vehicle.
2   Shock absorbers and/or suspension components worn or damaged. Check for worn bushings in the upper and lower links.
3   Wheel lug nuts loose.
4   Incorrect tire pressures.
5   Excessively worn or damaged tire.
6   Loosely mounted steering gear housing.

7   Steering gear improperly adjusted.
8   Loose, worn or damaged steering components.
9   Damaged idler arm.
10   Worn balljoint.

78   Excessive pitching and/or rolling around corners, or during braking

1   Defective shock absorbers. Replace as a set.
2   Broken or weak leaf springs and/or suspension components.
3   Worn or damaged stabilizer bar or bushings.

79   Wandering or general instability

1   Improper tire pressures.
2   Worn or damaged upper and lower link or tension rod bushings.
3   Incorrect front end alignment.
4   Worn or damaged steering linkage or suspension components.
5   Improperly adjusted steering gear.
6   Out of balance wheels.
7   Loose wheel lug nuts.
8   Worn rear shock absorbers.
9   Fatigued or damaged rear leaf springs.

80   Excessively-stiff steering

1   Lack of lubricant in power steering fluid reservoir, where appropriate (Chapter 1).
2   Incorrect tire pressures (Chapter 1).
3   Lack of lubrication at balljoints (Chapter 1).
4   Front end out of alignment.
5   Steering gear out of adjustment or lacking lubrication.
6   Improperly adjusted wheel bearings.
7   Worn or damaged steering gear.
8   Interference of steering column with turn signal switch.
9   Low tire pressures.
10   Worn or damaged balljoints.
11   Worn or damaged steering linkage.
12   See also Section 79.

81   Excessive play in steering

1   Loose wheel bearings (Chapter 1 or 8).
2   Excessive wear in suspension bushings (Chapter 1).
3   Steering gear improperly adjusted.
4   Incorrect wheel alignment.
5   Steering gear mounting bolts loose.
6   Worn steering linkage.

82   Lack of power assistance

1   Steering pump drivebelt faulty or not adjusted properly (Chapter 1).
2   Fluid level low (Chapter 1).
3   Hoses or pipes restricting the flow. Inspect and replace parts as necessary.
4   Air in power steering system. Bleed system.
5   Defective power steering pump.

83   Steering wheel fails to return to straight-ahead position

1   Incorrect front end alignment.
2   Tire pressures low.

3   Steering gears improperly engaged.
4   Steering column out of alignment.
5   Worn or damaged balljoint.
6   Worn or damaged steering linkage.
7   Improperly lubricated idler arm.
8   Insufficient oil in steering gear.
9   Lack of fluid in power steering pump.

84   Steering effort not the same in both directions (power system)

1   Leaks in steering gear.
2   Clogged fluid passage in steering gear

85   Noisy power steering pump

1   Insufficient oil in pump.
2   Clogged hoses or oil filter in pump.
3   Loose pulley.
4   Improperly adjusted drivebelt (Chapter 1).
5   Defective pump.

86   Miscellaneous noises

1   Improper tire pressures.
2   Insufficiently lubricated balljoint or steering linkage.
3   Loose or worn steering gear, steering linkage or suspension components.
4   Defective shock absorber.
5   Defective wheel bearing.
6   Worn or damaged suspension bushings.
7   Damaged leaf spring.

8   Loose wheel lug nuts.
9   Worn or damaged rear axleshaft spline.
10   Worn or damaged rear shock absorber mounting bushing.
11   Incorrect rear axle end play.
12   See also causes of noises at the rear axle and driveshaft.

87   Excessive tire wear (not specific to one area)

1   Incorrect tire pressures.
2   Tires out of balance. Have them balanced on the vehicle.
3   Wheels damaged. Inspect and replace as necessary.
4   Suspension or steering components worn (Chapter 1).

88   Excessive tire wear on outside edge

1   Incorrect tire pressure.
2   Excessive speed in turns.
3   Front end alignment incorrect (excessive toe-in).

89   Excessive tire wear on inside edge

1   Incorrect tire pressure.
2   Front end alignment incorrect (toe-out).
3   Loose or damaged steering components (Chapter 1).

90   Tire tread worn in one place

1   Tires out of balance. Have them balanced on the vehicle.
2   Damaged or buckled wheel. Inspect and replace if necessary.
3   Defective tire.

MOT test checks

Introduction

Motor vehicle testing has been compulsory in Great Britain since 1960, when the Motor Vehicle (Tests) Regulations were first introduced. At that time, testing was only applicable to vehicles ten years old or older, and the test itself only covered lighting equipment, braking systems and steering gear. Current vehicle testing is far more extensive and, in the case of private vehicles, is now an annual inspection commencing three years after the date of first registration. Test standards are becoming increasingly stringent; for details of changes, consult the latest edition of the MOT Inspection Manual (available from HMSO or bookshops).

This section is intended as a guide to getting your vehicle through the MOT test. It lists all the relevant testable items, how to check them yourself, and what is likely to cause the vehicle to fail. Obviously, it will not be possible to examine the vehicle to the same standard as the professional MOT tester, who will be highly experienced in this work, and will have all the necessary equipment available. However, working through the following checks will provide a good indication as to the condition of the vehicle, and will enable you to identify any problem areas before submitting the vehicle for the test. Where a component is found to need repair or renewal, reference should be made to the appropriate Chapter in the manual, where further information will be found.

The following checks have been sub-divided into four categories, as follows:

(a) Checks carried out from the driver's seat.
(b) Checks carried out with the vehicle on the ground.
(c) Checks carried out with the vehicle raised and with the wheels free to rotate.
(d) Exhaust emission checks.

In most cases, the help of an assistant will be necessary to carry out these checks thoroughly.

Checks carried out from the driver's seat

Handbrake (parking brake)

Test the operation of the handbrake by pulling on the lever until the handbrake is in the normal fully-applied position. Ensure that the travel of the lever (the number of clicks of the ratchet) is not excessive before full resistance of the braking mechanism is felt. If so, this would indicate a fault in the rear brakes and/or handbrake mechanism.

With the handbrake fully applied, tap the lever sideways and make sure that it does not release, which would indicate wear in the ratchet and pawl. Release the handbrake, and move the lever from side to side to check for excessive wear in the pivot bearing. Check the security of the lever mountings, and make sure that there is no corro-sion of any part of the body structure within 30 cm of the lever mounting. If the lever mountings cannot be readily seen from inside the vehicle, carry out this check later when working underneath.

Footbrake

Check that the brake pedal is sound, without visible defects such as excessive wear of the pivot bushes, or broken or damaged pedal pad. Check also for signs of fluid leaks on the pedal, floor or carpets, which would indicate failed seals in the brake master cylinder.

Depress the brake pedal slowly at first, then rapidly until sustained pressure can be held. Maintain this pressure, and check that the pedal does not creep down to the floor, which would again indicate problems with the master cylinder. Release the pedal, wait a few seconds, then depress it once until firm resistance is felt. Check that this resistance occurs near the top of the pedal travel. If the pedal travels nearly to the floor before firm resistance is felt, this would indicate incorrect brake adjustment, resulting in "insufficient reserve travel" of the footbrake. If firm resistance cannot be felt, ie the pedal feels spongy, this would indicate that air is present in the hydraulic system, which will necessitate complete bleeding of the system.

Check that the servo unit is operating correctly by depressing the brake pedal several times to exhaust the vacuum. Keep the pedal depressed, and start the engine. As soon as the engine starts, the brake pedal resistance will be felt to alter. If this is not the case, there may be a leak from the brake servo vacuum hose, or the servo unit itself may be faulty.

Steering wheel and column

Examine the steering wheel for fractures or looseness of the hub, spokes or rim. Move the steering wheel from side to side and then up and down, in relation to the steering column. Check that the steering wheel is not loose on the column, indicating wear in the column splines or a loose steering wheel retaining nut. Continue moving the steering wheel as before, but also turn it slightly from left to right. Check that there is no abnormal movement of the steering wheel, indicating excessive wear in the column upper support bearing, universal joint(s) or flexible coupling.

Windscreen and mirrors

The windscreen must be free of cracks or other damage which will seriously interfere with the driver's field of view, or which will prevent the windscreen wipers from operating properly. Small stone chips are acceptable. Any stickers, dangling toys or similar items must also be clear of the field of view.

Rear view mirrors must be secure, intact and capable of being adjusted. The nearside (passenger side) door mirror is not included in the test unless the interior mirror cannot be used - for instance, in the case of a van with blacked-out rear windows.

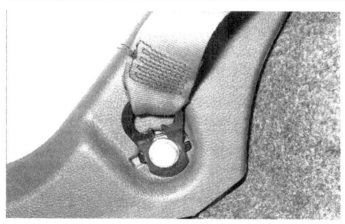

Check the security of all seat belt mountings

Seat belts and seats

Note: *The following checks are applicable to all seat belts, front and rear. Front seat belts must be of a type that will restrain the upper part of the body; lap belts are not acceptable. Various combinations of seat belt types are acceptable at the rear.*

Carefully examine the seat belt webbing for cuts, or any signs of serious fraying or deterioration. If the seat belt is of the retractable type, pull the belt all the way out, and examine the full extent of the webbing.

Fasten and unfasten the belt, ensuring that the locking mechanism holds securely, and releases properly when intended. If the belt is of the retractable type, check also that the retracting mechanism operates correctly when the belt is released.

Check the security of all seat belt mountings and attachments which are accessible, without removing any trim or other components, from inside the vehicle **(see illustration)**. Any serious corrosion, fracture or distortion of the body structure within 30 cm of any mounting point will cause the vehicle to fail. Certain anchorages will not be accessible or even visible from inside the vehicle; in this instance, further checks should be carried out later, when working underneath. If any part of the seat belt mechanism is attached to the front seat, then the seat mountings are treated as anchorages, and must also comply as above.

The front seats themselves must be securely attached so that they cannot move unexpectedly, and the backrests must lock in the upright position.

Doors

Both front doors must be able to be opened and closed from outside and inside, and must latch securely when closed. In the case of a pick-up, the tailgate must be securely attached, and capable of being securely fastened.

Electrical equipment

Switch on the ignition, and operate the horn. The horn must operate, and produce a clear sound audible to other road users. Note that a gong, siren or two-tone horn fitted as an alternative to the manufacturer's original equipment is not acceptable.

Check the operation of the windscreen washers and wipers. The washers must operate with adequate flow and pressure, and with the jets adjusted so that the liquid strikes the windscreen near the top of the glass.

Operate the windscreen wipers in conjunction with the washers, and check that the blades cover their designed sweep of the windscreen without smearing. The blades must effectively clean the glass so that the driver has an adequate view of the road ahead, and to the front nearside and offside of the vehicle. If the screen smears or does not clean adequately, it is advisable to renew the wiper blades before the MOT test.

Depress the footbrake with the ignition switched on, and have

your assistant check that both rear stop-lights operate, and are extinguished when the footbrake is released. If one stop-light fails to operate, it is likely that a bulb has blown or there is a poor electrical contact at, or near, the bulbholder. If both stop-lights fail to operate, check for a blown fuse, faulty stop-light switch, or possibly two blown bulbs. If the lights stay on when the brake pedal is released, it is possible that the switch is at fault.

Checks carried out with the vehicle on the ground

Vehicle identification

Front and rear number plates must be in good condition, securely fitted and easily read. Letters and numbers must be correctly spaced, with the gap between the group of numbers and the group of letters at least double the gap between adjacent numbers and letters.

The vehicle identification number on the plate under the bonnet must be legible. It will be checked during the test, as part of the measures taken to prevent the fraudulent acquisition of certificates.

Electrical equipment

Switch on the sidelights, and check that both front and rear sidelights and the number plate lights are illuminated, and that the lenses and reflectors are secure and undamaged. This is particularly important at the rear, where a cracked or damaged lens would allow a white light to show to the rear, which is unacceptable. Note in addition that any lens that is excessively dirty, either inside or out, such that the light intensity is reduced, could also constitute a fail.

Switch on the headlights, and check that both dipped beam and main beam units are operating correctly and at the same light intensity. If either headlight shows signs of dimness, this is usually attributable to a poor earth connection or severely-corroded internal reflector. Inspect the headlight lenses for cracks or stone damage. Any damage to the headlight lens will normally constitute a fail, but this is very much down to the tester's discretion. Bear in mind that with all light units, they must operate correctly when first switched on. It is not acceptable to tap a light unit to make it operate.

The headlights must not only be aligned so as not to dazzle other road users when switched to dipped beam, but also so as to provide adequate illumination of the road. This can only be accurately checked using optical beam-setting equipment, so if you have any doubts about the headlight alignment, it is advisable to have this professionally checked and if necessary reset, before the MOT test.

With the ignition switched on, operate the direction indicators, and check that they show amber lights to the front and to the rear, that they flash at the rate of between one and two flashes per second, and that the "tell-tale" on the instrument panel also functions. Operation of the sidelights and stop-lights must not affect the indicators - if it does, the cause is usually a bad earth at the rear light cluster. Similarly check the operation of the hazard warning lights, which must work with the ignition on and off. Examine the lenses for cracks or damage as described previously.

Check the operation of the rear foglight(s). The test only concerns itself with the statutorily-required foglight, which is the one on the offside (driver's side). The light must be secure, and emit a steady red light. The warning light on the instrument panel (or in the switch) must also work.

Footbrake

From within the engine compartment, examine the brake pipes for signs of leaks, corrosion, insecurity, chafing or other damage. Check the master cylinder and servo unit for leaks, security of their mountings, or excessive corrosion in the vicinity of the mountings. The master cylinder reservoir must be secure; if it is of the translucent type, the fluid level must be between the upper and lower level markings.

Turn the steering as necessary so that the right-hand front brake flexible hose can be examined. Inspect the hose carefully for any sign of cracks or deterioration of the rubber. This will be most noticeable if the hose is bent in half, and is particularly common where the rubber portion enters the metal end fitting **(see illustration)**. Turn the steering onto full-left then full-right lock, and ensure that the hose does not

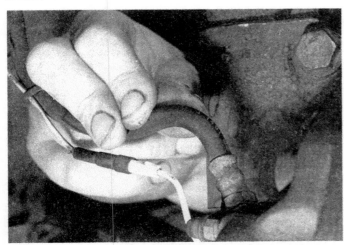

Check the braking system pipes and hoses for signs of damage
or deterioration

Shake the roadwheel vigorously to check for excess play in the
wheel bearing and suspension components

contact the wheel, tyre, or any part of the steering or suspension mechanism. While your assistant depresses the brake pedal firmly, check the hose for any bulges or fluid leaks under pressure. Now repeat these checks on the left-hand front hose. Should any damage or deterioration be noticed, renew the hose.

Steering mechanism and suspension

Have your assistant turn the steering wheel from side to side slightly, up to the point where the steering gear just begins to transmit this movement to the roadwheels. Check for excessive free play between the steering wheel and the steering gear, which would indicate wear in the steering column joints, wear or insecurity of the steering column-to-steering gear coupling, or insecurity, incorrect adjustment, or wear in the steering gear itself. Generally speaking, free play greater than 1.3 cm for vehicles with rack-and-pinion type steering (or 7.6 cm for vehicles with steering box mechanisms) should be considered excessive.

Have your assistant turn the steering wheel more vigorously in each direction, up to the point where the roadwheels just begin to turn. As this is done, carry out a complete examination of all the steering joints, linkages, fittings and attachments. Any component that shows signs of wear, damage, distortion, or insecurity should be renewed or attended to accordingly. On vehicles equipped with power steering, also check that the power steering pump is secure, that the pump drivebelt is in satisfactory condition and correctly adjusted, that there are no fluid leaks or damaged hoses, and that the system operates correctly. Additional checks can be carried out later with the vehicle raised, when there will be greater working clearance underneath.

Check that the vehicle is standing level and at approximately the correct ride height. Ensure that there is sufficient clearance between the suspension components and the bump stops to allow full suspension travel over bumps.

Shock absorbers

Depress each corner of the vehicle in turn, and then release it. If the shock absorbers are in good condition, the corner of the vehicle will rise and then settle in its normal position. If there is no noticeable damping effect from the shock absorber, and the vehicle continues to rise and fall, then the shock absorber is defective and the vehicle will fail. A shock absorber which has seized will also cause the vehicle to fail.

Exhaust system

Start the engine, and with your assistant holding a rag over the tailpipe, check the entire system for leaks, which will appear as a rhythmic fluffing or hissing sound at the source of the leak. Check the effectiveness of the silencer by ensuring that the noise produced is of a level to be expected from a vehicle of similar type. Providing that the

system is structurally sound, it is acceptable to cure a leak using a proprietary exhaust system repair kit or similar method.

Checks carried out with the vehicle raised and with the wheels free to rotate

Jack up the front and rear of the vehicle, and securely support it on axle stands positioned at suitable load-bearing points under the vehicle structure. Position the stands clear of the suspension assemblies, ensure that the wheels are clear of the ground, and that the steering can be turned onto full-right and full-left lock.

Steering mechanism

Examine the steering rack rubber gaiters for signs of splits, lubricant leakage or insecurity of the retaining clips. If power steering is fitted, check for signs of deterioration, damage, chafing, or leakage of the fluid hoses, pipes or connections. Also check for excessive stiffness or binding of the steering, a missing split pin or locking device, or any severe corrosion of the body structure within 30 cm of any steering component attachment point.

Have your assistant turn the steering onto full-left then full-right lock. Check that the steering turns smoothly, without undue tightness or roughness, and that no part of the steering mechanism, including a wheel or tyre, fouls any brake flexible or rigid hose or pipe, or any part of the body structure.

On vehicles with four-wheel steering, similar considerations apply to the rear wheel steering linkages. However, it is permissible for a rear wheel steering system to be inoperative, provided that the rear wheels are secured in the straight-ahead position, and that the front wheel steering system is operating effectively.

Front and rear suspension and wheel bearings

Starting at the front right-hand side of the vehicle, grasp the roadwheel at the 3 o'clock and 9 o'clock positions, and shake it vigorously. Check for any free play at the wheel bearings, suspension balljoints, or suspension mountings, pivots and attachments. Check also for any serious deterioration of the rubber or metal casing of any mounting bushes, or any distortion, deformation or severe corrosion of any components. Look for missing split pins, tab washers or other locking devices on any mounting or attachment, or any severe corrosion of the vehicle structure within 30 cm of any suspension component attachment point.

If any excess free play is suspected at a component pivot point, this can be confirmed by using a large screwdriver or similar tool, and levering between the mounting and the component attachment. This will confirm whether the wear is in the pivot bush, its retaining bolt or in the mounting itself (the bolt holes can often become elongated).

Now grasp the wheel at the 12 o'clock and 6 o'clock positions, shake it vigorously and repeat the previous inspection (**see illustra-**

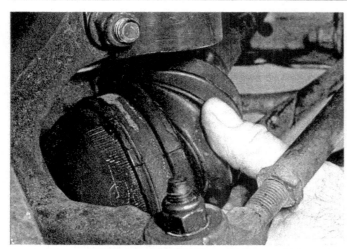

Inspect the constant velocity joint gaiters (4WD models) for splits
or damage

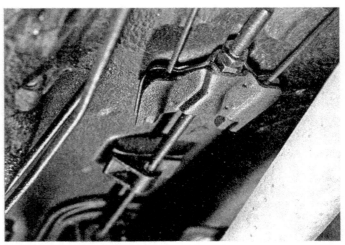

Check the handbrake mechanism - typical example shown - for
signs of frayed or broken cables, or insecurity of the linkage

tion). Rotate the wheel, and check for roughness or tightness of the
front wheel bearing such that imminent failure of the bearing is indicated.

Carry out all the above checks at the other front wheel, and then
at both rear wheels.

Roadsprings and shock absorbers

On vehicles with strut type suspension units, examine the strut
assembly for signs of serious fluid leakage, corrosion or severe pitting
of the piston rod, or damage to the casing. Check also for security of
the mounting points.

If coil springs are fitted, check that the spring ends locate correctly in their spring seats, that there is no severe corrosion of the
spring, and that it is not cracked, broken, or in any way damaged.

If the vehicle is fitted with leaf springs, check that all leaves are intact, that the axle is securely attached to each spring, and that there is
no wear or deterioration of the spring eye mountings, bushes, and
shackles.

The same general checks apply to vehicles fitted with other suspension types, such as torsion bars, hydraulic displacer units, etc. In
all cases, ensure that all mountings and attachments are secure, that
there are no signs of excessive wear, corrosion, cracking, deformation
or damage to any component or bush, and that there are no fluid leaks,
or damaged hoses or pipes (hydraulic types).

Inspect the shock absorbers for signs of serious fluid leakage.
(Slight seepage of fluid is normal for some types of shock absorber,
and is not a reason for failing.) Check for excessive wear of the mounting bushes or attachments, or damage to the body of the unit.

Driveshafts - 4WD models (referred to as driveaxles in US)

With the steering turned to full lock, rotate each front wheel in
turn, and inspect the constant velocity joint gaiters for splits or damage
(see illustration). Also check the gaiter is securely attached to its respective housings by clips or other methods of retention.

Continue turning the wheel, and check that each driveshaft is
straight, with no sign of damage.

Braking system

If possible, without dismantling, check the brake pads and the
condition of the discs. Ensure that the friction lining material has not
worn excessively, and that the discs are not fractured, pitted, scored,
or worn excessively.

Carefully examine all the rigid brake pipes underneath the vehicle,
and the flexible hoses at the rear. Look for signs of excessive corrosion, chafing or insecurity of the pipes, and for signs of bulging under
pressure, chafing, splits, or deterioration of the flexible hoses.

Look for signs of hydraulic fluid leaks at the brake calipers or on
the brake backplates, indicating failed hydraulic seals in the components concerned.

Slowly spin each wheel, while your assistant depresses the footbrake then releases it. Ensure that each brake is operating, and that
the wheel is free to rotate when the pedal is released. It is not possible
to test brake efficiency without special equipment, but (traffic and local
conditions permitting) a road test can be carried out to check that the
vehicle pulls up in a straight line.

Examine the handbrake mechanism, and check for signs of
frayed or broken cables, excessive corrosion, or wear or insecurity of
the linkage **(see illustration)**. Have your assistant operate the handbrake, while you check that the mechanism works on each relevant
wheel, and releases fully without binding.

Fuel and exhaust systems

Inspect the fuel tank, fuel pipes, hoses and unions (including the
unions at the pump, filter and carburetor). All components must be secure, and free from leaks. The fuel filler cap must also be secure, and
of an appropriate type.

Examine the exhaust system over its entire length, checking for
any damaged, broken or missing mountings, security of the pipe retaining clamps, and condition of the system with regard to rust and
corrosion **(see illustration)**.

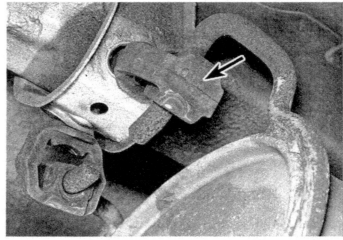

Check the condition of the exhaust system - typical example
shown - paying particular attention to the mountings

Wheels and tyres

Carefully examine each tyre in turn, on both the inner and outer walls, and over the whole of the tread area. Check for signs of cuts, tears, lumps, bulges, separation of the tread, and exposure of the ply or cord due to wear or other damage. Check also that the tyre bead is correctly seated on the wheel rim, and that the tyre valve is sound and properly seated. Spin the wheel, and check that it is not excessively distorted or damaged, particularly at the bead rim.

Check that the tyres are of the correct size for the vehicle, and that they are of the same size and type on each axle. (Having a "space saver" spare tyre in use is not acceptable.) The tyres should also be inflated to the specified pressures (see Chapter 10 Specifications).

Using a suitable gauge, check the tyre tread depth. The current legal requirement states that the tread pattern must be visible over the whole tread area, and must be of a minimum depth of 1.6 mm over at least three-quarters of the tread width. It is acceptable for some wear of the inside or outside edges of the tyre to be apparent, but this wear must be in one even circumferential band, and the tread must be visible. Any excessive wear of this nature may indicate incorrect front wheel alignment, which should be checked before the tyre becomes excessively worn. See the appropriate Chapters for further information on tyre wear patterns and front wheel alignment.

Body corrosion

Check the condition of the entire vehicle structure for signs of corrosion in any load-bearing areas. For the purpose of the MOT test, all chassis box sections, side sills, crossmembers, pillars, suspension, steering, braking system and seat belt mountings and anchorages, should all be considered as load-bearing areas. As a general guide, any corrosion which has seriously reduced the metal thickness of a load-bearing area to weaken it, is likely to cause the vehicle to fail. Should corrosion of this nature be encountered, professional repairs are likely to be needed.

Body damage or corrosion which causes sharp or otherwise dangerous edges to be exposed will also cause the vehicle to fail.

Exhaust emission checks

Have the engine at normal operating temperature, and make sure that the preliminary conditions for checking idle speed and mixture (ignition system in good order, air cleaner element in good condition, etc) have been met.

Before any measurements are carried out, raise the engine speed to around 2500 rpm, and hold it at this speed for 20 seconds. Allow the engine speed to return to idle, and watch for smoke emissions from the exhaust tailpipe. If the idle speed is obviously much too high, or if dense blue or clearly-visible black smoke comes from the tailpipe for more than 5 seconds, the vehicle will fail. As a rule of thumb, blue smoke signifies oil being burnt (worn valve stem oil seals, valve guides, piston rings or bores) while black smoke signifies unburnt fuel (dirty air cleaner element, mixture extremely rich, or other carburetor or fuel injection system fault).

If idle speed and smoke emission are satisfactory, an exhaust gas analyser capable of measuring carbon monoxide (CO) and hydrocarbons (HC) is now needed. The following paragraphs assume that such an instrument can be hired or borrowed - it is unlikely to be economic for the home mechanic to buy one. Alternatively, a local garage may agree to perform the check for a small fee.

CO emissions (mixture)

Current MOT regulations specify a maximum CO level at idle of 4.5% for vehicles first used after August 1983. The CO level specified by the vehicle maker is well inside this limit.

If the CO level cannot be reduced far enough to pass the test (and assuming that the fuel and ignition systems are otherwise in good condition) it is probable that the carburetor is badly worn, or that there is some problem in the fuel injection system. On carburetors with an automatic choke, it may be that the choke is not releasing as it should.

It is possible for the CO level to be within the specified maximum for MOT purposes, but well above the maximum specified by the manufacturer. The tester is entitled to draw attention to this, but it is not in itself a reason for failing the vehicle.

HC emissions

With the CO emissions within limits, HC emissions must be no more than 1200 ppm (parts per million). If the vehicle fails this test at idle, it can be re-tested at around 2000 rpm; if the HC level is then 1200 ppm or less, this counts as a pass.

Excessive HC emissions can be caused by oil being burnt, but they are more likely to be due to unburnt fuel. Possible reasons include:

(a) Spark plugs in poor condition or incorrectly-gapped.
(b) Ignition timing incorrect.
(c) Valve clearances incorrect.
(d) Engine compression low.

Note that excessive HC levels in the exhaust gas can cause premature failure of the catalytic converter (when fitted).

UK Specifications

Note: *The following general specifications are applicable to UK models, and supersede the relevant information appearing in the main Chapter Specifications. In cases where no information is given below, the main Chapter Specifications can be regarded as being applicable to UK models. Refer also to the "Notes for UK readers" Section at the start of this manual.*

Tune-up and routine maintenance
Clutch pedal height .... 183 to 188 mm (7.2 to 7.4 in)

Engine
Capacity
    Shogun 4-cylinder (4G54) .... 2555 cc
    Shogun 6-cylinder (6G72) .... 2972 cc
    L200 and 4WD Pick-ups (4G63-3) .... 1997 cc
Compression ratio/pressure
    Shogun 4-cylinder to 1989 (4G54) .... 8.3 : 1/10.3 bars
    Shogun 4-cylinder from 1989 (4G54 with hydraulic
    adjusters)... 8.4 : 1/8.2 bars
    Shogun 6-cylinder (6G72) .... 8.9 : 1/8.4 bars
    L200 and 4WD Pick-ups (4G63-3) .... 8.6 : 1/9.6 bars
Valve clearances (hot)
    4-cylinder engines (except 4G54 with hydraulic adjusters)
        Inlet .... 0.15 mm (0.006 in)
        Exhaust .... 0.25 mm (0.010 in)
Firing order (for cylinder numbering, see Chapter 2)
    4-cylinder 1-3-4-2
    6-cylinder 1-2-3-4-5-6

Cooling system
Thermostat opening temperature (all engines)......................... 88 °C
Radiator cap pressure (all engines)... 0.76 to 1.04 bars (11 to 15 lbf/in2)

Fuel system
Idle speed
    Shogun 4-cylinder to 1989 (4G54) .... 800 ± 50 rpm
    Shogun 4-cylinder from 1989 (4G54 with
    hydraulic adjusters) .... 700 ± 50 rpm
    Shogun 6-cylinder (6G72) .... 700 ± 100 rpm (for reference only)
    L200 and 4WD Pick-ups (4G63-3) .... 800 ± 50 rpm
CO% at idle speed (3000 rpm)
    Shogun 4-cylinder (4G54) .... 1.0 ± 0.5
    Shogun 6-cylinder (6G72) .... 1.5 ± 0.5
    L200 and 4WD Pick-ups (4G63-3) .... 1.0 ± 0.5
Carburettor
    Shogun 4-cylinder to 1989 (4G54) .... Mikuni 30-32 DIDTA-165
    Shogun 4-cylinder from 1989 (4G54 with
    hydraulic adjusters) .... Mikuni 32-35 DIDTA-389
    L200 and 4WD Pick-ups (4G63-3) .... Aisan 3EZA.2V
Fuel injection system
    Shogun 6-cylinder (6G72) .... Mitsubishi ECI.AC54-102
Fuel pump pressure
    Shogun 6-cylinder (6G72) .... 3.3 to 3.7 bars (48 to 54 lbf/in2)
    L200 and 4WD Pick-ups (4G63-3) .... 0.32 to 0.42 bars (4.6 to 6.1 lbf/in2)

Ignition system

Shogun 4-cylinder to 1989 (4G54)
  Type .... Contact breaker
  Ignition coil primary resistance .... 1.4 ohms
  Distributor type... Mitsubishi
  Points gap .... 0.45 to 0.55 mm (0.018 to 0.022 in)
  Dwell angle... 29° to 35°
  Distributor rotation .... Clockwise
  Ignition timing (without vacuum) .... 5° ± 2° BTDC @ idle
  Spark plug type... NGK BPR6ES or Champion RN9YCC
  Spark plug electrode gap... 0.7 to 0.8 mm (0.028 to 0.032 in)
Shogun 4-cylinder from 1989 (4G54 with hydraulic adjusters)
  Type .... Electronic
  Ignition coil primary resistance .... 1.08 to 1.32 ohms
  Ballast resistor resistance .... 1.22 to 1.48 ohms
  Distributor type... Mitsubishi
  Distributor rotation .... Clockwise
  Ignition timing (without vacuum) .... 5° ± 2° BTDC @ idle
  Spark plug type... NGK BPR5ES
  Spark plug electrode gap.. 0.7 to 0.8 mm (0.028 to 0.032 in)
Shogun 6-cylinder (6G72)
  Type .... Electronic
  Ignition coil primary resistance .... 0.72 to 0.88 ohms
  Distributor type... Mitsubishi
  Distributor rotation .... Clockwise
  Ignition timing (without vacuum) .... 5° ± 2° BTDC @ 700 ± 100 rpm
  Spark plug type... NGK BPR5ES-11 or Champion RN9YCC4
  Spark plug electrode gap.. 1.0 to 1.1 mm (0.039 to 0.043 in)
L200 and 4WD Pick-ups (4G63-3)
  Type .... Electronic
  Ignition coil primary resistance .... 1.2 ohms
  Distributor type... Mitsubishi
  Air gap .... 0.80 mm (0.032 in)
  Distributor rotation .... Clockwise
  Ignition timing (without vacuum) .... 13 ± 1° BTDC @ idle
  Spark plug type... NGK BPR6ES
  Spark plug electrode gap.. 0.7 to 0.8 mm (0.028 to 0.032 in)

Braking system

Minimum friction material thickness
  Shogun 4-cylinder (to 1987)... 1.0 mm (0.04 in) front and rear
  Shogun 4-cylinder (1988 on) .... 2.0 mm (0.08 in) front, 1.0 mm (0.04 in) rear
  Shogun 6-cylinder.. 2.0 mm (0.08 in) front and rear
  L200 and 4WD Pick-ups .... 2.0 mm (0.08 in) front, 1.0 mm (0.04 in) rear
Rear disc brakes
  Disc thickness (new)... 18.0 mm (0.71 in)
  Disc thickness (minimum) .... 16.0 mm (0.63 in)

Tyres

Size
  Shogun.. 215 x 15 or 205 x 16
  L200 and 4WD Pick-ups .... 185 x 14 or 205 x 16
Pressure
  185 x 14 (2WD)... 1.8 bars/26 lbf/in2 (front), 2.2 bars/32 lbf/in2 (rear)
  205 x 16 (2WD)... 1.8 bars/26 lbf/in2 (front), 2.2 bars/32 lbf/in2 (rear)
  205 x 16 (4WD)... 2.1 bars/31 lbf/in2 (front), 2.4 bars/35 lbf/in2 (rear)
  215 x 15 (2WD)... 1.6 bars/23 lbf/in2 (front), 2.0 bars/29 lbf/in2 (rear)
  215 x 15 (4WD)... 1.8 bars/26 lbf/in2 (front), 1.8 bars/26 lbf/in2 (rear)

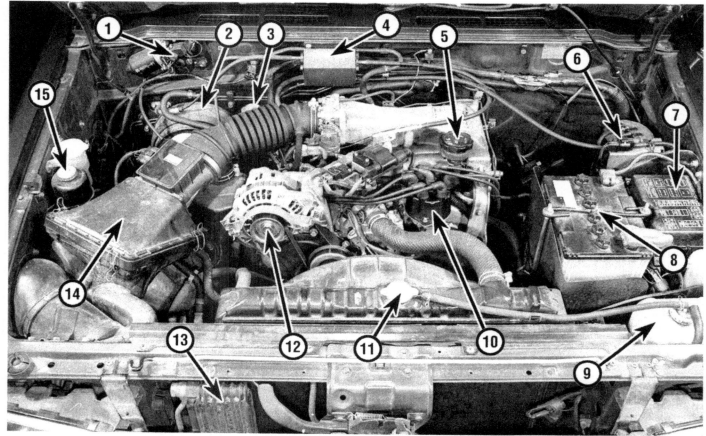

Engine compartment components (late 1991 GLS model with 3.0 litre V6 engine)

1   Wiper motor
2   Brake servo unit (brake fluid reservoir hidden behind hose)
3   Clutch fluid reservoir
4   Cruise control unit
5   Engine oil filler cap
6   Evaporative emissions system charcoal canister
7   Fusebox
8   Battery
9   Coolant reservoir
10 Distributor cap
11 Radiator filler cap
12 Alternator
13 Engine oil cooler
14 Air cleaner assembly
15 Power steering fluid reservoir

Front underside components (late 1991 GLS model with 3.0 litre V6 engine)

1	Manual transmission	7	Cooling fan
2	Exhaust pipe	8	Front axle differential check/fill plug
3	Front suspension crossmember	9	Front axle differential drain plug
4	Lower control arm	10	Torsion bar
5	Driveaxle	11	Front driveshaft
6	Steering relay rod	12	Transfer box

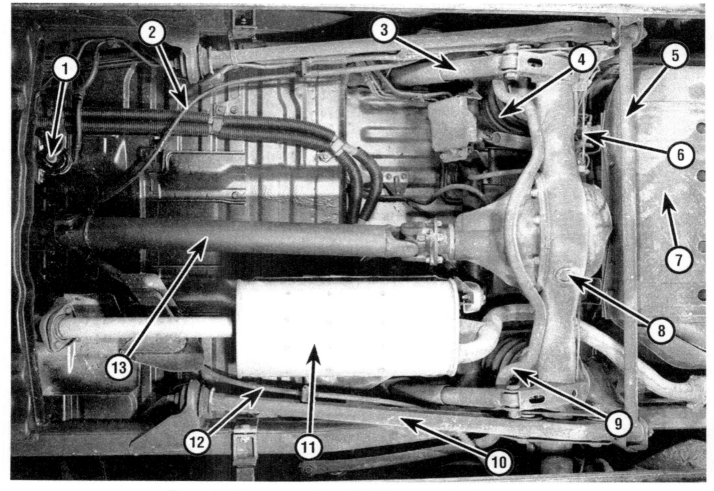

Rear underside components (late 1991 GLS model with 3.0 litre V6 engine)

1	Fuel filter	8	Rear axle differential drain plug
2	Handbrake cable (left-hand side)	9	Rear stabiliser bar
3	Shock absorber	10	Rear suspension trailing arm
4	Coil spring	11	Muffler
5	Rear suspension lateral rod	12	Handbrake cable (right-hand side)
6	Brake proportioning valve	13	Rear driveshaft
7	Fuel tank		

Chapter 1   Tune-up and routine maintenance

Contents

Specifications

Recommended lubricants and fluids*

Engine oil	
Type	API SG
Viscosity	See accompanying chart
Capacity (with new oil filter)	
2.0L four-cylinder engine	4.5 qts
2.4L four-cylinder engine	5.0 qts
2.6L four-cylinder engine	6.0 qts
3.0L V6 engine	
All Monteros and 1990 and earlier pick-ups	6.0 qts
1991 and later pick-ups	5.0 qts
Automatic transmission fluid	
Type	Dexron II or Mercon Automatic Transmission Fluid (ATF)
Capacity (approximate)**	
1983 through 1986 models	4.0 qts
1987 through 1989 models	5.0 qts
1990 and later models	
Pick-up	2.0 qts
Montero	5.3 qts

*All capacities approximate. Add as necessary to bring to appropriate level
**When refilling with automatic transmission fluid after overhaul or removing the pan, add fluid a little at a time, checking the fluid level after each addition. Do not drive the vehicle until you're certain the fluid level is correct. Normally, much more fluid is required after an overhaul than after a fluid change, since the torque converter is drained during an overhaul, but not during a normal fluid change.

Recommended lubricants and fluids (continued)

Manual transmission lubricant
    Type . . . . SAE 80/90W GL-5 gear lubricant
    Capacity (approximate) . . . . 2.6 qts
Differential lubricant
    Type . . . . SAE 80/90W GL-5 gear lubricant
    Capacity (approximate) . . . . 2.75 qts
Transfer case lubricant
    Type . . . . SAE 80/90W GL-5 gear lubricant
    Capacity (approximate) . . . . 2.5 qts
Power steering fluid type . . . . Dexron II or Mercon
Brake fluid type . . . . DOT 3 brake fluid
Clutch fluid type . . . . DOT 3 brake fluid
Coolant
    Type . . . . 50/50 mixture of ethylene glycol-based antifreeze and water
    Capacity (approximate)
        1986 and earlier models . . . . 9.0 qts
        1987 through 1989 models . . . . 8.0 qts
        1990 and later, except 1991 and later 4WD models . . . . 6.4 qts
        1991 and later 4WD models . . . . 9.0 qts
Chassis grease . . . . NLGI no. 2 chassis grease
Hood and door hinges . . . . Engine oil

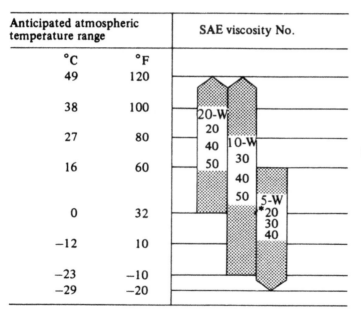

ENGINE OIL VISCOSITY

For best fuel economy and cold starting, select the lowest SAE viscosity grade oil for the expected temperature range

* SAE 5W-20 not recommended for sustained high speed vehicle operation.

Tune-up informatiormation

Firing order
    Four-cylinder engines 1-3-4-2
    V6 engine 1-2-3-4-5-6
Cylinder numbers/locations . . . . See Chapter 2
Spark plug type and gap*
    Type
        2.0L four-cylinder engine . . . . NGK BPR5ES-11, BP5ES-11
        2.4L four-cylinder engine . . . . NGK BPR6ES-11, BP6ES-11
        2.6L four-cylinder engine . . . . NGK BPR5ES-11, BP5ES-11
        3.0L engine . . . . NGK BPR5ES-11, BP5ES-11
    Gap
        US . . . . 0.39 to 0.43 inch
        Canada . . . . 0.28 to 0.31 inch

Tune-up informatiormation (continued)

Ignition timing*
2.0L and 2.4L four-cylinder engines	3-degrees to 7-degrees BTDC
2.6L four-cylinder engine	
1989 and earlier	3-degrees to 7-degrees BTDC
1990 and later	6-degrees to 10-degrees BTDC
3.0L V6 engine	3-degrees to 7-degrees BTDC

*Refer to the Vehicle Emission Control Information label in the engine compartment: use the information there if it differs from that listed here

Valve clearances (engine at normal operating temperature)

Intake valves	0.006 inch
Exhaust valves	0.010 inch
Jet valve	
1983 and earlier	0.006 inch
984 and later	0.010 inch

Note: When assembling valve train components after they've been removed, use the following cold clearance settings for initial start-up, then adjust the valves again after the engine warms up to normal operating temperature

Intake valves (engine cold)	0.004 inch
Exhaust and Jet valves (engine cold)	0.007 inch

Clutch

Pedal freeplay	
Cable-operated clutch	3/4 inch
Hydraulic clutch	5/8 inch
Pedal height	
2.4L four-cylinder and all V6 engines	6 1/2 inches
2.6L four-cylinder engine	7 inches
Cable freeplay (measured at firewall)	15/64 inch

Brake

Parking brake adjustment	
Umbrella-type handle	16 to 17 clicks
Lever-type handle	4 to 6 clicks
Pedal height	
Trucks	6 1/2 to 7 inches
Monteros	7 1/2 to 7 3/4 inches
Pedal freeplay	
1986 and earlier	13/32 to 9/16 inch
1987 and later	1/8 to 5/16 inch
Brake shoe lining wear limit	3/64 inch
Brake pad lining wear limit	3/32 inch

Torque specifications

	Ft-lbs (unless otherwise indicated)
Spark plugs	10
Engine oil drain plug	96 to 120 in-lbs
Valve cover bolts	96 to 120 in-lbs
Manual transmission check/fill and drain plugs	22 to 35
Differential check/fill and drain plugs . . . . , ...	29 to 43
Transfer case check/fill and drain plugs	14 to 29
Oxygen sensor	30 to 37
Wheel lug nuts	80 to 95

---

1   Introduction

This Chapter is designed to help the home mechanic maintain the Mitsubishi mini-pickups and Montero with the goals of maximum performance, economy, safety and reliability in mind.

Included is a master maintenance schedule (page 1-7), followed by procedures dealing specifically with every item on the schedule. Visual checks, adjustments, component replacement and other helpful items are included. Refer to the accompanying illustrations of the engine compartment and the under side of the vehicle for the locations of various components.

Servicing your vehicle in accordance with the planned mileage/time maintenance schedule and the step-by-step procedures should result in maximum reliability and extend the life of your vehicle. Keep in mind that it's a comprehensive plan – maintaining some items but not others at the specified intervals will not produce the same results.

As you perform routine maintenance procedures, you'll find that many can, and should, be grouped together because of the nature of the procedures or because of the proximity of two otherwise unrelated components or systems.

For example, if the vehicle is raised for chassis lubrication, you should inspect the exhaust, suspension, steering and fuel systems while you're under the vehicle. When you're rotating the tires, it makes good sense to check the brakes since the wheels are already removed. Finally, let's suppose you have to borrow or rent a torque wrench. Even if you only need it to tighten the spark plugs, you might as well check the torque of as many critical fasteners as time allows.

The first step in this maintenance program is to prepare yourself before the actual work begins. Read through all the procedures you're planning to do, then gather up all the parts and tools needed. If it looks like you might run into problems during a particular job, seek advice from a mechanic or experienced do-it-yourselfer.

Typical engine compartment components (2.6L engine shown)

1   Battery
2   Air cleaner housing assembly
3   Brake fluid reservoir
4   Clutch fluid reservoir

5   Upper radiator hose
6   Engine oil filler cap
7   Radiator cap
8   Engine oil filter
9   Engine oil dipstick

10   Evaporative emissions system
      charcoal canister
11   Coolant reservoir
12   Windshield washer fluid reservoir

Typical engine compartment underside components (4WD model shown)

1   Engine drivebelt
2   Radiator
3   Differential check/fill plug (4WD
    models only)
4   Differential drain plug (4WD
    models only)
5   Brake disc
6   Driveshaft (4WD models only)
7   Manual transmission drain plug
8   Exhaust pipe
9   Driveaxle boot (4WD models only)

Typical rear underside components

1   Fuel tank
2   Shock absorber
3   Drum brake assembly
4   Muffler
5   Differential drain plug
6   Driveshaft universal joint

Mitsubishi Pick-ups and Montero
Maintenance schedule

The following maintenance intervals are based on the assumption that the vehicle owner will be doing the maintenance or service work, as opposed to having a dealer service department do the work. Although the time/mileage intervals are loosely based on factory recommendations, most have been shortened to ensure, for example, that such items as lubricants and fluids are checked/changed at intervals that promote maximum engine/driveline service life. Also, subject to the preference of the individual owner interested in keeping his or her vehicle in peak condition at all times, and with the vehicle's ultimate resale in mind, many of the maintenance procedures may be performed more often than recommended in the following schedule. We encourage such owner initiative.

When the vehicle is new it should be serviced initially by a factory authorized dealer service department to protect the factory warranty. In many cases the initial maintenance check is done at no cost to the owner (check with your dealer service department for more information).

Every 250 miles or weekly, whichever comes first

Check the engine oil level (Section 4)
Check the engine coolant level (Section 4)
Check the windshield washer fluid level (Section 4)
Check the brake and clutch fluid levels (Section 4)
Check the automatic transmission fluid level (Section 5)
Check the power steering fluid level (Section 6)
Check the tires and tire pressures (Section 7)

Every 5000 miles or 4 months, whichever comes first

All items listed above plus:
Check and service the battery (Section 8)
Check the cooling system (Section 9)
Inspect and replace if necessary the windshield wiper blades (Section 10)
Inspect and replace if necessary all underhood hoses (Section 11)
Check and lubricate the accelerator linkage (Section 12)
Change the engine oil and filter (Section 13)*
Rotate the tires (Section 14)

Every 15,000 miles or 12 months, whichever comes first

All items listed above plus:
Adjust the valves (four-cylinder models) (Section 15)
Lubricate the chassis components (Section 16)
Inspect the suspension and steering components (Section 17)*
Inspect the exhaust system (Section 18)*
Check and adjust if necessary, the clutch pedal freeplay (Section 19)
Check the manual transmission lubricant (Section 20)*
Check the transfer case lubricant level (4WD models) (Section 21)*
Check the differential lubricant level (Section 22)*
Check the brakes (Section 23)*
Inspect the fuel system (Section 24)
Check the operation of the thermostatic air cleaner system (Section 25)
Check the engine drivebelts (Section 26)
Check the seat belts (Section 27)
Check and adjust, if necessary, the idle speed – 2.6L engines (see Chapter 4)

Every 30,000 miles or 24 months, whichever comes first

Check the carburetor/fuel injection throttle body nut/bolt torque (Section 28)
Replace the air filter (Section 29)
Replace the fuel filter (Section 30)
Check and adjust, if necessary, the brake pedal height (Section 31)
Check the distributor advance mechanism (Chapter 6)
Inspect the evaporative emissions system (Section 32)

Check the operation of the carburetor choke (Section 33)
Check and adjust if necessary, the idle speed (carbureted models except 2.6L engine) (see Chapter 4)
Change the manual transmission lubricant (Section 36)
Change the transfer case lubricant (4WD models) (Section 35)**
Change the differential lubricant (Section 37)**
Change the automatic transmission fluid and filter (Section 38)**
Check, repack and adjust the front wheel bearings (Section 39)**
Service the cooling system (drain, flush and refill) (Section 40)
Inspect the Positive Crankcase Ventilation (PCV) system (Section 41)
Replace the spark plugs (Section 42)
Inspect the spark plug wires, distributor cap and rotor (Section 43)
Check and adjust, if necessary, the ignition timing (Section 44)
Check the Exhaust Gas Recirculation (EGR) system (Section 45)
Replace the Solenoid valve air filter (1985 through 1989 models) (Section 46)
Replace the drive belt for the water pump and alternator (see Section 26)

Every 50,000 miles or 24 months, whichever comes first

Replace the oxygen sensor (1988 and earlier models so equipped) (Section 47)
Replace the EGR Valve (2.6L models, except California) (see Chapter 6)

Every 60,000 miles or 24 months, whichever comes first

Replace the timing belt (V6 and timing belt-equipped four-cylinder engines) (Chapter 2)

Every 80,000 miles or 24 months

Replace the oxygen sensor (1989 and later models) (Section 47)

* This item is affected by "severe" operating conditions as described below. If your vehicle is operated under severe conditions, perform all maintenance indicated with an asterisk (*) at 3000 mile/3 month intervals.

Severe conditions are indicated if you mainly operate your vehicle under one or more of the following:
In dusty areas
Off road use
Towing a trailer
Idling for extended periods and/or low speed operation
When outside temperatures remain below freezing and most trips are less than 4 miles

** If operated under one or more of the following conditions, perform the indicated maintenance item every 15,000 miles:
In heavy city traffic where the outside temperature regularly reaches 90-degrees F (32-degrees C) or higher
In hilly or mountainous terrain
Frequent trailer pulling
Frequent off road use

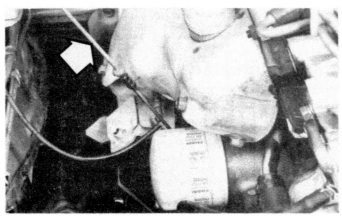

4.2   The engine oil dipstick (arrow) is located on the right (passenger's) side of the engine compartment

3   Tune-up general information

The term tune-up is used in this manual to represent a combination of individual operations rather than one specific procedure.

If, from the time the vehicle is new, the routine maintenance schedule is followed closely and frequent checks are made of fluid levels and high wear items, as suggested throughout this manual, the engine will be kept in relatively good running condition and the need for additional work will be minimized.

More likely than not, however, there will be times when the engine is running poorly due to lack of regular maintenance. This is even more likely if a used vehicle, which has not received regular and frequent maintenance checks, is purchased. In such cases, an engine tune-up will be needed outside of the regular routine maintenance intervals.

The first step in any tune-up or diagnostic procedure to help correct a poor running engine is a cylinder compression check. A compression check (see Chapter 2 Part D) will help determine the condition of internal engine components and should be used as a guide for tune-up and repair procedures. If, for instance, a compression check indicates serious internal engine wear, a conventional tune-up will not improve the performance of the engine and would be a waste of time and money. Because of its importance, the compression check should be done by someone with the right equipment and the knowledge to use it properly.

The following procedures are those most often needed to bring a generally poor running engine back into a proper state of tune.

Minor tune-up

Check all engine related fluids
Clean and check the battery (Section 8)
Check and adjust the drivebelts (Section 26)
Replace the spark plugs (Section 42)
Check the cylinder compression (Chapter 2)
Inspect the distributor cap and rotor (Section 43)
Inspect the spark plug and coil wires (Section 43)
Replace the air filter (Section 29)
Check and adjust the idle speed (Section 34)
Check and adjust the ignition timing (Section 44)
Replace the fuel filter (Section 30)
Check the PCV system (Section 41)
Adjust the valve clearances (Section 15)
Check and service the cooling system (Section 40)

Major tune-up

All items listed under Minor tune-up plus . . .
Check the EGR system (Section 45 and Chapter 6)
Check the charging system (Chapter 5)
Check the ignition system (Chapter 5)
Check the fuel system (Section 24 and Chapter 4)

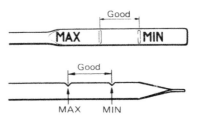

4.4   The oil level should be between the two marks or notches, if it's below the MIN line or lower notch, add enough oil to bring the level into the operating range

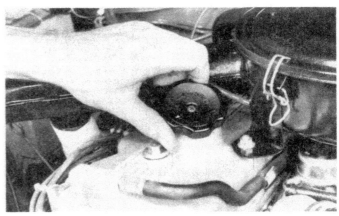

4.6   Unscrew the oil filler cap to remove it – make sure the area around the opening is clean before unscrewing the cap; this will prevent dirt from entering the engine

4.8   The coolant reservoir is located in the front corner of the engine compartment – the level must be maintained between the upper and lower marks

Replace the spark plugs (Section 42)
Replace the spark plug wires, distributor cap and rotor (Section 43)

4   Fluid level checks

Note: *The following are fluid level checks to be done on a 250 mile or weekly basis. Additional fluid level checks can be found in specific maintenance procedures which follow. Regardless of how often the fluid levels are checked, watch for puddles under the vehicle – if leaks are noted, make repairs immediately.*

1   Fluids are an essential part of the lubrication, cooling, brake, clutch and windshield washer systems. Because the fluids gradually become depleted and/or contaminated during normal operation of the vehicle, they

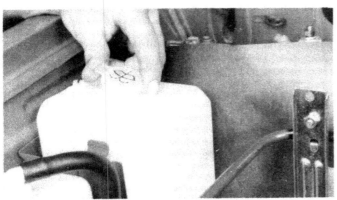

4.14a   The reservoir for the windshield washer fluid is located on the right side of the engine compartment and fluid is added after flipping the top up – how often you use the washers will dictate how often you need to check the reservoir

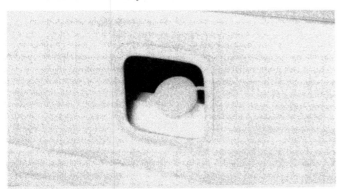

4.14c   The rear washer fluid reservoir is located in the rear cargo area, behind a cover

must be periodically replenished. See *Recommended lubricants and fluids* at the beginning of this Chapter before adding fluid to any of the following components. **Note:** *The vehicle must be on level ground when fluid levels are checked.*

Engine oil

Refer to illustrations 4.2, 4.4 and 4.6

2   The engine oil level is checked with a dipstick that extends through a tube and into the oil pan at the bottom of the engine **(see illustration)**.
3   The oil level should be checked before the vehicle has been driven, or about 15 minutes after the engine has been shut off. If the oil is checked immediately after driving the vehicle, some of the oil will remain in the upper engine components, resulting in an inaccurate reading on the dipstick.
4   Pull the dipstick from the tube and wipe all the oil from the end with a clean rag or paper towel. Insert the clean dipstick all the way back into the tube, then pull it out again. Note the oil at the end of the dipstick. Add oil as necessary to keep the level between the MAX and MIN marks or within the hatched area on the dipstick **(see illustration)**.
5   Don't overfill the engine by adding too much oil since this may result in oil fouled spark plugs, oil leaks or oil seal failures.
6   Oil is added to the engine after removing a threaded cap from the valve cover **(see illustration)**. An oil can spout or funnel may help to reduce spills.
7   Checking the oil level is an important preventive maintenance step. A consistently low oil level indicates oil leakage through damaged seals, defective gaskets or past worn rings or valve guides. If the oil looks milky in color or has water droplets in it, the cylinder head gasket(s) may be blown or the head(s) or block may be cracked. The engine should be checked immediately. The condition of the oil should also be checked. Whenever you check the oil level, slide your thumb and index finger up the dipstick before wiping off the oil. If you see small dirt or metal particles clinging to the dipstick, the oil should be changed (Section 13).

4.14b   On headlight washer-equipped models, flip up the cap to add fluid

Engine coolant

Refer to illustration 4.8

Warning: *Don't allow antifreeze to come in contact with your skin or painted surfaces of the vehicle. Flush contaminated areas immediately with plenty of water. Don't store new coolant or leave old coolant lying around where it's accessible to children or pets – they're attracted by its sweet taste. Ingestion of even a small amount of coolant can be fatal! Wipe up garage floor and drip pan coolant spills immediately. Keep antifreeze containers covered and repair leaks in your cooling system immediately.*

8   All vehicles covered by this manual are equipped with a pressurized coolant recovery system. A white plastic coolant reservoir located in the engine compartment is connected by a hose to the radiator filler neck **(see illustration)**. If the engine overheats, coolant escapes through a valve in the radiator cap and travels through the hose into the reservoir. As the engine cools, the coolant is automatically drawn back into the cooling system to maintain the correct level.
9   The coolant level in the reservoir should be checked regularly. **Warning:** *Do not remove the radiator cap to check the coolant level when the engine is warm. The level in the reservoir varies with the temperature of the engine. When the engine is cold, the coolant level should be at or slightly above the lower mark on the reservoir. Once the engine has warmed up, the level should be at or near the upper mark. If it isn't, allow the engine to cool, then remove the cap from the reservoir and add a 50/50 mixture of ethylene glycol-based antifreeze and water.*
10   Drive the vehicle and recheck the coolant level. If only a small amount of coolant is required to bring the system up to the proper level, water can be used. However, repeated additions of water will dilute the antifreeze and water solution. In order to maintain the proper ratio of antifreeze and water, always top up the coolant level with the correct mixture. An empty plastic milk jug or bleach bottle makes an excellent container for mixing coolant. Do not use rust inhibitors or additives.
11   If the coolant level drops consistently, there may be a leak in the system. Inspect the radiator, hoses, filler cap, drain plugs and water pump (see Section 9). If no leaks are noted, have the radiator cap pressure tested by a service station.
12   If you have to remove the radiator cap, wait until the engine has cooled, then wrap a thick cloth around the cap and turn it to the first stop. If coolant or steam escapes, let the engine cool down longer, then remove the cap.
13   Check the condition of the coolant as well. It should be relatively clear. If it's brown or rust colored, the system should be drained, flushed and refilled. Even if the coolant appears to be normal, the corrosion inhibitors wear out, so it must be replaced at the specified intervals.

Windshield, headlight and rear washer fluid

Refer to illustrations 4.14a, 4.14b and 4.14c

14   Fluid for the windshield washer system is stored in a plastic reservoir located on the passenger's side of the engine compartment **(see illustration)**. If necessary, refer to the underhood component illustration(s) at the beginning of this Chapter to locate the reservoir. Some models are equipped with headlight washers. The fluid reservoir is located on the left side of the engine compartment and should be kept filled the upper mark **(see illustration)**. On vehicles with rear window washers, the fluid reservoir is located under a cover on the right side of the cargo area **(see illustration)**.

4.19   Keep the brake and clutch fluid levels near the upper or MAX marks on the reservoir – fluid can be added after unscrewing the cap

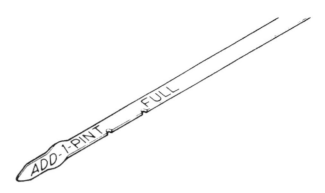

5.6   The automatic transmission fluid level must be between the two notches in the dipstick with the fluid at normal operating temperature

15   In milder climates, plain water can be used in the reservoir, but it should be kept no more than 2/3 full to allow for expansion if the water freezes. In colder climates, use windshield washer system antifreeze, available at any auto parts store, to lower the freezing point of the fluid. Mix the antifreeze with water in accordance with the manufacturer's directions on the container. **Caution:** *Don't use cooling system antifreeze – it will damage the vehicle's paint.*

16   To help prevent icing in cold weather, warm the windshield with the defroster before using the washer.

Battery electrolyte

17   To check the electrolyte level in the battery on conventional batteries, remove all of the cell caps. If the level is low, add distilled water until it's above the plates. Most aftermarket replacement batteries have a split-ring indicator in each cell to help you judge when enough water has been added – don't overfill the cells!

Brake and clutch fluid

Refer to illustration 4.19

18   The brake master cylinder is mounted on the front of the power booster unit in the engine compartment. The clutch cylinder used on some models with manual transmissions is mounted adjacent to it on the firewall.

19   The fluid inside is readily visible. The level should be between the upper and lower marks on the reservoirs **(see illustration)**. If a low level is indicated, be sure to wipe the top of the reservoir cover with a clean rag to prevent contamination of the brake and/or clutch system before removing the cover.

20   When adding fluid, pour it carefully into the reservoir to avoid spilling it onto surrounding painted surfaces. Be sure the specified fluid is used, since mixing different types of brake fluid can cause damage to the system. See *Recommended lubricants and fluids* at the front of this Chapter or your owner's manual. **Warning:** *Brake fluid can harm your eyes and damage painted surfaces, so be very careful when handling or pouring it. Don't use brake fluid that's been standing open or is more than one year old. Brake fluid absorbs moisture from the air. Excess moisture can cause a dangerous loss of brake efficiency.*

21   At this time the fluid and master cylinder can be inspected for contamination. The system should be drained and refilled if deposits, dirt particles or water droplets are seen in the fluid.

22   After filling the reservoir to the proper level, make sure the cover is on tight to prevent fluid leakage.

23   The brake fluid level in the master cylinder will drop slightly as the pads and the brake shoes at each wheel wear down during normal operation. If the master cylinder requires repeated additions to keep it at the proper level, it's an indication of leakage in the brake system, which should be corrected immediately. Check all brake lines and connections (see Section 23 for more information).

24   If, upon checking the master cylinder fluid level, you discover one or both reservoirs empty or nearly empty, the brake system should be bled (Chapter 9).

---

5   Automatic transmission fluid level check

Refer to illustration 5.6

1   The automatic transmission fluid level should be carefully maintained. Low fluid level can lead to slipping or loss of drive, while overfilling can cause foaming and loss of fluid.

2   With the parking brake set, start the engine, then move the shift lever through all the gear ranges, ending in Neutral. The fluid level must be checked with the vehicle level and the engine running at idle. **Note:** *Incorrect fluid level readings will result if the vehicle has just been driven at high speeds for an extended period, in hot weather in city traffic, or if it has been pulling a trailer. If any of these conditions apply, wait until the fluid has cooled (about 30 minutes).*

3   With the transmission at normal operating temperature, remove the dipstick from the filler tube. The dipstick is located at the rear of the engine compartment on the passenger's side.

4   Wipe the fluid from the dipstick with a clean rag and push it back into the filler tube until the cap seats.

5   Pull the dipstick out again and note the fluid level.

6   The level should be between the two notches **(see illustration)**.

7   If additional fluid is required, add it directly into the tube using a funnel. It takes about one pint to raise the level from the lower notch to the FULL notch with a hot transmission, so add the fluid a little at a time and keep checking the level until it's correct.

8   The condition of the fluid should also be checked along with the level. If the fluid at the end of the dipstick is a dark reddish-brown color, or if it smells burned, it should be changed. If you are in doubt about the condition of the fluid, purchase some new fluid and compare the two for color and smell.

---

6   Power steering fluid level check

Refer to illustration 6.5

1   Unlike manual steering, the power steering system relies on fluid which may, over a period of time, require replenishing.

2   The fluid reservoir for the power steering pump is located remotely from the pump on the passenger's side of the engine compartment.

3   For the check, the front wheels should be pointed straight ahead and the engine should be off. The power steering fluid should be checked after the vehicle has been driven and the fluid is at normal operating temperature.

4   Clean the cap and the area around the to prevent contamination of the fluid.

6.5   Unscrew the cap on the power steering fluid reservoir and check the fluid level on the dipstick

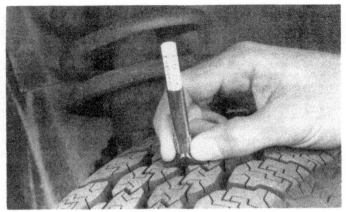

7.2   Use a tire tread depth indicator to monitor tire wear – they are available at auto parts stores and service stations and cost very little

Condition	Probable cause	Corrective action	Condition	Probable cause	Corrective action
Shoulder wear	• Underinflation (both sides wear) • Incorrect wheel camber (one side wear) • Hard cornering • Lack of rotation	• Measure and adjust pressure. • Repair or replace axle and suspension parts. • Reduce speed. • Rotate tires.	Feathered edge **Toe wear**	• Incorrect toe	• Adjust toe-in.
Center wear	• Overinflation • Lack of rotation	• Measure and adjust pressure. • Rotate tires.	**Uneven wear**	• Incorrect camber or caster • Malfunctioning suspension • Unbalanced wheel • Out-of-round brake drum • Lack of rotation	• Repair or replace axle and suspension parts. • Repair or replace suspension parts. • Balance or replace. • Turn or replace. • Rotate tires.

7.3   This chart will help you determine the condition of the tires, the probable cause(s) of abnormal wear and the corrective action necessary

5   Twist off the reservoir cap which has a built-in dipstick attached to it (**see illustration**). Wipe off the dipstick with a clean rag, reinstall it and remove it to get an accurate reading. The fluid level should be between the MIN and MAX marks on the dipstick.

6   If additional fluid is required, pour the specified type directly into the reservoir, using a funnel to prevent spills.

7   If the reservoir requires frequent fluid additions, all power steering hoses, hose connections and the power steering pump should be carefully checked for leaks.

7   Tire and tire pressure checks

Refer to illustrations 7.2, 7.3, 7.4a, 7.4b and 7.8

1   Periodic inspection of the tires may spare you the inconvenience of being stranded with a flat tire. It can also provide you with vital information regarding possible problems in the steering and suspension systems before major damage occurs.

2   The original tires on this vehicle are equipped with wear indicator bars that will appear when tread depth reaches a predetermined limit, usually 1/16-inch, but they don't appear until the tires are worn out. Tread wear can be monitored with a simple, inexpensive device known as a tread depth indicator (**see illustration**).

3   Note any abnormal tread wear (**see illustration**). Tread pattern irregularities such as cupping, flat spots and more wear on one side than the other are indications of front end alignment and/or balance problems. If any of these conditions are noted, take the vehicle to a tire shop or service station to correct the problem.

4   Look closely for cuts, punctures and embedded nails or tacks. Sometimes a tire will hold air pressure for a short time or leak down very slowly after a nail has embedded itself in the tread. If a slow leak persists, check the valve stem core to make sure it's tight (**see illustration**). Examine the tread for an object that may have embedded itself in the tire or for a "plug"

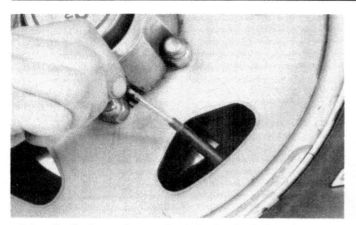

7.4a   If a tire loses air on a steady basis, check the valve core first to make sure it's snug (special inexpensive wrenches are commonly available at auto parts stores)

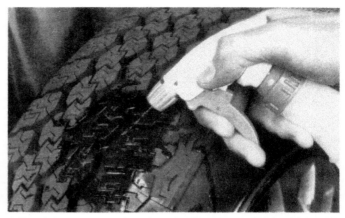

7.4b   If the valve core is tight, raise the corner of the vehicle with the low tire and spray a soapy water solution onto the tread as the tire is turned slowly – leaks will cause small bubbles to appear

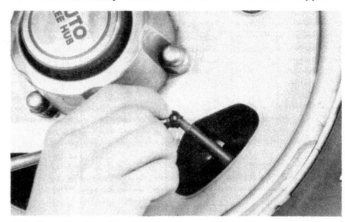

7.8   To extend the life of the tires, check the air pressure at least once a week with an accurate gauge (don't forget the spare!)

that may have begun to leak (radial tire punctures are repaired with a plug that's installed in a puncture). If a puncture is suspected, it can be easily verified by spraying a solution of soapy water onto the puncture area **(see illustration)**. The soapy solution will bubble if there's a leak. Unless the puncture is unusually large, a tire shop or service station can usually repair the tire.

5   Carefully inspect the inner sidewall of each tire for evidence of brake fluid leakage. If you see any, inspect the brakes immediately.

6   Correct air pressure adds miles to the lifespan of the tires, improves mileage and enhances overall ride quality. Tire pressure cannot be accurately estimated by looking at a tire, especially if it's a radial. A tire pressure gauge is essential. Keep an accurate gauge in the vehicle. The pressure gauges attached to the nozzles of air hoses at gas stations are often inaccurate.

7   Always check tire pressure when the tires are cold. Cold, in this case, means the vehicle has not been driven over a mile in the three hours preceding a tire pressure check. A pressure rise of four to eight pounds is not uncommon once the tires are warm.

8   Unscrew the valve cap protruding from the wheel or hubcap and push the gauge firmly onto the valve stem **(see illustration)**. Note the reading on the gauge and compare the figure to the recommended tire pressure shown on the placard on the glove compartment door. Be sure to reinstall the valve cap to keep dirt and moisture out of the valve stem mechanism. Check all four tires and, if necessary, add enough air to bring them up to the recommended pressure.

9   Don't forget to keep the spare tire inflated to the specified pressure (refer to your owner's manual or the tire sidewall).

---

8   Battery check, maintenance and charging

Refer to illustrations 8.1, 8.6, 8.7a, 8.7b and 8.7c

Warning: *Certain precautions must be followed when checking and servicing the battery. Hydrogen gas, which is highly flammable, is always present in the battery cells, so keep lighted tobacco and all other open flames and sparks away from the battery. The electrolyte inside the battery is actually dilute sulfuric acid, which will cause injury if splashed on your skin or in your eyes. It will also ruin clothes and painted surfaces. When removing the battery cables, always detach the negative cable first and hook it up last!*

Check and maintenance

1   Battery maintenance is an important procedure which will help ensure that you aren't stranded because of a dead battery. Several tools are required for this procedure **(see illustration)**.

2   When checking/servicing the battery, always turn the engine and all accessories off.

3   A sealed (sometimes called maintenance-free), battery is standard equipment on some vehicles. The cell caps cannot be removed, no electrolyte checks are required and water cannot be added to the cells. However, if a standard aftermarket battery has been installed, the following maintenance procedure can be used.

4   Remove the caps and check the electrolyte level in each of the battery cells (see Section 4). It must be above the plates. There's usually a split-ring indicator in each cell to indicate the correct level. If the level is low, add distilled water only, then reinstall the cell caps. **Caution:** *Overfilling the cells may cause electrolyte to spill over during periods of heavy charging, causing corrosion and damage to nearby components.*

5   The external condition of the battery should be checked periodically. Look for damage such as a cracked case.

6   Check the tightness of the battery cable bolts **(see illustration)** to ensure good electrical connections. Inspect the entire length of each cable, looking for cracked or abraded insulation and frayed conductors.

7   If corrosion (visible as white, fluffy deposits) **(see illustration)** is evident, remove the cables from the terminals, clean them with a battery brush and reinstall them **(see illustrations)**. Corrosion can be kept to a minimum by applying a layer of petroleum jelly or grease to the terminals.

8   Make sure the battery carrier is in good condition and the hold-down clamp is tight. If the battery is removed (see Chapter 5 for the removal and installation procedure), make sure that no parts remain in the bottom of the carrier when it's reinstalled. When reinstalling the hold-down clamp, don't overtighten the nuts.

9   Corrosion on the carrier, battery case and surrounding areas can be removed with a solution of water and baking soda. Apply the mixture with a small brush, let it work, then rinse it off with plenty of clean water.

10   Any metal parts of the vehicle damaged by corrosion should be coated with a zinc-based primer, then painted.

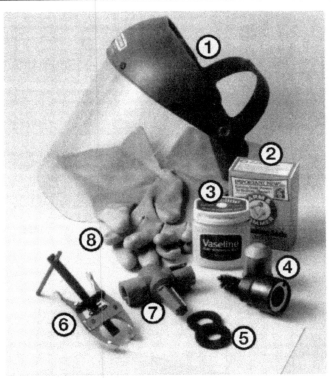

8.1   Tools and materials required for battery maintenance

1   *Face shield/safety goggles* – *When removing corrosion with a brush, the acidic particles can easily fly up into your eyes*
2   *Baking soda* – *A solution of baking soda and water can be used to neutralize corrosion*
3   *Petroleum jelly* – *A layer of this on the battery posts will help prevent corrosion*
4   *Battery post/cable cleaner* – *This wire brush cleaning tool will remove all traces of corrosion from the battery posts and cable clamps*
5   *Treated felt washers* – *Placing one of these on each post, directly under the cable clamps, will help prevent corrosion*
6   *Puller* – *Sometimes the cable clamps are very difficult to pull off the posts, even after the nut/bolt has been completely loosened. This tool pulls the clamp straight up and off the post without damage.*
7   *Battery post/cable cleaner* – *Here is another cleaning tool which is a slightly different version of number 4 above, but it does the same thing*
8   *Rubber gloves* – *Another safety item to consider when servicing the battery; remember that's acid inside the battery!*

11   Additional information on the battery and jump starting can be found in the front of this manual and in Chapter 5.

Charging

12   Remove all of the cell caps (if equipped) and cover the holes with a clean cloth to prevent spattering electrolyte. Disconnect the negative battery cable and hook the battery charger leads to the battery posts (positive to positive, negative to negative), then plug in the charger. Make sure it is set at 12 volts if it has a selector switch.
13   If you're using a charger with a rate higher than two amps, check the battery regularly during charging to make sure it doesn't overheat. If you're using a trickle charger, you can safely let the battery charge overnight after you've checked it regularly for the first couple of hours.
14   If the battery has removeable cell caps, measure the specific gravity with a hydrometer every hour during the last few hours of the charging cycle. Hydrometers are available inexpensively from auto parts stores – follow the instructions that come with the hydrometer. Consider the battery

8.6   Removing the cable from a battery post with a wrench – sometimes a special battery pliers is required for this procedure if corrosion has caused deterioration of the nut hex (always remove the ground cable first and hook it up last!)

8.7a   Battery terminal corrosion usually appears as light, fluffy powder

8.7b   When cleaning the cable clamps, all corrosion must be removed (the inside of the clamp is tapered to match the taper on the post, so don't remove too much material)

charged when there's no change in the specific gravity reading for two hours and the electrolyte in the cells is gassing (bubbling) freely. The specific gravity reading from each cell should be very close to the others. If not, the battery probably has a bad cell(s).
15   Some batteries with sealed tops have built-in hydrometers on the top that indicate the state of charge by the color displayed in the hydrometer window. Normally, a bright-colored hydrometer indicates a full charge and a dark hydrometer indicates the battery still needs charging. Check the battery manufacturer's instructions to be sure you know what the colors mean.
16   If the battery has a sealed top and no built-in hydrometer, you can hook up a digital voltmeter across the battery terminals to check the

8.7c   Regardless of the type of tool used on the battery posts, a clean, shiny surface should be the result

10.5   Depress the tab (arrow) and pull the blade assembly off the wiper arm

charge. A fully charged battery should read 12.6 volts or higher.

17   Further information on the battery and jump starting can be found in Chapter 5 and at the front of this manual.

9   Cooling system check

Refer to illustration 9.4

1   Many major engine failures can be attributed to a faulty cooling system. If the vehicle is equipped with an automatic transmission, the cooling system also cools the transmission fluid, prolonging transmission life.

2   The cooling system should be checked with the engine cold. Do this before the vehicle is driven for the day or after it has been shut off for at least three hours.

3   Remove the radiator cap by turning it counterclockwise until it reaches a stop. If you hear a hissing sound (indicating there's still pressure in the system), wait until it stops. Now press down on the cap with the palm of your hand and continue turning until it can be removed. Thoroughly clean the cap, inside and out, with clean water. Also clean the filler neck on the radiator. All traces of corrosion should be removed. The coolant inside the radiator should be relatively transparent. If it's rust colored, the system should be drained and refilled (Section 40). If the coolant level is not up to the top, add additional antifreeze/coolant mixture (see Section 4).

4   Carefully check the large upper and lower radiator hoses along with the smaller diameter heater hoses which run from the engine to the firewall. Inspect each hose along its entire length, replacing any hose that's cracked, swollen or deteriorated. Cracks may become more apparent if the hose is squeezed **(see illustration)**. Regardless of condition, it's a good idea to replace hoses with new ones every two years. Make sure that all hose connections are tight. A leak in the cooling system will usually show up as white or rust colored deposits on the areas adjoining the leak. If wire-type clamps are used at the ends of the hoses, it may be a good idea

ALWAYS CHECK hose for chafed or burned areas that may cause an untimely and costly failure.

SOFT hose indicates inside deterioration. This deterioration can contaminate the cooling system and cause particles to clog the radiator.

HARDENED hose can fail at any time. Tightening hose clamps will not seal the connection or stop leaks.

SWOLLEN hose or oil soaked ends indicate danger and possible failure from oil or grease contamination. Squeeze the hose to locate cracks and breaks that cause leaks.

9.4   Hoses, like drivebelts, have a habit of failing at the worst possible time – to prevent the inconvenience of a blown radiator or heater hose, inspect them carefully as shown here

to replace them with more secure screw-type clamps.

5   Use compressed air or a soft brush to remove bugs, leaves, etc. from the front of the radiator or air conditioning condenser. Be careful not to damage the delicate cooling fins or cut yourself on them.

6   Every other inspection, or at the first indication of cooling system problems, have the cap and system pressure tested. If you don't have a pressure tester, most gas stations and repair shops will do this for a minimal charge.

10   Wiper blade inspection and replacement

Refer to illustrations 10.5, 10.6a, 10.6b and 10.8

1   The windshield wiper blades should be inspected periodically for damage, loose components and cracked or worn blade elements (the rubber portions).

2   Road film can build up on the blade elements and can affect their efficiency, so they should be washed regularly with a mild detergent solution.

3   The action of the wiping mechanism can loosen bolts, nuts and fasteners, so they should be checked and tightened, as necessary, at the same time the wiper blade elements are checked.

4   If the wiper blade elements are cracked, worn or warped, or no longer clean adequately, they should be replaced with new ones

5   The wiper blade is removed by depressing the release tab at the center of the wiper arm and pulling the blade off the arm **(see illustration)**.

6   Bend the element end out of the way, use needle-nose pliers to pull the two support rods out, then slide the element out of the wiper bridge **(see illustrations)**.

7   Slide the new element into place and insert the rods to lock it in place.

8   When installing the wiper blade on the arm, place the plastic clip in position on the arm, then slide the blade into position over it until it locks **(see illustration)**.

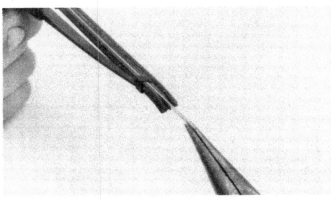

10.6a   Use needle-nose pliers to pull the two support rods out of the blade element

10.6b   With the rods out, it's an easy job to remove the element from the frame

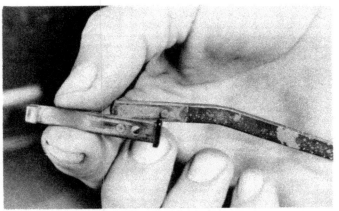

10.8   Place the plastic clip in position, then insert the blade onto the wiper arm

11   Underhood hose check and replacement

General

Caution: *Replacement of air conditioning hoses must be left to a dealer service department or air conditioning shop that has the equipment to depressurize the system safely. Never remove air conditioning components or hoses until the system has been depressurized.*

1   High temperatures in the engine compartment can cause the deterioration of the rubber and plastic hoses used for engine, accessory and emission systems operation. Periodic inspection should be made for cracks, loose clamps, material hardening and leaks. Information specific to the cooling system hoses can be found in Section 9.

2   Some, but not all, hoses are secured to the fittings with clamps. Where clamps are used, check to be sure they haven't lost their tension, allowing the hose to leak. If clamps aren't used, make sure the hose has not expanded and/or hardened where it slips over the fitting, allowing it to leak.

Vacuum hoses

3   It's quite common for vacuum hoses, especially those in the emissions system, to be color coded or identified by colored stripes molded into them. Various systems require hoses with different wall thicknesses, collapse resistance and temperature resistance. When replacing hoses, be sure the new ones are made of the same material.

4   Often the only effective way to check a hose is to remove it completely from the vehicle. If more than one hose is removed, be sure to label the hoses and fittings to ensure correct installation.

5   When checking vacuum hoses, be sure to include any plastic T-fittings in the check. Inspect the fittings for cracks and the hose where it fits over the fitting for distortion, which could cause leakage.

6   A small piece of vacuum hose (1/4-inch inside diameter) can be used as a stethoscope to detect vacuum leaks. Hold one end of the hose to your ear and probe around vacuum hoses and fittings, listening for the "hissing" sound characteristic of a vacuum leak. **Warning:** *When probing with the vacuum hose stethoscope, be very careful not to come into contact with moving engine components such as the drivebelts, cooling fan, etc.*

Fuel hose

Warning: *There are certain precautions which must be taken when inspecting or servicing fuel system components. Work in a well ventilated area and don't allow open flames (cigarettes, appliance pilot lights, etc.) or bare light bulbs near the work area. Mop up any spills immediately and don't store fuel soaked rags where they could ignite. On vehicles equipped with fuel injection, the fuel system is under pressure, so if any fuel lines are to be disconnected, the pressure in the system must be relieved first (see Chapter 4 for more information).*

7   Check all rubber fuel lines for deterioration and chafing. Check carefully for cracks in areas where the hose bends and where it's attached to fittings.

8   High quality fuel line, usually identified by the word Fluroelastomer printed on the hose, should be used for fuel line replacement. **Warning:** *Never, under any circumstances, use unreinforced vacuum line, clear plastic tubing or water hose for fuel lines!*

9   Spring-type clamps are commonly used on fuel lines. They often lose their tension over a period of time, and can be "sprung" during removal. Replace all spring-type clamps with screw clamps whenever a hose is replaced.

Metal lines

10   Sections of metal line are often used for fuel line between the fuel pump and carburetor or fuel injection unit. Check carefully to be sure the line has not been bent or crimped and look for cracks.

11   If a section of metal fuel line must be replaced, only seamless steel tubing should be used, since copper and aluminum tubing don't have the strength necessary to withstand normal engine vibration.

12   Check the metal brake lines where they enter the master cylinder and brake proportioning unit (if used) for cracks in the lines and loose fittings. Any sign of brake fluid leakage means an immediate thorough inspection of the brake system should be done.

12 Accelerator linkage check and lubrication

1   At the specified intervals, inspect the accelerator linkage and check it for free movement to make sure it is not binding.

2   Lubricate the linkage with a few drops of oil.

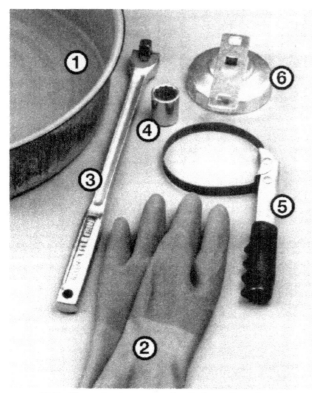

13.3   These tools are required when changing the engine oil and filter

1   *Drain pan* – *It should be fairly shallow in depth, but wide to prevent spills*
2   *Rubber gloves* – *When removing the drain plug and filter, you will get oil on your hands (the gloves will prevent burns)*
3   *Breaker bar* – *Sometimes the oil drain plug is tight and a long breaker bar is needed to loosen it*
4   *Socket* – *To be used with the breaker bar or a ratchet (must be the correct size to fit the drain plug – six-point preferred)*
5   *Filter wrench* – *This is a metal band-type wrench, which requires clearance around the filter to be effective*
6   *Filter wrench* – *This type fits on the bottom of the filter and can be turned with a ratchet or breaker bar (different size wrenches are available for different types of filters)*

13   Engine oil and filter change

Refer to illustrations 13.3, 13.9, 13.14 and 13.18

1   Frequent oil changes are the most important preventive maintenance procedures that can be done by the home mechanic. As engine oil ages, it becomes diluted and contaminated, which leads to premature engine wear.

2   Although some sources recommend oil filter changes every other oil change, the minimal cost of an oil filter and the fact that it's easy to install dictate that a new filter be used every time the oil is changed.

3 Gather all necessary tools and materials before beginning this procedure **(see illustration)**.

4   You should have plenty of clean rags and newspapers handy to mop up any spills. Access to the underside of the vehicle is greatly improved if the vehicle can be lifted on a hoist, driven onto ramps or supported by jackstands. **Warning:** *Do not work under a vehicle which is supported only by a bumper, hydraulic or scissors-type jack!*

5   If this is your first oil change, get under the vehicle and familiarize yourself with the locations of the oil drain plug and the oil filter. The engine and exhaust components will be warm during the actual work, so note how they're situated to avoid touching them when working under the vehicle.

13.9   The engine oil drain plug is located at the rear of the oil pan – it's usually fairly tight, so use a box-end wrench or six-point socket to avoid rounding off the corners of the plug

13.14   The oil filter is usually on very tight and will require a special wrench for removal – DO NOT use the wrench to tighten the new filter!

6   Warm the engine to normal operating temperature. If the new oil or any tools are needed, use the warm-up time to obtain everything necessary for the job. The correct oil for your application can be found in *Recommended lubricants and fluids* at the beginning of this Chapter.

7   With the engine oil warm (warm engine oil will drain better and more built-up sludge will be removed with it), raise and support the vehicle. Make sure it's safely supported!

8   Move all necessary tools, rags and newspapers under the vehicle. Set the drain pan under the drain plug. Keep in mind that the oil will initially flow from the pan with some force; position the pan accordingly.

9   Being careful not to touch any of the hot exhaust components, use a wrench to remove the drain plug near the bottom of the oil pan **(see illustration)**. Depending on how hot the oil is, you may want to wear gloves while unscrewing the plug the final few turns.

10   Allow the old oil to drain into the pan. It may be necessary to move the pan as the oil flow slows to a trickle.

11   After all the oil has drained, wipe off the drain plug with a clean rag. Small metal particles may cling to the plug and would immediately contaminate the new oil.

12   Clean the area around the drain plug opening and reinstall the plug. Tighten the plug securely with the wrench. If a torque wrench is available, use it to tighten the plug.

13   Move the drain pan into position under the oil filter.

14   Use the filter wrench to loosen the oil filter **(see illustration)**. Chain or metal band filter wrenches may distort the filter canister, but it doesn't matter since the filter will be discarded anyway.

15   Completely unscrew the old filter. Be careful; it's full of oil. Empty the oil inside the filter into the drain pan.

13.18   Lubricate the oil filter gasket with clean engine oil before installing the filter on the engine

15.1   The rocker arms on engines that do not require valve adjustment look like these (arrows) – they don't have adjustment screws (if the rocker arms do have adjustment screws for the intake and exhaust or smaller jet valves, follow the procedure in the text)

16   Compare the old filter with the new one to make sure they're the same type.
17   Use a clean rag to remove all oil, dirt and sludge from the area where the oil filter mounts to the engine. Check the old filter to make sure the rubber gasket isn't stuck to the engine. If the gasket is stuck to the engine, remove it.
18   Apply a light coat of clean oil to the rubber gasket on the new oil filter **(see illustration)**.
19   Attach the new filter to the engine, following the tightening directions printed on the filter canister or packing box. Most filter manufacturers recommend against using a filter wrench due to the possibility of overtightening and damage to the seal.
20   Remove all tools, rags, etc. from under the vehicle, being careful not to spill the oil in the drain pan, then lower the vehicle.
21   Move to the engine compartment and locate the oil filler cap.
22   Pour the fresh oil into the filler opening. A funnel may be used.
23   Pour three or four quarts of fresh oil into the engine. Wait a few minutes to allow the oil to drain into the pan, then check the level on the oil dipstick (see Section 4 if necessary). If the oil level is above the L mark, start the engine and allow the new oil to circulate.
24   Run the engine for only about a minute and then shut it off. Immediately look under the vehicle and check for leaks at the oil pan drain plug and around the oil filter. If either one is leaking, tighten it a little more.
25   With the new oil circulated and the filter now completely full, recheck the level on the dipstick and add more oil as necessary.
26   During the first few trips after an oil change, make it a point to check frequently for leaks and correct oil level.
27   The old oil drained from the engine cannot be reused in its present state and should be disposed of. Oil reclamation centers, auto repair shops and gas stations will normally accept the oil, which can be refined

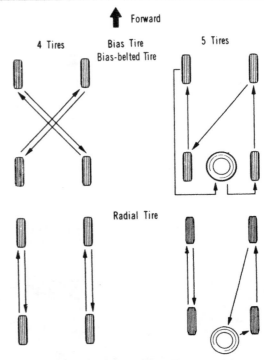

14.2   The rotation diagram for these models

and used again. After the oil has cooled it can be poured into a container (capped plastic jugs or bottles, milk cartons, etc.) for transport to a disposal site.

14   Tire rotation

Refer to illustration 14.2
1   The tires should be rotated at the specified intervals and whenever uneven wear is noticed.
2   Refer to the accompanying illustration for the preferred tire rotation pattern.
3   Refer to the information in Jacking and towing at the front of this manual for the proper procedures to follow when raising the vehicle and changing a tire. If the brakes are to be checked, don't apply the parking brake as stated. Make sure the tires are blocked to prevent the vehicle from rolling as it's raised.
4   Preferably, the entire vehicle should be raised at the same time. This can be done on a hoist or by jacking up each corner and then lowering the vehicle onto jackstands placed under the frame rails. Always use four jackstands and make sure the vehicle is safely supported.
5   After rotation, check and adjust the tire pressures as necessary and be sure to check the lug nut tightness.
6   For additional information on the wheels and tires, refer to Chapter 11.

15   Valve clearance check and adjustment (four-cylinder engines only)

Refer to illustrations 15.1, 15.5, 15.7 and 15.12
1   The valve clearances must be checked and adjusted at the specified intervals with the engine at normal operating temperature. Not all models require valve adjustment, while others require only adjustment of the jet valves. Consult your owner's manual or dealer to determine if your vehicle requires valve adjustment. If this information is not readily available, the only sure way to tell that adjustment is required is to remove the engine valve cover. Valves that do not require adjustment have no adjusting screws **(see illustration)**.

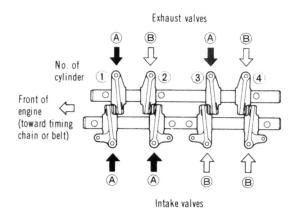

15.5 With the number one piston at Top Dead Center (TDC), adjust the valves marked A – with the number four piston at TDC, adjust the valves marked B

15.7 There should be a slight drag as the feeler gauge is pulled between the jet valve adjustment screw and the valve stem

15.12 T o make sure the adjusting screw doesn't move when the locknut is tightened, use a box-end wrench and have a good grip on the screwdriver

2   On carbureted models, remove the air cleaner assembly (see Chapter 4).

3   Remove the valve cover (see Chapter 2).

4   Place the number one piston at Top Dead Center (TDC) on the compression stroke (see Chapter 2). The number one cylinder rocker arms (closest to the timing chain or belt end of the engine) should be loose (able to move up and down slightly) and the camshaft lobes should be facing away from the rocker arms.

5   With the crankshaft in this position the valves labeled A (plus the jet valves adjacent to the intake valves) can be checked and adjusted **(see illustration)**. Always check and adjust the jet valve clearance first.

6   The intake valve and jet valve adjusting screws are located on a common rocker arm. Make sure the intake valve adjusting screw has been backed off two full turns, then loosen the locknut on the jet valve adjusting screw.

7   Turn the jet valve adjusting screw counterclockwise and insert the appropriate size feeler gauge (see this Chapter's Specifications) between the valve stem and the adjusting screw. Carefully tighten the adjusting screw until you can feel a slight drag on the feeler gauge as you withdraw it from between the stem and adjusting screw **(see illustration)**.

8   Since the jet valve spring is relatively weak, use special care not to force the jet valve open. Be particularly careful if the adjusting screw is hard to turn. Hold the adjusting screw with a screwdriver (to keep it from turning) and tighten the locknut. Recheck the clearance to make sure it hasn't changed.

9   Next, check and adjust the intake valve clearance. Insert the appropriate size feeler gauge between the intake valve stem and the adjusting screw. Carefully tighten the adjusting screw until you can feel a slight drag on the feeler gauge as you withdraw it from between the stem and adjust-

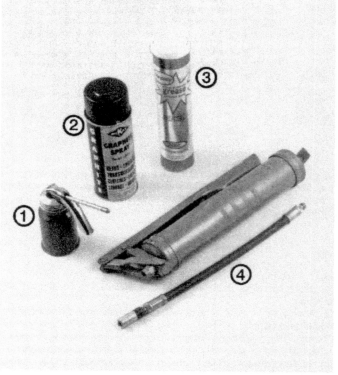

16.1 Materials required for chassis and body lubrication

1   **Engine oil** – *Light engine oil in a can like this can be used for door and hood hinges*
2   **Graphite spray** – *Used to lubricate lock cylinders*
3   **Grease** – *Grease, in a variety of types and weights, is available for use in a grease gun. Check the Specifications for your requirements.*
4   **Grease gun** – *A common grease gun, shown here with a detachable hose and nozzle, is needed for chassis lubrication. After use, clean it thoroughly!*

ing screw.

10   Hold the adjusting screw with a screwdriver (to keep it from turning) and tighten the locknut. Recheck the clearance to make sure it hasn't changed.

11   Loosen the locknut on the exhaust valve adjusting screw. Turn the adjusting screw counterclockwise and insert the appropriate size feeler gauge between the valve stem and the adjusting screw. Carefully tighten

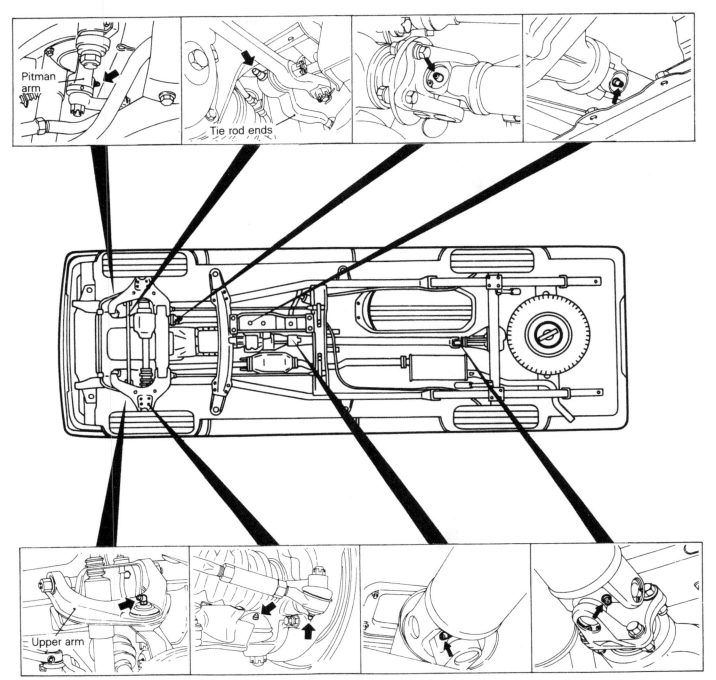

16.2a   Typical pickup chassis lubrication points

the adjusting screw until you can feel a slight drag on the feeler gauge as you withdraw it from between the stem and adjusting screw.

12   Hold the adjusting screw with a screwdriver (to keep it from turning) and tighten the locknut **(see illustration)**. Recheck the clearance to make sure it hasn't changed.

13   Rotate the crankshaft until the number four piston is at TDC on the compression stroke. The number four cylinder rocker arms (closest to the rear end of the engine) should be loose with the camshaft lobes facing away from the rocker arms.

14   Adjust the valves labelled B as described above **(see illustration 15.5).**

15   Install the valve cover and the air cleaner assembly.

16   Chassis lubrication

Refer to illustrations 16.1, 16.2a and 16.2b

1   A grease gun and cartridge filled with the recommended grease are the only items required for chassis lubrication other than some clean rags and equipment needed to raise and support the vehicle safely **(see illustration)**.

2   There are several points on the vehicle's suspension, steering and drivetrain components that must be periodically lubricated with lithium-based multi-purpose grease, depending on model and year. Included are the upper and lower suspension balljoints, the swivel joints on the steering

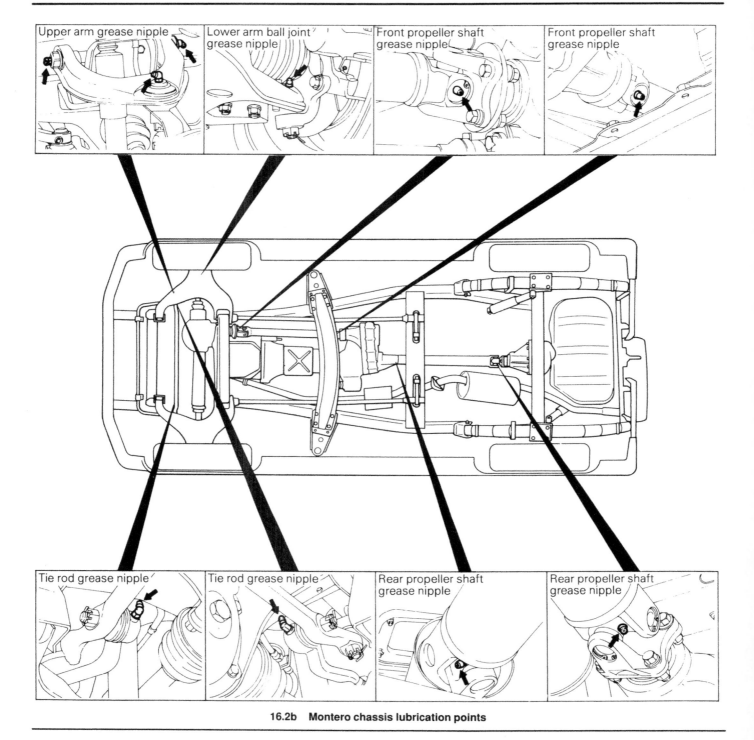

16.2b   **Montero chassis lubrication points**

linkage and, on 4WD models, the front and rear driveshafts **(see illustrations)**.

3   The grease point for each upper suspension balljoint (if equipped) is on top of the balljoint and is accessible by removing the front wheel and tire. The steering linkage swivel joints on some models are designed to be lubricated and the driveshaft universal joints require lubrication as well.

4   For easier access under the vehicle, raise it with a jack and place jackstands under the frame. Make sure the vehicle is safely supported on the stands!

5   If grease fittings aren't already installed, the plugs will have to be removed and fittings screwed into place.

6   Force a little of the grease out of the gun nozzle to remove any dirt, then wipe it clean with a rag.

7   Wipe the grease fitting and push the nozzle firmly over it. Squeeze the trigger on the grease gun to force grease into the component. Both the balljoints and swivel joints should be lubricated until the rubber reservoir is firm to the touch. Don't pump too much grease into the fittings or it could rupture the reservoir. If the grease seeps out around the grease gun nozzle, the fitting is clogged or the nozzle isn't seated all the way. Resecure the gun nozzle to the fitting and try again. If necessary, replace the fitting.

8   Wipe excess grease from the components and the grease fittings.

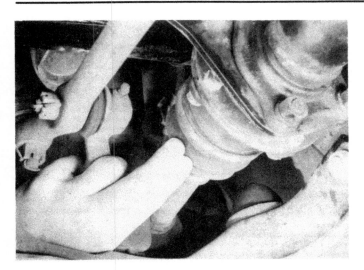

17.11   Push on the CV joint boot to check for cracks or lubricant leaks (4WD models)

9   While you're under the vehicle, clean and lubricate the parking brake cable along with the cable guides and levers. This can be done by smearing some of the chassis grease onto the cable and its related parts with your fingers.

10   Lower the vehicle to the ground for the remaining body lubrication process.

11   Open the hood and rear gate and smear a little chassis grease on the latch mechanisms. Have an assistant pull the release knob from inside the vehicle as you lubricate the cable at the latch.

12   Lubricate all the hinges (door, hood, hatch) with a few drops of light engine oil to keep them in proper working order.

13   The key lock cylinders can be lubricated with spray-on graphite, which is available at auto parts stores.

17   Suspension and steering check

Refer to illustration 17.11

1   Whenever the front of the vehicle is raised for any reason, it's a good idea to visually check the suspension and steering components for wear.

2   Indications of steering or suspension problems include excessive play in the steering wheel before the front wheels react, excessive swaying around corners or body movement over rough roads and binding at some point as the steering wheel is turned.

3   Before the vehicle is raised for inspection, test the shock absorbers by pushing down aggressively at each corner. If the vehicle doesn't come back to a level position within one or two bounces, the shocks are worn and should be replaced. As this is done listen for squeaks and other noises from the suspension components. Information on shock absorber and suspension components can be found in Chapter 10.

4   Raise the front end of the vehicle and support it on jackstands. Make sure it's safely supported!

5   Crawl under the vehicle and check for loose bolts, broken or disconnected parts and deteriorated rubber bushings on all suspension and steering components. Look for grease or fluid leaking from around the steering gear assembly and shock absorbers. If equipped, check the power steering hoses and connections for leaks.

6   The balljoint boots should be checked at this time. This includes not only the upper and lower suspension balljoints, but those connecting the steering linkage parts as well. After cleaning around the balljoints, inspect the seals for cracks and damage.

7   Grip the top and bottom of each wheel and try to move it in and out. It won't take a lot of effort to be able to feel any play in the wheel bearings. If the play is noticeable it would be a good idea to adjust it right away or it could confuse further inspections.

8   Grip each side of the wheel and try rocking it laterally. Steady pressure will, of course, turn the steering, but back-and-forth pressure will reveal a loose steering joint. If some play is felt it would be easier to get assistance from someone so while one person rocks the wheel from side to side, the other can look at the joints, bushings and connections in the steering linkage. Generally speaking, there are eight places where the play may occur. The two outer balljoints on the tie-rods are the most likely, followed by the two inner joints on the same rods, where they join to the center rod. Any play in them means replacement of the tie-rod end. Next are two swivel bushings, one at each end of the center gear rod. Finally, check the steering gear arm balljoint and the one on the idler arm which supports the center rod on the side opposite the steering box. This unit is bolted to the side of the frame member and any play calls for replacement of the bushings.

9   To check the steering box, first make sure the bolts holding the steering box to the frame are tight. Then get another person to help examine the mechanism. One should look at, or hold onto, the arm at the bottom of the steering box while the other turns the steering wheel a little from side to side. The amount of lost motion between the steering wheel and the gear arm indicates the degree of wear in the steering box mechanism. This check should be carried out with the wheels first in the straight ahead position and then at nearly full lock on each side. If the play only occurs noticeably in the straight ahead position then the wear is most likely in the worm and/or nut. If it occurs at all positions, then the wear is probably in the sector shaft bearing. Oil leaks from the unit are another indication of such wear. In either case the steering box will need removal for closer examination and repair.

10   Moving to the vehicle interior, check the play in the steering wheel by turning it slowly in both directions until the wheels can just be felt turning. The steering wheel free play should be less than 1-3/8 inch (35 mm). Excessive play is another indication of wear in the steering gear or linkage. The steering box can be adjusted for wear (see Chapter 10).

11   On 4WD models, inspect the front driveaxle CV joint boots for tears and leakage of grease **(see illustration)**.

12   Following the inspection of the front, a similar inspection should be made of the rear suspension components, again checking for loose bolts, damaged or disconnected parts and deteriorated rubber bushings.

18   Exhaust system check

1   With the engine cold (at least three hours after the vehicle has been driven), check the complete exhaust system from the manifold to the end of the tailpipe. Be careful around the catalytic converter, which may be hot even after three hours. The inspection should be done with the vehicle on a hoist to permit unrestricted access. If a hoist isn't available, raise the vehicle and support it securely on jackstands.

2   Check the exhaust pipes and connections for signs of leakage and/or corrosion indicating a potential failure. Make sure that all brackets and hangers are in good condition and tight.

3   Inspect the underside of the body for holes, corrosion, open seams, etc. which may allow exhaust gases to enter the passenger compartment. Seal all body openings with silicone sealant or body putty.

4   Rattles and other noises can often be traced to the exhaust system, especially the hangers, mounts and heat shields. Try to move the pipes, mufflers and catalytic converter. If the components can come in contact with the body or suspension parts, secure the exhaust system with new brackets and hangers.

19   Clutch pedal height and freeplay check and adjustment

Refer to illustrations 19.2, 19.3, 19.4 and 19.5

1   On vehicles equipped with a manual transmission, the clutch pedal height and freeplay must be correctly adjusted.

2   The height of the clutch pedal is the distance the pedal sits off the floor **(see illustration)**. This distance should be as listed in this Chapter's specifications. If the pedal height is not within the specified range, loosen the locknut on the clutch stopper bolt located on the pedal bracket and turn the

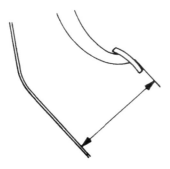

19.2   The clutch pedal height is measured from the top of the pedal to the floor

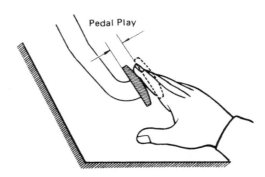

19.3   To check clutch pedal freeplay, measure the distance from the natural resting place of the pedal to the point at which resistance is felt

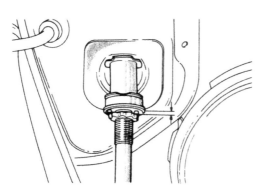

19.4   On cable-operated models, adjust the clutch cable to achieve the specified play between the nut and rubber cushion

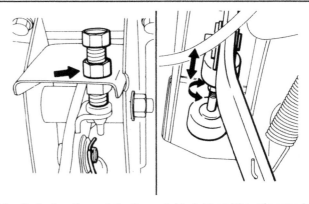

19.5   On hydraulic models, the pedal height and freeplay can be adjusted at the stopper bolt (left) or pushrod (right) – be careful not to push the pushrod toward the master cylinder during the adjustment

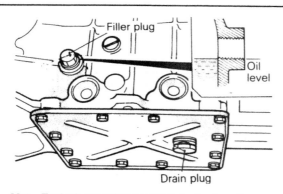

20.1   Typical manual transmission plug locations

bolt in or out until the pedal height is correct. Retighten the locknut. On hydraulic clutch models, there is provision for adjustment of the clutch master cylinder pushrod. Loosen the locknut and back the stopper bolt or switch out for clearance, then loosen the locknut on the clutch pushrod and turn the pushrod to adjust it.

3   The freeplay is the pedal slack, or the distance the pedal can be depressed before it begins to have any effect on the clutch **(see illustration)**. The distance should be as listed in this Chapter's specifications. It it isn't, it must be adjusted, as discussed under the appropriate heading below.

Cable actuated clutch

4   Working in the engine compartment, loosen the locknut, pull the outer cable toward the front of the vehicle and turn the adjusting nut in until the washer damper rubber contacts the firewall. Depress and release the

clutch pedal several times. Pull the cable forward again, tighten the adjusting nut, then back it off to provide the specified amount of play **(see illustration)**. Tighten the locknut.

Hydraulic clutch

5   The freeplay is adjusted by turning the stopper bolt or adjustable clutch master cylinder pushrod **(see illustration)**. Loosen the locknut or the pushrod or bolt. Turn the pushrod to achieve the proper freeplay, then retighten the locknut. If the freeplay and height are not as specified after adjustment, it may mean there is air in the system and it should be bled (see Chapter 8).

---

20   Manual transmission lubricant level check

Refer to illustration 20.1

1   Manual transmissions don't have a dipstick. The lubricant level is checked by removing a filler plug from the side of the transmission case **(see illustration)**. Locate the plug and use a rag to clean the plug and the area around it. If the vehicle is raised to gain access to the plug, be sure to support it safely on jackstands – DO NOT crawl under the vehicle when it's supported only by a jack!

2   With the engine and transmission cold, remove the plug. If lubricant immediately starts leaking out, thread the plug back into the transmission – the level is correct. If it doesn't, reach inside the hole with your little finger. The level should be even with the bottom of the plug hole.

3   If the transmission needs more lubricant, use a syringe or small pump to add it through the plug hole.

4   Thread the plug back into the transmission and tighten it securely. Drive the vehicle, then check for leaks around the plug.

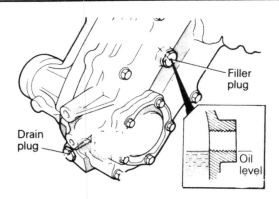

21.2   Transfer case plug locations

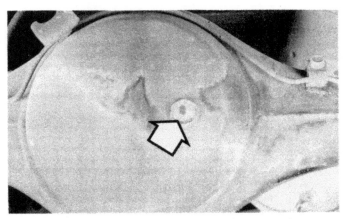

22.2a   Rear differential check/fill plug location (arrow) – use a box-end wrench to remove and install the plug to avoid rounding off the hex

22.2b   On 4WD models, also check the front differential lubricant level – remove the check/fill plug (arrow)

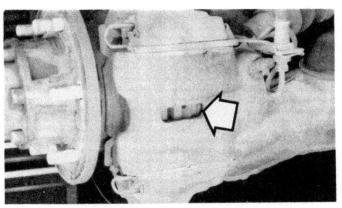

23.6   You'll find an inspection hole like this in each front caliper – placing a steel rule across the hole should enable you to determine the thickness of the remaining lining material for both inner and outer pads – the lining can also be inspected by looking through each end of the caliper

21   Transfer case lubricant level check (4WD models)

Refer to illustration 21.2

1   If necessary, remove the transfer case rock guard (if equipped). The lubricant level is checked by removing a filler plug from the side of the case. If the vehicle is raised to gain access to the plug, be sure to support it safely on jackstands – DO NOT crawl under the vehicle when it's supported only by a jack!

2   With the engine and transfer case cold, remove the plug **(see illustration)**. If lubricant immediately starts leaking out, thread the plug back into the case – the level is correct. If it doesn't, completely remove the plug and reach inside the hole with your little finger. The level should be even with the bottom of the plug hole.

3   If more lubricant is needed, use a syringe or small pump to add it through the opening.

4   Thread the plug back into the case and tighten it securely. Drive the vehicle, then check for leaks around the plug. Install the rock guard.

22   Differential lubricant level check

Refer to illustrations 22.2a and 22.2b

1 The differential has a check/fill plug which must be removed to check the lubricant level. If the vehicle is raised to gain access to the plug, be sure to support it safely on jackstands – DO NOT crawl under the vehicle when it's supported only by a jack.

2 Remove the check/fill plug from the differential **(see illustrations)**.

3 The lubricant level should be at the bottom of the plug opening. If not, use a syringe to add the recommended lubricant until it just starts to run out of the opening.

4 Install the plug and tighten it securely.

23   Brake check

Refer to illustrations 23.6, 23.13 and 23.15

Note: *For detailed photographs of the brake system, refer to Chapter 9.*

Warning: *Brake system dust may contain asbestos, which is hazardous to your health. DO NOT blow it out with compressed air and DO NOT inhale it. DO NOT use gasoline or solvents to remove the dust. Use brake system cleaner or denatured alcohol only!*

1   In addition to the specified intervals, the brakes should be inspected every time the wheels are removed or whenever a defect is suspected.

2   To check the brakes, the vehicle must be raised and supported securely on jackstands.

Disc brakes

3   Disc brakes are used on the front wheels. Extensive rotor damage can occur if the pads are allowed to wear beyond the specified limit.

4   Raise the vehicle and support it securely on jackstands, then remove the wheels (see *Jacking and Towing* at the front of the manual if necessary).

5   The disc brake calipers, which contain the pads, are visible with the wheels removed. There's an outer pad and an inner pad in each caliper. All pads should be inspected.

6   Each caliper has an opening, which allows you to inspect the pads **(see illustration)**. If the pad material has worn below the limit listed in this Chapter's Specifications, the pads should be replaced.

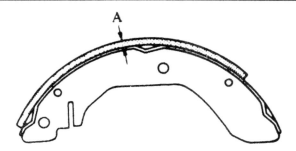

23.13   If the lining is bonded to the brake shoe, measure the lining thickness from the outer surface to the metal shoe, as shown here; if the lining is riveted to the shoe, measure from the lining outer surface to the rivet head

7   If you're unsure about the exact thickness of the remaining lining material, remove the pads for further inspection or replacement (refer to Chapter 9).

8   Before installing the wheels, check for leakage and/or damage (cracks, splitting, etc.) around the brake hose connections. Replace the hose or fittings as necessary, referring to Chapter 9.

9   Check the condition of the rotor. Look for score marks, deep scratches and burned spots. If these conditions exist, the hub/rotor assembly should be removed for servicing – Section 39 (2WD models) or Chapter 9 (4WD models).

Drum brakes

10   On rear brakes, remove the drum (see Chapter 9). If it's stuck, make sure the parking brake is released, then squirt penetrating oil into the joint between the hub and drum. Allow the oil to soak in and try to pull the drum off again.

11   If the drum still can't be pulled off, the brake shoes will have to be adjusted. This is done by first removing the cover in the backing plate, inserting a screwdriver into the opening and lifting the adjustment lever off the star wheel adjuster and backing the adjuster off to move the shoes away from the drum.

12   With the drum removed, be careful not to touch any brake dust (see the Warning at the beginning of this Section).

13   Note the thickness of the lining material on both the front and rear brake shoes. If the material has worn away to below the specified thickness above the recessed rivets or metal shoe, the shoes should be replaced **(see illustration)**. The shoes should also be replaced if they're cracked, glazed (shiny surface) or contaminated with brake fluid.

14   Make sure that all the brake assembly springs are connected and in good condition.

15   Check the brake components for signs of fluid leakage. Carefully pry back the rubber cups on the wheel cylinders located at the top of the brake shoes with your finger or a small screwdriver **(see illustration)**. Any leakage is an indication that the wheel cylinders should be overhauled immediately (see Chapter 9). Also check brake hoses and connections for leakage.

16   Wipe the inside of the drum with a clean rag and brake cleaner or denatured alcohol. Again, be careful not to breathe the asbestos dust.

17   Check the inside of the drum for cracks, score marks, deep scratches and hard spots, which will appear as small discolorations. If imperfections cannot be removed with fine emery cloth, the drum must be taken to a machine shop equipped to turn the drums.

18   If after the inspection process all parts are in good working condition, reinstall the brake drum.

19   Install the wheels and lower the vehicle.

Parking brake

20   The parking brake is operated by an umbrella type handle next to the steering column or a center-mounted lever and locks the rear brake system. The easiest, and perhaps most obvious method of periodically checking the operation of the parking brake assembly is to park the vehicle on a steep hill with the parking brake set and the transmission in Neutral. If

23.15   Pry the wheel cylinder boot back carefully to check for fluid leakage

the parking brake cannot prevent the vehicle from rolling within 16 to 17 (umbrella-type) or 4 to 6 (lever) clicks, it's in need of adjustment (see Chapter 9).

---

24   Fuel system check

Warning: *Gasoline is extremely flammable, so take extra precautions when you work on any part of the fuel system. Don't smoke or allow open flames or bare light bulbs near the work area, and don't work in a garage where a natural gas-type appliance (such as a water heater or clothes dryer) with a pilot light is present. If you spill any fuel on your skin, rinse it off immediately with soap and water. When you perform any kind of work on the fuel tank, wear safety glasses and have a Class B type fire extinguisher on hand. On fuel-injected models, no components should be disconnected until the pressure has been relieved (see Chapter 4).*

1   On most models, the fuel tank is located at the rear of the vehicle.

2   The fuel system should be checked with the vehicle raised on a hoist so the components underneath the vehicle are readily visible and accessible.

3   If the smell of gasoline is noticed while driving or after the vehicle has been in the sun, the system should be thoroughly inspected immediately.

4   Remove the gas tank cap and check for damage, corrosion and an unbroken sealing imprint on the gasket. Replace the cap with a new one if necessary.

5   With the vehicle raised, check the gas tank and filler neck for punctures, cracks and other damage. The connection between the filler neck and the tank is especially critical. Sometimes a rubber filler neck will leak due to loose clamps or deteriorated rubber, problems a home mechanic can usually rectify. **Warning:** *Do not, under any circumstances, try to repair a fuel tank yourself (except rubber components). A welding torch or any open flame can easily cause the fuel vapors to explode if the proper precautions are not taken!*

6   Carefully check all rubber hoses and metal lines leading away from the fuel tank. Look for loose connections, deteriorated hoses, crimped lines and other damage. Follow the lines to the front of the vehicle, carefully inspecting them all the way. Repair or replace damaged sections as necessary.

7   If a fuel odor is still evident after the inspection, refer to Section 32 and check the evaporative emissions system.

---

25   Thermostatic air cleaner check (carbureted models)

1   Carbureted models are equipped with a thermostatically controlled air cleaner, which draws air to the carburetor from different locations depending on engine temperature.

2   This is a simple visual check. However, if access is tight, a small mirror may have to be used.

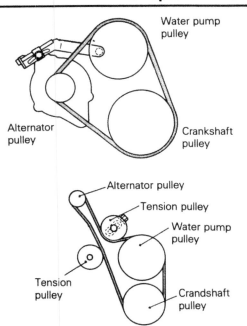

26.2   Drivebelt routing – top is a typical four-cylinder engine; bottom is a typical V6 engine

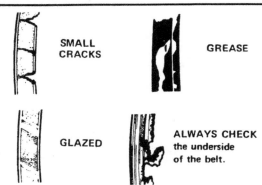

26.4a   Here are some of the more common problems associated with drivebelts (check the belts very carefully to prevent an untimely breakdown)

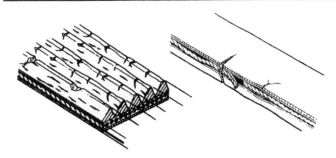

26.4b   On V-ribbed belts, look for signs of wear like these

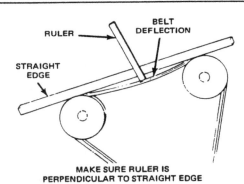

26.5   Measuring drivebelt deflection with a straightedge and ruler

3   Open the hood and find the air control valve on the air cleaner assembly. It's located inside the long snorkel portion of the metal air cleaner housing.

4   If there's a flexible air duct attached to the end of the snorkel, disconnect it so you can look through the end of the snorkel and see the air control valve inside. A mirror may be needed if you can't safely look directly into the end of the snorkel.

5   The check should be done when the engine and outside air are cold. Start the engine and watch the air control valve, which should move up and close off the snorkel air passage. With the valve closed, air can't enter through the end of the snorkel, but instead enters the air cleaner through the hot air duct attached to the exhaust manifold.

6   As the engine warms up to operating temperature, the valve should open to allow air through the snorkel end. Depending on outside air temperature, this may take 10 to 15 minutes. To speed up the check you can reconnect the snorkel air duct, drive the vehicle and then check the position of the valve.

7   If the thermostatic air cleaner isn't operating properly, see Chapter 6 for more information.

26   Drivebelt check, adjustment and replacement

Refer to illustrations 26.2, 26.4a, 26.4b, 26.5, 26.7a and 26.7b

1   The accessory drivebelts are located at the front of the engine. The belts drive the water pump, alternator, power steering pump and air conditioning compressor. The condition and tension of the drivebelts are critical to the operation of the engine and accessories. Excessive tension causes bearing wear, while insufficient tension produces slippage, noise, component vibration and belt failure. Because of their composition and the high stress to which they are subjected, drivebelts stretch and continue to deteriorate as they get older. As a result, they must be periodically checked and adjusted.

Check

2   The number, type and routing of belts used on a particular vehicle depends on the engine, model year and accessories installed **(see illustration)**.

3   Various types of drivebelts are used on these models. Some components are driven by V-belts (these are the conventional type). Others are driven by V-ribbed belts. Some models use a single V-ribbed belt to drive all of the accessories. This is known as a "serpentine" belt because of the winding path it follows between various drive, accessory and idler pulleys.

4   With the engine off, open the hood and locate the drivebelt(s) at the front of the engine. With a flashlight, check each belt for separation of the rubber plies from each side of the core, a severed core, separation of the ribs from the rubber, cracks, torn or worn ribs and cracks in the inner ridges of the ribs. Also check for fraying and glazing, which gives the belt a shiny appearance **(see illustrations)**. Cracks in the rib side of V-ribbed belts are acceptable, as are small chunks missing from the ribs. If a V-ribbed belt has lost chunks bigger than 1/2-inch (13 mm) from two adjacent ribs, or if the missing chunks cause belt noise, the belt should be replaced. Both sides of each belt should be inspected, which means you'll have to twist them to check the undersides. Use your fingers to feel a belt where you can't see it. If any of the above conditions are evident, replace the belt as described below.

5   To check the tension of the belts, the following "rule of thumb" method is recommended. Lay a straightedge across the longest free span (the distance between two pulleys) of the belt. Push down firmly on the belt at a point half way between the pulleys and see how much the belt moves (deflects). Measure the deflection with a ruler **(see illustration)**. The belt

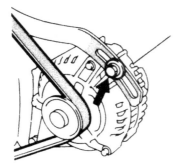

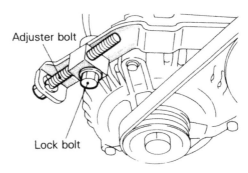

26.7a   On earlier models, to adjust the alternator belt, loosen this locking bolt (arrow) and the pivot bolt or nut at the bottom of the alternator

26.7b   On later models, after loosening the pivot bolt or nut at the bottom of the alternator, loosen this lock bolt and turn the adjuster bolt

should deflect 1/8 to 1/4-inch if the distance from pulley center-to-pulley center is less than 12 inches; it should deflect from 1/8 to 3/8-inch if the distance from pulley center-to-pulley center is over 12 inches.

Adjustment

6   To adjust belt tension on serpentine belts, turn the adjusting screw on the tension pulley **(see illustration 26.2)**. To adjust all except serpentine belts, move the belt-driven accessory on the bracket, as follows:

7   For each accessory, there will be a locking bolt and a pivot bolt or nut **(see illustrations)**. Both must be loosened slightly to enable you to move the component.

8   After the two bolts have been loosened, move the component away from the engine (to tighten the belt) or toward the engine (to loosen the belt). Some models have an adjuster bolt which is turned to move the component. Some other accessories are equipped with a square hole designed to accept a 1/2-inch square drive breaker bar. The bar can be used to lever the component and tension the drivebelt. Others have a cast lug which is designed to accept an open-end wrench, which can be used to pry the accessory. **Caution:** *If it's necessary to pry against an accessory to tighten a drivebelt, be very careful not to damage the accessory or the point the prybar rests against.*

9   Hold the accessory in position and check the belt tension. If it's correct, tighten the two bolts until snug, then recheck the tension. If it's alright, tighten the two bolts completely.

Replacement

10   Follow the above procedures for drivebelt adjustment, but loosen the belt until it will slip off the pulleys, then remove it. On some models, it may be necessary to remove forward belts to replace a rearward belt. Since belts tend to wear out at the same time, it's a good idea to replace all of them at the same time. Mark each belt and the corresponding pulley grooves so the belt can be reinstalled properly.

27   Seat belt check

1   Check the seat belts, buckles, latch plates and guide loops for any obvious damage or signs of wear.

2   Make sure the seat belt reminder light comes on when the key is turned on.

3   The seat belts are designed to lock up during a sudden stop or impact, yet allow free movement during normal driving. The retractors should hold the belt against your chest while driving and rewind the belt when the buckle is unlatched.

4   If any of the above checks reveal problems with the seat-belt system, replace parts as necessary.

28   Carburetor/throttle body mounting nut/bolt torque check

1   Nuts or bolts attach the carburetor to the intake manifold or the fuel injection system throttle body to the air intake plenum. The bolts or nuts

can sometimes work loose during normal engine operation and cause a vacuum leak.

2   To properly tighten the mounting bolts or nuts, a torque wrench is necessary. If you do not own one, they can usually be rented on a daily basis.

3   Remove the air cleaner or intake hose assembly (see Chapter 4).

4   Locate the mounting bolts/nuts at the base of the carburetor/throttle body. Decide what special tools or adaptors will be be necessary, if any, to tighten the bolts/nuts with a socket and the torque wrench.

5   Tighten the bolts/nuts to the torque specified in Chapter 4. Do not overtighten the bolts/nuts, as the threads may strip.

6   If you suspect a vacuum leak exists at the bottom of the carburetor/throttle body obtain a short length of rubber hose. Start the engine and place one end of the hose next to your ear as you probe around the base of the carburetor/throttle body with the other end. You should hear a hissing sound if a leak exists.

7   If, after the bolts/nuts are properly tightened, a vacuum leak still exists, the carburetor/throttle body must be removed and a new gasket installed. See Chapter 4 for more information.

8   After tightening the bolts/nuts, reinstall the air cleaner housing or intake hose.

29   Air filter replacement

1   At the specified intervals, the air filter should be replaced with a new one. A thorough program of preventive maintenance would also call for the filter to be inspected periodically between changes, especially if the vehicle is often driven in dusty conditions.

2   The air filter is located inside the air cleaner housing, which is mounted on top of the carburetor or at the right front corner of the engine compartment on fuel-injected models.

Carbureted models

Refer to illustrations 29.3a, 29.3b and 29.4

3   Release the clips, remove the wing nut and lift the top plate off the air cleaner housing **(see illustrations)**.

4   Lift the air filter out of the housing **(see illustration)**. If it's covered with dirt, it should be replaced.

5   Wipe the inside of the air cleaner housing with a rag.

6   Place the old filter (if in good condition) or the new filter (if replacement is necessary) into the air cleaner housing.

7   Reinstall the top plate on the air cleaner, then tighten the wing nut and snap the clips into place.

Fuel-injected models

Round filter housing

Refer to illustrations 29.9a, 29.9b and 29.10

8   Detach the air intake hose.

9   Release the clips and pull the air flow sensor out of the air cleaner housing **(see illustrations)**.

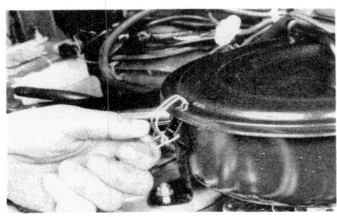

29.3a   Pull up on the clips to detach them

29.3b   Remove the wing nut so the top cover can be lifted off

29.4   Lift the air filter out – it should be replaced with a new one
if it's dirty

29.9a   Detach the round filter housing clips by lifting up

29.9b   Be careful when pulling the air flow sensor out of the air
cleaner housing

29.10   Support the air flow sensor and lift the filter element out

10   Remove the old filter element **(see illustration)**. If it is covered with
dirt, it should be replaced.

11   Insert the filter element in the air cleaner housing and align the tabs,
the install the air flow sensor body and secure it with the clips.

12   Connect the air intake hose securely, making sure there are no air
leaks.

Rectangular filter housing
Refer to illustration 29.13

13   Detach the clips, pull the cover up and lift the filter out of the housing
(see illustration). If the filter is covered with dirt, it should be replaced.

14   Wipe the inside of the air cleaner housing with a rag.

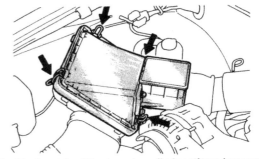

29.13   Rectangular filter housing clip locations (arrows)

**30.4   Disconnect the hoses (A), then detach the fuel filter (B)
from the clip (C)**

15   Place the old filter (if in good condition) or the new filter (if replacement is necessary) into the air cleaner housing. Set the cover in place and attach the clips.

30   Fuel filter replacement

Warning: *Gasoline is extremely flammable, so take extra precautions when you work on any part of the fuel system. Don't smoke or allow open flames or bare light bulbs near the work area, and don't work in a garage where a natural gas-type appliance (such as a water heater or clothes dryer) with a pilot light is present. If you spill any fuel on your skin, rinse it off immediately with soap and water. When you perform any kind of work on the fuel tank, wear safety glasses and have a Class B type fire extinguisher on hand.*

1   This job should be done with the engine cold (after sitting at least three hours). Place a metal container, rags or newspapers under the filter to catch spilled fuel.

2   **Warning:** *Before attempting to remove the fuel filter, disconnect the negative cable from the battery and position it out of the way so it can't accidentally contact the battery post.*

Carbureted models

Refer to illustration 30.4

3   The fuel filter is located either adjacent to the fuel tank or in the engine compartment, below the carburetor. Clamp the inlet hose before disconnecting the filter, otherwise fuel will continue to drain from the tank.

4   Loosen the clamps and slide them down the filter, past the fittings on the filter, then detach the filter from the clip **(see illustration)**.

5   Carefully twist and pull on the hoses to separate them from the filter. If the hoses are in bad shape, now would be a good time to replace them with new ones.

6   Connect the filter to the hoses and tighten the clamps securely. If spring-type clamps were originally installed, it would be a good idea to replace them with screw-type clamps. Push the filter back into the clip. Start the engine and check carefully for leaks at the filter hose connections.

Fuel-injected models

Refer to illustration 30.9

7   Depressurize the fuel system (Chapter 4).

8   The fuel filter is located under the vehicle, adjacent to the fuel tank. Raise the vehicle and support it securely on jackstands. Remove the filter protector plate (if equipped).

9   Using two wrenches, remove the high-pressure hose **(see illustration)**.

10   Loosen the output hose bolt or fitting and detach it. If the hoses are in bad shape, now would be a good time to replace them with new ones.

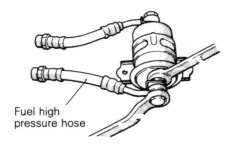

Fuel high
pressure hose

**30.9   Use two wrenches when removing the fuel hoses – an open
end to steady the filter and a box-end to loosen the bolt without
rounding it off**

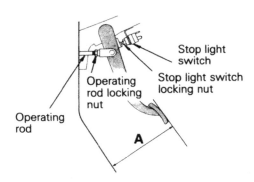

Stop light
switch

Operating
rod locking
nut

Stop light switch
locking nut

Operating
rod

A

31.1a   Brake pedal height adjustment details

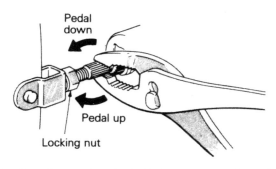

Pedal
down

Pedal up

Locking nut

**31.1b   Use pliers to turn the brake booster operating rod to
adjust the pedal height and freeplay**

11   Remove the bolts and detach the filter, noting the direction in which it was installed.

12   Install the new filter in the bracket, making sure the filter is properly oriented.

13   Connect the hoses to the new filter and tighten the bolts or fitting securely. On bolt-type (banjo) connections, use new sealing washers.

14   Start the engine and check carefully for leaks at the filter hose connections.

31   Brake pedal height and freeplay check and adjustment

Refer to illustrations 31.1a and 31.1b

1   Brake pedal height is the distance the pedal sits away from the floor **(see illustration)**. The distance should be as specified (see this Chapter's Specifications). If the pedal height is not within the specified range, loosen the locking nut and back the stop light switch off until it doesn't contact the brake pedal arm. Loosen the brake booster operating rod locking nut and turn rod in or out until the pedal height is correct **(see illustration)**. Retighten the locking nut.

32.2   The charcoal canister is attached to the fenderwell in the engine compartment – check the canister housing and hoses for damage

2   Brake pedal freeplay is the distance the pedal can be depressed before it begins to have any effect on the brakes. Measure the freeplay with the engine off after stepping on the brake pedal five times. The freeplay should be as specified. If it isn't, loosen the locknut, back off the brake light switch and adjust the brake booster rod until the freeplay is correct, then retighten the locknut.
3   After adjustment, turn the stop light switch until it contacts the brake pedal arm, then back it off about one turn and tighten the locknut.

32   Evaporative emissions system check

Refer to illustration 32.2
1   The function of the evaporative emissions system is to draw fuel vapors from the fuel tank, store them in a charcoal canister and burn them during normal engine operation.
2   The most common symptom of a fault in the evaporative emissions system is a strong fuel odor in the engine compartment. If a fuel odor is detected, inspect the charcoal canister, located in the engine compartment. Check the canister and all hoses for damage and deterioration **(see illustration).**
3   The canister is held to the fenderwell by a spring clip, secured around the the outside of the canister body. The canister is removed by marking and disconnecting the hoses, disengaging the clamp and lifting the canister out.
4   The evaporative emissions control system is explained in more detail in Chapter 6.

33   Carburetor choke check

1   The choke operates only when the engine is cold, so this check should be performed before the engine has been started for the day.
2   Open the hood and remove the top plate of the air cleaner assembly. It's held in place by one or two wing nuts at the center and several spring clips around the edge. If any vacuum hoses must be disconnected, tag them to ensure reinstallation in their original positions.
3   Look at the center of the air cleaner housing. You'll notice a flat plate at the carburetor opening.
4   Have an assistant press the throttle pedal to the floor. The plate should close completely. Start the engine while you watch the plate at the carburetor. Don't position your face near the carburetor, as the engine could backfire, causing serious burns! When the engine starts, the choke plate should open slightly.

5   Allow the engine to continue running at an idle speed. As the engine warms up to operating temperature, the plate should slowly open, allowing more air to enter through the top of the carburetor.
6   After a few minutes, the choke plate should be completely open to the vertical position. Tap the accelerator to make sure the fast idle cam disengages.
7   You'll notice that engine speed corresponds to the plate opening. With the plate closed, the engine should run at a fast idle speed. As the plate opens and the throttle is moved to disengage the fast idle cam, the engine speed will decrease.
8   With the engine off and the throttle held half-way open, open and close the choke several times. Check the linkage to see if it's hooked up correctly and make sure it doesn't bind.
9   If the choke or linkage binds, sticks or works sluggishly, clean it with choke cleaner (an aerosol spray available at auto parts stores). If the condition persists after cleaning, replace the troublesome parts.
10   Visually inspect all vacuum hoses to be sure they're securely connected and look for cracks and deterioration. Replace as necessary.
11   If the choke fails to operate normally, but no mechanical causes can be found, check the choke electrical circuits.

34   Idle speed check and adjustment (carbureted models only)

Refer to the carburetor adjustment procedures in Chapter 4.

35   Transfer case lubricant change (4WD models)

1   Drive the vehicle for at least 15 minutes in 4WD to warm up the lubricant in the case.
2   Raise the vehicle and support it securely on jackstands.
3   Move a drain pan, rags, newspapers and tools under the vehicle.
4   Remove the filler plug (see Section 21).
5   Remove the drain plug from the lower part of the case and allow the old lubricant to drain completely.
6   Carefully clean and install the drain plug after the case is completely drained. Tighten the plug to the torque listed in this Chapter's Specifications.
7   Fill the case with the specified lubricant until it's level with the lower edge of the filler hole.
8   Install the filler plug and tighten it securely.
9   Check carefully for leaks around the drain plug after the first few miles of driving.

36   Manual transmission lubricant change

1   Drive the vehicle for a few miles to thoroughly warm up the transmission lubricant.
2   Raise the vehicle and support it securely on jackstands.
3   Move a drain pan, rags, newspapers and tools under the vehicle. With the drain pan and newspapers in position under the transmission, loosen the drain plug located in the bottom of the transmission case.
4   Once loosened, carefully unscrew it with your fingers until you can remove it from the transmission. Allow all of the oil to drain into the pan. If the plug is too hot to touch, use the wrench to remove it.
5   Clean the drain plug, then reinstall it in the transmission and tighten it to the specified torque.
6   Remove the transmission lubricant filler plug (see Section 20). Using a hand pump or syringe, fill the transmission with the correct amount and grade of lubricant, until the level is just at the bottom of the plug hole.
7   Reinstall the filler plug and tighten it securely.

37   Differential lubricant change

Note: *The following procedure can be used for the rear differential as well as the front differential used on 4WD vehicles.*

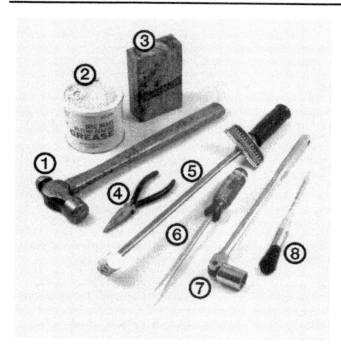

39.1   Tools and materials needed for front wheel bearing maintenance

1   **Hammer** – *A common hammer will do just fine*
2   **Grease** – *High-temperature grease that is formulated specially for front wheel bearings should be used*
3   **Wood block** – *If you have a scrap piece of 2x4, it can be used to drive the new seal into the hub*
4   **Needle-nose pliers** – *Used to straighten and remove the cotter pin in the spindle*
5   **Torque wrench** – *This is very important in this procedure; if the bearing is too tight, the wheel won't turn freely – if it's too loose, the wheel will "wobble" on the spindle. Either way, it could mean extensive damage.*
6   **Screwdriver** – *Used to remove the seal from the hub (a long screwdriver would be preferred)*
7   **Socket/breaker bar** – *Needed to loosen the nut on the spindle if it's extremely tight*
8   **Brush** – *Together with some clean solvent, this will be used to remove old grease from the hub and spindle*

1   Drive the vehicle for several miles to warm up the differential lubricant, then raise the vehicle and support it securely on jackstands.
2   Move a drain pan, rags, newspapers and a 1/2-inch drive breaker bar or ratchet with an extension under the vehicle.
3   With the drain pan under the differential, use the breaker bar or ratchet and extension to loosen the drain plug. It's the lower of the two plugs.
4   Once loosened, carefully unscrew it with your fingers until you can remove it from the case.
5   Allow all of the lubricant to drain into the pan, then replace the drain plug and tighten it to the torque listed in this Chapter's Specifications.
6   Feel with your hands along the bottom of the drain pan for any metal bits that may have come out with the lubricant. If there are any, it's a sign of excessive wear, indicating that the internal components should be carefully inspected in the near future.
7   Using a hand pump, syringe or funnel, fill the differential with the correct amount and grade of lubricant until the level is just at the bottom of the fill plug hole.
8   Reinstall the plug and tighten it securely.
9   Lower the vehicle. Check for leaks after the first few miles of driving.

38   Automatic transmission fluid and filter change

1   At the specified time intervals, the transmission fluid should be drained and replaced. Since the fluid should be hot when it's drained, drive the vehicle for 15 or 20 minutes before proceeding.
2   Before beginning work, purchase the specified transmission fluid and filter (if equipped). Most models with drain plugs do not have filter, so it's important before starting the job to determine whether your model requires a replacement filter.
3   Other tools necessary for this job include jackstands to support the vehicle in a raised position, a drain pan capable of holding at least eight pints, newspapers and clean rags.
4   Raise the vehicle and support it securely on jackstands.
5   Move the drain pan and necessary tools under the vehicle, being careful not to touch any of the hot exhaust components.

Drain plug-equipped models

6   Place the pan under the drain plug in the transmission pan and remove the plug. Be sure the drain pan is in position, as fluid will come out with some force. Once the fluid is drained, reinstall the drain plug securely.

Models without drain plugs

7   Place the drain pan in position under the rear of the transmission pan. Loosen the front transmission pan bolts about one turn and remove the rest of the bolts. Carefully pry the rear of the pan loose with a screwdriver and allow the fluid to drain. Remove the front pan bolts and remove the pan.
8   Remove the filter retaining bolts and lower the filter from the transmission. Be careful when lowering the filter as it contains residual fluid.
9   Place the new filter in position and install the bolts. Tighten the bolts securely.
10   Carefully clean the gasket surface of the transmission to remove all traces of the old gasket and sealant.
11   Drain any remaining fluid from the transmission pan, clean it with solvent and dry it with compressed air. Clean the pan magnet and install it in the pan so it will be directly below the filter.
12   Apply a thin layer of RTV sealant to the transmission case side of the new gasket.
13   Make sure the gasket surface on the transmission pan is clean, then apply a thin layer of RTV sealant to it and position the new gasket on the pan. Put the pan in place against the transmission, install the bolts and, working around the pan, tighten each bolt a little at a time until it's snug (do not over torque).

All models

14   Lower the vehicle and add new automatic transmission fluid through the filler tube (Section 5). The amount should be slightly less than the amount of fluid that was drained (you don't want to overfill it).
15   With the transmission in Park and the parking brake set, run the engine at a fast idle, but don't race it.
16   Move the gear selector through each range and back to Park, then check the fluid level (Section 5). Add more fluid as required. Add the fluid a little at a time, continually checking the level so you don't overfill the transmission.
17   Check under the vehicle for leaks during the first few miles of driving.

39   Front wheel bearing check, repack and adjustment (2WD models only)

Refer to illustrations 39.1 and 39.6
Note: *For 4WD vehicles, see Chapter 8.*

1   In most cases the front wheel bearings will not need servicing until the brake pads are changed. However, the bearings should be checked whenever the front of the vehicle is raised for any reason. Several items, including a torque wrench and special grease, are required for this procedure **(see illustration)**.
2   With the vehicle securely supported on jackstands, spin each wheel and check for noise, rolling resistance and freeplay.

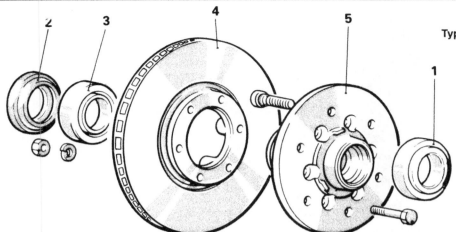

**Typical 2WD front hub components –
exploded view**

1 Outer bearing
2 Grease seal
3 Inner bearing
4 Brake disc
5 Hub

3   Grasp the top of each tire with one hand and the bottom with the other. Move the wheel in-and-out on the spindle. If there's any noticeable movement, the bearings should be checked and then repacked with grease or replaced if necessary.
4   Remove the wheel(s).
5   Remove the brake caliper (Chapter 9) and hang it out of the way on a piece of wire.
6   Pry the grease cap out of the hub **(see illustration)**.
7   Straighten the bent ends of the cotter pin, then pull the cotter pin out of the adjusting nut cap. Discard the cotter pin and use a new one during reassembly.
8   Remove the adjusting nut and washer from the end of the spindle.
9   Pull the hub out slightly, then push it back into its original position. This should force the outer wheel bearing off the spindle enough so it can be removed.
10   Pull the hub off the spindle.
11   Use a screwdriver to pry the grease seal out of the rear of the hub. As this is done, note how the seal is installed.
12   Remove the inner wheel bearing from the hub.
13   Use solvent to remove all traces of the old grease from the bearings, hub and spindle. A small brush may prove helpful; however make sure no bristles from the brush embed themselves inside the bearing rollers. Allow the parts to air dry.
14   Carefully inspect the bearings for cracks, heat discoloration, worn rollers, etc. Check the bearing races inside the hub for wear and damage. If the bearing races are defective, the hubs should be taken to a machine shop with the facilities to remove the old races and press new ones in. Note that the bearings and races come as matched sets and old bearings should never be installed on new races.
15   Use high-temperature front wheel bearing grease to pack the bearings. Work the grease completely into the bearings, forcing it between the rollers, cone and cage from the back side.
16   Apply a thin coat of grease to the spindle at the outer bearing seat, inner bearing seat, shoulder and seal seat.
17   Put a small quantity of grease behind each bearing race inside the hub. Using your finger, form a dam at these points to provide for extra grease and to keep thinned grease from flowing out of the bearing.
18   Place the grease-packed inner bearing into the rear of the hub and put a little more grease outside of the bearing. Place 1/2 oz of grease inside the end of the grease cap.
19   Place a new seal over the inner bearing and tap the seal evenly into place with a hammer and block of wood until it's flush with the hub.
20   Carefully place the hub assembly onto the spindle and push the grease-packed outer bearing into position.
21   Install the washer and adjusting nut. Tighten the nut to about 22 ft-lbs.
22   Loosen the nut, then tighten it to 6 ft-lbs.
23   Install the the cotter pin, taking care not to back it off more than 30-degrees to align the slot with the hole in the spindle.
24   Bend the ends of the cotter pin until they're flat against the nut. Cut off any extra length which could interfere with the grease cap.

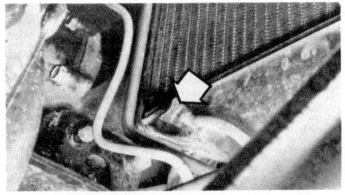

40.4   The radiator drain plug (arrow) is located at the bottom of the radiator

25   Install the grease cap, tapping it into place with a hammer.
26   Install the caliper (see Chapter 9).
27   Install the tire/wheel assembly on the hub and tighten the lug nuts.
28   Grasp the top and bottom of the tire and check the bearings in the manner described earlier in this Section.
29   Lower the vehicle.

40   Cooling system servicing (draining, flushing and refilling)

Refer to illustration 40.4
Warning: *Antifreeze is a corrosive and poisonous solution, so be careful not to spill any of the coolant mixture on the vehicle's paint or your skin. If you do, rinse it off immediately with plenty of clean water. Consult local authorities regarding proper disposal of antifreeze before draining the cooling system. In many areas, reclamation centers have been established to collect used oil and coolant mixtures.*

1   Periodically, the cooling system should be drained, flushed and refilled to replenish the antifreeze mixture and prevent formation of rust and corrosion, which can impair the performance of the cooling system and cause engine damage. When the cooling system is serviced, all hoses and the radiator cap should be checked and replaced if necessary.
2   Apply the parking brake and block the wheels. If the vehicle has just been driven, wait several hours to allow the engine to cool down before beginning this procedure.
3   Once the engine is completely cool, remove the radiator cap. Place the heater temperature control in the maximum heat position.
4   Move a large container under the radiator drain to catch the coolant, then unscrew the drain plug (a pair of pliers may be required to turn it) **(see illustration)**.
5   After the coolant stops flowing out of the radiator, move the container under the engine block drain plug(s) (on four-cylinder engines there is one

41.5   On models with a PCV valve, pull off the hose and use a wrench to unscrew the PCV valve from the valve cover

41.6   With the engine running, suction should be felt at the threaded end of the PCV valve

plug on the side of the block; on V6 engines there are two plugs, located on each side of the block). Remove the plug(s) and allow the coolant in the block to drain.

6   While the coolant is draining, check the condition of the radiator hoses, heater hoses and clamps (refer to Section 9 if necessary).

7   Replace any damaged clamps or hoses.

8   Once the system is completely drained, flush the radiator with fresh water from a garden hose until it runs clear at the drain. The flushing action of the water will remove sediments from the radiator but will not remove rust and scale from the engine and cooling tube surfaces.

9   These deposits can be removed with a chemical cleaner. Follow the procedure outlined in the manufacturer's instructions. If the radiator is severely corroded, damaged or leaking, it should be removed (Chapter 3) and taken to a radiator repair shop.

10   Remove the overflow hose from the coolant recovery reservoir. Drain the reservoir and flush it with clean water, then reconnect the hose.

11   Reinstall and tighten the radiator drain plug. Install and tighten the block drain plug(s).

12   Slowly add new coolant (a 50/50 mixture of water and antifreeze) to the radiator until it's full. Add coolant to the reservoir up to the lower mark.

13   Leave the radiator cap off and run the engine in a well-ventilated area until the thermostat opens (coolant will begin flowing through the radiator and the upper radiator hose will become hot).

14   Turn the engine off and let it cool. Add more coolant mixture to bring the level back up to the lip on the radiator filler neck.

15   Squeeze the upper radiator hose to expel air, then add more coolant mixture if necessary. Replace the radiator cap.

16   Start the engine, allow it to reach normal operating temperature and check for leaks.

---

41   Positive Crankcase Ventilation (PCV) system check

Refer to illustrations 41.5 and 41.6

1   The Positive Crankcase Ventilation (PCV) system directs blowby gases from the crankcase back into the intake manifold so they can be burned in the engine.

2   Rough idling or high idle speed and stalling are symptoms of faults in the PCV system.

3   The system on these models consists of a hose leading from the valve cover to the intake manifold and a fresh air hose between the air cleaner assembly and the valve cover. Gases from the crankcase are carried by the hose through a PCV valve or orifice in the hose into the intake manifold.

4   Check the system hoses for cracks, leaks and clogging. On orifice-type systems, check the orifice carefully for clogging. Clean the hoses if they are clogged and replace any which are damaged.

5   On models with a PCV valve, remove the valve **(see illustration)**.

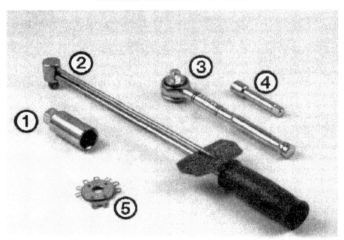

42.2   Tools required for changing spark plugs

1   **Spark plug socket** – This will have special padding inside to protect the spark plug's porcelain insulator
2   **Torque wrench** – Although not mandatory, using this tool is the best way to ensure the plugs are tightened properly
3   **Ratchet** – Standard hand tool to fit the spark plug socket
4   **Extension** – Depending on model and accessories, you may need special extensions and universal joints to reach one or more of the plugs
5   **Spark plug gap gauge** – This gauge for checking the gap comes in a variety of styles. Make sure the gap for your engine is included.

6   Start the engine and verify that air can be heard passing through the valve and a suction should be felt, indicating it is operating properly **(see illustration)**.

7   Shut off the engine and blow though the valve from the threaded end. If air will not pass through, replace the valve with a new one.

8   More information on the PCV system can be found in Chapter 6.

---

42   Spark plug replacement

Refer to illustrations 42.2, 42.5a, 42.5b, 42.6, 42.8 and 42.10

1   Replace the spark plugs with new ones at the intervals recommended in the Maintenance schedule.

2   In most cases, the tools necessary for spark plug replacement include a spark plug socket which fits onto a ratchet (spark plug sockets are padded inside to prevent damage to the porcelain insulators on the new plugs), various extensions and a gap gauge to check and adjust the gaps on the new plugs **(see illustration)**. A special plug wire removal tool is

42.5a   Spark plug manufacturers recommend using a wire type gauge when checking the gap – if the wire does not slide between the electrodes with a slight drag, adjustment is required

42.5b   To change the gap, bend the *side* electrode only, as indicated by the arrows, and be very careful not to crack or chip the porcelain insulator surrounding the center electrode

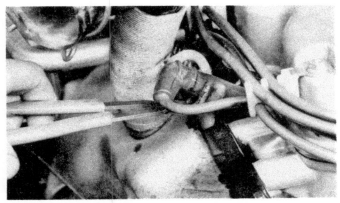

42.6   When removing the spark plug wires, pull only on the boot and twist it back-and-forth – a spark plug wire removal tool makes this job easier

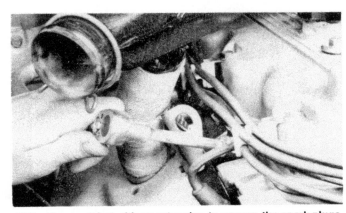

42.8   Use a ratchet with an extension to remove the spark plugs

available for separating the wire boots from the spark plugs, but it isn't absolutely necessary. A torque wrench should be used to tighten the new plugs.

3   The best approach when replacing the spark plugs is to purchase the new ones in advance, adjust them to the proper gap and replace them one at a time. When buying the new spark plugs, be sure to obtain the correct plug type for your particular engine. This information can be found on the Emission Control Information label located under the hood and in the factory owner's manual. If differences exist between the plug specified on the emissions label and in the owner's manual, assume the emissions label is correct.

4   Allow the engine to cool completely before attempting to remove any of the plugs. While you're waiting for the engine to cool, check the new plugs for defects and adjust the gaps.

5   The gap is checked by inserting the proper thickness gauge between the electrodes at the tip of the plug **(see illustration)**. The gap between the electrodes should be the same as the one specified on the Emissions Control Information label. The wire should just slide between the electrodes with a slight amount of drag. If the gap is incorrect, use the adjuster on the gauge body to bend the curved side electrode slightly until the proper gap is obtained **(see illustration)**. If the side electrode is not exactly over the center electrode, bend it with the adjuster until it is. Check for cracks in the porcelain insulator (if any are found, the plug shouldn't be used).

6   With the engine cool, remove the spark plug wire from one spark plug. Pull only on the boot at the end of the wire – don't pull on the wire. A plug wire removal tool should be used if available **(see illustration)**.

7   If compressed air is available, use it to blow any dirt or foreign material away from the spark plug hole. A common bicycle pump will also work. The

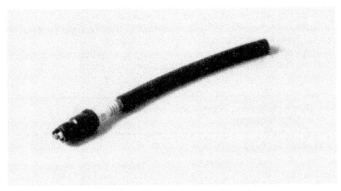

42.10   A length of 3/16-inch ID rubber hose will save time and prevent damaged threads when installing the spark plugs

idea here is to eliminate the possibility of debris falling into the cylinder as the spark plug is removed.

8   Place the spark plug socket over the plug and remove it from the engine by turning it in a counterclockwise direction **(see illustration)**.

9   Compare the spark plug to those shown in the accompanying photos to get an indication of the general running condition of the engine.

10   Thread one of the new plugs into the hole until you can no longer turn it with your fingers, then tighten it with a torque wrench (if available) or the ratchet. It might be a good idea to slip a short length of rubber hose over the end of the plug to use as a tool to thread it into place **(see illustration)**. The hose will grip the plug well enough to turn it, but will start to slip if the plug

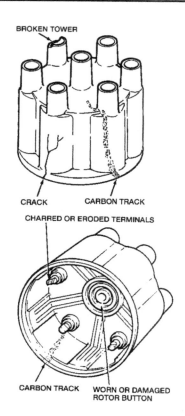

BROKEN TOWER

CRACK   CARBON TRACK

CHARRED OR ERODED TERMINALS

CARBON TRACK   WORN OR DAMAGED ROTOR BUTTON

43.11   Shown here are some of the common defects to look for when inspecting the distributor cap (if in doubt about its condition, install a new one)

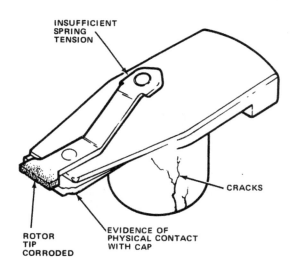

INSUFFICIENT SPRING TENSION

CRACKS

ROTOR TIP CORRODED

EVIDENCE OF PHYSICAL CONTACT WITH CAP

43.12   The ignition rotor should be checked for wear and corrosion as indicated here (if in doubt about its condition, buy a new one)

begins to cross-thread in the hole – this will prevent damaged threads and the accompanying repair costs.

11   Before pushing the spark plug wire onto the end of the plug, inspect it following the procedures outlined in Section 43.

12   Attach the plug wire to the new spark plug, again using a twisting motion on the boot until it's seated on the spark plug.

13   Repeat the procedure for the remaining spark plugs, replacing them one at a time to prevent mixing up the spark plug wires.

43   Spark plug wire, distributor cap and rotor check and replacement

Refer to illustrations 43.11 and 43.12

1   The spark plug wires should be checked whenever new spark plugs are installed.

2   Begin this procedure by making a visual check of the spark plug wires while the engine is running. In a darkened garage (make sure there is ventilation) start the engine and observe each plug wire. Be careful not to come into contact with any moving engine parts. If there is a break in the wire, you will see arcing or a small spark at the damaged area. If arcing is noticed, make a note to obtain new wires, then allow the engine to cool and check the distributor cap and rotor.

3   The spark plug wires should be inspected one at a time to prevent mixing up the order, which is essential for proper engine operation. Each original plug wire should be numbered to help identify its location. If the number is illegible, a piece of tape can be marked with the correct number and wrapped around the plug wire.

4   Disconnect the plug wire from the spark plug. A removal tool can be used for this purpose or you can grasp the rubber boot, twist the boot half a turn and pull the boot free. Do not pull on the wire itself **(see illustration 42.6).**

5   Check inside the boot for corrosion, which will look like a white crusty powder.

6   Push the wire and boot back onto the end of the spark plug. It should fit tightly onto the end of the plug. If it doesn't, remove the wire and use pliers to carefully crimp the metal connector inside the wire boot until the fit is snug.

7   Using a clean rag, wipe the entire length of the wire to remove built-up dirt and grease. Once the wire is clean, check for burns, cracks and other damage. Do not bend the wire sharply, because the conductor within the wire might break.

8   Disconnect the wire from the distributor. Again, pull only on the rubber boot. Check for corrosion and a tight fit. Press the wire back into the distributor.

9   Inspect the remaining spark plug wires, making sure that each one is securely fastened at the distributor and spark plug when the check is complete.

10   If new spark plug wires are required, purchase a set for your specific engine model. Pre-cut wire sets with the boots already installed are available. Remove and replace the wires one at a time to avoid mix-ups in the firing order.

11   Detach the distributor cap by prying off the two cap retaining clips or removing the two screws. Look inside it for cracks, carbon tracks and worn, burned or loose contacts **(see illustration).**

12   Remove the rotor from the distributor shaft. On some models there is a screw on the side of the rotor that must be removed. On other models, simply pull the rotor off the shaft. Examine the rotor for cracks and carbon tracks **(see illustration).** Replace the cap and rotor if any damage or defects are noted.

13   It is common practice to install a new cap and rotor whenever new spark plug wires are installed, but if you wish to continue using the old cap, clean the terminals first.

14   When installing a new cap, remove the wires from the old cap one at a time and attach them to the new cap in the exact same location – do not simultaneously remove all the wires from the old cap or firing order mix-ups may occur.

44   Ignition timing check and adjustment

Refer to illustrations 44.1, 44.6a, 44.6b, 44.7 and 44.10

Note: *If the information in this Section differs from the Vehicle Emission Control Information label in the engine compartment, the information on the label should be considered correct.*

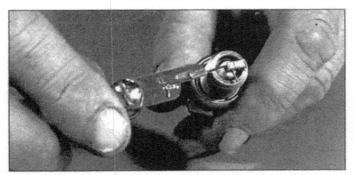

Electrode gap check - use a wire type gauge for best results

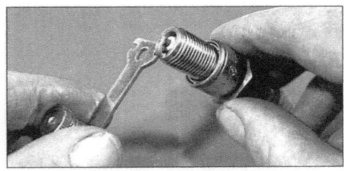

Electrode gap adjustment - bend the side electrode using the correct tool

Normal condition - A brown, tan or grey firing end indicates that the engine is in good condition and that the plug type is correct

Ash deposits - Light brown deposits encrusted on the electrodes and insulator, leading to misfire and hesitation. Caused by excessive amounts of oil in the combustion chamber or poor quality fuel/oil

Carbon fouling - Dry, black sooty deposits leading to misfire and weak spark. Caused by an over-rich fuel/air mixture, faulty choke operation or blocked air filter

Oil fouling - Wet oily deposits leading to misfire and weak spark. Caused by oil leakage past piston rings or valve guides (4-stroke engine), or excess lubricant (2-stroke engine)

Overheating - A blistered white insulator and glazed electrodes. Caused by ignition system fault, incorrect fuel, or cooling system fault

Worn plug - Worn electrodes will cause poor starting in damp or cold weather and will also waste fuel

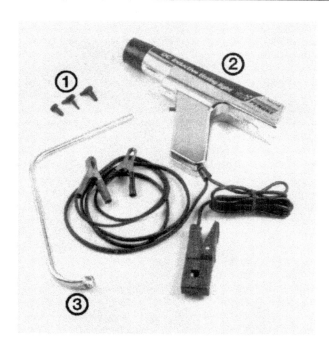

44.1   Tools needed to check and adjust the ignition timing

1   *Vacuum plugs* – *Vacuum hoses will, in most cases, have to be disconnected and plugged. Molded plugs in various shapes and sizes are available for this.*
2   *Inductive pick-up timing light* – *Flashes a bright concentrated beam of light when the number one spark plug fires. Connect the leads according to the instructions supplied with the light.*
3   *Distributor wrench* – *On some models, the hold-down bolt for the distributor is difficult to reach and turn with conventional wrenches or sockets. A special wrench like this must be used.*

1   The proper ignition timing setting for your vehicle is printed on the VECI label located in the engine compartment. Some special tools will be required for this procedure **(see illustration)**.
2   Locate the timing plate on the front of the engine, near the crankshaft pulley. The T or 0 mark is Top Dead Center (TDC). To locate which mark the notch in the pulley must line up with for the timing to be correct, count back from the T or 0 mark the number of degrees BTDC (Before Top Dead Center) noted on the VECI label.
3   Locate the timing notch in the pulley and mark it with a dab of paint or chalk so it'll be visible under the strobe light. To locate the notch it may be necessary to have an assistant temporarily turn the ignition key to Start in short bursts to turn the crankshaft. **Warning:** *Stay clear of all moving engine components if the engine is turned in this manner!*
4   Connect a tachometer according to the manufacturer's instructions and make sure the idle speed is correct (carbureted models). Adjust it, if necessary, as described in Chapter 4.
5   Allow the engine to reach normal operating temperature. Be sure the air conditioner, if equipped, and all other accessories are off.
6   With the ignition switch off, connect the pick-up lead of the timing light to the number one spark plug wire. On four-cylinder engines, it's the front one. On V6 engines it's the first spark plug on the right side as viewed from the driver's seat. Use either a jumper lead between the wire and plug or an inductive-type pick up. Don't pierce the wire or attempt to insert a wire between the boot and plug wire. Connect the timing light power leads according to the manufacturer's instructions. On fuel-injected models, should it be necessary to connect a tachometer (to verify the idle speed is correct), insert a paper clip into the wire side of the fuel injector connector – without disconnecting it – **(see illustrations)**. Connect the tachometer between the paper clip and ground.

2.4L Engine

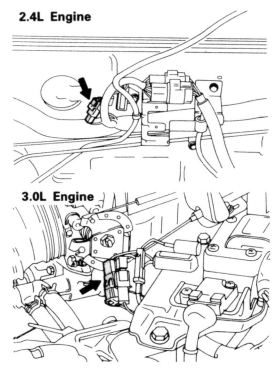

3.0L Engine

44.6a   To connect a tachometer on fuel-injected models, locate the fuel injector connector (arrows) . . .

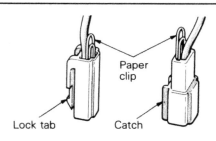

Paper clip

Lock tab   Catch

Female connector   Male connector

44.6b . . . and insert a paper clip as shown into the connector – the tachometer is then connected between the paper clip and ground

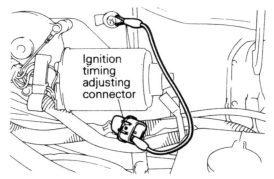

Ignition timing adjusting connector

44.7   On fuel-injected models, connect a jumper wire between the ignition timing adjusting connector and ground (Montero model shown)

7   On fuel-injected models, remove the waterproof cover from the ignition timing adjusting connector (in the engine compartment) and connect a wire with alligator clips between the terminal in the connector and ground

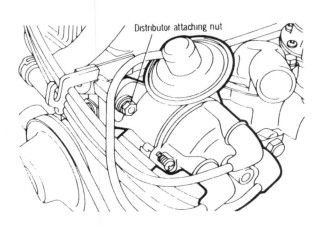

44.10   Loosen the distributor attaching/hold-down nut (arrow) and turn the distributor to adjust the ignition timing

45.2   Locate the EGR valve (arrow) and check the hoses leading to it for damage

46.2   Detach the altitude compensator for access to the solenoid air valve cover (arrow)

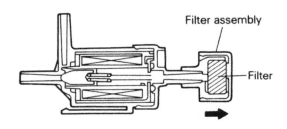

46.3   Solenoid valve air filter details

(see illustration). Do this before starting the engine to check the ignition timing.

8   Make sure the wiring for the timing light is clear of all moving engine components, then start the engine. Race the engine two or three times, then allow it to idle for a minute.

9   Point the flashing timing light at the timing marks, again being careful not to come in contact with moving parts. The marks you highlighted should appear stationary. If the marks are in alignment, the timing is correct. If the marks aren't aligned, turn off the engine.

10   Loosen the distributor attaching/hold-down bolt/nut until the distributor can be rotated (see illustration).

11   Start the engine and slowly rotate the distributor either left or right until the timing marks are aligned.

12   Shut off the engine and tighten the mounting bolt/nut, being careful not to move the distributor.

13   Restart the engine and recheck the timing to make sure the marks are still in alignment.

14   Disconnect the timing light and jumper wire.

15   Race the engine two or three times, then allow it to run at idle. Recheck the idle speed with the tachometer. If it has changed from the correct setting, readjust it (carbureted models only).

16   Drive the vehicle and listen for "pinging" noises. They'll be noticeable when the engine is hot and under load (climbing a hill, accelerating from a stop). If you hear engine pinging, the ignition timing is too far advanced (Before Top Dead Center). Reconnect the timing light and turn the distributor to move the mark 1 or 2-degrees in the retard direction (counterclockwise). Road test the vehicle again to check for proper operation.

17   To keep "pinging" at a minimum, yet still allow you to operate the vehicle at the specified timing setting, use gasoline of the same octane at all times. Switching fuel brands and octane levels can decrease performance and economy, and possibly damage the engine.

45   Exhaust Gas Recirculation (EGR) system check

Refer to illustration 45.2

1   The EGR valve is located on the intake manifold. Most of the time, when a problem develops in the emissions system, it is due to a stuck or corroded EGR valve.

2   With the engine cold to prevent burns, check the EGR valve hoses for damage (see illustration). Pull the hoses off and inspect for clogging.

3   If the hoses are cracked or clogged, replace them with new ones.

4   Refer to Chapter 6 for more information on the EGR system.

46   Solenoid valve air filter replacement (1985 through 1989 models)

Refer to illustrations 46.2 and 46.3

1   The solenoid valve air filter on 1985 through 1989 models must be replaced at the specified intervals or it will become clogged, causing rough idling. The solenoid valve is located in the engine compartment on the driver's side inner fender, under a cover.

2   Remove cover for access (see illustration).

3   Pull the filter out of the assembly and push a new one securely into place (see illustration).

47   Oxygen sensor replacement

1   The oxygen (exhaust gas) sensor used on later models should be replaced at the specified intervals.

48.2   On later models, the reset switch for the maintenance reminder light is located on the lower right corner of the instrument cluster

2   The sensor is threaded into the exhaust manifold and can be identified by the wire attached to it. Replacement consists of disconnecting the wire harness and unthreading the sensor from the manifold. Apply anti-seize compound to the threads of the new sensor (some new sensors may already have anti-seize compound on the threads). Tighten the new sensor to the torque listed in this Chapter's Specifications, then reconnect the wire harness.

3   refer to the next section for the emissions maintenance reminder light resetting procedure.

48   Emissions maintenance reminder light resetting

Refer to illustration 48.2

1   At certain mileage intervals, an emissions maintenance reminder light on the instrument cluster will illuminate, alerting the driver that it's time to check the EGR system and/or replace the oxygen sensor (see the *Maintenance schedule* at the beginning of this Chapter).

2   After performing the required service, a switch on the instrument cluster must be moved from one position to the other, which will reset the mileage counter. On some models the switch is located behind the instrument cluster, near the speedometer cable (see Chapter 12 for the instrument cluster removal procedure). On other models the switch is located on the front of the cluster, at the lower right corner **(see illustration)**. To gain access to this type, only the instrument panel trim has to be removed.

3   If the service being performed is at the 120,000–mile interval, remove the maintenance reminder light bulb from the instrument cluster.

Chapter 2 Part A   2.6L four-cylinder engine

Contents

Specifications

General

Firing order 1-3-4-2
Cylinder numbers (front-to-rear) 1–2–3–4
Bore . . . . 3.59 inches
Stroke . . . . 3.86 inches
Displacement . . . . 155.9 cubic inches

Camshaft

Endplay . . . . 0.004 to 0.008 inch
Runout . . . . 0.03 inch
Lobe height
  1983 through 1986 pick-up . . . . 1.6730 inch
  1983 and 1984 Montero . . . . 1.6730 inch
  1987 pick-up and 1985 through 1987 Montero . . . . 1.6693 inch
  1988 on (all models) . . . . 1.6705 inch
Lobe wear (maximum) . . . . 0.020 inch

Cylinder head warpage limit . . . . 0.008 inch

Intake/exhaust manifold warpage limit . . . . 0.006 inch per foot of manifold length

Oil pump

Drive gear-to-bearing clearance
  1983 through 1986 . . . . 0.0016 to 0.0028 inch
  1987 on . . . . 0.0020 to 0.0043 inch

Oil pump (continued)

Driven gear-to-bearing clearance

    1983 through 1986 . . . . 0.0008 to 0.0020 inch

    1987 on . . . . 0.0016 to 0.0039 inch

Drive gear-to-housing clearance . . . . 0.0043 to 0.0059 inch

Driven gear-to-housing clearance . . . . 0.0043 to 0.0059 inch

Drive gear endplay . . . . 0.0020 to 0.0043 inch

Driven gear endplay . . . . 0.0016 to 0.0039 inch

Relief spring free length

    1983 through 1986 . . . . 1.85 inch

    1987 on . . . . 1.835 inch

Torque specifications

Ft-lbs (unless otherwise indicated)

Camshaft bearing cap bolts

    Long (70 mm bolts) 15

    Short (25 mm bolts) 18

Valve cover bolts/nuts . . . . 60 in-lbs

Silent shaft chain guides **(see illustration 9.8)**

    Chain guide A bolts . . . . 156 in-lbs

    Chain guide B bolts

        Bolt A . . . . 12 in-lbs

        Bolt B 14

    Chain guide C bolts . . . . 156 in-lbs

Timing chain guides bolts . . . . 156 in-lbs

Exhaust manifold shield . . . . 132 in-lbs

Engine mount – pick-up **(see illustration 19.4a)**

    Insulator nuts 14

    Rear mount-to-crossmember bolts 18

Engine mount – Montero **(see illustration 19.4b)**

    Stopper bolts 29

    Insulator nuts 15

Camshaft sprocket bolt 40

Crankshaft sprocket bolt 87

Cylinder head bolts – *(use the tightening sequence shown in Section 14)*

    First step (engine cold) 34

    Second step (engine cold) 69

    Third step (engine hot) 75

Cylinder head bolt (M8) 15

Driveplate-to-crankshaft bolts 50

Flywheel-to-crankshaft bolts 60

Intake manifold bolts 14

Exhaust manifold nuts 14

Silent shaft sprocket bolt 48

Oil pan-to-engine block fasteners . . . . 60 in-lbs

Oil pick-up tube bolts 15

Oil pump sprocket bolt 50

Oil pump mounting bolts . . . . 96 in-lbs

Oil pump cover bolts . . . . 96 in-lbs

Oil pump driven gear bolt 50

Rear main oil seal housing bolts . . . . 105 in-lbs

Timing chain cover bolts . . . . 120 in-lbs

1   General information

This Part of Chapter 2 is devoted to in-vehicle repair procedures for the 2.6L timing chain engines. All information concerning engine removal and installation and engine block and cylinder head overhaul can be found in Part D of this Chapter.

The following repair procedures are based on the assumption that the engine is installed in the vehicle. If the engine has been removed from the vehicle and mounted on a stand, many of the steps outlined in this Part of Chapter 2 will not apply.

The Specifications included in this Part of Chapter 2 apply only to the procedures contained in this Part. Part D of Chapter 2 contains the Specifications necessary for cylinder head and engine block rebuilding.

The 2.6L engine is an inline vertical four, with a chain-driven overhead camshaft and a silent shaft counterbalancing system which cancels the engine's power pulses and produces relatively vibration-free operation. The crankshaft rides in five renewable insert-type main bearings, with the center bearing (the thrust bearing) assigned the additional task of controlling crankshaft endplay.

The pistons have two compression rings and one oil control ring. The semi-floating piston pins are press fitted into the small end of the connecting rod. The connecting rod big ends are also equipped with renewable insert-type plain bearings.

The engine is liquid-cooled, utilizing a centrifugal impeller-type pump, driven by a belt from the camshaft, to circulate coolant around the cylinders and combustion chambers and through the intake manifold.

Lubrication is handled by a gear-type oil pump mounted on the front of the engine under the timing chain cover. It is driven by the silent shaft-chain. The oil is filtered continuously by a cartridge-type filter mounted on the radiator side of the engine.

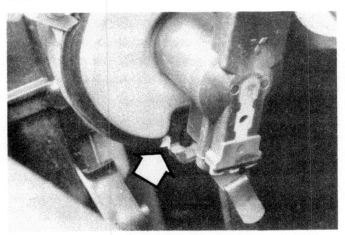

3.6   Mark the distributor housing directly beneath the number one spark plug wire terminal (double check the distributor cap to verify the rotor points to the number 1 cylinder spark plug wire)

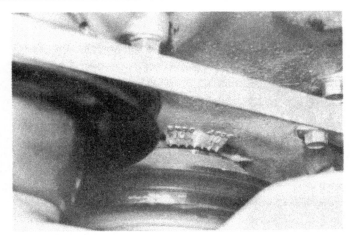

3.8   Align the notch in the pulley with the 0 on the timing plate, then check to see if the distributor rotor is pointing to number 1 cylinder (if not, the camshaft is 180-degrees out of time [number 4 is at TDC] – the crankshaft will have to be rotated 360-degrees)

2   Repair operations possible with the engine in the vehicle

Many major repair operations can be accomplished without removing the engine from the vehicle.

Clean the engine compartment and the exterior of the engine with some type of degreaser before any work is done. It will make the job easier and help keep dirt out of the internal areas of the engine.

Depending on the components involved, it may be helpful to remove the hood to improve access to the engine as repairs are performed (refer to Chapter 11 if necessary). Cover the fenders to prevent damage to the paint. Special pads are available, but an old bedspread or blanket will also work.

If vacuum, exhaust, oil or coolant leaks develop, indicating a need for gasket or seal replacement, the repairs can generally be made with the engine in the vehicle. The intake and exhaust manifold gaskets, oil pan gasket, crankshaft oil seals and cylinder head gasket are all accessible with the engine in place.

Exterior engine components, such as the intake and exhaust manifolds, the oil pan, the water pump, the starter motor, the alternator, the distributor and the fuel system components can be removed for repair with the engine in place.

Since the cylinder head can be removed without pulling the engine, camshaft and valve component servicing can also be accomplished with the engine in the vehicle. Replacement of the timing chain and sprockets is also possible with the engine in the vehicle.

In extreme cases caused by a lack of necessary equipment, repair or replacement of piston rings, pistons, connecting rods and rod bearings is possible with the engine in the vehicle. However, this practice is not recommended because of the cleaning and preparation work that must be done to the components involved.

3   Top Dead Center (TDC) for number one piston – locating

Refer to illustrations 3.6 and 3.8

Note: *The following procedure is based on the assumption that the spark plug wires and distributor are correctly installed. If you are trying to locate TDC to install the distributor correctly, piston position must be determined by feeling for compression at the number one spark plug hole, then aligning the ignition timing marks as described in Step 8.*

1   Top Dead Center (TDC) is the highest point in the cylinder that each piston reaches as it travels up-and-down when the crankshaft turns. Each piston reaches TDC on the compression stroke and again on the exhaust stroke, but TDC generally refers to piston position on the compression stroke.

2   Positioning the piston(s) at TDC is an essential part of many procedures such as camshaft and timing chain/sprocket removal and distributor removal.

3   Before beginning this procedure, be sure to place the transmission in Neutral and apply the parking brake or block the rear wheels. Also, disable the ignition system by detaching the coil wire from the center terminal of the distributor cap and grounding it on the block with a jumper wire. Remove the spark plugs (see Chapter 1).

S4   In order to bring any piston to TDC, the crankshaft must be turned using one of the methods outlined below. When looking at the front of the engine, normal crankshaft rotation is clockwise.

   a)   The preferred method is to turn the crankshaft with a socket and ratchet attached to the bolt threaded into the front of the crankshaft.

   b)   A remote starter switch, which may save some time, can also be used. Follow the instructions included with the switch. Once the piston is close to TDC, use a socket and ratchet as described in the previous paragraph.

   c)   If an assistant is available to turn the ignition switch to the Start position in short bursts, you can get the piston close to TDC without a remote starter switch. Make sure your assistant is out of the vehicle, away from the ignition switch, then use a socket and ratchet as described in Paragraph a) to complete the procedure.

5   Note the position of the terminal for the number one spark plug wire on the distributor cap. If the terminal isn't marked, follow the plug wire from the number one cylinder spark plug to the cap.

6   Mark the distributor body directly under the terminal **(see illustration)**.

7   Detach the cap from the distributor and set it aside (see Chapter 1 if necessary).

8   Locate the timing marks on the front cover. You'll see the timing increments directly above the front pulley. Turn the crankshaft (see Paragraph 3 above) until the TDC mark (zero) on the front cover is aligned with the groove in the front pulley **(see illustration)**.

9   Look at the distributor rotor – it should be pointing directly at the mark you made on the distributor body. If the rotor is pointing at the mark, go to Step 12. If it isn't, go to Step 10.

10   If the rotor is 180-degrees off, the number one piston is at TDC on the exhaust stroke.

11   To get the piston to TDC on the compression stroke, turn the crankshaft one complete turn (360-degrees) clockwise. The rotor should now be pointing at the mark on the distributor. When the rotor is pointing at the number one spark plug wire terminal in the distributor cap and the ignition timing marks are aligned, the number one piston is at TDC on the compression stroke.

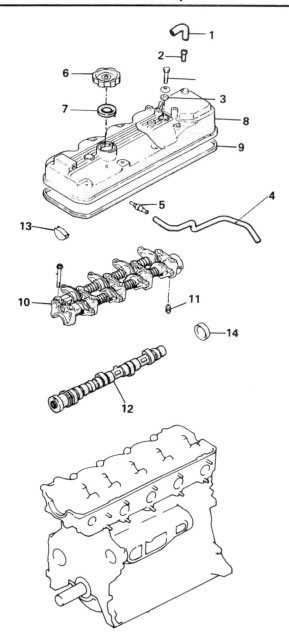

4.7a   An exploded view of the valve cover and related components

1	Breather hose	8	Valve cover
2	Fitting	9	Valve cover gasket
3	Oil seal	10	Rocker arm assembly
4	PCV hose	11	Hydraulic lash adjuster
5	PCV valve	12	Camshaft
6	Oil filter cap	13	Semi-circular plug
7	Oil filter cap seal	14	Camshaft plug

12   After the number one piston has been positioned at TDC on the compression stroke, TDC for any of the remaining pistons can be located by turning the crankshaft and following the firing order. Mark the remaining spark plug wire terminal locations on the distributor body just like you did for the number one terminal, then number the marks to correspond with the cylinder numbers. As you turn the crankshaft, the rotor will also turn. When it's pointing directly at one of the marks on the distributor, the piston for that particular cylinder is at TDC on the compression stroke.

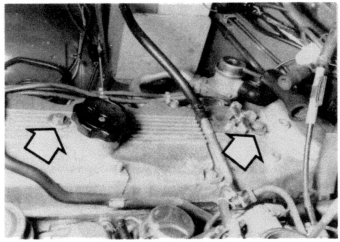

4.7b   Remove the two bolts (arrows) from the valve cover and lift the cover off the engine

---

4   Valve cover – removal and installation

Removal

Refer to illustrations 4.7a and 4.7b

1   Detach the cable from the negative battery terminal.
2   Remove the air cleaner inlet hose and housing assembly from the carburetor and the top of the valve cover (see Chapter 4).
3   Remove the distributor cap and wires from the cylinder head (see Chapter 1). Be sure to mark each wire for correct installation.
4   Remove any fuel lines or vent lines from the carburetor or fuel filter that will interfere with the removal of the valve cover.
5   Disconnect any electrical connections from the carburetor that will interfere with the removal of the valve cover.
6   Wipe off the valve cover thoroughly to prevent debris from falling onto the exposed cylinder head or camshaft/valve train assembly.
7   Remove the valve cover bolts **(see illustrations)**.
8   Carefully lift off the valve cover and gasket. If the gasket is stuck to the cylinder head, tap it with a rubber mallet to break the seal. Do not pry between the cover and cylinder head or you'll damage the gasket mating surfaces.

Installation

Refer to illustrations 4.11

9   Use a gasket scraper to remove all traces of old gasket material from the gasket mating surfaces of the cylinder head and the valve cover. Clean the surfaces with a rag soaked in lacquer thinner or acetone.
10   Be sure to install the semi-circular seal (camshaft plug) on top of the cylinder head near the camshaft sprocket. Apply beads of RTV sealant to the points where the seal meets the valve cover mating surfaces.
11   Install a new gasket onto the valve cover. Install the molded rubber gasket onto the cover by pushing the new gasket into the slot that circles the valve cover perimeter. Apply beads of RTV sealant where the cylinder head and camshaft bearing cap meet **(see illustration)**. Wait five minutes or so and let the RTV "set-up" (slightly harden) and then install the cover and bolts and tighten them to the torque listed in this Chapter's Specifications.
12   The remainder of installation is the reverse of removal.

---

5   Rocker arm assembly – removal, inspection and installation

---

Note 1: *The camshaft bearing caps are removed together with the rocker arm assembly. To prevent the opposite end (transmission end) of the camshaft from popping up (from timing-chain tension) after the assembly is removed, have an assistant hold the opposite end of the camshaft down,*

4.11 Apply a small amount of RTV sealant to the corners of the cylinder head next to the camshaft bearing cap

5.3 Remove the rocker arm assembly bolts (arrows)

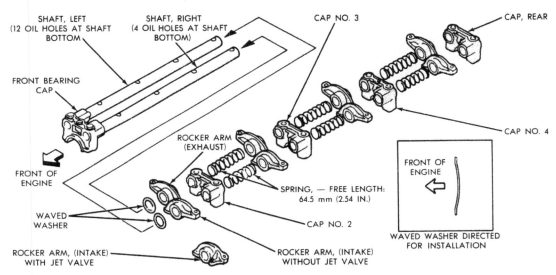

5.5 An exploded view of the rocker arms and shafts (typical)

then reinstall the main bearing cap on that end to hold it in place until reassembly.

Note 2: While the camshaft bearing caps are off, inspect them, as well as the camshaft bearing journals, as described in Section 13.

Removal

Refer to illustration 5.3

1   Remove the valve cover (see Section 4).

2   Position the number one piston at Top Dead Center (see Section 3).

3   Have an assistant hold down the transmission end of the camshaft, then loosen the camshaft bearing cap bolts 1/4-turn at a time until the spring pressure is relieved **(see illustration)**. Do not remove the bolts.

4   Lift the rocker arms and shaft assembly from the cylinder head. Reinstall the bearing cap at the transmission end to hold the camshaft in place.

Inspection

Refer to illustrations 5.5 and 5.6

5   If you wish to disassemble and inspect the rocker arm assemblies (a good idea as long as you have them off), remove the retaining bolts and slip the rocker arms, springs and bearing caps off the shafts **(see illustration)**. Keep the parts in order so you can reassemble them in the same positions. **Note**: *If the engine is equipped with hydraulic lash adjusters, refer to Chapter 2B, Section 7 for the inspection procedure.*

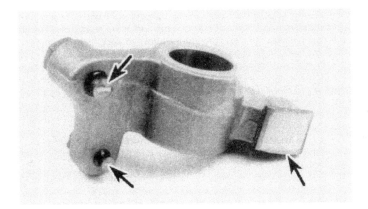

5.6 Check the contact faces and adjusting screw tips (arrows)

6   Thoroughly clean the parts and inspect them for wear and damage. Check the rocker arm faces that contact the camshaft and the adjusting screw tips **(see illustration)**. Check the surfaces of the shafts that the rocker arms ride on, as well as the bearing surfaces inside the rocker

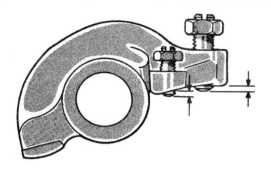

5.7   Back off the adjusters until they only protrude 1 mm (0.040 in)

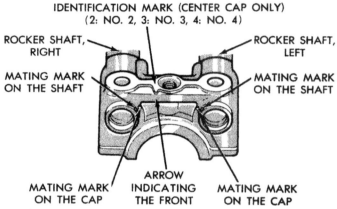

5.8b   Be sure the mating mark on the cap is aligned with the mating mark on the shaft

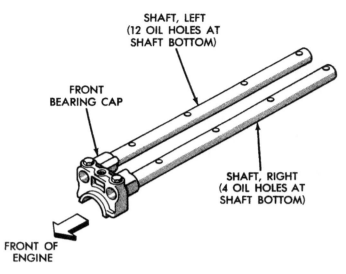

5.8a   Install the rocker shafts into the front bearing cap

6.4   This is what the air hose adapter that threads into the spark plug hole looks like – they're commonly available from auto parts stores

arms, for scoring and excessive wear. Replace any parts that are damaged or excessively worn. Also, make sure the oil holes in the shafts are not plugged.

Installation
Refer to illustrations 5.7, 5.8a and 5.8b

7   Loosen the locknuts and back off the adjusters until they only protrude 1 mm (0.040-inch) **(see illustration)**.
8   Lubricate all components with assembly lube or engine oil and reassemble the shafts. When installing the rocker arms, shafts and springs, note the markings and the difference between the left and right side parts **(see illustration)**. Place the marks in the end of the shaft directly in line with the marks on the caps **(see illustration)** to keep them aligned until they are ready to be installed onto the cylinder head.
9   Position the rocker arm assemblies on the cylinder head and install the mounting bolts finger tight. **Note:** *Check the numbered markings on the caps to make sure the caps are in the correct numerical sequence.*
10   Tighten the camshaft bearing cap bolts 1/4-turn at a time, starting from the middle and working out toward the ends, until the torque listed in this Chapter's Specifications is reached.
11   Adjust the valve clearances (cold) as described in Chapter 1.
12   Temporarily install the valve cover and run the engine until it is fully warmed up.
13   Readjust the valves while the engine is still warm (see Chapter 1).
14   Reinstall the remaining parts in the reverse order of removal.
15   Run the engine and check for oil leaks and proper operation.

---

6   Valve springs, retainers and seals – replacement

Refer to illustrations 6.4, 6.9 and 6.17
Note 1: *Broken valve springs and defective valve stem seals can be re-*

placed without removing the cylinder heads. Two special tools and a compressed air source are normally required to perform this operation, so read through this Section carefully and rent or buy the tools before beginning the job. If compressed air isn't available, a length of nylon rope can be used to keep the valves from falling into the cylinder during this procedure.
Note 2: *Some models are equipped with a jet valve that is mounted directly beside each intake valve. Refer to Chapter 2D, Section 11 for the jet valve servicing procedure.*

1   Refer to Section 4 and remove the valve cover from the affected cylinder head. If all of the valve stem seals are being replaced, remove both valve covers.
2   Remove the spark plug from the cylinder which has the defective component. If all of the valve stem seals are being replaced, all of the spark plugs should be removed.
3   Turn the crankshaft until the piston in the affected cylinder is at top dead center on the compression stroke (refer to Section 3 for instructions). If you're replacing all of the valve stem seals, begin with cylinder number one and work on the valves for one cylinder at a time. Move from cylinder-to-cylinder following the firing order sequence (see this Chapter's Specifications).
4   Thread an adapter into the spark plug hole and connect an air hose from a compressed air source to it **(see illustration)**. Most auto parts stores can supply the air hose adapter. **Note:** *Many cylinder compression gauges utilize a screw-in fitting that may work with your air hose quick-disconnect fitting.*
5   Remove the rocker arms and shafts (see Section 5).

6.9   Use needle nose pliers or a small magnet to remove the valve spring keepers – be careful not to drop them down into the engine

6.17   Apply a small dab of grease to each keeper as shown here before installation – it'll hold them in place on the valve stem as the spring is released

6   Apply compressed air to the cylinder. **Warning:** *The piston may be forced down by compressed air, causing the crankshaft to turn suddenly. If the wrench used when positioning the number one piston at TDC is still attached to the bolt in the crankshaft nose, it could cause damage or injury when the crankshaft moves.*

7   The valves should be held in place by the air pressure. If the valve faces or seats are in poor condition, leaks may prevent air pressure from retaining the valves – refer to the alternative procedure below.

8   If you don't have access to compressed air, an alternative method can be used. Position the piston at a point just before TDC on the compression stroke, then feed a long piece of nylon rope through the spark plug hole until it fills the combustion chamber. Be sure to leave the end of the rope hanging out of the engine so it can be removed easily. Use a large ratchet and socket to rotate the crankshaft in the normal direction of rotation until slight resistance is felt.

9   Stuff shop rags into the cylinder head holes above and below the valves to prevent parts and tools from falling into the engine, then use a valve spring compressor to compress the spring **(see illustration)**. Remove the keepers with small needle-nose pliers or a magnet.

10   Remove the spring retainer, shield and valve spring, then remove the umbrella type guide seal. **Note:** *If air pressure fails to hold the valve in the closed position during this operation, the valve face or seat is probably damaged. If so, the cylinder head will have to be removed for additional repair operations.*

11   Wrap a rubber band or tape around the top of the valve stem so the valve won't fall into the combustion chamber, then release the air pressure. **Note:** *If a rope was used instead of air pressure, turn the crankshaft slightly in the direction opposite normal rotation.*

12   Inspect the valve stem for damage. Rotate the valve in the guide and check the end for eccentric movement, which would indicate that the valve is bent.

13   Move the valve up-and-down in the guide and make sure it doesn't bind. If the valve stem binds, either the valve is bent or the guide is damaged. In either case, the head will have to be removed for repair.

14   Reapply air pressure to the cylinder to retain the valve in the closed position, then remove the tape or rubber band from the valve stem. If a rope was used instead of air pressure, rotate the crankshaft in the normal direction of rotation until slight resistance is felt.

15   Lubricate the valve stem with engine oil and install a new guide seal.

16   Install the spring(s) in position over the valve.

17   Install the valve spring retainer. Compress the valve spring and carefully position the keepers in the groove. Apply a small dab of grease to the inside of each keeper to hold it in place **(see illustration)**.

18   Remove the pressure from the spring tool and make sure the keepers are seated.

19   Disconnect the air hose and remove the adapter from the spark plug hole. If a rope was used in place of air pressure, pull it out of the cylinder.

20   Refer to Section 5 and install the rocker arm assembly.

21   Install the spark plug(s) and hook up the wire(s).

22   Refer to Section 4 and install the valve cover.

23   Start and run the engine, then check for oil leaks and unusual sounds coming from the valve cover area.

7   Intake manifold – removal and installation

Warning: *Gasoline is extremely flammable, so take extra precautions when you work on any part of the fuel system. Don't smoke or allow open flames or bare light bulbs near the work area, and don't work in a garage where a natural gas-type appliance (such as a water heater or clothes dryer) with a pilot light is present. If you spill any fuel on your skin, rinse it off immediately with soap and water. When you perform any kind of work on the fuel system, wear safety glasses and have a Class B type fire extinguisher on hand.*

Removal

1   Detach the cable from the negative battery terminal.

2   Drain the cooling system (see Chapter 1).

3   Remove the air cleaner (see Chapter 4).

4   Clearly label and detach all vacuum lines, electrical wiring and fuel lines.

5   Detach the accelerator cable from the throttle linkage (see Chapter 4).

6   Remove the drivebelts (see Chapter 1).

7   Remove the carburetor or throttle body unit from the intake manifold (see Chapter 4).

8   Remove the coolant hoses from the intake manifold.

9   Disconnect the fuel inlet line at the fuel filter (see Chapter 4).

10   Remove the fuel pump and fuel filter and lay them aside (see Chapter 4).

11   Remove the intake manifold bolts and remove the manifold from the engine.

Installation

12   Clean the manifold bolts with solvent and dry them with compressed air. **Warning:** *Wear eye protection!*

13   Check the mating surfaces of the manifold for flatness with a precision straightedge and feeler gauges. Refer to this Chapter's Specifications for the warpage limit.

14   Inspect the manifold for cracks and distortion.

15   If the manifold is cracked or warped, replace it or see if it can be resurfaced/repaired at an automotive machine shop.

16   Check carefully for any stripped or broken intake manifold bolts. Replace any defective bolts with new parts.

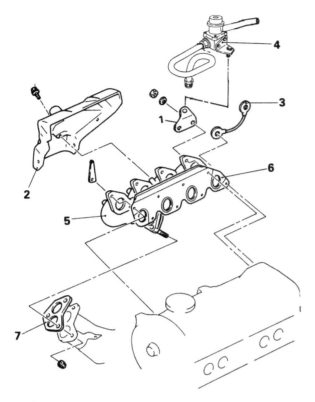

8.9   Remove the exhaust manifold nuts from the exhaust manifold. Be sure to soak the nuts with penetrating oil before attempting to remove them.

1	Reed valve bracket	5	Exhaust manifold
2	Heat shield	6	Exhaust manifold gasket
3	Ground cable	7	Exhaust manifold-to-exhaust
4	Reed valve assembly		pipe gasket

17   Using a scraper, remove all traces of old gasket material from the cylinder head and manifold mating surfaces. Clean the surfaces with lacquer thinner or acetone.

18   Install the intake manifold with a new gasket and tighten the bolts finger-tight. Starting at the center and working out in both directions, tighten the bolts in a criss-cross pattern until the torque listed in this Chapter's Specifications is reached.

19   The remainder of the installation procedure is the reverse of removal.

---

8   Exhaust manifold – removal and installation

Removal

Refer to illustration 8.9

1   Disconnect the negative battery cable from the battery.
2   Drain the cooling system (see Chapter 1).
3   Remove the air cleaner (see Chapter 4).
4   Loosen the power steering pump and remove the belt (see Chapter 1).
5   Raise the front of the vehicle and support it securely on jackstands. Detach the exhaust pipe from the exhaust manifold (see Chapter 4). Apply penetrating oil to the fastener threads if they are difficult to remove.
6   Disconnect the air injection tube assembly (pulse air feeder) if equipped, and move the tube assembly to one side.
7   Remove the power steering pump (if equipped) and set it aside (see Chapter 10).
8   Remove the heat shield from the exhaust manifold. Be sure to soak the bolts and nuts with penetrating oil before attempting to remove them

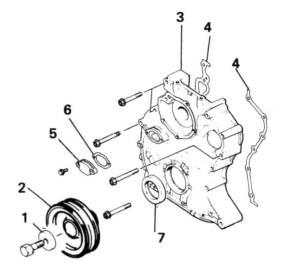

9.6   Timing chain cover installation details

1	Pulley bolt and washer	4	Gasket
	assembly	5	Access cover
2	Pulley	6	Gasket
3	Timing chain cover	7	Front seal

from the manifold.
9   Remove the exhaust manifold nuts **(see illustration)** and detach the exhaust manifold.
10   Separate the front catalytic converter from the exhaust manifold.

Installation

11   Discard the old gaskets and use a scraper to clean the gasket mating surfaces on the manifold and head, then clean the surfaces with a rag soaked in lacquer thinner or acetone.
12   Place the exhaust manifold and converter assembly in position on the cylinder head and install the nuts. Starting at the center, tighten the nuts in a criss-cross pattern until the torque listed in this Chapter's Specifications is reached.
13   The remainder of installation is the reverse of removal.
14   Start the engine and check for exhaust leaks between the manifold and the cylinder head and between the manifold and the exhaust pipe.

---

9   Silent shaft chain/sprockets – removal, inspection and installation

Note: *When a loose silent shaft drive chain is suspected as the cause of excessive noise, the tension must be adjusted. It is possible to do this procedure without removing the timing chain cover (see Step 17).*

Removal

Refer to illustrations 9.6 and 9.8

1   Before attempting to remove the silent shaft chain and sprockets, you must remove the cylinder head and the oil pan (Sections 14 and 15).
2   Remove the drivebelts (see Chapter 1).
3   Raise the vehicle and support it securely on jackstands. Remove the splash guard. Remove the large bolt at the front of the crankshaft and slide the pulley off. **Note:** *To keep the crankshaft from turning while you're removing this bolt, remove the starter (see Chapter 5) and wedge a large screwdriver into the flywheel/driveplate ring gear. Note: If the pulley does not come off easily, pullers are available at auto parts stores that will make removal easy.*
4   Remove the cooling fan and the water pump assembly (see Chapter 3).

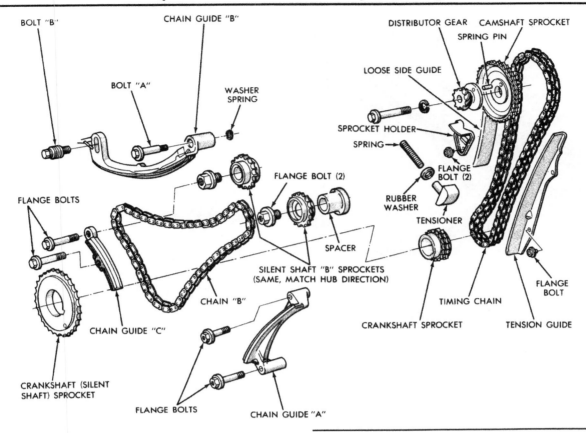

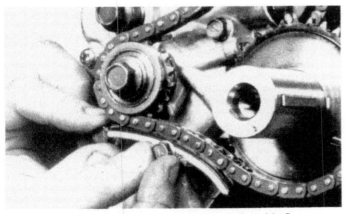

9.16a Installing the silent shaft chain guide C

left silent shaft.

10 Slide the crankshaft sprocket, the silent shaft sprockets and the chain off the engine as an assembly. Leave the bolt in the end of the crankshaft in place. Do not lose the keys that index the sprockets to the shafts.

Inspection

11 Check the sprocket teeth for wear and damage. Check the sprocket cushion rings and ring guides (silent shaft sprockets only) for wear and damage. Rotate the cushion rings and check for smooth operation. Inspect the chain for cracked side plates and pitted or worn rollers. Replace any defective or worn parts with new ones.

Installation

Refer to illustrations 9.16a, 9.16b, 9.16c and 9.17

12 Before installing the silent shaft chain and sprockets, the timing chain must be properly installed and the Number One piston must be at TDC on the compression stroke. Both silent shafts and the oil pump must also be in place.

13 Slide the crankshaft sprocket part way onto the front of the crankshaft by lining up the keyway in the sprocket with the key on the shaft.

14 Install the front silent shaft sprocket part way. The dished or recessed side of the front silent shaft sprocket must face out. Install the silent shaft chain onto the crankshaft sprocket and the front silent shaft sprocket. Line up the plated links on the chain with the mating marks stamped into the sprockets **(see illustration 9.16c).**

15 With the dished or recessed side facing in, slide rear silent shaft sprocket part way onto the lower oil pump gear shaft. Line up the plated link on the chain with the mating mark on the sprocket. Push the silent shaft sprockets all the way onto their respective shafts, lining up the keyways in the sprockets with the keys on the shafts. Simultaneously, push the crankshaft sprocket back until it bottoms on the crankshaft timing chain sprocket. Recheck the position of the mating marks on the chain and sprockets, then install the silent shaft sprocket bolts and tighten them to the torque listed in illustration 9.8.

16 Install the chain guides labeled A, B and C **(see illustrations)** and tighten the mounting bolts for chain guides A and C securely (leave the

5 Remove the alternator and brackets from the timing chain cover.

6 Remove the bolts attaching the timing chain cover to the engine block **(see illustration)**. Draw a simple diagram showing the location of each of the bolts so they can be returned to the same holes from which they were removed.

7 Tap the timing chain cover with a soft-faced hammer to break the gasket seal, then remove the cover from the engine block. **Caution:** *Prying between the cover and the engine block can damage the gasket sealing surfaces.*

8 Remove the chain guides labeled A, B and C **(see illustration)**. Each guide is held in place by two bolts. Again, draw a simple diagram showing the location of each bolt so they can be returned to the same holes from which they were removed.

9 Reinstall the large bolt in the end of the crankshaft. Hold it in place with a wrench to prevent the crankshaft from turning while loosening the bolt on the end of the right (passenger side) silent shaft, the bolt attaching the right silent shaft drive sprocket to the oil pump shaft and the bolt in the end of the

9.16b   Installing the silent shaft chain guide B

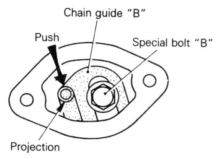

9.17   Use your finger to push the projection against the chain

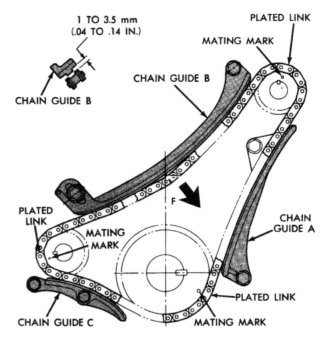

9.16c   Push in the direction of arrow F to remove the slack from the silent shaft chain

mounting bolts for chain guide B finger-tight). Note the difference between the upper and lower chain guide B mounting bolts. Make sure they are installed in the proper location.

17   Adjust the chain slack as follows: rotate the right (passenger side) silent shaft clockwise and the left (driver's side) silent shaft counterclockwise so the chain slack is collected at point F **(see illustration 9.16c).** Pull the chain with your finger tips in the direction of arrow F, then move the lower end of chain guide B up or down, as required, until the clearance between the chain and the guide (chain slack) is as specified **(see illustration 9.16c).** Tighten the mounting bolts for chain guide B securely, then recheck the slack to make sure it hasn't changed. If the chain is not tensioned properly, engine noise will result. **Note:** *To adjust the chain without removing the timing chain cover, remove the access cover mounted on the front of the timing chain cover* **(see illustration 9.6).** *Loosen bolt "B"* **(see illustration)** *and using your finger push the projection in the direction of the arrow. Do not use a screwdriver or other implement. Tighten bolt "B" and reinstall the access cover.*

18   Apply a coat of moly-based grease to the chain and chain guides.

19   Using a hammer and punch, drive the oil seal out of the timing chain case (see Section 12).

20   Lay a new seal in place – make sure the lip faces inward – and tap around its circumference with a block of wood and a hammer until it is properly seated.

21   Using a new gasket and RTV sealant, install the timing chain cover onto the engine **(see illustration 9.6).** Install the bolts in a criss-cross pattern and tighten them to the torque listed in this Chapter's Specifications. If the gasket protrudes beyond the top or bottom of the case and engine block, trim off the excess with a razor blade.

22   Apply a thin layer of clean moly-based grease to the seal contact surface of the crankshaft pulley, then slide it onto the crankshaft. Install the bolt and tighten it finger-tight only. **Note:** *The bolt should be tightened to the specified torque only after the cylinder head and camshaft have been installed.*

23   The remainder of installation is the reverse of removal.

10   Timing chain and sprockets – removal, inspection and installation

Refer to illustrations 10.6, 10.7, 10.8, 10.9a and 10.9b

Removal

1   Remove the silent shaft chain and sprockets for access to the timing chain assembly (see Section 9).

2   Remove the camshaft sprocket holder and the right and left timing chain guides from the front of the engine block **(see illustration 9.8).**

3   Depress the timing chain tensioner plunger on the oil pump and slide the camshaft sprocket, the crankshaft sprocket and the timing chain off the engine as an assembly. Do not lose the key that indexes the crankshaft sprocket in the proper place. Remove the timing chain tensioner plunger and spring from the oil pump.

Inspection

4   Inspect the sprocket teeth for wear and damage. Check the chain for cracked plates and pitted or worn rollers. Check the chain tensioner rubber shoe for wear and the tensioner spring for cracks and deterioration. Check the chain guides for wear and damage. Replace any defective parts with new ones.

Installation

5   Install the sprocket holder and the right and left timing chain guides onto the engine block. Tighten the bolts securely. The upper bolt in the left timing chain guide should be installed finger-tight only. Then coat the entire length of the chain contact surfaces of the guides with clean, high-quality moly-based grease.

6   Turn the crankshaft bolt with a large wrench until the Number One piston is at Top Dead Center (TDC) (see Section 3). Apply a layer of clean moly-based grease or engine assembly lube to the timing chain tensioner plunger and install the tensioner spring and plunger loosely into the oil pump body **(see illustration).** **Note:** *Chrysler Corporation officially recognizes a problem with the timing chain at start-up. Because of insufficient oil pressure, the timing chain will make a knocking noise when the engine is first started. This will not harm the engine, but it is necessary to update the tensioner. Purchase from a dealership parts department a rubber spacer and insert it into the tensioner spring. This spacer will prevent the oil from flowing out of the tensioner and back into the oil pump.*

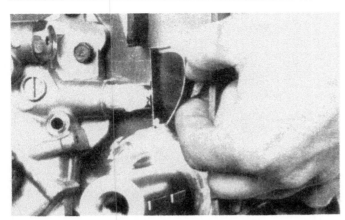

10.6 Lubricate the timing chain tensioner plunger and install it in the oil pump bore

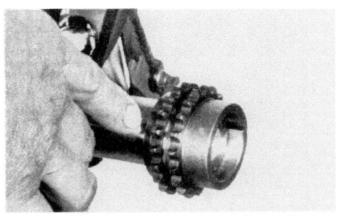

10.7 Install the timing chain sprocket on the end of the crankshaft with the wide shoulder facing out

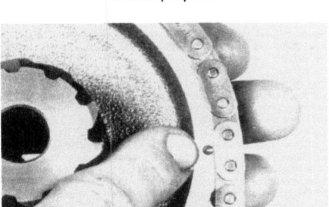

10.8 Mesh the camshaft sprocket and the timing chain with the mark on the sprocket directly opposite the plated link on the chain

10.9a Installing the timing chain on the crankshaft sprocket (note that the sprocket mark and the plated link are opposite each other)

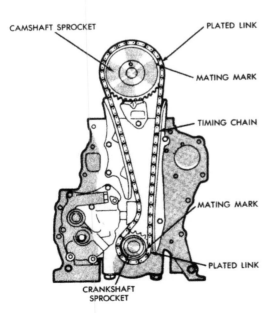

10.9b Correct timing chain and sprocket relationship

7 Position the timing chain sprocket on the end of the crankshaft with the wide shoulder facing out (see illustration). Line up the keyway in the sprocket with the key on the crankshaft.

8 Install the camshaft sprocket onto the chain, lining up the plated link on the chain with the marked tooth on the sprocket (see illustration).

9 Slip the chain over the crankshaft sprocket, lining up the plated link on the chain with the marked tooth on the sprocket (see illustration). Slide the crankshaft sprocket all the way onto the crankshaft while depressing the chain tensioner so the chain fits into place in the guides. Rest the camshaft sprocket on the sprocket holder (see illustration) and make sure the plated links and mating marks are aligned properly. Caution: *Do not rotate the crankshaft for any reason until the cylinder head and camshaft have been properly installed.*

10 The remainder of installation is the reverse of removal.

11 Camshaft oil plug – replacement

1 Remove the cylinder head from the engine (see Section 14).

2 The camshaft oil plug is serviced the same as an engine freeze plug (see Chapter 2D, Section 14). Be sure to use a small amount of sealant around the circumference of the new oil plug. Use a large socket to install the plug by tapping on it gently with a hammer. Note: *If necessary, have the camshaft oil plug removed and installed by an automotive machine shop.*

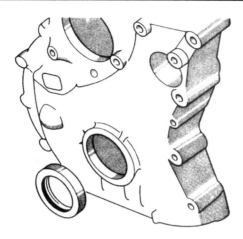

12.3   Crankshaft front oil seal installation – exploded view

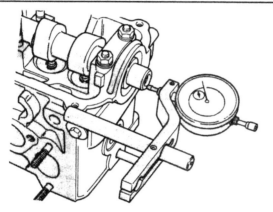

13.7   To check camshaft endplay, set up a dial indicator like this, with the gauge plunger touching the nose of the camshaft

12   Crankshaft front oil seal – replacement

Refer to illustration 12.3

1   Remove the drivebelts (see Chapter 1).
2   Remove the crankshaft pulley.
3   Carefully pry the seal out of the front cover **(see illustration)** with a seal removal tool or a screwdriver. Don't scratch the seal bore or damage the crankshaft in the process (if the crankshaft is damaged, the new seal will end up leaking).
4   Clean the bore in the timing chain cover and coat the outer edge of the new seal with engine oil or multi-purpose grease. Using a socket with an outside diameter slightly smaller than the outside diameter of the seal, carefully drive the seal into place with a hammer. If a socket is not available, a short section of a large diameter pipe will work. Check the seal after installation to be sure the spring did not pop out.
5   Install the crankshaft pulley.
6   Run the engine and check for leaks.

13   Camshaft – removal, inspection and installation

Removal

Refer to illustration 13.5

1   Remove the valve cover (see Section 4).
2   Remove the distributor (see Chapter 5).
3   Set the engine at TDC for cylinder number one (see Section 3), then remove the rocker arm assembly (see Section 5). If the camshaft bearing

13.5   Remove the camshaft sprocket bolt and detach the sprocket and distributor drive gear from the camshaft (the oil shield is used on early models only)

caps do not have numbers on them, number them before removal. Be sure to put the marks on the same ends of all the caps to prevent incorrect orientation of the caps during installation.
4   In order to keep the tensioner from collapsing once the sprocket has been removed, install a special retaining tool between the timing chain, near the tensioner **(see illustration 14.7)**. The tool will extend down into the timing chain cover, so be sure the strap or wire hanger on the tool does not fall into the cover or it will be very difficult to remove the tool when the camshaft has been installed.
5   Remove the camshaft sprocket bolt and distributor drive gear **(see illustration)**. **Note:** *Prevent the camshaft from turning by locking it in place with a large pair of Vise-grips or adjustable pliers. Fasten the tool onto the camshaft without contacting the camshaft lobes. Position the tool only on the spaces between the lobes that are equipped with a notched relief specifically designed for retaining the camshaft. Detach the timing chain and camshaft sprocket from the camshaft. Suspend the camshaft sprocket, with the chain still attached, out of the way.*
6   Lift out the camshaft, wipe it off with a clean shop towel and set it aside.

Inspection

Refer to illustrations 13.7 and 13.10

7   To check camshaft endplay:
   a) Install the camshaft and secure it with caps 1 and 5.
   b) Mount a dial indicator on the head **(see illustration)**.
   c) Using a large screwdriver as a lever at the opposite end, move the camshaft forward-and-backward and note the dial indicator reading.
   d) Compare the reading with the endplay listed in this Chapter's Specifications.
   e) If the indicated reading is higher, either the camshaft or the head is worn. Replace parts as necessary.
8   To check camshaft runout:
   a) Support the camshaft with a pair of V-blocks and attach a dial indicator with the stem resting against the center bearing journal on the camshaft.
   b) Rotate the camshaft and note the indicated runout.
   c) Compare the results to the camshaft runout listed in this Chapter's Specifications.
   d) If the indicated runout exceeds the specified runout, replace the camshaft.
9   Check the camshaft bearing journals and caps for scoring and signs of wear. If they are worn, replace the cylinder head with a new or rebuilt unit. Measure the journals on the camshaft with a micrometer, comparing your readings with this Chapter's Specifications. If the diameter of any of the journals is out of specification, replace the camshaft.
10   Check the cam lobes for wear:
   a) Check the toe and ramp areas of each cam lobe for score marks and uneven wear. Also check for flaking and pitting.

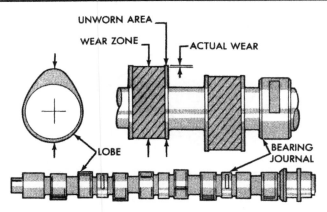

13.10   Measure the height of the camshaft lobes at the wear zone and unworn area, then subtract the wear zone measurement from the unworn area measurement to get the actual wear – compare the wear to the limit listed in this Chapter's Specifications

14.7   Before removing the camshaft sprocket, position the tensioner locking tool between the chain, at the tensioner – be sure the tool has a cord or wire attached to the end of it so it can be easily removed after the job – if the tool is not available, a block of wood and a length of mechanic's wire will also work

b) If there's wear on the toe or the ramp, replace the camshaft, but first try to find the cause of the wear. Look for abrasive substances in the oil and inspect the oil pump and oil passages for blockage. Lobe wear is usually caused by inadequate lubrication or dirty oil.

c) Using a micrometer, calculate the lobe wear **(see illustration)**. If the lobe wear is greater than listed in this Chapter's Specifications, replace the camshaft.

11   Inspect the rocker arms for wear, galling and pitting of the contact surfaces.

12   If any of the conditions described above are noted, the cylinder head is probably getting insufficient lubrication or dirty oil, so make sure you track down the cause of this problem (low oil level, low oil pump capacity, clogged oil passage, etc.) before installing a new head, camshaft or rocker arms.

Installation

Refer to illustration 13.14

13   Thoroughly clean the camshaft, the bearing surfaces in the head and caps and the rocker arms. Remove all sludge and dirt. Wipe off all components with a clean, lint-free cloth.

14   Lubricate the camshaft bearing surfaces in the head and the bearing journals and lobes on the camshaft with assembly lube or moly-base grease. Carefully lower the camshaft into position with the dowel pin pointing up **(see illustration)**. **Caution:** *Failure to adequately lubricate the camshaft and related components can cause serious damage to bearing*

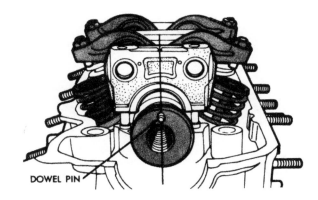

13.14   Install the camshaft with the dowel pin pointing up

and friction surfaces during the first few seconds after engine start-up, when the oil pressure is low or nonexistent.

15   Coat the outside diameter of the circular plug with RTV sealant. Install the plug to the rear of the cylinder head.

16   Apply a thin coat of assembly lube or moly-base grease to the bearing surfaces of the camshaft bearing caps.

17   Install the rocker arm shaft assembly. Tighten the camshaft bearing cap bolts 1/4-turn at a time, starting from the middle and working out to the ends, until the torque listed in this Chapter's Specifications is reached.

18   Install the camshaft sprocket and timing chain and related components (see Section 10). If you suspended the camshaft sprocket out the way and didn't disturb the timing chain or sprockets, the valve timing should still be correct. Rotate the camshaft as necessary to reattach the sprocket to the camshaft. If the timing was disturbed, align the sprockets and install the chain as described in section 10.

19   Remove the spark plugs and rotate the crankshaft by hand to make sure the valve timing is correct. After two revolutions, the timing marks on the sprockets should still be aligned. If they're not, re-index the timing chain to the sprockets (see Section 10). **Note:** *If you feel resistance while rotating the crankshaft, stop immediately and check the valve timing by referring to Section 10.*

20   Adjust the valve clearances as described in Chapter 1.

21   Install the semi-circular plug to the front of the cylinder head and apply sealant to the top of the semi-circular plug.

22   Install the valve cover and gasket.

23   The remainder of installation is the reverse of removal.

14   Cylinder head – removal and installation

Caution: *Allow the engine to cool completely before beginning this procedure.*

Removal

Refer to illustrations 14.7 and 14.8

1   Position the number one piston at Top Dead Center (see Section 3).

2   Disconnect the negative cable from the battery.

3   Drain the cooling system and remove the spark plugs (see Chapter 1).

4   Remove the intake and exhaust manifold (see Sections 7 and 8). **Note:** *If you're only replacing the cylinder head gasket, it isn't necessary to remove the manifolds. If you leave the manifolds attached, you may need an assistant to help lift the head off the engine, since it will be quite heavy.*

5   Remove the valve cover (see Section 4).

6   Remove the distributor (see Chapter 5), including the cap and wires.

7   Remove the silent shaft chain and sprockets (see Section 9) and the timing chain and sprocket (see Section 10). **Note:** *It is possible to use a tensioner locking tool (see illustration) to hold the chain and tensioner in place while the cylinder head is off the engine. This will save time you by*

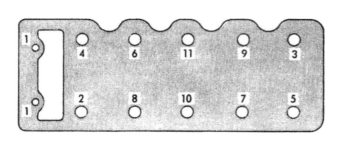

14.8   Loosen the head bolts 1/4-turn at a time, in the sequence shown, until they can be removed by hand

94 N•m (69 FT. LBS.) COLD ENGINE
103 N•m (75 FT. LBS.) HOT ENGINE

18 N•m (156 IN. LBS.)

14.16   Cylinder head bolt TIGHTENING sequence

not having to remove the timing chain and silent shaft chain assemblies. Be sure to install the tool very tightly to prevent it from popping out when the engine is shaken or jarred.

8   Loosen the head bolts in 1/4-turn increments until they can be removed by hand. Follow the recommended sequence to avoid warping the head (see illustration). Note where each bolt goes so it can be returned to the same location on installation.

9   Lift the head off the engine. If resistance is felt, don't pry between the head and block gasket mating surfaces – damage to the mating surfaces will result. Instead, pry against the casting protrusions on the sides of the cylinder head. Set the head on blocks of wood to prevent damage to the gasket sealing surfaces.

10   Cylinder head disassembly and inspection procedures are covered in detail in Chapter 2, Part D. It's a good idea to have the head checked for warpage, even if you're just replacing the gasket.

Installation

Refer to illustration 14.16

11   The mating surfaces of the cylinder head and block must be perfectly clean when the head is installed.

12   Use a gasket scraper to remove all traces of carbon and old gasket material, then clean the mating surfaces with lacquer thinner or acetone. If there's oil on the mating surfaces when the head is installed, the gasket may not seal correctly and leaks may develop. When working on the block, stuff the cylinders with clean shop rags to keep out debris. Use a vacuum cleaner to remove material that falls into the cylinders. Since the head is made of aluminum, aggressive scraping can cause damage. Be extra careful not to nick or gouge the mating surfaces with the scraper.

13   Check the block and head mating surfaces for nicks, deep scratches and other damage. If damage is slight, it can be removed with a file; if it's excessive, machining may be the only alternative.

14   Use a tap of the correct size to chase the threads in the head bolt holes. Mount each head bolt in a vise and run a die down the threads to remove corrosion and restore the threads. Dirt, corrosion, sealant and damaged threads will affect torque readings.

15   Place a new gasket on the block. Check to see if there are any markings (such as "TOP") on the gasket that say how it is to be installed. Those identification marks must face UP. Also, apply sealant to the edges of the timing cover where it mates with the engine block. Set the cylinder head in position.

16   Install the bolts. They must be tightened in a specific sequence (see illustration), in the stages and to the torques listed in this Chapter's Specifications. Note: *Use the first and second ("engine cold") and third ("engine hot") steps in the Specifications.*

17   Reinstall the timing chain and silent shaft chain, if removed. If a tensioner locking tool was used, attach the camshaft sprocket and remove the tool.

18   Reinstall the remaining parts in the reverse order of removal.

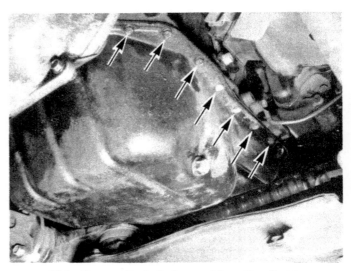

15.4   Remove the bolts (arrows) from the oil pan (Montero shown)

19   Be sure to refill the cooling system and check all fluid levels.

20   Rotate the crankshaft clockwise slowly by hand through two complete revolutions. Recheck the camshaft timing marks (see Section 10). Caution: *If you feel any resistance while turning the engine over, stop and re-check the camshaft timing. The valves may be hitting the pistons.*

21   Start the engine and check the ignition timing (see Chapter 1).

22   Run the engine until normal operating temperature is reached. Check for leaks and proper operation.

23   Remove the valve cover and re-tighten the cylinder head bolts while the engine is hot (use Step 3 in the Specifications), then re-install the valve cover.

15   Oil pan – removal and installation

Refer to illustration 15.4

Note: *The following procedure is based on the assumption that the engine is in the vehicle.*

1   Warm up the engine, then drain the oil and replace the oil filter (see Chapter 1).

2   Detach the cable from the negative battery terminal.

3   Raise the vehicle and support it securely on jackstands. **Note:** *On some models it may be necessary to unbolt the engine mounts and raise the engine several inches to make additional clearance for the oil pan. If*

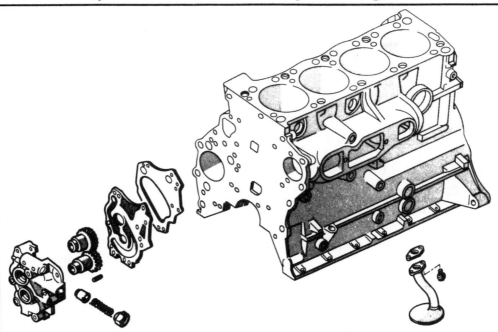

16.3   An exploded view of the oil pump assembly and the pick-up tube

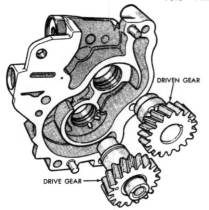

16.5   Check oil pump bearing clearance on each gear

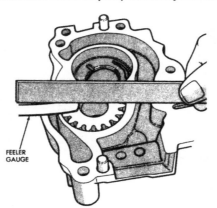

16.6a   Use a straightedge and a feeler gauge to check the endplay on the driven gear

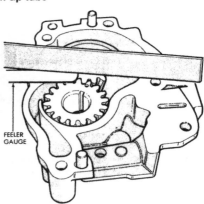

16.6b   Use a straightedge and a feeler gauge to check the endplay on the drive gear

this is the case, be sure to place wood blocks between the engine mounts and the frame while the engine is in the raised position.

4   Remove the bolts securing the oil pan to the engine block **(see illustration)**.

5   Tap on the pan with a soft-face hammer to break the gasket seal, then detach the oil pan from the engine. Don't pry between the block and oil pan mating surfaces.

6   Using a gasket scraper, remove all traces of old gasket and/or sealant from the engine block and oil pan. Remove the seals from each end of the engine block or oil pan. Clean the mating surfaces with lacquer thinner or acetone. Make sure the threaded bolt holes in the block are clean.

7   Clean the oil pan with solvent and dry it thoroughly. Check the gasket flanges for distortion, particularly around the bolt holes. If necessary, place the pan on a block of wood and use a hammer to flatten and restore the gasket surfaces.

8   Install the oil pan end seals, then apply a 1/8-inch wide bead of RTV sealant to the oil pan gasket surfaces. Continue the bead across the end seals. Make sure the sealant is applied to the inside edge of the bolt holes.

9   Carefully place the oil pan in position.

10   Install the bolts and tighten them in 1/4-turn increments to the torque listed in this Chapter's Specifications. Start with the bolts closest to the center of the pan and work out in a spiral pattern. Don't overtighten them or

leakage may occur.

11   Add oil, run the engine and check for oil leaks.

16   Oil pump – removal, inspection and installation

Removal
Refer to illustration 16.3

1   Remove the timing chain (see Section 10).

2   Remove the oil pan (see Section 15).

3   Remove the oil pump mounting bolts **(see illustration)** and remove the oil pump assembly.

Inspection
Refer to illustrations 16.5, 16.6a, 16.6b, 16.7, 16.8, 16.9 and 16.11

4   Remove the bolts and lift off the oil pump cover.

5   Check the oil pump bearing clearance on each gear **(see illustration)**.

6   Using feeler gauges and a straightedge, check the endplay of the driven gear and the drive gear **(see illustrations)**.

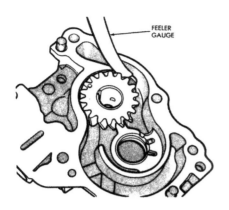

16.7   Check the driven gear-to-housing clearance

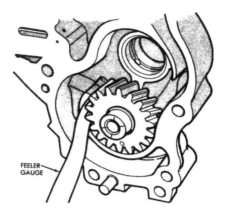

16.8   Check the drive gear-to-housing clearance

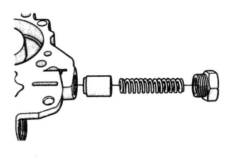

16.9   Remove the oil pressure relief valve spring and measure its free length

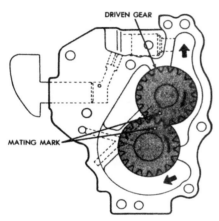

16.11   Be sure the mating marks on the oil pump gears are set when assembling the oil pump

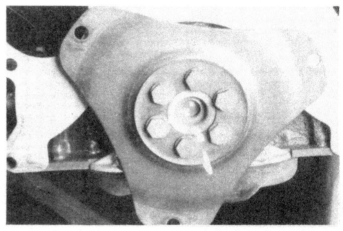

17.3   On engines with a symmetrical bolt pattern, be sure to mark the flywheel/driveplate to the crankshaft

7   Check the clearance between the driven gear and the pump housing with feeler gauges **(see illustration)**.
8   Check the clearance between the drive gear and the pump housing with feeler gauges **(see illustration)**.
9   Extract the spring and oil pump relief valve from the pump housing **(see illustration)**. Measure the free length of the oil pressure relief valve spring.
10   Compare the measurements to the oil pump Specifications at the beginning of this Chapter. If any of them are outside the limits, replace the pump.
11   Install the gears with the mating marks aligned together **(see illustration)**. Install the oil pressure relief valve and spring assembly. Install the pump cover and tighten the bolts to the torque listed in this Chapter's Specifications.

Installation

12   Apply a thin coat of RTV sealant to the mating surface of the pump and place the pump in position. Rotate it back-and-forth a little to ensure there's positive contact between the pump and the engine block.
13   Coat the threads of the mounting bolts with RTV sealant and, while holding the pump securely in place, install the bolts. Tighten them to the torque listed in this Chapter's Specifications.
14   Install a new gasket on the oil pick-up tube, if removed **(see illustration 16.3)** and install the oil pick-up tube and screen. Tighten the bolts to the torque listed in this Chapter's Specifications.
15   Install the oil pan (see Section 15).

17   Flywheel/driveplate – removal and installation

Removal

Refer to illustrations 17.3 and 17.4
1   Raise the vehicle and support it securely on jackstands, then refer to Chapter 7 and remove the transmission. If it's leaking, now would be a very good time to replace the front pump seal/O-ring (automatic transmission only).
2   Remove the pressure plate and clutch disc (see Chapter 8) (manual transmission equipped vehicles). Now is a good time to check/replace the clutch components and pilot bearing.
3   Make alignment marks on the flywheel/driveplate and crankshaft to ensure correct alignment during reinstallation **(see illustration)**.
4   Remove the bolts that secure the flywheel/driveplate to the crankshaft **(see illustration)**. If the crankshaft turns, remove the starter (see Chapter 5) and wedge a screwdriver in the flywheel ring gear teeth.
5   Remove the flywheel/driveplate from the crankshaft. Since the flywheel is fairly heavy, be sure to support it while removing the last bolt.
6   Clean the flywheel to remove grease and oil. Inspect the surface for cracks, rivet grooves, burned areas and score marks. Light scoring can be removed with emery cloth. Check for cracked and broken ring gear teeth. Lay the flywheel on a flat surface and use a straightedge to check for warpage.
7   Clean and inspect the mating surfaces of the flywheel/driveplate and the crankshaft. If the crankshaft rear seal is leaking, replace it before reinstalling the flywheel/driveplate.

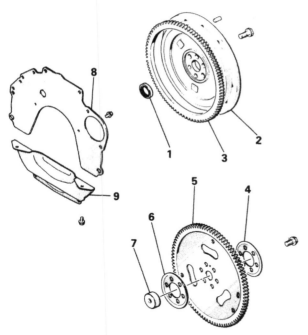

17.4 Flywheel/driveplate and related components – exploded view

1	Pilot bearing	6	Crankshaft adapter
2	Flywheel	7	Crankshaft bushing
3	Ring gear	8	Rear plate
4	Adapter plate	9	Bell housing cover
5	Driveplate		

Installation

8   Position the flywheel/driveplate against the crankshaft. Be sure to align the marks made during removal. Note that some engines have an alignment dowel or staggered bolt holes to ensure correct installation. Before installing the bolts, apply thread locking compound to the threads.

9   Wedge a screwdriver through the starter motor opening to keep the flywheel/driveplate from turning as you tighten the bolts to the torque listed in this Chapter's Specifications.

10   The remainder of installation is the reverse of the removal procedure.

---

18   Rear main oil seal – replacement

Refer to illustrations 18.2a, 18.2b, 18.5 and 18.6

1   The transmission must be removed from the vehicle for this procedure (see Chapter 7).

2   The seal can be replaced without removing the oil pan or seal retainer. However, this method is not recommended because the lip of the seal is quite stiff and it's possible to cock the seal in the retainer bore or damage it during installation. If you want to take the chance, pry out the old seal (**see illustration**). Apply a film of clean oil to the crankshaft seal journal and the lip of the new seal and carefully tap the new seal into place (**see illustration**). The lip is stiff so carefully work it onto the seal journal of the crankshaft with a smooth object like the end of an extension as you tap the seal into place. Don't rush it or you may damage the seal.

3   The following method is recommended but requires removal of the oil pan (see Section 15) and the seal retainer.

4   After the oil pan has been removed, remove the bolts, detach the seal retainer and peel off all the old gasket material.

5   Position the seal and retainer assembly on a couple of wood blocks on a workbench and drive the old seal out from the back side with a punch and hammer (**see illustration**).

18.2a   The quick (but not recommended) way to replace the rear main oil seal is to simply pry the old one out – other models may require removal of the rear main seal retainer

18.2b   Lubricate the crankshaft journal and the lip of the new seal with engine oil and tap the new seal into place – the seal lip is stiff and can be easily damaged during installation if you're not careful

18.5   After removing the retainer from the engine, support it on wood blocks and drive out the old seal with a punch and hammer

18.6   Drive the new seal into the retainer with a block of wood or a section of pipe, if you have one large enough – make sure you don't cock the seal in the retainer bore

6   Drive the new seal into the retainer with a block of wood **(see illustration)** or a section of pipe slightly smaller in diameter than the outside diameter of the seal.
7   Lubricate the crankshaft seal journal and the lip of the new seal with clean engine oil. Position a new gasket on the engine block.

8   Slowly and carefully push the seal onto the crankshaft. The seal lip is stiff, so work it onto the crankshaft with a smooth object such as the end of an extension as you push the retainer against the block.
9   Install and tighten the retainer bolts to the torque listed in this Chapter's Specifications. The bottom sealing flange of the retainer must not extend below the bottom sealing flange (oil pan rail) of the block.
10   The remaining steps are the reverse of removal.
11   Run the engine and check for oil leaks.

---

19   Engine mounts – check, replacement and adjustment

---

1   Engine mounts seldom require attention, but broken or deteriorated mounts should be replaced immediately or the added strain placed on the driveline components may cause damage or wear.

Check

Refer to illustrations 19.4a and 19.4b
2   During the check, the engine must be raised slightly to remove the weight from the mounts.
3   Raise the vehicle and support it securely on jackstands, then position a jack under the engine oil pan. Place a large block of wood between the jack head and the oil pan, then carefully raise the engine just enough to take the weight off the mounts. **Warning:** *DO NOT place any part of your body under the engine when it's supported only by a jack!*
4   Check the mount insulators **(see illustrations)** to see if the rubber is cracked, hardened or separated from the metal plates. Sometimes the rubber will split right down the center.

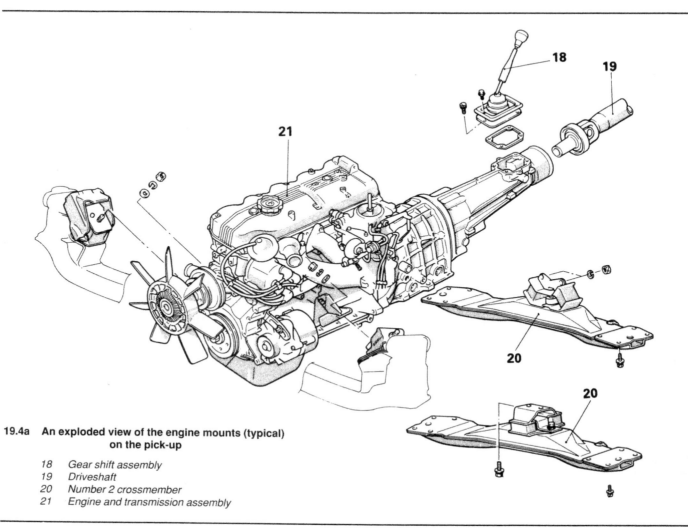

19.4a   An exploded view of the engine mounts (typical) on the pick-up

18   *Gear shift assembly*
19   *Driveshaft*
20   *Number 2 crossmember*
21   *Engine and transmission assembly*

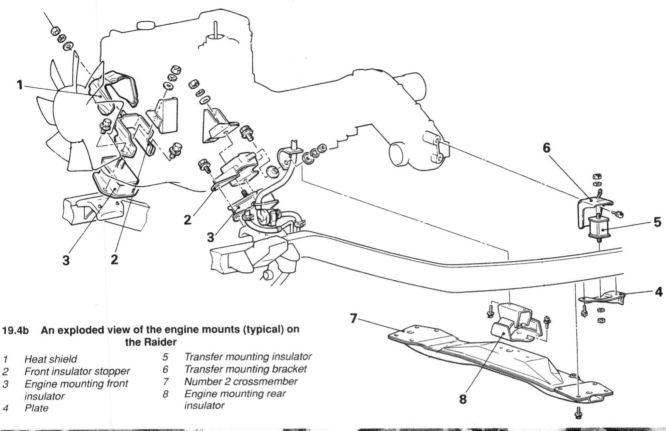

19.4b   An exploded view of the engine mounts (typical) on the Raider

1   Heat shield
2   Front insulator stopper
3   Engine mounting front insulator
4   Plate
5   Transfer mounting insulator
6   Transfer mounting bracket
7   Number 2 crossmember
8   Engine mounting rear insulator

19.8a   Removing the mount (note the alignment pin)

19.8b   Separating the roll restrictor and mount

19.8c   Removing the motor mount brackets

5   Check for relative movement between the mount plates and the engine or frame (use a large screwdriver or prybar to attempt to move the mounts). If movement is noted, lower the engine and tighten the mount fasteners.

6   Rubber preservative should be applied to the insulators to slow deterioration.

Replacement

Refer to illustrations 19.8a, 19.8b and 19.8c

7   Disconnect the negative battery cable from the battery, then raise the vehicle and support it securely on jackstands (if not already done).

8   Remove the fasteners and detach the mount from the frame bracket **(see illustrations)**.

9   Raise the engine slightly with a jack or hoist. Remove the insulator-to-engine bolts and detach the insulator.

10   Installation is the reverse of removal. Use thread locking compound on the mount bolts and be sure to tighten them securely.

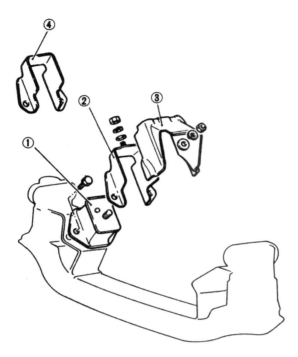

19.11   Don't tighten the engine mounts until the correct clearance has been attained

1	*Front insulator*	*3*	*Heat deflection plate*
2	*Roll restrictor*	*4*	*Roll restrictor (Canada)*

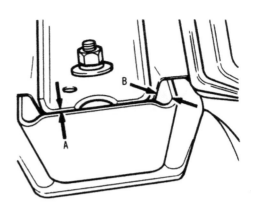

19.12   Before tightening the roll restrictor, check clearance A (0.4 inch [10.0 mm]) and clearance B (0.3 inch [7.5 mm])

Adjustment

Refer to illustrations 19.11 and 19.12

11   When installing the roll restrictor to the front insulator, adjust the clearance between the roll restrictor and the side of the insulator **(see illustration)**.

12   Position the roll restrictor and leave the nut loose until the correct clearance **(see illustration)** has been attained.

13   Tighten all the engine mounts securely.

Chapter 2 Part B
2.0L and 2.4L four-cylinder engines

Contents

Specifications

General

Firing order	1-3-4-2
Cylinder numbers (drivebelt end-to-transmission end)	1–2–3–4
Displacement	
2.0L	121.9 cubic inches
2.4L	143.4 cubic inches
Bore	
2.0L	3.35 inches
2.4L	3.41 inches
Stroke	
2.0L	3.46 inches
2.4L	3.94 inches

Camshaft

Camshaft endplay	0.004 to 0.008 in
Lobe height (standard)	
2.0L (1983 and 1984)	1.661 inch
2.0L (1985)	1.657 inch
2.0L (1986 on)	1.6565 inch
2.4L	1.6693 inch
Wear limit	0.020 inch
Camshaft bearing oil clearance	0.002 to 0.0035 inch

Cylinder head

Warpage limit	0.002 inch

Timing belt

Timing belt deflection	Tension automatically adjusted
Clearance between timing belt and seal line	Approx. 9/16-inch

Oil pump

Clearances	
Tip clearance	
Drive gear	0.0063 to 0.0083 inch
Driven gear	0.0051 to 0.0071 inch
Side clearance	
Drive gear	0.0031 to 0.0055 inch
Driven gear	0.0024 to 0.0047 inch
Pressure relief spring	
Free length	1.834 inch
Load	13.4 lb @ 1.579 inch

Torque specifications

	Ft-lbs (unless otherwise indicated)
Valve cover bolts	48 to 60 in-lbs
Intake/exhaust manifold nuts/bolts	132 to 168 in-lbs
Camshaft sprocket bolt	58 to 72

Camshaft bearing cap bolts

8X25	15 to 19
8X65	14 to 15

Cylinder head bolts

1992 and earlier

Cold engine	65 to 72
Warm engine	73 to 80

1993

Step 1	58
Step 2	Loosen all bolts 3 turns in sequence **(see illustration 13.10)**
Step 3	14
Step 4	Turn an additional 90-degrees
Step 5	Turn an additional 90-degrees

Crankshaft pulley bolts	15 to 21
Crankshaft pulley center bolt	80 to 94

Engine mounts

Front insulator nuts	14 to 22
Front stopper bolts	72 to 108 in-lbs
Rear insulator-to-transmission	14 to 17

Rear insulator-to-number 2 crossmember

Manual transmission	108 to 168 in-lbs
Automatic transmission	14 to 18
Rear stopper	25 to 40

Oil pump sprocket nut	36 to 43
Oil pump cover bolts	132 to 156 in-lbs
Oil pan bolts	48 to 72 in-lbs
Oil pan drain bolt	26 to 32
Oil seal retainer bolts	84 to 108 in-lbs
Flywheel/driveplate bolts	94 to 101
Silent Shaft sprocket nut	25 to 28
Automatic tensioner bolt	14 to 20
Timing belt tensioner bolt	32 to 40
Tensioner "B" bolt	11 to 15
Timing belt cover bolts	84 to 108 in-lbs

1   General information and engine identification

This Part of Chapter 2 is devoted to in-vehicle engine repair procedures for the 2.0L and 2.4L four-cylinder engines. Information concerning engine removal and installation and engine block and cylinder head overhaul can be found in Part D of this Chapter.

The following repair procedures are based on the assumption that the engine is installed in the vehicle. If the engine has been removed from the vehicle and mounted on a stand, many of the steps outlined in this Part of Chapter 2 will not apply.

The Specifications included in this Part of Chapter 2 apply only to the procedures contained in this Part. Part D of Chapter 2 contains the Specifications necessary for cylinder head and engine block rebuilding.

2   Repair operations possible with the engine in the vehicle

Many major repair operations can be accomplished without removing the engine from the vehicle.

Clean the engine compartment and the exterior of the engine with some type of degreaser before any work is done. It will make the job easier and help keep dirt out of the internal areas of the engine.

Depending on the components involved, it may be helpful to remove the hood to improve access to the engine as repairs are performed (refer to Chapter 11 if necessary). Cover the fenders to prevent damage to the paint. Special pads are available, but an old bedspread or blanket will also work.

If vacuum, exhaust, oil or coolant leaks develop, indicating a need for gasket or seal replacement, the repairs can generally be made with the engine in the vehicle. The intake and exhaust manifold gaskets, oil pan gasket, crankshaft oil seals and cylinder head gasket are all accessible with the engine in place.

Exterior engine components, such as the intake and exhaust manifolds, the oil pan (and the oil pump), the water pump, the starter motor,

4.3   Carefully disconnect the spark plug wires from the clips

the alternator, the distributor and the fuel system components can be removed for repair with the engine in place.

Since the camshaft and cylinder head can be removed without pulling the engine, valve component servicing can also be accomplished with the engine in the vehicle. Replacement of the timing belt and sprockets is also possible with the engine in the vehicle.

In extreme cases caused by a lack of necessary equipment, repair or replacement of piston rings, pistons, connecting rods and rod bearings is possible with the engine in the vehicle. However, this practice is not recommended because of the cleaning and preparation work that must be done to the components involved.

3   Top Dead Center (TDC) for number 1 piston – locating

This procedure is essentially the same as for the 2.6L engine. Refer to Part A, Section 3 and follow the procedure outlined there.

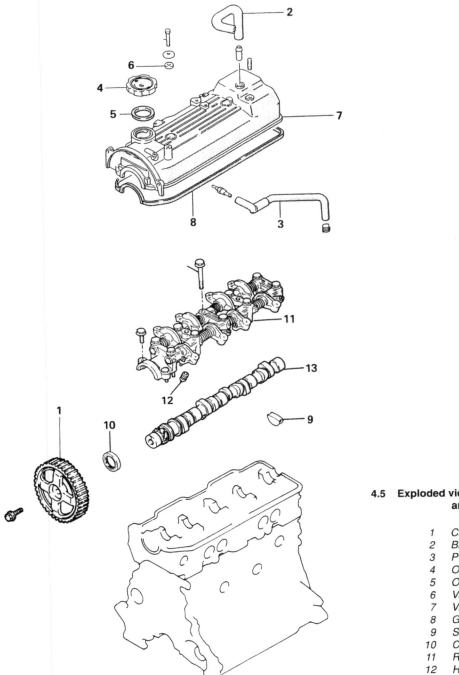

4.5   **Exploded view of the 2.0L valve cover, rocker arms and camshaft**

1   Camshaft sprocket
2   Breather hose
3   PCV hose
4   Oil filler cap
5   Oil filler cap seal
6   Valve cover bolt seal
7   Valve cover
8   Gasket
9   Semi-circular seal
10   Camshaft oil seal
11   Rocker arm assembly
12   Hydraulic lash adjuster
13   Camshaft

4   Valve cover – removal and installation

Refer to illustrations 4.3 and 4.5

1   Disconnect the negative cable from the battery.
2   Remove the air cleaner assembly (see Chapter 4).
3   Detach the spark plug wires and cable brackets from the valve cover **(see illustration)**.
4   Clearly label and then disconnect any emission hoses and cables which connect to or cross over the valve cover.
5   Remove the valve cover bolts **(see illustration)** and lift the cover off. If the cover sticks to the cylinder head, tap on it with a soft-face hammer or place a block of wood against the cover and tap on the wood with a hammer.
6   Thoroughly clean the valve cover and remove all traces of old gasket material.
7   Install a new gasket on the cover, using RTV to hold it in place. Place the cover on the engine and install the cover bolts. **Note:** *Be sure to install a new semi-circular seal* **(see illustration 4.5)** *into the cylinder head. Apply a small amount of sealant to the bottom of the seal and, after it has been installed, to the top of the seal, at the seal-to-head joint.*
8   Tighten the bolts to the torque listed in this Chapter's Specifications. The remaining steps are the reverse of removal. When finished, run the engine and check for oil leaks.

5.3   Remove the rocker arm assembly bolts (arrows) – 2.0L engine shown

---

5   Rocker arm assembly – removal, inspection and installation

Removal

Refer to illustration 5.3

1   Remove the valve cover (see Section 4).
2   Position the number one piston at Top Dead Center, compression (see Section 3).
3   Loosen the rocker arm shaft mounting bolts, 1/4-turn at a time each, until the spring pressure is relieved **(see illustration)**. Remove the bolts.
4   Lift the rocker arms and shaft assembly, or the individual rocker arms, from the cylinder head. If you're working on an engine with hydraulic lash adjusters, be sure not to let the adjusters fall out of the rocker arms. Wrap pieces of tape around the ends of the rocker arms to keep the adjusters in place.

Inspection

Refer to illustrations 5.5 and 5.6

5   If you wish to disassemble and inspect the rocker arm assemblies (a

good idea as long as you have them off), remove the retaining bolts and slip the rocker arms and springs off the shafts **(see illustration)**. Keep the parts in order so you can reassemble them in the same positions.
6   Thoroughly clean the parts and inspect them for wear and damage. Check the rocker arm faces that contact the camshaft and the adjusting screw tips **(see illustration)**. Replace any parts that are damaged or excessively worn. Also, make sure the oil holes in the shafts are not plugged.

Installation

Refer to illustrations 5.7, 5.8a, 5.8b and 5.8c

7   On rocker arms with adjusting screws, loosen the locknuts and back off the adjusters **(see illustration)** until they only protrude 1 mm (0.040-inch).
8   Lubricate all components with assembly lube or engine oil and reassemble the shafts. When installing the rocker arms, shafts and springs, note the markings and the difference between the left and right side parts **(see illustrations)**. Place the notches in the end of the shaft up **(see illustration)** and install the bolts through the cap into the shafts to keep them aligned until they are ready to be installed onto the cylinder head.
9   If removed, insert the hydraulic lash adjusters into the rocker arms and wrap tape around the ends of the rocker arms to prevent the adjusters from falling out. **Note:** *New adjusters are primed with diesel oil. To make sure the oil is not spilled from the adjuster while handling, avoid tilting the adjuster as much as possible. If the oil is spilled from the adjuster, bleed the adjuster as described in Section 7.*
10   Position the rocker arm assemblies on the cylinder head and install the mounting bolts finger tight. Check the markings on the caps to identify the correct journal number and intake/exhaust position. On models with hydraulic lash adjusters, remove the tape from the rocker arms.
11   Tighten the bolts in several stages until the torque listed in this Chapter's Specifications is reached. Tighten the bearing caps a little at a time, starting with the center journals and working toward the ends of the camshaft.
12   On adjustable-type rocker arms, adjust the valve clearances (cold) as described in Chapter 1.
13   Temporarily install the valve cover and run the engine until it is fully warmed up.
14   Readjust the valves while the engine is still warm (see Chapter 1).
15   Reinstall the remaining parts in the reverse order of removal.
16   Run the engine and check for oil leaks and proper operation.

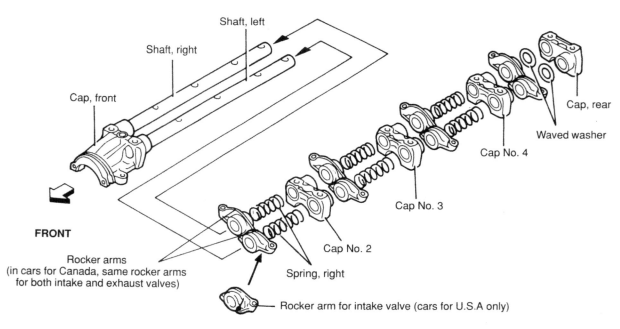

5.5   Exploded view of the rocker arms and shafts (typical)

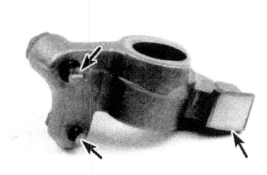

5.6   Check the contact faces and adjusting screw tips (arrows)

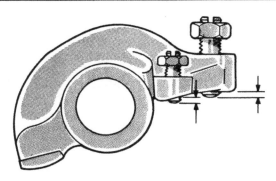

5.7   On adjustable-type rocker arms, back off the adjusters until they only protrude 1 mm (0.040 in)

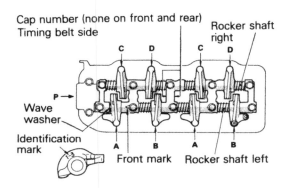

5.8a   Rocker arms marked A or B belong on the intake side while rockers marked C or D belong on the exhaust side

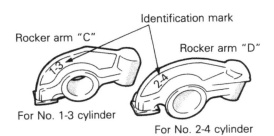

5.8b   Exhaust-side rocker arms marked 1 – 3 are in the C positions in illustration 5.8a, while exhaust rockers marked 2 – 4 are installed in the D positions

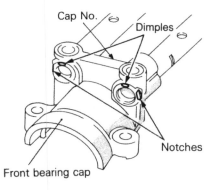

5.8c   On 2.4L engines, align the dimples offset to the notches on the bearing cap

6.1   Remove the valve guide seal with a pair of pliers

---

6   Valve springs, retainers and seals – replacement

Refer to illustrations 6.1 and 6.2

Note: *The jet valve is mounted directly beside each intake valve. Refer to Chapter 2D for the jet valve servicing procedure.*

This procedure is essentially the same as for the 2.6L engine covered in Chapter 2, Part A. Refer to Part A, Section 6 and follow the procedure outlined there (but also refer to the illustrations accompanying this Section).

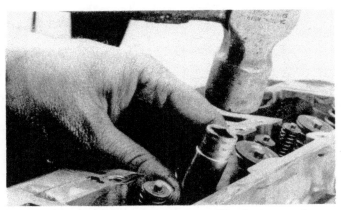

6.2   Gently tap the seal into place with a hammer and deep socket

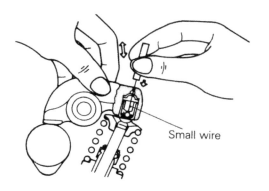

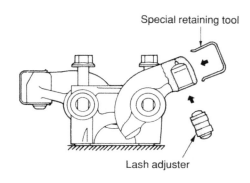

7.1   When performing the freeplay test, make sure the adjuster that is being tested has the corresponding camshaft lobe pointing away from the rocker arm (closed valve)

7.4   The hydraulic lash adjusters are precision units installed in the machined openings in the rocker arms

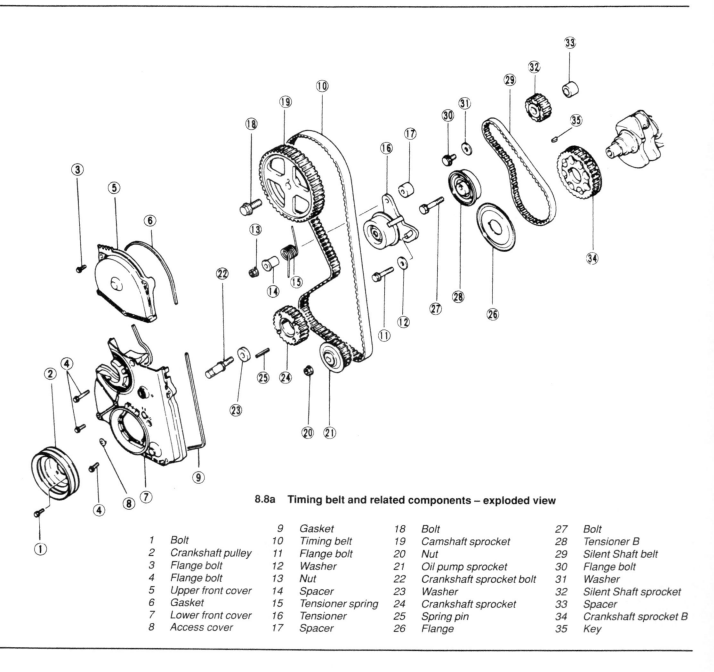

8.8a   Timing belt and related components – exploded view

1	Bolt	9	Gasket	18	Bolt	27	Bolt
2	Crankshaft pulley	10	Timing belt	19	Camshaft sprocket	28	Tensioner B
3	Flange bolt	11	Flange bolt	20	Nut	29	Silent Shaft belt
4	Flange bolt	12	Washer	21	Oil pump sprocket	30	Flange bolt
5	Upper front cover	13	Nut	22	Crankshaft sprocket bolt	31	Washer
6	Gasket	14	Spacer	23	Washer	32	Silent Shaft sprocket
7	Lower front cover	15	Tensioner spring	24	Crankshaft sprocket	33	Spacer
8	Access cover	16	Tensioner	25	Spring pin	34	Crankshaft sprocket B
		17	Spacer	26	Flange	35	Key

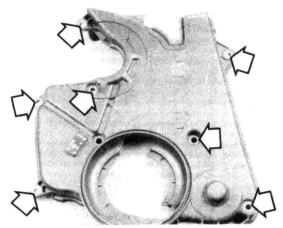

8.8b   The upper timing belt cover is attached with three bolts (arrows) (2.0L engine shown)

8.8c   Arrows point to the locations of the lower timing belt cover bolts (cover removed for clarity) (2.0L engine shown)

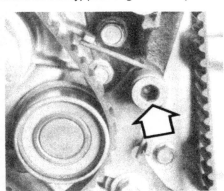

8.9   If you plan to reuse the belt, paint an arrow on it to indicate direction of rotation (clockwise)

8.10a   Loosen the belt tensioner bolt (arrow) and pry the tensioner towards the water pump (belt removed for clarity)

8.10b   Some engines use an Allen-head bolt (arrow) to retain the tensioner

---

7   Hydraulic lash adjusters – removal, inspection and installation

Check

Refer to illustration 7.1

1   Check the hydraulic lash adjusters for freeplay by inserting a small wire through the air bleed hole in the rocker arm while lightly pushing the check ball down **(see illustration)**.
2   While lightly holding the check ball down, move the rocker arm up and down to check for freeplay. There should be a small amount of movement. If there is no freeplay, replace the adjuster with a new unit.

Removal

Refer to illustration 7.4

3   Remove the valve cover (see Section 4) and the rocker arm shaft components (see Section 5).
4   Remove the hydraulic lash adjuster(s) from the rocker arm(s) **(see illustration)**. **Note:** *Be sure to label each rocker arm and adjuster and place them in a partitioned box or something suitable to keep them from getting mixed up.*
5   Installation is the reverse of removal.

---

8   Timing belt, Silent Shaft belt and sprockets – removal, inspection and installation

Caution: *Do not try to turn the crankshaft with the camshaft sprocket bolt and do not rotate the crankshaft counterclockwise. Also, don't turn the*

crankshaft after the timing belt has been removed.
1   Position the number one piston at Top Dead Center (see Section 3).
2   Disconnect the negative cable from the battery.
3   Remove the air cleaner assembly and associated hoses (see Chapter 4).
4   Set the parking brake and block the rear wheels. Raise the front of the vehicle and support it securely on jackstands.
5   Remove the power steering pump drivebelt (see Chapter 1) and the air conditioner drivebelt and tensioner (see Chapter 3).

Removal

Refer to illustrations 8.8a, 8.8b, 8.8c, 8.9, 8.10a, 8.10b, 8.14 and 8.15

6   Loosen the water pump pulley bolts and remove the remaining drivebelts (see Chapter 1).
7   Unbolt and remove the water pump pulley (see Chapter 3).
8   Remove the bolts that secure the timing belt upper cover **(see illustrations)** and lift the cover off. Remove the bolts that secure the lower cover **(see illustration)** and lift it off.
9   If you plan to reuse the timing belt, draw an arrow on it **(see illustration)** to indicate the direction of rotation (clockwise).
10   Loosen the adjusting bolt and move the timing belt tensioner towards the water pump as far as possible **(see illustrations)**. Temporarily secure the tensioner by tightening the bolt.
11   Remove the splash pan from beneath the engine, then remove the large center bolt from the crankshaft pulley. **Note:** *Some models secure the crankshaft pulley with four bolts. It's very tight – to break it loose, wrap a rag around the pulley and attach a chain wrench. Slip a socket onto the bolt and insert an extension through the hole in the inner fender. Turn the extension with a breaker bar.*

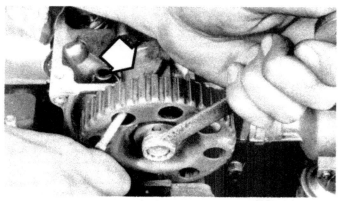

8.14   Slip a screwdriver through the sprocket to prevent the camshaft from turning – be sure to pad the gasket surface (arrow) to prevent damage to the head

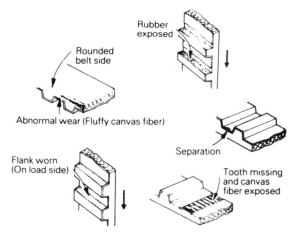

8.20   Carefully inspect the timing belt for the conditions shown here

12   If you are unable to loosen the bolt due to the chain wrench slipping, you can prevent the crankshaft from turning by having an assistant wedge a flat-blade screwdriver in the flywheel/driveplate ring gear teeth. To do this, you must first remove the flywheel/driveplate cover (described in the transaxle removal procedures in Chapter 7).

13   Make sure the tensioner bolts are loose and slip the timing belt off the sprockets and set it aside.

14   If you intend to remove the camshaft, unscrew the camshaft sprocket bolt and slide the sprocket off – a large screwdriver inserted through a hole in the sprocket will keep it from turning while you remove the bolt **(see illustration)**. Also, remove the oil pump sprocket at this time and inspect the oil pump seal for leaks or apparent damage.

15   Remove the plug at the left side of the cylinder block and insert a screwdriver or a long punch to hold the Silent Shaft stationary **(see illustration)**. The screwdriver or punch should have an approximate diameter of 5/16-inch and a length of 2 3/8-inches.

16   Loosen the bolt that retains the Silent Shaft sprocket.

17   Loosen the Silent Shaft belt tensioner **(see illustration 8.8b)** and remove the Silent Shaft belt (timing belt B). **Caution:** *Do not attempt to loosen the sprocket bolt by holding the sprocket stationary with pliers.*

18   If you intend to replace the crankshaft front oil seal, slide off the crankshaft sprocket and the belt guide flange (if equipped) located behind the crankshaft sprocket. When removing the flange, note the way it's installed (the chamfered side faces out).

Inspection

Refer to illustration 8.20

19   Rotate the tensioner pulley by hand and move it side-to-side to detect roughness and excess play. Visually inspect the sprockets for any signs of

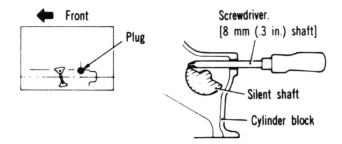

8.15   A screwdriver is used to keep the Silent Shaft from turning as the oil pump is loosened

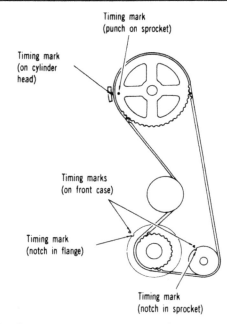

8.22   Camshaft and crankshaft sprocket alignment marks

damage and wear. Replace parts as necessary.

20   Inspect the timing belt for cracks, separation, wear, missing teeth and oil contamination **(see illustration)**. Replace the belt if it's in questionable condition.

Installation

Refer to illustrations 8.22, 8.23, 8.24, 8.25a, 8.25b, 8.29 and 8.30

21   Reinstall the timing belt sprockets, if they were removed. Note that the camshaft sprocket is indexed by punch marks. Slip the belt guide flange onto the crankshaft before installing the lower sprocket – the chamfered side of the flange faces out.

22   Align the timing marks located on the camshaft, crankshaft and oil pump sprockets with the marks on the cylinder head and the front case **(see illustration)**. **Note:** *Different engines have different types of alignment marks. Some alignment marks are notches or raised arrows and some are punch indentations. Identify the exact type and location of the alignment marks on each sprocket before continuing the procedure. When aligning the oil pump sprocket marks, it is critical that the silent shaft (if equipped) has the weighted portion at the bottom of the shaft (it is possible to align the marks with the Silent Shaft weight at the top; if you do this accidentally, severe engine vibration will result). Before installing the timing belt, slightly rock the oil pump sprocket by hand and watch carefully that the sprocket has the tendency to remain stationary (return to approximately the marks-aligned position) when the sprocket is rotated. This means the sprocket is CORRECTLY timed. If the sprocket has the tendency to rotate clockwise when spun lightly, the shaft is INCORRECTLY timed. If there is any doubt about whether or not the silent shaft is in the correct position, insert a screwdriver through the hole in the left side of the*

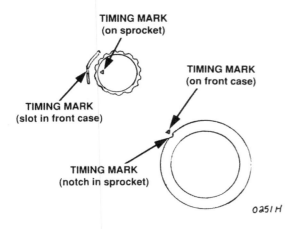

8.23 Align the marks as shown before installing timing belt B

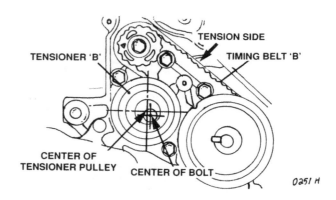

8.24 Make sure the tension side of the belt is drawn tight when initially installing the timing belt – also, the tensioner pulley must be positioned as shown

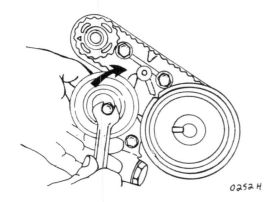

8.25a Rotate the tensioner clockwise and up to apply tension to the belt

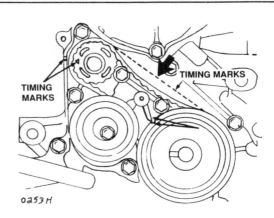

8.25b Press on the center of the belt to check tension

8.29 Since you must view the camshaft sprocket marks at an angle, it may help to use a pointer to avoid mistakes

cylinder block **(see illustration 8.15)**. *Make sure the screwdriver extends approximately two inches into the hole and also make sure the sprocket cannot be rotated with the screwdriver in place; now you can be sure the timing is correct.*

23 Install timing belt B. Align the timing marks on each sprocket with the timing marks on the front case **(see illustration)**.

24 After installing timing belt B, make sure the tension side has no slack **(see illustration)**.

25 Make sure the tensioner sprocket for timing belt B has the center located just to the left side of the mounting bolt with the pulley directed to the front of the engine **(see illustration 8.24).** Lift the tensioner up with one finger to tighten the belt **(see illustration)** and tighten the tensioner bolt to the torque listed in this Chapter's Specifications. **Note:** *Use the index finger and press firmly on the timing belt* **(see illustration)**. *The belt deflection should be 13/64 to 9/32-inch (5.0 to 7.0 mm).*

26 Slip the timing belt onto the crankshaft sprocket. While maintaining tension on the rear (firewall) side of the belt, slip the belt onto the camshaft sprocket.

27 Release the tensioner hold-down bolt to apply spring tension against the belt. Retighten the bolt.

28 Install the crankshaft pulley, taking care to align the locating pin with the small hole in the pulley (if equipped). Install the crankshaft pulley bolts (both the pulley securing bolts and the center bolt) and tighten them to the torques listed in this Chapter's Specifications. When tightening the bolts, hold the crankshaft in place using one of the methods discussed in Steps 11 and 12.

29 Using the bolt in the center of the crankshaft pulley, turn the crankshaft clockwise through six complete revolutions. **Note:** *The camshaft, crankshaft and right Silent Shaft sprocket marks will align every two revolutions of the crankshaft; however, since the left (oil pump) sprocket turns at 2/3 crankshaft speed, its marks will only align every six crankshaft revolutions. Recheck the alignment of the timing marks* **(see illustration)**. *If the marks do not align properly, loosen the tensioner, slip the belt off the camshaft sprocket, align the marks, reinstall the belt, and check the alignment marks again.*

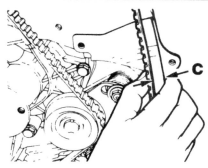

8.30   Squeeze the timing belt and case and observe the distance between the belt and Line C to measure the belt deflection

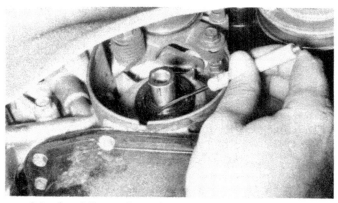

9.2   Carefully pry the seal out with a small screwdriver

10.12   Measure the camshaft lobe heights

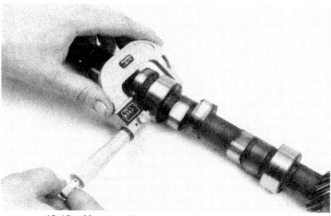

10.13   Measure the camshaft journal diameters

30   If it is too tight or too loose, loosen the tensioner bolts and adjust the tensioner. Squeeze the timing belt and the cover **(see illustration)**, and measure the distance between the timing belt and Line C. The distance should be approximately 9/16-inch.

31   Tighten the tensioner bolts to the torque listed in this Chapter's Specifications, starting with the adjustment bolt; then tighten the bolt which goes through the tension spring.

32   Reinstall the remaining parts in the reverse order of removal. Note that the timing belt cover bolts come in different lengths.

33   Start the engine, set the ignition timing (see Chapter 1) and road test the vehicle.

---

9   Crankshaft front oil seal – replacement

Refer to illustration 9.2

1   Remove the timing belt, Silent Shaft belt and the crankshaft sprockets (see Section 8).

2   Wrap the tip of a small screwdriver with tape. Working from below the left inner fender, use the screwdriver to pry the seal out of its bore **(see illustration)**. Take care to prevent damaging the crankshaft and the seal bore.

3   Thoroughly clean and inspect the seal bore and sealing surface on the crankshaft. Minor imperfections can be removed with emery cloth. If there is a groove worn in the crankshaft sealing surface (from contact with the seal), installing a new seal will probably not stop the leak. Such wear normally indicates the internal engine components are also worn. Consider overhauling the engine.

4   Lubricate the new seal with engine oil and drive the seal into place with a hammer and socket.

5   Reinstall the sprockets, the timing belt, the Silent Shaft belt and related components as described in Section 8.

6   Run the engine and check for oil leaks.

---

10   Camshaft – removal, inspection and installation

Removal

1   Position the number one piston at Top Dead Center (see Section 3).

2   Disconnect the negative cable from the battery.

3   Remove the valve cover (see Section 4).

4   Remove the distributor (see Chapter 5).

5   Drain the cooling system (see Chapter 1) and disconnect the upper radiator hose from the thermostat housing.

6   Remove the fuel pump (carbureted models only) (see Chapter 4).

7   Remove the timing belt and camshaft sprocket (see Section 8).

8   Detach the rocker arm assembly (see Section 5).

9   Lift the camshaft from the cylinder head **(see illustration 4.5)**.

Inspection

Refer to illustrations 10.12, 10.13 and 10.15

10   Thoroughly clean the camshaft and the gasket surfaces.

11   Visually inspect the camshaft for wear and/or damage to the distributor drive gear, lobe surfaces, bearing journals and seal contact surfaces. Visually inspect the camshaft bearing surfaces in the cylinder head for scoring and other damage.

12   Measure the camshaft lobe heights **(see illustration)** and compare them to this Chapter's Specifications.

13   Measure the camshaft bearing journal diameters **(see illustration)**, then measure the inside diameter of the camshaft bearing surfaces in the cylinder head, using a telescoping gauge (you'll have to reinstall the camshaft bearing caps). Subtract the journal measurement from the bearing measurement to obtain the camshaft bearing oil clearance. Compare this clearance with this Chapter's Specifications.

14   Replace the camshaft if it fails any of the above inspections. **Note:** *If the distributor drive gear is faulty, replace the driven gear also. If the lobes are worn, replace the rocker arms along with the camshaft. Cylinder head replacement may be necessary if the camshaft bearing surfaces in the head are damaged or excessively worn.*

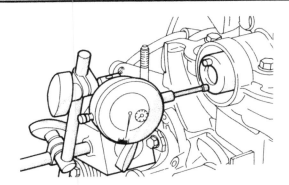

10.15 To measure camshaft endplay, set up a dial indicator with the plunger of the indicator in line with the camshaft, as shown – gently pry the camshaft all the way to the rear, zero the indicator, then pry the camshaft all the way to the front – the reading on the indicator is the endplay measurement

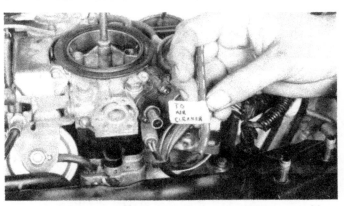

11.4 Carefully label the wires and hoses to aid in reassembly

15 Remove the rocker arms and shafts from the camshaft bearing caps (see Section 5). Temporarily install the bearing caps, in their proper positions, and tighten the bolts to the torque listed in this Chapter's Specifications. Using a dial indicator, check the camshaft endplay **(see illustration)** and compare it to this Chapter's Specifications.
16 If the endplay is excessive, replace the camshaft and/or the cylinder head.

Installation

17 Liberally coat the journals and thrust portions of the camshaft with assembly lube or engine oil.
18 Carefully install the camshaft in the cylinder head. **Caution:** *If the camshaft was not properly marked before removal, install it with the lobes facing DOWN or away from the rocker arms. This will set the engine at TDC number 1 (provided the crankshaft hasn't been rotated since Step 1).*
19 Coat a new camshaft oil seal with engine oil and press it into place with a hammer and a deep socket.
20 Assemble and install the rocker arm assembly, tightening the bolts to the torque listed in this Chapter's Specifications (see Section 5).
21 Install the camshaft sprocket and tighten the bolt to the torque listed in this Chapter's Specifications.
22 Install the timing belt (see Section 8).

23 Temporarily set the valve clearances prior to engine start-up (see Chapter 1). **Note:** *Later models use hydraulic lash adjusters on the intake and exhaust valves but the jet valve must still be adjusted manually.*
24 Reinstall the remaining parts in the reverse order of removal.
25 Start the engine and allow it to warm up, then adjust the ignition timing (see Chapter 1).
26 Readjust the valve clearances as described in Chapter 1.
27 Reinstall the valve cover and run the engine while checking for oil leaks.

11 Intake manifold – removal and installation

1 Relieve the fuel system pressure (see Chapter 4), then disconnect the negative cable from the battery.
2 Drain the cooling system (see Chapter 1).

Removal

Carbureted models

Refer to illustrations 11.4 and 11.8

3 Remove the air cleaner (see Chapter 4).
4 Clearly label **(see illustration)** and disconnect all hoses, wires, brackets and emission lines which run to the carburetor and intake manifold. Several components may be slipped out of brackets and laid over the carburetor **(see illustration)**.

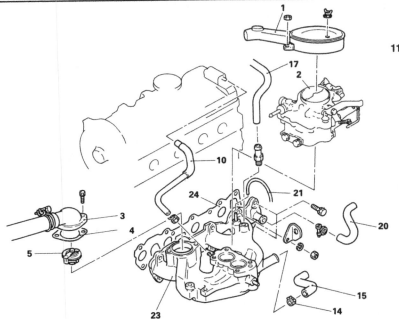

11.8 Exploded view of the intake manifold and components on a carbureted engine

1	Air cleaner
2	Carburetor
3	Thermostat housing
4	Gasket
5	Thermostat
10	Breather hose
14	Heater hose clamp
15	Heater hose
17	Brake booster vacuum line
20	Water hose
21	Vacuum connector hose
23	Intake manifold
24	Intake manifold gasket

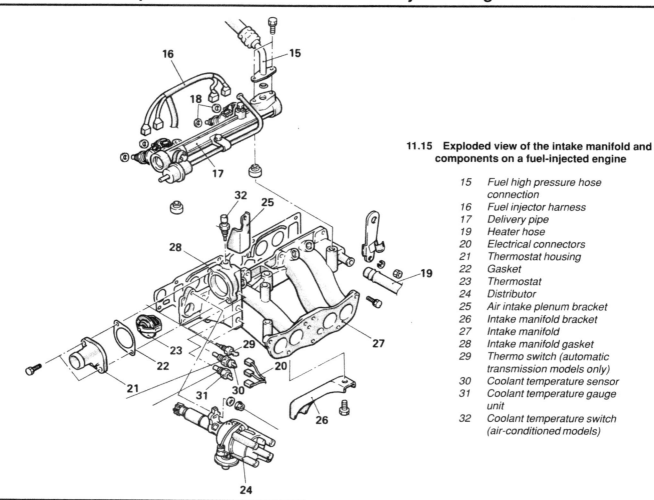

11.15 Exploded view of the intake manifold and components on a fuel-injected engine

15	Fuel high pressure hose connection
16	Fuel injector harness
17	Delivery pipe
19	Heater hose
20	Electrical connectors
21	Thermostat housing
22	Gasket
23	Thermostat
24	Distributor
25	Air intake plenum bracket
26	Intake manifold bracket
27	Intake manifold
28	Intake manifold gasket
29	Thermo switch (automatic transmission models only)
30	Coolant temperature sensor
31	Coolant temperature gauge unit
32	Coolant temperature switch (air-conditioned models)

5   Disconnect the fuel lines from the carburetor and cap the fittings to prevent leakage (see Chapter 4).

6   Disconnect the throttle cable from the carburetor (see Chapter 4).

7   Detach the cable which runs from the carburetor to the transmission (automatic transmission models only) and the cruise control cable, on vehicles so equipped.

8   Unbolt the intake manifold and remove it from the engine **(see illustration)**. If it sticks, tap the manifold with a soft-face hammer. **Caution:** *Do not pry between gasket sealing surfaces or tap on the carburetor.*

Fuel-injected models
Refer to illustration 11.15

9   Remove the air intake hose (see Chapter 4).

10   Clearly label and disconnect all hoses, wires, brackets and emission lines which run to the fuel injection system and intake manifold.

11   Remove the distributor (see Chapter 5) and the accelerator cable(s) (see Chapter 4).

12   Remove the bolts that retain the air intake plenum to the intake manifold (see Chapter 4). Remove the plenum.

13   Remove the bolts that hold the fuel rail to the intake manifold then remove the fuel rail (see Chapter 4).

14   Raise the vehicle and support it securely on jackstands.

15   Remove the bolts that retain the lower intake manifold bracket to the engine **(see illustration)**.

16   Unbolt the intake manifold and remove it from the engine. If it sticks, tap the manifold with a soft-face hammer or carefully pry it from the head. **Caution:** *Do not pry between gasket sealing surfaces.*

Installation

17   Thoroughly clean the manifold and cylinder head mating surfaces, re-

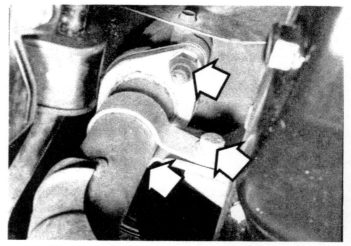

12.3 Working under the vehicle, apply penetrating oil to the threads and remove the nuts (arrows) – note that one is hidden from view

moving all traces of gasket material.

18   Install the manifold, using a new gasket. Tighten the nuts in several stages, working from the center out, until the torque listed in this Chapter's Specifications is reached.

19   Reinstall the remaining parts in the reverse order of removal.

20   Add coolant, run the engine and check for leaks and proper operation.

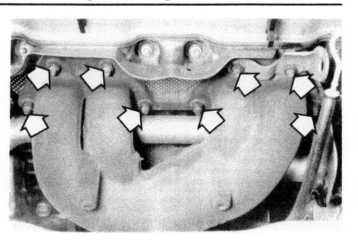

12.7   Remove the bolts from the heat shield (arrows) (2.0L engine shown)

12.8   Remove the exhaust manifold mounting nuts (arrows) (2.0L engine shown)

12   Exhaust manifold – removal and installation

Warning: *Allow the engine to cool completely before beginning this procedure.*

Removal

Refer to illustrations 12.3, 12.7 and 12.8

1   Disconnect the negative cable from the battery.
2   Set the parking brake and block the rear wheels. Raise the vehicle and support it securely on jackstands.
3   Working from under the vehicle, remove the nuts that secure the exhaust system to the bottom of the exhaust manifold **(see illustration)**. Apply penetrating oil to the threads to make removal easier.
4   On carbureted engines, remove the air cleaner assembly (see Chapter 4).
5   Unplug the oxygen sensor wire (see chapter 6).
6   If equipped with an secondary air system, apply penetrating oil and unscrew the flare nuts on the air injection tube. Remove the tube from the manifold.
7   Remove the three bolts that secure the heat shield **(see illustration)** to the exhaust manifold. Lift the heat shield off.
8   Apply penetrating oil to the threads and remove the exhaust manifold mounting nuts **(see illustration)**, brackets and emission components.
9   Slip the manifold off the studs and remove it from the engine compartment.

Installation

Refer to illustration 12.8

10   Clean and inspect all threaded fasteners and repair as necessary.
11   Remove any traces of gasket material from the mating surfaces and inspect them for wear and cracks.
12   Place a new gasket over the studs **(see illustration)**, install the manifold and tighten the nuts in several stages, working from the center out, to the torque listed in this Chapter's Specifications.

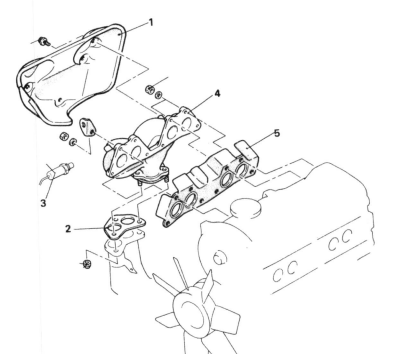

12.12   Exhaust manifold mounting details

1   *Heat shield*
2   *Gasket*
3   *Oxygen sensor*
4   *Exhaust manifold*
5   *Exhaust manifold gasket*

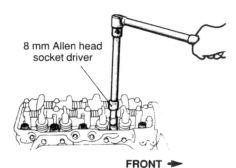

8 mm Allen head
socket driver

FRONT →

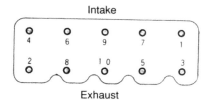

Intake

| 4 | 6 | 9 | 7 | 1 |
| 2 | 8 | 10 | 5 | 3 |

Exhaust

13.10   Cylinder head bolt LOOSENING sequence

13   Reinstall the remaining parts in the reverse order of removal.
14   Run the engine and check for exhaust leaks.

13   Cylinder head – removal and installation

Caution: *Allow the engine to cool completely before following this procedure.*

Removal

Refer to illustrations 13.10, 13.11 and 13.12
1   Position the number one piston at Top Dead Center (TDC) (see Section 3).
2   Disconnect the negative cable from the battery.
3   Drain the cooling system and remove the spark plugs (see Chapter 1).
4   Remove the intake manifold (see Section 11).
5   Remove the exhaust manifold (see Section 12).
6   Remove the distributor (see Chapter 5), including the cap and wires.
7   On carbureted models, remove the fuel pump (see Chapter 4).
8   Remove the timing belt (see Section 8). **Note:** *On some models it is possible to remove the cylinder head without removing the timing belt. Hang the sprocket with a piece of wire attached to the hood of the vehicle –*

make sure the belt does not lose tension after the camshaft sprocket has been detached from the camshaft.
9   Remove the valve cover (see Section 4).
10   Using an 8 mm Allen head socket, loosen the cylinder head bolts, 1/4-turn at a time, in the sequence shown **(see illustration)** until they can be removed by hand.
11   Carefully lift the cylinder head straight up and place it on wood blocks to prevent damage to the sealing surfaces. If the head sticks to the engine block, dislodge it by placing a block of wood against the head casting and tapping the wood with a hammer or by prying the head with a prybar placed carefully on a casting protrusion **(see illustration)**. Cylinder head disassembly and inspection procedures are covered in Chapter 2, Part D. It's a good idea to have the head checked for warpage, even if you're just replacing the gasket.
12   Remove all traces of old gasket material from the block and head **(see illustration)**. Do not allow anything to fall into the engine. Clean and inspect all threaded fasteners and be sure the threaded holes in the block are clean and dry.

Installation

Refer to illustrations 13.13 and 13.14
13   Place a new gasket and the cylinder head in position. **Note:** *Position the identification mark facing up and at the front of the engine block* **(see illustration)**.
14   The cylinder head bolts should be tightened in several stages following the proper sequence **(see illustration)** to the torque listed in this Chapter's Specifications.
15   Reinstall the timing belt (see Section 8).
16   Reinstall the remaining parts in the reverse order of removal.
17   Be sure to refill the cooling system and check all fluid levels. Rotate the crankshaft clockwise slowly by hand through two complete revolutions. Recheck the camshaft timing marks (see Section 8).
18   Start the engine and set the ignition timing (see Chapter 1). Run the engine until normal operating temperature is reached. Check for leaks and proper operation. Shut off the engine. Remove the valve cover and retighten the cylinder head bolts, unless the gasket manufacturer states otherwise. Recheck the valve adjustment if the engine is not equipped with hydraulic lash adjusters.

14   Oil pan – removal and installation

Refer to illustration 14.7

Removal

1   Disconnect the negative cable from the battery.
2   Raise the vehicle and support it securely on jackstands.
3   Remove the splash pan under the engine, then remove the dipstick and drain the engine oil (see Chapter 1).

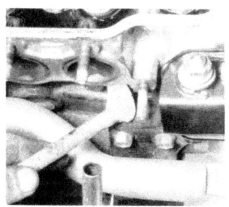

13.11   Pry on an area of the cylinder head that won't be damaged when pressure is applied

13.12   Use a gasket scraper to remove all traces of the old gasket

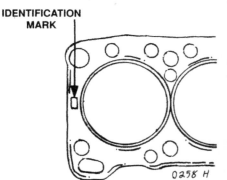

IDENTIFICATION
MARK

0258 H

13.13   The identification mark should face up and be positioned next to the camshaft sprocket

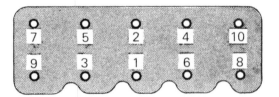

Timing belt side ➡

13.14   Cylinder head bolt TIGHTENING sequence

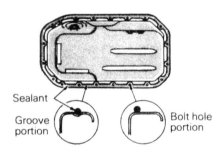

Sealant
Groove portion
Bolt hole portion

14.7   If the oil pan was sealed with RTV sealant only, apply RTV sealant in the groove and to the inside of the bolt holes

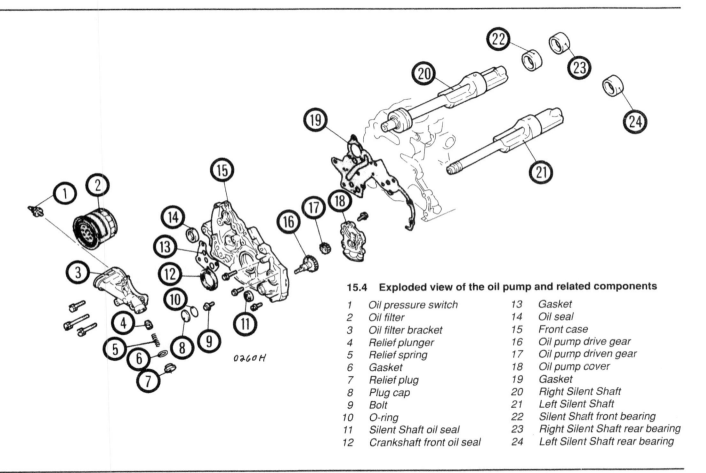

15.4   Exploded view of the oil pump and related components

1	Oil pressure switch	13	Gasket
2	Oil filter	14	Oil seal
3	Oil filter bracket	15	Front case
4	Relief plunger	16	Oil pump drive gear
5	Relief spring	17	Oil pump driven gear
6	Gasket	18	Oil pump cover
7	Relief plug	19	Gasket
8	Plug cap	20	Right Silent Shaft
9	Bolt	21	Left Silent Shaft
10	O-ring	22	Silent Shaft front bearing
11	Silent Shaft oil seal	23	Right Silent Shaft rear bearing
12	Crankshaft front oil seal	24	Left Silent Shaft rear bearing

4   Unbolt the exhaust pipe from the exhaust manifold (see illustration 12.3).
5   Remove the bolts and lower the oil pan from the vehicle. If the pan is stuck, tap it with a soft-face hammer or place a block of wood against the pan and tap the wood with a hammer. Note: If necessary, for additional clearance for the oil pan, remove the engine mounts and raise the engine a few inches.
6   Thoroughly clean the oil pan and sealing surfaces. Remove all traces of old gasket material. Check the oil pan sealing surface for distortion. Straighten or replace as necessary.

Installation

7   If the oil pan was sealed with RTV sealant only (no gasket), apply a 4 mm bead of RTV sealant to the oil pan flange (see illustration). If you are using a gasket, apply a thin coat of RTV sealant to the oil pan flange and affix the gasket.

8   Place the oil pan into position and install the bolts finger tight. Working side-to-side from the center out, tighten the bolts to the torque listed in this Chapter's Specifications.
9   Reinstall the remaining parts in the reverse order of removal.
10   Refill the crankcase with the proper quantity and grade of oil (see Chapter 1) and run the engine, checking for leaks. Road test the vehicle and check for leaks again.

15   Oil pump – removal, inspection and installation

Removal

Refer to illustration 15.4

1   Remove the timing belt and crankshaft sprocket (see Section 8).
2   Remove the oil pan (see Section 14).

15.10a   Measure the driven gear-to-tip clearance

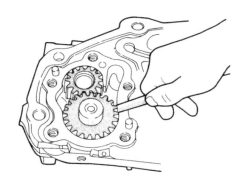

15.10b   Measure the drive gear-to-tip clearance

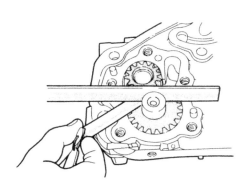

15.10c   Measure the side clearance (endplay) using a
straightedge and feeler gauge

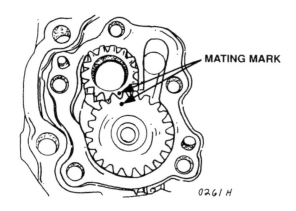

15.10d   Install the gears with the marks aligned and
facing out

3   Unbolt the oil pickup tube (screen) from the bottom of the pump housing.
4   Remove the pressure relief plug, spring and plunger **(see illustration)**.
5   Remove the timing belt tensioner (see Section 8).
6   Remove the oil pump-to-block bolts noting the different lengths and locations of the bolts. Carefully separate the front case from the engine.
7   Detach the cover from the rear of the case **(see illustration 15.4)** and remove the inner and outer oil pump gears.
8   Remove the crankshaft oil seal from the front case (see Section 9).

Inspection

Refer to illustrations 15.10a, 15.10b, 15.10c and 15.10d

9   Clean all parts thoroughly and remove all traces of old gasket material from the sealing surfaces. Visually inspect all parts for wear, cracks and other damage. Replace parts as necessary.
10   Install the oil pump outer and inner gears and measure the clearances **(see illustrations)**. Compare the clearances to the values listed in this Chapter's Specifications. Measure the free length of the pressure relief spring and compare the measurement to this Chapter's Specifications. Replace parts as necessary. Pack the pump cavity with petroleum jelly and install the cover. Tighten the bolts to the torque listed in this Chapter's Specifications. **Note:** *Be sure to install the gears with the mating marks in the correct place* **(see illustration)**.

Installation

11   Install a new crankshaft front oil seal (see Section 9).
12   Install the pressure relief valve components and tighten the plug securely.

13   Using a new gasket, position the pump on the engine. Install the bolts in their proper locations, according to length. Tighten the bolts to the torque listed in this Chapter's Specifications.
14   Reinstall the remaining parts in the reverse order of removal.
15   Add oil, start the engine and check for oil pressure and leaks.

16   Flywheel/driveplate – removal and installation

This procedure is essentially the same for all engines. Refer to Chapter 2 Part A, Section 17, and follow the procedure outlined there.

17   Rear main oil seal – replacement

This procedure is essentially the same for all engines. Refer to Chapter 2 Part A, Section 18, and follow the procedure outlined there.

18   Engine mounts – check and replacement

1   Engine mounts seldom require attention, but broken or deteriorated mounts should be replaced immediately or the added strain placed on the driveline components may cause damage or wear.

Check

2   During the check, the engine must be raised slightly to remove the weight from the mounts.

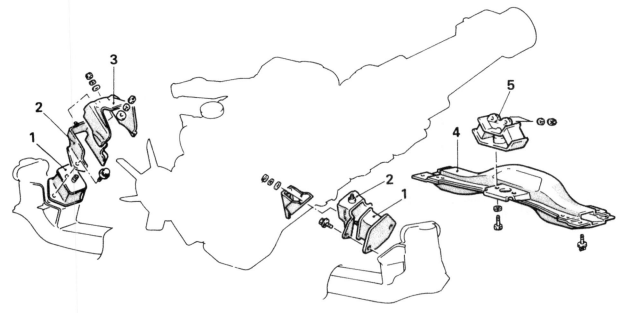

18.8a   Engine mount details (typical 2WD model)

1   Front insulator   3   Heat protector   5   Rear insulator
2   Insulator stopper   4   Number 2 crossmember

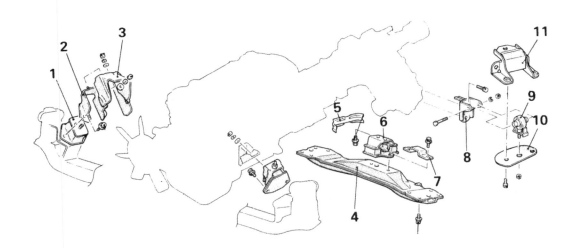

18.8b   Engine mount details on a 4WD pick-up

1   Front insulator   4   Number 2 crossmember   7   Stopper   10   Plate assembly
2   Insulator stopper   5   Heat protector   8   Transfer mounting bracket   11   Transfer support bracket
3   Heat protector   6   Rear insulator   9   Transfer support insulator

3   Raise the vehicle and support it securely on jackstands, then position a jack under the engine oil pan. Place a large block of wood between the jack head and the oil pan, then carefully raise the engine just enough to take the weight off the mounts. **Warning:** *DO NOT place any part of your body under the engine when it's supported only by a jack!*
4   Check the mounts to see if the rubber is cracked, hardened or separated from the metal backing. Sometimes the rubber will split right down

the center. Check that the rod on the front mount is not bent.
5   Check for relative movement between the mount plates and the engine or frame (use a large screwdriver or pry bar to attempt to move the mounts). If movement is noted, lower the engine and tighten the mount fasteners.
6   Rubber preservative may be applied to the mounts to slow deterioration.

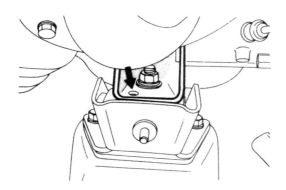

18.8c   Be sure to align the locating boss and hole in the engine mount

Replacement

Refer to illustrations 18.8a, 18.8b and 18.8c

7   Disconnect the negative battery cable from the battery, then raise the vehicle and support it securely on jackstands (if not already done).

8   Remove the fasteners and detach the mount from the frame and engine **(see illustrations)**. Do not disconnect more than one mount at a time, except during engine removal.

9   Installation is the reverse of removal. Use thread locking compound on the mount bolts and be sure to tighten them securely.

Chapter 2 Part C   3.0L V6 engine

Contents

Specifications

General

Displacement	181 cubic inches (3.0 liters)
Bore	3.587 inch
Stroke	2.992 inch
Compression ratio	8.85:1
Firing order	1-2-3-4-5-6
Cylinder numbers (front to rear)	
Right (passenger's side)	1–3–5
Left (driver's side)	2–4–6

Camshaft and related components

Camshaft runout limit	0.004 inch
Lobe height	1.624 inch
Lobe wear limit	0.02 inch

Oil pump

Case-to-outer rotor clearance	0.004 to 0.007 inch
Rotor end clearance	0.0015 to 0.0035 inch
Case-to-inner rotor clearance (maximum wear limit)	0.006 inch

Torque specifications

Ft-lbs (unless otherwise indicated)

Rocker arm shaft bolts	180 in-lbs
Intake manifold nuts/bolts	168 in-lbs
Distributor drive adapter bolts	132 in-lbs
Engine mounts **(see illustration 21.1)**	
Stopper bolts	29
Front insulator bolts	22
Rear insulator-to-crossmember bolts	40
Heat shield bolts	108 in-lbs
Transfer support bracket bolts	18
Exhaust manifold nuts	180 in-lbs
Exhaust manifold heat shield bolts	132 in-lbs
Exhaust pipe-to-manifold bolts	25
Crankshaft vibration damper-to-crankshaft bolt	112
Camshaft sprocket bolt	70
Timing belt cover bolts **(see illustration 10.13)**	
A (M6 X 20)	115 in-lbs
B (M6 X 55)	115 in-lbs
C (M6 X 25)	115 in-lbs
D (M6 X 10)	115 in-lbs
Timing belt tensioner locking nut or bolt	20
Cylinder head bolt	
Pick-ups	65 to 72
Montero	
1990 and earlier	65 to 72
1991 and later	76 to 83
Flywheel/driveplate mounting bolts*	72 to 80
Oil pan mounting bolts	72 in-lbs
Oil pump assembly mounting bolts	120 in-lbs
Oil pump relief plug	36
Oil pick-up tube-to-pump bolts	180 in-lbs
Oil pump cover bolts	120 in-lbs
Valve cover bolts	84 in-lbs

Apply a thread locking compound to the threads prior to installation

---

1   General information

This Part of Chapter 2 is devoted to in-vehicle repair procedures for the 3.0L V6 engine. All information concerning engine removal and installation and engine block and cylinder head overhaul can be found in Part D of this Chapter.

The following repair procedures are based on the assumption that the engine is installed in the vehicle. If the engine has been removed from the vehicle and mounted on a stand, many of the steps outlined in this Part of Chapter 2 will not apply.

The Specifications included in this Part of Chapter 2 apply only to the procedures contained in this Part. Part D of Chapter 2 contains the Specifications necessary for cylinder head and engine block rebuilding.

The 60-degree V6 has a cast iron block and aluminum heads with a camshaft in each head. The block has thin walled sections for light weight. A "cradle frame" main bearing casting – the main bearing caps are cast as a unit, with a bridge, or truss, connecting them – supports the cast ductile iron crankshaft.

Both camshafts are driven off the crankshaft by a cog belt. A spring loaded tensioner, adjusted by an eccentric type locknut, maintains belt tension. Each camshaft actuates two valves per cylinder through hydraulic lash adjusters and shaft-mounted forged aluminum rocker arms.

Each cast aluminum three-ring piston has two compression rings and a three-piece oil control ring. The piston pins are pressed into forged steel connecting rods. The flat-topped pistons produce a 8.85:1 compression ratio.

The distributor (or crank angle sensor), which is mounted on the drivebelt end of the front cylinder head, is driven by a helical gear on the cam-shaft. The water pump, which is bolted to the timing belt end of the block, is driven off the crankshaft by a drivebelt and pulley. The gear type oil pump is mounted in the oil pump case and attached to the timing belt cover. It is driven by the crankshaft.

From the oil pump, oil travels through the filter to the main oil gallery, from which it is routed either directly to the main bearings, crankshaft, connecting rod bearings and pistons and cylinder walls or to the cylinder heads.

---

2   Repair operations possible with the engine in the vehicle

Many major repair operations can be accomplished without removing the engine from the vehicle.

Clean the engine compartment and the exterior of the engine with some type of degreaser before any work is done. It will make the job easier and help keep dirt out of the internal areas of the engine.

Depending on the components involved, it may be helpful to remove the hood to improve access to the engine as repairs are performed (refer to Chapter 11 if necessary). Cover the fenders to prevent damage to the paint. Special pads are available, but an old bedspread or blanket will also work.

If vacuum, exhaust, oil or coolant leaks develop, indicating a need for gasket or seal replacement, the repairs can generally be made with the engine in the vehicle. The intake and exhaust manifold gaskets, oil pan gasket, camshaft and crankshaft oil seals and cylinder head gaskets are all accessible with the engine in place.

4.3   An exploded view of the left side valve cover, rocker arm assembly and cylinder head

19   Spark plug wire connections
      (nos. 2, 4 and 6)
20   Distributor
21   EGR pipe
22   EGR gasket
23   Heat protector
24   Air intake plenum bracket
25   Bracket
26   Exhaust manifold
27   Gasket
28   Valve cover
29   Valve cover gasket
30   Air intake plenum gasket rear
31   Cylinder head
32   Cylinder head gasket
33   Timing belt rear cover

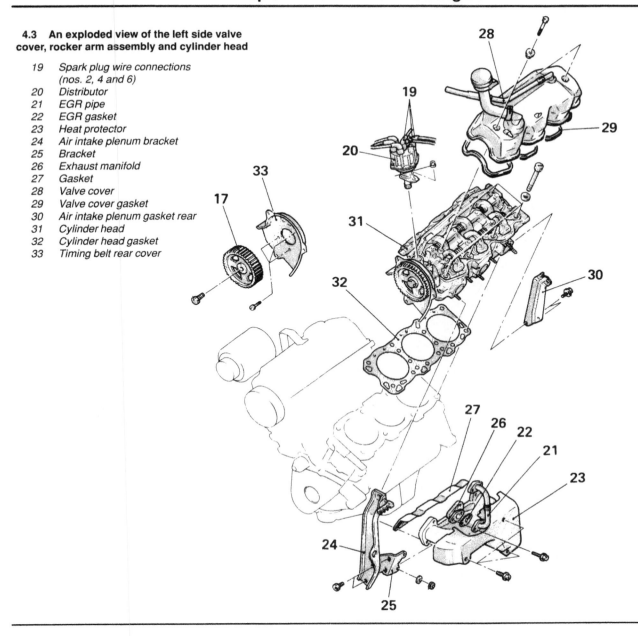

Exterior engine components, such as the intake and exhaust manifolds, the oil pan (and the oil pump), the water pump, the starter motor, the alternator, the distributor and the fuel system components can be removed for repair with the engine in place.

Since the cylinder heads can be removed without pulling the engine, camshaft and valve component servicing can also be accomplished with the engine in the vehicle. Replacement of the timing belt and sprockets is also possible with the engine in the vehicle.

In extreme cases caused by a lack of necessary equipment, repair or replacement of piston rings, pistons, connecting rods and rod bearings is possible with the engine in the vehicle. However, this practice is not recommended because of the cleaning and preparation work that must be done to the components involved.

---

3   Top Dead Center (TDC) for number one piston – locating

This procedure is essentially the same for all engines. Refer to Chapter 2, Part A, Section 3 and follow the procedure outlined there.

---

4   Valve covers – removal and installation

Refer to illustrations 4.3, 4.8 and 4.16

Removal
1   Relieve the fuel system pressure (see Chapter 4).
2   Disconnect the negative cable from the battery.

Left side cover
3   Remove the breather hose from the valve cover **(see illustration)**.
4   Remove the spark plug wires from the spark plugs. Mark them clearly with pieces of masking tape to prevent confusion during installation.
5   Remove air intake plenum (see Chapter 4).
6   Remove the valve cover bolts and washers.
7   Detach the valve cover. **Caution:** *If the cover is stuck to the head, bump one end with a block of wood and a hammer to jar it loose. If that doesn't work, try to slip a flexible putty knife between the head and cover to break the gasket seal. Don't pry at the cover-to-head joint or damage to the sealing surfaces may occur (leading to oil leaks in the future).*

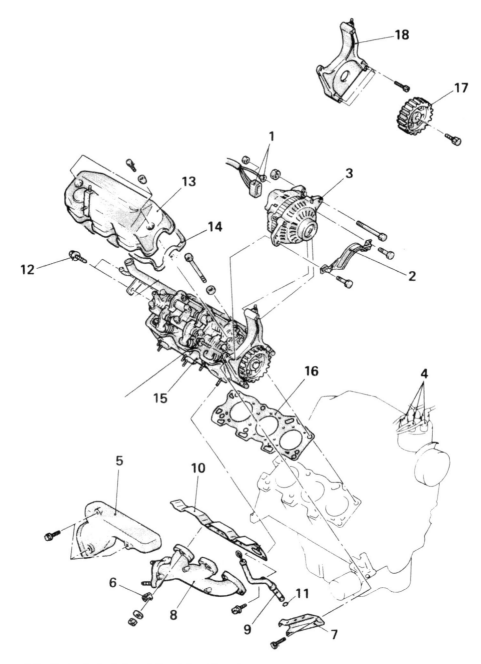

4.8   An exploded view of the right side valve cover, rocker arm assembly and cylinder head

1	Alternator connectors	5	Heat shield	10	Gasket	15	Cylinder head assembly
2	Alternator cover	6	Engine removal bracket	11	O-ring	16	Cylinder head gasket
3	Alternator	7	Alternator bracket	12	Bolt	17	Camshaft sprocket
4	Spark plug wire connections	8	Exhaust manifold	13	Valve cover	18	Alternator bracket
	(nos. 1, 3 and 5)	9	Oil level gauge guide	14	Valve cover gasket		

Right side cover

8   Remove the breather hose from the cover **(see illustration)**.
9   Tag and detach the spark plug wires.
10   Disconnect the electrical connectors and vacuum hoses necessary for removal. Label and move the wiring and hoses aside.
11   Remove the air cleaner assembly (see Chapter 4).
12   Remove the air intake plenum (see Chapter 4).

13   Remove the valve cover bolts and washers and lift off the valve cover. Read the Caution in Step 7.

Installation

14   The mating surfaces of each cylinder head and valve cover must be perfectly clean when the covers are installed. Use a gasket scraper to remove all traces of sealant and old gasket material, then clean the mating

surfaces with lacquer thinner or acetone. If there's sealant or oil on the mating surfaces when the cover is installed, oil leaks may develop.

15   If necessary, clean the mounting screw threads with a die to remove any corrosion and restore damaged threads. Make sure the threaded holes in the head are clean – run a tap into them to remove corrosion and restore damaged threads.

16   The gaskets should be mated to the covers before the covers are installed. Apply a bead of RTV sealant to the cover in the areas indicated **(see illustration)**, then position the gasket inside the cover and allow the sealant to set up so the gasket adheres to the cover. If the sealant isn't allowed to set, the gasket may fall out of the cover as it's installed on the engine.

17   Carefully position the cover on the head and install the bolts.

18   Tighten the bolts in three or four steps to the torque listed in this Chapter's Specifications.

19   The remaining installation steps are the reverse of removal.

20   Start the engine and check carefully for oil leaks as the engine warms up.

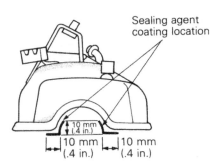

4.16   It's not necessary to use RTV gasket sealer on the inside of the gasket if the gasket is a tight fit and does not budge once it is installed inside the valve cover – it is necessary to apply RTV to the edges (arrows) on the outside of the gasket where it mates with the camshaft seals

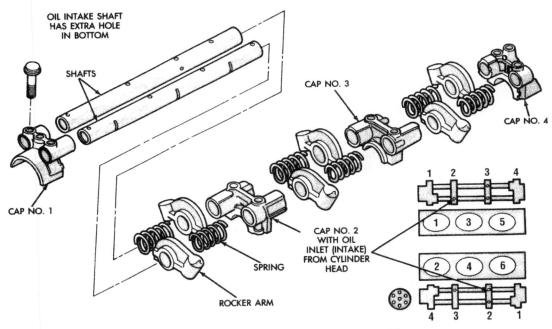

5.2   An exploded view of the rocker arm assembly

5   Rocker arm components – removal and installation

Refer to illustrations 5.2, 5.4 and 5.5

1   Position the engine at TDC compression for the number 1 cylinder (see Section 3). Remove the valve cover (see Section 4).

2   Loosen the rocker arm shaft bolts **(see illustration)** in two or three stages, working your way from the ends toward the middle of the shafts. **Caution:** *Some of the valves will be open when you loosen the rocker arm shaft bolts and the rocker arm shafts will be under a certain amount of valve spring pressure. Therefore, the bolts must be loosened gradually. Loosening a bolt all at once near a rocker arm under spring pressure could bend or break the rocker arm shaft.*

3   Prior to removal, scribe or paint identifying marks on the rockers to ensure they will be installed in their original locations.

4   Remove the bolts and lift off the rocker arm shaft assemblies one at a time. Lay them down on a nearby workbench in the same relationship to each other that they're in when installed. They must be reinstalled on the same cylinder head. Note the location of the stamped bearing cap number and the position of the notches **(see illustration)**.

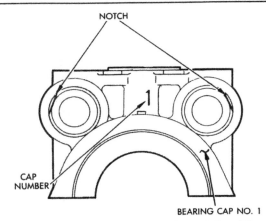

5.4   Check each bearing cap stamped numeral and the position of the notches to aid in correct assembly

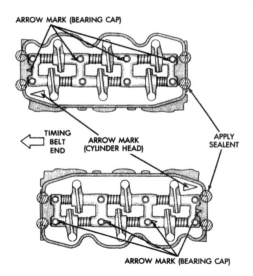

5.5 The   **arrows on the bearing caps should point in the same direction as the arrows on the cylinder heads**

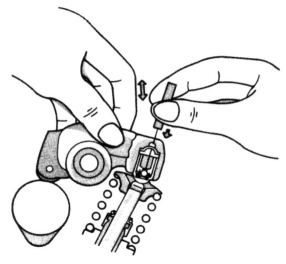

6.1   When performing the freeplay test, make sure the adjuster that is being tested has the corresponding camshaft lobe pointing away from the rocker arm (closed valve)

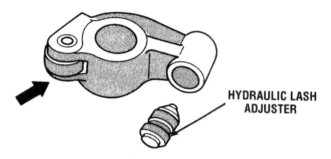

6.4   The hydraulic lash adjusters are precision units installed in the machined openings in the rocker arm assemblies

5   Installation is the reverse of the removal procedure. **Note:** *Be sure the arrows stamped into the cylinder head and the bearing caps* **(see illustration)** *are pointing in the same direction. Tighten the rocker arm shaft bolts, in several steps, to the torque listed in this Chapter's Specifications. Work from the ends of the shafts toward the middle.*

6   Hydraulic lash adjusters – check, removal and installation

Check

Refer to illustration 6.1

1   Check the hydraulic lash adjusters for freeplay by inserting a small wire through the air bleed hole in the rocker arm while lightly pushing the check ball down **(see illustration)**.
2   While lightly holding the check ball down, move the rocker arm up and down to check for freeplay. There should be a small amount of movement. If there is no freeplay, replace the adjuster with a new unit.

Removal

Refer to illustration 6.4

3   Remove the valve cover(s) (see Section 4) and the rocker arm shaft components (see Section 5).
4   Pull the hydraulic lash adjuster(s) out of the rocker arm(s) **(see illustration)**. **Note:** *Be sure to label each rocker arm and adjuster and place them in a partitioned box or something suitable to keep them from getting mixed with each other.*
5   Installation is the reverse of removal.

7   Intake manifold – removal and installation

Removal

Refer to illustration 7.13

1   Relieve the fuel system pressure (see Chapter 4).
2   Disconnect the cable from the negative terminal of the battery.
3   Drain the cooling system (don't forget to drain the cylinder block) (see Chapter 1).
4   Remove the air cleaner-to-throttle body inlet hose (see Chapter 4).
5   Remove the spark plug wires and distributor cap. Be sure to mark the spark plug wires for proper reinstallation (see Chapter 1).
6   Remove the throttle cable and transmission kickdown linkage (see Chapter 4 and 7B).
7   Remove the Idle Speed Control (ISC) motor and throttle position sensor (TPS) electrical connectors from the throttle body.
8   Remove the EGR tube flange from the air intake plenum.
9   Label and detach any vacuum lines from the throttle body.
10   Detach the fuel lines from the fuel rail (see Chapter 4).
11   Remove the throttle body, air intake plenum and the fuel injectors (see Chapter 4).
12   Label and remove any remaining hoses, wires or cables attached to the intake manifold or its components.
13   Loosen the manifold mounting bolts/nuts in 1/4-turn increments until they can be removed by hand. Loosen the outer bolts first, then the inner bolts **(see illustration)**.
14   The manifold will probably be stuck to the cylinder heads and force may be required to break the gasket seal. **Caution:** *Don't pry between the manifold and the heads or damage to the gasket sealing surfaces may occur, leading to vacuum leaks.*

Installation

Note: *The mating surfaces of the cylinder heads and manifold must be perfectly clean when the manifold is installed. Gasket removal solvents in aerosol cans are available at most auto parts stores and may be helpful when removing old gasket material that's stuck to the heads and manifold (since they're made of aluminum, aggressive scraping can cause damage). Be sure to follow the directions printed on the container.*

15   Use a gasket scraper to remove all traces of sealant and old gasket material, then clean the mating surfaces with lacquer thinner or acetone. If there's old sealant or oil on the mating surfaces when the manifold is installed, oil or vacuum leaks may develop. Use a vacuum cleaner to remove any material that falls into the intake ports in the heads.

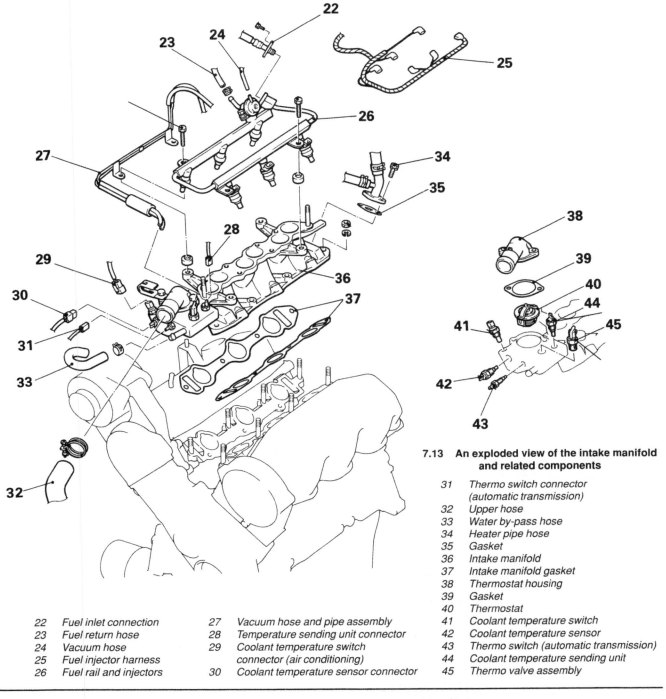

7.13   An exploded view of the intake manifold and related components

31	Thermo switch connector (automatic transmission)
32	Upper hose
33	Water by-pass hose
34	Heater pipe hose
35	Gasket
36	Intake manifold
37	Intake manifold gasket
38	Thermostat housing
39	Gasket
40	Thermostat
41	Coolant temperature switch
42	Coolant temperature sensor
43	Thermo switch (automatic transmission)
44	Coolant temperature sending unit
45	Thermo valve assembly

22	Fuel inlet connection	27	Vacuum hose and pipe assembly
23	Fuel return hose	28	Temperature sending unit connector
24	Vacuum hose	29	Coolant temperature switch connector (air conditioning)
25	Fuel injector harness	30	Coolant temperature sensor connector
26	Fuel rail and injectors		

16   Use a tap of the correct size to chase the threads in the bolt holes, then use compressed air (if available) to remove the debris from the holes. **Warning:** *Wear safety glasses or a face shield to protect your eyes when using compressed air!*

17   Position the gaskets on the cylinder heads. No sealant is required; however, follow the instructions included with the new gaskets.

18   Make sure all intake port openings, coolant passage holes and bolt holes are aligned correctly.

19   Carefully set the manifold in place. Be careful not to disturb the gaskets.

20   Install the nuts/bolts and tighten them to the torque listed in this Chapter's Specifications starting with the inner bolts and working your way to the outer bolts. Work up to the final torque in two steps.

21   Install the air intake plenum (see Chapter 4).

22   The remaining installation steps are the reverse of removal. Start the engine and check carefully for oil and coolant leaks at the intake manifold joints.

8   Exhaust manifolds – removal and installation

Refer to illustration 8.3

Note: *The engine must be completely cool when this procedure is done.*

1   Disconnect the negative cable from the battery. Raise the vehicle and support it securely on jackstands.

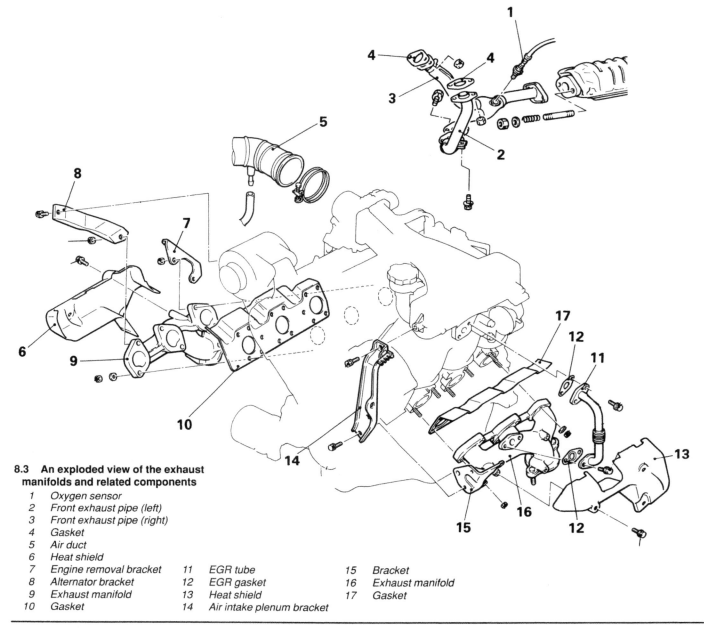

8.3   An exploded view of the exhaust manifolds and related components

1	Oxygen sensor				
2	Front exhaust pipe (left)				
3	Front exhaust pipe (right)				
4	Gasket				
5	Air duct				
6	Heat shield				
7	Engine removal bracket	11	EGR tube	15	Bracket
8	Alternator bracket	12	EGR gasket	16	Exhaust manifold
9	Exhaust manifold	13	Heat shield	17	Gasket
10	Gasket	14	Air intake plenum bracket		

2   Spray penetrating oil on the exhaust manifold fasteners and allow it to soak in. Disconnect the oxygen sensor electrical connector.
3   Remove the bolts and nuts that retain the front exhaust pipes to the manifolds **(see illustration)** and lower the pipes.
4   Remove the bolts and detach the EGR tube from the left manifold.
5   Remove the nuts retaining the heat shield(s) to the manifold(s) near the cylinder head and slip it off the mounting studs **(see illustration 8.3).**
6   Remove the nuts that retain the manifold to the cylinder head and lift the exhaust manifold off.
7   Carefully inspect the manifolds and fasteners for cracks and damage.
8   Use a scraper to remove all traces of old gasket material and carbon deposits from the manifold and cylinder head mating surfaces. If the gasket was leaking, have the manifold checked for warpage at an automotive machine shop and resurfaced if necessary.
9   Position new gaskets over the cylinder head studs. **Note:** *If the new gasket is marked, install the gasket with the numbers 1-3-5 on the top onto the right cylinder head and install the gasket with the numbers 2-4-6 onto the left cylinder head.*
10   Install the manifold and thread the mounting nuts into place.

11   Working from the center out, tighten the nuts to the torque listed in this Chapter's Specifications in three or four equal steps.
12   Reinstall the remaining parts in the reverse order of removal. Use new gaskets when connecting the exhaust pipes.
13   Run the engine and check for exhaust leaks.

9   Crankshaft pulley/vibration damper – removal and installation

Removal

1   Disconnect the negative cable from the battery.
2   Raise the front of the vehicle and support it securely on jackstands.
3   Remove the drivebelts (see Chapter 1).
4   Remove the bolts that retain the pulley to the vibration damper. Remove the pulley from the engine.
5   Wrap a cloth around the vibration damper to protect the belt surface and attach a chain wrench to the pulley. Hold the crankshaft from turning

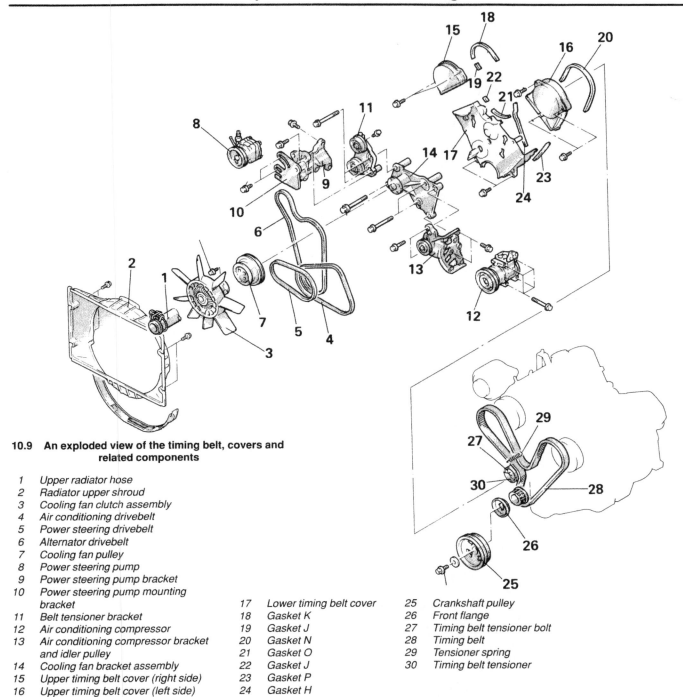

10.9   An exploded view of the timing belt, covers and related components

1   Upper radiator hose
2   Radiator upper shroud
3   Cooling fan clutch assembly
4   Air conditioning drivebelt
5   Power steering drivebelt
6   Alternator drivebelt
7   Cooling fan pulley
8   Power steering pump
9   Power steering pump bracket
10 Power steering pump mounting bracket
11 Belt tensioner bracket
12 Air conditioning compressor
13 Air conditioning compressor bracket and idler pulley
14 Cooling fan bracket assembly
15 Upper timing belt cover (right side)
16 Upper timing belt cover (left side)
17 Lower timing belt cover
18 Gasket K
19 Gasket J
20 Gasket N
21 Gasket O
22 Gasket J
23 Gasket P
24 Gasket H
25 Crankshaft pulley
26 Front flange
27 Timing belt tensioner bolt
28 Timing belt
29 Tensioner spring
30 Timing belt tensioner

and use a socket wrench to loosen the bolt.

6   Install a special tool (vibration damper/steering wheel puller) to the damper and slowly draw the vibration damper off.

Installation

7   Lightly lubricate the seal contact surface with engine oil and position it on the nose of the crankshaft. Align the keyway in the pulley with the key in the crankshaft and push the pulley into place by hand. If necessary, tap lightly on the damper using a block of wood and a hammer.

8   Prevent the crankshaft from turning as described in Step 5, then install the bolt and tighten it to the torque listed in this Chapter's Specifications.

9   Reinstall the remaining parts in the reverse order of removal.

10   Timing belt – removal, installation and adjustment

Removal

Refer to illustration 10.9, 10.13 and 10.14

1   Disconnect the cable from the negative terminal of the battery.

2   If equipped, unbolt the cruise control servo and set it aside, without disconnecting the wires or cables.

3   Drain the coolant from the system (see Chapter 1) and remove the coolant reservoir (see Chapter 3).

4   Remove the radiator shroud and the radiator (see Chapter 3).

5   Raise the front of the vehicle and support it securely on jackstands.

6   Remove the splash pan from under the engine.

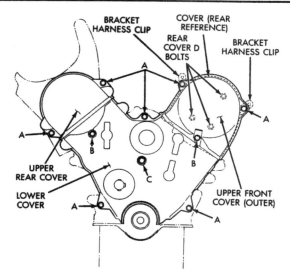

10.13   Be sure to mark each bolt with the correct size and location for proper reassembly

7   Remove the cooling fan and clutch assembly (see Chapter 3).
8   Position the number one piston at TDC on the compression stroke (see Section 3). Remove the spark plugs (see Chapter 1).
9   Remove the drivebelts (see Chapter 1) **(see illustration)**.
10   Remove the power steering pump (see Chapter 10) without disconnecting the lines. Also remove the power steering pump bracket and the belt tensioner bracket.
11   Remove the air conditioning compressor (see Chapter 3), bracket and idler pulley **(see illustration 10.9).** Do not disconnect the refrigerant lines from the compressor. Remove the cooling fan bracket assembly.
12   Remove the crankshaft pulley (see Section 9), the vibration damper

and crankshaft sprocket flange. **Note:** *Don't allow the crankshaft to rotate during removal of the pulley. If the crankshaft moves, the number one piston will no longer be at TDC.*
13   Remove the bolts securing the timing belt upper and lower covers **(see illustration)**. Note the various type and sizes of bolts by recording a diagram or making specific notes while the timing belt cover is being removed. The bolts must be reinstalled in their original locations.
14   Confirm that the number one piston is still at TDC on the compression stroke by verifying that the timing marks on all three timing belt sprockets are aligned with their respective stationary timing marks **(see illustration)**.
15   Relieve tension on the timing belt by loosening the nut or bolt on the timing belt tensioner **(see illustration 10.14).**
16   Check to see that the timing belt is marked with an arrow as to which side faces out. If there isn't a mark, paint one on (only if the same belt will be reinstalled). Slide the timing belt off the sprockets. Check the condition of the tensioner.

Installation

Refer to illustrations 10.17a and 10.17b

17   Prepare to install the timing belt by prying the tensioner away from the spring to the end of the adjustment slot **(see illustration)**, then temporarily tightening the locking nut or bolt. Make sure the tensioner spring is positioned properly **(see illustration)**.
18   Install the belt on the crankshaft sprocket first, and simultaneously keep the belt tight on the tension side **(see illustration 10.14).**
19   Install the belt on the left camshaft sprocket and then onto the water pump pulley and finally the right camshaft sprocket and timing belt tensioner. Be careful not to nudge the camshaft sprocket(s) or crankshaft gear off the timing marks. Install the timing belt with the directional arrow pointing away from the engine.
20   Align the factory-made white lines on the timing belt with the punch mark on each of the camshaft sprockets and the crankshaft sprocket. Make sure all three sets of timing marks are properly aligned **(see illustration 10.14). Note:** *Be sure to install the crankshaft sprocket flange onto the crankshaft sprocket* **(see illustration 10.9).**

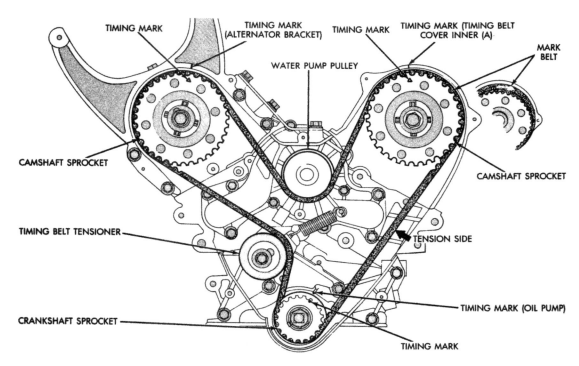

10.14   Timing belt alignment marks

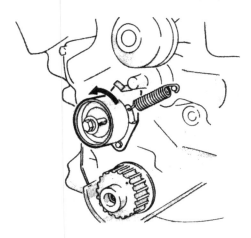

10.17a   Temporarily tighten the tensioner after moving it to the end of the slot

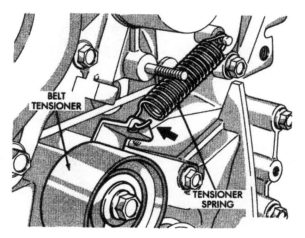

10.17b   Correct spring position on the tensioner

11.4   If the sprocket is stuck, drill and tap two holes and remove it with a bolt-type puller

11.7   Apply a film of grease to the lips of the new seal before installing it (if you apply a small amount of grease to the outer edge, it will be easier to push into the bore

11.8a   Fabricate a seal installation tool from a piece of pipe and a large washer . . .

Adjustment

21   Loosen the tensioner nut or bolt and let the tensioner assembly spring toward the belt – the spring tension will automatically apply the proper amount of tension to the belt. Tighten the tensioner nut or bolt to the torque listed in this Chapter's Specifications while keeping the tensioner steady with your hand.

22   Slowly turn the crankshaft clockwise two full revolutions, returning the number one piston to TDC on the compression stroke. **Caution:** *If excessive resistance is felt wile turning the crankshaft, it's an indication that the pistons are coming into contact with the valves. Go back over the procedure to correct the situation before proceeding.*

23   Check to be sure all timing marks are still aligned **(see illustration 10.14).** Check the deflection of the timing belt by observing the force the tensioner pulley applies to the timing belt. If the belt seems loose, replace the tensioner spring.

24   Install the various components removed during disassembly, referring to the appropriate Sections as necessary.

---

11   Crankshaft front oil seal – replacement

Refer to illustrations 11.4, 11.7, 11.8a and 11.8b

1   Disconnect the negative cable from the battery.

2   Remove the drivebelts (see Chapter 1), crankshaft pulley and timing belt (see Sections 9 and 10).

3   Wedge two screwdrivers behind the crankshaft sprocket. Carefully pry the sprocket off the crankshaft. Some timing belt sprockets can be pried off easily with screwdrivers. Others are more difficult to remove because corrosion fuses them onto the nose of the crankshaft. If the pulley on your engine is difficult to pry off, don't damage the oil pump with the screwdrivers.

4   If the sprocket won't come loose, drill and tap two holes into the face of the sprocket and use a bolt-type puller to slip it off the crankshaft **(see illustration). Caution:** *Do not reuse a drilled sprocket – replace it.*

5   Turn the bolt of the puller until the pulley comes off. Remove the timing belt plate.

6   Carefully pry the oil seal out with a screwdriver or seal removal tool. Don't scratch or nick the crankshaft in the process!

7   Before installation, apply a coat of multi-purpose grease to the inside of the seal **(see illustration).**

8   Fabricate a seal installation tool with a short length of pipe of equal or slightly smaller outside diameter than the seal itself. File the end of the pipe that will bear down on the seal until it's free of sharp edges. You'll also need a large washer, slightly larger in diameter than the pipe, on which the bolt head can seat **(see illustration).** Install the oil seal by pressing it into position with the seal installation tool **(see illustration).** When you

11.8b   ... to push the seal into the bore – the pipe must bear against the outer edge of the seal as the bolt is tightened

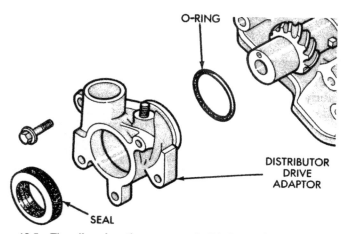

12.5   The oil seal on the rear camshaft is located inside the distributor drive adaptor

see and feel the seal stop moving, don't turn the bolt any more or you'll damage the seal.

9   Slide the timing belt plate onto the nose of the crankshaft.

10   Make sure the Woodruff key is in place in the crankshaft.

11   Apply a thin coat of assembly lube to the inside of the timing belt sprocket and slide it onto the crankshaft.

12   Installation of the remaining components is the reverse of removal. Be sure to refer to Section 10 for the timing belt installation and adjustment procedure. Tighten all bolts to the torque values listed in this Chapter's Specifications.

12   Camshaft oil seal – replacement

Refer to illustration 12.5

Note: *The 3.0L engine is equipped with two camshaft oil seals on the front as well as two camshaft oil plugs on the rear of the engine.*

1   Disconnect the negative battery cable from the battery.

2   Remove the drivebelts (see Chapter 1), crankshaft pulley (see Section 9) and timing belt (see Section 10).

3   Insert a screwdriver through a hole in the camshaft sprocket to lock it in place while loosening the mounting bolt.

4   Once the bolt is out, the sprocket can be removed by hand. **Note:** *If you're removing both camshaft sprockets, don't mix them up. Mark each sprocket with either an R (for Right) or L (for Left).*

5   Carefully remove the old oil seal with a screwdriver **(see illustration)**. Don't nick or scratch the camshaft in the process. Refer to Steps 6, 7 and 8 in Section 11. The same seal installation tool used for the crankshaft seal can be used for both camshaft seals.

6   Install the sprocket. Make sure the R or L mark faces out! The side of the sprocket with the deep recess must face the engine, which means the shallow recess must face out.

7   Insert a screwdriver through the top hole in the camshaft sprocket to lock it in place while you tighten the bolt to the torque listed in this Chapter's Specifications.

8   Installation of the remaining components is the reverse of removal.

13   Valve spring, retainer and seals – replacement

This procedure is essentially the same as for the 2.6 liter four-cylinder engine. Refer to Part A, Section 6 and follow the procedure outlined there.

14   Cylinder head(s) – removal and installation

Note: *Allow the engine to cool completely before beginning this procedure.*

Removal

1   Position the engine at TDC on the compression stroke for the number 1 cylinder (see Section 3). Drain the engine coolant (see Chapter 1).

2   Remove the timing belt cover, timing belt, camshaft sprockets and camshafts (see Sections 10, 12 and 15).

3   Remove the intake manifold (see Section 7).

4   Remove the rocker arm components (see Section 5) and hydraulic lash adjusters (see Section 6).

5   Remove the exhaust manifold(s) as described in Section 8. **Note:** *If desired, each manifold may remain attached to the cylinder head until after the head is removed from the engine. However, the manifold must still be disconnected from the exhaust system.*

Left (driver's side) cylinder head

6   Remove the distributor (crank angle sensor) (see Chapter 5).

7   Remove the air conditioning compressor from the bracket without disconnecting any hoses (see Chapter 3) and set it aside. It may be helpful to secure the compressor to the vehicle with rope or wire to make sure it doesn't hang by its hoses.

8   Remove the air conditioning compressor bracket (see Chapter 3).

Right (passenger's side) cylinder head

9   Detach the heater hoses and brackets from the rear of the head.

10   Remove the air cleaner housing from the engine compartment (see Chapter 4).

11   Remove the alternator and bracket from the cylinder head (see Chapter 5).

Both sides

Refer to illustration 14.12

12   Loosen the cylinder head bolts with a 10 mm hex drive tool in 1/4-turn increments until they can be removed by hand. Be sure to follow the proper numerical sequence **(see illustration)**.

13   Head bolts must be reinstalled in their original locations. To keep them from getting mixed up, store them in cardboard holders marked to indicate the bolt pattern. Mark the holders L (left) and R (right) and indicate the timing belt end of the engine.

14   Lift the head off the block. If resistance is felt, dislodge the head by striking it with a wood block and hammer. If prying is required, pry only on a casting protrusion – be very careful not to damage the head or block!

15   If necessary, remove the camshaft(s) as described in Section 15.

Installation

Refer to illustration 14.23

16   Remove all traces of old gasket material from the cylinder heads and the engine block. The mating surfaces of the cylinder heads and block

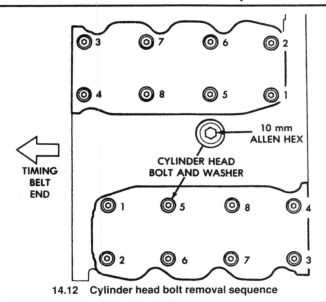

14.12   Cylinder head bolt removal sequence

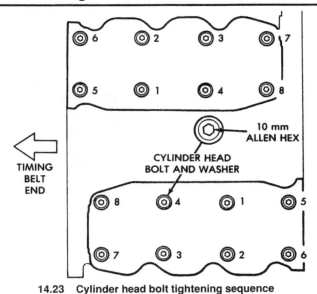

14.23   Cylinder head bolt tightening sequence

must be perfectly clean when the heads are installed.

17   Use a gasket scraper to remove all traces of carbon and old gasket material, then clean the mating surfaces with lacquer thinner or acetone. If there's oil on the mating surfaces when the heads are installed, the gaskets may not seal correctly and leaks may develop. Use a vacuum cleaner to remove any debris that falls into the cylinders.

18   Check the block and head mating surfaces for nicks, deep scratches and other damage. If damage is slight, it can be removed with a file – if it's excessive, machining may be the only alternative.

19   Use a tap of the correct size to chase the threads in the head bolt holes. Mount each bolt in a vise and run a die down the threads to remove corrosion and restore the threads. Dirt, corrosion, sealant and damaged threads will affect torque readings. Ensure that the threaded holes in the block are clean and dry.

20   Position the new gaskets over the dowel pins on the block.

21   Carefully position the heads on the block without disturbing the gaskets.

22   Lightly oil the threads and install the bolts in their original locations. Tighten them finger tight.

23   Follow the recommended sequence and tighten the bolts in three steps to the torque listed in this Chapter's Specifications **(see illustration)**.

24   The remaining installation steps are the reverse of removal.

25   Add coolant and change the engine oil and filter (see Chapter 1), then start the engine and check carefully for oil and coolant leaks.

15   Camshaft(s) – removal and installation

Removal

1   Position the engine at TDC on the compression stroke for the number 1 cylinder (see Section 3). Remove the timing belt and camshaft sprockets (see Sections 10 and 12). **Note:** *If you're only removing one camshaft and you want to save time by not removing and installing the timing belt and re-timing the engine, you can unfasten the camshaft sprocket and suspend it out of the way – with the belt still attached – by a piece of rope. Be sure the rope keeps firm tension on the belt so the belt won't become disengaged from any of the sprockets.*

2   If you're removing the left (driver's side) cylinder head, remove the bolts and gently pry off the distributor drive adapter **(see illustration 12.5).**

3   Remove the rocker arm assembly (see Section 5).

4   Carefully pry the camshaft plugs from the rear section of the cylinder head. Don't scratch or nick the camshaft in the process!

5   Carefully lift the camshaft from the cylinder head. Inspect the camshaft as described in Section 16.

16.2   A dial indicator and V-blocks are needed to check camshaft runout

Installation

6   Lubricate the camshaft bearing journals and lobes with moly-base grease or engine assembly lube, then install it carefully in the head. Don't scratch the bearing surfaces with the cam lobes!

7   Install the distributor drive adapter retaining bolts and tighten them to the torque listed in this Chapter's Specifications.

8   Check to make sure the mark on the crankshaft sprocket is still aligned with its mark on the oil pump. Slide the camshaft sprockets onto the camshafts and align the marks on the sprockets with their corresponding marks on the cylinder heads.

9   The remaining steps are the reverse of the removal procedure.

16   Camshaft and bearing surfaces – inspection

Refer to illustrations 16.2 and 16.3

1   Visually check the camshaft bearing surfaces for pitting, score marks, galling and abnormal wear. If the bearing surfaces are damaged, the head will have to be replaced.

2   Check camshaft runout by placing the camshaft between two V-blocks and set up a dial indicator on the center journal **(see illustration)**. Zero the dial indicator. Turn the camshaft slowly and note the total indicator reading. Record your readings and compare them with the specified runout in this Chapter. If the measured runout exceeds the runout specified in this Chapter, replace the camshaft.

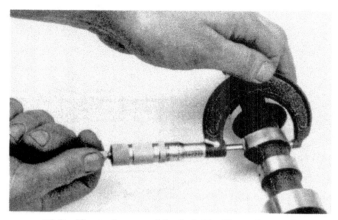

16.3   Measuring cam lobe height with a micrometer

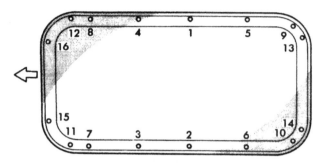

17.15   Oil pan bolt tightening sequence

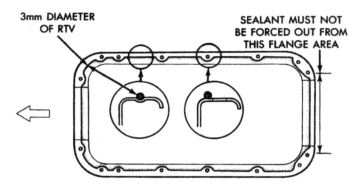

17.14   The bead of RTV sealant should not interfere with the holes for the oil pan bolts

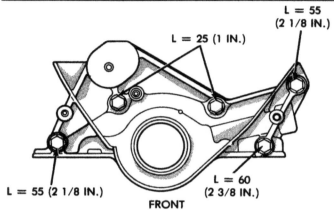

18.3   Be sure to mark the position of each bolt to aid in installation

3   Check the camshaft lobe height by measuring each lobe with a micrometer (see illustration). Compare the measurement to the cam lobe height specified in this Chapter. Then subtract the measured cam lobe height from the specified height to compute wear on the cam lobes. Compare it to the specified wear limit. If it's greater than the specified wear limit, replace the camshaft.

4   Inspect the contact and sliding surfaces of each hydraulic lash adjuster for scoring or damage (see Section 6). Replace any defective parts.

5   Check the rocker arms and shafts for abnormal wear, pits, galling, score marks and rough spots. Don't attempt to restore rocker arms by grinding the pad surfaces. Replace any defective parts.

17   Oil pan – removal and installation

Removal

1   Disconnect the negative cable from the battery.
2   Raise the vehicle and support it securely on jackstands.
3   Remove the under-vehicle splash pan.
4   Drain the engine oil and install a new oil filter (see Chapter 1).
5   Unbolt the exhaust pipe from the exhaust manifolds (see Section 8).
6   Support the engine/transmission securely with a hoist from above or a jack under the bellhousing. Protect the bellhousing by placing a wood block on the jack pad. **Warning:** *Be absolutely certain the engine/transmission is securely supported! DO NOT place any part of your body under the engine/transmission – it could crush you if the jack or hoist fails!*
7   Unbolt the engine mounts (see Section 21). Raise the engine/transmission assembly to provide clearance for oil pan removal.
8   Remove the oil pan bolts.
9   Detach the oil pan. Don't pry between the pan and block or damage to the sealing surfaces may result and oil leaks could develop. If the pan is stuck, dislodge it with a hammer and a block of wood.
10   Use a gasket scraper to remove all traces of old gasket material and sealant from the block and pan. Clean the mating surfaces with lacquer

thinner or acetone.
11   Unbolt the oil pick-up tube and screen assembly.

Installation

Refer to illustrations 17.14 and 17.15
12   Replace the gasket on the flange of the oil pick-up tube and reinstall the tube. Tighten the pick-up tube bolts to the torque listed in this Chapter's Specifications.
13   Ensure that the threaded holes in the block are clean (use a tap to remove any sealant or corrosion from the threads).
14   Apply a small amount of RTV sealant (or equivalent) to the oil pump-to-block and rear seal retainer-to-block junctions (see illustration) and apply a thin continuous bead along the circumference of the oil pan flange. **Note:** *Allow the sealant to "set-up" (slightly harden) before installing the gasket.*
15   Install the oil pan and tighten the bolts in three or four steps following the sequence shown (see illustration) to the torque listed in this Chapter's Specifications.
16   The remaining installation steps are the reverse of removal.
17   Allow at least 30 minutes for the sealant to dry. Fill the crankcase with oil (see Chapter 1), start the engine and check for oil pressure and leaks.

18   Oil pump – removal, inspection and installation

Removal

Refer to illustration 18.3
1   Remove the timing belt and the crankshaft sprocket (see Sections 10 and 11). Remove the oil pan and pick-up tube (see Section 17).
2   Unbolt the power steering pump (see Chapter 10) without disconnecting the hoses. Remove the power steering pump bracket.

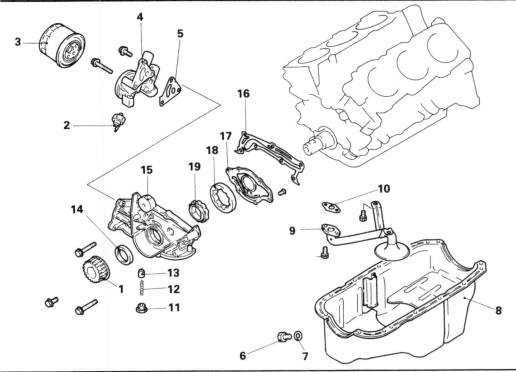

An exploded view of the oil pump

1   Crankshaft sprocket
2   Oil pressure switch
3   Oil filter
4   Oil filter bracket
5   Oil filter bracket gasket
6   Drain plug
7   Drain plug gasket
8   Oil pan
9   Oil screen
10 Oil screen gasket
11 Plug
12 Relief spring
13 Relief plunger
14 Front oil seal
15 Oil pump case
16 Oil pump gasket
17 Oil pump cover
18 Oil pump outer rotor
19 Oil pump inner rotor

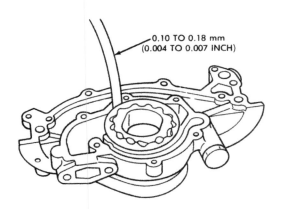

18.10a   Checking case-to-outer rotor clearance with a feeler gauge

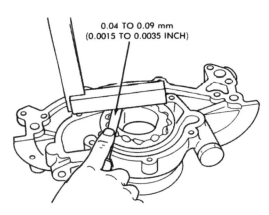

18.10b   Checking rotor end clearance with a straightedge and a feeler gauge

3   Remove the oil pump-to-engine block bolts from the front of the engine **(see illustration)**.

4   Use a block of wood and a hammer to break the oil pump loose.

5   Pull out on the oil pump to remove it from the engine block.

6   Use a scraper to remove old gasket material and sealant from the oil pump and engine block mating surfaces. Clean the mating surfaces with lacquer thinner or acetone.

Inspection

Refer to illustrations 18.7, 18.10a, 18.10b and 18.10c

7   Remove the screws holding the rear cover to the oil pump **(see illustration)**.

8   Clean all components with solvent, then inspect them for wear and damage.

9   Remove the oil pressure relief valve plug, washer, spring and valve (plunger). Check the oil pressure relief valve sliding surface and valve spring. If either the spring or the valve is damaged, they must be replaced as a set.

10 Check the following clearances **(see illustrations)** and compare the measurements to the clearances listed in this Chapter's Specifications:

   Case-to-outer rotor
   Rotor end clearance
   Case-to-inner rotor

   If any of the clearances are excessive, replace the entire oil pump assembly.

11 Pack the cavities of the oil pump with petroleum jelly to prime it. Assemble the oil pump and tighten the screws to the torque listed in this Chapter's Specifications. Install the oil pressure relief valve, spring and washer, then tighten the oil pressure relief valve plug to the torque listed in this Chapter's Specifications.

Installation

12 Apply a thin film of RTV sealant to the new oil pump gasket.

13 Installation is the reverse of the removal procedure. Align the flats on the crankshaft with the flats in the inner rotor of the oil pump. Tighten all fasteners to the torque values listed in this Chapter's Specifications.

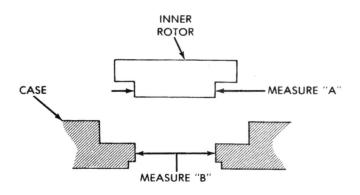

18.10c   Check for excessive clearance between the case and inner rotor

19   Flywheel/driveplate – removal and installation

This procedure is essentially the same for all engines. Refer to Part A and follow the procedure outlined there, but use the bolt torque listed in this Chapter's Specifications.

20   Rear main oil seal – replacement

This procedure is essentially the same for all engines. Refer to Part A and follow the procedure outlined there.

21   Engine mounts – check and replacement

Refer to illustration 21.1

This procedure is essentially the same for all engines. See Part A of this Chapter and follow the procedure outlined there, but use the torque values listed in this Chapter's Specifications. Use the accompanying exploded view for reference **(see illustration)**.

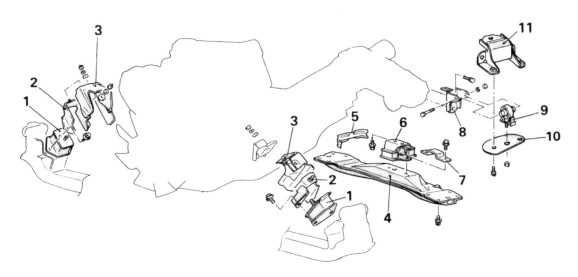

21.1   An exploded view of the engine mounts (4WD Montero shown, others similar)

1	Front insulator	4	Number 2 crossmember	7	Stopper	10	Plate assembly
2	Stopper	5	Heat shield	8	Transfer mounting bracket	11	Transfer support bracket
3	Heat shield	6	Rear insulator	9	Transfer support insulator		

Chapter 2 Part D
General engine overhaul procedures

Contents

Specifications

2.6L engine

General

Displacement	155.9 cubic inches
Bore	3.59 inches
Stroke	3.86 inches
Cylinder compression pressure	130 to 150 psi at 250 rpm
Oil pressure (at 3000 rpm)	25 to 90 psi

Engine block

Cylinder taper limit	0.0008 inch
Cylinder out-of-round limit	0.0008 inch

2.6L engine (continued)

Pistons and rings

Piston diameter	3.5866 inches
Piston ring side clearance	
1983 through 1986	
Top compression ring	
Standard	0.002 to 0.004 inch
Service limit	Not available
Second compression ring	
Standard	0.001 to 0.002 inch
Service limit	Not available
1987 on	
Top compression ring	
Standard	0.0020 to 0.0035 inch
Service limit	0.0047 inch
Second compression ring	
Standard	0.0008 to 0.0024 inch
Service limit	0.0039 inch
Piston ring end gap	
1983 models only	
Top compression ring	
Standard	0.010 to 0.015 inch
Service limit	Not available
Second compression ring	
Standard	0.010 to 0.018 inch
Service limit	Not available
Oil ring	
Standard	0.012 to 0.024 inch
Service limit	Not available
1984 through 1986	
Top compression ring	
Standard	0.012 to 0.018 inch
Service limit	Not available
Second compression ring	
Standard	0.010 to 0.015 inch
Service limit	Not available
Oil ring	
Standard	0.012 to 0.024 inch
Service limit	Not available
1987 on	
Top compression ring	
Standard	0.0118 to 0.0177 inch
Service limit	0.031 inch
Second compression ring	
Standard	0.0098 to 0.0157 inch
Service limit	0.031 inch
Oil ring	
Standard	0.0118 to 0.0315 inch
Service limit	0.039 inch

Crankshaft and connecting rods

Endplay (standard)	0.002 to 0.007 inch
Main bearing journal	
Diameter	2.3622 inches
Taper limit	
1983 through 1986	0.0004 inch
1987 on	0.0002 inch
Out-of-round limit	
1983 through 1986	0.0004 inch
1987 on	0.0006 inch
Connecting rod journal	
Diameter	2.086 inches
Taper limit	
1983 through 1986	0.0004 inch
1987 on	0.0002 inch
Out-of-round limit	
1983 through 1986	0.0004 inch
1987 on	0.0006 inch

Main bearing oil clearance
   1983 through 1986
      Standard .... 0.0008 to 0.0020 inch
      Service limit .... 0.004 inch
   1987 on
      Standard .... 0.0008 to 0.0018 inch
      Service limit .... 0.004 inch
Connecting rod bearing oil clearance
   1983 through 1987
      Standard .... 0.0008 to 0.0024 inch
      Service limit .... 0.004 inch
   1988 on
      Standard .... 0.0007 to 0.0022 inch
      Service limit .... 0.004 inch
Connecting rod endplay (side clearance) .... 0.004 to 0.010 inch

Camshaft
Endplay .... 0.004 to 0.008 inch

Silent shafts
1983 through 1986
   Front bearing journal diameter .... 0.906 inch
   Front bearing oil clearance .... 0.0008 to 0.0024 inch
   Rear bearing journal diameter .... 1.693 inch
   Rear bearing oil clearance .... 0.0024 to 0.0039 inch
1987 on
   Right silent shaft
      Front bearing journal diameter .... 0.830 inch
      Front bearing oil clearance .... Not available
      Rear bearing journal diameter .... 1.693 inch
      Rear bearing oil clearance .... 0.0039 to 0.0053 inch
   Left silent shaft
      Front bearing journal diameter .... 0.906 inch
      Front bearing oil clearance .... 0.0008 to 0.0024 inch
      Rear bearing journal diameter .... 1.693 inch
      Rear bearing oil clearance .... 0.0039 to 0.0053 inch

Cylinder head and valves
Head warpage limit .... 0.004 inch
Valve seat angle 45-degrees
Valve face angle 45-degrees
Valve margin width
   Intake
      Standard .... 0.047 inch
      Service limit .... 0.028 inch
   Exhaust
      Standard .... 0.079 inch
      Service limit (1983 through 1986) .... Not available
      Service limit (1987 on) .... 0.059 inch
Valve stem-to-guide clearance
   Intake
      Standard .... 0.0012 to 0.0024 inch
      Service limit .... 0.004 inch
   Exhaust
      Standard .... 0.0020 to 0.0035 inch
      Service limit .... 0.006 inch
Valve spring free length
   1983 and 1984
      Standard .... 1.869 inch
      Service limit .... 1.479 inch
   1985 on
      Standard .... 1.961 inch
      Service limit .... 1.922 inch
Valve spring installed height
   Standard .... 1.590 inch
   Service limit .... 1.629 inch
Jet valves
   Stem diameter .... 0.1693 inch
   Seat angle 45-degrees
   Spring free length .... 1.165 inch
   Spring pressure .... 7.7 lbs. at 0.846 inch

2.6L engine (continued)

Torque specifications*   **Ft-lbs** (unless otherwise indicated)
Jet valves   14
Main bearing cap bolts   58
Connecting rod bearing cap nuts   34

* Note: Refer to Part A for additional torque specifications.

2.0L and 2.4L engines

General
Displacement
  2.0L . . . .   121.9 cubic inches
  2.4L . . . .   143.4 cubic inches
Bore
  2.0L . . . .   3.35 inches
  2.4L . . . .   3.41 inches
Stroke
  2.0L . . . .   3.46 inches
  2.4L . . . .   3.94 inches
Cylinder compression pressure . . . .   130 to 150 psi at 250 rpm
Oil pressure (at 3000 rpm) . . . .   25 to 90 psi

Cylinder head and valves
Head warpage limit
  Standard . . . .   0.002 inch
  Service limit . . . .   0.008 inch
Valve margin width
  Intake
    Standard . . . .   0.047 inch
    Service limit . . . .   0.028 inch
  Exhaust
    Standard . . . .   0.079 inch
    Service limit . . . .   0.059 inch
Valve stem diameter (intake and exhaust) . . . .   0.3100 inch
Valve stem-to-guide clearance
  1987 only
    Intake
      Standard . . . .   0.0012 to 0.0020 inch
      Service limit . . . .   Not available
    Exhaust
      Standard . . . .   0.0020 to 0.0031 inch
      Service limit . . . .   Not available
  All others
    Intake
      Standard . . . .   0.0012 to 0.0024 inch
      Service limit . . . .   0.004 inch
    Exhaust
      Standard . . . .   0.0020 to 0.0035 inch
      Service limit . . . .   0.006 inch
Valve spring
  Out-of-square limit 3-degrees
  Pressure . . . .   72 lbs (322 N)
  Installed height . . . .   1.591 inch
  Free length
    1983 and 1984
      Standard . . . .   1.870 inch
      Service limit . . . .   Not available
    1985 on
      Standard . . . .   1.960 inch
      Service limit . . . .   1.921 inch
Jet valves
  Stem diameter
    1987 through 1989 . . . .   0.1693 inch
    All others . . . .   Not available
  Face/seat angle
    1987 through 1989 . . . .   45-degrees
    All others . . . .   Not available

Spring
   Free length
      1987 through 1989 .... 1.165 inch
      All others .... Not available
   Load
      1987 through 1989 .... 7.7 lbs at 0.846 in
      All others .... Not available

Crankshaft and connecting rods

Connecting rod journal
   1983 through 1987
      Diameter .... 1.7720 inch
      Out-of-round/taper limits .... 0.0004 inch
      Bearing oil clearance .... 0.0008 to 0.0020 inch
   1988 on
      Diameter .... 1.7720 inch
      Out-of-round .... 0.0006 inch
      Taper limits .... 0.0002 inch
      Bearing oil clearance .... 0.0006 to 0.0020 inch
Connecting rod endplay (side clearance) .... 0.004 to 0.010 inch
Main bearing journal
   1983 through 1987
      Diameter .... 2.2440 inches
      Out-of-round limits/taper limits .... 0.0004 inch
      Bearing oil clearance .... 0.0008 to 0.0020 inch
   1988 on
      Diameter .... 2.2440 inches
      Out-of-round limits .... 0.0006 inch
      Taper limit .... 0.0002 inch
      Bearing oil clearance .... 0.0008 to 0.0020 inch
Crankshaft endplay .... 0.002 to 0.007 inch

Cylinder bore

Diameter (nominal)
   2.0L engines .... 3.346 inches
   2.4L engines .... 3.406 inches
Out-of-round/taper limits .... 0.0008 inches

Pistons and rings

Piston diameter (nominal)*
   2.0L .... 3.346 inches
   2.4L .... 3.406 inches
Piston-to-bore clearance
   2.0L .... 0.0004 to 0.0012 inch
   2.4L .... 0.0008 to 0.0016 inch
Piston ring end gap
   1983 and 1984
      Number 1 (top) compression ring
         Standard .... 0.010 to 0.018 inch
         Service limit .... Not available
      Number 2 compression ring
         Standard .... 0.008 to 0.016 inch
         Service limit .... Not available
      Oil ring
         Standard .... 0.008 to 0.020 inch
         Service limit .... Not available
   1985 and 1986
      Number 1 compression ring
         Standard .... 0.010 to 0.018 inch
         Service limit .... Not available
      Number 2 compression ring
         Standard .... 0.008 to 0.016 inch
         Service limit .... Not available
      Oil ring
         Standard .... 0.008 to 0.028 inch
         Service limit .... Not available
   1987 on
      Number 1 compression ring
         Standard .... 0.010 to 0.016 inch
         Service limit .... 0.031 inch

2.0L and 2.4L engines (continued)

Number 2 compression ring (2.0L only)
Standard . . . . 0.008 to 0.014 inch
Service limit . . . . 0.031 inch
Number 2 compression ring (2.4L only)
Standard . . . . 0.008 to 0.016 inch
Service limit . . . . 0.031 inch
Oil ring
Standard . . . . 0.008 to 0.028 inch
Service limit . . . . 0.039 inch
Piston ring side clearance
1986 and earlier
No. 1 (top) compression ring
Standard . . . . 0.002 to 0.004 inch
Service limit . . . . Not available
No. 2 compression ring
Standard . . . . 0.001 to 0.002 inch
Service limit . . . . Not available
1987 on
No. 1 (top) compression ring
Standard . . . . 0.0012 to 0.0028 inch
Service limit . . . . 0.004 inch
No. 2 compression ring
Standard . . . . 0.0008 to 0.0024 inch
Service limit . . . . 0.004 inch

* Measured 5/64-inch up from bottom of skirt*

Silent shafts

Right silent shaft
Front bearing journal diameter . . . . 1.650 inch
Front bearing oil clearance
1987 only . . . . 0.0031 to 0.0043 inch
All others . . . . 0.0008 to 0.0024 inch
Rear bearing journal diameter . . . . 1.610 inch
Rear bearing oil clearance
1987 only . . . . 0.0043 to 0.0055 inch
All others . . . . 0.0020 to 0.0036 inch
Left silent shaft
Front bearing journal diameter . . . . 0.728 inch
Front bearing oil clearance
1983 through 1986 . . . . 0.0008 to 0.0020 inch
1987 only . . . . 0.0008 to 0.0021 inch
All others . . . . 0.0008 to 0.0024 inch
Rear bearing journal diameter . . . . 1.610 inch
Rear bearing oil clearance
1987 only . . . . 0.0043 to 0.0055 inch
All others . . . . 0.0020 to 0.0036 inch

Torque specifications*   **Ft-lbs**

Main bearing cap bolts . . . . 37 to 39
Connecting rod cap nuts . . . . 37 to 38
Jet valves . . . . 13 to 16

* Note: Refer to Part B for additional torque specifications.*

3.0L engine

General

Displacement . . . . 181 cubic inches
Bore . . . . 3.587 inches
Stroke . . . . 2.992 inches
Cylinder compression pressure . . . . 119 at 250 rpm
Oil pressure . . . . 11.4 psi at idle

Engine block

Inside diameter . . . . 3.586 to 3.587 inches
Cylinder taper limit . . . . 0.0008 inch
Cylinder out-of-round limit . . . . 0.0008 inch

Pistons and rings

Piston diameter	3.587 inches
Piston ring side clearance	
Top compression ring	
Standard	0.0012 to 0.0035 inch
Service limit	0.004 inch
Second compression ring	
Standard	0.0008 to 0.0024 inch
Service limit	0.004 inch
Piston ring end gap	
Top compression ring	
Standard	0.0118 to 0.0177 inch
Service limit	0.031 inch
Second compression ring	
Standard	0.0098 to 0.0157 inch
Service limit	0.031 inch
Oil ring	
Standard	0.0079 to 0.0276 inch
Service limit	0.040 inch

Crankshaft and connecting rods

Endplay	
Standard	0.002 to 0.010 inch
Service limit	0.012 inch
Main bearing journal	
Diameter	2.361 to 2.362 inches
Taper limit	0.0002 inch
Out-of-round limit	0.001 inch
Connecting rod journal	
Diameter	1.968 to 1.969 inch
Taper limit	0.0002 inch
Out-of-round limit	0.001 inch
Main bearing oil clearance	0.0008 to 0.0019 inch
Connecting rod bearing oil clearance	0.0006 to 0.0018 inch
Connecting rod endplay (side clearance)	
Standard	0.004 to 0.010 inch
Service limit	0.016 inch

Cylinder head and valves

Head warpage limit	0.002 inch
Valve seat angle	45-degrees
Valve face angle	45-degrees
Valve margin width	
Intake	
Standard	0.047 inch
Service limit	0.027 inch
Exhaust	
Standard	0.079 inch
Service limit	0.059 inch
Valve stem-to-guide clearance	
Intake	
Standard	0.0012 to 0.0024 inch
Service limit	0.004 inch
Exhaust	
Standard	0.0020 to 0.0035 inch
Service limit	0.006 inch
Valve spring free length	
Standard	1.988 inch
Service limit	1.949 inch
Valve spring installed height	
Standard	1.591 inch
Service limit	1.630 inch
Valve stem diameter	
Intake	0.313 to 0.314 inch
Exhaust	0.312 to 0.313 inch

Torque specifications

	Ft-lbs (unless otherwise indicated)
Main bearing cap bolts	60
Connecting rod bearing cap nuts	34

Note: Refer to Part C for additional torque specifications.

Four cylinder and V-6 engines

Model	Engine number (Displacement)	Valve type
Pick-up		
G63B	(2.0L) (1983-1984)	Adjustable w/Jet valve
G63B	(2.0L) (1985-1989)	Hydraulic w/Jet valve
G54B	(2.6L) (1983-1984)	Adjustable w/Jet valve
G54B	(2.6L) (1985-1989)	Hydraulic w/Jet valve
4G64	(2.4L) (1990 on)	Hydraulic wo/Jet valve
6G72	(3.0L) (1990 on)	Hydraulic wo/Jet valve
Montero		
6G72	(3.0L) (1989 on)	Hydraulic wo/Jet valve
G54B	(2.6L)	Hydraulic w/Jet valve

1.4   Engine Identification Chart

2.4a   Remove the oil pressure sending unit (switch) and install a pressure gauge in its place (2.6L engine shown)

1   General information

Included in this portion of Chapter 2 are the general overhaul procedures for the cylinder head(s) and internal engine components.

The information ranges from advice concerning preparation for an overhaul and the purchase of replacement parts to detailed, step-by-step procedures covering removal and installation of internal engine components and the inspection of parts.

The following Sections have been written based on the assumption the engine has been removed from the vehicle. For information concerning in-vehicle engine repair, as well as removal and installation of the external components necessary for the overhaul, see Part A (2.6L engine), Part B (2.0L and 2.4L engines) or Part C (3.0L V6 engine) of this Chapter.

The Specifications included in this Part are only those necessary for the inspection and overhaul procedures which follow. Refer to Parts A, B and C for additional Specifications.

2   Engine overhaul – general information

Refer to illustrations 2.4a, 2.4b and 2.4c

It's not always easy to determine when, or if, an engine should be completely overhauled, as a number of factors must be considered.

High mileage isn't necessarily an indication an overhaul is needed, while low mileage doesn't preclude the need for an overhaul. Frequency of servicing is probably the most important consideration. An engine that's had regular and frequent oil and filter changes, as well as other required maintenance, will most likely give many thousands of miles of reliable service. Conversely, a neglected engine may require an overhaul very early in its life.

Excessive oil consumption is an indication that piston rings, valve seals and/or valve guides are in need of attention. Make sure oil leaks aren't responsible before deciding the rings and/or guides are bad. Perform a cylinder compression check to determine the extent of the work required (see Section 3).

Remove the oil pressure sending unit and check the oil pressure with a gauge installed in its place **(see illustrations)**. Compare the results to this Chapter's Specifications. As a general rule, engines should have ten psi oil pressure for every 1,000 rpm's. If the pressure is extremely low, the bearings and/or oil pump are probably worn out.

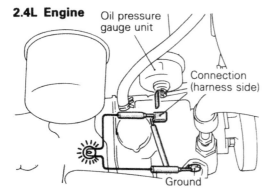

2.4b   Location of the oil pressure sending unit on 2.4L engines

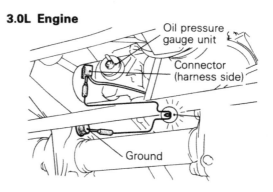

2.4c   Location of the oil pressure sending unit on 3.0L engines

Loss of power, rough running, knocking or metallic engine noises, excessive valve train noise and high fuel consumption rates may also point to the need for an overhaul, especially if they're all present at the same time. If a complete tune-up doesn't remedy the situation, major mechanical work is the only solution.

An engine overhaul involves restoring the internal parts to the specifications of a new engine. During an overhaul, the piston rings are replaced and the cylinder walls are reconditioned (rebored and/or honed). If a rebore is done by an automotive machine shop, new oversize pistons will also be installed. The main bearings, connecting rod bearings and camshaft bearings are generally replaced with new ones and, if necessary, the crankshaft may be reground to restore the journals. Generally, the valves are serviced as well, since they're usually in less-than-perfect condition at this point. While the engine is being overhauled, other components, such as the starter and alternator, can be rebuilt as well. The end result should be a like-new engine that will give many trouble free miles. **Note:** *Critical cooling system components such as the hoses, drivebelts, thermostat and water pump MUST be replaced with new parts when an engine is overhauled. The radiator should be checked carefully to ensure it isn't clogged or leaking (see Chapter 3). Also, we don't recommend overhauling the oil pump – always install a new one when an engine is rebuilt.*

Before beginning the engine overhaul, read through the entire procedure to familiarize yourself with the scope and requirements of the job. Overhauling an engine isn't particularly difficult, if you follow all of the instructions carefully, have the necessary tools and equipment and pay close attention to all specifications; however, it can be time consuming. Plan on the vehicle being tied up for a minimum of two weeks, especially if parts must be taken to an automotive machine shop for repair or reconditioning. Check on availability of parts and make sure any necessary special tools and equipment are obtained in advance. Most work can be done with typical hand tools, although a number of precision measuring tools are required for inspecting parts to determine if they must be replaced. Often an automotive machine shop will handle the inspection of parts and offer advice concerning reconditioning and replacement. **Note:** *Always wait until the engine has been completely disassembled and all components, especially the engine block, have been inspected before deciding what service and repair operations must be performed by an automotive machine shop.* Since the block's condition will be the major factor to consider when determining whether to overhaul the original engine or buy a rebuilt one, never purchase parts or have machine work done on other components until the block has been thoroughly inspected. As a general rule, time is the primary cost of an overhaul, so it doesn't pay to install worn or substandard parts.

As a final note, to ensure maximum life and minimum trouble from a rebuilt engine, everything must be assembled with care in a spotlessly clean environment.

3 Cylinder compression check

Refer to illustration 3.6

1 A compression check will tell you what mechanical condition the upper end (pistons, rings, valves, head gaskets) of the engine is in. Specifically, it can tell you if the compression is down due to leakage caused by worn piston rings, defective valves and seats or a blown head gasket. **Note:** *The engine must be at normal operating temperature and the battery must be fully charged for this check.*

2 Begin by cleaning the area around the spark plugs before you remove them. Compressed air should be used, if available, otherwise a small brush or even a bicycle tire pump will work. The idea is to prevent dirt from getting into the cylinders as the compression check is being done.

3 Remove all of the spark plugs from the engine (see Chapter 1).

4 Block the throttle wide open.

5 Disable the fuel system by removing the fuel pump fuse (see Chapter 4).

6 Install the compression gauge in the number one spark plug hole **(see illustration)**.

7 Crank the engine over at least seven compression strokes and watch the gauge. The compression should build up quickly in a healthy engine.

Low compression on the first stroke, followed by gradually increasing pressure on successive strokes, indicates worn piston rings. A low compression reading on the first stroke, which doesn't build up during successive strokes, indicates leaking valves or a blown head gasket (a cracked head could also be the cause). Deposits on the undersides of the valve heads can also cause low compression. Record the highest gauge reading obtained.

8 Repeat the procedure for the remaining cylinders and compare the results to this Chapter's Specifications.

9 If the readings are below normal, add some engine oil (about three squirts from a plunger-type oil can) to each cylinder, through the spark plug hole, and repeat the test.

10 If the compression increases after the oil is added, the piston rings are definitely worn. If the compression doesn't increase significantly, the leakage is occurring at the valves or head gasket. Leakage past the valves may be caused by burned valve seats and/or faces or warped, cracked or bent valves.

11 If two adjacent cylinders have equally low compression, there's a strong possibility the head gasket between them is blown. The appearance of coolant in the combustion chambers or the crankcase would verify this condition.

12 If one cylinder is about 20-percent lower than the others, and the engine has a slightly rough idle, a worn exhaust lobe on the camshaft could be the cause.

13 If the compression is unusually high, the combustion chambers are probably coated with carbon deposits. If that's the case, the cylinder head(s) should be removed and decarbonized.

14 If compression is way down or varies greatly between cylinders, it would be a good idea to have a leak-down test performed by an automotive repair shop. This test will pinpoint exactly where the leakage is occurring and how severe it is.

4 Engine removal – methods and precautions

If you've decided the engine must be removed for overhaul or major repair work, several preliminary steps should be taken.

Locating a suitable place to work is extremely important. Adequate work space, along with storage space for the vehicle, will be needed. If a shop or garage isn't available, at the very least a flat, level, clean work surface made of concrete or asphalt is required.

Cleaning the engine compartment and engine before beginning the removal procedure will help keep tools clean and organized.

An engine hoist or A-frame will also be necessary. Make sure the equipment is rated in excess of the combined weight of the engine and its

3.6 A compression gauge with a threaded fitting for the spark plug hole is preferred over the type that requires hand pressure to maintain the seal

accessories. Safety is of primary importance, considering the potential hazards involved in lifting the engine out of the vehicle.

If the engine is being removed by a novice, a helper should be available. Advice and aid from someone more experienced would also be helpful. There are many instances when one person cannot simultaneously perform all of the operations required when lifting the engine out of the vehicle.

Plan the operation ahead of time. Arrange for or obtain all of the tools and equipment you'll need prior to beginning the job. Some of the equipment necessary to perform engine removal and installation safely and with relative ease are (in addition to an engine hoist) a heavy duty floor jack, complete sets of wrenches and sockets as described in the front of this manual, wooden blocks and plenty of rags and cleaning solvent for mopping up spilled oil, coolant and gasoline. If the hoist must be rented, be sure to arrange for it in advance and perform all of the operations possible without it beforehand. This will save you money and time.

Plan for the vehicle to be out of use for quite a while. A machine shop will be required to perform some of the work which the do-it-yourselfer can't accomplish without special equipment. These shops often have a busy schedule, so it would be a good idea to consult them before removing the engine in order to accurately estimate the amount of time required to rebuild or repair components that may need work.

Always be extremely careful when removing and installing the engine. Serious injury can result from careless actions. Plan ahead, take your time and a job of this nature, although major, can be accomplished successfully.

---

5   Engine – removal and installation

Refer to illustration 5.5

Warning: *Gasoline is extremely flammable, so take extra precautions when you work on any part of the fuel system. Don't smoke or allow open flames or bare light bulbs near the work area, and don't work in a garage where a natural gas-type appliance (such as a water heater or clothes dryer) with a pilot light is present. If you spill any fuel on your skin, rinse it off immediately with soap and water. When you perform any kind of work on the fuel system, wear safety glasses and have a Class B type fire extinguisher on hand. Also, the air conditioning system is under high pressure – have a dealer service department or service station discharge the system before disconnecting any of the hoses or fittings.*

Note: *Read through the following steps carefully and familiarize yourself with the procedure before beginning work.*

Removal

1   On air conditioned models only, have the air conditioning system discharged by a dealer service department or service station.
2   Refer to Chapter 4 and relieve the fuel system pressure, then disconnect the negative cable from the battery.
3   Cover the fenders and cowl and remove the hood (see Chapter 11). Special pads are available to protect the fenders, but an old bedspread or blanket will also work.
4   Remove the air cleaner assembly (see Chapter 4).
5   Label the vacuum lines, emissions system hoses, electrical connectors, ground straps and fuel lines to ensure correct reinstallation, then detach them. Pieces of masking tape with numbers or letters written on them work well **(see illustration)**. If there's any possibility of confusion, make a sketch of the engine compartment and clearly label the lines, hoses and wires.
6   Raise the vehicle and support it securely on jackstands. Drain the cooling system (see Chapter 1).
7   Label and detach all coolant hoses from the engine.
8   Remove the coolant reservoir, cooling fan, shroud and radiator (see Chapter 3).
9   Remove the drivebelt(s) and idler, if equipped (see Chapter 1).
10   Disconnect the fuel lines running from the engine to the chassis (see Chapter 4). Plug or cap all open fittings/lines.
11   Disconnect the throttle linkage (and TV linkage/cruise control cable, if equipped) from the engine (see Chapters 4 and 7).

12   Unbolt the power steering pump and set it aside (see Chapter 10). Leave the lines/hoses attached and make sure the pump is kept in an upright position in the engine compartment.
13   Unbolt the air conditioning compressor (see Chapter 3) and set it aside. Do not disconnect the hoses.
14   Drain the engine oil and remove the filter (see Chapter 1).
15   Remove the starter and the alternator (see Chapter 5).
16   Check for clearance and remove the brake master cylinder, if necessary, to allow clearance for the engine (see Chapter 9).
17   Disconnect the exhaust system from the engine (see Chapter 4).
18   If the vehicle is equipped with an automatic transmission, remove the torque converter bolts (see Chapter 7, Part B). Do not remove any of the transmission-to-engine mounting bolts.
19   Support the transmission with a jack. Position a block of wood on the jack head to prevent damage to the transmission.
20   Attach an engine sling or a length of chain to the lifting brackets on the engine.
21   Roll the hoist into position and connect the sling to it. Take up the slack in the sling or chain, but don't lift the engine. **Warning:** *DO NOT place any part of your body under the engine when it's supported only by a hoist or other lifting device.*
22   Remove the driveshaft(s) (see Chapter 8).
23   Remove the engine mount-to-chassis bolts. Refer to the appropriate Chapter (2A, 2B or 2C) for the complete illustrations of the engine mounts.
24   Remove the engine-to-transmission bellhousing bolts.
25   Recheck to be sure nothing is still connecting the engine to the transmission. Disconnect anything still remaining.
26   Raise the engine slightly to disengage the mounts. Also, slightly raise the jack supporting the transmission. Move the engine forward, disengaging it from the transmission. If the vehicle is equipped with a manual transmission, be sure the clutch pressure plate is clear of the transmission input shaft. If the vehicle is equipped with an automatic transmission, make sure the torque converter stays with the transmission and doesn't stick to the driveplate. Slowly raise the engine out of the vehicle. Check carefully to make sure nothing is hanging up as the hoist is raised.
27   Once the engine assembly is out of the vehicle, be sure the torque converter (automatic transmission) stays in place (clamp a pair of vise-grips to the housing to keep the converter from sliding out).
28   Lower the engine to the ground and support it with blocks of wood. Remove the clutch and flywheel or driveplate and mount the engine on an engine stand.

Installation

29   Check the engine and transmission mounts. If they're worn or damaged, replace them.
30   If you're working on a manual transmission equipped vehicle, install the clutch and pressure plate (see Chapter 7). Now is a good time to install a new clutch. Apply a dab of high-temperature grease to the input shaft.

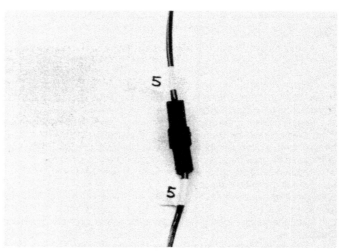

5.5   Label each wire before unplugging the connector

31   Carefully lower the engine into the engine compartment and mate it to the transmission. **Caution:** *DO NOT use the bellhousing bolts to force the transmission and engine together.* If you're working on an automatic transmission equipped vehicle, take great care when installing the torque converter, following the procedure outlined in Chapter 7B. Line up the holes in the engine mounts with the holes in the frame and install the bolts, tightening them securely.
32   Add coolant, oil, power steering and transmission fluid as needed. If the brake master cylinder was removed, bleed the brakes (see Chapter 9). Recheck the fluid level and test the brakes.
33   Run the engine and check for leaks and proper operation of all accessories, then install the hood and test drive the vehicle.
34   If the air conditioning system was discharged, have it evacuated, recharged and leak tested by the shop that discharged it.

6   Engine rebuilding alternatives

The home mechanic is faced with a number of options when performing an engine overhaul. The decision to replace the engine block, piston/connecting rod assemblies and crankshaft depends on a number of factors, with the number one consideration being the condition of the block. Other considerations are cost, access to machine shop facilities, parts availability, time required to complete the project and the extent of prior mechanical experience.

Some of the rebuilding alternatives include:

Individual parts – If the inspection procedures reveal the engine block and most engine components are in reusable condition, purchasing individual parts may be the most economical alternative. The block, crankshaft and piston/connecting rod assemblies should all be inspected carefully. Even if the block shows little wear, the cylinder bores should be surface honed.

Short block – A short block consists of an engine block with a crankshaft and piston/connecting rod assemblies already installed. All new bearings are incorporated and all clearances will be correct. The existing camshaft, valve train components, cylinder head(s) and external parts can be bolted to the short block with little or no machine shop work necessary.

Long block – A long block consists of a short block plus an oil pump, oil pan, cylinder head(s), valve cover(s), camshaft and valve train components, timing sprockets and chain and timing chain cover. All components are installed with new bearings, seals and gaskets incorporated throughout. The installation of manifolds and external parts is all that's necessary.

Give careful thought to which alternative is best for you and discuss the situation with local automotive machine shops, auto parts dealers and experienced rebuilders before ordering or purchasing replacement parts.

7   Engine overhaul – disassembly sequence

Refer to illustrations 7.5a, 7.5b and 7.5c

1   It's much easier to disassemble and work on the engine if it's mounted on a portable engine stand. A stand can often be rented quite cheaply from an equipment rental yard. Before it's mounted on a stand, the flywheel/driveplate should be removed from the engine.
2   If a stand isn't available, it's possible to disassemble the engine with it blocked up on the floor. Be extra careful not to tip or drop the engine when working without a stand.
3   If you're going to obtain a rebuilt engine, all external components must come off first, to be transferred to the replacement engine, just as they will if you're doing a complete engine overhaul yourself. These include:

Alternator and brackets
Emissions control components
Ignition coil/module assembly, spark plug wires and spark plugs
Thermostat and housing cover
Water pump
Carburetor/EFI components
Intake/exhaust manifolds
Oil filter
Engine mounts
Clutch and flywheel/driveplate

Note: *When removing the external components from the engine, pay close attention to details that may be helpful or important during installation. Note the installed position of gaskets, seals, spacers, pins, brackets, washers, bolts and other small items.*

4   If you're obtaining a short block, which consists of the engine block, crankshaft, pistons and connecting rods all assembled, then the cylinder head(s), oil pan and oil pump will have to be removed as well. See Engine rebuilding alternatives for additional information regarding the different possibilities to be considered.
5   If you're planning a complete overhaul, the engine must be disassembled and the internal components removed in the following general order **(see illustrations on following page)**:

2.6L engine
Valve cover
Cylinder head and camshaft
Timing chain housing
Silent shaft chain and sprockets
Timing chain and sprockets
Oil pan
Oil pump
Piston/connecting rod assemblies
Rear main oil seal housing
Crankshaft and main bearings

2.0L and 2.4L engines
Valve cover
Intake/exhaust manifolds
Rocker arm assembly
Hydraulic lash adjusters (if equipped)
Camshaft
Timing belt cover
Timing belt and sprockets
Cylinder head
Oil pan
Oil pump
Piston/connecting rod assemblies
Crankshaft and main bearings

3.0L V6 engine
Valve covers
Exhaust manifolds
Rocker arm assemblies and camshafts
Rocker arms
Intake manifold
Timing belt cover
Timing belt and sprockets
Cylinder heads
Oil pan
Oil pump
Piston/connecting rod assemblies
Rear main oil seal housing
Crankshaft and main bearings

6   Before beginning the disassembly and overhaul procedures, make sure the following items are available. Also, refer to Engine overhaul – reassembly sequence for a list of tools and materials needed for engine reassembly.

Common hand tools
Small cardboard boxes or plastic bags for storing parts
Gasket scraper
Ridge reamer
Vibration damper puller
Micrometers
Telescoping gauges
Dial indicator set
Valve spring compressor
Cylinder surfacing hone
Piston ring groove cleaning tool

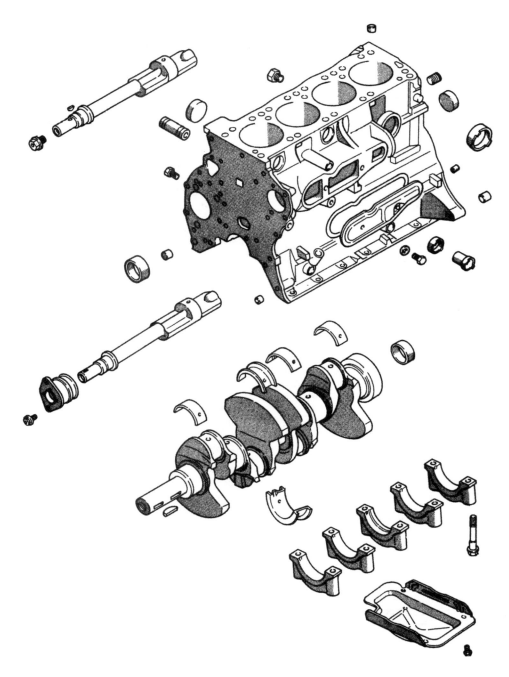

7.5a   Exploded view of the cylinder block and internal engine components (2.6L engine)

Electric drill motor
Tap and die set
Wire brushes
Oil gallery brushes
Cleaning solvent

8   Cylinder head – disassembly

Refer to illustrations 8.2, 8.3 and 8.4
Note: *New and rebuilt cylinder heads are commonly available for most en-*

gines at dealerships and auto parts stores. Due to the fact that some specialized tools are necessary for the disassembly and inspection procedures, and replacement parts aren't always readily available, it may be more practical and economical for the home mechanic to purchase replacement head(s) rather than taking the time to disassemble, inspect and recondition the original(s).

1   Cylinder head disassembly involves removal of the intake and exhaust valves and related components. The rocker arm assemblies and camshaft(s) must be removed before beginning the cylinder head disassembly procedure (see Part A, B or C of this Chapter). Label the parts or store them separately so they can be reinstalled in their original locations.

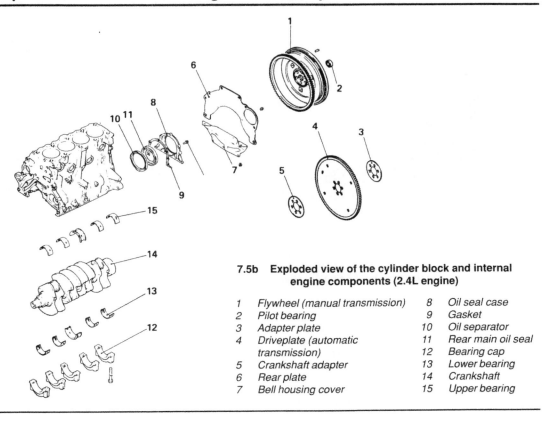

7.5b Exploded view of the cylinder block and internal engine components (2.4L engine)

1	Flywheel (manual transmission)	8	Oil seal case
2	Pilot bearing	9	Gasket
3	Adapter plate	10	Oil separator
4	Driveplate (automatic transmission)	11	Rear main oil seal
5	Crankshaft adapter	12	Bearing cap
6	Rear plate	13	Lower bearing
7	Bell housing cover	14	Crankshaft
		15	Upper bearing

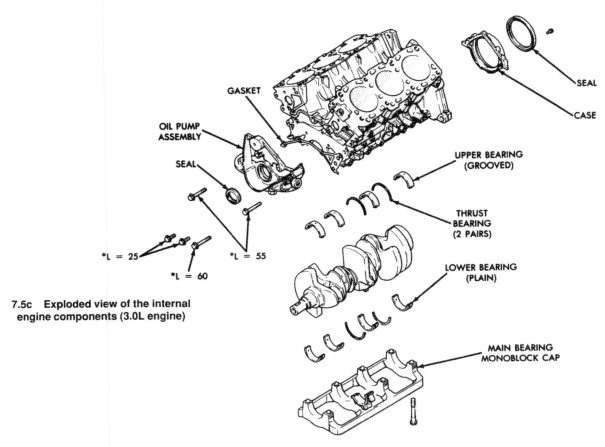

7.5c Exploded view of the internal engine components (3.0L engine)

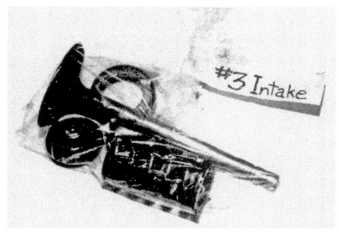

8.2   A small plastic bag, with an appropriate label, can be used to store the valve train components so they can be kept together and reinstalled in the original location

2   Before the valves are removed, arrange to label and store them, along with their related components, so they can be kept separate and re-installed in their original locations **(see illustration)**.
3   Compress the springs on the first valve with a spring compressor and remove the keepers **(see illustration)**. Carefully release the valve spring compressor and remove the retainer, the spring and the spring seat (if used).
4   Pull the valve out of the head, then remove the oil seal from the guide. If the valve binds in the guide (won't pull through), push it back into the head and deburr the area around the keeper groove with a fine file or whet-stone **(see illustration)**.
5   Repeat the procedure for the remaining valves. Remember to keep all the parts for each valve together so they can be reinstalled in the same locations.
6   Once the valves and related components have been removed and stored in an organized manner, the head should be thoroughly cleaned and inspected. If a complete engine overhaul is being done, finish the en-gine disassembly procedures before beginning the cylinder head cleaning and inspection process.

---

9   Cylinder head – cleaning and inspection

---

1   Thorough cleaning of the cylinder head(s) and related valve train components, followed by a detailed inspection, will enable you to decide how much valve service work must be done during the engine overhaul. **Note:** *If the engine was severely overheated, the cylinder head is probably warped.*

Cleaning

2   Scrape all traces of old gasket material and sealant off the head gas-ket, intake manifold and exhaust manifold mating surfaces. Be very care-ful not to gouge the cylinder head. Special gasket removal solvents that soften gaskets and make removal much easier are available at auto parts stores.
3   Remove all built-up scale from the coolant passages.
4   Run a stiff wire brush through the various holes to remove deposits that may have formed in them.
5   Run an appropriate size tap into each of the threaded holes to remove corrosion and thread sealant that may be present. If compressed air is available, use it to clear the holes of debris produced by this operation. **Warning:** *Wear eye protection when using compressed air!*
6   Clean the camshaft bearing cap bolt threads with a wire brush.
7   Clean the cylinder head with solvent and dry it thoroughly. Com-pressed air will speed the drying process and ensure that all holes and re-cessed areas are clean. **Note:** *Decarbonizing chemicals are available and*

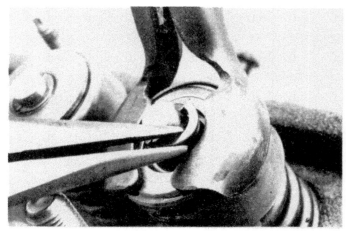

8.3   Use a valve spring compressor to compress the spring, then remove the keepers from the valve stem

8.4   If the valve won't pull through the guide, deburr the edge of the stem end and the area around the top of the keeper groove with a file or whetstone

may prove very useful when cleaning cylinder heads and valve train com-ponents. They're very caustic and should be used with caution. Be sure to follow the instructions on the container.
8   Clean the rocker arms and bearing caps with solvent and dry them thoroughly (don't mix them up during the cleaning process). Compressed air will speed the drying process and can be used to clean out the oil pas-sages.
9   Clean all the valve springs, spring seats, keepers and retainers with solvent and dry them thoroughly. Do the components from one valve at a time to avoid mixing up the parts.
10   Scrape off any heavy deposits that may have formed on the valves, then use a motorized wire brush to remove deposits from the valve heads and stems. Again, make sure the valves don't get mixed up.

Inspection

Refer to illustrations 9.12, 9.14, 9.15, 9.16, 9.17, and 9.18
Note: *Be sure to perform all of the following inspection procedures before concluding machine shop work is required. Make a list of the items that need attention.*

Cylinder head

11   Inspect the head very carefully for cracks, evidence of coolant leak-age and other damage. If cracks are found, check with an automotive ma-chine shop concerning repair. If repair isn't possible, a new cylinder head should be obtained.

9.12 Check the cylinder head gasket surface for warpage by trying to slip a feeler gauge under the straightedge (see this Chapter's Specifications for the maximum warpage allowed and use a feeler gauge of that thickness)

9.14 A dial indicator can be used to determine the valve stem-to-guide clearance (move the valve stem as indicated by the arrows)

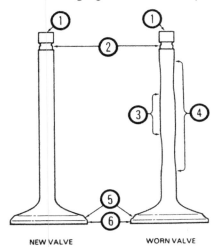

9.15 Check for valve wear at the points shown here

1	Valve tip	4	Stem (most worn area)
2	Keeper groove	5	Valve face
3	Stem (least worn area)	6	Margin

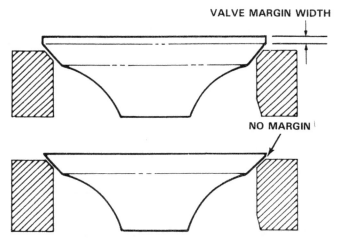

9.16 The margin width on each valve must be as specified (if no margin exists, the valve cannot be reused)

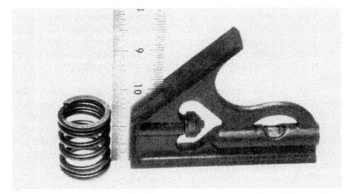

9.17 Measure the free length of each valve spring with a dial or vernier caliper

12 Using a straightedge and feeler gauge, check the head gasket mating surface for warpage **(see illustration)**. If the warpage exceeds the limit in this Chapter's Specifications, it can be resurfaced at an automotive machine shop. **Note:** *If the V6 engine heads are resurfaced, the intake manifold flanges will also require machining.*

13 Examine the valve seats in each of the combustion chambers. If they're pitted, cracked or burned, the head will require valve service that's beyond the scope of the home mechanic.

14 Check the valve stem-to-guide clearance by measuring the lateral movement of the valve stem with a dial indicator attached securely to the head **(see illustration)**. The valve must be in the guide and approximately 1/16-inch off the seat. The total valve stem movement indicated by the gauge needle must be divided by two to obtain the actual clearance. After this is done, if there's still some doubt regarding the condition of the valve guides, they should be checked by an automotive machine shop (the cost should be minimal).

Valves

15 Carefully inspect each valve face for uneven wear, deformation, cracks, pits and burned areas. Check the valve stem for scuffing and galling and the neck for cracks. Rotate the valve and check for any obvious indication that it's bent. Look for pits and excessive wear on the end of the

stem. The presence of any of these conditions **(see illustration)** indicates the need for valve service by an automotive machine shop.

16 Measure the margin width on each valve **(see illustration)**. Any valve with a margin narrower than specified in this Chapter will have to be replaced with a new one.

Valve components

17 Check each valve spring for wear (on the ends) and pits. Measure the free length and compare it to this Chapter's Specifications **(see illustra-**

9.18   Check each valve spring for squareness

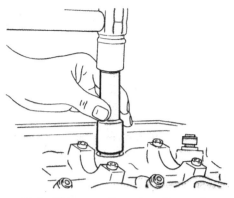

11.4   Make sure the valve stem seals are installed evenly and carefully to avoid damage

11.6   Apply a small dab of grease to each keeper as shown here before installation – it'll hold them in place on the valve stem as the spring is released

tion). Any springs that are shorter than specified have sagged and shouldn't be reused. The tension of all springs should be checked with a special fixture before deciding they're suitable for use in a rebuilt engine (take the springs to an automotive machine shop for this check).

18   Stand each spring on a flat surface and check it for squareness **(see illustration)**. If any of the springs are distorted or sagged, replace all of them with new parts.

19   Check the spring retainers and keepers for obvious wear and cracks. Any questionable parts should be replaced with new ones, as extensive damage will occur if they fail during engine operation.

20   If the inspection process indicates the valve components are in generally poor condition and worn beyond the limits specified, which is usually the case in an engine that's being overhauled, reassemble the valves in the cylinder head and refer to Section 11 for valve servicing recommendations.

10   Valves – servicing

1   Because of the complex nature of the job and the special tools and equipment needed, servicing of the valves, the valve seats and the valve guides, commonly known as a valve job, should be done by a professional.

2   The home mechanic can remove and disassemble the head, do the initial cleaning and inspection, then reassemble and deliver it to a dealer service department or an automotive machine shop for the actual service work. Doing the inspection will enable you to see what condition the head and valvetrain components are in and will ensure that you know what work and new parts are required when dealing with an automotive machine shop.

3   The dealer service department, or automotive machine shop, will remove the valves and springs, recondition or replace the valves and valve seats, recondition the valve guides, check and replace the valve springs, rotators, spring retainers and keepers (as necessary), replace the valve seals with new ones, reassemble the valve components and make sure the installed spring height is correct. The cylinder head gasket surface will also be resurfaced if it's warped.

4   After the valve job has been performed by a professional, the head will be in like new condition. When the head is returned, be sure to clean it again before installation on the engine to remove any metal particles and abrasive grit that may still be present from the valve service or head resurfacing operations. Use compressed air, if available, to blow out all the oil holes and passages.

11   Cylinder head – reassembly

Refer to illustrations 11.4, 11.6, 11.8, 11.9 and 11.12

1   Regardless of whether or not the head was sent to an automotive re-

pair shop for valve servicing, make sure it's clean before beginning reassembly.

2   If the head was sent out for valve servicing, the valves and related components will already be in place. Begin the reassembly procedure with Step 8.

3   Install the spring seats or valve rotators (if equipped) before the valve seals.

4   Install new seals on each of the valve guides. Using a hammer and a deep socket or seal installation tool, gently tap each seal into place until it's completely seated on the guide **(see illustration)**. Don't twist or cock the seals during installation or they won't seal properly on the valve stems.

5   Beginning at one end of the head, lubricate and install the first valve. Apply moly-base grease or clean engine oil to the valve stem.

6   Position the valve springs (and shims, if used) over the valves. Compress the springs with a valve spring compressor and carefully install the keepers in the groove, then slowly release the compressor and make sure the keepers seat properly. Apply a small dab of grease to each keeper to hold it in place if necessary **(see illustration)**.

7   Repeat the procedure for the remaining valves. Be sure to return the components to their original locations – don't mix them up!

8   Check the installed valve spring height with a ruler graduated in 1/32-inch increments or a dial caliper. If the head was sent out for service work, the installed height should be correct (but don't automatically assume it is). The measurement is taken from the top of each spring seat to the bottom of the retainer **(see illustration)**. If the height is greater than listed in this Chapter's Specifications, shims can be added under the springs to correct it. **Caution:** *Do not, under any circumstances, shim the*

11.8   Be sure to check the valve spring installed height (the distance from the top of the seat/shims to the top of the spring)

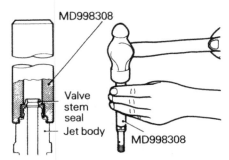

11.9   A special tool is available for jet valve stem seal replacement

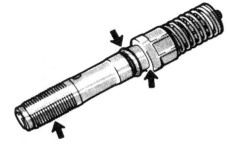

12.12   Be sure to use new O-rings when reinstalling the jet valves and apply engine oil to the O-rings, threads and seat area (arrows)

springs to the point where the installed height is less than specified.

9   If the engine is equipped with jet valves (refer to the chart in Section 1), install new valve stem seals and O-rings onto each assembly. Using the special tool, drive the jet valve stem seal into place on the valve body **(see illustration)**. If the special tool isn't available, a deep socket of the appropriate size can be used if you're careful. Do not reuse the old seals and don't try to install the seals with any other type of tool.

10   Apply engine oil to the jet valve stem when installing it in the valve body. Take care not to damage the valve stem seal lip. Make sure the jet valve stem slides smoothly in the body.

11   Compress the spring with special tool and install it together with the valve spring retainer. Install the retainer lock. Be careful not to damage the valve stem seal with the bottom of the retainer.

12   Install a new O-ring in the jet valve body groove and apply a thin coat of engine oil to it **(see illustration)**. Apply oil to the threads and seat as well.

13   Reinstall the jet valves and tighten them to the specified torque.

14   Apply moly-base grease to the rocker arm faces, the camshaft and the rocker shafts, then install the camshaft, rocker arms and shafts (refer to Part A).

15   Install the camshafts, hydraulic lash adjusters and rocker arm assemblies onto the head.

16   Apply moly-base grease to the rocker arm faces and the pivot balls, then install the rocker arm assembly on the cylinder head.

12   Pistons and connecting rods – removal

Refer to illustrations 12.1, 12.3 and 12.6

Note: *Prior to removing the piston/connecting rod assemblies, remove the*

cylinder head(s), the oil pan and the oil pump by referring to the appropriate Sections in Parts A, B or C of Chapter 2.

1   Use your fingernail to feel if a ridge has formed at the upper limit of ring travel (about 1/4-inch down from the top of each cylinder). If carbon deposits or cylinder wear have produced ridges, they must be completely removed with a special tool **(see illustration)**. Follow the manufacturer's instructions provided with the tool. Failure to remove the ridges before attempting to remove the piston/connecting rod assemblies may result in piston breakage.

2   After the cylinder ridges have been removed, turn the engine upside-down so the crankshaft is facing up.

3   Before the connecting rods are removed, check the endplay with feeler gauges. Slide them between the first connecting rod and the crankshaft throw until the play is removed **(see illustration)**. The endplay is equal to the thickness of the feeler gauge(s). If the endplay exceeds the service limit, new connecting rods will be required. If new rods (or a new crankshaft) are installed, the endplay may fall under the minimum listed in this Chapter's Specifications (if it does, the rods will have to be machined to restore it – consult an automotive machine shop for advice if necessary). Repeat the procedure for the remaining connecting rods.

4   Check the connecting rods and caps for identification marks. If they aren't plainly marked, use a small center punch to make the appropriate number of indentations on each rod and cap (1, 2, 3, etc., depending on the engine type and cylinder they're associated with).

5   Loosen each of the connecting rod cap nuts 1/2-turn at a time until they can be removed by hand. Remove the number one connecting rod cap and bearing insert. Don't drop the bearing insert out of the cap.

6   Slip a short length of plastic or rubber hose over each connecting rod cap bolt to protect the crankshaft journal and cylinder wall as the piston is removed **(see illustration)**.

12.1   A ridge reamer is required to remove the ridge from the top of each cylinder – do this before removing the pistons!

12.3   Check the connecting rod side clearance with a feeler gauge as shown

12.6   To prevent damage to the crankshaft journals and cylinder walls, slip sections of rubber or plastic hose over the rod bolts before removing the pistons

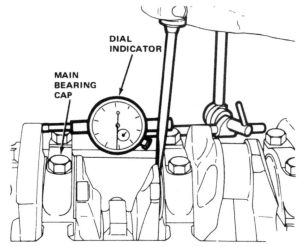

13.1   Checking crankshaft endplay with a dial indicator

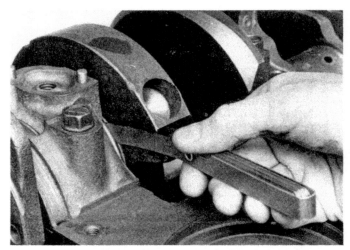

13.3   Checking crankshaft endplay with a feeler gauge

13.4a   Use a center punch or number stamping dies to mark the main bearing caps to ensure installation in their original locations on the block (make the punch marks near one of the bolt heads)

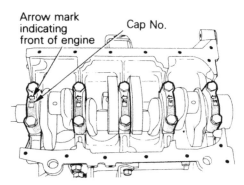

13.4b   The main bearing cap numerals (arrows) are easily visible on the 2.4L engine

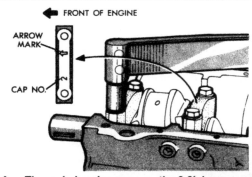

13.4c   The main bearing caps on the 2.6L have arrows that point to the front of the engine

7   Remove the bearing insert and push the connecting rod/piston assembly out through the top of the engine. Use a wooden or plastic hammer handle to push on the upper bearing surface in the connecting rod. If resistance is felt, double-check to make sure all of the ridge was removed from the cylinder.

8   Repeat the procedure for the remaining cylinders.

9   After removal, reassemble the connecting rod caps and bearing inserts in their respective connecting rods and install the cap nuts finger tight. Leaving the old bearing inserts in place until reassembly will help prevent the connecting rod bearing surfaces from being accidentally nicked or gouged.

10   Don't separate the pistons from the connecting rods (see Section 17 for additional information).

13   Crankshaft – removal

Refer to illustrations 13.1, 13.3, 13.4a, 13.4b and 13.4c

Note: *The crankshaft can be removed only after the engine has been removed from the vehicle. It's assumed the flywheel or driveplate, crankshaft balancer/vibration damper, timing chain or belt, oil pan, oil pump and piston/connecting rod assemblies have already been removed. The rear main oil seal housing must be unbolted and separated from the block before proceeding with crankshaft removal.*

1   Before the crankshaft is removed, check the endplay. Mount a dial indicator with the stem in line with the crankshaft and touching one of the crank throws **(see illustration)**.

2   Push the crankshaft all the way to the rear and zero the dial indicator. Next, pry the crankshaft to the front as far as possible and check the reading on the dial indicator. The distance it moves is the endplay. If it's greater than specified in this Chapter, check the crankshaft thrust surfaces for wear. If no wear is evident, new main bearings should correct the endplay.

3   If a dial indicator isn't available, feeler gauges can be used. Gently pry or push the crankshaft all the way to the front of the engine. Slip feeler gauges between the crankshaft and the front face of the thrust main bearing to determine the clearance **(see illustration)**.

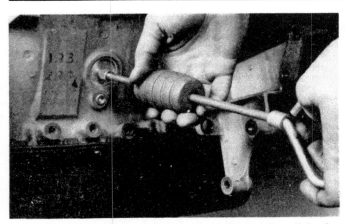

14.4   The core plugs should be removed with a puller – if they're driven into the block, they may be impossible to retrieve

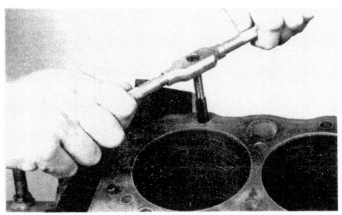

14.8   All bolt holes in the block – particularly the main bearing cap and head bolt holes – should be cleaned and restored with a tap (be sure to remove debris from the holes after this is done)

14.10   A large socket on an extension can be used to drive the new core plugs into the bores

4   Check the main bearing caps to see if they're marked to indicate their locations. They should be numbered consecutively from the front of the engine to the rear. If they aren't, mark them with number stamping dies or a center punch **(see illustrations)**. Main bearing caps generally have a cast-in arrow, which points to the front of the engine **(see illustration)**. Loosen the main bearing cap bolts 1/4-turn at a time each, until they can be removed by hand. Note if any stud bolts are used and make sure they're returned to their original locations when the crankshaft is reinstalled.

5   Gently tap the caps with a soft-face hammer, then separate them from the engine block. If necessary, use the bolts as levers to remove the caps. Try not to drop the bearing inserts if they come out with the caps.

6   Carefully lift the crankshaft out of the engine. It may be a good idea to have an assistant available, since the crankshaft is quite heavy. With the bearing inserts in place in the engine block and main bearing caps, return the caps to their respective locations on the engine block and tighten the bolts finger tight.

14   Engine block – cleaning

Refer to illustrations 14.4, 14.8 and 14.10

1   Remove the main bearing caps and separate the bearing inserts from the caps and the engine block. Tag the bearings, indicating which cylinder they were removed from and whether they were in the cap or the block, then set them aside.

2   Using a gasket scraper, remove all traces of gasket material from the

engine block. Be very careful not to nick or gouge the gasket sealing surfaces.

3   Remove all of the covers and threaded oil gallery plugs from the block. The plugs are usually very tight – they may have to be drilled out and the holes retapped. Use new plugs when the engine is reassembled.

4   Drill a small hole in the center of each core plug and pull them out with an auto body type dent puller **(see illustration)**. **Caution:** *The core plugs (also known as freeze or soft plugs) may be difficult or impossible to retrieve if they're driven into the block coolant passages.*

5   If the engine is extremely dirty, it should be taken to an automotive machine shop to be steam cleaned or hot tanked.

6   After the block is returned, clean all oil holes and oil galleries one more time. Brushes specifically designed for this purpose are available at most auto parts stores. Flush the passages with warm water until the water runs clear, dry the block thoroughly and wipe all machined surfaces with a light, rust preventive oil. If you have access to compressed air, use it to speed the drying process and blow out all the oil holes and galleries. **Warning:** *Wear eye protection when using compressed air!*

7   If the block isn't extremely dirty or sludged up, you can do an adequate cleaning job with hot soapy water and a stiff brush. Take plenty of time and do a thorough job. Regardless of the cleaning method used, be sure to clean all oil holes and galleries very thoroughly, dry the block completely and coat all machined surfaces with light oil.

8   The threaded holes in the block must be clean to ensure accurate torque readings during reassembly. Run the proper size tap into each of the holes to remove rust, corrosion, thread sealant or sludge and restore damaged threads **(see illustration)**. If possible, use compressed air to clear the holes of debris produced by this operation. Now is a good time to clean the threads on the head bolts and the main bearing cap bolts as well.

9   Reinstall the main bearing caps and tighten the bolts finger tight.

10   After coating the sealing surfaces of the new core plugs with Permatex no. 2 sealant, install them in the engine block **(see illustration)**. Make sure they're driven in straight and seated properly or leakage could result. Special tools are available for this purpose, but a large socket, with an outside diameter that will just slip into the core plug, a 1/2-inch drive extension and a hammer will work just as well.

11   Apply non-hardening sealant (such as Permatex no. 2 or Teflon pipe sealant) to the new oil gallery plugs and thread them into the holes in the block. Make sure they're tightened securely.

12   If the engine isn't going to be reassembled right away, cover it with a large plastic trash bag to keep it clean.

15   Engine block – inspection

Refer to illustrations 15.4a, 15.4b and 15.4c

1   Before the block is inspected, it should be cleaned as described in Section 14.

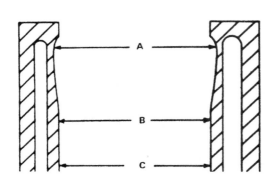

15.4a   Measure the diameter of each cylinder just under the wear ridge (A), at the center (B) and at the bottom (C)

15.4b   The ability to "feel" when the telescoping gauge is at the correct point will be developed over time, so work slowly and repeat the check until you're satisfied the bore measurement is accurate

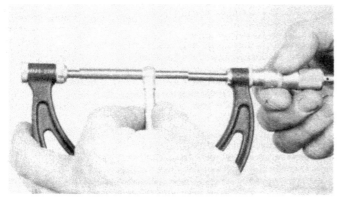

15.4c   The gauge is then measured with a micrometer to determine the bore size

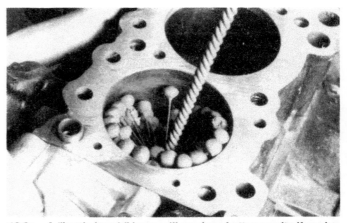

16.3a   A "bottle brush" hone will produce better results if you've never honed cylinders before

2   Visually check the block for cracks, rust and corrosion. Look for stripped threads in the threaded holes. It's also a good idea to have the block checked for hidden cracks by an automotive machine shop that has the special equipment to do this type of work. If defects are found, have the block repaired, if possible, or replaced.

3   Check the cylinder bores for scuffing and scoring.

4   Measure the diameter of each cylinder at the top (just under the ridge area), center and bottom of the cylinder bore, parallel to the crankshaft axis **(see illustrations)**. **Note:** *These measurements should not be made with the bare block mounted on an engine stand – the cylinders will be distorted and the measurements will be inaccurate.*

5   Next, measure each cylinder's diameter at the same three locations across the crankshaft axis. Compare the results to this Chapter's Specifications.

6   If the required precision measuring tools aren't available, the piston-to-cylinder clearances can be obtained, though not quite as accurately, using feeler gauge stock. Feeler gauge stock comes in 12-inch lengths and various thicknesses and is generally available at auto parts stores.

7   To check the clearance, select a feeler gauge and slip it into the cylinder along with the matching piston. The piston must be positioned exactly as it normally would be. The feeler gauge must be between the piston and cylinder on one of the thrust faces (90-degrees to the piston pin bore).

8   The piston should slip through the cylinder (with the feeler gauge in place) with moderate pressure.

9   If it falls through or slides through easily, the clearance is excessive and a new piston will be required. If the piston binds at the lower end of the cylinder and is loose toward the top, the cylinder is tapered. If tight spots are encountered as the piston/feeler gauge is rotated in the cylinder, the cylinder is out-of-round.

10   Repeat the procedure for the remaining pistons and cylinders.

11   If the cylinder walls are badly scuffed or scored, or if they're out-of-

round or tapered beyond the limits given in this Chapter's Specifications, have the engine block rebored and honed at an automotive machine shop. If a rebore is done, oversize pistons and rings will be required.

12   If the cylinders are in reasonably good condition and not worn to the outside of the limits, and if the piston-to-cylinder clearances can be maintained properly, they don't have to be rebored. Honing is all that's necessary (see Section 16).

16   Cylinder honing

Refer to illustrations 16.3a and 16.3b

1   Prior to engine reassembly, the cylinder bores must be honed so the new piston rings will seat correctly and provide the best possible combustion chamber seal. **Note:** *If you don't have the tools or don't want to tackle the honing operation, most automotive machine shops will do it for a reasonable fee.*

2   Before honing the cylinders, install the main bearing caps and tighten the bolts to the specified torque.

3   Two types of cylinder hones are commonly available – the flex hone or "bottle brush" type and the more traditional surfacing hone with spring-loaded stones. Both will do the job, but for the less experienced mechanic the "bottle brush" hone will probably be easier to use. You'll also need some honing oil (kerosene will work if honing oil isn't available), rags and an electric drill motor. Proceed as follows:

  a) Mount the hone in the drill motor, compress the stones and slip it into the first cylinder **(see illustration)**. Be sure to wear safety goggles or a face shield!

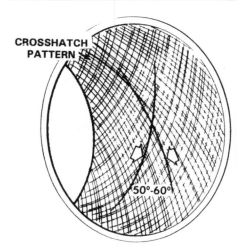

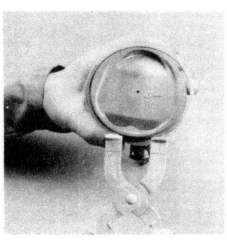

16.3b   The cylinder hone should leave a smooth, crosshatch pattern with the lines intersecting at approximately a 60-degree angle

17.2   Use a special tool to remove the piston rings from the piston

17.4a   The piston ring grooves can be cleaned with a special tool, as shown here, . . .

6   After rinsing, dry the block and apply a coat of light rust preventive oil to all machined surfaces. Wrap the block in a plastic trash bag to keep it clean and set it aside until reassembly.

17   Pistons and connecting rods – inspection

Refer to illustrations 17.2, 17.4a, 17,4b, 17.10 and 17.11

1   Before the inspection process can be carried out, the piston/connecting rod assemblies must be cleaned and the original piston rings removed from the pistons. **Note:** *Always use new piston rings when the engine is reassembled.*
2   Using a piston ring installation tool **(see illustration)**, carefully remove the rings from the pistons. Be careful not to nick or gouge the pistons in the process.
3   Scrape all traces of carbon from the top of the piston. A hand held wire brush or a piece of fine emery cloth can be used once the majority of the deposits have been scraped away. Do not, under any circumstances, use a wire brush mounted in a drill motor to remove deposits from the pistons. The piston material is soft and may be eroded away by the wire brush.
4   Use a piston ring groove cleaning tool to remove carbon deposits from the ring grooves. If a tool isn't available, a piece broken off the old ring will do the job. Be very careful to remove only the carbon deposits – don't remove any metal and do not nick or scratch the sides of the ring grooves **(see illustrations)**.
5   Once the deposits have been removed, clean the piston/rod assemblies with solvent and dry them with compressed air (if available). **Warning:** *Wear eye protection. Make sure the oil return holes in the back sides of the ring grooves are clear.*
6   If the pistons and cylinder walls aren't damaged or worn excessively, and if the engine block isn't rebored, new pistons won't be necessary. Normal piston wear appears as even vertical wear on the piston thrust surfaces and slight looseness of the top ring in its groove. New piston rings, however, should always be used when an engine is rebuilt.
7   Carefully inspect each piston for cracks around the skirt, at the pin bosses and at the ring lands.
8   Look for scoring and scuffing on the thrust faces of the skirt, holes in the piston crown and burned areas at the edge of the crown. If the skirt is scored or scuffed, the engine may have been suffering from overheating and/or abnormal combustion, which caused excessively high operating temperatures. The cooling and lubrication systems should be checked thoroughly. A hole in the piston crown is an indication that abnormal combustion (preignition) was occurring. Burned areas at the edge of the piston crown are usually evidence of spark knock (detonation). If any of the above problems exist, the causes must be corrected or the damage will

17.4b   . . . or a section of a broken ring

b) Lubricate the cylinder with plenty of honing oil, turn on the drill and move the hone up-and-down in the cylinder at a pace that will produce a fine crosshatch pattern on the cylinder walls. Ideally, the crosshatch lines should intersect at approximately a 60-degree angle **(see illustration)**. Be sure to use plenty of lubricant and don't take off any more material than is absolutely necessary to produce the desired finish. **Note:** *Piston ring manufacturers may specify a smaller crosshatch angle than the traditional 60-degrees – read and follow any instructions included with the new rings.*
c) Don't withdraw the hone from the cylinder while it's running. Instead, shut off the drill and continue moving the hone up-and-down in the cylinder until it comes to a complete stop, then compress the stones and withdraw the hone. If you're using a "bottle brush" type hone, stop the drill motor, then turn the chuck in the normal direction of rotation while withdrawing the hone from the cylinder.
d) Wipe the oil out of the cylinder and repeat the procedure for the remaining cylinders.
4   After the honing job is complete, chamfer the top edges of the cylinder bores with a small file so the rings won't catch when the pistons are installed. Be very careful not to nick the cylinder walls with the end of the file.
5   The entire engine block must be washed again very thoroughly with warm, soapy water to remove all traces of the abrasive grit produced during the honing operation. **Note:** *The bores can be considered clean when a lint-free white cloth – dampened with clean engine oil- used to wipe them out doesn't pick up any more honing residue, which will show up as gray areas on the cloth. Be sure to run a brush through all oil holes and galleries and flush them with running water.*

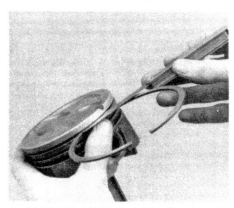

17.10   Check the ring side clearance with a feeler gauge at several points around the groove

17.11   Measure the piston diameter at a 90-degree angle to the piston pin and in line with it

18.1   The oil holes should be chamfered so sharp edges don't gouge or scratch the new bearings

occur again. The causes may include intake air leaks, incorrect fuel/air mixture, low octane fuel, ignition timing and EGR system malfunctions.

9   Corrosion of the piston, in the form of small pits, indicates coolant is leaking into the combustion chamber and/or the crankcase. Again, the cause must be corrected or the problem may persist in the rebuilt engine.

10   Measure the piston ring side clearance by laying a new piston ring in each ring groove and slipping a feeler gauge in beside it **(see illustration)**. Check the clearance at three or four locations around each groove. Be sure to use the correct ring for each groove – they are different. If the side clearance is greater than specified in this Chapter, new pistons will have to be used.

11   Check the piston-to-bore clearance by measuring the bore (see Section 15) and the piston diameter. Make sure the pistons and bores are correctly matched. Measure the piston across the skirt, at a 90-degree angle to the piston pin **(see illustration)** below the axis of the piston pin.

12   Subtract the piston diameter from the bore diameter to obtain the clearance. If it's greater than listed in this Chapter's Specifications, the block will have to be rebored and new pistons and rings installed.

13   Check the piston-to-rod clearance by twisting the piston and rod in opposite directions. Any noticeable play indicates excessive wear, which must be corrected. The piston/connecting rod assemblies should be taken to an automotive machine shop to have the pistons and rods resized and new pins installed.

14   If the pistons must be removed from the connecting rods for any reason, they should be taken to an automotive machine shop. While they are there have the connecting rods checked for bend and twist, since automotive machine shops have special equipment for this purpose. **Note:** *Unless new pistons and/or connecting rods must be installed, do not*

disassemble the pistons and connecting rods.

15   Check the connecting rods for cracks and other damage. Temporarily remove the rod caps, lift out the old bearing inserts, wipe the rod and cap bearing surfaces clean and inspect them for nicks, gouges and scratches. After checking the rods, replace the old bearings, slip the caps into place and tighten the nuts finger tight. **Note:** *If the engine is being rebuilt because of a connecting rod knock, be sure to install new rods.*

18   Crankshaft – inspection

Refer to illustrations 18.1, 18.2, 18.4, 18.6 and 18.8

1   Remove all burrs from the crankshaft oil holes with a stone, file or scraper **(see illustration)**.

2   Clean the crankshaft with solvent and dry it with compressed air (if available). **Warning:** *Wear eye protection when using compressed air. Be sure to clean the oil holes with a stiff brush **(see illustration)** and flush them with solvent.*

3   Check the main and connecting rod bearing journals for uneven wear, scoring, pits and cracks.

4   Rub a penny across each journal several times **(see illustration)**. If a journal picks up copper from the penny, it's too rough and must be reground.

5   Check the rest of the crankshaft for cracks and other damage. It should be magnafluxed to reveal hidden cracks – an automotive machine shop will handle the procedure.

6   Using a micrometer, measure the diameter of the main and connecting rod journals and compare the results to this Chapter's Specifications

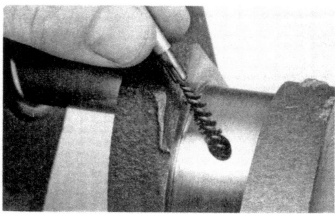

18.2   Use a wire or stiff plastic bristle brush to clean the oil passages in the crankshaft

18.4   Rubbing a penny lengthwise on each journal will reveal its condition – if copper rubs off and is embedded in the crankshaft, the journals should be reground

18.6   Measure the diameter of each crankshaft journal at several points to detect taper and out-of-round conditions

18.8   If the seals have worn grooves in the crankshaft journals, or if the seal contact surfaces are nicked or scratched, the new seals will leak

(see illustration). By measuring the diameter at a number of points around each journal's circumference, you'll be able to determine whether or not the journal is out-of-round. Take the measurement at each end of the journal, near the crank throws, to determine if the journal is tapered.

7   If the crankshaft journals are damaged, tapered, out-of-round or worn beyond the limits given in the Specifications, have the crankshaft reground by an automotive machine shop. Be sure to use the correct size bearing inserts if the crankshaft is reconditioned.

8   Check the oil seal journals at each end of the crankshaft for wear and damage. If the seal has worn a groove in the journal, or if it's nicked or scratched **(see illustration)**, the new seal may leak when the engine is reassembled. In some cases, an automotive machine shop may be able to repair the journal by pressing on a thin sleeve. If repair isn't feasible, a new or different crankshaft should be installed.

9   Refer to Section 19 and examine the main and rod bearing inserts.

19   Main and connecting rod bearings – inspection

Refer to illustration 19.1

1   Even though the main and connecting rod bearings should be replaced with new ones during the engine overhaul, the old bearings should be retained for close examination, as they may reveal valuable information about the condition of the engine **(see illustration)**.

2   Bearing failure occurs because of lack of lubrication, the presence of dirt or other foreign particles, overloading the engine and corrosion. Regardless of the cause of bearing failure, it must be corrected before the engine is reassembled to prevent it from happening again.

3   When examining the bearings, remove them from the engine block, the main bearing caps, the connecting rods and the rod caps and lay them out on a clean surface in the same general position as their location in the engine. This will enable you to match any bearing problems with the corresponding crankshaft journal.

4   Dirt and other foreign particles get into the engine in a variety of ways. It may be left in the engine during assembly, or it may pass through filters or the PCV system. It may get into the oil, and from there into the bearings. Metal chips from machining operations and normal engine wear are often present. Abrasives are sometimes left in engine components after reconditioning, especially when parts aren't thoroughly cleaned using the proper cleaning methods. Whatever the source, these foreign objects often end up embedded in the soft bearing material and are easily recognized. Large particles won't embed in the bearing and will score or gouge the bearing and journal. The best prevention for this cause of bearing failure is to clean all parts thoroughly and keep everything spotlessly clean during engine assembly. Frequent and regular engine oil and filter changes are also recommended.

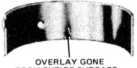

19.1   Typical bearing failures

5   Lack of lubrication (or lubrication breakdown) has a number of interrelated causes. Excessive heat (which thins the oil), overloading (which squeezes the oil from the bearing face) and oil leakage or throw off (from excessive bearing clearances, worn oil pump or high engine speeds) all contribute to lubrication breakdown. Blocked oil passages, which usually are the result of misaligned oil holes in a bearing shell, will also oil starve a bearing and destroy it. When lack of lubrication is the cause of bearing failure, the bearing material is wiped or extruded from the steel backing of the bearing. Temperatures may increase to the point where the steel backing turns blue from overheating.

6   Driving habits can have a definite effect on bearing life. Full throttle,

21.3   When checking piston ring end gap, the ring must be square in the cylinder bore (this is done by pushing the ring down with the top of a piston as shown)

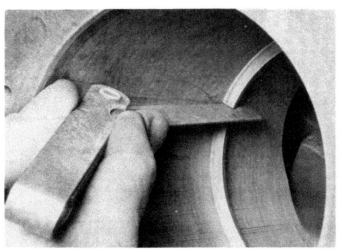

21.4   With the ring square in the cylinder, measure the end gap with a feeler gauge

low speed operation (lugging the engine) puts very high loads on bearings, which tends to squeeze out the oil film. These loads cause the bearings to flex, which produces fine cracks in the bearing face (fatigue failure). Eventually the bearing material will loosen in pieces and tear away from the steel backing. Short trip driving leads to corrosion of bearings because insufficient engine heat is produced to drive off the condensed water and corrosive gases. These products collect in the engine oil, forming acid and sludge. As the oil is carried to the engine bearings, the acid attacks and corrodes the bearing material.

7   Incorrect bearing installation during engine assembly will lead to bearing failure as well. Tight fitting bearings leave insufficient oil clearance and will result in oil starvation. Dirt or foreign particles trapped behind a bearing insert result in high spots on the bearing which lead to failure.

---

20   Engine overhaul – reassembly sequence

---

1   Before beginning engine reassembly, make sure you have all the necessary new parts, gaskets and seals as well as the following items on hand:

Common hand tools
Torque wrench (1/2-inch drive)
Piston ring installation tool
Piston ring compressor
Vibration damper installation tool
Short lengths of rubber or plastic hose to fit over connecting rod bolts
Plastigage
Feeler gauges
Fine-tooth file
New engine oil
Engine assembly lube or moly-base grease
Gasket sealant
Thread locking compound

2   In order to save time and avoid problems, engine reassembly must be done in the following general order:

2.6L engine
Crankshaft and main bearings
Rear main oil seal housing
Piston/connecting rod assemblies
Oil pump
Oil pan
Timing chain housing
Timing chain and sprockets
Silent shaft chain and sprockets
Intake and exhaust manifolds
Cylinder head, camshaft and rocker arms

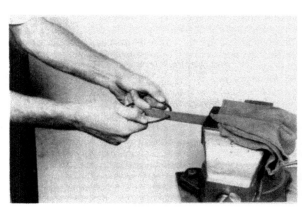

21.5   If the end gap is too small, clamp a file in a vise and file the ring ends (from the outside in only) to enlarge the gap slightly

Valve cover
Flywheel/driveplate

2.0L and 2.4L engines
Crankshaft and main bearings
Rear main oil seal housing
Piston/connecting rod assemblies
Oil pump
Timing belt and sprockets
Timing belt cover
Oil pan
Cylinder head, camshaft and rocker arms
Intake/exhaust manifolds
Valve cover
Engine rear plate (if equipped)
Flywheel/driveplate

3.0L V6 engine
Crankshaft and main bearings
Rear main oil seal housing
Piston/connecting rod assemblies
Oil pump
Oil pan
Timing belt cover
Timing belt and sprockets
Cylinder heads, camshafts and rocker arms
Intake and exhaust manifolds
Valve covers
Flywheel/driveplate

21.9a   Installing the spacer/expander in the oil control ring groove

21.9b   DO NOT use a piston ring installation tool when installing the oil ring side rails

21   Piston rings – installation

Refer to illustrations 21.3, 21.4, 21.5, 21.9a, 21.9b, 21.11 and 21.12

1   Before installing the new piston rings, the ring end gaps must be checked. It's assumed the piston ring side clearance has been checked and verified correct (see Section 17).

2   Lay out the piston/connecting rod assemblies and the new ring sets so the ring sets will be matched with the same piston and cylinder during the end gap measurement and engine assembly.

3   Insert the top (number one) ring into the first cylinder and square it up with the cylinder walls by pushing it in with the top of the piston **(see illustration)**. The ring should be near the bottom of the cylinder, at the lower limit of ring travel.

4   To measure the end gap, slip feeler gauges between the ends of the ring until a gauge equal to the gap width is found **(see illustration)**. The feeler gauge should slide between the ring ends with a slight amount of drag. Compare the measurement to this Chapter's Specifications. If the gap is larger or smaller than specified, double-check to make sure you have the correct rings before proceeding.

5   If the gap is too small, it must be enlarged or the ring ends may come in contact with each other during engine operation, which can cause serious engine damage. The end gap can be increased by filing the ring ends very carefully with a fine file. Mount the file in a vise equipped with soft jaws, slip the ring over the file with the ends contacting the file teeth and slowly move the ring to remove material from the ends. When performing this operation, file only from the outside in **(see illustration)**.

6   Excess end gap isn't critical unless it's greater than 0.040-inch.

Again, double-check to make sure you have the correct rings for the engine.

7   Repeat the procedure for each ring that will be installed in the first cylinder and for each ring in the remaining cylinders. Remember to keep rings, pistons and cylinders matched up.

8   Once the ring end gaps have been checked/corrected, the rings can be installed on the pistons.

9   The oil control ring (lowest one on the piston) is usually installed first. It's composed of three separate components. Slip the spacer/expander into the groove **(see illustration)**. If an anti-rotation tang is used, make sure it's inserted into the drilled hole in the ring groove. Next, install the lower side rail. Don't use a piston ring installation tool on the oil ring side rails, as they may be damaged. Instead, place one end of the side rail into the groove between the spacer/expander and the ring land, hold it firmly in place and slide a finger around the piston while pushing the rail into the groove **(see illustration)**. Next, install the upper side rail in the same manner.

10   After the three oil ring components have been installed, check to make sure both the upper and lower side rails can be turned smoothly in the ring groove.

11   The number two (middle) ring is installed next. It's usually stamped with a mark, which must face up, toward the top of the piston **(see illustration)**. **Note:** *Always follow the instructions printed on the ring package or box – different manufacturers may require different approaches. Don't mix up the top and middle rings, as they have different cross sections.*

12   Use a piston ring installation tool and make sure the identification mark is facing the top of the piston, then slip the ring into the middle groove on the piston **(see illustration)**. Don't expand the ring any more than necessary to slide it over the piston.

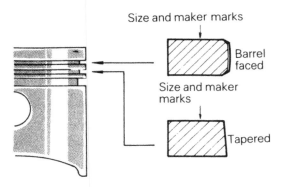

21.11   The number 1 (top) and number 2 compression rings have different cross-sections – be sure to install them in the correct locations with the marks facing UP

Size and maker marks

Barrel faced

Size and maker marks

Tapered

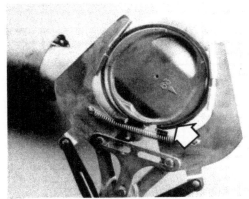

21.12   Installing the compression rings with a ring expander – the mark (arrow) must face up

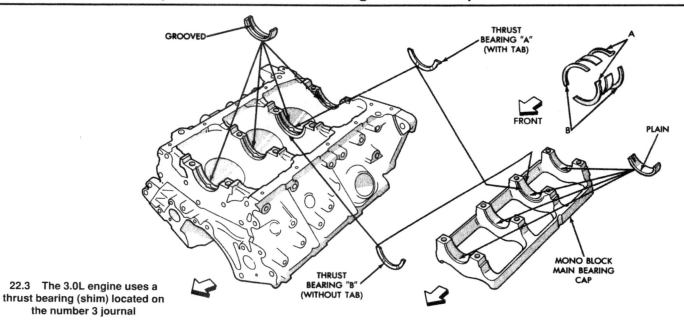

22.3 The 3.0L engine uses a thrust bearing (shim) located on the number 3 journal

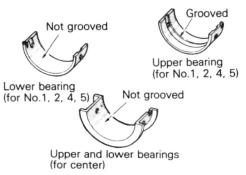

22.6 Main bearing designations for the 2.0L and 2.4L engines – the thrust bearing is installed in the number three cap and saddle

22.11 Lay the Plastigage strips (arrow) on the main bearing journals, parallel to the crankshaft centerline

13 Install the number one (top) ring in the same manner. Make sure the mark is facing up. Be careful not to confuse the number one and number two rings.

14 Repeat the procedure for the remaining pistons and rings.

22 Crankshaft – installation and main bearing oil clearance check

Refer to illustrations 22.3, 22.6, 22.11, 22.13 and 22.15

1 Crankshaft installation is the first step in engine reassembly. It's assumed at this point that the engine block and crankshaft have been cleaned, inspected and repaired or reconditioned.

2 Position the engine with the bottom facing up.

3 Remove the main bearing cap bolts and lift out the caps. Lay them out in the proper order to ensure correct installation (**see illustration**).

4 If they're still in place, remove the original bearing inserts from the block and the main bearing caps. Wipe the bearing surfaces of the block and caps with a clean, lint-free cloth. They must be kept spotlessly clean.

Main bearing oil clearance check

Note: *Don't touch the faces of the new bearing inserts with your fingers. Oil and acids from your skin can etch the bearings.*

5 Clean the back sides of the new main bearing inserts and lay one in each main bearing saddle in the block. If one of the bearing inserts from each set has a large groove in it, make sure the grooved insert is installed in the block. Lay the other bearing from each set in the corresponding main bearing cap. Make sure the tab on the bearing insert fits into the recess in the block or cap. **Caution:** *The oil holes in the block must line up with the oil holes in the bearing inserts. Do not hammer the bearing into place and don't nick or gouge the bearing faces. No lubrication should be used at this time.*

6 The flanged thrust bearing must be installed in the number two cap and saddle (counting from the front of the engine) on 2.6L engines. On the 2.0L, 2.4L (**see illustration**) and 3.0L engines the thrust bearing must be installed in the number three (center) cap and saddle.

7 Clean the faces of the bearings in the block and the crankshaft main bearing journals with a clean, lint-free cloth.

8 Check or clean the oil holes in the crankshaft, as any dirt here can go only one way – straight through the new bearings.

9 Once you're certain the crankshaft is clean, carefully lay it in position in the main bearings.

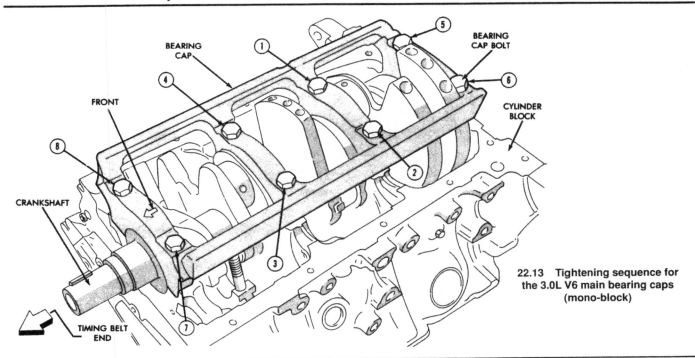

22.13 Tightening sequence for the 3.0L V6 main bearing caps (mono-block)

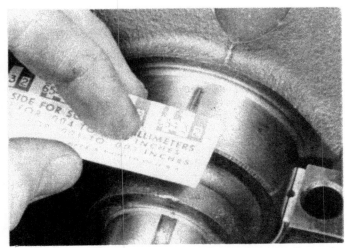

22.15 Compare the width of the crushed Plastigage to the scale on the envelope to determine the main bearing oil clearance (always take the measurement at the widest point of the Plastigage); be sure to use the correct scale – standard and metric ones are included

10 Before the crankshaft can be permanently installed, the main bearing oil clearance must be checked.

11 Cut several pieces of the appropriate size Plastigage (they should be slightly shorter than the width of the main bearings) and place one piece on each crankshaft main bearing journal, parallel with the journal axis (**see illustration**).

12 Clean the faces of the bearings in the caps and install the caps in their original locations (don't mix them up) with the arrows pointing toward the front of the engine. Don't disturb the Plastigage.

13 Starting with the center main and working out toward the ends, tighten the main bearing cap bolts, in three steps, to the torque figure listed in this Chapter's Specifications. Don't rotate the crankshaft at any time during this operation. **Note:** *On 3.0L V6 engines, torque bolts on the mono-block in the proper sequence* (**see illustration**).

14 Remove the bolts and carefully lift off the main bearing caps. Keep them in order. Don't disturb the Plastigage or rotate the crankshaft. If any

of the main bearing caps are difficult to remove, tap them gently from side-to-side with a soft-face hammer to loosen them.

15 Compare the width of the crushed Plastigage on each journal to the scale printed on the Plastigage envelope to obtain the main bearing oil clearance (**see illustration**). Check the Specifications at the beginning of this Chapter to make sure it's correct.

16 If the clearance is not as specified, the bearing inserts may be the wrong size (which means different ones will be required). Before deciding different inserts are needed, make sure no dirt or oil was between the bearing inserts and the caps or block when the clearance was measured. If the Plastigage was wider at one end than the other, the journal may be tapered (see Section 18).

17 Carefully scrape all traces of the Plastigage material off the main bearing journals and/or the bearing faces. Use your fingernail or the edge of a credit card – don't nick or scratch the bearing faces.

Final crankshaft installation

18 Carefully lift the crankshaft out of the engine.

19 Clean the bearing faces in the block, then apply a thin, uniform layer of moly-base grease or engine assembly lube to each of the bearing surfaces. Be sure to coat the thrust faces as well as the journal face of the thrust bearing.

20 Make sure the crankshaft journals are clean, then lay the crankshaft back in place in the block.

21 Clean the faces of the bearings in the caps, then apply lubricant to them.

22 Install the caps in their original locations with the arrows pointing toward the front of the engine.

23 Install the bolts.

24 Tighten all except the thrust bearing cap bolts to the torque listed in this Chapter's Specifications (work from the center out and approach the final torque in three steps).

25 Tighten the thrust bearing cap bolts to 10-to-12 ft-lbs.

26 Tap the ends of the crankshaft forward and backward with a lead or brass hammer to line up the main bearing and crankshaft thrust surfaces.

27 Retighten all main bearing cap bolts to the torque listed in this Chapter's Specifications, starting with the center main and working out toward the ends.

28 Rotate the crankshaft a number of times by hand to check for any obvious binding.

29 The final step is to check the crankshaft endplay with feeler gauges or

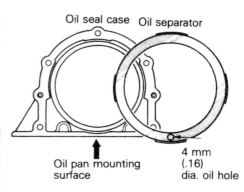

23.1   To remove the old seal, support the housing on a pair of wood blocks and drive out the seal with a punch or screwdriver and hammer – make sure you don't damage the seal bore

23.2a   To install the new rear seal in the housing, simply lay the housing on a clean, flat workbench, lay a block of wood on the seal and carefully tap it into place with a hammer

23.2b   Be sure to mount the oil separator with the oil hole positioned at the bottom

a dial indicator as described in Section 13. The endplay should be correct if the crankshaft thrust faces aren't worn or damaged and new bearings have been installed.

30   Refer to Section 23 and install the new rear main oil seal.

23   Rear main oil seal – installation

Refer to illustrations 23.1, 23.2a, 23.2b and 23.3

Note: *The crankshaft must be installed and the main bearing caps bolted in place before the new seal and housing assembly can be bolted to the block.*

1   Remove the old seal from the housing with a hammer and punch by driving it out from the back side **(see illustration)**. Be sure to note how far it's recessed into the housing bore before removing it; the new seal will have to be recessed an equal amount. Be very careful not to scratch or otherwise damage the bore in the housing or oil leaks could develop.

2   Make sure the housing is clean, then apply a thin coat of engine oil to the outer edge of the new seal. The seal must be pressed squarely into the housing bore, so hammering it into place isn't recommended. If you don't have access to a press, sandwich the housing and seal between two smooth pieces of wood and press the seal into place with the jaws of a

large vise. If you don't have a vise big enough, lay the housing on a work-bench and drive the seal into place with a block of wood and hammer **(see illustration)**. The pieces of wood must be thick enough to distribute the force evenly around the entire circumference of the seal. Work slowly and make sure the seal enters the bore squarely. **Note:** *On 2.0L and 2.4L engines, after the oil seal has been installed press the oil separator into the housing making sure the oil hole is positioned at the bottom* **(see illustration)**

3   Lubricate the seal lips with moly-based grease or engine assembly lube before you slip the seal/housing over the crankshaft and bolt it to the block. Apply anaerobic sealer on the upper portion of the retainer **(see illustration)** before installing the housing.

4   Tighten the housing bolts a little at a time until they're all snug.

24   Pistons and connecting rods – installation and rod bearing oil clearance check

Refer to illustrations 24.4, 24.5, 24.9a, 24.9b, 24.11, 24.13, 24.14 and 24.17

1   Before installing the piston/connecting rod assemblies, the cylinder walls must be perfectly clean, the top edge of each cylinder must be chamfered, and the crankshaft must be in place.

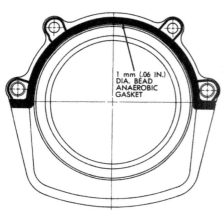

23.3   Apply anaerobic sealer onto the upper portion of the retainer

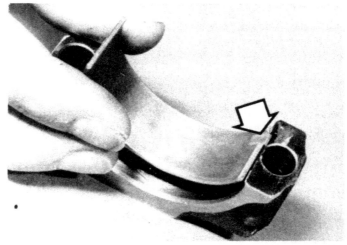

24.4   The tab on the bearing (arrow) must fit into the cap recess so the bearing will seat properly

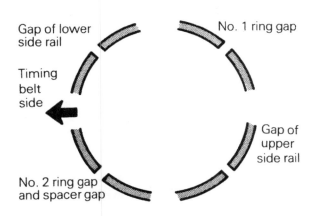

24.5 **Position the ring gaps as shown here before installing the piston/connecting rod assemblies in the engine**

24.9a **On four-cylinder engines, the arrow on the piston must face the front of the engine**

2   Remove the cap from the end of the number one connecting rod (check the marks made during removal). Remove the original bearing inserts and wipe the bearing surfaces of the connecting rod and cap with a clean, lint-free cloth. They must be kept spotlessly clean.

Connecting rod bearing oil clearance check

Note: *Don't touch the faces of the new bearing inserts with your fingers. Oil and acids from your skin can etch the bearings.*

3   Clean the back side of the new upper bearing insert, then lay it in place in the connecting rod. Make sure the tab on the bearing fits into the recess in the rod. Don't hammer the bearing insert into place and be very careful not to nick or gouge the bearing face. Don't lubricate the bearing at this time.

4   Clean the back side of the other bearing insert and install it in the rod cap. Again, make sure the tab on the bearing fits into the recess in the cap **(see illustration)**, and don't apply any lubricant. It's critically important that the mating surfaces of the bearing and connecting rod are perfectly clean and oil free when they're assembled.

5   Position the piston ring gaps at 120-degree intervals around the piston **(see illustration)**.

6   Slip a section of plastic or rubber hose over each connecting rod cap bolt.

7   Lubricate the piston and rings with clean engine oil and attach a piston ring compressor to the piston. Leave the skirt protruding about 1/4-inch to

guide the piston into the cylinder. The rings must be compressed until they're flush with the piston.

8   Rotate the crankshaft until the number one connecting rod journal is at BDC (bottom dead center) and apply a coat of engine oil to the cylinder walls.

9   With the mark or notch on top of the piston facing the front of the engine **(see illustrations)**, gently insert the piston/connecting rod assembly into the number one cylinder bore and rest the bottom edge of the ring compressor on the engine block.

10   Tap the top edge of the ring compressor to make sure it's contacting the block around its entire circumference.

11   Gently tap on the top of the piston with the end of a wooden or plastic hammer handle **(see illustration)** while guiding the end of the connecting rod into place on the crankshaft journal. The piston rings may try to pop out of the ring compressor just before entering the cylinder bore, so keep some downward pressure on the ring compressor. Work slowly, and if any resistance is felt as the piston enters the cylinder, stop immediately. Find out what's hanging up and fix it before proceeding. Do not, for any reason, force the piston into the cylinder – you might break a ring and/or the piston.

12   Once the piston/connecting rod assembly is installed, the connecting rod bearing oil clearance must be checked before the rod cap is permanently bolted in place.

13   Cut a piece of the appropriate size Plastigage slightly shorter than the width of the connecting rod bearing and lay it in place on the number one

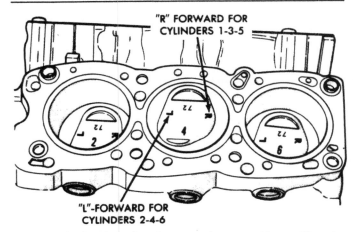

24.9b **On the V6 engine, the proper letter must be positioned towards the front of the engine (R for cylinders 1, 3 and 5; L for cylinders 2, 4 and 6)**

24.11 **Drive the piston gently into the cylinder bore with the end of a wooden or plastic hammer handle**

24.13   Lay the Plastigage strips on each rod bearing journal, parallel to the crankshaft centerline

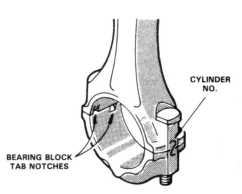

24.14   Match up the cylinder number marks and the bearing tab notches when installing the connecting rod caps

24.17   Measuring the width of the crushed Plastigage to determine the rod bearing oil clearance (be sure to use the correct scale – standard and metric ones are included)

connecting rod journal, parallel with the journal axis **(see illustration)**.

14   Clean the connecting rod cap bearing face, remove the protective hoses from the connecting rod bolts and install the rod cap. Make sure the mating mark on the cap is on the same side as the mark on the connecting rod **(see illustration)**.

15   Install the nuts and tighten them to the torque listed in this Chapter's Specifications. Work up to it in three steps. **Note:** *Use a thin-wall socket to avoid erroneous torque readings that can result if the socket is wedged between the rod cap and nut. If the socket tends to wedge itself between the nut and the cap, lift up on it slightly until it no longer contacts the cap.* Do not rotate the crankshaft at any time during this operation.

16   Remove the nuts and detach the rod cap, being very careful not to disturb the Plastigage.

17   Compare the width of the crushed Plastigage to the scale printed on the Plastigage envelope to obtain the oil clearance **(see illustration)**. Compare it to this Chapter's Specifications to make sure the clearance is correct.

18   If the clearance is not as specified, the bearing inserts may be the wrong size (which means different ones will be required). Before deciding different inserts are needed, make sure no dirt or oil was between the bearing inserts and the connecting rod or cap when the clearance was measured. Also, recheck the journal diameter. If the Plastigage was wider at one end than the other, the journal may be tapered (see Section 18).

Final connecting rod installation

19   Carefully scrape all traces of the Plastigage material off the rod journal and/or bearing face. Be very careful not to scratch the bearing – use your fingernail or the edge of a credit card.

20   Make sure the bearing faces are perfectly clean, then apply a uniform layer of clean moly-base grease or engine assembly lube to both of them. You'll have to push the piston into the cylinder to expose the face of the bearing insert in the connecting rod – be sure to slip the protective hoses over the rod bolts first.

21   Slide the connecting rod back into place on the journal, remove the protective hoses from the rod cap bolts, install the rod cap and tighten the nuts to the torque specified in this Chapter. Again, work up to the torque in three steps. **Note:** *Again, make sure the mating mark on the cap is on the same side as the mark on the connecting rod* **(see illustration 24.14)**.

22   Repeat the entire procedure for the remaining pistons/connecting rods.

23   The important points to remember are . . .
   a) Keep the back sides of the bearing inserts and the insides of the connecting rods and caps perfectly clean when assembling them.
   b) Make sure you have the correct piston/rod assembly for each cylinder.
   c) The arrow or mark on the piston must face the front (timing chain end) of the engine.

   d) Lubricate the cylinder walls with clean oil.
   e) Lubricate the bearing faces when installing the rod caps after the oil clearance has been checked.

24   After all the piston/connecting rod assemblies have been properly installed, rotate the crankshaft a number of times by hand to check for any obvious binding.

25   As a final step, the connecting rod endplay must be checked. Refer to Section 12 for this procedure.

26   Compare the measured endplay to this Chapter's Specifications to make sure it's correct. If it was correct before disassembly and the original crankshaft and rods were reinstalled, it should still be right. If new rods or a new crankshaft were installed, the endplay may be inadequate. If so, the rods will have to be removed and taken to an automotive machine shop for resizing.

---

25   Initial start-up and break-in after overhaul

Warning: *Have a fire extinguisher handy when starting the engine for the first time.*

1   Once the engine has been installed in the vehicle, double-check the engine oil and coolant levels.

2   With the spark plugs out of the engine and the ignition system disabled (see Section 3), crank the engine until oil pressure registers on the gauge or the light goes out.

3   Install the spark plugs, hook up the plug wires and restore the ignition system functions (see Section 3).

4   Start the engine. It may take a few moments for the fuel system to build up pressure, but the engine should start without a great deal of effort. **Note:** *If backfiring occurs through the carburetor or throttle body, recheck the valve timing and ignition timing.*

5   After the engine starts, it should be allowed to warm up to normal operating temperature. While the engine is warming up, make a thorough check for fuel, oil and coolant leaks.

6   Shut the engine off and recheck the engine oil and coolant levels.

7   Drive the vehicle to an area with minimum traffic, accelerate at full throttle from 30 to 50 mph, then allow the vehicle to slow to 30 mph with the throttle closed. Repeat the procedure 10 or 12 times. This will load the piston rings and cause them to seat properly against the cylinder walls. Check again for oil and coolant leaks.

8   Drive the vehicle gently for the first 500 miles (no sustained high speeds) and keep a constant check on the oil level. It isn't unusual for an engine to use oil during the break-in period.

9   At approximately 500 to 600 miles, change the oil and filter.

10   For the next few hundred miles, drive the vehicle normally. Don't pamper it or abuse it.

11   After 2000 miles, change the oil and filter again and consider the engine broken in.

Chapter 3   Cooling, heating and air conditioning systems

Contents

Specifications

General

Coolant type and capacity	See Chapter 1
Thermostat opening temperature	180 to 195-degrees F
Radiator cap pressure rating	12 to 15 psi
Refrigerant capacity	Approx. 25 to 30 ounces

Torque specifications

Ft-lbs (unless otherwise indicated)

Cooling fan bolts	84 to 108 in-lbs
Fan clutch bolts	72 to 84 in-lbs
Water pump bolts	
Small bolts	108 to 132 in-lbs
Large bolts	15 to 20
Coolant temperature switch	22 to 29
Coolant temperature sensor	14 to 29

cold

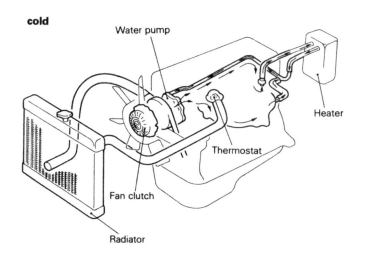

Water pump

Heater

Thermostat

Fan clutch

Radiator

hot

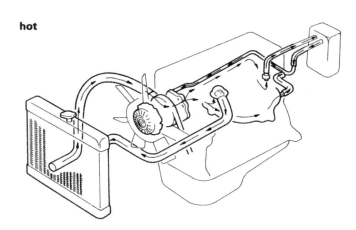

1.2   Coolant flow with the engine cold and hot

1   General information

Refer to illustration 1.2

Engine cooling system

All vehicles covered by this manual employ a pressurized engine cooling system with thermostatically controlled coolant circulation. An impeller-type water pump mounted on the front of the block pumps coolant through the engine. The coolant flows around each cylinder and toward the rear of the engine. Cast-in coolant passages direct coolant around the intake and exhaust ports, near the spark plug areas and in close proximity to the exhaust valve guides.

A wax pellet-type thermostat is located in a housing near the front of the engine. During warm-up, the closed thermostat prevents coolant from circulating through the radiator. As the engine nears normal operating temperature, the thermostat opens and allows hot coolant to travel through the radiator, where it's cooled before returning to the engine **(see illustration)**.

The cooling system is sealed by a pressure type radiator cap, which raises the boiling point of the coolant and increases the cooling efficiency of the radiator. If the system pressure exceeds the cap pressure relief value, the excess pressure in the system forces the spring-loaded valve inside the cap off its seat and allows the coolant to escape through the overflow tube into a coolant reservoir. When the system cools the excess coolant is automatically drawn from the reservoir back into the radiator.

The coolant reservoir does double duty as both the point at which fresh coolant is added to the cooling system to maintain the proper fluid level and as a holding tank for overheated coolant.

This type of cooling system is known as a closed design because coolant that escapes past the pressure cap is saved and reused.

Heating system

The heating system consists of a blower fan and heater core located in the heater box, the hoses connecting the heater core to the engine cooling system and the heater/air conditioning control head on the dashboard. Hot engine coolant is circulated through the heater core. When the heater mode is activated, a flap door opens to expose the heater box to the passenger compartment. A fan switch on the control head activates the blower motor, which forces air through the core, heating the air.

Air conditioning system

The air conditioning system consists of a condenser mounted in front of the radiator, an evaporator mounted adjacent to the heater core, a compressor mounted on the engine, a receiver/drier which contains a high-pressure relief valve and the plumbing connecting all of the above components.

A blower fan forces the warmer air of the passenger compartment through the evaporator core (sort of a radiator-in-reverse), transferring the heat from the air to the refrigerant. The liquid refrigerant boils off into low pressure vapor, taking the heat with it when it leaves the evaporator.

2   Antifreeze – general information

Warning: *Do not allow antifreeze to come in contact with your skin or painted surfaces of the vehicle. Rinse off spills immediately with plenty of water. If consumed, antifreeze can be fatal; children and pets are attracted by its sweet taste, so wipe up garage floor and drip pan coolant spills immediately. Keep antifreeze containers covered and repair leaks in your cooling system as soon as they are noticed.*

The cooling system should be filled with a water/ethylene glycol-based antifreeze solution, which will prevent freezing down to at least -20-degrees F, or lower if local climate requires it. It also provides protection against corrosion and increases the coolant boiling point.

The cooling system should be drained, flushed and refilled at the specified intervals (see Chapter 1). Old or contaminated antifreeze solutions are likely to cause damage and encourage the formation of rust and scale in the system. Use distilled water with the antifreeze.

Before adding antifreeze, check all hose connections, because antifreeze tends to leak through very minute openings. Engines don't normally consume coolant, so if the level goes down, find the cause and correct it.

The exact mixture of antifreeze-to-water which you should use depends on the relative weather conditions. The mixture should contain at least 50 percent antifreeze, but should never contain more than 70 percent antifreeze. Consult the mixture ratio chart on the antifreeze container before adding coolant. Hydrometers are available at most auto parts stores to test the coolant. Use antifreeze which meets the vehicle manufacturer's specifications.

3   Thermostat – check and replacement

Warning: *Do not remove the radiator cap, drain the coolant or replace the thermostat until the engine has cooled completely.*

Check

1   Before assuming the thermostat is to blame for a cooling system problem, check the coolant level, water pump (see Section 7), drivebelt tension (see Chapter 1) and temperature gauge (or light) operation.

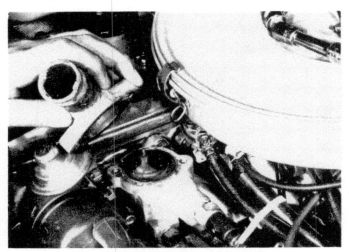

3.10a   Removing the thermostat housing

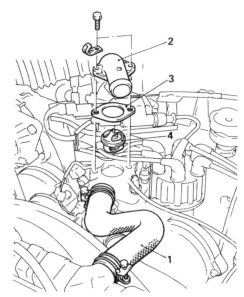

3.10c   Thermostat installation details (3.0L engine)

1 Upper radiator hose	3 Gasket
2 Thermostat housing	4 Thermostat

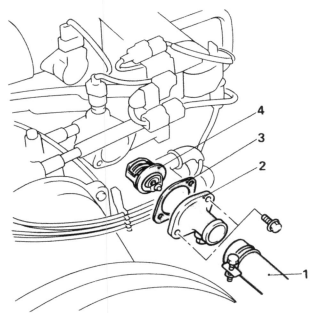

3.10b   Thermostat installation details (2.0L and 2.4L engines)

1 Upper radiator hose	3 Gasket
2 Thermostat housing	4 Thermostat

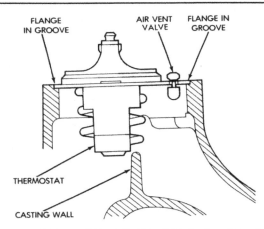

3.13   Thermostat installation (2.6L engine shown)

2   If the engine seems to be taking a long time to warm up (based on heater output or temperature gauge operation), the thermostat is probably stuck open. Replace the thermostat with a new one.

3   If the engine runs hot, use your hand to check the temperature of the upper radiator hose. If the hose isn't hot, but the engine is, the thermostat is probably stuck closed, preventing the coolant inside the engine from escaping to the radiator. Replace the thermostat. **Caution:** *Don't drive the vehicle without a thermostat. The computer may stay in open loop and emissions and fuel economy will suffer.*

4   If the upper radiator hose is hot, it means that the coolant is flowing and the thermostat is open. Consult the *Troubleshooting* Section at the front of this manual for cooling system diagnosis.

Replacement

Refer to illustrations 3.10a, 3.10b, 3.10c and 3.13

5   Disconnect the negative battery cable from the battery.

6   Drain the cooling system (see Chapter 1). If the coolant is relatively new or in good condition (see Chapter 1), save it and reuse it.

7   Follow the upper radiator hose to the engine to locate the thermostat housing.

8   Loosen the hose clamp, then detach the hose from the fitting. If it's stuck, grasp it near the end with a pair of Channelock pliers and twist it to break the seal, then pull it off. If the hose is old or deteriorated, cut it off and install a new one.

9   If the outer surface of the large fitting that mates with the hose is deteriorated (corroded, pitted, etc.) it may be damaged further by hose removal. If it is, the thermostat housing cover will have to be replaced.

10   Remove the bolts and detach the housing cover **(see illustrations)**. If the cover is stuck, tap it with a soft-face hammer to jar it loose. Be prepared for some coolant to spill as the gasket seal is broken.

11   Note how it's installed (which end is facing up), then remove the thermostat.

12   Stuff a rag into the engine opening, then remove all traces of old gasket material and sealant from the housing and cover with a gasket scraper. Remove the rag from the opening and clean the gasket mating surfaces with lacquer thinner or acetone.

13   Install the new thermostat in the housing. Make sure the correct end faces up – the spring end is normally directed into the engine **(see illustration)**.

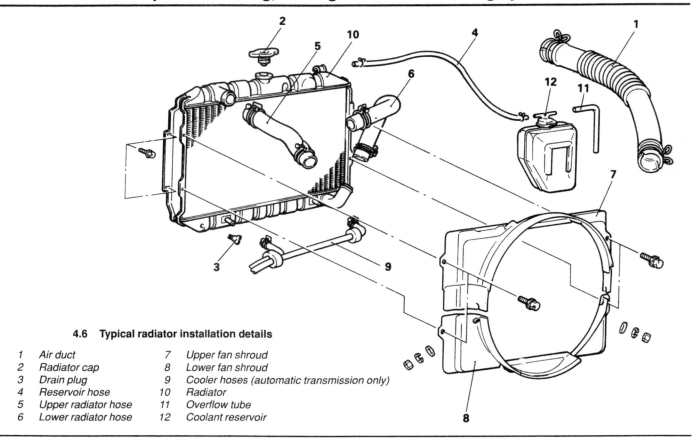

4.6 Typical radiator installation details

1	Air duct	7	Upper fan shroud
2	Radiator cap	8	Lower fan shroud
3	Drain plug	9	Cooler hoses (automatic transmission only)
4	Reservoir hose	10	Radiator
5	Upper radiator hose	11	Overflow tube
6	Lower radiator hose	12	Coolant reservoir

14   Apply a thin, uniform layer of RTV sealant to both sides of the new gasket and position it on the housing.
15   Install the cover and bolts. Tighten the bolts to the torque listed in this Chapter's Specifications.
16   Reattach the hose to the fitting and tighten the hose clamp securely.
17   Refill the cooling system (see Chapter 1).
18   Start the engine and allow it to reach normal operating temperature, then check for leaks and proper thermostat operation (as described in Steps 2 through 4).

4   Radiator – removal and installation

Refer to illustration 4.6
Warning: *Wait until the engine is completely cool before beginning this procedure.*
1   Disconnect the negative battery cable from the battery.
2   Drain the cooling system (see Chapter 1). If the coolant is relatively new or in good condition, save it and reuse it. If necessary for clearance, remove the air duct.
3   Loosen the hose clamps, then detach the radiator hoses from the fittings. If they're stuck, grasp each hose near the end with a pair of adjustable pliers and twist it to break the seal, then pull it off – be careful not to distort the radiator fittings! If the hoses are old or deteriorated, cut them off and install new ones.
4   Disconnect the reservoir hose from the radiator filler neck.
5   If equipped, remove the screws that attach the upper fan shroud to the radiator and slide the shroud toward the engine. Remove the lower shroud, on models so equipped.
6   If the vehicle is equipped with an automatic transmission, disconnect the cooler hoses from the radiator **(see illustration)**. Use a drip pan to catch spilled fluid.
7   Plug the lines and fittings
8   Remove the radiator mounting bolts.

9   Carefully lift out the radiator. Don't spill coolant on the vehicle or scratch the paint.
10   With the radiator removed, it can be inspected for leaks and damage. If it needs repair, have a radiator shop or dealer service department perform the work as special techniques are required.
11   Bugs and dirt can be removed from the radiator with compressed air and a soft brush. Don't bend the cooling fins as this is done.
12   Check the radiator mounts for deterioration and make sure there's nothing in them when the radiator is installed.
13   Installation is the reverse of the removal procedure.
14   After installation, fill the cooling system with the proper mixture of antifreeze and water. Refer to Chapter 1 if necessary.
15   Start the engine and check for leaks. Allow the engine to reach normal operating temperature, indicated by the upper radiator hose becoming hot. Recheck the coolant level and add more if required.
16   If you're working on an automatic transmission equipped vehicle, check and add fluid as needed.

5   Engine cooling fan and clutch – check and replacement

Warning: *To avoid possible injury or damage, DO NOT operate the engine with a damaged fan. Do not attempt to repair fan blades – replace a damaged fan with a new one.*

Check

1   Disconnect the negative battery cable and rock the fan back and forth by hand to check for excessive bearing play.
2   With the engine cold, turn the fan blades by hand. The fan should turn freely.
3   Visually inspect for substantial fluid leakage from the clutch assembly. If problems are noted, replace the clutch assembly.
4   With the engine completely warmed up, turn off the ignition switch and disconnect the negative battery cable from the battery. Turn the fan by hand. Some drag should be evident. If the fan turns easily, replace the fan clutch.

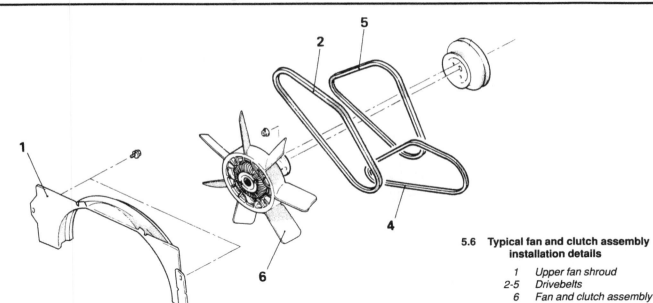

5.6   **Typical fan and clutch assembly installation details**

    1   Upper fan shroud
    2-5 Drivebelts
    6   Fan and clutch assembly

Replacement

Refer to illustration 5.6

5   Disconnect the negative battery cable. Remove the fan shroud mounting screws and detach the shroud **(see illustration 4.6)**.

6   Remove the bolts/nuts attaching the fan/clutch assembly to the water pump hub **(see illustration)**.

7   Lift the fan/clutch assembly (and shroud, if necessary) out of the engine compartment.

8   Carefully inspect the fan blades for damage and defects. Replace it if necessary.

9   At this point, the fan may be unbolted from the clutch, if necessary. If the fan clutch is stored, position it with the radiator side facing down.

10   Installation is the reverse of removal Be sure to tighten the fan and clutch mounting nuts/bolts evenly and securely.

6   Coolant reservoir – removal and installation

1   The coolant reservoir is located on the right fenderwell. It should be removed periodically and checked for cracks and other damage, and flushed with clean water. **Note:** *On 1990 and later models, the reservoir is located on the left fenderwell.*

2   To remove the reservoir, carefully pry off the cap with the hose attached and lay the cap aside.

3   Pull out the reservoir and simultaneously pull up and slide the reservoir off its mount.

4   To install the reservoir, line it up with the mount and push down until it is properly seated. Don't forget to install the cap.

7   Water pump – check

Refer to illustration 7.5

1   A failure in the water pump can cause serious engine damage due to overheating.

2   There are three ways to check the operation of the water pump while it's installed on the engine. If the pump is defective, it should be replaced with a new or rebuilt unit.

3   With the engine running at normal operating temperature, squeeze the upper radiator hose. If the water pump is working properly, a pressure surge should be felt as the hose is released. **Warning:** *Keep your hands away from the fan blades!*

7.5   **Grasp the water pump flange and try to rock the shaft back and forth to check for play (fan and pulley shown removed for clarity)**

4   Water pumps are equipped with weep or vent holes. If a failure occurs in the pump seal, coolant will leak from the hole. In most cases you'll need a flashlight to find the hole on the water pump from underneath to check for leaks.

5   If the water pump shaft bearings fail, there may be a howling sound at the front of the engine while it's running. Shaft wear can be felt if the water pump pulley is rocked up and down **(see illustration)**. Don't mistake drivebelt slippage, which causes a squealing sound, for water bearing failure.

8   Water pump – replacement

2.6L engine

Removal

Refer to illustration 8.8

Warning: *Wait until the engine is completely cool before beginning this procedure.*

1   Disconnect the negative battery cable from the battery.

2   Drain the cooling system (see Chapter 1). If the coolant is relatively new or in good condition, save it and reuse it.

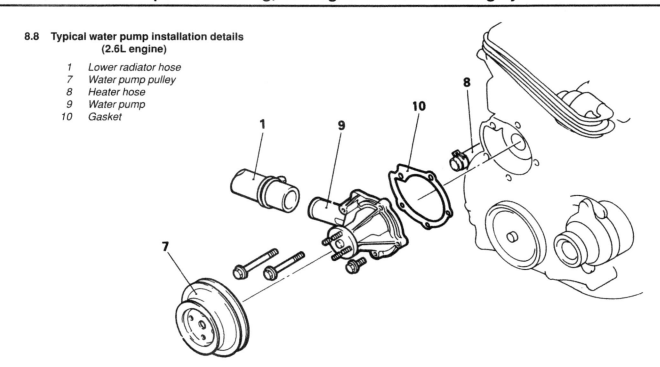

8.8   Typical water pump installation details (2.6L engine)

1   Lower radiator hose
7   Water pump pulley
8   Heater hose
9   Water pump
10 Gasket

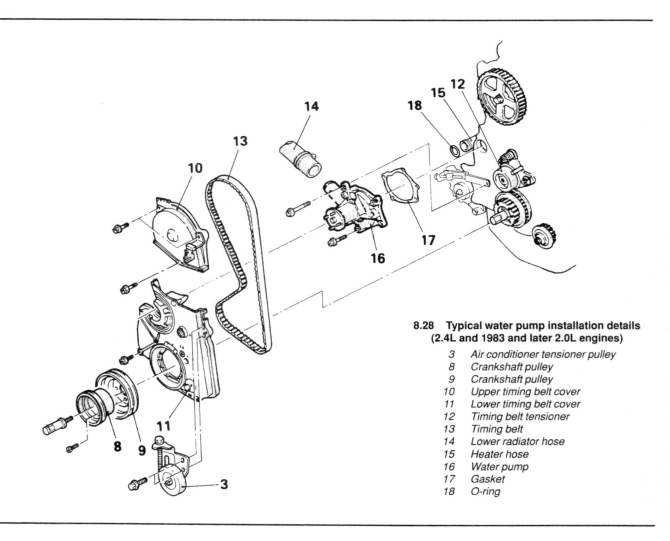

8.28   Typical water pump installation details (2.4L and 1983 and later 2.0L engines)

3   Air conditioner tensioner pulley
8   Crankshaft pulley
9   Crankshaft pulley
10 Upper timing belt cover
11 Lower timing belt cover
12 Timing belt tensioner
13 Timing belt
14 Lower radiator hose
15 Heater hose
16 Water pump
17 Gasket
18 O-ring

3   Remove the cooling fan and clutch assembly (see Section 5).
4   Disconnect and remove the lower radiator hose and heater hose.
5   Remove the drivebelts (see Chapter 1). **Note:** *To remove the air conditioning belt, completely remove the adjustment bracket assembly.*
6   Remove the cooling fan and water pump pulley.
7   Remove the alternator bracket from the water pump.
8   Remove the bolts and detach the water pump from the engine. Note the locations of the various lengths and different types of bolts as they're removed to ensure correct installation **(see illustration)**.

Installation

9   Clean the bolt threads and the threaded holes in the engine to remove corrosion and sealant.
10   Compare the new pump to the old one to make sure they're identical.
11   Remove all traces of old gasket material from the engine with a gasket scraper.
12   Clean the engine and new water pump mating surfaces with lacquer thinner or acetone.
13   Apply a thin coat of RTV sealant to the engine side of the new gasket and to the gasket mating surface of the new pump, then carefully mate the gasket and the pump. Slip a couple of bolts through the pump mounting holes to hold the gasket in place.
14   Carefully attach the pump and gasket to the engine and thread the bolts into the holes finger tight. Note that the bolt on the left side of the pump (that attaches the alternator brace) is longer than the other four bolts. Be sure to install the bolt(s) with the correct length into the corresponding water pump holes.
15   Place the alternator bracket in position, install the bolts and tighten all the bolts to the torque listed in this Chapter's Specifications in 1/4-turn increments. Don't overtighten them or the pump may be distorted.
16   Reinstall all parts removed for access to the pump.
17   Refill the cooling system and check the drivebelt tension (see Chapter 1). Run the engine and check for leaks.

2.0L, 2.4L and 3.0L engines

Removal

Refer to illustration 8.28

Warning: *Wait until the engine is completely cool before beginning this procedure.*

18   Disconnect the negative battery cable from the battery.
19   Drain the cooling system (see Chapter 1). If the coolant is relatively new or in good condition, save it and reuse it.
20   Remove the radiator fan shroud (see Section 4).
21   Remove the drivebelts (see Chapter 1).
22   Remove the air conditioner tensioner pulley.
23   Remove the fan and fan clutch (see Section 5).
24   Remove the water pump pulley.
25   Remove the crankshaft pulleys (see Chapter 2, Part B).
26   Remove the timing belts (see Chapter 2, Part B).
27   Remove the lower radiator hose from the water pump. If it's stuck, grasp it near the end with a pair of adjustable pliers and twist it to break the seal, then pull it off. If the hose is old or deteriorated, cut it off and install a new one.
28   Remove the bolts and detach the water pump **(see illustration)**. Note the locations and various lengths and different types of bolts as they're removed to ensure correct installation.

Installation

29   Clean the bolt threads and the threaded holes in the engine to remove any corrosion and sealant.
30   Compare the new pump to the old one to make sure they're identical.
31   Remove all traces of old gasket material from the engine with a gasket scraper.
32   Clean the engine and new water pump mating surfaces with lacquer thinner or acetone.
33   Install a new O-ring in the groove at the front end of the coolant pipe and lubricate the O-ring with coolant.

34   Apply a thin coat of RTV sealant to the engine side of the new gasket and to the gasket mating surface of the new pump, then carefully mate the gasket and the pump. Slip a couple of bolts through the pump mounting hole to hold the gasket in place.
35   Carefully attach the pump and gasket to the engine and thread the bolts into the holes finger tight. Be sure to install the bolts with the correct length into the corresponding water pump holes.
36   Tighten all bolts to the torque listed in this Chapter's Specifications in 1/4-turn increments. Don't overtighten them or the pump may be distorted.
37   Refer to Chapter 2, part B for the installation of the timing belt(s).
38   Installation of all parts removed is the reverse of removal.
39   Refill the cooling system and check the drivebelt tension (see Chapter 1). Run the engine and check for leaks.

9   Coolant temperature gauge sending unit – check and replacement

Warning: *Wait until the engine is completely cool before beginning this procedure.*

1   The coolant temperature indicator system is composed of a light or temperature gauge mounted in the instrument panel and a coolant temperature sending unit mounted on the engine. Some vehicles have more than one sending unit, but only one is used for the indicator system.
2   If an overheating indication occurs, check the coolant level in the system and then make sure the wiring between the light or gauge and the sending unit is secure and all fuses are intact.
3   When the ignition switch is turned on and the starter motor is turning, the indicator light should be on (overheated engine indication).
4   If the light is not on, the bulb may be burned out, the ignition switch may be faulty or the circuit may be open. Test the circuit by grounding the wire to the sending unit while the ignition is on (engine not running for safety). If the gauge deflects full scale or the light comes on, replace the sending unit.
5   As soon as the engine starts, the light should go out and remain out unless the engine overheats. Failure of the light to go out may be due to a grounded wire between the light and the sending unit, a defective sending unit or a faulty ignition switch. Check the coolant to make sure it's the proper type. Plain water may have too low a boiling point to activate the sending unit.
6   If the sending unit must be replaced, simply unscrew it from the engine and install the replacement. Use sealant on the threads. Make sure the engine is cool before removing the defective sending unit. There will be some coolant loss as the unit is removed, so be prepared to catch it. Check the level after the replacement has been installed.

10   Heating system – general information

Refer to illustrations 10.1a and 10.1b

The main components of the heating system include the heater unit (which contains the heater core and cable-operated valves) the blower motor, the control assembly (mounted in the dash) and the air ducts which deliver the air to the various outlet locations **(see illustrations)**.

Either outside air or interior (recirculated) air (depending on the settings) is drawn into the system through the blower unit. From there the blower motor forces the air into the heater unit.

The lever settings on the control assembly operate the valves in the heater unit, which determines the mix of heated and outside air by regulating how much air is passed through the heater core. The hotter the setting the more air is passed through core.

The air ducts carry the heated air from the heater unit to the desired location. Again, valves within the duct system regulate where in the vehicle the air will be delivered.

The heater core is heated by engine coolant passing through it. The heater hoses carry the coolant from the engine to the heater core and then back again.

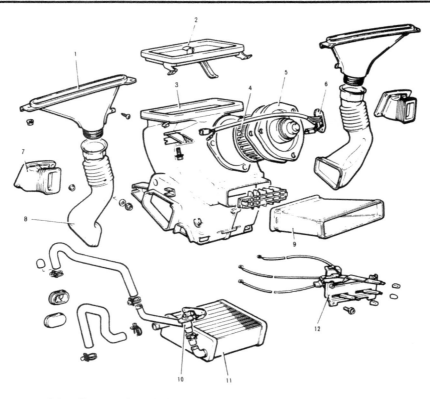

10.1a   Heater unit and related components (1987 and earlier models)

1	Defroster nozzle	4	Turbo fan	7	Side ventilator duct	10	Water valve
2	Ventilator bezel	5	Blower motor	8	Defroster duct	11	Heater core
3	Heater assembly	6	Heater resistor	9	Center ventilator duct	12	Heater control panel assembly

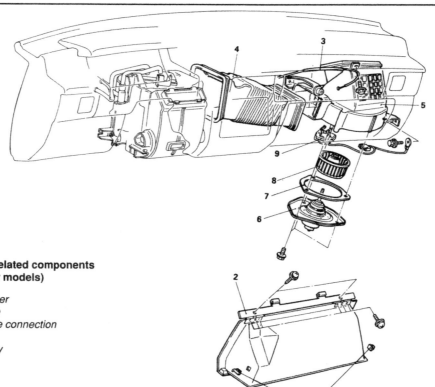

10.1b   Heater unit and related components
(1988 and later models)

1   Glove box stopper
2   Glove box frame
3   Air selection wire connection
4   Duct
5   Blower assembly
6   Blower motor
7   Gasket
8   Fan
9   Resistor block

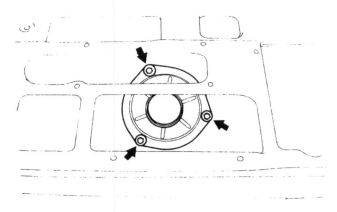

11.4   The blower motor is secured by three bolts (arrows)

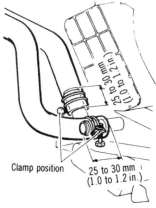

12.7   Heater hose connections (pre-1988 models)

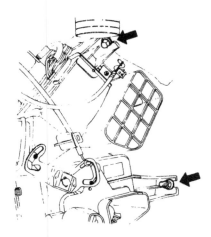

12.9   Heater assembly attaching bolts and nuts (arrows) (pre-1988 models)

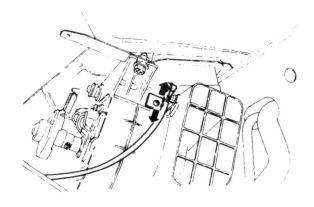

12.14a   To adjust the INSIDE/OUTSIDE air control cable, move the cable housing in the securing clip (pre-1988 models)

11   Blower motor – removal and installation

Refer to illustration 11.4

1   The blower motor is attached to the heater assembly so it is automatically removed when the heater assembly is removed. It can also be taken out as a separate unit.
2   On 1987 and earlier models, remove the center console (if so equipped – see Chapter 11), the center panel and the center ventilator grille and duct **(see illustration 10.1a)**. On 1988 and later models, it may be necessary to remove the glove box for access to the blower motor **(see illustration 10.1b)**.
3   Unplug the motor electrical connector(s).
4   Remove the three bolts attaching the motor to the heater assembly, then lift out the motor and fan **(see illustration)**.
5   Installation is the reverse of removal.

12   Heater core – removal and installation

1987 and earlier models

Refer to illustrations 12.7, 12.9, 12.14a, 12.14b and 12.14c

1   To gain access to the heater core, the heater assembly should be removed from the vehicle.
2   Disconnect the negative battery cable from the battery.
3   Drain the cooling system (see Chapter 1).

4   Remove the center console (see Chapter 11).
5   Remove the center panel and the center ventilator bezel **(see illustration 10.1a)**.

6   Disconnect the heater control cables at the heater assembly (not at the control assembly).
7   Disconnect the heater hoses at the heater core. Use some rags near the hoses when disconnecting the hoses to catch any coolant that may run out **(see illustration)**. Then plug the hoses and the inlets and outlets on the heater core.
8   Unplug the blower motor wiring connectors.
9   Remove the two mounting bolts from the top and the two mounting nuts from the center of the heater assembly **(see illustration)**.
10   Carefully lift out the heater assembly out of its mounting position.
11   Use a flat-bladed screwdriver to remove the clips holding the heater assembly together, then remove the heater core.
12   Repair and cleaning of the heater core should be done by a radiator repair shop, or replace it with a new one.
13   Installation is the reverse of removal.
14   Adjust the heater control cables **(see illustrations)**.
15   After the heater assembly is in place, fill the cooling system (see Chapter 1).
16   Place the heater control in the HOT position. Start the engine and allow it to run to circulate the coolant to eliminate any air from the cooling system.
17   Add coolant as the level drops. Once the level has stabilized install the radiator pressure cap and check for leaks.

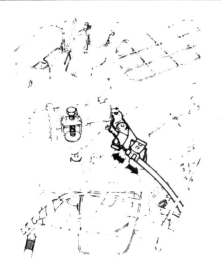

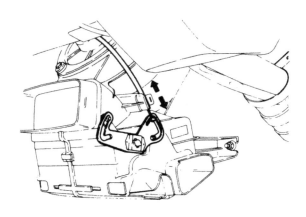

12.14b   The control valve should be fully closed (lever "up") with the heater control lever in the OFF position (move the cable housing in the securing clip to adjust it) (pre-1988 models)

12.14c   To adjust the DEF-HEAT-VENT damper, move the cable housing in the securing clip (pre-1988 models)

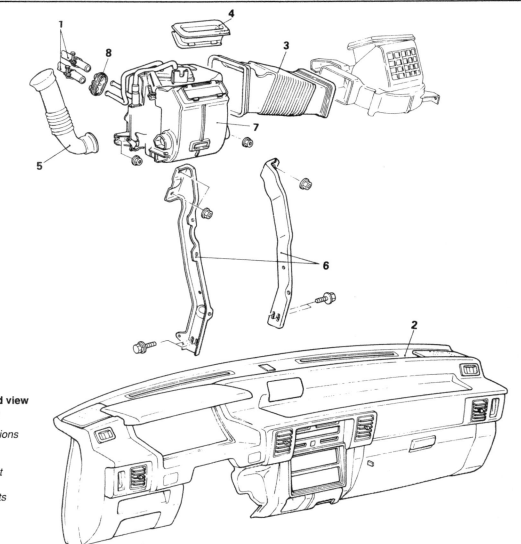

12.19   Heater unit – exploded view (1988 and later models)

1   Heater hose connections
2   Instrument panel
3   Main duct
4   Center ventilator duct
5   Defroster duct
6   Center reinforcements
7   Heater unit
8   Grommet

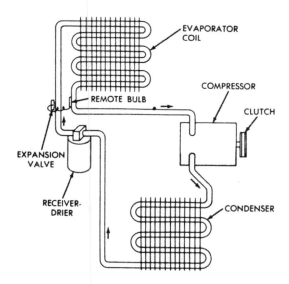

13.3 A typical air conditioning system schematic

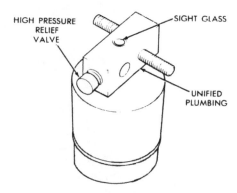

14.7 Watch the receiver/drier sight glass and see if it looks clear inside (which is normal) – if it's foamy inside, the system needs recharging

1988 and later models

Refer to illustration 12.19

18 To remove the heater core, the heater unit must be removed from the vehicle.

19 Working inside the engine compartment, disconnect the heater hoses from the heater unit **(see illustration)**. Place rags under the hose connections to catch spilled coolant. After disconnecting the hoses, plug them and the heater unit tubes.

20 Remove the instrument panel (see Chapter 11).

21 Remove the main duct.

22 Remove the center ventilator duct.

23 Remove the defroster duct.

24 Unbolt the center reinforcements (four bolts at the bottom and four nuts at the top) and remove the heater unit

25 If the heater unit is a split-type, remove the clips that hold the two halves of the heater unit together, then separate the halves and remove the heater core.

26 If the heater unit cannot be split, remove the bolt from the joint hose clamp, cut off the joint hose and remove the heater core.

27 Installation is the reverse of removal.

28 After the heater assembly is in place, fill the cooling system (see Chapter 1).

29 Place the heater control in the HOT position. Start the engine and allow it to run to circulate the coolant to eliminate any air from the cooling system.

30 Add coolant as the level drops. Once the level has stabilized install the radiator pressure cap and check for leaks.

13 Air conditioning system – general information

Refer to illustration 13.3

Warning: *The air conditioning system is under high pressure. Do not loosen any hose fitting or remove any components until after the system has been discharged by a service station or automotive air conditioning shop. Always wear eye protection when disconnecting air conditioning fittings.*

The air conditioning system used in these vehicles maintains proper temperature by cycling the compressor on and off according to the pressure within the system, and by maintaining a mix of cooled, outside and heated air, using the same blower, heater core and outlet duct system that the heating system uses.

A fast-idle control device regulates idle speed when the air conditioner is operating.

The main components of the system include a belt-driven compressor, a condenser (mounted in front of the radiator), a receiver/drier and an evaporator **(see illustration)**.

The system operates by air (outside or recirculated) entering the evaporator core by the action of the blower motor, where it receives cooling. When the air leaves the evaporator, it enters the heater/air conditioner duct assembly and, by means of a manually controlled deflector, either passes through or bypasses the heater core in the correct proportions to provide the desired vehicle temperature.

Distribution of this air into the vehicle is regulated by a manually operated deflector, and is directed either to the floor vents, dash vents or defroster vents according to settings.

14 Air conditioning system – check and maintenance

Refer to illustrations 14.7 and 14.12

Warning: *The air conditioning system is under high pressure. Do not loosen any fittings or remove any components until after the system has been discharged. Air conditioning refrigerant should be properly discharged into an EPA-approved container at a dealer service department or an automotive air conditioning repair facility. Always wear eye protection when disconnecting air conditioning system fittings*

1 The following maintenance checks should be performed on a regular basis to ensure that the air conditioner continues to operate at peak efficiency.

   a) Check the compressor drivebelt. If it's worn or deteriorated, replace it (see Chapter 1).

   b) Check the drivebelt tension and, if necessary, adjust it (see Chapter 1).

   c) Check the system hoses. Look for cracks, bubbles, hard spots and deterioration. Inspect the hoses and all fittings for oil bubbles and seepage. If there's any evidence of wear, damage or leaks, replace the hose(s).

   d) Inspect the condenser fins for leaves, bugs and other debris. Use a "fin comb" or compressed air to clean the condenser.

   e) Make sure the system has the correct refrigerant charge.

2 It's a good idea to operate the system for about 10 minutes at least once a month, particularly during the winter. Long term non-use can cause hardening, and subsequent failure, of the seals.

3 Because of the complexity of the air conditioning system and the special equipment necessary to service it, in-depth troubleshooting and repairs are not included in this manual. However, simple checks and component replacement procedures are provided in this Chapter. For more complete information on the air conditioning system, refer to the *Haynes automotive heating and air conditioning* manual.

14.12   Place a thermometer in the right-side dashboard vent to monitor cooling

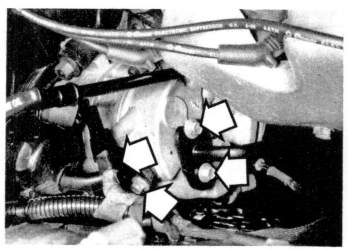

16.5a   Remove these four bolts (arrows) to disconnect the refrigerant lines from the compressor (far left bolt hidden from view by connector) (1987 and earlier models)

4   The most common cause of poor cooling is simply a low system refrigerant charge. If a noticeable drop in cool air output occurs, the following quick check will help you determine if the refrigerant level is low.

5   Warm the engine up to normal operating temperature.

6   Place the air conditioning temperature selector at the coldest setting and put the blower at the highest setting. Open the doors (to make sure the air conditioning system doesn't cycle off as soon as it cools the passenger compartment).

7   With the compressor engaged – the clutch will make an audible click and the center of the clutch will rotate – inspect the sight glass, if equipped, which is located on the receiver/drier **(see illustration)**. If the refrigerant looks foamy, it's low. Have a dealer service department or licensed air conditioning repair facility charge the system.

8   If there's no sight glass, feel the inlet and outlet pipes at the compressor. One side should be cold and one hot. If there's no perceptible difference between the two pipes, there's something wrong with the compressor or the system. It might be a low charge – it might be something else. Take the vehicle to a dealer service department or an automotive air conditioning shop.

---

15   Air conditioning receiver/drier – removal and installation

---

Warning: *The air conditioning system is under high pressure. DO NOT disassemble any part of the system (hoses, compressor, line fittings, etc.) until after the system has been depressurized by a dealer service department or service station.*

1   The receiver/drier, which acts as a reservoir for the refrigerant, is the cannister-shaped object mounted either in the engine compartment or in front of the condenser **(see illustration 14.7)**.

2   Before removing the receiver/drier, the system must be discharged by an conditioning technician (see *Warning* above). DO NOT attempt to do this yourself; the refrigerant used in the system can cause serious injuries and respiratory irritation.

3   Loosen the hose clamps and remove both hoses from the receiver/drier.

4   loosen the clamp and pull up on the receiver/receiver to remove it from its mount.

5   When installing the receiver/drier, lubricate the inside surfaces of the hoses and the outside of the fittings with refrigerant oil. Be sure the hose clamps are properly located by the clamp finders and securely tightened.

6   Have the system evacuated, recharged and leak tested by the shop that discharged it.

---

16   Air conditioning system compressor – removal and installation

---

Refer to illustrations 16.5a and 16.5b

Warning: *The air conditioning system is under high pressure. DO NOT disassemble any part of the system (hoses, compressor, line fittings, etc.) until after the system has been depressurized by a dealer service department or service station.*

1   Have the air conditioning system discharged (see *Warning* above).

2   Disconnect the negative battery cable from the battery.

3   Disconnect the compressor clutch wiring harness.

4   Remove the drivebelt (see Chapter 1).

5   Disconnect the refrigerant lines from the rear of the compressor. Plug the open fittings to prevent entry of dirt and moisture **(see illustrations)**.

6   Unbolt the compressor from the mounting brackets and lift it out of the vehicle.

7   If a new compressor is being installed, follow the directions with the compressor regarding the draining of excess oil prior to installation.

8   The clutch may have to be transferred from the original to the new compressor.

9   Installation is the reverse of removal. Replace all O-rings with new ones specifically made for air conditioning system use and lubricate them with refrigerant oil.

10   Have the system evacuated, recharged and leak tested by the shop that discharged it.

---

17   Air conditioning system condenser – removal and installation

---

Warning: *The air conditioning system is under high pressure. DO NOT disassemble any part of the system (hoses, compressor, line fittings, etc.) until after the system has been depressurized by a dealer service department or service station.*

1   Have the air conditioning system discharged (see *Warning* above).

2   Remove the battery (see Chapter 5).

3   Drain the cooling system (see Chapter 1).

4   Remove the radiator (see Chapter 3).

5   Disconnect the refrigerant lines from the condenser **(see illustration 16.5b)**.

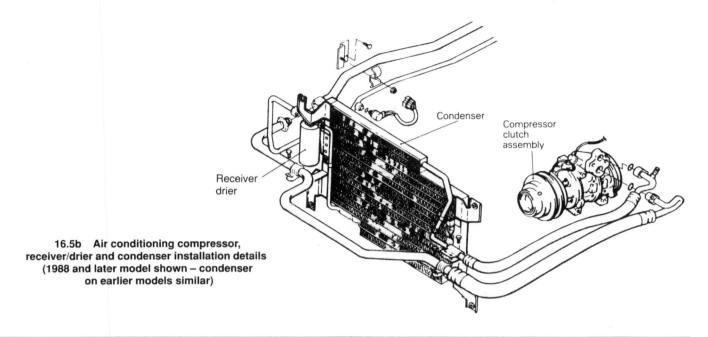

16.5b   Air conditioning compressor, receiver/drier and condenser installation details (1988 and later model shown – condenser on earlier models similar)

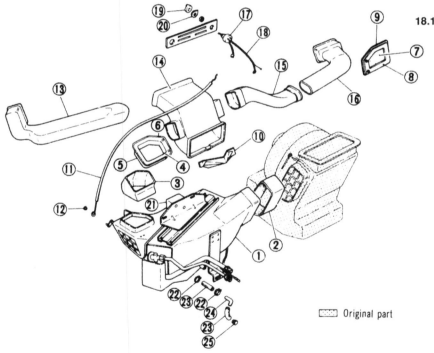

Original part

18.1a   Evaporator assembly and related components (pre-1988 models)

1   Evaporator assembly
2   Sleeve duct
3   Fresh air duct
4   Fresh air cover gasket (right)
5   Fresh air cover (right)
6   Original part
7   Fresh air cover (left)
8   Fresh air cover gasket (left)
9   Original part
10   Baffle
11   Cable
12   Clip
13   Duct (right)
14   Center duct
15   Left lower duct
16   Left upper duct
17   Fan and temperature switch
18   Wiring harness
19   Fan knob
20   Temperature knob
21   Thermistor control box
22   Drain clamp
23   Drain hose
24   90-degree elbow
25   Drain restrictor

6   Remove the mounting bolts from the condenser brackets.
7   Lift the condenser out of the vehicle and plug the lines to keep dirt and moisture out.
8   If the original condenser will be reinstalled, store it with the line fittings on top to prevent oil from draining out.
9   If a new condenser is being installed, pour one ounce of refrigerant oil into it prior to installation.
10   Reinstall the components in the reverse order of removal. Be sure the rubber pads are in place under the condenser.
11   Have the system evacuated, recharged and leak tested by the shop that discharged it.

18   Air conditioning system evaporator – removal and installation

Refer to illustrations 18.1a, 18.1b, 18.9a and 18.9b

1   The air conditioner evaporator is combined with the heater assembly and is mounted under the right side of the vehicle dashboard (**see illustrations**).
2   Before removing the evaporator, the system must be depressurized by an air conditioning technician. DO NOT attempt to do this yourself; the refrigerant used in the system can cause serious injuries and respiratory irritation.

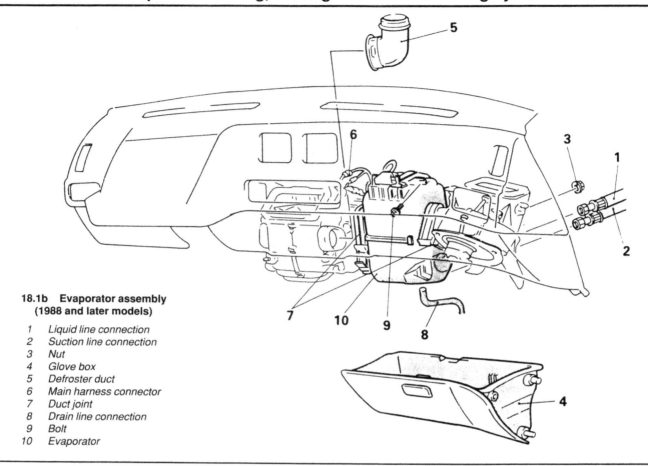

**18.1b   Evaporator assembly
(1988 and later models)**

1   Liquid line connection
2   Suction line connection
3   Nut
4   Glove box
5   Defroster duct
6   Main harness connector
7   Duct joint
8   Drain line connection
9   Bolt
10   Evaporator

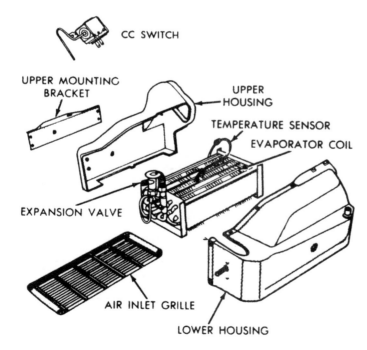

**18.9c   Evaporator assembly – exploded view
(pre-1988 models)**

3   On later models, remove the glove box (see Chapter 11).
4   Loosen the hose clamps and remove the hoses from the evaporator fittings inside the engine compartment.
5   Disconnect the control cable from the damper lever at the right side of the evaporator.
6   Slide back the hose clamp and remove the drain hose from the spigot at the rear of the evaporator.
7   Peel off the sealing compound around the evaporator inlet and outlet tubes at the vehicle fire wall
8   Remove the bolts attaching the evaporator to the dashboard and firewall and carefully move it down and out from the dashboard. Do not misplace the plastic duct that fits between the heater assembly and the evaporator.
9   Use a flat-bladed screwdriver to remove the clips from the evaporator housing and remove the evaporator **(see illustrations)**.
10   Installation is the reverse of removal. Be sure to position the plastic ducts before slipping the evaporator into place. When installing the hoses, lubricate their surfaces and the outside of the fittings with refrigerant oil. The hoses must be positioned properly with the clamp finders and tightened securely. Do not forget to install the drain hose and the sealing compound.
11   Have the system evacuated and recharged by the shop that discharged it.

**19   Heater/air conditioning control assembly – removal
and installation**

Refer to illustrations 19.3, 19.4, 19.6 and 19.7

1   Pull off the radio knobs and remove the nuts from from the control shafts. Lift off the radio trim panel.
2   Pull off the heater fan control knob and the heater control lever ends. Remove the nut from the fan control knob.

18.9b   Evaporator assembly – exploded view (1988 and later models)

1   Upper evaporator case
2   Clip
3   ECCS
4   Evaporator assembly
5   Expansion valve
6   Lower evaporator case

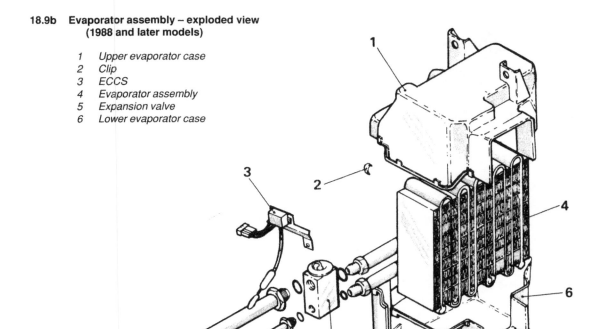

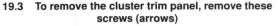

19.3   To remove the cluster trim panel, remove these screws (arrows)

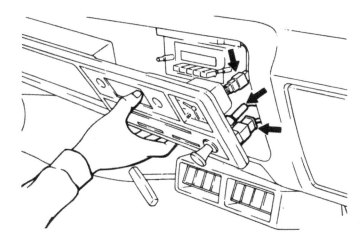

19.4   Removing the cluster trim panel – be sure to unplug the electrical connectors (arrows)

3   Pull out the ashtray, and remove the bracket attaching screws. Then remove the cluster trim panel attaching screws **(see illustration)**.
4   Remove the screws from the cluster trim panel and lift it out of place by carefully prying out on the lower left corner **(see illustration)**.
5   Disconnect the electrical connectors at the right of the cluster trim panel.
6   Disconnect the control cable from the heater (not from the control as-sembly) **(see illustration)**.

7   Remove the four screws attaching the control assembly and remove it from the dashboard **(see illustration)**.
8   Minor repairs, such as cleaning and lubrication of the pivots and cables, can be performed on the heater control assembly. But it would be a good idea to replace it with a new one if it is not operating properly.
9   Installation is the reverse of the removal. Remember to plug in the electrical connectors before installing the instrument cluster trim panel.

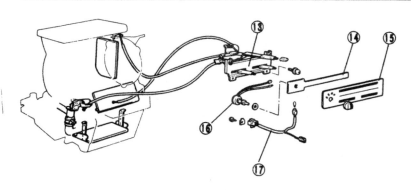

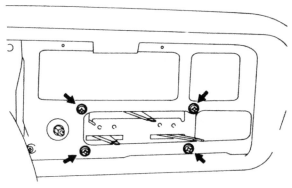

19.6   Heater control assembly details

13	Heater control assembly	16	Heater fan switch
14	Heater control panel lens	17	Control illumination harness
15	Heater control panel		

19.7   To remove the heater control assembly from the dashboard, remove these four screws (arrows)

Chapter 4 Fuel and exhaust systems

Contents

Specifications

Accelerator cable freeplay

Carbureted engines	0.00 to 0.04 inch
Fuel-injected engines	
2.4L engine	
Manual transmission	0.04 to 0.08 inch
Automatic transmission	0.12 to 0.20 inch
3.0L engine	0.04 to 0.08 inch

Fuel pressure

Carbureted models	4.6 to 6 psi
Fuel-injected models	
Vacuum hose connected to pressure regulator	38 psi at curb idle
Vacuum hose disconnected from regulator	47 to 53 psi at curb idle

Fuel injector resistance . . . .   13 to 16 ohms

Idle speed
1983 and 1984 models
  Federal
    2.0L engine
      Five-speed manual transmission . . . .   700 ± 100 rpm
      Automatic and four-speed manual transmission . . . .   750 ± 100 rpm
    2.6L engine
      Manual transmission . . . .   750 ± 100 rpm
      Automatic transmission . . . .   800 ± 100 rpm
1983 and 1984 models
  California
    2.0L engine . . . .   750 ± 100 rpm
    2.6L engine
      Manual transmission . . . .   750 ± 100 rpm
      Automatic transmission . . . .   800 ± 100 rpm
  Canada
    2.0L engine . . . .   850 ± 50 rpm
    2.6L engine . . . .   850 ± 50 rpm
1985 and 1986 models
  Federal and California
    2.0L engine . . . .   750 ± 100 rpm
    2.6L engine
      Manual transmission . . . .   750 ± 100 rpm
      Automatic transmission . . . .   800 ± 100 rpm
  Canada
    Manual transmission . . . .   750 ± 50 rpm
    Automatic transmission . . . .   800 ± 50 rpm
1987 through 1989 models
  2.0L engine . . . .   750 ± 100 rpm
  2.6L engine . . . .   800 ± 100 rpm
1990 and later models
  2.4L engine . . . .   750 ± 50 rpm
  3.0L engine . . . .   700 ± 50 rpm

Idle-up (throttle opener) engine speed
  (carbureted air-conditioned models) . . . .   850 to 950 rpm

Float level (1986 and earlier models) . . . .   0.787 in ± 0.0394 in

Dashpot speed (1987 through 1989 models)
Manual transmission . . . .   2000 rpm
Automatic transmission . . . .   1500 rpm

Slow Cut Solenoid Valve (SCSV) resistance
  (1987 through 1989 models) . . . .   48 to 60 ohms

Fast idle opening
1985 and 1986 models
  2.0L engine with manual transmission . . . .   0.025 inch
  2.0L engine with automatic transmission and
  2.6L engine with manual transmission . . . .   0.028 inch
  2.6L engine with automatic transmission . . . .   0.031 inch
1987 models
  Manual transmission
    2.0L engine . . . .   0.0394 inch
    2.6L engine . . . .   0.0476 inch
  Automatic transmission
    2.0L engine . . . .   0.0433 inch
    2.6L engine . . . .   0.0520 inch
1988 models
  Manual transmission . . . .   0.031 inch
  Automatic transmission . . . .   0.035 inch

Fast idle opening (continued)

1989 models
Manual transmission
    2.0L engine .... 0.025 inch
    2.6L engine .... 0.031 inch
Automatic transmission
    2.0L engine .... 0.028 inch
    2.6L engine .... 0.035 inch

Choke valve-to-choke bore clearance (1987 through 1989 models)

Unloader opening .... 0.075 to 0.083 inch
Choke breaker
1987 models
First stage
    2.0L engine .... 0.087 to 0.094 inch
    2.6L engine .... 0.098 to 0.106 inch
Second stage
    2.0L engine .... 0.114 to 0.122 inch
    2.6L engine .... 0.126 to 0.133 inch
1988 models
First stage .... 0.091 to 0.098 inch
Second stage .... 0.118 to 0.126 inch
1989 models
First stage
    2.0L engine .... 0.079 to 0.087 inch
    2.6L engine .... 0.091 to 0.098 inch
Second stage
    2.0L engine .... 0.114 to 0.122 inch
    2.6L engine .... 0.118 to 0.126 inch

Idle Speed Control (ISC) servo coil resistance

2.4L engine .... 5 to 35 ohms
3.0L engine .... 28 to 33 ohms

Torque specifications

Ft-lbs (unless otherwise indicated)

Carburetor mounting bolts/nuts .... 132 to 168 in-lbs
Throttle body mounting nuts
    1991 3.0L engine .... 84 to 108 in-lbs
    All others .... 11 to 16
Idle Speed Control (ISC) servo mounting screws .... 22 to 38 in-lbs
Air intake plenum mounting bolts .... 11 to 14
Fuel high-pressure hose attaching bolts .... 12 to 24 in-lbs
Fuel pressure regulator mounting bolts .... 60 to 96 in-lbs

1   General information

Fuel system

The fuel system consists of the fuel tank, a mechanical or electric fuel pump, an air cleaner, either a carburetor or a fuel injection system and the hoses and lines which connect these components.

All 1983 through 1988 and some 1989 models are carbureted. These models have a mechanical fuel pump mounted on the cylinder head. The pump is driven by an eccentric on the camshaft. Beginning in 1985, carburetors began being equipped with Feedback Control (FBC) systems which utilize sensors and solenoid actuators, controlled by the engine's electronic control module, to control emissions.

Some 1989 and all 1990 and later models are fuel-injected. A multipoint (one injector per cylinder) Electronic Fuel Injection (EFI) system is used on both 3.0L and 2.4L engines. All fuel-injected models use an in-tank electric fuel pump. For more information regarding the EFI system, refer to Section 18.

Exhaust system

The exhaust system consists of the exhaust manifold(s), exhaust pipes, catalytic converter and muffler. For information regarding the removal and installation of the exhaust manifold(s), refer to Chapter 2, Part

A. For information regarding exhaust system and catalytic converter servicing, refer to the last Section in this Chapter. For further information regarding the catalytic converter, refer to Chapter 6.

2   Fuel pressure relief procedure (fuel-injected models)

Refer to illustration 2.1

1   Disconnect the electrical connector for the fuel pump harness at the rear side of the fuel tank **(see illustration)**.
2   Start the engine, let it run until it stalls and turn off the ignition switch.
3   Detach the cable from the negative terminal of the battery and re-connect it after repairs are complete.

3   Fuel pump/fuel pressure – check

Warning: *Gasoline is extremely flammable, so take extra precautions when you work on any part of the fuel system. Don't smoke or allow open flames or bare light bulbs near the work area, and don't work in a garage where a natural gas-type appliance (such as a water heater or clothes dryer) with a pilot light is present. If you spill any fuel on your skin, rinse it off*

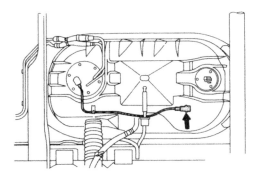

2.1   The electrical connector (arrow) for the fuel pump harness is located on the rear side of the fuel tank

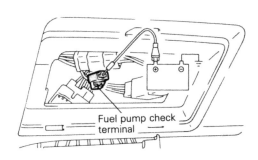

3.11a   The check connector for the fuel pump (located on the rear side of the fuse block) (1990 pick-up models)

immediately with soap and water. When you perform any kind of work on the fuel system, wear safety glasses and have a Class B type fire extinguisher on hand.

Carbureted models

1   Before deciding that the fuel pump is defective, it should be tested for correct pressure while still in the vehicle.
2   To check the fuel pump pressure, you will need a 'T' fitting, a length of hose (with the same inside diameter as the fuel hoses), a fuel pressure gauge and a tachometer.
3   Loosen the hose clamp and pull the fuel hose off the fuel pump outlet fitting. Insert one end of the 'T' fitting into the hose that was disconnected from the pump and tighten the hose clamp. Cut a short length of hose, slip one end over the 'T' fitting and the other end onto the fuel pump outlet fitting.
4   Connect another length of hose (approximately six inches long) between the fuel pressure gauge and the remaining end of the 'T' fitting. Install hose clamps on all the connections.
5   Loosen the hose clamps and disconnect the fuel return hose, which returns fuel to the fuel tank from the carburetor. Slip a short length of hose, which has been plugged, onto the fitting and install the hose clamp.
6   Connect the tachometer according to the instructions provided by the manufacturer.
7   Start the engine and allow it to run for a few moments before taking the pressure reading. This will allow any air in the pump to be vented, which will ensure an accurate reading.
8   Make sure the engine idle speed is correct, then note the pressure reading on the gauge and compare it to this Chapter's Specifications.
9   Stop the engine and observe the gauge. The pressure should remain constant or return to zero slowly.

10   If the pressure was higher or lower than specified, or if it dropped to zero instantly when the engine was shut off, the fuel pump is defective and should be replaced with a new one.

Fuel-injected models

Fuel pump check (2.4L models only)
Refer to illustrations 3.11a, 3.11b, 3.11c and 3.11d

11   Turn the ignition switch to Off, open the fuel tank filler cap, apply battery voltage directly to the check connector for the fuel pump **(see illustrations)** and listen for the whirring sound of the electric pump through the filler port. Now squeeze the fuel high-pressure hose – you should be able to feel pressure in the hose. If you cannot hear whirring, the fuel pump or its circuit is defective. If you can hear whirring, but pressure does not develop in the fuel high-pressure hose, the fuel pump is defective.

Fuel pressure check
Refer to illustrations 3.13a, 3.13b, 3.14a, 3.14b, 3.18a, 3.18b, 3.22 and 3.23

12   Relieve the system fuel pressure (see Section 2), detach the cable from the negative battery terminal and reconnect the electrical connector for the fuel pump.
13   Disconnect the fuel high-pressure hose at the delivery pipe **(see illustrations)**. Cover the connection with shop rags to absorb any fuel that leaks out.
14   Attach your fuel pressure gauge (it must have a range through 50 psi) to the special adapter (MD998700 or equivalent) as shown **(see illustration)**. On 3.0L models, attach the special hose (MD998753 or equivalent) to the adapter as shown **(see illustration)**.
15   Attach the gauge with adapter to the fuel delivery pipe.
16   Reconnect the battery terminal.

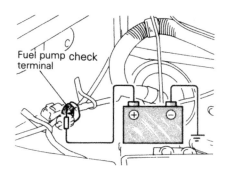

3.11b   The check connector for the fuel pump (located on the right side of the engine compartment) (1991 and later pick-up models)

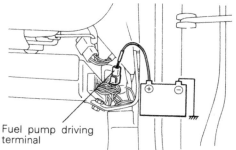

3.11c   Fuel pump driving terminal (check connector) location on 1989 and 1990 Montero models

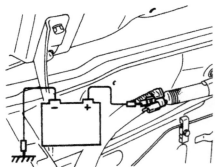

3.11d   The check connector on 1991 and later Montero models is located at the right center of the engine firewall

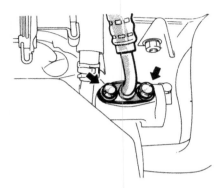

3.13a   To disconnect the fuel high-pressure hose flange from a 2.4L engine, remove these two bolts (arrows)

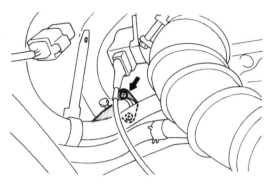

3.13b   To disconnect the fuel high-pressure hose flange from a 3.0L engine, remove these two bolts (arrow)

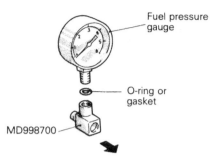

3.14a   To measure the fuel pressure on a fuel-injected engine, attach a fuel pressure gauge to the special adapter (MD998700 or equivalent) – be sure to seal the two parts with an O-ring or gasket as shown

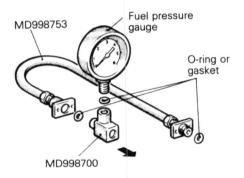

3.14b   On 3.0L engines, you'll also need to attach a special hose (MD998753 or equivalent) to the adapter as shown – be sure to seal both hose flanges with O-rings or gaskets as shown

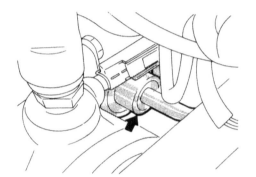

3.18a   Fuel pressure regulator/vacuum hose (2.4L engine) (arrow)

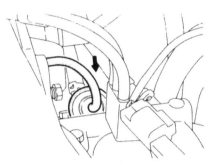

3.18b   Fuel pressure regulator/vacuum hose (3.0L engine) (arrow)

Symptom	Probable cause	Remedy
Fuel pressure is lower than standard value	Clogged fuel strainer	Replace fuel strainer
	Faulty pressure regulator	Replace pressure regulator
	Faulty fuel pump	Replace fuel pump
Fuel pressure is higher than standard value	Faulty pressure regulator	Replace pressure regulator
	Clogged fuel return hose or pipe	Clean or replace hose or pipe
Fuel pressure does not vary even if the vacuum hose is connected	Leakage around vacuum hose	Replace the vacuum hose

3.22   Fuel pressure troubleshooting table for fuel-injected engines

Symptom	Probable cause	Remedy
Fuel pressure drops slowly after engine is stopped	Faulty injector (leaks)	Replace injector
Fuel pressure drops sharply immediately after engine is stopped	Faulty fuel pump (pump inside check valve binding)	Replace fuel pump

3.23   Fuel pressure drop troubleshooting table for fuel-injected engines

17   Apply battery voltage to the fuel pump check connector **(see illustrations 3.11a, 3.11b and 3.11c)** and activate the fuel pump. Make sure there's no fuel leaking from the pressure gauge/adapter setup.
18   Start the engine and run it at curb idle speed, measure the fuel pressure with the vacuum hose connected to the pressure regulator **(see illustrations)** and compare your reading to the pressure listed in this Chapter's Specifications.
19   Detach the vacuum hose from the pressure regulator, plug the hose, measure the fuel pressure again and compare this reading to the pressure listed in this Chapter's Specifications.
20   Race the engine two or three times in quick succession, then recheck the fuel pressure to verify it doesn't fall when the engine runs at idle.
21   Gently squeeze the fuel return hose with your fingers while repeatedly racing the engine to verify fuel pressure in the return hose. If the volume of fuel flow is insufficient, there won't be any fuel pressure in the return hose.
22   If the results of your readings aren't within the specified values, use the accompanying table **(see illustration)** to determine the probable cause and make the necessary repairs.
23   Stop the engine and verify that the reading on the fuel pressure gauge doesn't drop. If it does drop, note the rate of drop and use the accompanying table **(see illustration)** to determine the cause and make the necessary repairs.
24   Relieve the system fuel pressure (see Section 2).
25   Cover the fuel high-pressure hose connection with a shop towel to absorb leaking fuel, disconnect the fuel high-pressure hose, remove the fuel gauge/adapter assembly, install a new O-ring in the groove in the end of the high-pressure hose fitting and reconnect the hose. Tighten the attaching screws for the fuel high-pressure hose fitting to the torque listed in this Chapter's Specifications.
26   Apply battery voltage to the fuel pump terminal, operate the pump and check the fuel high-pressure hose for leaks.

4   Fuel pump – removal and installation

Warning: *Gasoline is extremely flammable, so take extra precautions when you work on any part of the fuel system. Don't smoke or allow open flames or bare light bulbs near the work area, and don't work in a garage where a natural gas-type appliance (such as a water heater or clothes dryer) with a pilot light is present. If you spill any fuel on your skin, rinse it off immediately with soap and water. When you perform any kind of work on the fuel system, wear safety glasses and have a Class B type fire extinguisher on hand.*

Carbureted engines

Refer to illustration 4.6

1   The fuel pump is mounted on the cylinder head immediately in front of the carburetor. It is held in place with two nuts.
2   Pull the coil high-tension lead out of the distributor and ground it on the engine block. Remove the spark plugs and place your thumb over the number one cylinder spark plug hole.
3   Rotate the crankshaft in a clockwise direction (with a wrench on the large bolt attaching the pulley to the front of the crankshaft) until you can feel the compression pressure rising in the number one cylinder.

4   Continue rotating the crankshaft until the notch on the crankshaft pulley lines up with the 'T' on the timing mark tab on the timing chain case. At this point, the lift of the fuel pump drive cam is reduced to a minimum, which will make the pump easier to remove.
5   Install the spark plugs and hook up the wires. Do not forget the coil high-tension lead.
6   Loosen the hose clamps and remove the fuel hoses from the pump fittings **(see illustration)**. Plug the ends of the hoses.
7   Remove the fuel pump mounting bolts and pull the pump off the engine. You may have to tap the pump body with a soft-faced hammer to break the gasket seal.
8   If the pump is difficult to remove, take off the valve cover (see Chapter 2) and guide the pump rocker arm out of the head from the inside.
9   Remove the insulator block and scrape off all traces of the old gaskets and sealer. Clean the mating surfaces on the head and insulator block with lacquer thinner or acetone.
10   Before installing the new pump ensure that the rocker arm moves up and down without binding or sticking.
11   Coat both sides of the new gaskets with silicone-type gasket sealer before installation.
12   Slip the first gasket, the insulator block and the second gasket (in that order) onto the fuel pump mounting studs.
13   Install the fuel pump. It may be necessary to guide the rocker arm into place from inside the head. Work slowly; there is not much clearance between the rocker arm and the valve gear.
14   Once the fuel pump is properly seated, install the mounting nuts and tighten them evenly. Do not overtighten them or the insulator block may be cracked.
15   Install the valve cover if it was removed.
16   Install the hoses (after inspecting them for cracks) and the hose clamps.
17   Start the engine and check for fuel leaks at the hose fittings. Check for oil leaks where the fuel pump mounts on the cylinder head.

Fuel-injected engines

18   Remove the fuel tank (see Section 5).
19   Remove the six fuel pump retaining nuts and pull the pump assembly out of the fuel tank **(see illustration 5.4b)**.
20   Installation is the reverse of removal. Be sure the gasket between the fuel pump assembly and the fuel tank is in good shape. If not, replace it.
21   Install the fuel tank (see Section 5).

5   Fuel tank – removal and installation

Refer to illustrations 5.3, 5.4a, 5.4b, 5.6, 5.7a, 5.7b and 5.8
Warning: *Gasoline is extremely flammable, so take extra precautions when you work on any part of the fuel system. Don't smoke or allow open flames or bare light bulbs near the work area, and don't work in a garage where a natural gas-type appliance (such as a water heater or clothes dryer) with a pilot light is present. If you spill any fuel on your skin, rinse it off immediately with soap and water. When you perform any kind of work on the fuel system, wear safety glasses and have a Class B type fire extinguisher on hand.*

1   Before doing any work around the fuel tank, make sure that the ignition switch is off and remove the key from the ignition lock. Block the front

2.0L engine

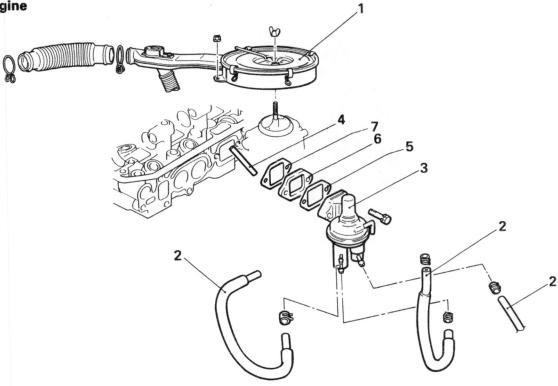

2.6L engine

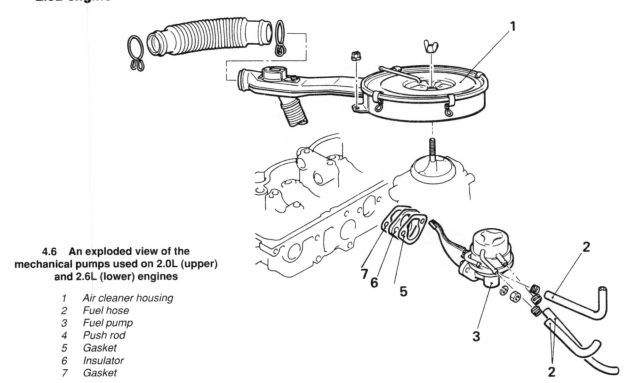

4.6   An exploded view of the mechanical pumps used on 2.0L (upper) and 2.6L (lower) engines

1   Air cleaner housing
2   Fuel hose
3   Fuel pump
4   Push rod
5   Gasket
6   Insulator
7   Gasket

5.3   Remove the drain plug to drain the fuel from the fuel tank

wheels to keep the vehicle from rolling, then raise the rear of the vehicle and set it on jack stands.

2   Remove the tank filler cap so any pressure in the tank can escape.

3   Position a suitable container (large enough to hold the fuel that it is in the tank) under the tank. Remove the drain plug **(see illustration)** and allow the fuel to drain into the container. Be very careful when working around gasoline; it is highly explosive. After the fuel has drained complete-

ly, reinstall the drain plug.

4   Loosen the hose clamps on the main, return and vapor fuel hoses, then pull the hoses off the tank **(see illustrations)**.

5   Unplug the electrical wires from the fuel pump (fuel-injected models) and fuel level sending unit.

6   Remove the filler neck mud shield from the inside of the left rear wheel well. It is held in place with three bolts **(see illustration)**.

7   Loosen the hose clamps on the filler connecting hose (large) and the breather hose (small) where they attach to the tank **(see illustrations)**. Pull the hoses off the tank. (Be careful not to damage them in the process).

8   Support the fuel tank, preferably with a portable jack and a block of wood. Remove the four mounting nuts **(see illustration)**, lower the tank carefully and move it out from under the vehicle.

9   Check the tank interior for rust and corrosion. If the tank is not extremely corroded, it can be cleaned and reused. Special solvents made especially for cleaning fuel tanks are available. If you use one, be sure to follow the directions on the container. The inside of the tank is plated with zinc so be sure to use a cleaner that will not harm it in any way.

10   If the tank is severely corroded, replace it with a new one or a clean used one.

11   Look for evidence of leaks and cracks. If any are found, take the tank to a repair shop to have it fixed.

12   Inspect all fuel and breather hoses for cracks and deterioration. Check all hose clamps for damage and proper operation.

13   Installation of the tank is basically the reverse of removal. Be sure to double check all hoses for proper routing. Also, if you have not already done so, be sure to tighten the drain plug securely.

14   Fill the tank with fuel and check for leaks. After the engine has been run, make a second check for leaks, particularly at the hose fittings that were removed.

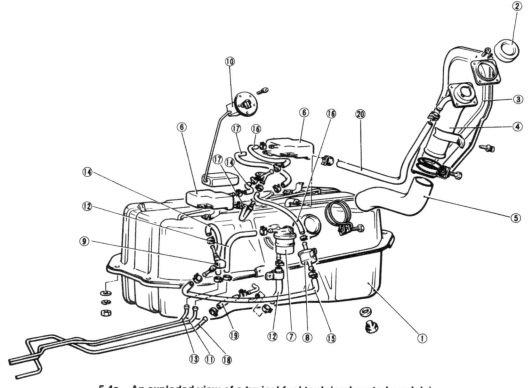

5.4a   An exploded view of a typical fuel tank (carbureted models)

1	Fuel tank	5	Connecting hose	9	Check valve	13	Fuel vapor pipe	17	Vapor hose
2	Fuel filler cap	6	Separator tank (two pieces)	10	Fuel gauge unit	14	Vapor hose	18	Fuel return pipe
3	Filler hose protector	7	Fuel filter	11	Fuel main pipe	15	Vapor hose	19	Soft vinyl tube
4	Filler neck	8	Two-way valve	12	Soft vinyl tube	16	Vapor hose	20	Breather hose

Standard body

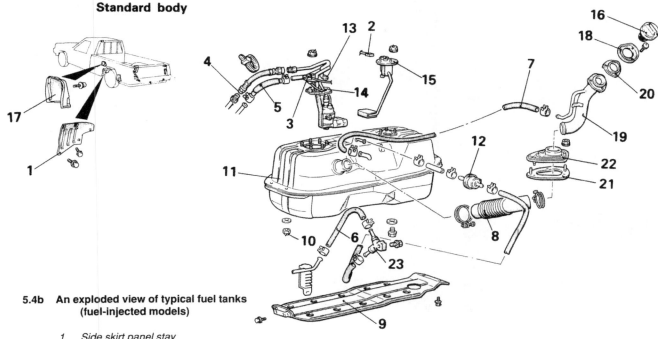

5.4b An exploded view of typical fuel tanks (fuel-injected models)

1	Side skirt panel stay
2	Fuel gauge unit connector
3	Fuel pump connector
4	Main hose connection
5	Return hose connection
6	Vapor hose connection
7	Breather hose connection
8	Fuel filler hose connection
9	Fuel tank protector (4WD)
10	Fuel tank mounting nut
11	Fuel tank
12	Overfill limiter (two-way valve)
13	Fuel pump assembly
14	Packing
15	Fuel gauge unit
16	Fuel filler cap
17	Filler neck cover
18	Reinforcement
19	Filler neck
20	Packing
21	Retainer
22	Grommet
23	Check valve

Long body and extended cab

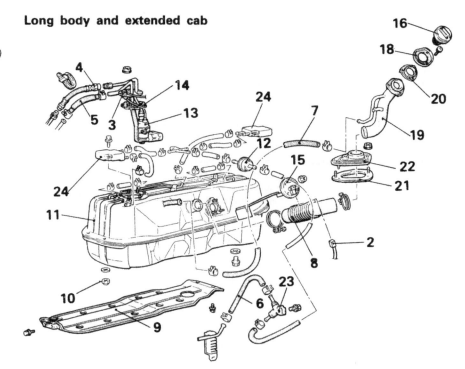

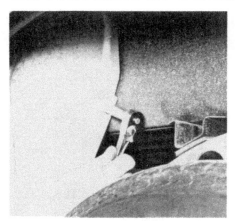

5.6   Remove the filler neck mud shield

5.7a   Filler connecting hose clamp location

5.7b   Breather hose clamp location

5.8   Remove the four fuel tank mounting nuts while supporting the tank securely

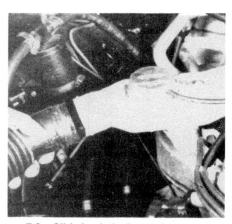

7.2   Slide back the hose clamp and remove the snorkel tube (carbureted engines)

7.3   Pull off the crankcase breather hose (carbureted engines)

6   Fuel tank cleaning and repair – general information

1   All repairs to the fuel tank or filler neck should be carried out by a professional who has experience in this critical and potentially dangerous work. Even after cleaning and flushing of the fuel system, explosive fumes can remain and ignite during repair of the tank.
2   If the fuel tank is removed from the vehicle, it shouldn't be placed in an area where sparks or open flames could ignite the fumes coming out of the tank. Be especially careful inside garages where a natural gas-type appliance is located, because the pilot light could cause an explosion.

7   Air cleaner assembly – removal and installation

1   The air cleaner assembly must be removed in order to perform many maintenance repair and adjustment procedures. It is very important to remove and install it carefully and correctly to ensure proper engine operation.

Carbureted engines
Refer to illustrations 7.2, 7.3, 7.4, 7.5, 7.7, 7.8a and 7.8b
2   Remove the snorkel tube (connected between the air cleaner and the headlight brace) from the air cleaner **(see illustration)**.
3   Pull off the crankcase breather hose (if equipped) from the front of the air cleaner housing **(see illustration)**.

4   Remove the large hose leading to the secondary air supply system valve **(see illustration)**.
5   Slide back the hose clamp and remove the hose that leads to the purge control valve from the air cleaner housing **(see illustration)**.
6   Remove the top cover (it is held in place with four spring clips and a wing nut) and lift out the filter element.
7   Remove the two nuts, lock washers and flat washers attaching the air cleaner housing to the valve cover **(see illustration)**.
8   Carefully lift up on the housing and disconnect the hot-air duct between the exhaust manifold and air cleaner housing **(see illustration)** and the vacuum hose leading to the air bleed valve in the housing. (The hose is color coded white) **(see illustration)**.
9   Install the air cleaner by reversing the removal procedure. Be sure to line up the arrows on the top cover and the housing before setting the cover in place.

Fuel-injected engines
Refer to illustrations 7.10a and 7.10b
10   Remove the air intake hose **(see illustrations)**.
11   Unplug the electrical connector for the air flow sensor assembly.
12   On 1991 models, remove the mounting nuts and remove the air flow sensor (on 1990 models, the air flow sensor is an integral part of the air cleaner housing mounted on the inside of the air cleaner cover).
13   Remove the air cleaner housing mounting bolts and remove the housing.
14   Installation is the reverse of removal.

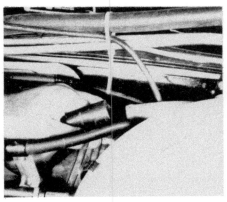

7.4   Remove the large hose leading to the secondary air supply system reed valve (carbureted engines)

7.5   Remove the hose that leads to the purge control valve (carbureted engines)

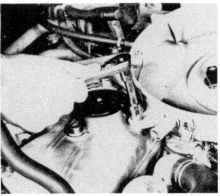

7.7   Remove the two nuts, lock washers and flat washers (carbureted engines)

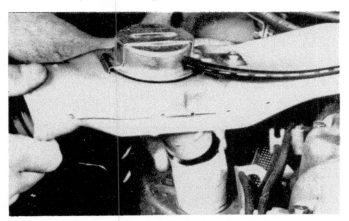

7.8a   Disconnect the hot air duct (carbureted engines)

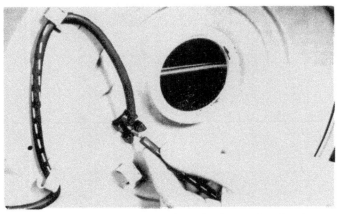

7.8b   Remove the vacuum hose (carbureted engines)

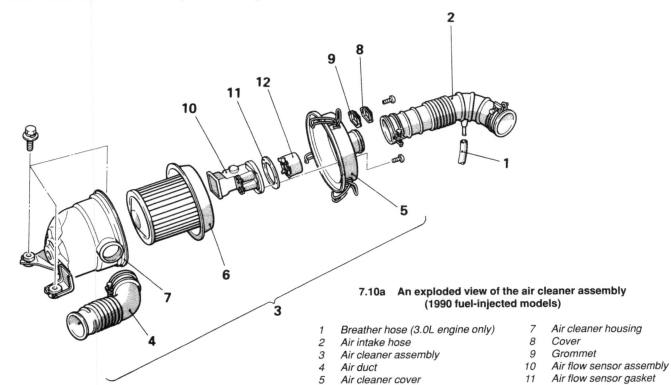

7.10a   An exploded view of the air cleaner assembly (1990 fuel-injected models)

1	Breather hose (3.0L engine only)	7	Air cleaner housing
2	Air intake hose	8	Cover
3	Air cleaner assembly	9	Grommet
4	Air duct	10	Air flow sensor assembly
5	Air cleaner cover	11	Air flow sensor gasket
6	Air cleaner filter element	12	Noise reduction filter

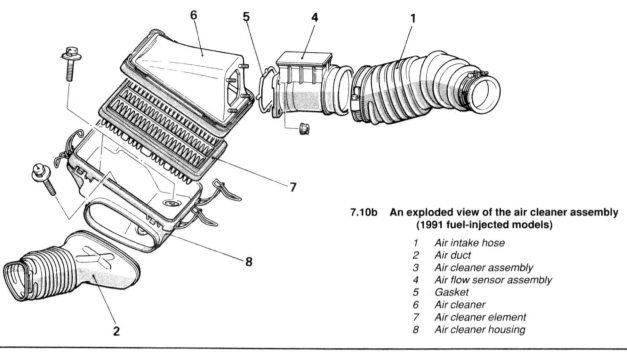

7.10b   An exploded view of the air cleaner assembly (1991 fuel-injected models)

1   Air intake hose
2   Air duct
3   Air cleaner assembly
4   Air flow sensor assembly
5   Gasket
6   Air cleaner
7   Air cleaner element
8   Air cleaner housing

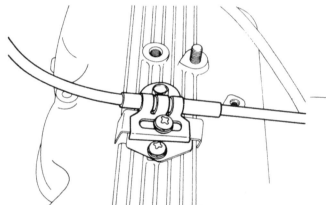

8.2   Detach this accelerator cable clamp from the valve cover to replace the cable – or loosen the screw and slide the clamp back and forth to adjust the cable (earlier carbureted engines)

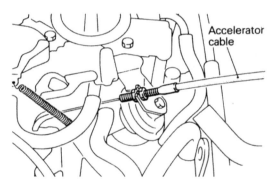

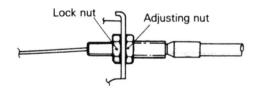

8.3   Typical accelerator cable support bracket with locknut and adjusting nut arrangement (used on later carbureted engines and on 2.4L fuel-injected engines)

8   Accelerator cable – replacement and adjustment

Refer to illustrations 8.2, 8.3 and 8.4

Removal and installation

1   Remove the air cleaner housing (see Section 7).
2   On carbureted engines, loosen the cable clamp on top of the valve cover **(see illustration)** and detach the cable from the valve cover. On 3.0L engines, remove the two cable adjusting bolts from the air intake plenum and detach the cable from the plenum.
3   If the cable has a support bracket at the carburetor or throttle body, loosen the locknut at the bracket **(see illustration)** and detach the cable from the bracket.
4   Working inside the vehicle, under the dash, unhook the throttle return spring, pull out the cotter pin and disconnect the accelerator cable from the accelerator pedal assembly **(see illustration)**.

5   Detach the cable guide from the firewall. Earlier guides are threaded into the firewall; later units are attached to the firewall with two bolts.
6   Disconnect the cable from the throttle lever at the carburetor or throttle body and remove the cable.
7   Installation is the reverse of removal.

Adjustment

8   To adjust the cable on carbureted engines, loosen the cable clamp on the valve cover (earlier engines) or the locknut at the cable support bracket (later engines). Move the cable toward or away from the carburetor until there's just enough freeplay to allow the throttle valve to close freely when

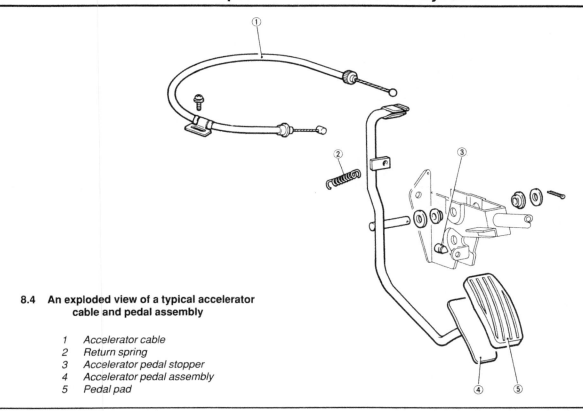

8.4 **An exploded view of a typical accelerator cable and pedal assembly**

1 *Accelerator cable*
2 *Return spring*
3 *Accelerator pedal stopper*
4 *Accelerator pedal assembly*
5 *Pedal pad*

the accelerator pedal is released, with a little bit of slack. Pull the cable (clamp-type) or turn the adjustment nut (support bracket type) until the cable starts to lift the throttle lever off its stop, then let the cable come back slightly (clamp-type) or back off the adjustment nut one turn (support bracket type). To ensure the correct gap between the throttle lever and its stopper, insert a feeler gauge between the lever and the stopper. The correct gap is listed in this Chapter's Specifications. Tighten the clamp bolts or support bracket locknut.

9   Before adjusting the accelerator cable freeplay on fuel-injected engines, turn off the air conditioner and all lights, warm up the engine, verify the idle speed is correct (see Section 13, 15 or 17), stop the engine (ignition switch off) and make sure there are no sharp bends in the accelerator cable. Then, before checking the cable freeplay, turn the ignition switch to On (with the engine stopped) and keep it in that position for 15 seconds. This 15-second key-on/engine off interval fully extends the probe for the idle speed control actuator.

10   The cable on 2.4L fuel-injected engines is adjusted basically the same way as later carbureted engines with a support bracket, locknut and adjustment nut. The cable on 3.0L fuel-injected engines is adjusted basically the same way as earlier carbureted engines with a clamp on the valve cover, except it uses two bolts and slotted clips on top of the air intake plenum. To ensure the correct gap between the throttle lever and its stopper, insert a feeler gauge between the lever and the stopper. The correct gap is listed in this Chapter's Specifications. Tighten the locknut (2.4L) or adjustment bolts (3.0L) securely.

11   Now check the accelerator pedal: It should operate smoothly and the throttle valve must open fully by the time the accelerator pedal has been depressed as far as it will go.

12   Periodically, apply a thin coat of multi-purpose grease to the accelerator pedal pivot points.

***

9   **Fuel hoses and vapor separator – replacement**

Warning: *Gasoline is extremely flammable, so take extra precautions when you work on any part of the fuel system. Don't smoke or allow open flames or bare light bulbs near the work area, and don't work in a garage where a natural gas-type appliance (such as a water heater or clothes dryer) with a pilot light is present. If you spill any fuel on your skin, rinse it off immediately with soap and water. When you perform any kind of work on the fuel system, wear safety glasses and have a Class B type fire extinguisher on hand.*

Note: *Since the fuel injection system is under considerable pressure, always replace all clamps released or removed with new ones.*

Fuel hoses

1   Periodically, check all rubber fuel hoses and metal fuel lines for cracks, bends, deformation, deterioration or clogging.
2   Remove the air cleaner assembly.
3   On fuel-injected engines, relieve the fuel system pressure (see Section 2).
4   Disconnect the negative cable from the battery.
5   Loosen the hose clamps or bolts (if equipped), wrap a cloth around each end of the hose to catch the residual fuel and twist and pull (clamped on type), pull straight off (bolted-on type) or unscrew the hose (screwed-in type) to remove the hose.
6   When replacing hoses, always use original equipment-type replacement hose and use new hose clamps or O-rings. Pressure hoses for the fuel injection system are made from special materials to handle the high pressures – use only hoses made to the same high standards.
7   Connect the negative battery cable, start the engine and check for leaks.
8   Install the air cleaner assembly.

Vapor separator (carbureted models)

9   The vapor separator is the small canister mounted high on the left front fenderwell. It is mounted in the fuel system between the fuel pump and the carburetor and is designed to prevent vapor lock caused by high underhood temperatures.

10   The main fuel line from the fuel pump is connected to the middle fitting (color-coded red) leads to the carburetor accelerator pump housing (which is also color-coded red). The hose connected to the bottom fitting (color coded yellow) leads to the carburetor fuel inlet (also color-coded yellow).

11.5   Removing the float bowl vent tube from the carburetor

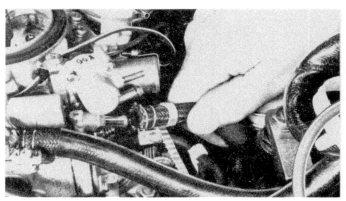

11.6   Remove and plug the three fuel hoses

11   The color-coded lines and fittings reduce the possibility of incorrect hose installation during carburetor servicing.

12   If the vapor separator is somehow damaged or begins to leak, it must be replaced with a new one. When installing a new vapor separator, position it so that the red fitting is at the top.

10   Carburetor – servicing

1   A thorough road test and check of carburetor adjustment should be done before any major carburetor service. Specifications for some adjustments are listed on the Vehicle Emissions Control Information label found in the engine compartment.

2   Some performance complaints directed at the carburetor are actually a result of loose, misadjusted or malfunctioning engine or electrical components. Others develop when vacuum hoses leak, are disconnected or are incorrectly routed. The proper approach to analyzing carburetor problems should include a routine check of the following areas:

3   Inspect all vacuum hoses and actuators for leaks and proper installation (see Chapter 6).

4   Tighten the intake manifold nuts and carburetor mounting nuts evenly and securely.

5   Perform a cylinder compression test (see Chapter 2).

6   Clean or replace the spark plugs as necessary.

7   Test the resistance of the spark plug wires (see Chapter 5).

8   Inspect the ignition primary wires and check the vacuum advance operation. Replace any defective parts.

9   Check the ignition timing with the vacuum advance line disconnected and plugged.

10   Set the carburetor idle mixture (see Section 13).

11   Check the fuel pump pressure (see Section 3).

12   Inspect the heat control valve in the air cleaner for proper operation (see Chapter 6).

13   Remove the carburetor air filter element and blow out any dirt with compressed air. If the filter is extremely dirty, replace it with a new one.

14   Inspect the crankcase ventilation system (see Chapter 6).

15   Carburetor problems usually show up as flooding, hard starting, stalling, severe backfiring, poor acceleration and lack of response to idle mixture screw adjustments. A carburetor that is leaking fuel and/or covered with wet-looking deposits definitely needs attention.

16   Diagnosing carburetor problems may require that the engine be started and run with the air cleaner removed. While running the engine without the air cleaner it is possible that it could backfire. A backfiring situation is likely to occur if the carburetor is malfunctioning, but removal of the air cleaner alone can lean the air/fuel mixture enough to produce an engine backfire.

17   Once it is determined that the carburetor is indeed at fault, it should be disassembled, cleaned and reassembled using new parts where necessary. Before dismantling the carburetor, make sure you have a carburetor rebuild kit, which will include all necessary gaskets and internal parts, carburetor cleaning solvent and some means of blowing out all the internal

passages of the carburetor. To do the job properly, you will also need a clean place to work and plenty of time and patience.

11   Carburetor – removal and installation

Refer to illustrations 11.5 and 11.6

Warning: *Gasoline is extremely flammable, so take extra precautions when you work on any part of the fuel system. Don't smoke or allow open flames or bare light bulbs near the work area, and don't work in a garage where a natural gas-type appliance (such as a water heater or clothes dryer) with a pilot light is present. If you spill any fuel on your skin, rinse it off immediately with soap and water. When you perform any kind of work on the fuel tank, wear safety glasses and have a Class B type fire extinguisher on hand.*

Removal

1   Remove the fuel filler cap to relieve fuel tank pressure and disconnect the negative battery cable from the battery.

2   Remove the air cleaner from the carburetor. Be sure to label all vacuum hoses attached to the air cleaner housing (see Section 7).

3   Disconnect the accelerator cable from the throttle lever on the carburetor (see Section 8).

4   If the vehicle is equipped with an automatic transmission, disconnect the TV (kickdown) cable from the throttle lever.

5   Clearly label all vacuum and coolant hoses and fittings, then disconnect the hoses **(see illustration)**.

6   Disconnect the fuel lines from the carburetor **(see illustration)**.

7   Label the wires and terminals, then unplug all electrical connectors.

8   Remove the nuts (there are five on most models) and lock washers attaching the carburetor to the intake manifold. Removal of the idle speed adjusting screws (SAS) from the carburetor body will make access to the left rear mounting nut less restricted. Remove the carburetor mounting gasket. Stuff a shop rag into the intake manifold openings.

Installation

9   Use a gasket scraper to remove all traces of gasket material and sealant from the intake manifold (and the carburetor, if it's being reinstalled), then remove the shop rag from the manifold openings. Clean the mating surfaces with lacquer thinner or acetone.

10   Place a new gasket on the intake manifold.

11   Position the carburetor on the gasket and install the mounting nuts.

12   To prevent carburetor distortion or damage, tighten the nuts in a crisscross pattern, 1/4-turn at a time, to the torque listed in this Chapter's Specifications.

13   The remaining installation steps are the reverse of removal.

14   Check and, if necessary, adjust the idle speed (see Section 13, 15 or 17).

15   If the vehicle is equipped with an automatic transmission, refer to Chapter 7B for the TV (kickdown) cable adjustment procedure.

16   Start the engine and check carefully for fuel leaks.

12.1a   Remove the air cleaner hold-down stud

12.1b   Slide back the hose clamps and remove the coolant hose

12.2a   Remove the spring clip, then pry the throttle opener rod out of the throttle lever (air conditioned models only)

12.2b   The throttle opener is held in place with two screws

12.3a   Remove the fuel cut-off solenoid ground wire

12.3b   Remove the solenoid retaining screw

---

12   Carburetor (32-35 DIDTA) (1983 and 1984 non-FBC models) – overhaul

Warning: *Gasoline is extremely flammable, so take extra precautions when you work on any part of the fuel system. Don't smoke or allow open flames or bare light bulbs near the work area, and don't work in a garage where a natural gas-type appliance (such as a water heater or clothes dryer) with a pilot light is present. If you spill any fuel on your skin, rinse it off immediately with soap and water. When you perform any kind of work on the fuel system, wear safety glasses and have a Class B type fire extinguisher on hand.*

Note: *The following overhaul procedure is for an early model carburetor. The procedure for carburetors installed on later models is essentially the same, but slight detail changes made to these models may slightly affect the disassembly and reassembly sequence.*

Disassembly

Refer to illustrations 12.1a, 12.1b, 12.2a, 12.2b, 12.3a, 12.3b, 12.3c, 12.4a, 12.4b, 12.5a, 12.5b, 12.5c, 12.5d, 12.5e, 12.6a, 12.6b, 12.7a, 12.7b, 12.8a, 12.8b, 12.8c, 12.9, 12.10, 12.11, 12.12a, 12.12b, 12.12c, 12.12d, 12.13a, 12.13b, 12.13c, 12.14a, 12.14b, 12.15, 12.16, 12.17, 12.18, 12.19, 12.20a, 12.20b, 12.21a, 12.21b, 12.21c, 12.21d, 12.22a, 12.22b, 12.23, 12.24a, 12.24b, 12.24c. 12.25, 12.26a, 12.26b, 12.26c, 12.26d, 12.26e, 12.26f, 12.27a, 12.27b and 12.28

1   Remove the carburetor (see Section 11). Remove the air cleaner hold-down stud **(see illustration)** and the air cleaner gasket from the top of the carburetor. Pull back the hose clamp and remove the coolant hose from the back of the carburetor **(see illustration)**.

2   Remove the spring clip and carefully pry the throttle opener actuating rod out of the primary throttle shaft lever (air conditioned models only) **(see illustration)**. Remove the throttle opener from the carburetor body; it is held in place with two screws **(see illustration)**.

3   Disconnect the fuel cut-off solenoid ground wires from the carburetor body **(see illustration)**. Remove the solenoid retaining screw **(see illustration)** and lift the solenoid away from the carburetor **(see illustration)**. Do not lose the O-ring on the solenoid body.

4   Unscrew and remove the idle mixture screw, the spring, the washer and rubber seal **(see illustrations)**.

5   Disconnect the linkage at the sub EGR valve by prying off the spring clip **(see illustration)** and removing the pin **(see illustration)**. Slide the linkage out of position and remove the spring and ball from the end of the sub EGR plunger. Using a screwdriver, unsnap the accelerator pump linkage from the throttle shaft arm **(see illustration)** and remove the accelerator pump from the carburetor body. It is held in place with four screws **(see illustration)**. Disassemble the pump and inspect the parts **(see illustration)**.

8   Remove the vent system ground wire **(see illustration)** and the three screws holding the solenoid to the carburetor body **(see illustration)**. Carefully lift the solenoid and the spring inside it away from the carburetor **(see illustration)**.

9   Remove the one remaining screw holding the vent system body to the carburetor **(see illustration)** and lift it off (don't forget to remove the rubber gasket from the carburetor body).

12.3c Carefully lift the solenoid away
from the carburetor

12.4a Remove the idle mixture screw

12.4b Idle mixture screw, spring,
washer and rubber seal

12.5a Pry the spring clip off the
sub-EGR valve linkage pin

12.5b Sub-EGR linkage pin

12.5c Unsnap the accelerator pump
linkage from the throttle shaft arm

12.5d Remove the accelerator pump
from the carburetor body

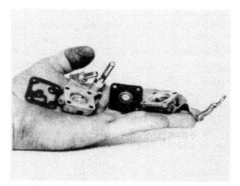

12.5e Accelerator pump components

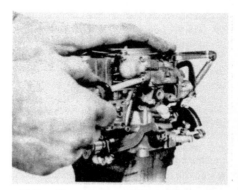

12.6a Remove the ASV housing screws

6   Remove the four screws holding the ASV housing in place **(see illus-tration)** and lift off the housing. Remove the spring, the spring cap, the spring guide and the diaphragm. Lay the parts out on a clean surface in the order of disassembly **(see illustration)**.

7   Remove the screw attaching the ASV body to the carburetor **(see il-lustration)** and carefully lift off the ASV body **(see illustration)**.

10   To disassemble the vent valve, remove the spring clip, the washer, the valve seal from the end of the plunger. Slip the O-ring off the body. The diaphragm and plunger (one piece) can now be withdrawn from the valve body. Lay the parts out on a clean surface in the order of disassembly **(see illustration)**.

11   Remove the enrichment system diaphragm housing. It is held in place by three screws. Remove the gasket, separate the two halves of the hous-ing, and lift out the spring and the diaphragm **(see illustration)**.

12   Remove the CAV housing. It is held in place by three screws **(see il-lustration)**. Lift out the spring guide, the springs, the spring cap and the diaphragm. Lay the parts out on a clean surface in the order of disassem-bly **(see illustration)**. Remove the three screws holding the choke un-loader diaphragm plate to the carburetor body **(see illustration)**. Lift off the plate and remove the spring **(see illustration)**.

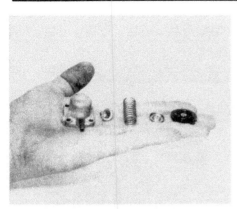

12.6b   ASV components

12.7a   Remove the ASV body attaching screws

12.7b   The ASV body

12.8a   Remove the vent system ground wire

12.8b   Remove the screws attaching the solenoid to the carburetor body

12.8c   The solenoid and spring

12.9   Remove the screw holding the vent system body to the carburetor

12.10   Vent system components

12.11   Enrichment system components

12.12a   Remove the CAV housing screws

12.12b   CAV components

12.12c   Remove the choke unloader diaphragm plate screws

12.12d   Choke unloader diaphragm plate and spring

12.13a   Pry the secondary diaphragm link out of the secondary throttle lever

12.13b   Pull the hose off the carburetor body

12.13c   Remove the secondary diaphragm mounting screws

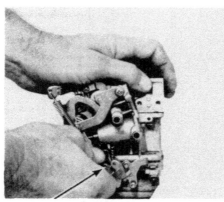

12.14a   Disconnect the throttle return spring from the primary throttle lever

12.14b   Note the reference lines on the upper choke pinion gear assembly mount

12.15   Remove the two screws holding the choke pinion gear assembly to the carburetor

12.16   Remove the screws attaching the choke plate to the choke shaft

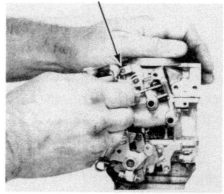

12.17   Remove the spring clip from the manual choke unloader linkage rod

13   Carefully pry the secondary diaphragm link out of the secondary throttle lever **(see illustration)** and pull the hose off the carburetor body **(see illustration)**. Remove the two mounting screws and lift off the diaphragm assembly **(see illustration)**.

14   Disconnect the throttle return spring from the primary throttle lever **(see illustration)**. The upper choke pinion gear assembly mount has a series of lines scribed on it. Note which one is lined up with the dot on the body **(see illustration)**.

15   Remove the two screws holding the choke pinion gear assembly to the carburetor body and carefully pull it free **(see illustration)**.

16   Separate the choke plate from the choke shaft. It is held in place with two small screws **(see illustration)**.

17   Remove the spring clip and carefully pry the manual choke unloader linkage rod out of the choke lever **(see illustration)**.

18   Using small pliers, pull out the pin holding the choke unloader diaphragm in alignment **(see illustration)**.

19   Remove the throttle return spring mount. It is held in place with one bolt **(see illustration)**.

20   Pull out the choke unloader diaphragm and linkage **(see illustration)**, then withdraw the choke shaft from the carburetor body **(see illustration)**.

12.18   Pull out the pin holding the choke unloader diaphragm in alignment

12.19   Remove the throttle return spring mount

12.20a   Pull out the choke unloader diaphragm and linkage

12.20b   Withdraw the choke shaft

12.21a   Unhook the secondary return spring

12.21b   Remove the two choke mechanism housing screws

12.21c   Lift the choke mechanism housing away from the carburetor body

12.21d   Separate the spacer and O-ring from the housing

12.22a   Remove the top cover screws

21   Unhook the secondary return spring from the choke mechanism housing **(see illustration)**. Remove the two screws **(see illustration)** and lift the choke mechanism housing away from the carburetor body **(see illustration)**. Separate the spacer and small O-ring from the housing **(see illustration)**.

22   Remove the four remaining screws **(see illustration)** and lift the top cover off the carburetor. Be careful not to bend or otherwise damage the float mechanism **(see illustration)**.

23   Before removing the float, invert the top cover and measure the distance from the float seam to the gasket surface of the top cover **(see illustration)**. Record the measurement for future reference.

24   Carefully slide out the pivot pin and separate the float and inlet needle from the top cover **(see illustration)**. Slip the needle out of its mount on the float **(see illustration)**. Unscrew and remove the inlet needle seat and washer **(see illustration)**.

25   Remove the top cover gasket from the carburetor body **(see illustration)**.

26   Hold your finger over the accelerator pump discharge plunger bore **(see illustration)**. Tip the carburetor upside down and let the steel ball from the anti-overflow mechanism in the bottom of the float bowl fall out **(see illustration)**. Next, remove the accelerator pump steel check ball and weight **(see illustration)**. Draw a simple diagram showing the sizes (stamped on the jets) and the locations of the primary and secondary main jets, then unscrew and remove them from the carburetor body **(see illustrations)**.

12.22b   Lift the top cover off; don't bend the float arm

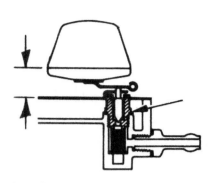

12.23   Measure the distance from the float seam to the gasket surface of the top cover

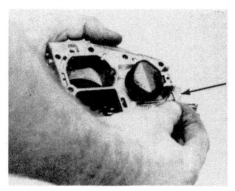

12.24a   Slide out the pivot pin

12.24b   Separate the float and needle from the top cover

12.24c   Remove the inlet needle seat

12.25   Remove the top cover gasket

12.26a   Accelerator pump discharge plunger bore

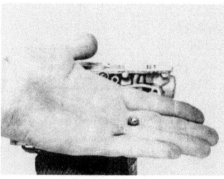

12.26b   Anti-overflow mechanism steel ball

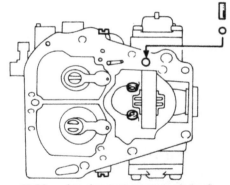

12.26c   Accelerator pump steel check ball and weight location

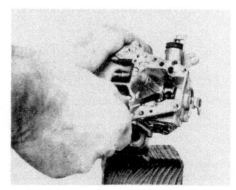

12.26d   Remove the primary main jet

12.26e   Remove the secondary main jet

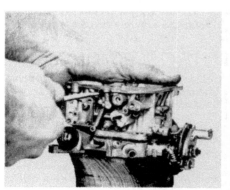

12.26f   Remove the idle jets

12.27a Remove the two screws attaching the throttle body to the carburetor body

12.27b Separate the throttle body from the carburetor body (don't disassemble the throttle shafts and linkages at this time)

27 Remove the two attaching screws **(see illustration)** and separate the throttle body from the carburetor body **(see illustration)**. Do not remove any plugs or fittings from the carburetor body that have been sealed with white paint.

28 Slip off the rubber boot and slide the sub-EGR valve plunger out of the throttle body **(see illustration)**.

Inspection

29 Once the carburetor has been completely disassembled, the parts should be thoroughly cleaned and inspected. There are many commercial carburetor cleaning solvents available which can be used with good results.

30 The diaphragms and some plastic parts of the carburetor can be damaged by solvents; avoid placing these parts in any liquid. Clean the external surfaces of these parts with a clean cloth or soft brush. Shake or wipe dirt and other foreign material from the stem plunger side of the diaphragm. Compressed air can be used to remove loose dirt, but should not be connected to the vacuum diaphragm fitting.

31 If the commercial solvent or cleaner recommends the use of water as a rinse, hot water will produce the best results. After rinsing, all traces of water must be blown from the passages using compressed air. Never clean jets with a wire, drill bit or other objects. The orifices may be enlarged, making the mixture too rich for proper performance.

32 When checking parts removed from the carburetor, it is often difficult to be sure they are serviceable. It is therefore recommended that new parts be installed, if available, when the carburetor is disassembled. The required parts should be included in the carburetor rebuild kit.

33 After all the parts have been cleaned and dried, check the throttle valve shaft and choke shaft for proper operation. If sticking or binding occurs, clean the shafts with solvent and lubricate them with engine oil.

34 Check the jets for damage or clogging. Replace them if damage is evident.

35 Inspect the idle mixture adjusting screw. The tapered portion of the screw must be straight and smooth. If the tapered portion is grooved or ridged replace the screw with a new one.

36 Check the strainer screen for clogging and damage.

37 Check the vacuum chamber. Push the vacuum chamber rod in, seal off the nipple and release the rod. If the rod does not return, the vacuum chamber is most likely in good condition. If the rod returns when released, the diaphragm is defective. The vacuum chamber should be replaced with a new one if this condition exists.

38 To check the fuel cut-off solenoid, connect a jumper lead to the positive (+) terminal of a 12-volt battery and the wire lead of the solenoid. Connect a second jumper lead to the negative (-) terminal of the battery and the solenoid ground wire. The needle should move in toward the solenoid when the battery is connected and out when the battery is disconnected. If it does, the fuel cut-off solenoid is good.

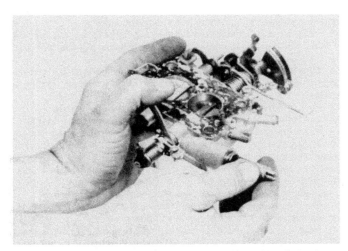

12.28 Slide the sub-EGR plunger out of the throttle body

Reassembly

Note: *The reassembly process will be easier if the sequenced photos in the disassembly section are followed in reverse.*

39 Using a new gasket, assemble the throttle body to the carburetor body and tighten the mounting screws securely.

40 Install the main and pilot jets in the carburetor body. Make sure they are installed in the correct bores.

41 Place the anti-overflow ball in place in the bottom of the float bowl and insert the accelerator pump steel check ball and weight into the accelerator pump bore.

42 Install the new inlet needle seat in place in the carburetor top cover; (don't forget to include a new washer). Assemble the new inlet needle to the float and attach the float to the top cover.

43 Invert the top cover and measure the distance from the float seam to the gasket surface of the top cover **(see illustration 12.23)**. If the measured distance is more or less than it was during disassembly, remove the float from the top cover, unscrew the inlet needle seat and add or remove washers (as necessary) to change the float height. Reassemble the inlet needle and float and recheck the measurement. Repeat the procedure as required until the distance is the same as it was during disassembly. When checking the float level on 1984 models, measure the distance from the bottom of the float to the gasket surface of the float chamber (it should be 0.787 + or – 0.394 inches).

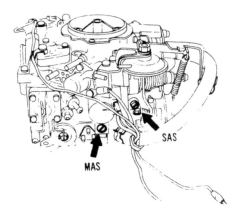

13.5 Idle speed (SAS) and mixture (MAS) adjustment screw locations

44 Gently lay the top cover in place using a new gasket and install the mounting screws. Tighten them evenly and securely.
45 Install the choke mechanism housing and tighten the screws securely. Make sure the manual choke unloader rod is facing in the proper direction.
46 Slide the choke shaft into place and install the choke plate. It is a very good idea to use a thread locking compound on the choke plate attaching screws.
47 Insert the manual choke unloader rod into the choke lever.
48 Install the choke unloader/diaphragm and push the pin into place.
49 Install the throttle return spring mount and tighten the screw securely.
50 Engage the spring loop on the choke pinion gear assembly, hold the choke plate closed and engage the plastic gear teeth of the choke pinion gear with the gear teeth on the choke set lever. Install the screws, move the pinion gear assembly to line up the marks exactly as they were before disassembly, then tighten the screws securely.
51 Install the secondary diaphragm assembly and hook up the hose. Slip the diaphragm link into the secondary throttle lever.
52 Install the choke unloader diaphragm plate and tighten the screws.
53 Install the CAV internal parts and housing then tighten the mounting screws evenly and securely.
54 Assemble the enrichment system components and install the housing in place on the carburetor body. (The wire clamp fits over the upper left mounting screw). Tighten the mounting screws securely.
55 Assemble the vent valve. Lubricate the O-ring on the valve body and slide the valve into place in the carburetor body. Tighten the mounting screws securely.
56 Install the vent valve solenoid and tighten the mounting screws. Attach the ground wire to the carburetor body.
57 Install the ASV housing (with the wire clamp on the longest screw) and tighten the mounting screws finger-tight. Assemble the ASV internal parts, install the housing and tighten the mounting screws.
58 Install the accelerator pump and hook the linkage to the throttle shaft arm.
59 Slip the small steel ball and the spring into place in the end of the sub-EGR valve plunger Install the rubber boot and push the plunger into place in the throttle body. Hold the linkage in place, install the pin and snap the spring clip into place on the end of the pin.
60 Make sure the O-ring is in place on the fuel cut-off solenoid body, then install the solenoid and tighten the mounting screws. Remove the short screw on the ASV body. Install the fuel cut-off solenoid ground wire and tighten both ASV body mounting screws securely.
61 Insert the throttle opener actuating rod into the primary throttle shaft lever. Install the spring clip and mount the throttle opener on the carburetor (air-conditioned models only).
62 Install the coolant hose and slide the hose clamps into place.
63 Double check all screws to make sure they are tight and the carburetor reassembly is complete.

13 Carburetor (32-35 DIDTA) (1983 and 1984 non-FBC models) – adjustments

Idle speed and mixture

1 An exhaust gas analyzer must be used to adjust the idle mixture. Since the average home mechanic doesn't have access to such equipment, we recommend the idle speed and mixture adjustments be done by a dealer service department or a suitably-equipped automotive tune-up facility perform.
2 However, you can do the basic adjustments for the idle speed and mixture without an exhaust gas analyzer if you follow the steps outlined here. Just remember that final adjustment must be done with the proper equipment to ensure compliance with emission standards.
3 Before making the idle speed and mixture adjustments, check the ignition system, including the ignition timing. Look for cracked or disconnected vacuum lines. Make sure the intake manifold and carburetor mounting nuts are tightened evenly and securely; any intake leaks must be fixed before proceeding. Also, the engine must be at normal operating temperature so the choke is completely open. Place the transmission in Neutral and set the parking brake. The air conditioner, lights and all accessories must be off.
4 Hook up a tachometer in accordance with the instructions provided by its manufacturer.

2.0L engine (49-states only)
Refer to illustration 13.5
5 With the engine running, carefully turn the idle mixture adjusting screw (MAS) **(see illustration)** clockwise, preferably by hand, until the engine starts to slow down or misfire. When this happens, slowly turn the MAS in the opposite direction (counterclockwise). The engine should start to speed up again. Then, as the MAS is turned farther, the engine should begin to slow down or misfire.
6 These two points are sometimes difficult to discern, so keep a close eye on the tachometer. The idle mixture adjusting screw should be turned approximately 1/16 of a turn each time, allowing about ten seconds for the engine speed to stabilize between adjustments.
7 Once you have determined how the engine reacts to changes of the MAS position, slowly turn it clockwise or counterclockwise, as necessary, until the smoothest, fastest idle speed is obtained.
8 Next, turn the idle speed adjusting screw (SAS) until the speed listed in this Chapter's Specifications is obtained.
9 Recheck the MAS to make sure it is still providing the smoothest, fastest idle speed at that position.
10 Slowly turn the MAS clockwise, while watching the tachometer, until the engine is idling at the specified idle speed. Turning the MAS clockwise leans the idle mixture, forcing it to fall into the emission specification range, and causes the engine to slow down. If the engine misfires badly, repeat the procedure, turning the MAS further counterclockwise initially.

2.0L engine (California only) and 2.6L engine (all)
11 Remove the air hose from the inlet of the secondary air supply system reed valve and plug the reed valve inlet.
12 With the engine running, carefully turn the idle mixture adjusting screw (MAS) **(see illustration 13.5)** clockwise, preferably by hand, until the engine starts to slow down or misfire. When this happens, slowly turn the MAS in the opposite direction (counterclockwise). The engine should start to speed up again. Then, as the MAS is turned further, it should begin to slow down or misfire.
13 These two points are sometimes difficult to discern, so keep a close eye on the tachometer. The MAS should be turned approximately 1/16 of a turn each time, allowing about ten seconds for the engine speed to stabilize between adjustments.
14 Once you have determined how the engine reacts to changes of the MAS position, slowly turn it clockwise or counterclockwise, as necessary, until the smoothest, fastest idle speed is obtained. Next turn the idle speed adjusting screw (SAS) until the idle speed listed in this Chapter's Specifications is obtained. Recheck the MAS to make sure it is still providing the smoothest, fastest idle speed at that position.
15 Unplug the reed valve inlet and hook up the air hose.

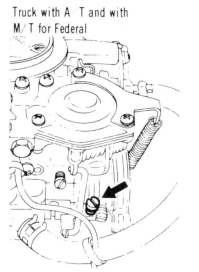
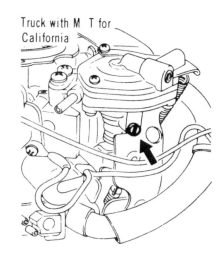

Truck with A T and with M/T for Federal

Truck with M T for California

13.19   Throttle opener (idle-up) adjusting screw location (air-conditioned models)

16   If the idle speed changes, return it to the specified rpm by turning the SAS in or out as necessary.

17   If the engine misfires badly, repeat the procedure, turning the MAS further counterclockwise initially.

Air-conditioned models

Refer to illustration 13.19

18   After the idle mixture and speed have been adjusted, an additional adjustment must be made to all air-conditioned models.

19   Turn off all accessories. Put the transmission in Neutral and apply the parking brake. If the vehicle has power steering, put the wheels in the straight ahead position so the power steering pump isn't loaded. Now turn the air conditioner control switch to On (this activates the throttle opener on the carburetor). Adjust the idle speed to the idle-up engine speed listed in this Chapter's Specifications by turning the throttle opener (idle-up) adjusting screw **(see illustration)** in or out as necessary.

20   When the speed has been set, turn off the air conditioner control switch – the engine should return to the specified idle speed.

Automatic choke

21   The choke valve is automatically operated by a wax element that senses the coolant temperature. This element allows the choke valve to close under spring pressure at low coolant temperatures and opens it through a set lever and a rack and pinion gear setup as the coolant temperature increases.

22   The wax element plunger pushes against an adjustable screw on the choke set lever. This screw is pre-set at the factory to provide for proper choke closing and opening and sealed with white paint. Do not tamper with it, as choke operation will be adversely affected.

23   The choke should not require any adjustment as long as the rack and pinion gears are properly oriented and the choke pinion gear assembly is adjusted so that the choke plate is lightly seated in the closed position when the choke linkage is installed.

---

14   Carburetor (FBC) (1985 and 1986 models) – overhaul

Warning: *Gasoline is extremely flammable, so take extra precautions when you work on any part of the fuel system. Don't smoke or allow open flames or bare light bulbs near the work area, and don't work in a garage where a natural gas-type appliance (such as a water heater or clothes dryer) with a pilot light is present. If you spill any fuel on your skin, rinse it off immediately with soap and water. When you perform any kind of work on the fuel system, wear safety glasses and have a Class B type fire extinguisher on hand.*

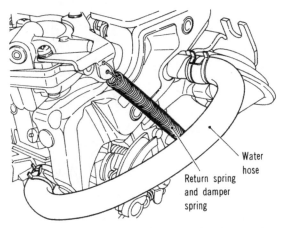

Water hose

Return spring and damper spring

14.1   Remove the coolant hose, throttle return spring and damper spring

Disassembly

Refer to illustrations 14.1, 14.3, 14.4, 14.5, 14.7, 14.8a, 14.8b, 14.10, 14.11, 14.12, 14.13, 14.14, 14.16, 14.17a, 14.17b, 14.18, 14.19a, 14.19b, 14.20, 14.21, 14.22 and 14.23

Note: *Do not remove the choke and throttle valves from the shafts.*

1   Remove the carburetor (see Section 11) and detach the coolant hose from the carburetor **(see illustration)**.

2   Remove the throttle return spring and the damper spring.

3   Grind off the heads on the choke cover screws **(see illustration)** with a hand grinder, then remove the cover.

4   Remove the Throttle Position Sensor (TPS) **(see illustration)**.

5   Remove the throttle opener/dashpot rod from the free lever, then remove the throttle opener/dashpot from the float chamber cover **(see illustration)**.

6   Unplug the wiring harness from the electrical connector.

7   Unscrew and remove the three solenoid valves – deceleration, enrichment and jet mixture – from the float chamber cover **(see illustration)**.

8   Remove the bowl vent solenoid and valve **(see illustrations)**.

9   Remove the vacuum hose from the depression chamber and the throttle body fitting.

10   Remove the screws and detach the choke breaker cover **(see illustration)**.

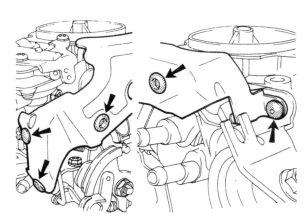

14.3   Grind off the heads on the choke cover screws (arrows) and remove the choke cover

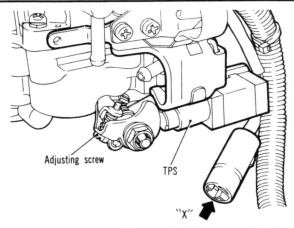

14.4   Remove the Throttle Position Sensor (TPS)

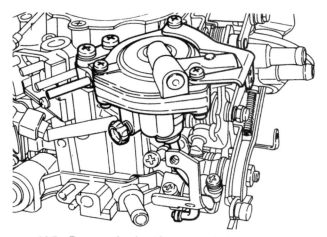

14.5   Remove the throttle opener/dashpot

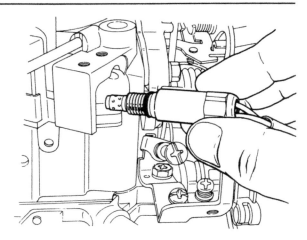

14.7   Remove the solenoid valves

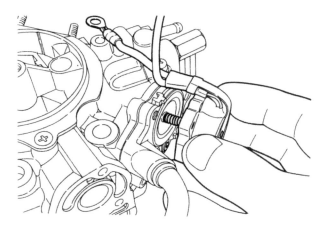

14.8a   Remove the bowl vent solenoid . . .

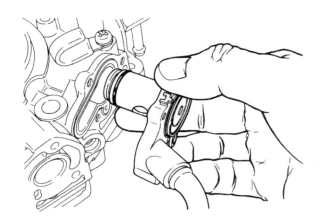

14.8b . . . and valve

11   Remove the depression chamber rod from the secondary throttle lever, then remove the depression chamber **(see illustration)**.

12   Detach the accelerator pump rod from the throttle lever **(see illustration)**.

13   Remove the snap-ring from the choke rod, then disconnect the rod from the choke lever **(see illustration)**.

14   Remove the float chamber cover screws (B) and remove the throttle body **(see illustration)**.

15   Remove the screws (A) and remove the float chamber cover from the main body.

16   Pull out the pin and remove the float and the needle **(see illustration)**.

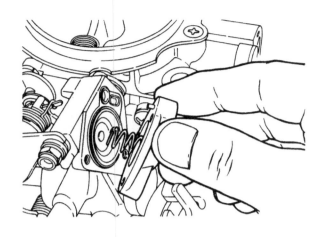

14.10   Remove the choke breaker cover

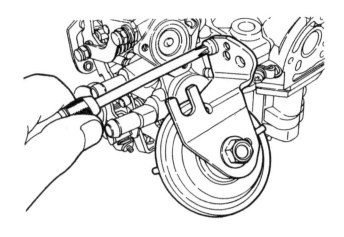

14.11   Remove the depression chamber

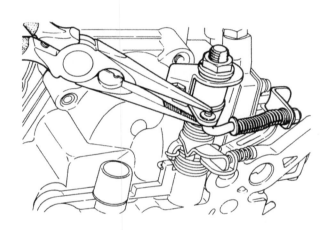

14.12   Remove the accelerator pump rod

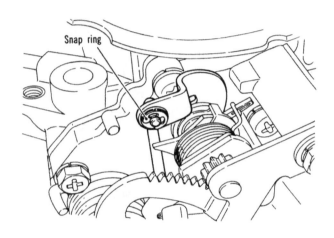

14.13   Remove the snap-ring, then remove the choke rod

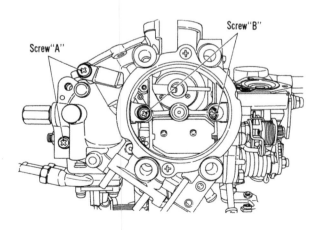

14.14   Remove the float chamber cover

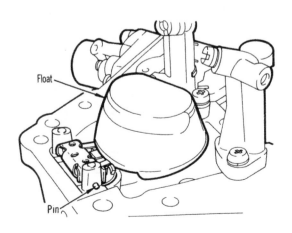

14.16   Remove the pin and the float, then remove the needle

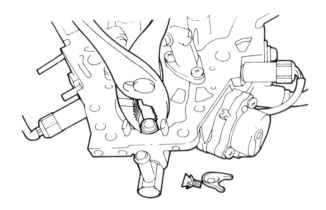

14.17a   When removing the needle seat, . . .

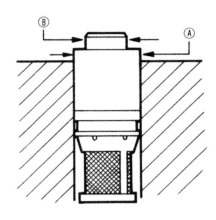

14.17b   . . . grasp the seat at area A, not in area B

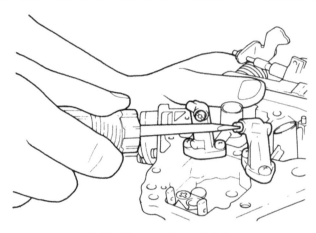

14.18   Remove the main jets

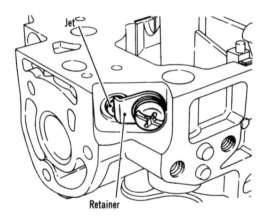

14.19a   To remove the pilot jet, remove the retainer, . . .

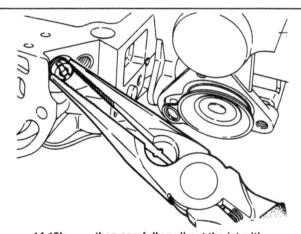

14.19b   . . . then carefully pull out the jet with needle-nose pliers

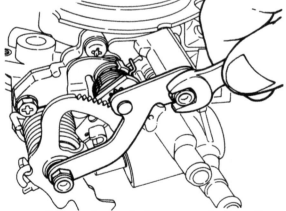

14.20   Remove the two lock screws and remove the choke pinion assembly

17   Unscrew the retainer and remove the needle seat with a pair of pliers **(see illustration). Caution:** *When removing the needle seat, clamp area A with pliers, not area B* **(see illustration).**

18   Using a screwdriver with the right size tip, remove the main jets from the jet blocks **(see illustration).**

19   Remove the pilot jet retainer and pull out the secondary pilot jet with pliers **(see illustrations).**

20   Remove the two lock screws and remove the choke pinion assembly **(see illustration).**

21   Remove the check weight and ball, and the steel ball of the anti-over-fill device **(see illustration).**

22   Remove the accelerator pump mounting screws and remove the pump cover link assembly, diaphragm, spring, body and gasket from the main body **(see illustration).**

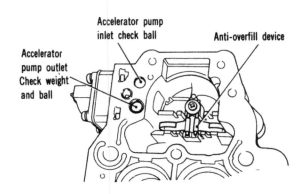

14.21   Remove the check weight and ball from the accelerator pump outlet and remove the steel ball of the anti-overfill device

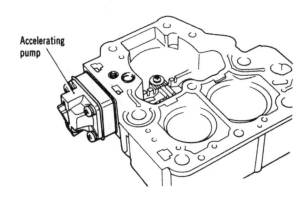

14.22   Remove the accelerator pump mounting screws and remove the pump cover link assembly, diaphragm, spring, body and gasket from the carburetor

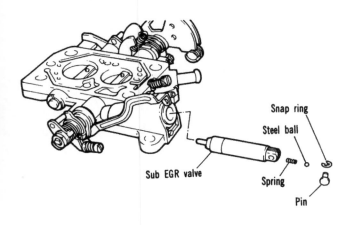

14.23   Remove the snap-ring from the sub-EGR control valve pin

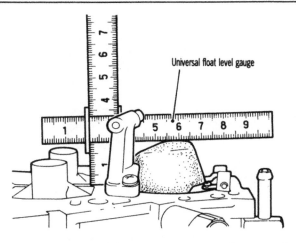

14.31   A universal float level gauge setup for measuring float height

23   Remove the snap-ring from the sub-EGR control valve pin (**see illustration**).
24   Remove the pin, then remove the link from the valve. Then take out the steel ball and spring from the sub-EGR control valve.
25   Remove the sub-EGR control valve from the throttle body.

Reassembly

26   Clean all parts thoroughly in solvent and blow out all air passages with compressed air before beginning reassembly.
27   Reassembly is the reverse of disassembly. Don't reuse any old gaskets or O-rings. Use the new ones in the carburetor rebuild kit.
28   When replacing jets, make sure the old jet and new jet are the same size (a No. is stamped on each jet).
29   Inspect the operation of the throttle and choke linkage, and the sub-EGR valve. They should operate smoothly.

Float adjustment

Refer to illustrations 14.31 and 14.32

30   Invert the float chamber cover assembly without a gasket.
31   Position a universal float level gauge, or equivalent instrument, as shown (**see illustration**). The float level (distance from the bottom of the float to the surface of the float chamber) should be within the dimension listed in this Chapter's Specifications.

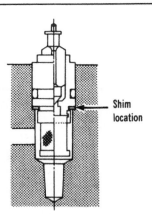

14.32   Shim location for float height adjustment shims

32   If it isn't, the shim under the needle seat (**see illustration**) must be changed. Shim kit MD606952 contains three shims (.0118 in., .0157 in. and .0196 in.). Adding or removing a shim changes the float level by three times the thickness of the shim you add or remove.

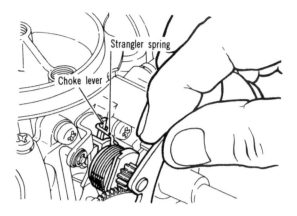

14.33   Fit the strangler spring to the choke lever

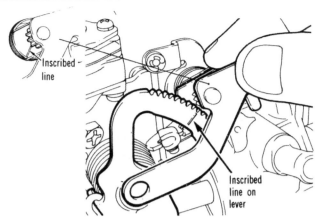

14.34   Align the inscribed line or black painted line of the choke pinion with the inscribed line on the cam lever

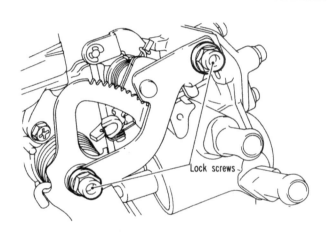

14.35   Temporarily tighten the new lock screws

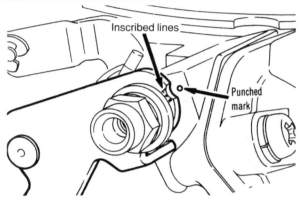

14.36   Set the choke valve by moving the pinion arm up or down, align a punched mark on the float chamber at the center of the three inscribed lines and secure the pinion arm with the lock screws

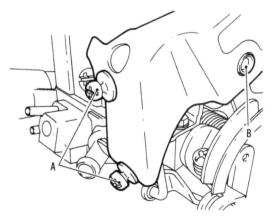

14.37a   After installing the choke cover and the new cover screws, cut off the heads of the A screws ...

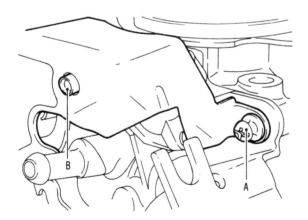

14.37b   ... and peen over the heads of the B screws

Choke valve setting
Refer to illustrations 14.33, 14.34, 14.35, 14.36, 14.37a, 14.37b

33   Fit the strangler spring to the choke lever **(see illustration)**.
34   Align the inscribed line or black painted line of the choke pinion with the inscribed line on the cam lever **(see illustration)**.
35   Temporarily tighten the new lock screws **(see illustration)**.

36   Set the choke valve by moving the pinion arm up or down, align a punched mark on the float chamber at the center of the three inscribed lines and secure the pinion arm with the lock screws **(see illustration)**.
37   Install the choke cover and tighten the lock screws **(see illustrations)**. Cut off the head of the A lock screws. Peen the heads of the B lock screws with a ball peen hammer or punch.

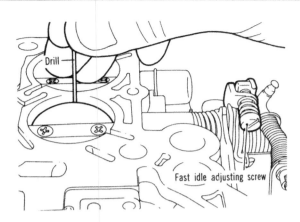

14.39 Using a drill bit of the specified diameter, measure the fast idle opening; if it's not correct, adjust it with the fast idle adjusting screw

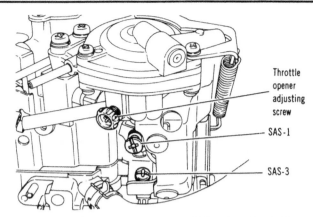

15.1a Idle speed adjusting screw (SAS-1) location (1985 and 1986 FBC carburetor) – don't touch the other idle speed adjusting screw (SAS-3); the throttle opener adjusting screw is for adjusting the air conditioning idle-up speed

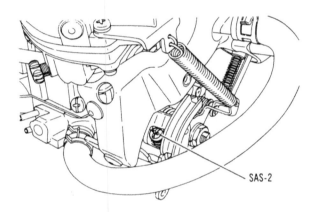

15.1b Don't touch idle speed adjusting screw (SAS-2) – it's preset at the factory (1985 and 1986 FBC carburetors)

Fast idle opening adjustment
Refer to illustration 14.39
38   The carburetor should sit in an ambient temperature of 73-degrees F. for an hour before adjusting the fast idle opening.
39   Using a drill bit of the specified diameter, measure the fast idle opening and compare it to the value listed in this Chapter's Specifications **(see illustration)**. If it's not correct, adjust it with the fast idle adjusting screw.

15   Carburetor (FBC) (1985 and 1986 models) – adjustments

Refer to illustrations 15.1a and 15.1b
The procedure for adjusting the idle speed and, on air-conditioned models, the idle-up speed, is essentially the same on models with FBC carburetors as it is on earlier models with non-FBC carburetors (see Section 13). However, the location of the adjusting screws is different **(see illustrations)**. **Caution:** *Don't touch idle speed adjusting screw No. 2 (SAS-2), which is preset at the factory. SAS-2 determines the relationship between the throttle valve and the free lever and has been accurately set at the factory. If this setting is disturbed, throttle opener adjustment and dashpot adjustment are impossible to set. There's a third idle screw known as SAS-3. Don't tamper with it either!*
The idle mixture is factory pre-set on these models and should not require adjustment under normal circumstances. If, however, you must adjust the mixture, you'll have to drill out and remove the concealment plug

over the mixture adjusting screw. Once this is done, follow the procedure in Section 13.
There's one other important carburetor adjustment on FBC carburetors – the Throttle Position Sensor (TPS) adjustment. You'll find the procedure for this adjustment in Chapter 6, in the "Information sensors" Section.

16   Carburetor (FBC) (1987 through 1989 models) – overhaul

Warning: *Gasoline is extremely flammable, so take extra precautions when you work on any part of the fuel system. Don't smoke or allow open flames or bare light bulbs near the work area, and don't work in a garage where a natural gas-type appliance (such as a water heater or clothes dryer) with a pilot light is present. If you spill any fuel on your skin, rinse it off immediately with soap and water. When you perform any kind of work on the fuel system, wear safety glasses and have a Class B type fire extinguisher on hand.*

Disassembly
Refer to illustrations 16.1, 16.5, 16.6, 16.7a, 16.7b, 16.8, 16.9, 16.10a, 16.10b, 16.11a, 16.11b, 16.18, 16.21 and 16.23
Caution: *When loosening a Phillips screw which is very tight, use a Phillips screwdriver that's an exact fit for the screw. Also, during the following disassembly procedure, don't disassemble the choke valve; the choke shaft and automatic choke device; the inner venturi; the throttle valve and throttle shaft; or the fuel inlet nipple.*
1   After removing the carburetor (see Section 11), remove the throttle return spring, damper spring and throttle return spring bracket **(see illustration)**.
2   Remove the throttle opener/dashpot.
3   Remove the accelerator cable bracket.
4   Remove the vacuum delay valve and both short sections of vacuum hose to which it's connected.
5   Using a pin or a small screwdriver with a thin, flat tip, push the stopper portion to remove each of the three TPS terminals from the rear of the electrical connector **(see illustration)**. Make sure the terminals aren't bent when the connectors are unplugged.
6   Remove the float chamber cover screws, the float chamber cover and the cover gasket. Don't try to force off the cover if it's stuck to the gasket. Insert a screwdriver between the enrichment cover and the float chamber cover, lightly pry and lift up the float chamber cover **(see illustration)**.
7   Remove the float pivot pin **(see illustrations)**, the float, the needle valve, the O-ring and the packing. Don't let the float drop and don't put a load on the float. And don't damage the end of the needle valve.
8   Using a pair of flat-bladed screwdrivers, pry up the needle valve seat at both edges **(see illustration)** and remove the seat. Don't damage the float chamber cover when pushing on the needle valve seat.

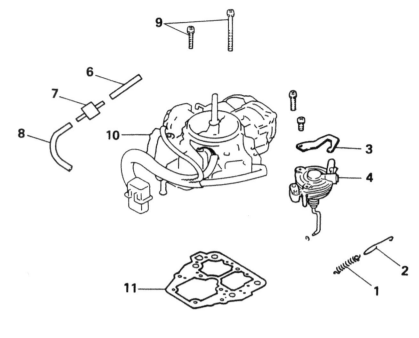

16.1   An exploded view of the two main components of the 1987 through 1989 FBC carburetor

1   Throttle return spring
2   Damper spring
3   Throttle return spring bracket
4   Throttle opener/dashpot
5   Bracket
6   Vacuum hose
7   Vacuum delay valve
8   Vacuum hose
9   Screw
10   Float chamber cover assembly
11   Float chamber cover gasket
12   Mixing body and throttle body assembly

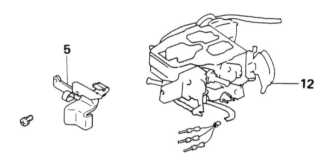

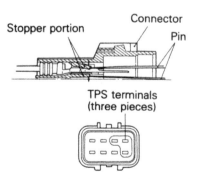

16.5   (above) Using a pin or small screwdriver with a thin, flat tip, push the stopper portion to remove the three TPS terminals from the rear of their respective connectors – (below) TPS terminal locations

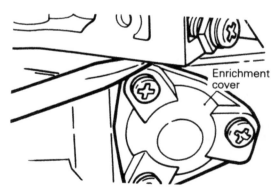

16.6   If the float chamber cover is stuck to the gasket, insert a screwdriver between the float chamber cover and the enrichment cover and pry the float chamber cover loose

9   Remove the retainer screw and retainer for the feedback solenoid. Using a pin or a small screwdriver with a thin, flat tip, push the stopper portion and remove the two terminals from behind the electrical connector **(see illustration)**, then remove the feedback solenoid and the O-rings (the feedback solenoid can't be removed until the the terminals are removed from the connector). Make sure you don't bend any terminals during removal of the connector. Remove the tube for the electrical harness.

10   Remove the retainer for the Slow Cut Solenoid Valve (SCSV) and remove the SCSV and O-rings. When removing the SCSV, grasp the valve body – not the leads **(see illustration)**. Using a pin or a small screwdriver with a thin, flat tip, push the stopper section and remove the two terminals from behind the connector **(see illustration)**.

16.7a   An exploded view of the float chamber assembly (1985 through 1987 FBC carburetor)

1	Float pivot pin	24	Body
2	Float	25	Spring
3	Needle valve	26	Diaphragm
4	Needle valve seat	27	Valve
5	O-ring	28	Mixture control valve (MCV) assembly
6	Packing	29	Gasket
7	Retainer	30	Cover
8	Feedback Solenoid Valve (FBSV)	31	Spring
9	O-ring	32	Diaphragm
10	O-ring	33	Body
11	Tube	34	Spring
12	Retainer	35	Diaphragm
13	Slow-cut solenoid valve (SCSV)	36	Bracket
14	O-ring	37	Cover
15	O-ring	38	Spring
16	Plate	39	Diaphragm
17	Bimetal assembly	40	Body
18	Packing	41	Primary main air jet
19	Connector	42	Primary pilot jet
20	Cover	43	Secondary pilot jet
21	Diaphragm	44	Float chamber cover
22	Spring seat		
23	Spring		

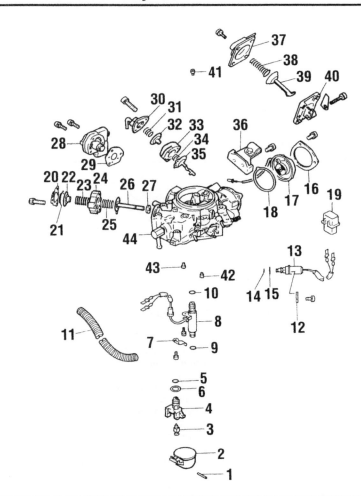

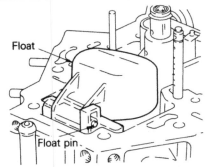

16.7b   To remove the float, knock out the float pivot pin

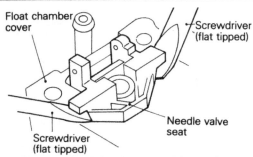

16.8   Using a pair of flat-bladed screwdrivers, pry up on the edges of the needle valve seat

16.9   FBSV terminal locations

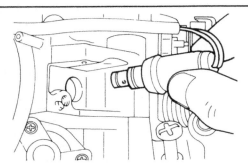

16.10a   Remove the retainer for the Slow Cut Solenoid Valve (SCSV) and remove the SCSV and O-rings

16.10b   SCSV terminal locations

16.11b   Bimetal terminal location

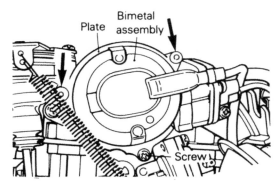

16.11a   To remove the bimetal assembly, grind off the heads of the two rivets (Canadian models have no rivets) and remove the screw (arrow)

11   Grind off the heads of the two rivets of the bimetal assembly with a hand grinder, remove the screw **(see illustration)**, remove the plate, the bimetal assembly and the packing. Knock out the remainder of each rivet body with a pin punch. Using a pin or a small screwdriver with a thin, flat tip, push the stopper section and remove the terminal from behind the electrical connector **(see illustration)**. Make sure you don't bend the terminal during connector removal. **Note:** *Canadian models don't have any rivets, just three screws, holding the bimetal assembly plate.*

12   Remove the cover, diaphragm, spring seat, spring, body, spring, diaphragm and valve from the carburetor (parts 20 through 27 in illustration 16.7a).

13   Remove the mixture control valve (MCV) assembly and the gasket.

14   Remove the cover, spring, diaphragm, body, spring and diaphragm (parts 30 through 35 in illustration 16.7a).

15   Remove the bracket (part 36 in illustration 16.7a).

16   Remove the cover, spring, diaphragm and body (parts 37 through 40 in illustration 16.7a).

17   Remove the primary main air jet, the primary pilot jet and the secondary pilot jet. When you remove jets, use a screwdriver that's an exact fit for their respective slots so you don't nick or gouge them during removal.

18   Remove the steel ball, weight, ball, plug, O-ring and ball **(see illustration)**.

19   Remove the screw(s) from the underside of the throttle body. Make sure the Phillips screwdriver you use is an exact fit to prevent stripping the crosshead out of the screw. Any burrs created in the head of this screw could produce a gap between the throttle body and the manifold surface.

20   Separate the throttle body from the mixing body. Discard the gasket between the two. Don't reuse it.

21   Remove the primary main jet and the secondary main jet **(see illustration)**. Again, use an appropriately sized screwdriver that fits tightly to prevent damage to the jets. The jets are stamped on top to indicate their size. Be sure to note which size jet goes where so they can be reassembled the same way.

22   Remove the cover, spring and diaphragm (parts 11 through 13 in illustration 16.18).

23   Remove the enrichment jet valve **(see illustration)**. **Caution:** *This valve has many small parts; don't lose even one of them! Again, use a screwdriver whose tip is an exact fit for the cross slots in the head of the jet to avoid damaging the jet during removal. Using a screwdriver, take out the enrichment jet, the spring and the ball from the enrichment jet valve.*

24   Remove the accelerator pump cover assembly, diaphragm, spring, pump body and gasket (parts 18 through 21 in illustration 16.18).

25   Remove the hose, auxiliary accelerator pump cover, spring, diaphragm and check valve (parts 23 through 27).

26   Remove the vacuum hose and detach the depression chamber (dashpot) (parts 28 and 29).

27   Remove the Throttle Position Sensor (TPS) (part 31).

28   Do NOT remove the throttle lever, cam follower, fast idle adjusting screw, free lever, apartment plate, idle speed adjusting screw (SAS-2), spring, secondary lever, idle speed adjusting screw (SAS-1), plug or mixture screw (parts 32 through 42).

Inspection

Refer to illustration 16.41

29   Wash the carburetor mixing body and throttle body thoroughly in fresh solvent and blow dry with compressed air.

30   Inspect all fuel circuits (jets) and air circuits (jets or orifices) for clogging. If a circuit is plugged, blow it out with compressed air – don't stick metal wires into circuits.

31   Inspect all diaphragms for tears and cracks. Replace as necessary.

32   Verify that the needle valve operates smoothly. If it's hard to slide or binds, repair or replace it. If the carburetor's been overflowing, the valve-to-seat contact is probably bad. Inspect this area thoroughly. Also check the fuel inlet filter immediately above the needle valve for clogging.

33   Check the operation of the float assembly. Look for any deformation in the float or lever. Replace as necessary.

34   Check the operation of the throttle valve, choke valve and link. If they don't operate smoothly, scrub and clean them with solvent, blow dry, apply new engine oil to the shaft and recheck. If the assembly still binds, replace it.

35   Inspect the float chamber and main body for damage and cracks.

36   Apply battery voltage directly to the Slow Cut Solenoid Valve (SCSV) terminals and verify that the valve clicks.

37   Using a self-powered test light or continuity checker, verify that there's no continuity between the solenoid valve body and the terminals.

38   Measure the resistance between the SCSV terminals. Compare your measurement to the value listed in this Chapter's Specifications.

39   Replace the SCSV if it fails any of the above tests.

40   Apply battery voltage directly to the Feedback Solenoid Valve (FBSV) terminals and verify that the valve clicks.

41   Inspect the jet in the FBSV **(see illustration)**. Make sure it's not clogged.

42   Using a self-powered test light or continuity checker, verify continuity between the FBSV body and the terminals.

43   Measure the resistance between the FBSV terminals.

44   Replace the FBSV if it fails any of the above tests.

45   Using a self-powered test light or continuity checker, measure the resistance between the terminal and body of the bimetal assembly. Resistance should be approximately 6 ohms.

46   Verify that the dashpot operates properly. Pull on the dashpot rod – you should feel a steady resistance. Release the rod – it should return quickly to its retracted position. If you feel no resistance when you pull on the rod, the diaphragm or check valve is broken. If the rod returns slowly to

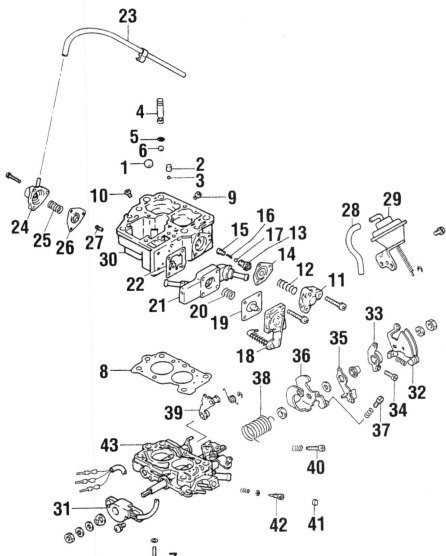

16.18   An exploded view of the mixing body and throttle body assemblies (1985 through 1987 FBC carburetor)

1   Steel ball
2   Weight
3   Ball
4   Plug
5   O-ring
6   Ball
7   Screw
8   Gasket
9   Primary main jet
10 Secondary main jet
11 Cover
12 Spring
13 Diaphragm
14 Enrichment jet valve
15 Enrichment jet
16 Spring
17 Ball
18 Pump cover assembly
19 Diaphragm
20 Spring
21 Pump body
22 Gasket
23 Vacuum hose
24 Auxiliary accelerator pump cover
25 Spring
26 Diaphragm
27 Check valve
28 Vacuum hose
29 Depression chamber (dashpot)
30 Mixing body
31 Throttle Position Sensor (TPS)
32 Throttle lever
33 Cam follower
34 Fast-idle adjustment screw
35 Free lever
36 Throttle linkage adjustment plate
37 Idle-speed adjustment screw (SAS-2)
38 Spring
39 Secondary lever
40 Idle-speed adjustment screw (SAS-1)
41 Concealment plug
42 Mixture-adjustment screw (MAS)
43 Throttle body

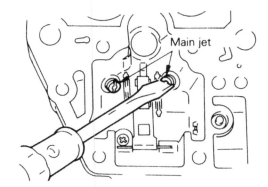

16.21   Remove the primary main jet and the secondary main jet with a small screwdriver – make sure the screwdriver tip fits snugly to prevent damage to the slots in the jets

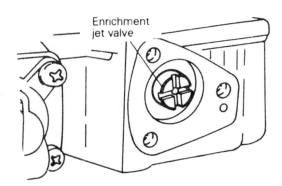

16.23   Remove the enrichment jet valve – again, use a screwdriver with a tip size that just fits into the cross slots in the head of the valve

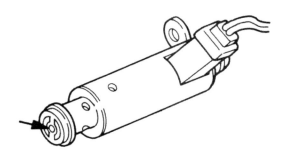

16.41　Inspect the jet (arrow) in the FBSV to make sure it's not clogged

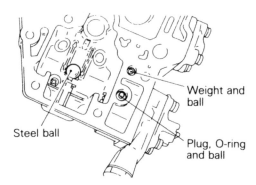

16.52　Install the ball, O-ring, plug, ball, weight and steel ball in their correct locations

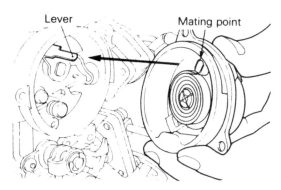

16.54a　Fit the bimetal end over the choke valve lever, . . .

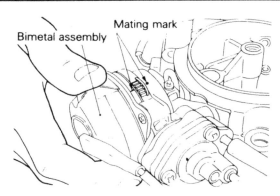

16.54b　. . . and install the plate and the screw, align the mating marks

its retracted position, the check valve is binding. In either case, replace the dashpot.

47　Inspect the depression chamber diaphragm for damage. First, push the rod all the way in, plug the vacuum pipe with your finger and release the rod. If the rod doesn't return to its initial position, the diaphragm is in good condition. If the rod returns, the diaphragm is broken. Replace the depression chamber.

48　Inspect the mixture adjusting screw (MAS) for any damage caused to its tapered end by overtightening.

49　Inspect the Throttle Position Sensor (see Chapter 6).

Reassembly

Refer to illustrations 16.52, 16.54a, 16.54b, 16.55 and 16.56

50　Reassembly is essentially the reverse of disassembly. But be sure to note the following points as you reassemble the carburetor.

51　The main jets are stamped on the top to indicate their size. Be sure the jets go back into their original locations.

52　Install the ball, O-ring, plug, ball, weight and steel ball in the correct sequence and at the correct locations **(see illustration)**.

53　Make sure you install the correct size secondary pilot jet, primary pilot jet and primary main air jet in the correct locations. The size of each jet is stamped on the side of the jet body.

54　Fit the bimetal end over the choke valve lever **(see illustration)**, install the plate, slightly tighten the screw, align the mating marks **(see illustration)**, put the rivets in position, install the bimetal assembly with a hand riveter, tighten the screw and install the terminal at the correct location in the electrical connector **(see illustration 16.11b)**. **Note:** *The bimetal assembly on Canadian models doesn't use rivets.*

55　When you install the Slow Cut Solenoid Valve (SCSV) and the Feedback Solenoid Valve (FBSV), make sure you install the terminals at their correct locations in the electrical connector **(see illustration)**.

56　After you've installed the float chamber cover assembly, install the

three Throttle Position Sensor (TPS) terminals at the correct locations in the electrical connector **(see illustration)**.

Fast idle opening adjustment

Refer to illustrations 16.57 and 16.58

57　Set the lever on the highest step of the fast idle cam (1987 models) or the second highest step (1988 and 1989 models) **(see illustration)**.

58　Using a drill bit, measure the primary valve-to-throttle bore clearance (fast idle opening) **(see illustration)** and compare your measurement with the value listed in this Chapter's Specifications. If the clearance is out of specification, adjust it with the the fast idle adjusting screw. If you turn the adjusting screw clockwise, the valve opening increases and the fast idle rpm increases; if you turn the screw counterclockwise, the valve opening decreases and the fast idle rpm decreases.

Unloader opening adjustment

Refer to illustrations 16.60 and 16.61

59　Lightly press the choke valve with your finger to close it all the way.

60　Fully open the throttle valve and measure the choke valve-to-choke bore clearance **(see illustration)**. Compare your measurement to the clearance listed in this Chapter's Specifications.

61　If the clearance is out of specification, bend the throttle lever at the indicated point **(see illustration)**. If you bend the lever up, the choke valve-to-choke bore clearance increases and response deteriorates; if you bend the lever down, the clearance decreases.

Choke breaker adjustment

Refer to illustration 16.64

62　Lightly press the choke valve with your finger to close it all the way.

63　Push the choke breaker rod toward the diaphragm and measure the choke valve-to-choke bore clearance. Compare your measurement to the clearance listed in this Chapter's Specifications.

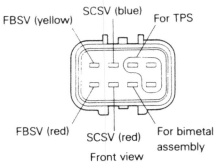

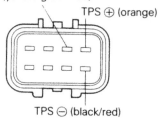

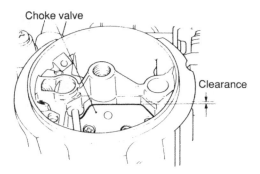

16.55 A terminal guide for installing the terminals of the Slow Cut Solenoid Valve (SCSV) and Feedback Solenoid Valve (FBSV)

16.56 A terminal guide for installing the terminals of the Throttle Position Sensor (TPS)

16.57 On 1988 and 1989 models, set the lever on the second highest step of the fast idle cam, as shown here; on 1987 models, set it on the highest step

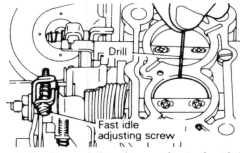

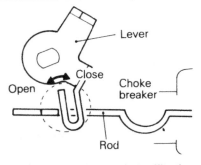

16.58 Measure the primary valve-to-throttle bore clearance (fast idle opening); if it's off, adjust it with the the fast idle adjusting screw – turning the adjusting screw clockwise increases the valve opening and the fast idle rpm; turning the screw counterclockwise decreases the valve opening and the fast idle rpm

16.60 Fully open the throttle valve and measure the choke valve-to-choke bore clearance

16.61 If the choke valve-to-choke bore clearance is incorrect, bend the throttle lever at the point indicated by the arrows – bending the lever up increases the choke valve-to-choke bore clearance; bending the lever down decreases clearance

16.64 If the clearance is out of specification, adjust it by bending the throttle lever at the indicated point – bending the lever open increases the choke valve-to-choke bore clearance, hurts startability and increases the likelihood that the engine will stall; bending the lever closed decreases clearance

64 If the clearance is out of specification, adjust it by bending the throttle lever at the indicated point (see illustration). If you bend the lever open, the choke valve-to-choke bore clearance increases, startability deteriorates and the engine is more likely to stall; if you bend the lever closed, clearance decreases.

Choke valve operation check

65 Operate the choke valve with a finger and check for freeplay, incorrect operation and binding.

66 If the choke doesn't operate smoothly and lightly, re-clean the area around the choke valve with fresh solvent, then apply a light coat of engine oil.
67 If the freeplay is excessive, replace the float chamber cover.

Secondary throttle valve operation check

68 Open the throttle valve all the way and operate the secondary throttle valve lever with your finger to check for freeplay, incorrect operation and binding.

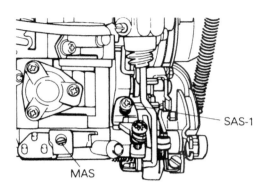

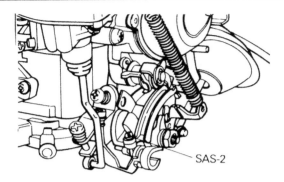

17.8a   If the idle speed isn't within the specified limits, readjust it by turning adjusting screw No. 1 (SAS-1)

17.8b   Don't touch SAS-2 – this screw, preset at the factory, establishes the relationship between the throttle valve and the free lever; if you alter this relationship, throttle opener and dashpot adjustments won't be accurate

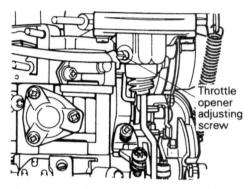

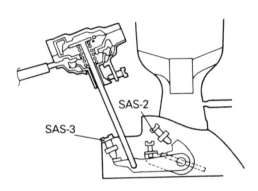

17.10   If the throttle opener speed is outside the specified limits, adjust it with the throttle opener adjusting screw

17.13   Open the throttle valve so the dashpot rod is extended the full length of its stroke and the free lever contacts SAS-3

69   If the valve doesn't operate smoothly, reclean the area around the valve and apply a thin coat of engine oil.
70   If freeplay is excessive, replace the throttle body.
Port check
71   Connect a hand-operated vacuum pump to each port and check for clogging of the passages.
72   If any port is clogged, reclean it and blow compressed air into the port.

---

17   Carburetor (FBC) (1987 through 1989 models) – adjustments

---

1   Make sure all lights and accessories are turned off. Place the transmission in Neutral. If the vehicle is equipped with power steering, center the steering wheel (wheels pointed straight ahead).
2   Hook up a timing light and tachometer in accordance with the manufacturer's instructions.
3   Start the engine and warm it up to its normal operating temperature.

Idle speed

Refer to illustrations 17.8a and 17.8b

4   Depress the accelerator pedal once to release the fast idle cam.
5   Check the ignition timing. Adjust it if necessary (see Chapter 1).
6   Run the engine at idle for two minutes.
7   Note the idle speed and compare your reading with the idle speed listed in this Chapter's Specifications.
8   If the idle speed isn't within the specified limits, readjust it by turning adjusting screw No. 1 (SAS-1) **(see illustration)**. **Caution:** *Don't touch SAS-2 **(see illustration)**. This screw, which is preset at the factory, esta-*

blishes the relationship between the throttle valve and the free lever. If this relationship is altered, the throttle opener and dashpot adjustments below won't be accurate.

Throttle opener (air-conditioned models)

Refer to illustration 17.10

Note: *Check and, if necessary, adjust the ignition timing (see Chapter 1) and idle speed (see above) before doing this adjustment. And see Steps 1 through 3.*

9   Turn on the air conditioner switch; this opens the solenoid valve, allowing intake manifold vacuum to actuate the throttle opener. Note what happens to engine speed when you turn on the switch. It should be within the range listed in this Chapter's Specifications.
10   If the engine speed is outside the specified limits, adjust it with the throttle opener adjusting screw **(see illustration)**.

Dashpot speed

Refer to illustration 17.13

11   Adjust the idle speed (see above). And see Steps 1 through 3.
12   Start the engine and run it at idle.
13   Open the throttle valve until the dashpot rod is extended the full length of its stroke and the free lever contacts SAS-3 **(see illustration)**.
14   Close the throttle lever until SAS-2 contacts the free lever and note the engine speed at that moment of contact. Compare your reading with the dashpot speed listed in this Chapter's Specifications.
15   If the dashpot speed isn't as specified, adjust the dashpot speed by turning SAS-3.
16   Release the free lever and verify that the engine returns to idle speed slowly.

18 Multi-Point Injection (MPI) – general information

Some 1989 and all 1990 and later models are equipped with an electronic fuel injection system known as Multi-Point Injection (MPI). Aside from slight differences in some emissions-related components, the MPI systems used on 2.4L and 3.0L engines are virtually identical. Both are computerized, electronically controlled fuel, ignition and emission control systems. Their important sub-systems include air induction, fuel delivery, fuel control, emission control and the engine control unit. Each system differs slightly in the type and location of these components.

Air induction system

The air induction system includes the air cleaner assembly, the throttle body, the ductwork between the air cleaner and the throttle body, the Throttle Position Sensor (TPS) and the Idle Speed Control (ISC) servo.

Fuel delivery system

The fuel delivery system provides fuel from the fuel tank into the fuel control system. It also returns any excess fuel back into the fuel tank. The system includes an in-tank electric fuel pump, fuel filter and return line.

Fuel control system

The fuel control system includes the fuel pressure regulator, the fuel rail and the fuel injectors. On MPI systems, the intake manifold supplies air only; fuel is sprayed directly into the ports by the fuel injectors.

Emission controls and the engine control unit

The oxygen sensor, airflow sensor, intake air temperature sensor, engine coolant temperature sensor, Throttle Position Sensor (TPS), idle position switch, crank angle sensor and barometric pressure sensor are all important to the proper operation of the MPI system, but they're more closely related to emissions than to fuel. If you'd like to know more about related emission control systems, particularly the information sensors and the engine control unit, refer to Chapter 6.

19 Fuel injection system – check

Note: *the following procedure is based on the assumption that the fuel pressure is adequate (see Section 3).*

1 Check all ground wire connections for tightness. Check all wiring harness connectors related to the MPI system. Loose connectors and poor grounds can cause many problems that resemble more serious malfunctions. Also check all vacuum connections and make sure all vacuum hoses are in good condition and not hardened, cracked or plugged.
2 Verify that the battery is fully charged; the engine control unit and the information sensors depend on an accurate supply voltage to function properly.
3 Check the air filter element – a dirty or partially blocked filter will severely impede performance and economy (see Chapter 1).
4 Check for blown fuses. If a blown fuse is found, replace it and see if it blows again. If it does, search the circuit for a short.
5 Look for leaks in the air intake duct between the air cleaner housing and the throttle body and at the gasket between the throttle body and the air intake plenum. Air leaks cause an excessively lean mixture. Also inspect all vacuum hoses connected to the throttle body and intake manifold.
6 Remove the air intake duct from the throttle body and check for dirt, carbon or other residue build-up. If the throttle body is dirty (pay particular attention to the area just inside the throttle plate), clean it with carburetor cleaner and a toothbrush.
7 With the engine running, place a screwdriver against each injector, one at a time, and listen through the handle for the clicking sound made by the solenoid inside. This sound should be clearly audible at idle.

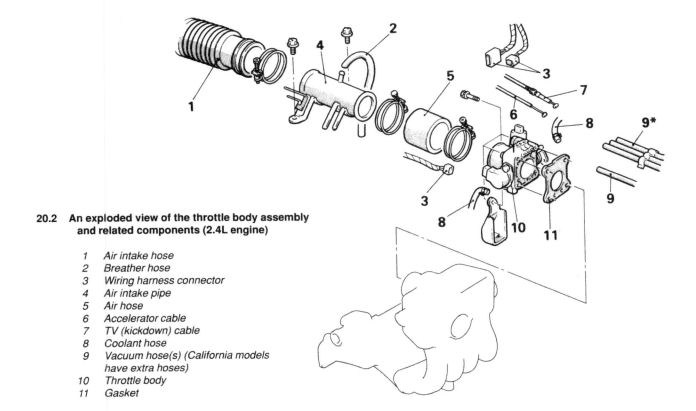

20.2 An exploded view of the throttle body assembly and related components (2.4L engine)

1 Air intake hose
2 Breather hose
3 Wiring harness connector
4 Air intake pipe
5 Air hose
6 Accelerator cable
7 TV (kickdown) cable
8 Coolant hose
9 Vacuum hose(s) (California models have extra hoses)
10 Throttle body
11 Gasket

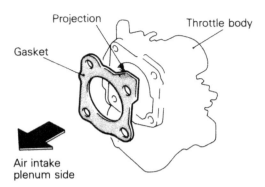

20.12   Be sure to install the throttle body gasket with the projection in the position shown – if gasket installation is incorrect, it can affect idle quality and cause other problems

20   Throttle body – removal and installation

2.4L engine

Refer to illustrations 20.2 and 20.12

1   Disconnect the negative cable from the battery.
2   Loosen the hose clamp and detach the air intake hose from the air intake pipe **(see illustration)**.
3   Detach the breather hose from the air intake pipe.
4   Unplug the wiring harness connector(s).
5   Remove the air intake pipe mounting bolts and remove the air intake pipe.
6   Remove the air hose.
7   Disconnect the accelerator cable (see Section 8).

8   Disconnect the TV (kickdown) cable (see Chapter 7, Part B).
9   Place some absorbent shop towels under the connections for the coolant hoses, then detach both hoses. Some coolant will be lost.
10   Detach the vacuum hose(s).
11   Remove the four throttle body mounting bolts, the throttle body and the gasket. Use a scraper to remove all traces of old gasket material from the throttle body and plenum mating surfaces. Wipe the surfaces with a rag soaked in lacquer thinner or acetone.
12   Installation is the reverse of removal. Be sure to install the gasket correctly **(see illustration)**. Tighten the throttle body mounting bolts to the torque listed in this Chapter's Specifications. Connect the negative battery cable and adjust the accelerator cable when you're through (see Section 8). Add coolant to replace the coolant lost when you disconnected the coolant hoses from the throttle body.

3.0L engine

Refer to illustration 20.14

13   Disconnect the negative cable from the battery. Disconnect the accelerator cable (see Section 8).
14   Detach the vacuum hose(s) **(see illustration)**.
15   Loosen the hose clamp and detach the air intake hose.
16   Unplug the Throttle Position Sensor (TPS) electrical connector.
17   Unplug the Idle Speed Control (ISC) servo electrical connector.
18   Place some absorbent shop towels under the connections for the coolant hoses, then detach both hoses. Some coolant will be lost.
19   Remove the throttle body mounting bolts, the throttle body and the gasket. Using a scraper, remove all traces of old gasket material from the throttle body and air intake plenum mating surfaces. Clean the surfaces with a rag soaked in lacquer thinner or acetone.
20   Installation is the reverse of removal. Be sure to tighten the throttle body mounting bolts to the torque listed in this Chapter's Specifications. Adjust the accelerator cable when you're through (see Section 8), and add coolant to replace the coolant lost when you disconnected the coolant hoses from the throttle body. Connect the negative battery cable.

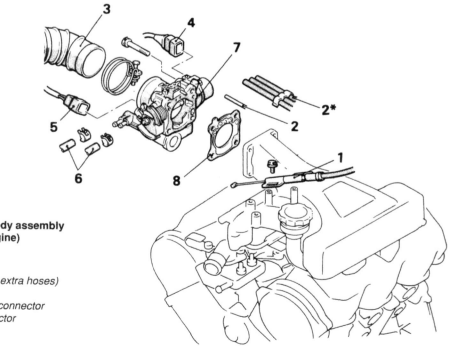

20.14   An exploded view of the throttle body assembly and related components (3.0L engine)

1   *Accelerator cable*
2   *Vacuum hose(s) (California models have extra hoses)*
3   *Air intake hose*
4   *Throttle Position Sensor (TPS) electrical connector*
5   *Idle Speed Control (ISC) electrical connector*
6   *Coolant hose*
7   *Throttle body*
8   *Gasket*

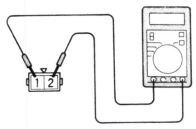

Idle speed control
servo connector

21.2   Using an ohmmeter or multimeter at the connector terminals, check the continuity of the ISC servo coil and compare your measurement with the resistance listed in this Chapter's Specifications (2.4L engine)

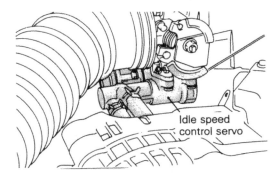

21.5   On the 3.0L engine, the ISC servo is located under the throttle body

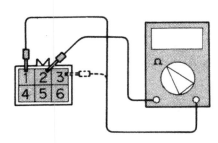

21.8   Using an ohmmeter or multimeter, check the continuity of the ISC servo connector at the indicated terminals and compare your measurements with the resistance listed in this Chapter's Specifications (3.0L engine)

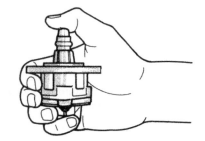

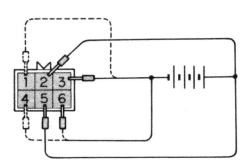

21.12   Holding the ISC servo as shown, power it up with a 6V DC battery by touching the terminals of the electrical connector in the sequence described in the accompanying text

21   Idle Speed Control (ISC) servo – check and replacement

Check

2.4L engine

Refer to illustration 21.2

1   Unplug the electrical connector for the Idle Speed Control (ISC) servo.

2   Using an ohmmeter or multimeter at the connector terminals (1 and 2), check the resistance of the ISC servo coil **(see illustration)**. Compare your measurement with the resistance listed in this Chapter's Specifications.

3   Hook up a 6V DC battery between terminal 1 and terminal 2 of the connector for the ISC servo and verify that the ISC servo is operating. **Caution:** *Don't use a more powerful battery or you may lock the gears inside the ISC servo.*

4   If the ISC servo fails to operate when powered up by a 6V DC battery, or if the indicated resistance is outside the specified resistance, replace the servo as an assembly.

3.0L engine

Refer to illustrations 21.5, 21.8 and 21.12

5   Listen to the ISC servo **(see illustration)** while an assistant turns the ignition switch to On (not to Start). The servo should make an audible sound.

6   If the servo is silent, inspect the electrical circuit. If the circuit is in good shape, the likely cause is a malfunction of the servo or the engine control unit.

7   Unplug the ISC servo electrical connector.

8   Measure the resistance between terminals 2 and 1, and between terminals 2 and 3 **(see illustration)** and compare your reading to the resistance listed in this Chapter's Specifications.

9   Measure the resistance between terminals 5 and 6, and between terminals 5 and 4 and compare your reading to the resistance listed in this Chapter's Specifications.

10   Remove the throttle body (see Section 20).

11   Remove the ISC servo (see below).

12   Hook up the positive terminal of a 6V DC battery to terminals 2 and 5 **(see illustration)**.

13   Holding the ISC servo as shown in the preceding illustration, hook up the negative terminal of the 6V DC battery to each terminal of the connector in the following sequence and note whether there's any vibration (a very slight shaking of the servo) as the motor is activated.

   1)   Connect the negative battery terminal to connector terminals 3 and 6.

   2)   Connect the negative battery terminal to connector terminals 1 and 6.

   3)   Connect the negative battery terminal to connector terminals 1 and 4.

   4)   Connect the negative battery terminal to connector terminals 3 and 4.

   5)   Connect the negative battery terminal to connector terminals 3 and 6.

   6)   Repeat the above five steps in the reverse sequence (5 through 1).

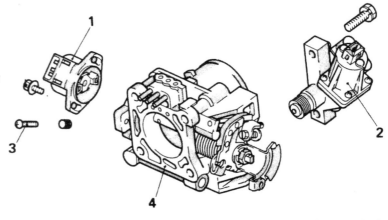

21.16a   An exploded view of the throttle body assembly (2.4L engine)

1   *Throttle Position Sensor (TPS)*
2   *Idle Speed Control (ISC) servo assembly*
3   *Throttle valve set screw*
4   *Throttle body*

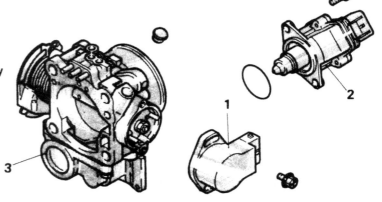

21.16b   An exploded view of the throttle body assembly (3.0L engine)

1   *Throttle Position Sensor (TPS)/ idle position switch assembly*
2   *Idle Speed Control (ISC) servo assembly*
3   *Throttle body*

14   If the servo vibrates slightly during these tests, it's okay; if it doesn't, replace it.

Replacement

Refer to illustrations 21.16a and 21.16b

15   Unplug the ISC servo electrical connector, if you haven't already done so.

16   Remove the ISC servo mounting screws **(see illustrations)**. The threads of these screws have been coated with adhesive, so make sure you don't strip out the heads trying to loosen them.

17   Remove the ISC servo unit.

18   Installation is the reverse of removal. Be sure to tighten the screws to the torque listed in this Chapter's Specifications.

22   Air intake plenum – removal and installation

2.4L engine

Refer to illustration 22.1

1   If you're planning to replace the air intake plenum assembly, remove the throttle body (see Section 20); if you're only removing the plenum to replace a gasket or service the cylinder head (i.e. if you intend to reinstall the same plenum assembly), the throttle body can remain attached. Detach all hoses, cables and connectors from the throttle body as if you were going to remove it, but leave it attached to the plenum **(see illustration)**.

2   Disconnect the PCV hose, brake booster vacuum hose and other vacuum hoses.

3   Remove the ignition coil (see Chapter 5).

4   Unbolt the air intake plenum assembly and remove it and the gasket.

5   Using a scraper, remove all traces of old gasket material from the ple-

num and intake manifold mating surfaces. Clean the surfaces with a rag soaked in lacquer thinner or acetone. Installation is the reverse of removal. Use a new gasket and tighten the plenum mounting bolts to the torque listed in this Chapter's Specifications in several stages, working from the center out.

3.0L engine

Refer to illustration 22.6

6   If you're planning to replace the air intake plenum assembly, remove the throttle body (see Section 20); if you're only removing the plenum to replace a gasket or service the cylinder head (i.e. if you intend to reinstall the same plenum assembly), the throttle body can remain attached. Detach all hoses, cables and connectors from the throttle body as if you were going to remove it, but leave it bolted to the plenum **(see illustration)**.

7   Unplug the electrical connector for the EGR temperature sensor.

8   Detach the brake booster vacuum hose, all other vacuum hoses and the PCV hose from the plenum.

9   Remove the ignition coil (see Chapter 5). Detach the accelerator and TV (kickdown) cable brackets from the plenum.

10   Detach the bracket for the engine oil filler neck.

11   Remove the EGR pipe attaching bolts and detach the EGR pipe from the plenum.

12   Unbolt and remove the plenum stays. Remove the mounting bolts for the plenum assembly.

13   Remove the plenum and gasket.

14   Using a scraper, remove all traces of old gasket material from the plenum and intake manifold mating surfaces. Wipe the mating surfaces clean with a rag soaked in lacquer thinner or acetone.

15   Installation is the reverse of removal. Use a new gasket and tighten the plenum mounting bolts in several stages, working from the center out, to the torque listed in this Chapter's Specifications.

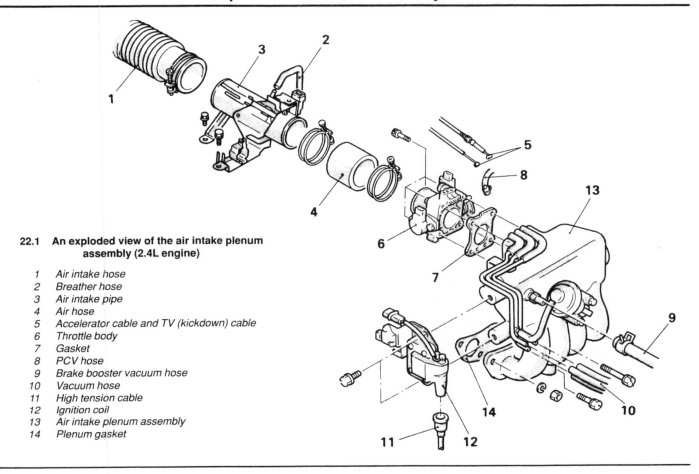

22.1 An exploded view of the air intake plenum assembly (2.4L engine)

1   Air intake hose
2   Breather hose
3   Air intake pipe
4   Air hose
5   Accelerator cable and TV (kickdown) cable
6   Throttle body
7   Gasket
8   PCV hose
9   Brake booster vacuum hose
10 Vacuum hose
11 High tension cable
12 Ignition coil
13 Air intake plenum assembly
14 Plenum gasket

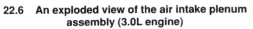
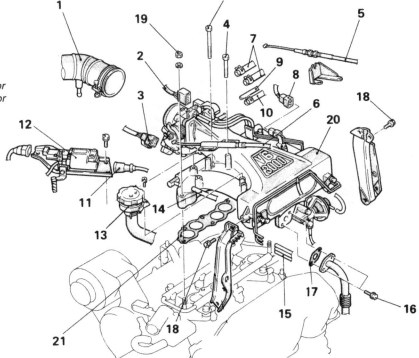

22.6 An exploded view of the air intake plenum assembly (3.0L engine)

1   Air intake hose
2   Throttle Position Sensor (TPS) electrical connector
3   Idle Speed Control (ISC) servo electrical connector
4   Accelerator cable adjusting bolt
5   TV (kickdown) cable
6   Accelerator cable
7   Coolant hoses
8   EGR temperature sensor electrical connector
9   Vacuum hose
10 Brake booster vacuum hose
11 High tension cable
12 Ignition coil
13 Engine oil filler neck bracket
14 PCV hose
15 Vacuum hoses
16 EGR pipe attaching bolt
17 Gasket
18 Plenum stay-to-plenum bolt
19 Bolt and nut
20 Air intake plenum assembly
21 Plenum gasket

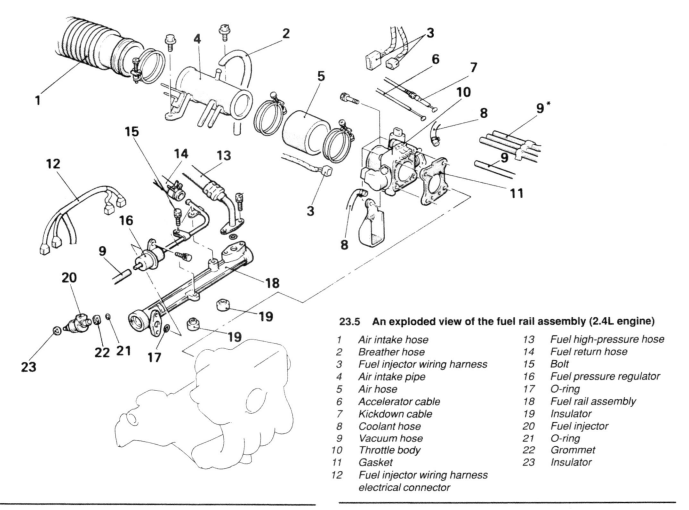

23.5   An exploded view of the fuel rail assembly (2.4L engine)

1	Air intake hose	13	Fuel high-pressure hose
2	Breather hose	14	Fuel return hose
3	Fuel injector wiring harness	15	Bolt
4	Air intake pipe	16	Fuel pressure regulator
5	Air hose	17	O-ring
6	Accelerator cable	18	Fuel rail assembly
7	Kickdown cable	19	Insulator
8	Coolant hose	20	Fuel injector
9	Vacuum hose	21	O-ring
10	Throttle body	22	Grommet
11	Gasket	23	Insulator
12	Fuel injector wiring harness electrical connector		

23   Fuel rail assembly – removal and installation

Warning: *Gasoline is extremely flammable, so take extra precautions when you work on any part of the fuel system. Don't smoke or allow open flames or bare light bulbs near the work area, and don't work in a garage where a natural gas-type appliance (such as a water heater or clothes dryer) with a pilot light is present. If you spill any fuel on your skin, rinse it off immediately with soap and water. When you perform any kind of work on the fuel system, wear safety glasses and have a Class B type fire extinguisher on hand.*

1   Relieve the fuel system pressure (see Section 2).
2   Disconnect the negative cable from the battery.
3   Disconnect all hoses, cables and connectors from the throttle body (see Section 20)
4   Remove the throttle body and air intake plenum as an assembly (see Section 22).

2.4L engine

Refer to illustration 23.5

5   Pull up the retaining clip on each injector electrical connector and unplug the connector from the fuel injector **(see illustration)**.
6   Cover the connection for the fuel high-pressure hose with a shop rag to absorb any spilled fuel (there's still residual pressure in the line, even after the fuel pressure has been relieved). Remove the fuel high-pressure hose attaching bolts and detach the high-pressure hose. Discard the old O-ring.
7   Loosen the hose clamp and disconnect the fuel return hose.
8   Detach the vacuum hose from the fuel pressure regulator.

9   Remove the bolt that attaches the metal pipe between the fuel pressure regulator and the fuel return hose.
10   Remove the bolts that attach the fuel pressure regulator to the fuel rail. Remove the fuel pressure regulator/metal pipe assembly. Discard the O-ring.
11   Remove the fuel rail assembly and the insulators. Pull gently up on the rail, using a rocking motion. Inspect the insulators. If they're in satisfactory condition, they can be reused. If they're cracked or damaged, replace them.
12   Installation is the reverse of removal. Do not reuse the O-rings for the fuel pressure regulator and the fuel high-pressure hose flange. Use new ones. Be sure to tighten the fuel pressure regulator mounting bolts and the fuel high-pressure hose attaching bolts to the torque listed in this Chapter's Specifications.

3.0L engine

Refer to illustrations 23.13 and 23.18

13   Cover the connection for the fuel high-pressure hose with a shop rag to absorb any spilled fuel (there's still residual pressure in the line, even after the fuel pressure has been relieved). Remove the fuel high-pressure hose attaching bolts **(see illustration)** and disconnect the hose. Discard the O-ring.
14   Loosen the hose clamp and disconnect the fuel return hose.
15   Detach the vacuum hose from the fuel pressure regulator and any other vacuum hoses in the way.
16   Pull up the retaining clip on each injector electrical connector and unplug the connector from the injector.

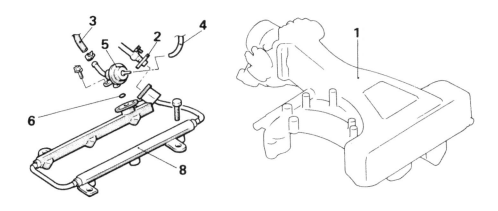

23.13 An exploded view of the fuel rail assembly (3.0L engine)

1   Air intake plenum assembly
2   Fuel high-pressure hose
3   Fuel return hose
4   Vacuum hose
5   Fuel pressure regulator
6   O-ring
7   Fuel injector wiring harness electrical connector
8   Fuel rail assembly
9   Fuel injector
10 O-ring
11 Grommet
12 Insulators
13 Insulator

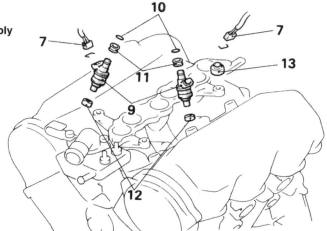

17   Remove the fuel rail mounting bolts and remove the fuel rail and the insulators. Pull gently up on the rail, using a rocking motion. Discard the insulators.

18   Installation is the reverse of removal. Be sure to use new insulators for the fuel rail **(see illustration)** and fuel injectors. Also, use a new O-ring for the fuel high-pressure hose connection and coat the O-ring with gasoline before installation. Tighten the fuel high-pressure hose attaching bolts to the torque listed in this Chapter's Specifications.

---

24   Fuel injector(s) – check, removal and installation

Warning: *Gasoline is extremely flammable, so take extra precautions when you work on any part of the fuel system. Don't smoke or allow open flames or bare light bulbs near the work area, and don't work in a garage where a natural gas-type appliance (such as a water heater or clothes dryer) with a pilot light is present. If you spill any fuel on your skin, rinse it off immediately with soap and water. When you perform any kind of work on the fuel system, wear safety glasses and have a Class B type fire extinguisher on hand.*

Check

Refer to illustration 24.2

1   With the engine running or cranking, listen to the sound from each injector with an automotive stethoscope and verify the injectors are all clicking the same. If you don't have a stethoscope, place the tip of a

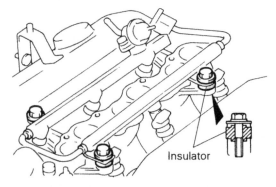

23.18   After installing the fuel rail and mounting bolts, verify that all four insulators are properly seated before tightening the bolts (3.0L engine)

Insulator

---

screwdriver against the injectors and press your ear against the handle of the screwdriver. Also feel the operation of each injector with your finger. It should sound/feel smooth and uniform and its sound/feel should rise and fall with engine RPM. If an injector isn't operating, or sounds/feels erratic, check the injector connector and the wire harness connector. If the connectors are snug, check for voltage to the injector, using a special injector harness test light (available at most auto parts stores).

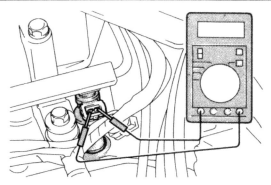

24.2　If the injector is malfunctioning, check the resistance across the terminals and compare your measurement to the resistance listed in this Chapter's Specifications – if the indicated resistance is outside specification, replace the injector

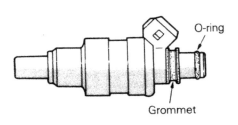

24.5　Make sure you install a new grommet and O-ring at the correct location on each injector

2　If there's voltage to the injector but it isn't operating, or if it sounds or feels erratic, check the injector's resistance **(see illustration)**. Compare your measurement to the resistance listed in this Chapter's Specifications. If the indicated resistance is outside the specified range, replace the injector.

Removal and installation

Refer to illustration 24.5

3　Remove the air intake plenum assembly (see Section 22) and the fuel rail assembly (see Section 23).

4　Place the fuel rail assembly on a clean work surface so the fuel injectors are accessible. To remove an injector from the fuel rail, gently pull it straight out. Twisting it slightly as you pull may help. Discard the old O-ring and grommet.

5　Installation is the reverse of removal. Install a new O-ring and grommet onto each injector **(see illustration)**. Apply a light coat of fresh gasoline to the O-ring to facilitate installation. To install an injector into the fuel rail, push it straight into its bore in the fuel rail, gently twisting it to the left and right as you push. Once the injector is fully seated, try to rotate it back and forth. It should turn smoothly if it's properly installed. If it doesn't, the O-ring may be pinched or jammed; remove the injector and check the O-ring. If it's okay, reinstall the injector; if the O-ring is damaged, replace it before installing the injector.

6　Install the fuel rail assembly with the injectors installed in the fuel rail (see Section 23). Install the air intake plenum assembly (see Section 22).

25　Fuel pressure regulator – removal and installation

Warning: *Gasoline is extremely flammable, so take extra precautions when you work on any part of the fuel system. Don't smoke or allow open flames or bare light bulbs near the work area, and don't work in a garage where a natural gas-type appliance (such as a water heater or clothes dryer) with a pilot light is present. If you spill any fuel on your skin, rinse it off immediately with soap and water. When you perform any kind of work on the fuel system, wear safety glasses and have a Class B type fire extinguisher on hand.*

1　Relieve the system fuel pressure (see Section 2).

2　Disconnect the cable from the negative battery terminal.

3　Remove the air intake plenum (see Section 22).

4　Detach the vacuum line from the fuel pressure regulator **(see illustration 23.5 or 23.13)**.

5　Loosen the hose clamp, slide it back on the fuel return hose and disconnect the fuel return hose from the metal tube attached to the fuel pressure regulator.

6　On 2.4L engines, remove the bolt that attaches the bracket for the metal pipe between the regulator and the fuel return hose.

7　Unbolt the fuel pressure regulator and detach it from the fuel rail. Discard the old O-ring.

8　Installation is the reverse of removal. Use a new O-ring and coat it with a light coat of fresh gasoline. Tighten the fuel pressure regulator mounting bolts to the torque listed in this Chapter's Specifications.

26　Exhaust system servicing – general information

Refer to illustrations 26.1a and 26.1b

Warning: *Inspection and repair of exhaust system components should be done only with the engine and exhaust components completely cool. Also, when working under the vehicle, make sure it's securely supported on jackstands.*

1　The exhaust system **(see illustrations)** consists of the exhaust manifold(s), the catalytic converter, the muffler, the tailpipe and all connecting pipes, brackets, hangers and clamps. The exhaust system is attached to the body with mounting brackets and rubber hangers. If any of the parts are improperly installed, excessive noise and vibration will be transmitted to the body.

2　Conduct regular inspections of the exhaust system to keep it safe and quiet. Look for any damaged or bent parts, open seams, holes, loose connections, excessive corrosion or other defects which could allow exhaust fumes to enter the vehicle. Deteriorated exhaust system components shouldn't be repaired; they should be replaced with new parts.

3　If the exhaust system components are extremely corroded or rusted together, welding equipment will probably be required to remove them. The convenient way to accomplish this is to have a muffler repair shop remove the corroded sections with a cutting torch. If, however, you want to save money by doing it yourself (and you don't have a welding outfit with a cutting torch), simply cut off the old components with a hacksaw. If you have compressed air, special pneumatic cutting chisels can also be used. If you do decide to tackle the job at home, be sure to wear safety goggles to protect your eyes from metal chips and work gloves to protect your hands.

4　Here are some simple guidelines to follow when repairing the exhaust system:

　a)　Work from the back to the front when removing exhaust system components.

　b)　Apply penetrating oil to the component fasteners to make them easier to remove.

　c)　Use new gaskets, hangers and clamps when installing exhaust system components.

　d)　Apply anti-seize compound to the threads of all exhaust system fasteners during reassembly.

　e)　Be sure to allow sufficient clearance between newly installed parts and all points on the underbody to avoid overheating the floor pan and possibly damaging the interior carpet and insulation. Pay particularly close attention to the catalytic converter and heat shields **(see illustration)**.

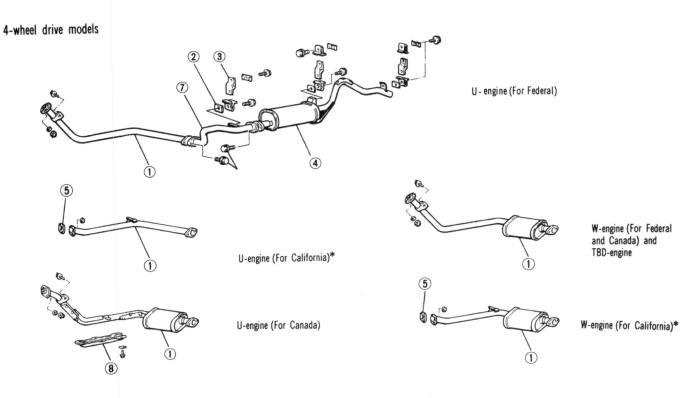

26.1a   An exploded view of typical pre-1987 exhaust systems

1	Front exhaust pipe	4	Main muffler	7	Center exhaust pipe
2	Asbestos plate	5	Gasket	8	Protector
3	Hanger	6	Suspender		

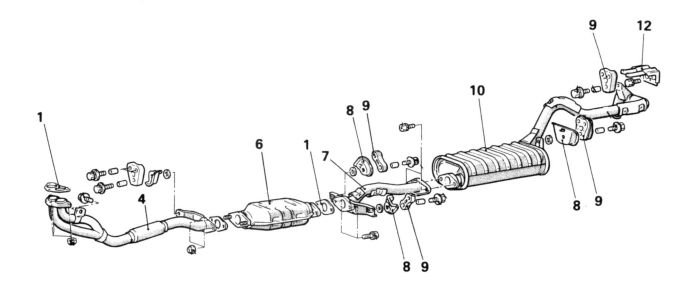

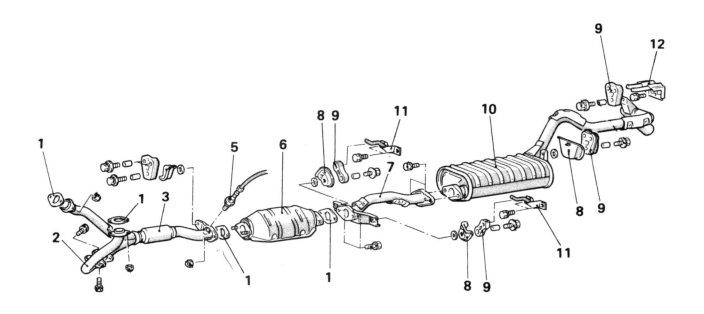

26.1b   An exploded view of typical exhaust systems used on 1987 and later models

1	Gasket	5	Oxygen sensor	9	Hanger
2	Front exhaust pipe (left)	6	Catalytic converter	10	Main muffler
3	Front exhaust pipe (right)	7	Center exhaust pipe	11	Catalytic converter hanger
4	Front exhaust pipe	8	Heat cover	12	Tail pipe hanger

Chapter 5   Engine electrical systems

Contents

Specifications

Distributor pick-up air gap

Note: *The air gap check and adjustment procedure is not applicable to 1990 and later models with 2.4L and 3.0L engines.*

1983 models	Not adjustable
1984 through 1989 Mitsubishi type	0.031 inch
1986 through 1989 Nippondenso type	0.008 to 0.015 inch

Ignition coil

Primary resistance
1983 through 1985 models	1.04 to 1.27 ohms
1986 through 1989 models	1.2 ohms
1990 and later models	0.72 to 0.88 ohms

Secondary resistance
1983 models	7.10 to 9.60 K-ohms
1984 and 1985 models	
Pick-up	7.10 to 9.60 K-ohms
Montero	11.6 to 15.8 K-ohms
1986 models	
Mitsubishi type (2.6L engine)	17.0 K-ohms
Nippondenso type (2.0L engine)	13.7 K-ohms

Ignition coil (continued)

1987 models . . . .   22.5 K-ohms
1988 and 1989 models
  Pick-up . . . .   27.0 K-ohms
  Montero . . . .   14.5 to 19.5 K-ohms
1990 and later models
  Pick-up . . . .   10.3 to 13.9 K-ohms
  Montero . . . .   14.5 to 19.5 K-ohms

Ballast resistor resistance

1983 through 1985 models . . . .   1.2 to 1.5 ohms
1986 and later models . . . .   1.35 ohms

Pick-up coil resistance

Note: *The pick-up coil resistance check is not applicable to 1990 and later models.*

1983 models . . . .   920 to 1,120 ohms
1984 through 1989 Mitsubishi type . . . .   920 to 1,120 ohms
1986 through 1989 Nippondenso type . . . .   140 to 180 ohms

---

1   General information

The engine electrical systems include all ignition, charging and starting components. Because of their engine-related functions, these components are discussed separately from chassis electrical devices such as the lights, the instruments, etc (which are included in Chapter 12).

Always observe the following precautions when working on the electrical systems:

a) Be extremely careful when servicing engine electrical components. They are easily damaged if checked, connected or handled improperly.
b) Never leave the ignition switch on for long periods of time with the engine off.
c) Don't disconnect the battery cables while the engine is running.
d) Maintain correct polarity when connecting a battery cable from another vehicle during jump starting.
e) Always disconnect the negative cable first and hook it up last or the battery may be shorted by the tool being used to loosen the cable clamps.

It's also a good idea to review the safety-related information regarding the engine electrical systems located in the *Safety first* section near the front of this manual before beginning any operation included in this Chapter.

---

2   Battery – emergency jump starting

Refer to the *Booster battery (jump) starting* procedure at the front of this manual.

---

3   Battery – removal and installation

Refer to illustration 3.1

1   **Caution:** *Always disconnect the negative cable first and hook it up last or the battery may be shorted by the tool being used to loosen the cable clamps. Disconnect both cables from the battery terminals* **(see illustration).**
2   Remove the battery hold-down clamp.
3   Lift out the battery. Be careful – it's heavy.
4   While the battery is out, inspect the carrier (tray) for corrosion (see Chapter 1).
5   If you are replacing the battery, make sure that you get one that's identical, with the same dimensions, amperage rating, cold cranking rating, etc.
6   Installation is the reverse of removal.

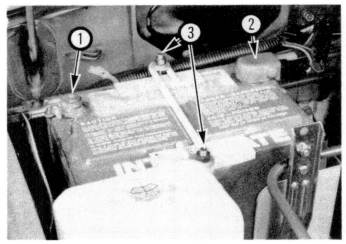

3.1   To remove the battery

1   *Detach the cable from the negative terminal*
2   *Detach the cable for the positive terminal*
3   *Remove the nuts and detach the hold-down clamp*

---

4   Battery cables – check and replacement

1   Periodically inspect the entire length of each battery cable for damage, cracked or burned insulation and corrosion. Poor battery cable connections can cause starting problems and decreased engine performance.
2   Check the cable-to-terminal connections at the ends of the cables for cracks, loose wire strands and corrosion. The presence of white, fluffy deposits under the insulation at the cable terminal connection is a sign that the cable is corroded and should be replaced. Check the terminals for distortion, missing mounting bolts and corrosion.
3   When removing the cables, always disconnect the negative cable first and hook it up last or the battery may be shorted by the tool used to loosen the cable clamps. Even if only the positive cable is being replaced, be sure to disconnect the negative cable from the battery first (see Chapter 1 for further information regarding battery cable removal).
4   Disconnect the old cables from the battery, then trace each of them to their opposite ends and detach them from the starter solenoid and ground terminals. Note the routing of each cable to ensure correct installation.
5   If you are replacing either one or both of the cables, take them with you when buying new cables. It is vitally important that you replace the

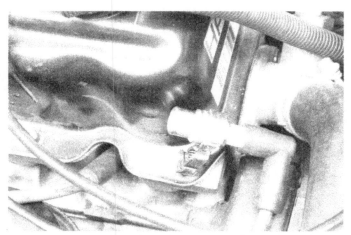

6.2   To use a calibrated ignition tester (available at most auto parts stores), simply disconnect a spark plug wire, attach the wire to the tester and clip the tester to a good ground – if there is enough power to fire the plug, sparks will be clearly visible between the electrode tip and the tester body as the engine is turned over

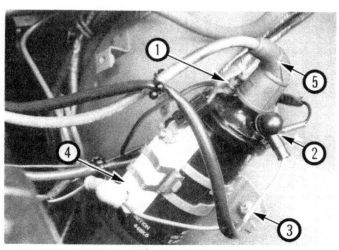

7.2   To remove a typical coil from the engine compartment, disconnect the primary wires and the high-voltage lead, then unbolt the bracket

1	Negative primary wire	4	Ballast resistor
2	Positive primary wire	5	High-voltage lead
3	Bracket		

cables with identical parts. Cables have characteristics that make them easy to identify: positive cables are usually red, larger in cross section and have a larger diameter battery post clamp; ground cables are usually black, smaller in cross-section and have a slightly smaller diameter clamp for the negative post.

6   Clean the threads of the solenoid or ground connection with a wire brush to remove rust and corrosion. Apply a light coat of battery terminal corrosion inhibitor, or petroleum jelly, to the threads to prevent future corrosion.

7   Attach the cable to the solenoid or ground connection and tighten the mounting nut/bolt securely.

8   Before connecting a new cable to the battery, make sure that it reaches the battery post without having to be stretched.

9   Connect the positive cable first, followed by the negative cable.

---

5   Ignition system – general information and precautions

When working on the ignition system, take the following precautions:
a) Do not keep the ignition switch on for more than 10 seconds if the engine will not start.
b) Always connect a tachometer in accordance with the manufacturer's instructions. Some tachometers may be incompatible with this ignition system. Consult a dealer service department before buying a tachometer for use with this vehicle.
c) Never allow the primary terminals of the ignition coil to touch ground.
d) Do not disconnect the battery when the engine is running.

The ignition system includes the ignition switch, the battery, the coil, the primary (low voltage) and secondary (high voltage) wiring circuits, the distributor and the spark plugs. On later distributors not using a vacuum or centrifugal advance, the ignition timing is controlled by the Electronic Control Unit (ECU).

---

6   Ignition system – check

Refer to illustration 6.2

Warning: *Because of the very high voltage generated by the ignition system, extreme care should be taken when this check is performed.*

1   If the engine turns over but won't start, disconnect the spark plug wire from any spark plug and attach it to a calibrated ignition tester (available at

most auto parts stores). **Note:** *Be sure to purchase the correct tester for either an electronic distributor or points distributor, depending which system the vehicle is equipped with.*

2   Connect the clip on the tester to a bolt or metal bracket on the engine **(see illustration)**. If you're unable to obtain a calibrated ignition tester, remove the wire from one of the spark plugs and, using an insulated tool, hold the end of the wire about 1/4-inch from a good ground.

3   Crank the engine and watch the end of the tester or spark plug wire to see if bright blue, well-defined sparks occur. If you're not using a calibrated tester, have an assistant crank the engine for you. **Warning:** *Keep clear of drivebelts and other moving engine components that could injure you.*

4   If sparks occur, sufficient voltage is reaching the plug to fire it (repeat the check at the remaining plug wires to verify the wires, distributor cap, rotor and coil are OK. However, the plugs themselves may be fouled, so remove them and check them as described in Chapter 1.

5   If no sparks or intermittent sparks occur, remove the distributor cap and check the cap and rotor as described in Chapter 1. If moisture is present, dry out the cap and rotor, then reinstall the cap.

6   If there is still no spark, detach the coil secondary wire from the distributor cap and hook it up to the tester (reattach the plug wire to the spark plug), then repeat the spark check. Again, if you don't have a tester, hold the end of the wire about 1/4 inch from a good ground. If sparks occur now, the distributor cap, rotor or plug wire(s) may be defective.

7   If no sparks occur, check the wire connections at the coil to make sure they're clean and tight. Check for voltage to the coil. Make any necessary repairs, then repeat the check again.

8   If there's still no spark, the coil-to-cap wire may be bad (check the resistance with an ohmmeter – it should be 7000 ohms per foot or less). If a known good wire doesn't make any difference in the test results, the ignition coil, module or pick-up coil may be defective.

---

7   Ignition coil and ballast resistor – check and replacement

Ignition coil

Refer to illustrations 7.2, 7.4a, 7.4b, 7.5a and 7.5b

1   Detach the cable from the negative battery terminal.

2   Mark the wires and terminals with pieces of numbered tape, then remove the primary wires and the high-voltage lead from the coil **(see illustration)**. Disconnect the coil mounting bracket, remove the coil/bracket assembly, clean the outer case and check it for cracks and other damage.

7.4a   To check the coil primary resistance on an earlier type coil, touch the leads of an ohmmeter to the positive and negative primary terminals (arrows) and compare your reading with the coil primary resistance listed in this Chapter's Specifications

3   Clean the coil primary terminals and check the coil tower terminal for corrosion. Clean it with a wire brush if any corrosion is found.
4   Check the coil primary resistance by attaching the leads of an ohmmeter to the positive and negative primary terminals **(see illustrations)**. Compare your readings to the primary resistance listed in this Chapter's Specifications.
5   Check the coil secondary resistance by hooking one of the ohmmeter leads to one of the primary terminals and the other ohmmeter lead to the large center terminal **(see illustrations)**. Compare your readings to the secondary resistance listed in this Chapter's Specifications.
6   If the measured resistances are not as specified, the coil is probably defective and should be replaced with a new one.
7   For proper ignition system operation, all coil terminals and wire leads must be kept clean and dry.
8   Install the coil in the vehicle and hook up the wires.

Ballast resistor

9   Some earlier models use a ballast resistor **(see illustration 7.2)** to protect the coil from excessive voltage during low-speed operation.
10   To check the ballast resistor, detach it from the coil or firewall, unplug the leads, touch the probes of an ohmmeter to the terminals of the resistor and compare your readings to the resistance listed in this Chapter's Specifications. If the resistance is not as specified, replace the resistor.

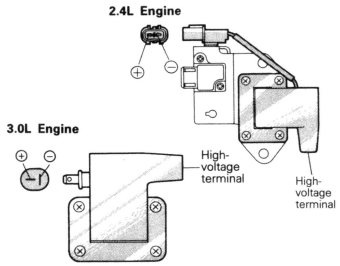

7.4b   To check the coil primary resistance on a later type coil, touch the leads of an ohmmeter to the positive and negative primary terminals and compare your reading with the coil primary resistance listed in this Chapter's Specifications

---

8   Distributor – removal and installation

Removal

Refer to illustrations 8.6a and 8.6b

1   Detach the cable from the negative battery terminal.
2   Unplug the coil high-voltage lead from the distributor cap.
3   Detach the vacuum hose(s) from the advance unit (if equipped).
4   Look for a raised "1" on the distributor cap. This marks the location for the number one cylinder spark plug wire terminal. If the cap does not have a mark for the number one terminal, locate the number one spark plug and trace the wire back to the terminal on the cap.
5   Remove the distributor cap (see Chapter 1) and turn the engine over until the rotor is pointing toward the number one spark plug terminal (see the locating TDC procedure in Chapter 2).
6   Make a mark on the edge of the distributor base directly below the rotor tip and in line with it **(see illustration)**. Also, mark the distributor base and the engine block to ensure that the distributor is installed correctly **(see illustration)**.
7   Remove the distributor hold-down nut and washer, then pull the distributor straight out to remove it. **Caution:** *DO NOT turn the crankshaft*

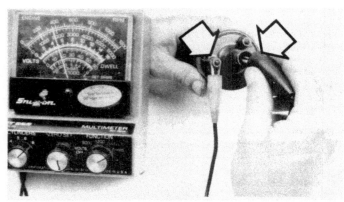

7.5a   To check the coil secondary resistance on an earlier type coil, touch one lead of the ohmmeter to one of the primary terminals and the other lead to the high-tension terminal (arrows), then compare your reading to the coil secondary resistance listed in this Chapter's Specifications

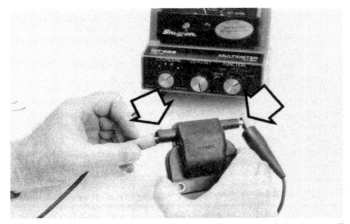

7.5b   Checking the coil secondary resistance on a later-type coil (2.0L engine shown)

8.6a   Before removing the distributor, paint or scribe an alignment mark on the edge of the distributor base directly beneath the rotor tip – DO NOT use a lead pencil

8.6b   Also paint an alignment mark on the engine and the distributor base to ensure the correct timing after the distributor is installed

while the distributor is out of the engine, or the alignment marks will be useless.
8   Detach the primary wiring from the distributor.

Installation

Note: *If the crankshaft has been moved while the distributor is out, the number one piston must be repositioned at TDC. This can be done by feeling for compression pressure at the number one plug hole as the crankshaft is turned. Once compression is felt, align the TDC marks on the drivebelt pulley and the timing cover.*

9   Insert the distributor into the engine in exactly the same relationship to the block that it was in when removed.
10   To mesh the helical gears on the camshaft and the distributor, it may be necessary to turn the rotor slightly. Recheck the alignment marks between the distributor base and the block to verify that the distributor is in the same position it was in before removal. Also check the rotor to see if it's aligned with the mark you made on the edge of the distributor base.
11   Loosely install the nut.
12   Reconnect the electrical leads.
13   Install the distributor cap.

14   Reattach the vacuum line(s) to the advance unit (if equipped).
15   Reattach the spark plug wires to the plugs (if removed).
16   Connect the cable to the negative terminal of the battery.
17   Check the ignition timing (see Chapter 1) and tighten the distributor hold-down nut securely.

9   Centrifugal advance assembly – check and replacement

Refer to illustrations 9.7a, 9.7b, 9.7c, 9.7d, and 9.7e
1   Detach the vacuum line(s) from vacuum advance unit on the distributor and plug them.
2   Connect a timing light according to it's manufacturer's instructions.
3   Start the engine.
4   While watching the timing marks with the use of the timing light, raise the engine speed while watching the timing marks advance.
5   The timing should advance smoothly.
6   If the timing does not advance smoothly, check the advance weights, springs and plate for damage or binding.
7   Replace parts as needed **(see illustrations)**.

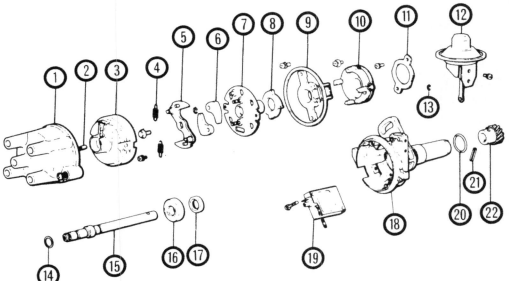

9.7a   An exploded view of the distributor on 1983 models

1   Breather
2   Cap
3   Contact carbon
4   Rotor
5   Centrifugal advance springs
6   Centrifugal advance plate
7   Centrifugal advance weights
8   Centrifugal advance base
9   Signal rotor
10   Pick-up coil
11   Ignitor
12   Breaker
13   Plate
14   Washer
15   Shaft
16   Bearing
17   Oil seal
18   Housing
19   O-ring
20   Spring pin
21   Gear
22   Vacuum control

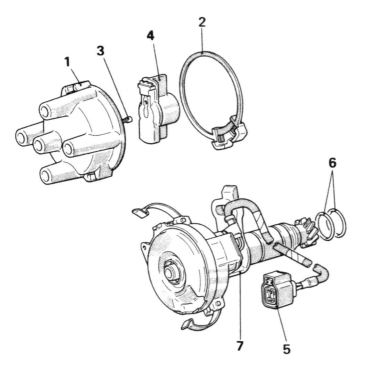

9.7b   An exploded view of the distributor on 1989 and later 2.4L engines

1   Distributor cap
2   Packing
3   Contact carbon
4   Rotor
5   Lead wire
6   O-rings
7   Housing and crank angle sensor assembly

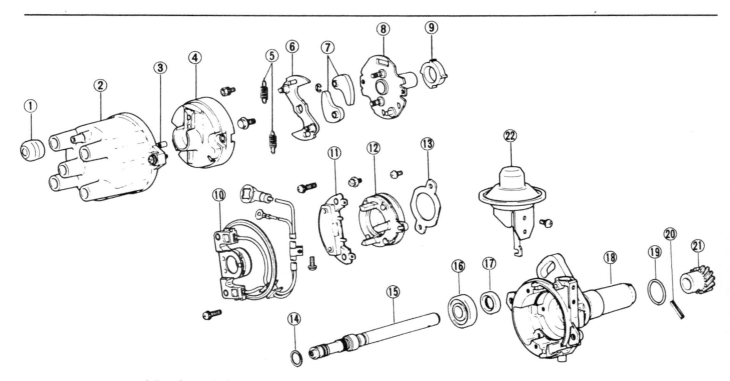

9.7c   An exploded view of the distributor on 1984 through 1989 models (Mitsubishi type)

1	Breather	7	Igniter	12	Vacuum advance unit	18	Oil seal
2	Cap	8	Dowel pin		(single-diaphragm type)	19	Packing
3	Contact carbon	9	Signal rotor	13	Rotor shaft	20	Housing
4	Rotor	10	Advance plate	14	Spring retainers	21	O-ring
5	Cable assembly	11	Vacuum advance unit	15	Centrifugal advance springs	22	Washer
6	Ground wire		(dual-diaphragm type)	16	Centrifugal advance weights	23	Driven gear
				17	Distributor shaft	24	Pin

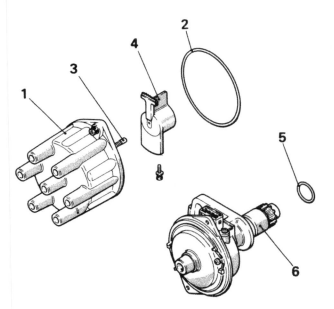

9.7d   An exploded view of the distributor on 1989 and later 3.0L engines

1   Distributor cap
2   O-ring
3   Contact carbon
4   Rotor
5   O-ring
6   Distributor housing assembly

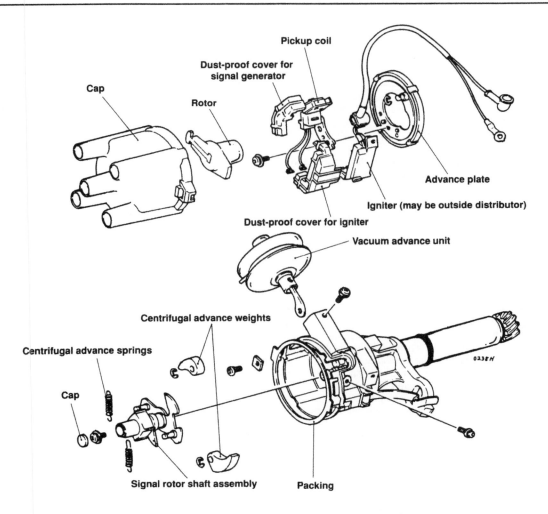

9.7e   An exploded view of the distributor on 1986 through 1989 models (Nippondenso type)

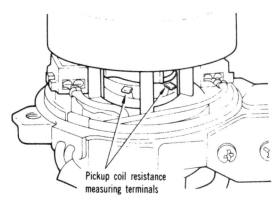

10.1   Use an ohmmeter to check the resistance of the pick-up coil

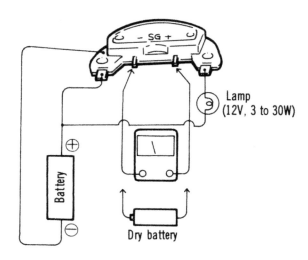

10.7   Set-up for checking the igniter on 1983 distributors

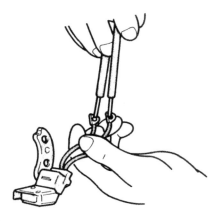

10.18   Depending on the year and model of the vehicle, the pick-up coil can be checked either in the distributor or removed.

10   Distributor electronic components – check and replacement (1983 through 1989 models only)

1983 models

Pick-up coil check and replacement
Refer to illustration 10.1

1   Using an ohmmeter, measure the resistance of the pick-up coil **(see illustration)**. Compare the measured resistance to the Specifications listed in this Chapter. If the resistance is not correct, replace the pick-up coil with a new unit. **Note:** *The resistance of the pick-up coil can be measured with the pick-up coil installed in the distributor.*
2   To remove the pick-up coil, remove the two mounting screws **(see illustration 9.7a)** and lift the rotor off the governor assembly.
3   Remove the bolt from the shaft and pull off the governor assembly. **Note:** *Before the governor weights and springs are removed, make marks on the pins and springs for reference on assembly. Also, handle the springs very carefully to avoid any deformation which could cause changes in the advance characteristics.*
4   Remove the screws attaching the pick-up coil to the distributor. The coil and cap gasket can now be lifted out.

Igniter check and replacement
Refer to illustration 10.7

5   Follow the procedure in Steps 2 through 4 and remove the igniter. Refer to illustration 9.7a if problems are encountered.

6   Be sure to mark the relationship between the drive gear and distributor shaft before driving out the roll pin.
7   The igniter (control unit) can be checked as follows. Connect jumper wires from the battery and a 12-volt test light to the igniter terminals **(see illustration)**.
8   Connect an ohmmeter or small dry cell to the remaining terminals as shown (this will apply a small signal to the igniter).
9   If the test light glows when the signal is applied and goes out when it is removed, the igniter is apparently working properly. If not, it is defective. **Note:** *Even if the test results are as specified, the igniter may be defective.*
10   When reassembling the distributor, be sure to align the mating marks on the gear and shaft before installing the roll pin.
11   The air gap between the signal rotor and pick-up coil must be adjusted after the distributor is reassembled (see Section 11).

1984 through 1989 Mitsubishi type

12   The pick-up coil can be checked as follows. Disconnect the electrical connectors from the coil. Connect an ohmmeter to the electrical terminals and check the resistance.
13   The resistance should be within the range listed in this Chapter's Specifications. If the test results are not within this range, replace the pick-up coil with a new unit.
14   To remove the pick-up coil, follow the procedure in Steps 3 through 6, but note that later model distributors differ in certain details. Refer to illustration 9.7c if problems are encountered.
15   The air gap between the signal rotor and pick-up coil must be adjusted after the distributor is reassembled (see Section 11).

1986 through 1989 Nippondenso type (2.0L engine)
Refer to illustration 10.18

16   Follow the procedure in Step 2 and remove the igniter (control unit), but note that later model distributors differ in certain details. Refer to illustration 9.7d if problems are encountered.
17   On most models, the distributor cap and rotor must be removed before the igniter can be removed.
18   The igniter (control unit) can be checked as follows: Connect an ohmmeter to the electrical terminals **(see illustration)** and check the resistance.
19   The resistance should be 140 to 180 ohms.
20   Reinstall the distributor cap and rotor.
21   The air gap between the signal rotor and pick-up coil must be adjusted after the distributor is reassembled (see Section 11).

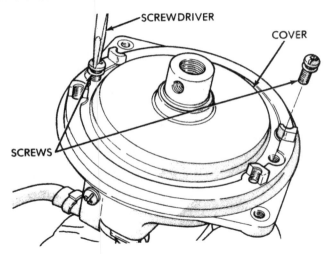

10.24   To get at the photo-optic sensing unit on a 3.0L distributor, remove these two screws (arrows) and this protective cover

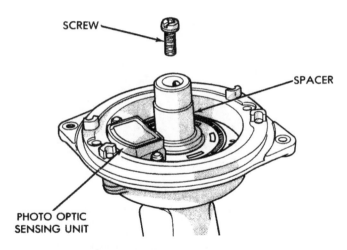

10.25   Remove the screw (arrow) from the spacer and remove the spacer

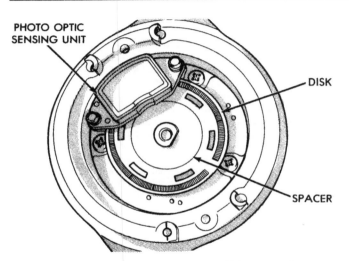

10.26a   Carefully remove the upper disk spacer, the disk and the lower disk spacer (underneath the disk, not visible in this illustration)

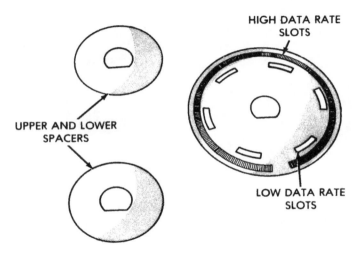

10.26b   Note how the upper and lower disk spacers and the disk itself are keyed to prevent incorrect reassembly

Photo-optic sensing unit (3.0L engine)

Refer to illustrations 10.24, 10.25, 10.26a, 10.26b and 10.28

22   Remove the distributor (see Section 8).

23   Remove the rotor (see Chapter 1).

24   Remove the protective cover from the distributor housing **(see illustration)**.

25   Remove the screw from the spacer **(see illustration)** and remove the spacer.

26   Carefully remove the upper disk spacer, the disk and the lower disk spacer **(see illustration)**. **Note:** *The disk and spacers are keyed to ensure proper reassembly* **(see illustration)**.

27   Check the disk for warpage, cracks or damaged slots. If any damage is evident, replace the disk.

28   Remove the bushing from the photo-optic sensing unit, remove the three screws from the sensing unit **(see illustration)** and remove the sensing unit.

29   Reassembly is the reverse of disassembly.

30   Install the distributor (see Section 8) and install the rotor and cap (see Chapter 1).

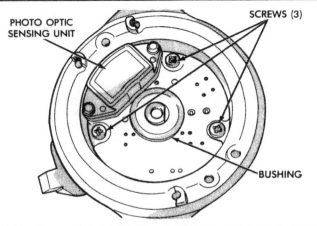

10.28   Remove the bushing (arrow) from the photo-optic sensing unit, remove these three screws (arrows) and remove the photo-optic sensing unit

11.2   To adjust the air gap between the pick-up and the signal rotor, loosen the pick-up mounting screws, insert a feeler gauge of the specified thickness between the pick-up and one of the signal rotor projections, push the pick-up against the gauge and tighten the mounting screws

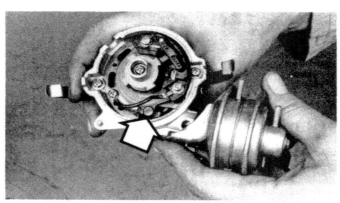

12.8   . . . then tilt it down, detach it from the pin (arrow) on the breaker base and pull it out

---

11   Distributor pick-up air gap – check and adjustment

Refer to illustration 11.2

Note: *This procedure does not apply to 1990 and later 2.4L four-cylinder and 3.0L V6 engines.*

1   Anytime you disturb the pick-up air gap in the distributor it must be properly adjusted.

2   Loosen the pick-up mounting screws. Place a feeler gauge of the thickness listed in this Chapter's Specifications between one of the projections on the signal rotor and the pick-up **(see illustration)**.

3   Gently push the pick-up toward the signal rotor until it's a snug – not tight – fit against the feeler gauge.

4   Tighten the pick-up mounting screws.

5   Check the adjustment by noting the amount of drag on the feeler gauge when you pull it out of the gap between the signal rotor and the pick-up. You should feel a slight amount of drag. If you feel excessive drag on the gauge, the gap is probably too small. If you don't feel any drag on the gauge when you pull it out, the air gap is too large.

---

12   Vacuum advance unit – check and replacement

Check

1   Remove the vacuum line from the vacuum advance unit and plug the line. If there are two lines, disconnect and plug the outer (furthest from the distributor) line.

2   Connect a timing light to the vehicle.

12.7   To detach the vacuum unit from the distributor remove the two screws (arrows) . . .

3   Attach a vacuum pump to the advance unit.

4   With the engine running, gradually apply vacuum to the advance unit while watching the timing marks with the timing light.

5   The timing should gradually advance. If it doesn't advance, but the unit holds vacuum, the advance plate in the distributor is binding. If it doesn't advance, and the unit does not hold vacuum, replace the unit.

Replacement

Refer to illustrations 12.7 and 12.8

6   Remove the distributor cap and rotor (see Chapter 1).

7   Remove the vacuum unit mounting screws **(see illustration)**.

8   Remove the vacuum unit link from the pin on the breaker base, then detach the vacuum unit **(see illustration)**.

9   Installation is the reverse of removal.

---

13   Charging system – general information and precautions

The charging system includes the alternator, with an integral voltage regulator, the battery, the fusible link(s) and wiring between all the components. The charging system supplies electrical power for the ignition system, the lights, the radio, etc. The alternator is driven by a drivebelt at the front of the engine.

The purpose of the voltage regulator is to limit the alternator's voltage to a preset value. This prevents power surges, circuit overloads, etc., during peak voltage output.

The fusible link can be either a short length of insulated wire integral with the engine compartment wiring harness or a fuse-like device installed in the underhood electrical panel. See Chapter 12 for additional information regarding fusible links.

The charging system doesn't ordinarily require periodic maintenance. However, the drivebelt, battery and wires and connections should be inspected at the intervals outlined in Chapter 1.

The dashboard warning light should come on when the ignition key is turned to Start, then go off immediately. If it remains on, there is a malfunction in the charging system (see Section 14).

Be very careful when making electrical circuit connections to a vehicle equipped with an alternator and note the following:

a) When reconnecting wires to the alternator from the battery, be sure to note the polarity.

b) Before using arc welding equipment to repair any part of the vehicle, disconnect the wires from the alternator and the battery terminals.

c) Never start the engine with a battery charger connected.

d) Always disconnect both battery leads before using a battery charger.

e) The alternator is turned by an engine drivebelt which could cause serious injury if your hands, hair or clothes become entangled in it with the engine running.

f) Because the alternator is connected directly to the battery, it could arc or cause a fire if overloaded or shorted out.

g) Wrap a plastic bag over the alternator and secure it with rubber-bands before steam cleaning the engine.

15.3 Loosen the adjustment bolt (arrow) and the pivot bolts to remove the drivebelt from the alternator pulley

14 Charging system – check

1   If a malfunction occurs in the charging circuit, don't automatically assume that the alternator is causing the problem. First check the following items:

a) Check the drivebelt tension and condition (Chapter 1). Replace it if it's worn or deteriorated.
b) Make sure the alternator mounting and adjustment bolts are tight.
c) Inspect the alternator wiring harness and the connectors at the alternator. They must be in good condition and tight.
d) Check the fusible link(s). If burned, determine the cause, repair the circuit and replace the link (the vehicle won't start and/or the accessories won't work if the fusible link blows). Sometimes a fusible link may look good, but still be bad. If in doubt, remove it and check for continuity.
e) Start the engine and check the alternator for abnormal noises (a shrieking or squealing sound indicates a bad bearing).
f) Check the specific gravity of the battery electrolyte. If it's low, charge the battery (doesn't apply to maintenance free batteries).
g) Make sure the battery is fully charged (one bad cell in a battery can cause overcharging by the alternator).
h) Disconnect the battery cables (negative first, then positive). Inspect the battery posts and the cable clamps for corrosion. Clean them thoroughly if necessary (see Chapter 1). Reconnect the cable to the positive terminal.
i) With the key off, connect a test light between the negative battery post and the disconnected negative cable clamp.
   1) If the test light does not come on, reattach the clamp and proceed to the next step.
   2) If the test light comes on, there is a short (drain) in the electrical system of the vehicle. The short must be repaired before the charging system can be checked.
   3) Disconnect the alternator wiring harness.
      (a) If the light goes out, the alternator is bad.
      (b) If the light stays on, pull each fuse until the light goes out (this will tell you which component is shorted).

2   Using a voltmeter, check the battery voltage with the engine off. If should be approximately 12-volts.

3   Start the engine and check the battery voltage again. It should now be approximately 14-to-15 volts.

4   Turn on the headlights. The voltage should drop, and then come back up, if the charging system is working properly.

5   If the voltage reading is more than the specified charging voltage, replace the voltage regulator (refer to Section 16). If the voltage is less, the alternator diode(s), stator or rectifier may be bad or the voltage regulator may be malfunctioning.

3.0L Engine

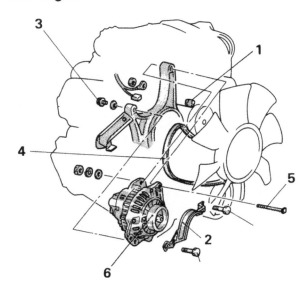

2.4L Engine

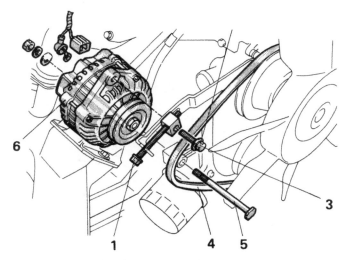

15.4a An exploded view of the mounting hardware for a typical 2.4L and 3.0L alternator installation

1 Alternator adjustment bolt   4 Alternator drive belt
2 Alternator cover   5 Alternator support bolt
3 Alternator brace bolt   6 Alternator

15 Alternator – removal and installation

Refer to illustrations 15.3, 15.4a and 15.4b

1   Detach the cable from the negative terminal of the battery.

2   Detach the electrical connector(s) from the alternator. Be sure to label each wire to avoid confusion during installation.

3   Loosen the alternator adjustment and pivot bolts and detach the drivebelt **(see illustration)**.

4   Remove the adjustment and pivot bolts and separate the alternator from the engine **(see illustrations)**.

2.0L engine

Vehicles without an air-conditioner

2.6L engine

Vehicles with an air condtioner

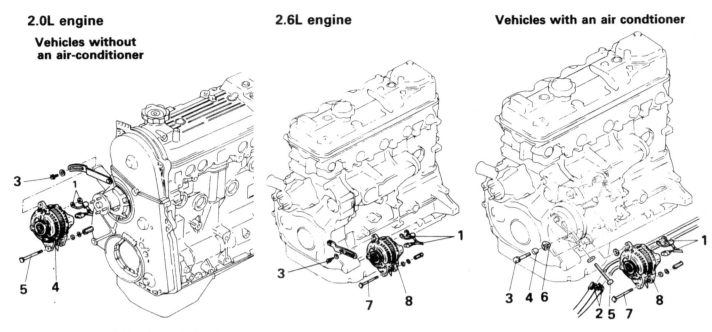

15.4b   An exploded view of the mounting hardware for a typical 2.0L and 2.6L alternator installation

1	Alternator connectors	3	Adjustment bolt	6	Tension plate
2	Automatic transmission oil cooler hoses	4	Spacer	7	Support plate
		5	Adjusting bolt	8	Alternator

16.2   To detach the voltage regulator/brush holder assembly, remove the two mounting screws (arrows) and pull the regulator/brush holder straight out

5   If you're replacing the alternator, take the old one with you when purchasing a replacement unit. Make sure the new/rebuilt unit looks identical to the old alternator. Look at the terminals – they should be the same in number, size and location as the terminals on the old alternator. Finally, look at the identification numbers – they will be stamped into the housing or printed on a tag attached to the housing. Make sure the numbers are the same on both alternators.

6   Many new/rebuilt alternators DO NOT have a pulley installed, so you may have to switch the pulley from the old unit to the new/rebuilt one. When buying an alternator, find out the shop's policy regarding pulleys – some shops will perform this service free of charge.

7   Installation is the reverse of removal.

8   After the alternator is installed, adjust the drivebelt tension (see Chapter 1).

9   Check the charging voltage to verify proper operation of the alternator (see Section 14).

16   Voltage regulator/alternator brushes – replacement

Bosch type

Refer to illustrations 16.2, 16.3 and 16.4

Note: *If you are replacing the brushes (but not the regulator itself), the following procedure requires that you unsolder the old brush leads from the regulator and solder the new ones into place. Unless you are skilled with a soldering gun, have this procedure performed by someone who is. If you overheat and damage the regulator, you could end up spending a lot more money than necessary.*

1   Remove the alternator (see Section 15).

2   Remove the voltage regulator mounting screws **(see illustration)**.

3   Remove the regulator/brush holder assembly and measure the length of the brushes **(see illustration)**. If they are less than 3/16-inch long, replace them with new ones. **Note:** *If you're simply replacing the voltage regulator, skip the next step – the new regulator assembly includes a new set of brushes so the following step is unnecessary.*

4   Unsolder the brush wiring connections **(see illustration)** and remove the brushes and springs.

5   Installation is the reverse of removal. Be sure to solder the new brush leads properly.

Melco type

Refer to illustrations 16.10a, 16.10b, 16.11, 16.12a, 16.12b, 16.13 and 16.14

6   Remove the alternator (see Section 15).

7   Remove the bolts retaining the two halves of the alternator together.

8   Mount the front of the alternator face down in a vise. Using rags as a cushion, clamp to the front case portion of the alternator.

9   Remove all nuts from the back of the alternator.

10   Using a 200-watt soldering iron, heat the rear bearing area (bearing box) of the rear case **(see illustration)**. Insert two standard screwdrivers carefully between the two halves of the alternator (not too deep or you will damage the stator) and pry the rear case off the alternator **(see illustration)**.**Caution:** *Pry gently or you'll break the delicate aluminum case.*

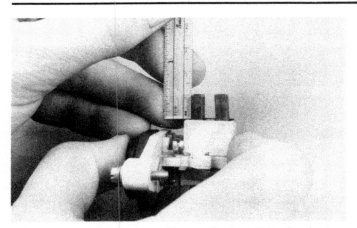

16.3   Measure the brushes with a small ruler – if they're shorter than 3/16 of an inch, install new ones

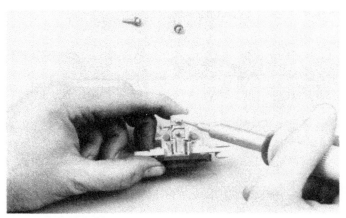

16.4   To detach worn brushes from the voltage regulator/brush holder assembly, carefully unsolder the brush leads and extract each brush and lead from the holder

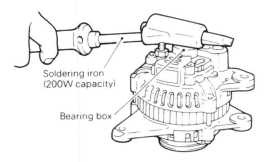

16.10a   Heating the rear bearing box of the alternator will make splitting the alternator easier

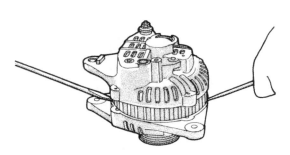

16.10b   Use two screwdrivers to split the alternator

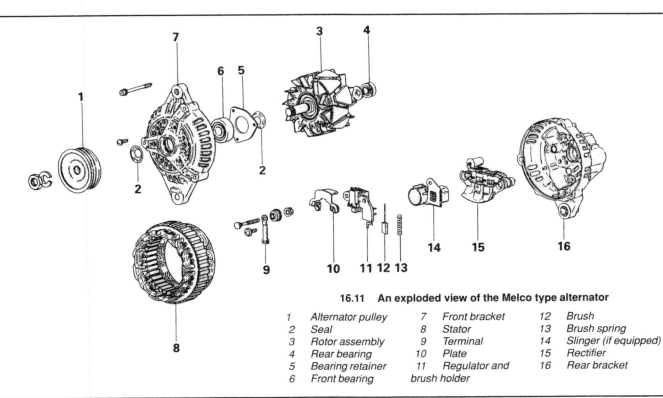

16.11   An exploded view of the Melco type alternator

1 Alternator pulley	7 Front bracket	12 Brush
2 Seal	8 Stator	13 Brush spring
3 Rotor assembly	9 Terminal	14 Slinger (if equipped)
4 Rear bearing	10 Plate	15 Rectifier
5 Bearing retainer	11 Regulator and	16 Rear bracket
6 Front bearing	brush holder	

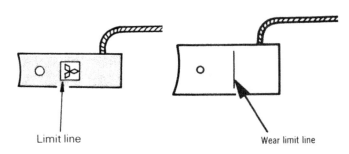

Limit line

Wear limit line

16.12a   If the brushes are worn past the wear limit line, they should be replaced

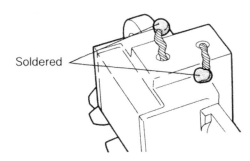

Soldered

16.12b   If the brushes are being replaced, unsolder and solder the pigtails at the area shown

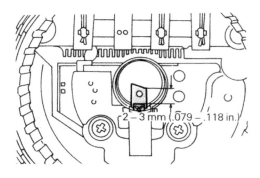

2 – 3 mm (.079 – .118 in.)

16.13   When installing new brushes, they should extend out of the holder the proper amount

11   Unsolder the regulator/brush holder **(see illustration)**. **Note:** *While applying heat to electrical components, it's a good idea to use a pair of needle-nose pliers as a heat sink. Don't apply heat for more than about five seconds.*
12   Inspect the brushes for excessive wear **(see illustration)** and replace them if necessary by unsoldering **(see illustration)**.
13   When installing new brushes, solder the pigtails so the brush limit line will be about 0.079 to 0.118 inch above the end of the brush holder **(see illustration)**.
14   To reassemble, compress the brushes into their holder and retain them with a straight piece of wire that can be pulled from the back of the alternator when reassembled **(see illustration)**.
15   To reassemble, reverse disassembly procedure.

17   Starting system – general information and precautions

The sole function of the starting system is to turn over the engine quickly enough to allow it to start.
The starting system consists of the battery, the starter motor, the starter solenoid and the wires connecting them. The solenoid is mounted directly on the starter motor.
The solenoid/starter motor assembly is installed on the transmission bellhousing.
When the ignition key is turned to the Start position, the starter solenoid is actuated through the starter control circuit. The starter solenoid then connects the battery to the starter. The battery supplies the electrical energy to the starter motor, which does the actual work of cranking the engine.

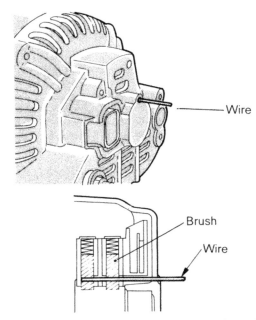

Wire

Brush

Wire

16.14   When placing the two covers together, use a piece of wire through the rear case and into the brush holder to retain the brushes in the holder

Always observe the following precautions when working on the starting system:
 a) Excessive cranking of the starter motor can overheat it and cause serious damage. Never operate the starter motor for more than 30 seconds at a time without pausing to allow it to cool for at least two minutes.
 b) The starter is connected directly to the battery and could arc or cause a fire if mishandled, overloaded or shorted out.
 c) Always detach the cable from the negative terminal of the battery before working on the starting system.

18   Starter motor – in-vehicle check

Note: *Before diagnosing starter problems, make sure the battery is fully charged.*

1   If the starter motor does not turn at all when the switch is operated, make sure that the shift lever is in Neutral or Park (automatic transmission) or that the clutch pedal is depressed (manual transmission).

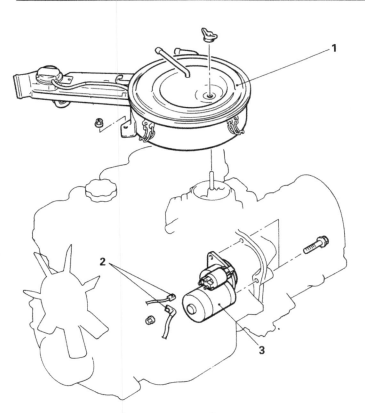

19.3   Typical mounting details for the starter motor

1   *Air cleaner housing*   3   *Starter motor*
2   *Electrical connections*

20.3   To separate the solenoid from the starter motor, remove the nut and detach the lead (arrow) . . .

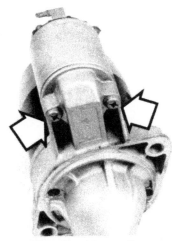

20.4   . . . then remove the solenoid mounting screws (arrows) and pull the solenoid straight off the starter flange

2   Make sure that the battery is charged and that all cables, both at the battery and starter solenoid terminals, are clean and secure.
3   If the starter motor spins but the engine is not cranking, the overrunning clutch in the starter motor is slipping and the stater motor must be replaced.
4   If, when the switch is actuated, the starter motor does not operate at all but the solenoid clicks, then the problem lies with either the battery, the main solenoid contacts or the starter motor itself (or the engine is seized).
5   If the solenoid plunger cannot be heard when the switch is actuated, the battery is bad, the fusible link is burned (the circuit is open) or the solenoid itself is defective.
6   To check the solenoid, connect a jumper lead between the battery (+) and the ignition switch wire terminal (the small terminal) on the solenoid. If the starter motor now operates, the solenoid is OK and the problem is in the ignition switch, neutral start switch or the wiring.
7   If the starter motor still does not operate, remove the starter/solenoid assembly for disassembly, testing and repair.
8   If the starter motor cranks the engine at an abnormally slow speed, first make sure that the battery is charged and that all terminal connections are tight. If the engine is partially seized, or has the wrong viscosity oil in it, it will crank slowly.
9   Run the engine until normal operating temperature is reached. Disconnect the coil wire from the distributor cap and ground it on the engine.
10   Connect a voltmeter positive lead to the positive battery post and connect the negative lead to the negative post.
11   Crank the engine and take the voltmeter readings as soon as a steady figure is indicated. Do not allow the starter motor to turn for more than 30 seconds at a time. A reading of 9 volts or more, with the starter motor turning at normal cranking speed, is normal. If the reading is 9 volts or more but the cranking speed is slo, the solenoid contacts are burned, there is a bad connection or the motor is faulty. If the reading is less than 9 volts and the cranking speed is slow, the starter motor is bad or the battery is discharged.

19   Starter motor – removal and installation

Refer to illustration 19.3

1   Detach the cable from the negative terminal of the battery.
2   Clearly label, then disconnect the wires from the terminals on the starter solenoid.
3   Remove the mounting bolts **(see illustration)** and remove the starter.
4   Installation is the reverse of removal.

20   Starter motor/solenoid/gear reduction assembly – replacement

1   Disconnect the cable from the negative terminal of the battery.
2   Remove the starter motor (see Section 19).

Direct drive type

Refer to illustrations 20.3, 20.4 and 20.5

3   Remove the field terminal nut, disconnect the field terminal lead and remove the washer **(see illustration)**.
4   Remove the solenoid mounting screws **(see illustration)**.

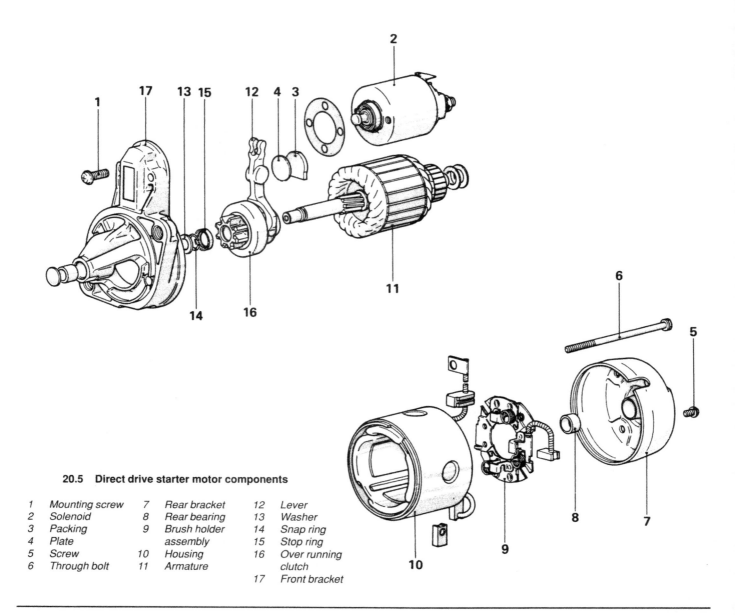

20.5   Direct drive starter motor components

1	Mounting screw	7	Rear bracket	12	Lever
2	Solenoid	8	Rear bearing	13	Washer
3	Packing	9	Brush holder	14	Snap ring
4	Plate		assembly	15	Stop ring
5	Screw	10	Housing	16	Over running
6	Through bolt	11	Armature		clutch
				17	Front bracket

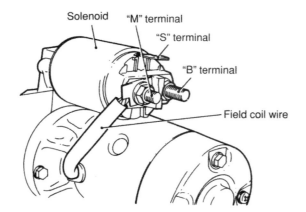

20.7   Disconnect the field coil wire from terminal M

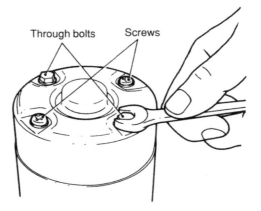

20.8a   Remove the through bolts from the starter housing

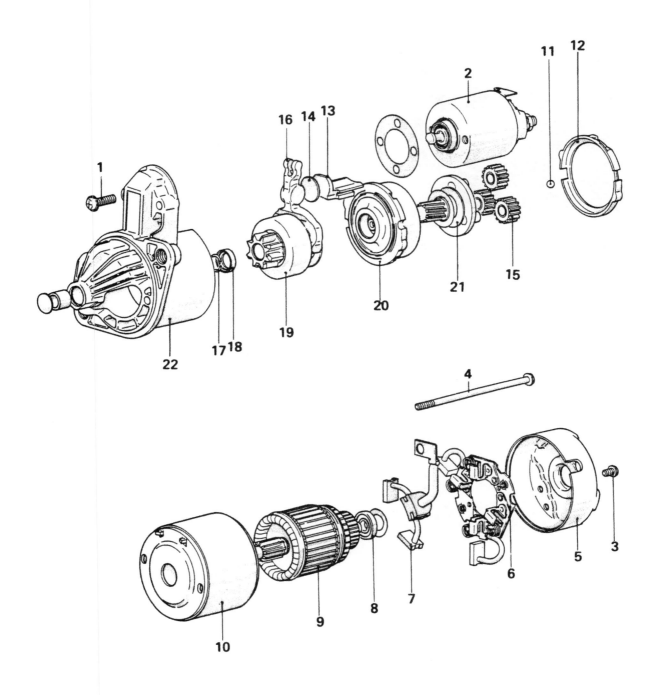

20.8b   Gear reduction starter motor components (later model shown)

1	Mounting screw	7	Brush	13	Packing B	18	Stop ring
2	Solenoid	8	Rear bearing	14	Plate	19	Over running clutch
3	Screw	9	Armature	15	Planetary gear	20	Integral gear
4	Screw	10	Housing	16	Lever	21	Planetary gear holder
5	Rear bracket	11	Ball	17	Snap-ring	22	Front bracket
6	Brush holder	12	Packing A				

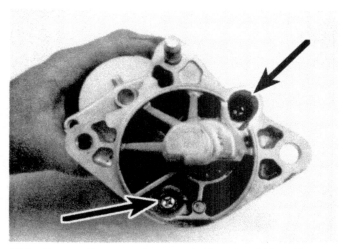

20.9   Remove the screws to separate the solenoid from the gear reduction assembly

5   Work the solenoid off the shift fork and detach it from the drive end housing **(see illustration)**.

6   Installation is the reverse of removal.

Gear reduction type

Refer to illustrations 20.7, 20.8a, 20.8b and 20.9

7   If you're replacing the starter motor or solenoid, disconnect the field coil wire from the solenoid terminal **(see illustration)**; if you're replacing the gear reduction assembly, skip this step and proceed to the next step.

8   To detach the starter motor from the gear reduction assembly, simply remove the two long through-bolts and pull off the starter **(see illustrations)**.

9   To detach the solenoid from the gear reduction assembly, remove the starter, then remove the two Phillips screws from the gear reduction assembly and pull off the solenoid **(see illustration)**.

10   Installation is the reverse of removal.

Chapter 6   Emissions control systems

Contents

Specifications

Dashpot adjustment

Engine set speed
    2.0L engine .... 2200 ± 100 rpm
    2.6L engine .... 1700 ± 100 rpm
Dashpot drop time .... Three to six seconds

Throttle position sensor

Output voltage
    2.4L engine .... 0.48 to 0.52 volts
    3.0L engine .... 0.4 to 1.0 volts
Resistance (at closed throttle) .... 3.5 to 6.5 k-ohms

EGR control solenoid valve resistance .... 36 to 44 ohms

Engine coolant temperature sensor resistance

32-degrees F. .... 5.9 k-ohms
68-degrees F. .... 2.5 k-ohms
104-degrees F. .... 1.1 k-ohms
176-degrees F. .... 0.3 k-ohms

Motor position sensor resistance (2.4L models) .... 4 to 6 k-ohms

Oxygen sensor output voltage

1990 2.4L models .... 1 volt
1991 2.4L and all 3.0L models .... 0.6 to 1 volt

Purge control solenoid valve resistance .... 36 to 44 ohms @ 68-degrees F

Torque specifications

	Ft-lbs
EGR valve bolts	12 to 18
EGR temperature sensor	7.3 to 8.6
Engine coolant temperature sensor	15 to 19

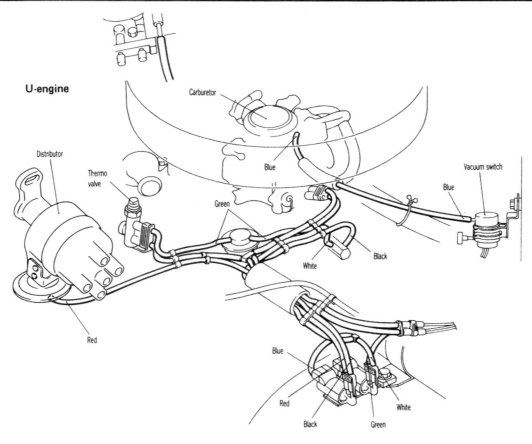

1.3a   Vacuum schematic (1985 and 1986 2.0L engine shown, 2.6L engine similar)

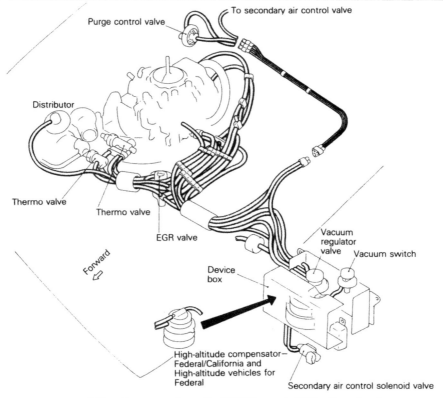

1.3b   Vacuum schematic (1987 through 1989, all engines)

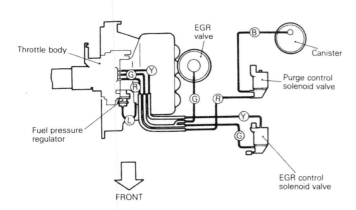

1.3c   Vacuum schematic (1990 and later 2.4L engines)

1   General information

Refer to illustrations 1.3a, 1.3b, 1.3c, 1.3d and 1.3e

To prevent pollution of the atmosphere from incompletely burned and evaporating gases, and to maintain good driveability and fuel economy, a number of emission control systems are incorporated. The principal systems are:

Air aspirator system
Catalytic converter
Deceleration system
Evaporative emission control system
Exhaust Gas Recirculation (EGR) system
Feedback carburetor (FBC) system
Heated air intake system
Jet air system
Multi-Port Injection (MPI) system
Oxygen sensor
Positive Crankcase Ventilation (PCV) system
Secondary Air Supply (SAS) system

The Sections in this Chapter include general descriptions, checking procedures within the scope of the home mechanic and component replacement procedures (when possible) for each of the systems listed above.

Before assuming an emissions control system is malfunctioning, check the fuel and ignition systems carefully. The diagnosis of some emis-

sion control devices requires specialized tools, equipment and training. If checking and servicing become too difficult or if a procedure is beyond your ability, consult a dealer service department. Remember, the most frequent cause of emissions problems is simply a loose or broken vacuum hose or wire, so always check the hose and wiring connections first **(see illustrations)**.

This doesn't mean, however, that emission control systems are particularly difficult to maintain and repair. You can quickly and easily perform many checks and do most of the regular maintenance at home with common tune-up and hand tools. **Note:** *Because of a Federally mandated extended warranty which covers the emission control system components, check with your dealer about warranty coverage before working on any emissions-related systems. Once the warranty has expired, you may wish to perform some of the component checks and/or replacement procedures in this Chapter to save money.*

Pay close attention to any special precautions outlined in this Chapter. It should be noted that the illustrations of the various systems may not exactly match the system installed on your vehicle because of changes made by the manufacturer during production or from year-to-year.

A Vehicle Emissions Control Information label is located in the engine compartment (usually on the underside of the hood). This label contains important emissions specifications and adjustment information. When servicing the engine or emissions systems, the VECI label in your particular vehicle should always be checked for up-to-date information.

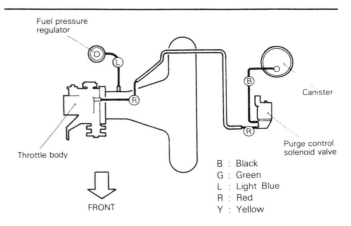

B : Black
G : Green
L : Light Blue
R : Red
Y : Yellow

1.3d   Vacuum schematic (1990 and later Federal and Canadian 3.0L engines)

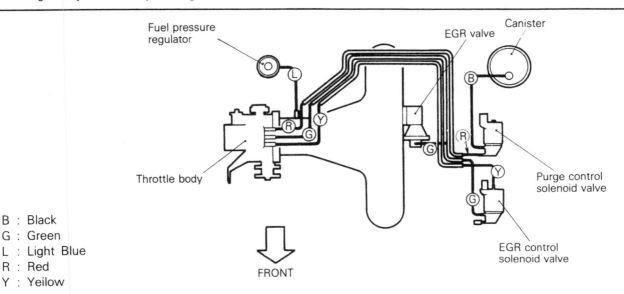

B : Black
G : Green
L : Light Blue
R : Red
Y : Yellow

1.3e   Vacuum schematic (1990 and later California 3.0L engines)

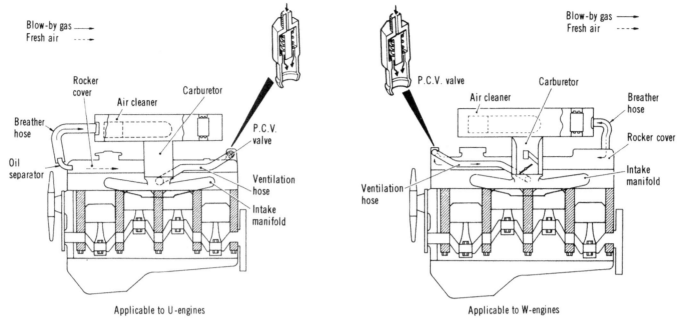

2.1a   Typical Positive Crankcase Ventilation (PCV) system (2.0L engine on left, 2.6L engine on right)

2.4L Engine   ## 3.0L Engine

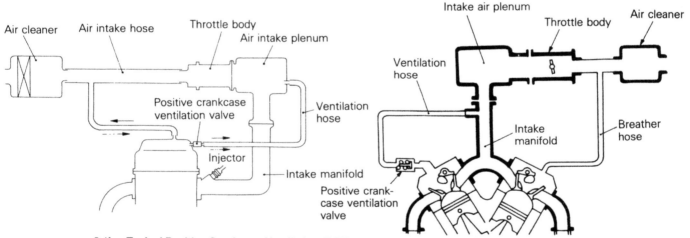

2.1b   Typical Positive Crankcase Ventilation (PCV) system (2.4L engine on left, 3.0L engine on right)

2   Positive Crankcase Ventilation (PCV) system

Refer to illustrations 2.1a and 2.1b

1   A closed-type crankcase ventilation system is utilized to prevent blow-by gases from escaping into the atmosphere. This system has a small orifice fixed at the intake manifold or at the valve cover **(see illustrations)**.

2   The blow-by gas is led through a rubber hose from the front of the valve cover into the air cleaner and through another hose from the rear of the cover into the intake manifold through the orifice. At narrow throttle openings, the blow-by gas is drawn from the rear of the cover into the intake manifold with fresh air entering from the air cleaner through the front of the valve cover. At wide open throttle, the blow-by gas is drawn through both passages.

3   Very little maintenance is required for the crankcase emission control system. Check the hoses for cracks and kinks. Replace them with new ones if they are deteriorated. Make sure that the orifice isn't clogged or poor crankcase ventilation will result.

3   Evaporative emissions control system

Refer to illustrations 3.2a, 3.2b, 3.2c and 3.2d

1   To prevent fuel vapors from escaping into the atmosphere from the fuel tank (due to normal vaporization) the vehicles in this manual are equipped with an evaporative emissions control system.

2   The evaporative emissions control system consists of one or two vapor/liquid separators (not used on all models), an overfill limiter (two-way valve), a fuel check valve, a purge control valve (carbureted models) or purge control solenoid valve (fuel-injected models), a charcoal-filled canister and lines and hoses connecting the components **(see illustrations)**. A carbon element, designed to store fuel vapors generated in the carburetor while the engine is off, is installed in the air cleaner on some models. No routine maintenance is required, but if the element appears to be clogged or dirty, replace it with a new one.

3   The charcoal-filled canister is installed between the fuel tank and the air cleaner. Gasoline vapors are routed to this canister for temporary storage. While the engine is running, outside air is drawn through the canister,

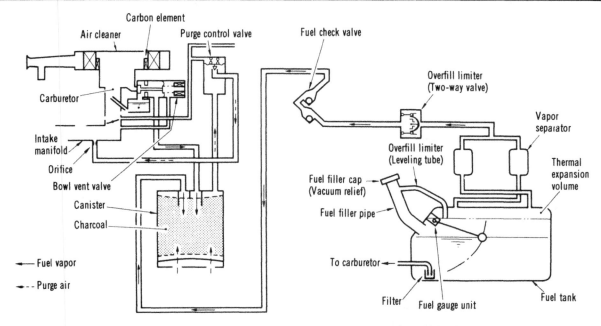

3.2a   Evaporative emissions control system (1983 through 1989 US models)

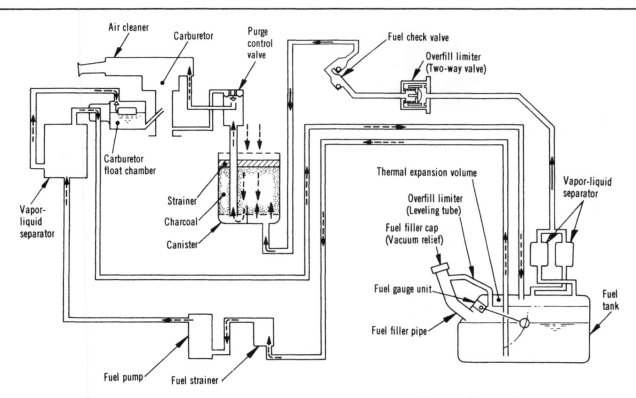

3.2b   Evaporative emissions control system (1983 through 1986 Canadian models)

purging the vapors from the charcoal. This air/vapor mixture is then routed to the engine combustion chambers (through the air cleaner) and burned.

4   The purge control valve is kept closed at idle speeds to prevent vaporized fuel from entering the air cleaner and causing high-idle carbon monoxide emissions.

5   The carburetor itself is vented internally or through the charcoal canister, depending on the temperature, which prevents the escape of gasoline vapors into the atmosphere from the carburetor.

6   When the engine is not running, gasoline vapors produced in the fuel tank (by an increase in atmospheric temperatures) are routed to the separator tank in which liquid gasoline formed by condensation of the vapors is separated. The remaining fuel vapor is led into a two-way valve. The two-way pressure valve is designed to open at a predetermined pressure, admitting the fuel vapors into the charcoal-filled canister, the vapors are trapped by the charcoal, preventing the discharge of raw hydrocarbons into the atmosphere.

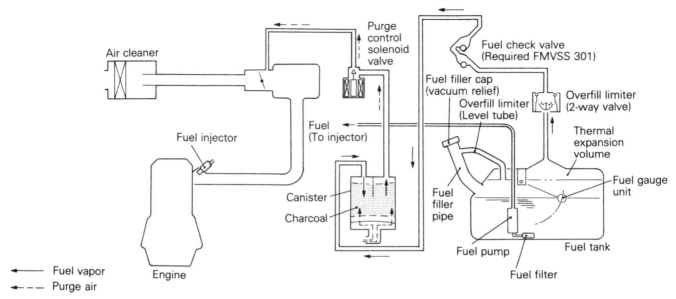

← ——— Fuel vapor
← – – – Purge air

3.2c   Evaporative emissions control system (1990 and later 2.4L model shown, 3.0L similar)

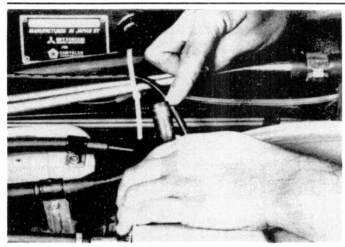

3.17   To check the operation of the purge control valve, disconnect the hose from the air cleaner housing and blow into it

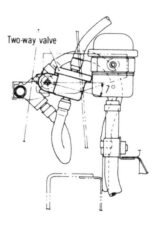

3.27   Install the two-way valve at a seven-degree angle (in relation to the tank)

7   While the engine is running, a vacuum is built above the canister (on the carburetor side) causing outside air to be drawn into the canister through the inlet holes in the case, then passing through the filter and the charcoal. As the outside air flows through, the vapors trapped by the charcoal are carried away, passing through the passage at the center of the canister into the air cleaner, the carburetor and ultimately the engine cylinders where they are burned.

8   During engine operation, vapors originating in the fuel tank are also routed directly into the canister (through the passage in the center of the canister) and fed into the engine for combustion.

9   As the fuel is used, a vacuum is produced inside the fuel tank. The two-way vacuum valve opens momentarily, drawing outside air through the air inlet hose of the canister into the fuel tank, thus maintaining normal pressure in the tank.

10   During filling of the fuel tank, the air in the tank flows through the leveling pipe and out into the atmosphere, venting the tank. When the fuel entering the tank has sealed off the leveling pipe opening in the tank, further filling cannot be done because of the air pressure inside the tank. If filling is continued, overflow of fuel will result.

Charcoal canister

11   Because of the fact that the canister inlet air hose and filter can be-

come clogged over a long period of time, it is recommended that the canister be replaced according to the mileage intervals listed in Chapter 1

12   Also, carefully inspect the rubber hoses attached to the canister. If they are cracked or otherwise deteriorated, replace them with new ones when the canister is replaced.

13   Refer to Chapter 1 for canister removal and installation procedures.

Purge control valve

Refer to illustration 3.17

14   The purge control valve is connected by hoses to the top of the ECS canister, the air cleaner and the carburetor.

15   It is a simple spring-loaded close valve, and its operation is controlled by negative pressure, generated at a port provided slightly above the carburetor throttle valve, which acts on a diaphragm in the valve. When the engine is idling, the valve and evaporated gas passage are closed. When the engine is running at 1500 rpm or more the valve is opened and the fuel vapors stored in the canister are drawn into the carburetor.

16   When inspecting the valve, the engine must be at normal operating temperature.

17   Disconnect the purge hose from the air cleaner **(see illustration)** and blow into it. If the valve is not open, it is in good condition. Next, start the engine and increase the engine speed to 1500 or 2000 rpm and blow into the purge hose again. If the valve is open, it is operating properly.

18   If the valve does not check out as described, replace it with a new one.

Fuel check valve

19   The fuel check valve, located just to the left of the fuel tank, is designed to prevent fuel leaks should the vehicle roll over during an accident. The check valve contains two balls. Under normal conditions the gasoline vapor passage in the valve is open, but if a roll-over occurs, either of the two balls will close the fuel passage and prevent fuel leaks.

20   Remove the hose clamps and disconnect the hoses from the check valve.

21   Remove the bolt attaching the fuel check valve to the rear body mounting bracket.

22   Check the hoses for cracks and replace them if they are deteriorated.

23   Installation of the valve is the reverse of removal.

Two-way valve

Refer to illustration 3.27

24   The two-way valve, located just to the left of the fuel tank, is composed of a pressure valve and a vacuum valve. The pressure valve is designed to open when the fuel tank internal pressure has increased over the normal pressure, which allows the fuel vapors to enter the charcoal canister for storage, and the vacuum valve opens when a vacuum has been produced in the tank.

25   Removal of the valve is quite simple. Loosen the hose clamps and pull off the two hoses, then remove the valve mounting bolt.

26   Blow lightly into the valve inlet. If there is an initial resistance followed by passage of air, the valve is in good condition. Repeat the check by blowing into the outlet.

27   Installation is the reverse of removal. The valve must tilt approximately 7-degrees **(see illustration)** in relation to the fuel tank when it is installed.

Vapor/liquid separator tank(s)

28   The function of the separator tank is to temporarily accommodate an increased volume of gasoline caused by expansion at high outside air temperatures. They also prevent liquid fuel from entering the vapor line during hard cornering.

29   Mark each fuel/vapor hose and its corresponding fitting with numbered pieces of tape.

30   Refer to Chapter 4 and remove the fuel tank.

31   The separator tanks are attached to the top of the fuel tank. They can be removed very easily once the fuel tank has been separated from the vehicle.

32   Replace any cracked or deteriorated fuel/vapor hoses.

33   Installation is basically the reverse of removal. Chapter 4 contains detailed fuel tank installation procedures.

Purge control system (fuel-injected models only)

Refer to illustrations 3.34 and 3.35

34   Detach the vacuum hose with the red stripes from the throttle body and attach it to a hand vacuum pump **(see illustration)**. Plug the vacuum pipe from which the hose was detached.

35   Follow the sequence of tests in the accompanying chart **(see illustration)**.

36   If the system doesn't perform as described, proceed to the following tests.

Purge port vacuum (fuel-injected models only)

Refer to illustrations 3.38

37   Start the engine and warm it up.

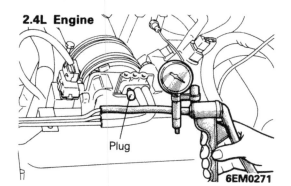

2.4L Engine

Plug

6EM0271

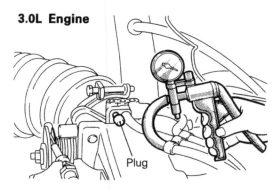

3.0L Engine

Plug

3.34   Detach the vacuum hose with the red stripes from the throttle body and attach it to a hand vacuum pump (plug the vacuum pipe from which the hose was detached) (fuel-injected models only)

When engine is cold

Engine operating condition	Applying vacuum	Result
Idling	400 mmHg (15.7 in.Hg.)	Vacuum is maintained
3,000 rpm		

When engine is warm

Engine operating condition	Applying vacuum	Result
Idling	400 mmHg (15.7 in.Hg.)	Vacuum is maintained
Within 3 minutes after engine start 3,000 rpm	Try applying vacuum	Vacuum leaks
After 3 minutes have passed after engine start 3,000 rpm	400 mmHg (15.7 in.Hg.)	Vacuum will be maintained momentarily, after which it will leak. NOTE: The vacuum will leak continuously if the altitude is 2,200 m (7,200 ft.) or higher, or the intake air temperature is 50°C (122°F) or higher.

3.35   Follow the sequence of tests in this chart to diagnose the purge control system (fuel-injected models only)

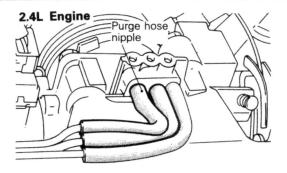

2.4L Engine

Purge hose nipple

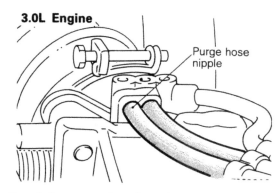

3.0L Engine

Purge hose nipple

3.38   Detach the vacuum hose from the throttle body purge hose nipple and connect a hand-held vacuum pump in its place (fuel-injected models)

38   Detach the vacuum hose from the throttle body purge hose nipple and connect a hand vacuum pump in its place **(see illustration)**.
39   Start the engine and verify that, after the engine rpm is raised by racing the engine, vacuum remains fairly constant.
40   If there's no vacuum created, the throttle body port may be clogged and require cleaning.

Purge control solenoid valve (fuel-injected models)
Refer to illustration 3.41
41   Detach the vacuum hose with the red stripe from the solenoid valve and attach a hand-held vacuum pump in its place **(see illustration)**.

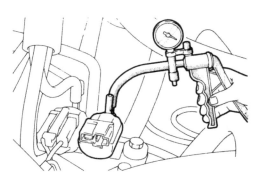

3.41   Detach the vacuum hose with the red stripe from the solenoid valve and attach a hand-held vacuum pump in its place (fuel-injected models)

42   Unplug the electrical connector from the solenoid valve.
43   Apply battery voltage (or any 12V DC source) to the purge control solenoid valve, apply a vacuum and verify that the valve leaks vacuum when voltage is applied; when voltage is discontinued, the valve should maintain vacuum.
44   Measure the resistance between the terminals of the solenoid valve and compare your reading to the range of acceptable resistance listed in this Chapter's Specifications.
45   If the purge control solenoid valve fails either of these tests, replace it.

4   Jet air system (carbureted models only)

Refer to illustration 4.1
1   The jet air system **(see illustration)** utilizes an additional inlet valve (jet valve) which provides for air, or a super lean mixture, to be drawn from the air intake into the cylinder. The jet valve is operated by the same cam as the inlet valve. They use a common rocker arm so the jet valve and the inlet valve open and close simultaneously.
2   On the intake stroke of the engine, fuel/air mixture flows through the intake ports into the combustion chamber. At the same time, jet air is forced into the combustion chamber because of the pressure difference between the jet intake in the throttle bore and the jet valve in the cylinder as

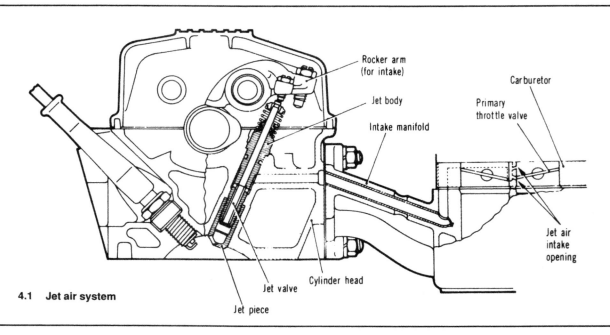

4.1   Jet air system

Rocker arm (for intake)

Jet body

Intake manifold

Carburetor

Primary throttle valve

Jet air intake opening

Cylinder head

Jet valve

Jet piece

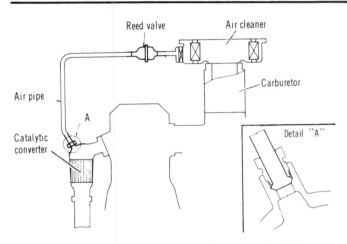

6.1 Secondary Air Supply (SAS) system (typical)

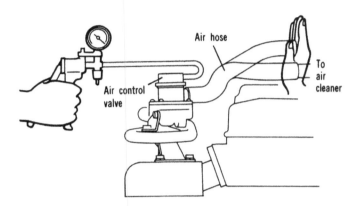

6.5 Checking the air control valve diaphragm on 1985 and later SAS systems

the piston moves down. At small throttle openings, there is a large pressure difference, giving the jet air a high velocity. This scavenges the residual gases around the spark plug and creates good ignition conditions. It also produces a strong swirl in the combustion chamber, which lasts throughout the compression stroke and improves flame propagation after ignition, assuring high combustion efficiency and lowering exhaust emissions. As the throttle opening is increased, less jet air is forced in and jet swirl diminishes but the increased flow through the intake valve ensures satisfactory combustion.

3 Incorrect valve clearances affect emission levels and can cause engine troubles. Refer to the valve clearance adjustment Section in Chapter 1 for the jet valve adjustment procedure.

4 Jet valve removal, inspection and installation procedures are covered in detail in Chapter 2, Part D.

5 Catalytic converter

1 The catalytic converter provides for the oxidizing of hydrocarbons and carbon monoxide in the exhaust system, which reduces the levels of these pollutants in the exhaust.

2 Its ceramic monolithic element, coated with a catalytic agent, is pressed into the exhaust manifold on early models. On later models it is a replaceable component located under the vehicle in the exhaust system.

3 The catalytic converter requires the use of the unleaded fuel only. Leaded gasoline will destroy the effectiveness of the catalyst as an emission control device.

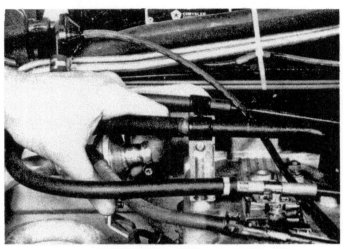

6.4 To check the operation of the SAS reed valve, place your finger over the valve inlet with the engine running

4 Under normal operating conditions, the catalytic converter will not require maintenance. However, it is important to keep the engine properly tuned. If the engine is not properly tuned, engine misfiring may cause overheating of the catalyst, which may damage the converter or other vehicle components. Heat damage can also occur during diagnostic testing if spark plug wires are removed and the engine is allowed to idle for a prolonged period of time.

5 **Caution:** *Vehicle operation, including idling, should be avoided if engine misfiring occurs. Under these conditions the exhaust system will operate at an abnormally high temperature and may cause damage to the catalyst or other underbody parts of the vehicle. Alteration or deterioration of the ignition or fuel systems, or any type of operating condition which results in engine misfiring, must be corrected to avoid overheating the catalytic converter.*

6 Secondary Air Supply (SAS) system (carbureted models only)

Description
Refer to illustration 6.1

1 The SAS system **(see illustration)** consists of reed valves and air pipes that supply secondary air into the exhaust manifold and exhaust pipe (at a point beyond the catalytic converter) for the purpose of promoting oxidation (or complete burning) of any remaining unburned fuel. The system used on 1985 and later models is somewhat more complex; it utilizes a secondary air control valve and a computer-controlled solenoid valve to control the flow of air through the reed valve and into the exhaust manifold.

2 The SAS is actuated by exhaust vacuum generated from pulsations in the exhaust manifold. Air is drawn through the air cleaner and directed into the manifold by the valve motion corresponding to the exhaust pulses.

Check
Refer to illustrations 6.4 and 6.5

3 Check the air hose and air pipe for damage and cracks. Check the air pipe connections for leakage.

4 Start and run the engine at idle. Disconnect the rubber air hose from the reed valve and place your hand over the intake port of the valve **(see illustration)**. If suction is felt, the reed valve is operating properly. If no suction is felt, or if pressure is felt, replace the reed valve with a new one.

5 To check the air control valve diaphragm on 1985 and later models, hook up a hand-operated vacuum pump to the valve fitting with a short section of hose and apply a vacuum of approximately 20 in-Hg **(see illustration)**. The pump gauge needle should remain stable.

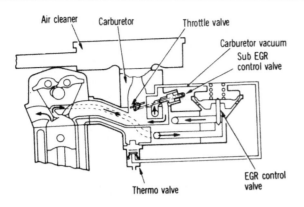

7.3a EGR system (49-state models)

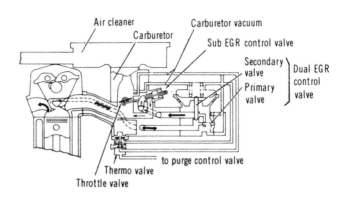

7.3b EGR system (California models)

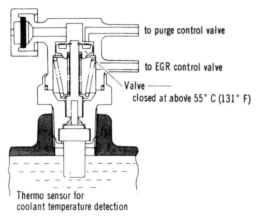

7.3c Thermo valve (49-state models)

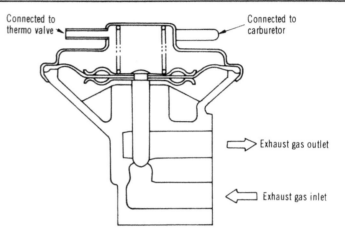

7.4a Dual EGR control valve (California models)

6　Now start the engine and allow it to idle, then apply a vacuum of 4.3 in-Hg or more to the air control valve with the pump. Disconnect the hose from the air cleaner and place your hand over the open end of the hose. You should feel suction.

Replacement

7　Removal of the reed valve is very simple. Pull the rubber hose off the inlet and unscrew the valve from the air pipe. Be sure to use a backup wrench on the pipe so it doesn't become twisted when the valve is unscrewed.
8　Installation is the reverse of removal.

7　Exhaust Gas Recirculation (EGR) system

Description (carbureted models)
US models
Refer to illustrations 7.3a, 7.3b, 7.3c, 7.4a, 7.4b, 7.5 and 7.6

1　The vehicles covered in this manual utilize an Exhaust Gas Recirculation (EGR) system to reduce oxides of nitrogen in the exhaust.
2　The stringent oxides of nitrogen emission standards require high rates of EGR flow, which adversely affects driveability of the vehicle. To solve this problem, it is necessary to increase EGR flow during high load vehicle operation and decrease EGR flow to improve driveability during low load operation.
3　To accomplish this, two different systems are in use; one for vehicles sold in California and one for vehicles sold in the remaining 49 states **(see illustrations)**. Both systems utilize an EGR control valve, a sub-EGR control valve and a thermal valve **(see illustration)**.

4　The California system has a dual EGR control valve (primary and secondary), which is controlled by different carburetor vacuums in response to throttle valve openings **(see illustration)**. The primary EGR valve controls EGR flow during relatively narrow throttle valve openings, while the secondary EGR valve takes over as the throttle valve is opened wider. EGR flow is suspended completely at idle and wide open throttle conditions. The thermal valve **(see illustration)**, which senses coolant temperature, controls the vacuum applied to the EGR control valve.

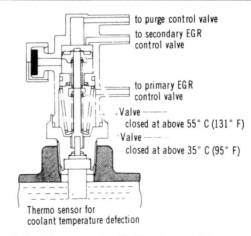

7.4b Thermo valve (California models)

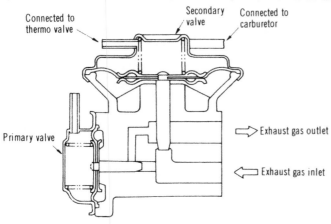

7.5 EGR control valve (49-state models)

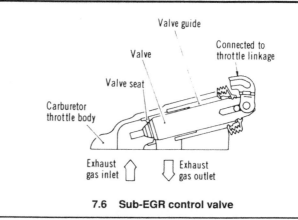

7.6 Sub-EGR control valve

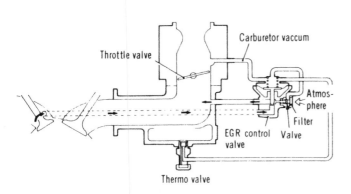

7.8 EGR system (Canadian models)

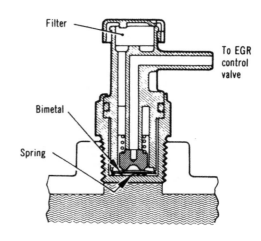

7.11 Thermo valve (Canadian models)

5   The 49 state EGR system utilizes a conventional-type EGR valve that is controlled by carburetor vacuum in response to various throttle valve openings **(see illustration)**. Again, EGR flow is suspended at idle and wide open throttle conditions. The thermal valve controls the vacuum applied to the EGR valve.

6   In both systems, the sub-EGR control valve **(see illustration)** is opened and closed by a linkage connected to the throttle valve. This enables the sub-EGR valve to closely modulate the EGR flow according to the size of the throttle valve opening.

Canadian models

Refer to illustrations 7.8 and 7.11

7   All engines built for use in Canada utilize an exhaust gas recirculation system to reduce oxides of nitrogen in the vehicle exhaust.

8   With this system **(see illustration)**, the exhaust gas is partially recirculated from an exhaust port in the cylinder head, through the EGR control valve, to a port located in the intake manifold below the carburetor.

9   EGR flow is controlled by the EGR control valve and is varied according to engine load. The flow is increased during high load vehicle operation and decreased to preserve driveability of the vehicle during low load operation.

10   With this arrangement, the EGR control valve is activated by carburetor vacuum, drawn from slightly above the throttle valve, so the EGR flow is modulated to attain effective oxides of nitrogen reduction and is suspended at idle and wide-open throttle conditions.

11   The vacuum to be applied on the EGR control valve is controlled by a thermal valve **(see illustration)**, which senses the coolant temperature and cuts off the vacuum when the engine is cold and a vacuum valve which respond to vehicle load by detecting engine manifold vacuum which responds to vehicle load by detecting engine manifold vacuum.

Fuel-injected models

Refer to illustrations 7.12a and 7.12b

12   The EGR system on fuel-injected models is essentially the same as the one on carbureted models. However, the EGR valve is computer-controlled via the EGR control solenoid valve **(see illustrations)**.

Check
Carbureted models
US models
Refer to illustrations 7.18, 7.19 and 7.20

13   Check all vacuum hoses for cracks and correct installation.

14   Start the engine (it must be completely cool) and run it at idle speed.

15   Touch the underside of the secondary EGR valve diaphragm and increase the engine speed from idle to approximately 2500 rpm. No movement of the secondary EGR diaphragm should be felt. If it does move, which means the secondary EGR valve is opening, replace the thermo valve with a new one. **Warning:** *The valve may be very hot – wear a glove or use a rag to prevent your hand from burns.*

16   Allow the engine to warm up until the coolant temperature exceeds 131-degrees F.

17   Again, touch the underside of the secondary EGR valve diaphragm and increase the engine speed from idle to approximately 2500 rpm. This time, the secondary EGR diaphragm should move. If it does not move, which means the secondary EGR valve is not opening, inspect the EGR control valve and the thermo valve.

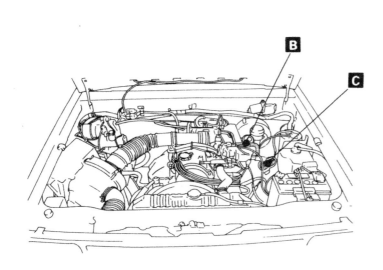

7.12a   EGR system component locations (2.4L engine)

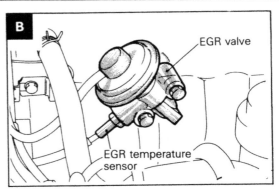

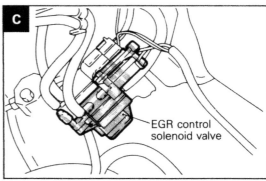

3.0L Engine

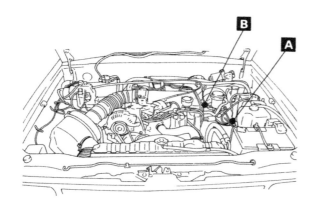

7.12b   EGR system component locations (3.0L engine)

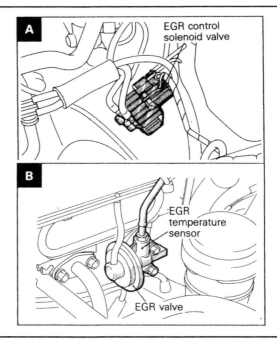

18 To check the thermo valve, disconnect the green-striped hose from the valve **(see illustration)**.

19 Connect the hand-held vacuum pump to the thermo valve and apply vacuum **(see illustration)**. If no vacuum can be held, the thermo valve is good.

20 To check the EGR control valve, disconnect the green-striped hose from the nipple on the carburetor and connect it to the hand-held vacuum pump **(see illustration)**.

21 Open the sub-EGR valve (by pulling on it by hand) and apply a vacuum to the EGR control valve with the pump.

22 If the idle speed becomes unstable, the EGR valve is operating properly. If the idle speeds remain the same, the valve is not operating properly and it should be replaced with a new one.

23 Pull on the sub-EGR valve and check for smooth operation. If the valve binds, it should be removed from its bore, cleaned thoroughly, lubricated with a small amount of light oil and reinstalled. If it still does not operate smoothly, replace it with a new one.

Canadian models

24 Check all vacuum hoses for cracks and proper installation.

25 Start the engine (it must be completely cool) and run it at idle speed. Touch the underside of the EGR control valve diaphragm and increase the engine speed from idle to 2500 rpm. **Warning:** *The valve may be very hot – wear a glove or use a rag to prevent your hand from burns. No movement of the diaphragm should be felt. If movement is felt, which means that the EGR valve is opening, check the green-striped vacuum hose to make sure it isn't clogged. If the hose is clear, the thermal valve is most likely defective*

7.18   Disconnect the green-striped hose from the thermo valve

7.19   Apply a vacuum to the thermo valve

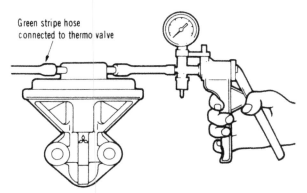

7.20   To check for proper operation of the EGR control valve, hook up a hand-operated vacuum pump/gauge to the carburetor side of the valve

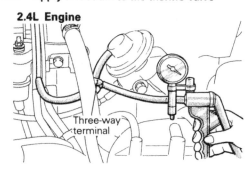

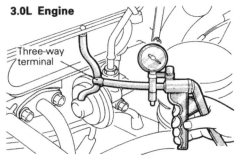

7.28   Disconnect the vacuum hose with the green stripe from the EGR valve and connect a hand-operated vacuum pump/gauge into the line with a three-way terminal

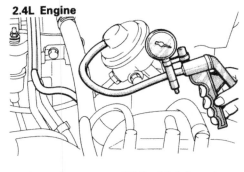

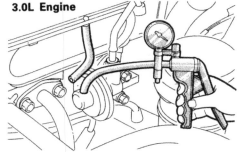

7.31   Disconnect the vacuum pump from the three-way terminal, remove the terminal and connect the vacuum pump directly to the EGR valve

and should be replaced with a new one.

26   If no movement was felt, allow the engine to warm up until the coolant temperature exceeds 104-degrees F.

27   Repeat the test outlined in Step 2. This time movement of the diaphragm should occur. If no movement is felt, the EGR control valve, the thermal valve and the vacuum hoses should be checked for leaks and other defects.

Fuel-injected models
EGR system inspection
Refer to illustrations 7.28 and 7.31

28   Disconnect the vacuum hose with the green stripe from the EGR valve and connect a hand-operated vacuum pump/gauge into the line with a three-way terminal **(see illustration)**.

29   Start the engine. While it's still cold, press down on the accelerator pedal abruptly and race the engine – there should be no vacuum indicated (atmospheric pressure).

30   After the engine is warmed up, press down suddenly on the accelerator again – the indicated vacuum should rise momentarily to about 5.9-in-Hg.

31   Disconnect the vacuum pump from the three-way terminal, remove the terminal and connect the vacuum pump directly to the EGR valve **(see**

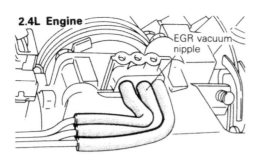

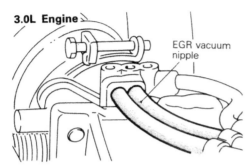

7.33   Disconnect the vacuum hose from the throttle body EGR vacuum nipple and hook up a hand-held vacuum pump in its place

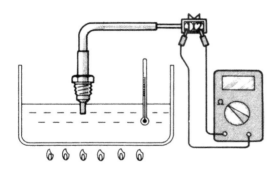

7.41   Measure the resistance of the temperature sensor at the temperatures specified in the text

illustration). With the engine at idle, apply a vacuum of 9.4 in-Hg and note whether the engine stalls or idles roughly (it should).

32   If there's a problem, proceed to the next Step.

EGR valve control vacuum
Refer to illustration 7.33

33   The engine should be warmed up for this test. Disconnect the vacuum hose from the throttle body EGR vacuum nipple **(see illustration)** and hook up a hand vacuum pump in its place.

34   Start the engine, race the engine and verify that vacuum rises in proportion to the rise in engine speed.

35   If it doesn't, the port in the throttle body may be clogged and require cleaning.

EGR valve
Refer to illustration 7.38

36   Remove the EGR valve and, through the open portion underneath, check the diaphragm for sticking. Look for carbon deposits inside the valve. If the valve is dirty, or the diaphragm is stuck, clean the valve with solvent and check it again. If it's still sticking, or clogged, replace it.

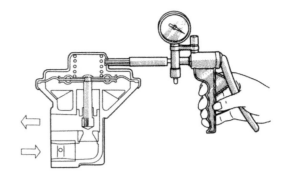

7.38   Apply less than 1.2 in-Hg and try to blow through the valve – you shouldn't be able to; now apply 9.5 or more in-Hg and try to blow through the valve again – this time you should be able to

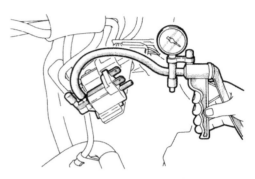

7.44   Disconnect the vacuum hose with the yellow and green stripes from the solenoid valve and connect a hand-operated vacuum pump in its place

37   Hook up a hand-operated vacuum pump to the EGR valve, apply a vacuum of 10 in-Hg and note whether the diaphragm leaks (the valve should hold the vacuum).

38   Release the vacuum applied in the previous Step. Apply less than 1.2 in-Hg and try to blow through the valve – you shouldn't be able to; now apply 9.5 or more in-Hg and try to blow through the valve again – this time you should be able to **(see illustration)**.

39   Install the EGR valve. Use a new gasket and tighten the EGR valve mounting bolts to the torque listed in this Chapter's Specifications.

EGR temperature sensor
Refer to illustration 7.41

40   Remove the EGR temperature sensor and place it in a pot of water. Use a thermometer to monitor the water temperature.

41   As you bring the water to a boil, measure the resistance between terminals 1 and 2 **(see illustration)**. Up to about 122-degrees F, the resistance between the terminals should be between 60 and 83 k-ohms; by the time the water is boiling (212-degrees F), the resistance should be between 11 and 14 k-ohms.

42   If the temperature sensor doesn't perform as described, replace it.

43   When you install the temperature sensor, coat the threads with sealant or Teflon tape and tighten the sensor to the torque listed in this Chapter's Specifications.

EGR control solenoid valve
Refer to illustration 7.44

44   Disconnect the vacuum hose with the yellow and green stripes from the solenoid valve and connect a hand-operated vacuum pump in its place **(see illustration)**.

45   Unplug the wiring harness electrical connector.

46   Apply battery voltage and vacuum to the EGR control solenoid simultaneously. With vacuum and voltage applied, the solenoid should maintain vacuum. When voltage is interrupted, the solenoid should leak vacuum.

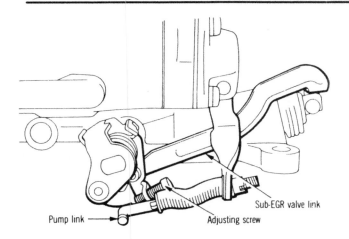

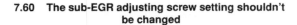

7.60 The sub-EGR adjusting screw setting shouldn't be changed

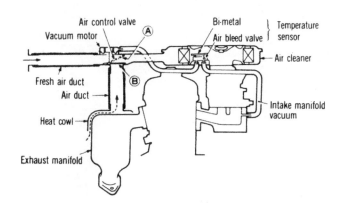

8.1 Typical heated air intake system

47   Measure the resistance between the terminals of the solenoid valve and compare your reading to the value listed in this Chapter's Specifications.

48   If the solenoid valve doesn't perform as described, replace it.

Component replacement

EGR control valve

49   The EGR valve is attached to the lower part of the intake manifold, directly under the carburetor.

50   Mark the vacuum hose and fittings with pieces of numbered tape, then disconnect the vacuum hoses from the EGR valve.

51   Remove the bolts attaching the EGR valve to the intake manifold and the valve can be lifted away. You may have to tap gently on the EGR body with a soft-faced hammer to break the gasket seal.

52   When installing the EGR valve, use a new gasket and tighten the mounting bolts evenly and securely. Also, be sure to install the vacuum hoses properly.

Sub-EGR valve

Refer to illustration 7.60

53   The sub-EGR valve is located on the base of the carburetor and is connected by a linkage to the throttle valve.

54   Carefully pry off the spring clip and remove the pin attaching the sub-EGR valve plunger to the linkage.

55   Hold the end of the linkage up and remove the spring and the steel ball from the end of the plunger. These parts are small and easily lost, so don't drop them.

56   Slip off the rubber boot and slide the plunger out of the carburetor throttle body.

57   Before installing the plunger, clean it with solvent to remove any deposits.

58   Lubricate the plunger with a small amount of light oil, slide it into place in the carburetor throttle body and install the rubber boot.

59   Install the steel ball and spring, hold the linkage in place and insert the pin. Carefully slide the spring clip in place, then check for smooth operation of the valve plunger.

60   The sub-EGR adjusting screw **(see illustration)** has been preset at the factory and should not be disturbed.

Thermal valve

61   The thermal valve is located just in front of the carburetor and is threaded into the coolant passage in the intake manifold.

62   Removal of the thermal valve is quite simple. Pull off the vacuum hoses that are connected to the thermal valve fittings, then unscrew the valve from the manifold.

63   When installing the thermal valve, be sure to use thread-sealing tape on the threads.

---

8   Heated air intake system (carbureted models only)

Description

Refer to illustration 8.1

1   Carbureted models are equipped with a temperature-regulated air cleaner **(see illustration)** so that the carburetor can be calibrated leaner to reduce carbon monoxide and hydrocarbon emissions. Improved engine warm-up characteristics and minimized carburetor icing can also be attained with this system.

2   The air cleaner is equipped with an air control valve inside the snorkel to modulate the temperature of carburetor intake air which flows through the intake. The air control valve is controlled by a vacuum motor/temperature sensor combination system which responds to the intake manifold vacuum and temperature inside the air cleaner.

3   When the bi-metal senses a temperature inside the air cleaner below about 84-degrees F, the air bleed valve of the temperature sensor assembly remains closed, causing intake manifold vacuum to be applied to the diaphragm of the vacuum motor. This in turn opens the air control valve and allows the preheated intake air to flow through the heat cowl and air duct into the air cleaner.

4   When the bi-metal senses that the temperature inside the air cleaner is above about 113-degrees F, the air bleed valve is fully open. As a result, the intake air to the carburetor comes directly through the fresh air duct, since the air control valve is positioned at 'B', as shown in illustration 8.1, regardless of the intake manifold vacuum.

5   At intermediate temperatures, the air entering the carburetor is a blend of fresh and preheated air as regulated by the thermostatically-actuated air control valve.

Check

Refer to illustrations 8.10 and 8.11

6   Make sure all vacuum hoses and the heat cowl-to-air cleaner air duct are properly attached and in good condition.

7   With the engine completely cold and the outside air temperature less than 84-degrees F, remove the rubber tube from the end of the air cleaner snorkel. Start the engine and look into the snorkel (be careful when working around moving engine parts). The air control valve should be in the 'Up' (Heat on) position.

8   With the engine running at normal operating temperatures, check the temperature of the air entering the end of the air cleaner snorkel. If the temperature is 113-degrees F or higher, the air control valve should be in the "down" (heat off) position.

9   To check the operation of the sensor and vacuum motor, you will need a hand-held vacuum pump.

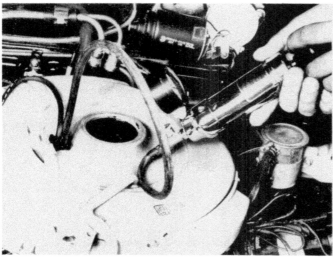

8.10   To check the temperature sensor for the heated air intake system, apply vacuum to the sensor – the air control valve should be in the "up" (heat on) position

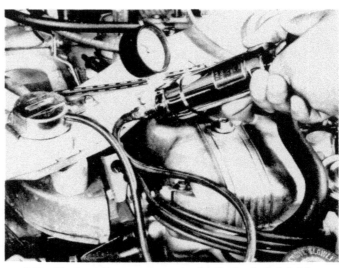

8.11   To check the vacuum motor for the heated air intake system, apply a vacuum to the motor inlet fitting – the air control valve should be in the "up" (heat on) position

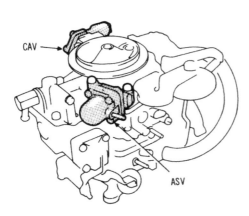

9.1   Deceleration system components

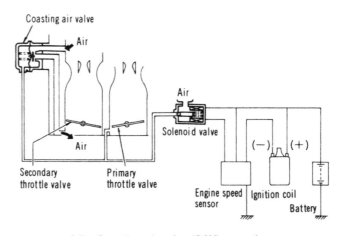

9.2   Coasting air valve (CAV) operation

10   Remove the air cleaner from the engine (see Chapter 4) and allow it to cool to below 84-degrees F. Hook the vacuum pump to the sensor hose and apply a vacuum to the sensor **(see illustration)**. The air control valve should be in the "up" (heat on) position. If it is not, check the vacuum motor for proper operation.

11   To check the vacuum motor, apply a vacuum directly to the motor inlet fitting **(see illustration)**. The air control valve should be in the "up" (heat on) position. If it is not, check to be sure it is not sticking. If the valve moves freely but will not operate properly when a vacuum is applied, the air cleaner housing will have to be replaced.

12   If the vacuum motor operates properly but the valve does not operate when vacuum is applied to the sensor, the sensor should be removed and replaced with a new one.

---

9   Deceleration systems (carbureted models only)

Description

Refer to illustrations 9.1, 9.2 and 9.3

1   The deceleration system **(see illustration)** decreases hydrocarbon emission during vehicle deceleration. It includes the Coasting Air Valve (CAV), the Air Switching Valve (ASV) and the fuel cut-off solenoid, which are built into the carburetor.

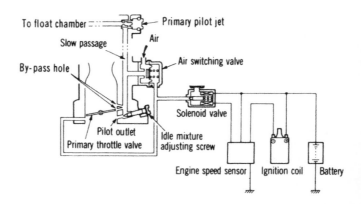

9.3   Air switching valve (ASV) operation

2   The CAV **(see illustration)**, which is activated by carburetor ported vacuum, supplies additional air into the intake manifold, leaning the fuel/air mixture.

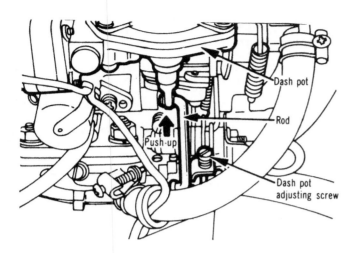

9.7   Dashpot adjustment (early Canadian models with automatic transmission)

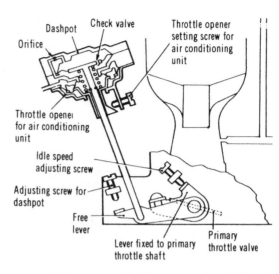

9.8a   Dashpot adjustment screw location (1983 and 1984, USA model shown)

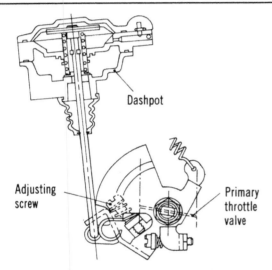

9.8b   Dashpot adjustment screw location (1985 through 1989, Canadian model shown)

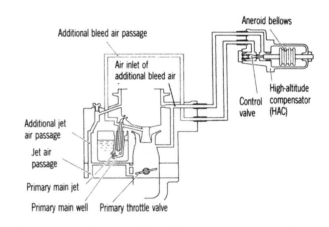

10.1   High altitude compensation system component layout

3   The ASV **(see illustration)**, which is also activated by carburetor ported vacuum, improves fuel economy by supplying additional air into the idle circuit slow passage.

4   In order to maintain smooth vehicle deceleration, and to prevent stalling, operation of the CAV and ASV is suspended by opening the solenoid valve (when the engine speed sensor detects engine speed at or below a specified value).

Dashpot systems

5   Carburetors on some early Canadian models with an automatic transmission, all Canadian and California models with a manual transmission from 1983 and all 1985 and later models, regardless of transmission type or destination, are equipped with a dashpot which delays the closing of the throttle valve during vehicle deceleration and reduces the hydrocarbon emissions.

Dashpot adjustment

Refer to illustrations 9.7, 9.8a and 9.8b

6   Before adjusting the dashpot, make sure the idle speed is set correctly. Use a tachometer connected according to the manufacturer's instructions.

7   Push the dashpot rod up through its entire stroke until it comes to a stop **(see illustration)**.

8   Check the engine speed (set speed) at this point and compare it to the specifications. If it is not correct, turn the dashpot adjusting screw, as necessary, until the set speed is as specified **(see illustrations)**.

9   Raise the engine speed, then release the throttle. If the engine speed drops too quickly (see this Chapter's Specifications), the dashpot should be replaced.

10   High altitude compensation system (carbureted models only)

Refer to illustration 10.1

1   The high altitude compensation system **(see illustration)** is installed on later model vehicles in order to maintain the appropriate fuel/air mixture at high altitudes. The system affects the primary metering system in the carburetor to alter the fuel/air mixture.

2   A small cylindrical bellows mounted on the fender well, along with several rubber hoses, are the only components of the system.

3   Maintenance consists of checking the hoses for cracks and other damage as well as secure connections.

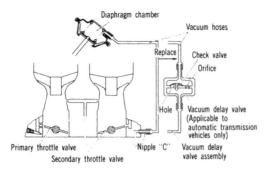

11.1 Vacuum delay valve component layout (some later models with automatic transmission)

11 Vacuum delay valve (carbureted models only)

Refer to illustration 11.1

1 Some later vehicles with an automatic transmission are equipped with a vacuum delay valve **(see illustration)**, which delays the opening of the secondary throttle valve and reduces CO and HC emissions during acceleration.

2 Periodically check the vacuum hoses for cracks, leaks and correct installation. The delay valve itself should be open when a vacuum is applied to one end and restricted when vacuum is applied to the other end.

12 Throttle opener (carbureted models only)

Refer to illustration 12.1

1 The throttle opener system **(see illustration)** is installed on all vehicles with air conditioning. It consists of a throttle opener assembly, a solenoid valve, an engine speed sensor and the compressor switch for the air conditioner.

2 The throttle opener opens the throttle slightly when the air conditioning system is turned on (which prevents stalling and increases emission due to the increased engine load).

3 The throttle opener adjustment is part of the idle speed adjustment procedure (see Chapter 4).

4 Maintenance consists of checking the vacuum hoses and wires for damage and correct installation and making sure the linkage is not binding in any way.

13 Feedback Carburetor (FBC) system

Description

Refer to illustration 13.1

1 An electronically controlled feedback carburetor (FBC) system **(see illustration)** is used on 1985 and later models. The fuel/air mixture delivered by the carburetor is controlled by solenoid valves, which are activated by the ECU (Electronic Control Unit). The ECU receives signals from several sensors, including the exhaust gas oxygen sensor, throttle position sensor, vacuum switch and intake air temperature sensor. Depending on the input from the various sensors, the ECU cycles the solenoid valves on the carburetor to regulate the fuel/air mixture to obtain the lowest emissions levels possible while maintaining an acceptable level of driveability.

2 The fuel inlet, primary metering, secondary metering, accelerator pump and choke systems are essentially the same as in a conventional carburetor. The jet (air) mixture, enrichment and fuel cut-off systems are electronically controlled.

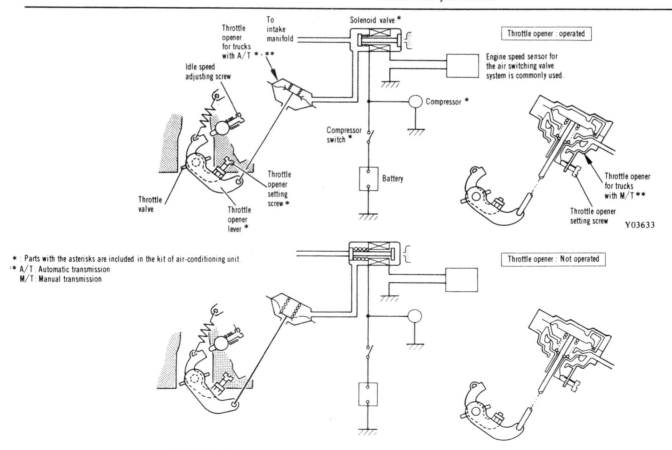

* : Parts with the asterisks are included in the kit of air-conditioning unit.
* * A/T : Automatic transmission
M/T : Manual transmission

12.1 Throttle opener system component layout (models with air conditioning)

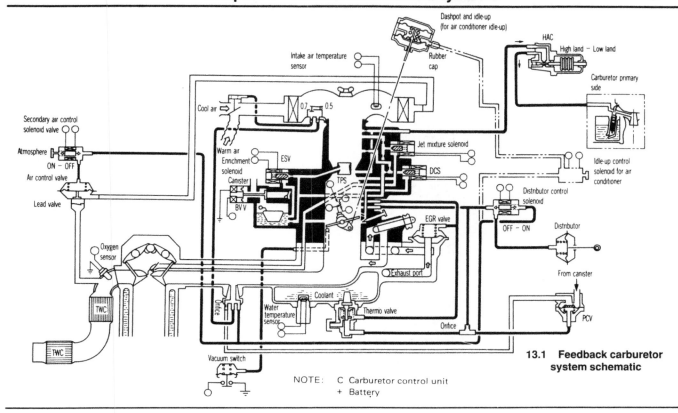

13.1 Feedback carburetor system schematic

NOTE: C Carburetor control unit
+ Battery

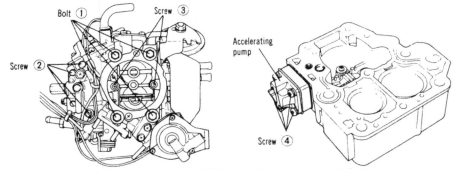

13.15 The carburetor fasteners must be checked to make sure they're tight or air/fuel leaks will occur

3   The jet mixture solenoid, which is controlled by the ECU, is used to enrich the mixture if the exhaust gas oxygen sensor detects a lean condition. As the mixture is restored to optimum, the jet mixture solenoid responds appropriately.
4   The enrichment system solenoid is activated in response to increased demand for rich fuel/air mixtures, such as during heavy acceleration or engine loads, cold start and warm-up operation. It provides additional fuel for the main metering system.
5   The fuel cut-off system deceleration solenoid cuts off fuel flow when the ignition key is turned off to prevent engine run-on (dieseling). Under certain deceleration conditions, the solenoid valve reduces fuel flow to decrease HC emissions and improve fuel economy.
6   Since the feedback carburetor is rather complex, major troubleshooting and testing of the system should be left to a dealer service department. However, the do-it-yourselfer can perform many of the maintenance checks and testing procedures without special equipment. Symptoms of a problem in the FBC include hard starting or failure to start, unstable idle and poor driveability. If a problem occurs, be sure to check the ignition system and engine mechanical condition before assuming that the FBC is at fault.

Throttle position system check

7   Remove the air cleaner from the engine and check the throttle position sensor plunger operation. Operate the throttle lever and see if the plunger follows the cam mounted on the throttle shaft.

8   Check the sensor body and plunger for damage and cracks.
9   Check the throttle sensor mounting screws to make sure they are tight (do not move the sensor or the fuel/air mixture will be adversely affected).
10   The sensor can be adjusted, but it should be done by a dealer service department (a digital voltmeter is required).

Solenoid valve/thermo valve air filter replacement

11   If the filters on the thermo valve and solenoid valve are clogged, driveability problems will result.
12   The thermo valve has a cap which fits over the filter. If the cap is removed by pulling out on it, the filter can be removed and a new one installed.
13   The solenoid valve filter is a one piece assembly which can be pulled off the valve and replaced with a new one.

Carburetor fastener check

Refer to illustration 13.15

14   To avoid mixture control problems resulting from air and fuel leaks, the carburetor fasteners must be checked and tightened at the recommended intervals.
15   Remove the air cleaner assembly and use a wrench, socket or screwdriver to check the tightness of the carburetor-to-intake manifold bolts, the float chamber cover screws and the accelerator pump mounting screws **(see illustration)**.

Check item	Condition		Check meter reading when normal	Terminal number of computer
Power supply	Ignition switch OFF → ON		11–13V	A-7
Distributor advance vacuum exchange solenoid valve	Idling		0–1V	B-7
	2000 rpm		13–15V	
Throttle position sensor (TPS)	Ignition switch OFF → ON	Accelerator closed	0.2–1.5V	A-13
		Accelerator wide opened	5V	
Coolant temperature sensor	Ignition switch OFF → ON	20°C (68°F)	2.4–2.6V	A-12
		40°C (104°F)	1.4–1.6V	
		80°C (176°F)	0.5–0.7V	
Intake air temperature sensor	Ignition switch OFF → ON	20°C (68°F)	2.4–2.6V	A-4
		40°C (104°F)	1.4–1.6V	
		80°C (176°F)	0.5–0.7V	
Vacuum switch	Ignition switch OFF → ON		9–11V	A-5
	Idling		0–1V	
Idle up control solenoid valve	Ignition switch OFF → ON		0–0.6V	B-3
Enrichment solenoid valve (ESV)	Ignition switch OFF → ON		11–13V	B-5
A/C cut relay	Ignition switch and A/C switch OFF → ON	Accelerator closed	0–0.6V	B-6
		Accelerator wide opened	11–15V	
Power supply for sensor	Ignition switch OFF → ON		4–5.5V	A-3
Secondary air control solenoid valve	Ignition switch OFF → ON	Coolant temp. 30–40°C (86–104°F)	0–0.6V	B-4
		Coolant temp. Less than 30°C (86°F) or more than 40°C (104°F)	11–13V	

Check item	Condition	Check meter reading when normal	Terminal number of computer
Jet mixture solenoid valve (JSV)	Ignition switch OFF → ON	11–13V	B-1
	Idling	2–10V	
Idle up control solenoid valve	2000 rpm with A/C switch ON	13–15V	B-3
Ignition pulse	Idling	5–7V	A-10
Power supply for back-up	Idling	13–15V	A-9
Deceleration solenoid valve (DSV)	Idling	0–0.6V	B-2
	Quick deceleration from 4000 rpm to idling with "P" or "N" position	Momentarily 13–15V	
Oxygen sensor	Keep 1300 rpm after warming up	0–1V ↕ Flashing 2.7V	A-1
Enrichment solenoid valve (ESV)	Idling after warming up	12–15V	B-5
	Quick acceleration from idling to 4000 rpm with "P" or "N" position	Momentarily approx. 5V	
Secondary air control solenoid valve	Idling after warming up	11–13V	B-4
	Quick deceleration from 2000 rpm to idling with "P" or "N" position	Momentarily 0–0.6V	

13.16a　FBC control unit voltage check table

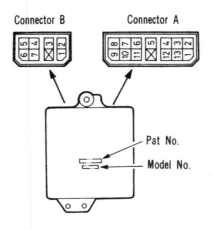

13.16b   FBC control unit connector terminal guide

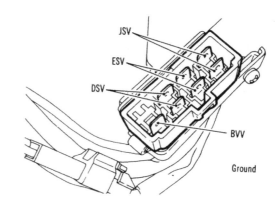

13.23   Solenoid valve terminal guide

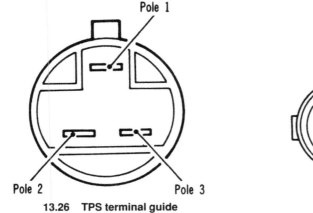

13.26   TPS terminal guide

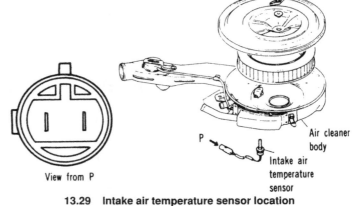

13.29   Intake air temperature sensor location

System check (ECU input/output signals)

Refer to illustrations 13.16a and 13.16b

16   The FBC system can be checked with a voltmeter by referring to the accompanying terminal identification guide and FBC control unit voltage check table **(see illustrations)**. The component is listed in the left column and the desired voltmeter reading is indicated in the second column from the right. Attach one voltmeter lead to the computer terminal indicated and the other lead to a good ground when making the check. Be sure to observe the conditions indicated in the chart.

Throttle opener check (air-conditioned models only)

17   Check the vacuum hoses and throttle opener control solenoid harness for correct installation.
18   Disconnect the vacuum hose from the fitting on the throttle opener and attach a hand-type vacuum pump to the fitting with a length of hose.
19   Start and run the engine at idle, then apply a vacuum of 11.8 in-Hg (300 mm-Hg) minimum with the pump. The engine speed should increase. If it doesn't, replace the throttle opener with a new one.

Throttle opener solenoid valve check

20   With the ignition switch off, disconnect the wires from the throttle opener solenoid valve.
21   Using an ohmmeter, check the resistance between the solenoid valve terminals (it should be approximately 40 ohms).

Solenoid valve check

Refer to illustration 13.23

22   With the ignition switch off, disconnect the wire harness from the solenoid valve.

23   Using an ohmmeter, check the resistance between the Deceleration (DSV), Enrichment (ESV) and Jet Mixture (JSV) solenoid valve terminals **(see illustration)**. It should be 49.7 ohms.
24   Check the resistance between the Bowl Vent Valve (BVV) terminal and ground. It should be 80 ohms.
25   If a valve is defective, it must be unscrewed from the carburetor and replaced with a new one.

Throttle position sensor check

Refer to illustration 13.26

26   Unplug the throttle position sensor connector and check the resistance between terminals two and three **(see illustration)** with an ohmmeter. When the throttle is closed, it should be approximately 1.2 K-ohms.
27   As the throttle is opened, the resistance should increase smoothly until it is approximately 4.9 K-ohms when the throttle is wide open.
28   If the sensor is defective, it should be replaced with a new one and adjusted by a dealer service department.

Intake air temperature sensor check

Refer to illustration 13.29

29   The intake air temperature sensor is mounted on the bottom of the air cleaner housing **(see illustration)**. Unplug the wiring harness connector and check the resistance between the sensor terminals.
30   It should be 2.45 K-ohms at 68-degrees F. If it is considerably larger or smaller than specified, the sensor is open or short-circuited and should be replaced with a new one.

Coolant temperature sensor check

31   If some means of monitoring the coolant temperature is available, the sensor can be checked in place by measuring the resistance between the sensor terminal and sensor body with an ohmmeter.

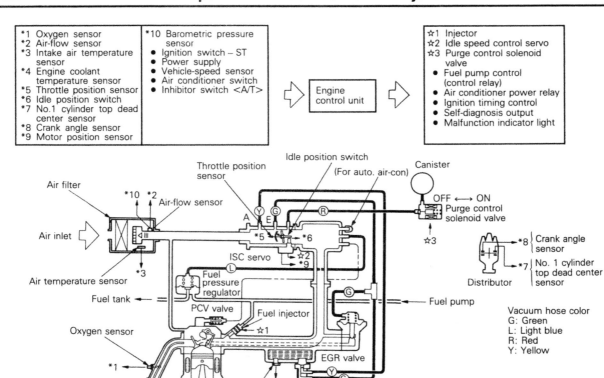

14.1a   Multi-Point Injection (MPI) system (2.4L Federal and Canadian models)

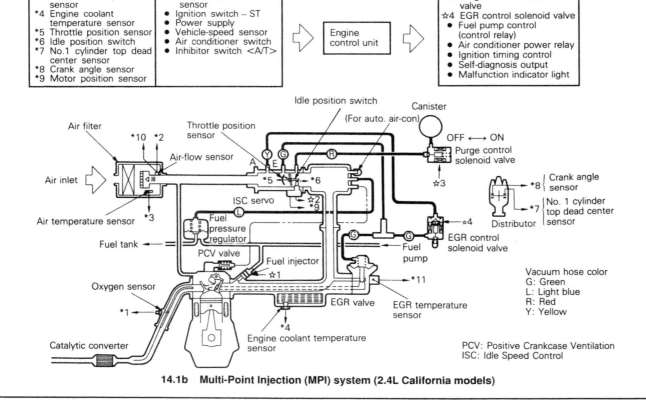

14.1b   Multi-Point Injection (MPI) system (2.4L California models)

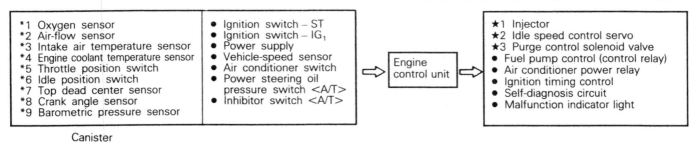

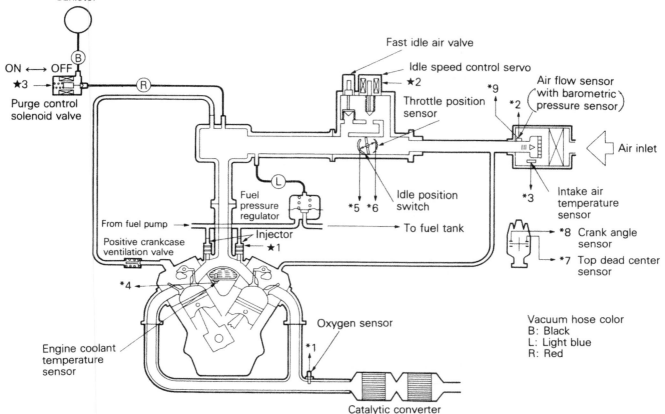

14.1c   Multi-Point Injection (MPI) system (3.0L Federal and Canadian models)

32   At 68-degrees F, the resistance should be 2.45 K-ohms. At 176-degrees F (coolant temperature), the resistance should be 296 ohms.

33   If the coolant temperature cannot be monitored closely, drain the cooling system (see Chapter 1), remove the sensor and heat the end in a pan of water to the specified temperatures, then take the resistance readings. If this is done, make sure the sensor body is at least 1/8-inch away from the water surface.

34   When reinstalling the sensor, use sealant on the threads and tighten it to the torque listed in this Chapter's Specifications.

Vacuum switch check

35   The vacuum switch is mounted on the right side of the firewall.

36   Unplug the wiring harness connector and attach the leads of an ohmmeter or self-powered test light to the switch terminals. No continuity should be indicated.

37   Disconnect the vacuum hose from the switch fitting and attach a hand-held vacuum pump to the fitting with a section of hose.

38   Apply a vacuum of 10.2 in-Hg (260 mm-Hg) or more and make sure continuity is indicated. Release the vacuum and verify that continuity is interrupted.

39   If the switch fails the check, replace it with a new one.

14   Multi-Point Injection (MPI) system

Refer to illustrations 14.1a, 14.1b, 14.1c, 14.1d, 14.3a and 14.3b

1   A Multi-Point Injection (MPI) system is used on all 1990 and later models. MPI is a computerized engine management system which controls all emission, fuel and ignition functions. The fuel control functions of the MPI system are covered in Chapter 4. The information in this Section concerns the electronic control unit (ECU), the information sensors it uses to monitor the MPI system and the emission devices it uses to adjust the system **(see illustrations)**.

2   The ECU is the "brain" of the MPI system. Its sophisticated network of information sensors monitor engine operation and transmit digital voltage signals to the ECU. The ECU analyzes this data, compares it to the "map" (program) stored in its memory and fine-tunes variables such as ignition timing, spark advance, fuel injector pulse width and idle speed by readjusting various devices such as the fuel injectors, the idle speed control servo, the purge control solenoid valve, etc. The result is an always correct air-fuel ratio under all driving conditions that lowers exhaust emissions and maintains good driveability.

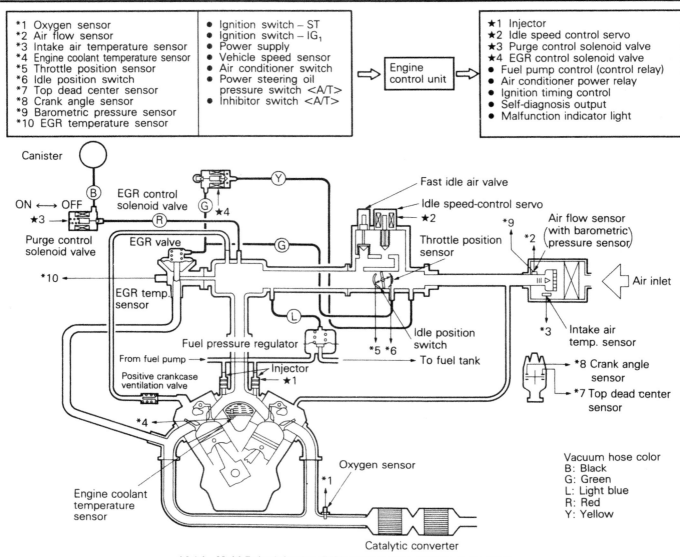

*1 Oxygen sensor	• Ignition switch – ST	★1 Injector
*2 Air flow sensor	• Ignition switch – IG₁	★2 Idle speed control servo
*3 Intake air temperature sensor	• Power supply	★3 Purge control solenoid valve
*4 Engine coolant temperature sensor	• Vehicle speed sensor	★4 EGR control solenoid valve
*5 Throttle position sensor	• Air conditioner switch	• Fuel pump control (control relay)
*6 Idle position switch	• Power steering oil	• Air conditioner power relay
*7 Top dead center sensor	pressure switch <A/T>	• Ignition timing control
*8 Crank angle sensor	• Inhibitor switch <A/T>	• Self-diagnosis output
*9 Barometric pressure sensor		• Malfunction indicator light
*10 EGR temperature sensor		

14.1d   Multi-Point Injection (MPI) system (3.0L California models)

3   Numerous sensors transmit data to the ECU; they include:

Air conditioner switch
Air-flow sensor
Barometric pressure sensor
Coolant temperature sensor
Crank angle sensor
EGR temperature sensor (California models)
Idle position switch
Ignition switch
Inhibitor switch (models equipped with an automatic transmission)
Intake air temperature sensor
Motor position sensor (2.4L engine)
Oxygen sensor
Throttle position sensor
Top dead center sensor
Vehicle speed sensor

You can locate these sensors and switches by referring to the accompanying illustrations **(see illustrations)**.

4   The ECU also monitors most of its own input and output circuits. If it detects a fault somewhere in the MPI system, it stores this information in its memory. You can often determine the location of a problem, or at least which circuit it's in, by outputting stored malfunction codes with a voltmeter. To learn how to output this information and display it on a voltmeter,

refer to Section 15.

5   Your first step should be a thorough visual inspection of the vacuum hoses and electrical connectors in the part of the MPI system that's malfunctioning. Make sure everything is properly connected and/or plugged in. The most common cause of a problem in an MPI system is a loose or corroded electrical connector or a loose vacuum line. If that doesn't solve the problem, you'll find simple tests of the important information sensors in Section 16.

---

15   Self-diagnosis and malfunction codes (fuel-injected models only)

Refer to illustrations 15.1, 15.6 and 15.7

1   When a malfunction in the MPI system is detected by the ECU, a malfunction indicator light **(see illustration)** on the instrument panel comes on. If the ECU detects that the trouble has disappeared before the ignition switch has been turned off, the light goes out. And even if the light remains on, it goes out when the ignition switch is turned off. The next time the ignition switch is turned on, the light doesn't come back on again unless the ECU has "memorized" the code(s) it stored the last time you operated the vehicle, or it detects the malfunction again. The light does, however, come

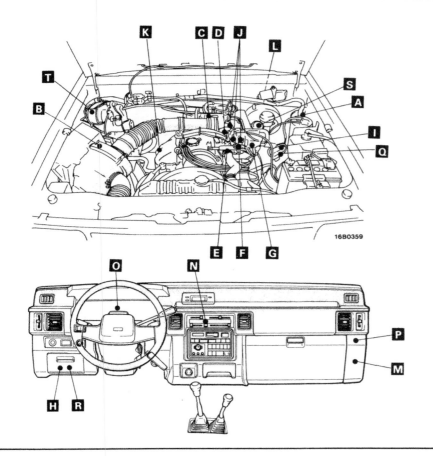

14.3a MPI system component location (2.4L models)

A   Air conditioner compressor power relay
B   Air flow sensor
C   Idle speed control servo (idle position switch, motor position sensor)
D   Throttle position sensor
E   Engine coolant temperature sensor
F   Ignition coil (power transistor)
G   Crank angle sensor and No. 1 cylinder Top Dead Center sensor
I   Purge control solenoid valve
J   Fuel injectors)
K   Oxygen sensor
L   Inhibitor switch (models with automatic transmission)
M   Engine control relay
N   Air conditioner switch
O   Vehicle speed sensor
P   Engine control unit (ECU)
Q   EGR control solenoid valve
R   Self-diagnosis connector
S   EGR temperature sensor (California models)
T   Ignition timing adjustment terminal

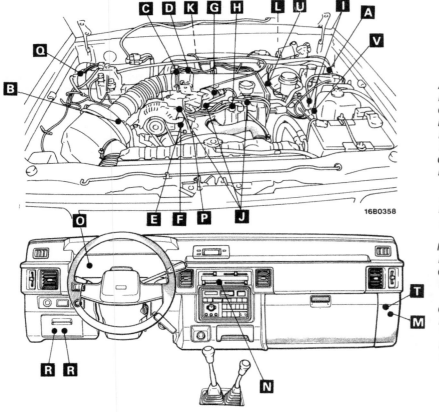

14.3b MPI system component location (3.0L models)

A   Air conditioner compressor power relay
B   Air flow sensor
C   Idle speed control (ISC) servo
D   Throttle position sensor (with idle position switch)
E   Air conditioner temperature sensor
F   Engine coolant temperature sensor
G   Ignition coil (power transistor)
H   Crank angle sensor
I   Purge control solenoid valve
J   Fuel injectors
K   Oxygen sensor
L   Inhibitor switch (models with automatic transmission)
M   Engine control relay
N   Air conditioner switch
O   Engine warning light (malfunction indicator light)
P   Power steering oil pressure switch (automatic transmission models)
Q   Ignition timing adjustment terminal
R   Self-diagnosis connector
T   Engine control unit
U   EGR temperature sensor (California models)
V   EGR control solenoid valve (California models)

Output preference order	Diagnosis item	Diagnosis code — Output signal pattern	No.	Memory	Check item (Remedy)
1	Engine control unit	H / L (12A0104)	–	–	(Replace engine control unit)
2	Oxygen sensor	H / L (12A0104)	11	Retained	• Harness and connector • Fuel pressure • Injectors (Replace if defective) • Intake air leaks • Oxygen sensor
3	Air flow sensor	H / L (12A0104)	12	Retained	• Harness and connector (If harness and connector are normal, replace air flow sensor assembly.)
4	Intake air temperature sensor	H / L (12A0104)	13	Retained	• Harness and connector • Intake air temperature sensor
5	Throttle position sensor	H / L (12A0104)	14	Retained	• Harness and connector • Throttle position sensor • Idle position switch
6	Motor position sensor	H / L (12A0104)	15	Retained	• Harness and connector • Motor position sensor • Throttle position sensor
7	Engine coolant temperature sensor	H / L (12A0107)	21	Retained	• Harness and connector • Engine coolant temperature sensor
8	Crank angle sensor	H / L (12A0107)	22	Retained	• Harness and connector (If harness and connector are normal, replace distributor assembly.)
9	No. 1 cylinder top dead center sensor	H / L (12A0107)	23	Retained	• Harness and connector (If harness and connector are normal, replace distributor assembly.)
10	Vehicle speed sensor (reed switch)	H / L (12A0107)	24	Retained	• Harness and connector • Vehicle speed sensor (reed switch)
11	Barometric pressure sensor	H / L (12A0107)	25	Retained	• Harness and connector (If harness and connector are normal, replace barometric pressure sensor assembly.)
12	Ignition timing adjustment signal	H / L	36	–	• Harness and connector
13	Injector	H / L (12A0105)	41	Retained	• Harness and connector • Injector coil resistance
14	Fuel pump	H / L (12A0105)	42	Retained	• Harness and connector • Control relay
15	EGR <California>	H / L (12A0105)	43	Retained	• Harness and connector • EGR temperature sensor • EGR valve • EGR valve control solenoid valve • EGR valve control vacuum
16	Normal state	H / L (12A0104)	–	–	–

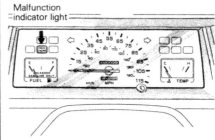

15.1   The malfunction indicator light (arrow) is located on the instrument cluster

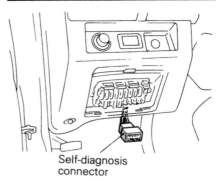

15.6   The self-diagnosis connector is located in the console, below the radio – to put the ECU into malfunction code output mode, simply hook up an analog voltmeter to the indicated terminals of the connector

15.7   Malfunction code and diagnosis table

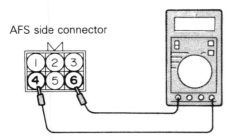

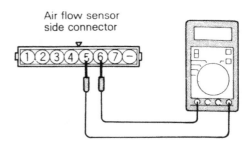

16.2a   To check the intake air temperature sensor on 1990 models, measure the resistance between terminals 4 and 6 of the air flow sensor

16.2b   To check the intake air temperature sensor on 1991 models, measure the resistance between terminals 5 and 6 of the air flow sensor

on for five seconds – then goes out – every time you turn on the ignition switch, to indicate that the malfunction indicator light circuit is operating normally.

2   The malfunction indicator light will comes on when any of the following components develop a problem:

   Air flow sensor
   Barometric pressure sensor
   Crank angle sensor
   EGR temperature sensor (California models)
   Engine control unit
   Engine coolant temperature sensor
   Fuel injector(s)
   Fuel pump
   Intake air temperature sensor
   Motor position sensor (2.4L engines)
   No. 1 cylinder TDC sensor
   Oxygen sensor
   Throttle position sensor

3   To check the malfunction indicator light, verify that the light comes on for five seconds when you turn on the ignition switch. If the light doesn't come on, check the indicator light circuit and the light bulb.

4   If the malfunction indicator light comes on – and stays on – when you start the car, or if it comes on while you're driving – and doesn't go off, drive the vehicle home and discontinue operation until you've outputted the malfunction code(s), identified the problem and fixed it.

5   Any malfunction codes memorized and stored by the ECU will remain in its memory even when the ignition switch is turned off, because the computer memory is battery-powered when the engine electrical system is shut off. But if the battery is disconnected, or the ECU is unplugged, memory is erased and any codes stored are lost. Because the ECU's memory is battery-powered when the engine is turned off, the battery must be fully charged and in good condition. If battery voltage is low, the ECU is unable to detect a malfunction or memorize and store a code.

6   To output the malfunction codes, hook up an analog voltmeter to the self-diagnosis connector as shown **(see illustration)**.

7   Turn the ignition switch to On. The ECU will begin displaying the contents of its memory immediately. Now refer to the accompanying malfunction code and diagnosis table **(see illustration)**. If the MPI system is operating normally and there are no problems, the needle on the voltmeter indicates a normal pattern of deflection; in other words, it deflects on and off at a regular rate – the "on" and "off" segments are equal in duration (see the "normal state" output signal pattern). However, if the ECU outputs a malfunction code, the deflection of the voltmeter needle will be long or short (sort of like Morse code). For example, if the oxygen sensor is malfunctioning, the needle will make one long deflection, followed by a one short deflection; if the air flow sensor is bad, the needle will make one long deflection, then two short ones; and so on.

8   Note that the actual malfunction code number on the accompanying table is not the same number as the output preference order (far left

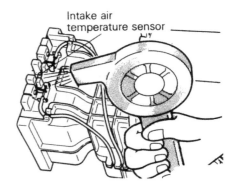

Intake air temperature sensor

16.3a   Heating the intake air temperature sensor on a 1990 model

column on the chart). That's because the ECU outputs any stored codes in a specific order to simplify your task of identifying each sequence of needle deflection patterns.

9   After you've outputted all stored codes and identified the general source of the problem(s), go to the next Section, or the indicated Chapter, check the suspected bad component or circuit and make the necessary repairs or replace the component.

10   After you've fixed the problem, check your work: Repeat the procedure above and verify that the malfunction code for the problem you fixed is no longer displayed. If the code is still displayed, you haven't fixed the problem (or the ECU itself is faulty, but don't replace an ECU until you're positive that everything in a circuit or system is functioning normally).

11   To erase the ECU's memory of any stored codes once the problem is fixed, simply disconnect the negative terminal of the battery for at least 10 seconds.

16   Information sensors (fuel-injected models only)

Intake air temperature sensor

Refer to illustrations 16.2a, 16.2b, 16.3a and 16.3b

1   Unplug the electrical connector from the intake air temperature sensor.

2   Measure the resistance between the indicated terminals **(see illustrations)**.

3   While heating the sensor with a hair drier **(see illustrations)**, measure the resistance and note how the resistance changes as the sensor heats up. At 32-degrees F, the resistance should be 6 k-ohms; at 68-degrees F, it should be 2.7 k-ohms; at 176-degrees F, it should be

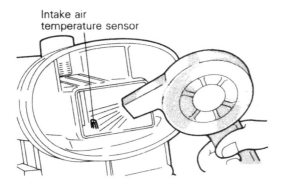

16.3b   Heating the intake air temperature sensor on a 1991 model

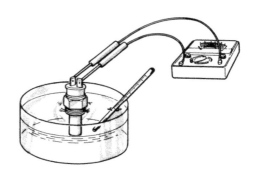

16.5   To check the engine coolant temperature sensor, immerse its sensing tip in a container of water and, as the water heats up, measure the resistance across the terminals

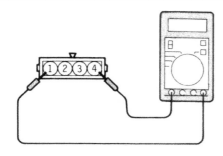

16.8   To check the throttle position sensor, measure the resistance between terminals 1 and 4

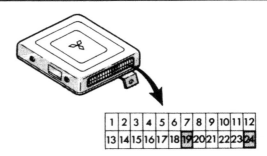

16.14   Hook up a voltmeter between terminal 19 (throttle position sensor output voltage) and terminal 24 (ground) of the engine control unit

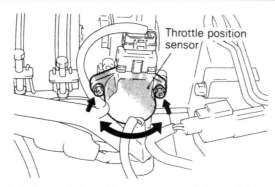

16.15   If the throttle position sensor on a 2.4L model is out of specification, adjust it by loosening the mounting screws and rotating the sensor – clockwise rotation increases the output voltage; counterclockwise decreases it

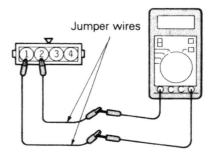

16.19   On 3.0L models, hook up an ohmmeter between terminals 1 and 2 with a pair of jumper wires

0.4 k-ohms. In other words, as the temperature goes up, the resistance should go down.

4   If your readings deviate significantly from these figures, replace the sensor. Don't forget to plug in the electrical connector.

Engine coolant temperature sensor

Refer to illustration 16.5

5   Unplug the electrical connector from the engine coolant temperature sensor, remove the sensor from the intake manifold and immerse its temperature sensing tip in a container of water. Place a thermometer in the water so you can monitor the temperature and hook up an ohmmeter to the terminals of the sensor. As the water heats up, measure the resistance

across the sensor terminals **(see illustration)**. Compare your measurements with the resistance values listed in this Chapter's Specifications.

6   If your readings deviate significantly from these figures, replace the sensor. Be sure to apply thread sealant or Teflon tape to the threads of the new unit to prevent leaks. Tighten the coolant temperature sensor to the torque listed in this Chapter's Specifications. Plug in the electrical connector.

Throttle position sensor

Refer to illustrations 16.8, 16.14, 16.15, 16.19, 16.20 and 16.21

7   Unplug the electrical connector from the throttle position sensor.

8   Measure the resistance between terminals 1 and 4 **(see illustration)** and compare your measurement with the resistance value listed in this

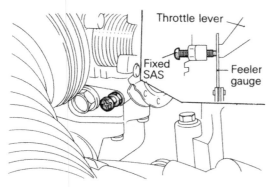

16.20   Insert feeler gauges with a combined thickness of 0.0256 in between the fixed SAS and the throttle lever (3.0L models)

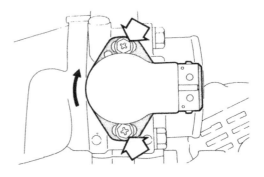

16.21   The TPS is located on the side of the throttle body – it's secured by two screws

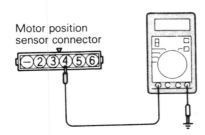

16.32   To check the idle position switch on 2.4L models, check the continuity between terminal 4 of the electrical connector and ground – with the accelerator pedal pressed down, there should be no continuity; with the pedal released, there should be continuity

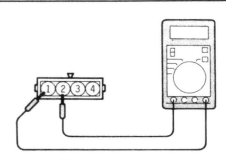

16.36   To check the idle position switch on 3.0L models, check the continuity between terminal 1 (sensor ground) and terminal 2 (idle position switch) of the electrical connector for the throttle position sensor

Chapter's Specifications. If the indicated resistance is outside this specification, replace the throttle position sensor.

9   Using an analog ohmmeter hooked up to terminals 2 and 4 (2.4L engine) or terminals 1 and 3 (3.0L engine), slowly open the throttle valve from its idle position all the way to the fully open position and verify that the resistance rises smoothly in proportion to the throttle valve opening angle.

10   If the indicated resistance doesn't fall within the specified values or operate as described above, replace the throttle position sensor.

11   Loosen the accelerator cable (see Chapter 4).

12   If you're adjusting the TPS on a 3.0L engine, proceed to Step 18. If you're adjusting the TPS on a 2.4L engine, follow Steps 13 through 17.

13   Plug in the electrical connector.

14   Connect a digital voltmeter between terminals 19 (TPS output voltage) and 24 (ground) of the engine control unit **(see illustration)**. Turn the ignition switch to On – don't start the engine – and verify that the output voltage from the throttle position sensor is within the range listed in this Chapter's Specifications.

15   If the throttle position sensor is out of specification, adjust it by loosening the mounting screws **(see illustration)** and rotating the sensor. Clockwise rotation increases the output voltage; counterclockwise decreases it.

16   After adjustment, tighten the screws securely.

17   Adjust the accelerator cable (see Chapter 4).

18   On 3.0L engines, unplug the electrical connector for the throttle position sensor.

19   Hook up an ohmmeter between terminals 1 and 2 with a pair of jumper wires **(see illustration)**.

20   Insert feeler gauges with a total combined thickness of 0.0256 in between the fixed SAS and the throttle lever **(see illustration)**.

21   Loosen the throttle position sensor mounting screws **(see illustration)**. 22

Turn the sensor clockwise as far as it will go, then check the continuity between terminals 1 and 2.

23   Slowly turn the throttle position sensor in the counterclockwise direction to the point at which there's no longer any continuity. Tighten the sensor mounting screws securely at this point.

24   Plug in the electrical connector for the throttle position sensor.

25   Hook up a voltmeter between terminal 19 (throttle position sensor output voltage) and terminal 24 (ground) of the engine control unit **(see illustration 16.14)**.

26   Turn the ignition switch to On (but don't start the engine), check the output voltage of the throttle position sensor and compare your reading to the standard value listed in this Chapter's Specifications.

27   If the indicated resistance is outside the specified value, check the throttle position sensor and the wiring harness.

28   Remove the feeler gauge.

29   Turn the ignition switch to Off.

30   Adjust the tension of the accelerator cable (see Chapter 4).

Idle position switch

2.4L engine

Refer to illustration 16.32

31   Unplug the electrical connector from the idle position switch.

32   Check the continuity between terminal 4 and ground **(see illustration)**. With the accelerator pedal pressed down, there shouldn't be any continuity (infinite resistance); with the pedal released, there should be continuity (zero resistance). If the idle position switch fails either test, replace it.

33   Plug in the connector.

3.0L engine

Refer to illustration 16.36

34   With the accelerator pedal released, verify that the throttle valve lever or the fixed SAS is pushed. If it isn't, adjust the fixed SAS (see Section 26 in Chapter 4).

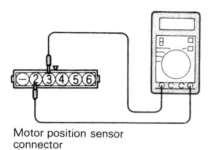

16.40   To check the motor position sensor (2.4 models only), measure the resistance between terminal 2 and terminal 3 of the electrical connector

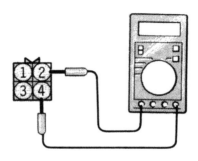

16.48   To check the oxygen sensor on 3.0L models, check the continuity between terminal 2 and terminal 4 of the connector

35   Unplug the electrical connector from the throttle position sensor.
36   Check the continuity between terminal 1 (sensor ground) and terminal 2 (idle position switch) of the throttle position sensor connector **(see illustration)**. With the accelerator pedal pushed down, there shouldn't be any continuity (infinite resistance); with the pedal released, there should be continuity (zero resistance). If there is no continuity when the accelerator pedal is returned, loosen the throttle position sensor mounting screws, turn the sensor as far as it will go in the clockwise direction and check again. If the throttle position sensor still fails either test, replace it (the idle position switch is inside the throttle position sensor, so you have to replace the throttle position sensor to replace the idle position switch).
37   If you install a new throttle position sensor/idle position switch unit, adjust it (see Steps 18 through 30) before tightening the throttle position sensor mounting screws securely.
38   Plug in the electrical connector.

Motor position sensor (2.4L engine only)

Refer to illustration 16.40

39   Unplug the electrical connector from the motor position sensor.
40   Measure the resistance between terminals 2 and 3 **(see illustration)**. Compare your measurement with the value listed in this Chapter's Specifications. If the indicated value isn't within this range, replace the motor position sensor.
41   Unplug the electrical connector from the idle-speed control servo.
42   Hook up a 6V DC battery between terminals 1 and 2 of the idle-speed control servo connector **(see illustration)**, then measure the resistance between terminals 3 and 5 of the motor position sensor connector while the idle-speed control servo is powered up by the 6V battery (it should expand and contract). If the motor position sensor is functioning properly, the indicated resistance should decrease smoothly as the idle speed control servo plunger contracts.
43   If the indicated resistance doesn't behave this way, or if the change isn't smooth, replace the idle speed control servo assembly.

Oxygen sensor

2.4L engine

44   Warm up the engine to its normal operating temperature.
45   Unplug the electrical connector to the oxygen sensor and hook up a digital voltmeter between the connector terminal and ground (1990 models) or between the connector terminals (1991 models).
46   Race the engine several times and note the oxygen sensor output voltage. Compare your measurement to the output voltage values listed in this Chapter's Specifications. If the indicated output voltage falls outside the specified value, replace the oxygen sensor (see Chapter 1).

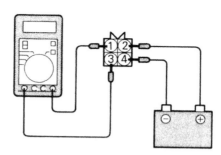

16.51   Connect terminal 2 and terminal 4 of the connector to the positive and negative battery terminals, respectively, with jumper wires, hook up a digital voltmeter to terminal 1 and terminal 3 of the connector, race the engine several times and measure the output voltage of the oxygen sensor

3.0L engine

Refer to illustrations 16.48 and 16.51

47   Unplug the electrical connector for the oxygen sensor.
48   Check the continuity between terminal 2 and terminal 4 of the connector **(see illustration)**. There should be about 20 ohms of resistance when the sensor is cool (approximately 68-degrees F).
49   If there's no continuity, replace the oxygen sensor (see Chapter 1).
50   Warm up the engine to normal operating temperature.
51   Connect terminal 2 and terminal 4 of the connector to the positive and negative battery terminals, respectively, with jumper wires **(see illustration)**. **Caution:** *Connecting the terminals on the connector to the battery terminals in the reverse order can damage the oxygen sensor.*
52   Hook up a digital voltmeter to terminal 1 and terminal 3 of the connector.
53   Race the engine several times and measure the output voltage of the oxygen sensor. Compare your measurement with the output voltage listed in this Chapter's Specifications. If the indicated voltage isn't within the specified voltage range, replace the oxygen sensor (see Chapter 1).

EGR temperature sensor (California models only)

54   See Section 7 for this procedure.

Chapter 7 Part A Manual transmission

Contents

Specifications

General

Lubricant type .... See Chapter 1

Torque specifications

	Ft-Lbs
Transmission-to-engine bolts	
Four-cylinder engines	40
V6 engine	60

---

1 General information

All vehicles covered in this manual come equipped with either a four-speed or five-speed manual transmission or an automatic transmission. All information on the manual transmissions is included in this part of Chapter 7. Information on the automatic transmission and transfer case can be found in Parts B and C of this Chapter.

The manual transmission used in these models is a four-speed or a five-speed unit, with fifth gear being an overdrive.

Due to the complexity, unavailability of replacement parts and the special tools necessary, internal repair by the home mechanic is not recommended. The information in this Chapter is limited to general information and removal and installation of the transmission.

Depending on the expense involved in having a faulty transmission overhauled, it may be a good idea to replace the unit with either a new or rebuilt one. Your local dealer or transmission shop should be able to supply you with information concerning cost, availability and exchange policy. Regardless of how you decide to remedy a transmission problem, you can still save a lot of money by removing and installing the unit yourself.

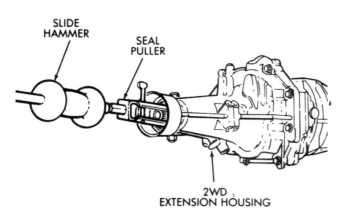

2.6   A slide hammer with a special seal puller may be required to remove the oil seal

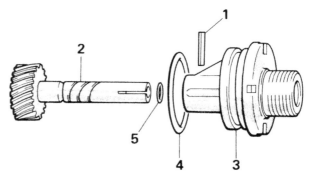

2.13   Exploded view of the speedometer driven gear assembly

1	Spring pin	4	O-ring
2	Driven gear	5	O-ring
3	Housing		

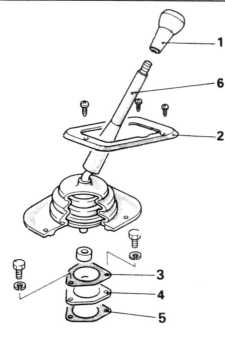

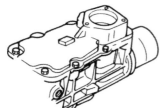

3.3   Shift lever details

1	Shift knob	4	Stopper plate
2	Shifter boot plate	5	Gasket
3	Gasket	6	Shift lever

2   Oil seals – replacement

Refer to illustrations 2.6 and 2.13

1   Oil leaks frequently occur due to wear of the extension housing oil seal and/or the speedometer drive gear oil seal and O-ring. Replacement of these seals is relatively easy, since the repairs can usually be performed without removing the transmission or transfer case (4WD models) from the vehicle.

2   The extension housing oil seal is located at the extreme rear of the transmission or transfer case, where the driveshaft is attached. If leakage at the seal is suspected, raise the vehicle and support it securely on jackstands. If the seal is leaking, transmission lubricant will be built up on the front of the driveshaft and may be dripping from the rear of the transmission or transfer case.

3   Refer to Chapter 8 and remove the driveshaft.

4   Using a soft-faced hammer, carefully tap the dust shield (if equipped) to the rear and remove it from the transmission. Be careful not to distort it.

5   Using a screwdriver or pry bar, carefully pry the oil seal out of the rear of the transmission or transfer case. Do not damage the splines on the transmission output shaft.

6   If the oil seal cannot be removed with a screwdriver or pry bar, a special oil seal removal tool (available at auto parts stores) will be required **(see illustration)**.

7   Using a large section of pipe or a very large deep socket as a drift, install the new oil seal. Drive it into the bore squarely and make sure it's completely seated.

8   Reinstall the dust shield (if equipped) by carefully tapping it into place. Lubricate the splines of the transmission output shaft and the outside of the driveshaft sleeve yoke with lightweight grease, then install the driveshaft. Be careful not to damage the lip of the new seal.

9   The speedometer gear housing is located on the side of the extension housing. Look for transmission lubricant around the housing to determine if the O-rings are leaking.

10   Unscrew the speedometer cable casing from the speedometer gear housing.

11   Mark the relationship of the speedometer gear housing to the extension housing.

12   Remove the bolt and withdraw the housing.

13   Install a new O-ring on the driven gear shaft and on the housing, then reinstall the housing **(see illustration)**.

3   Shift lever – removal and installation

Refer to illustration 3.3

Removal

1   Disconnect the negative cable from the battery.

2   If your vehicle is equipped with a center console, remove it (see Chapter 11).

3   Remove the screws that attach the shifter boot plate to the tunnel **(see illustration)**. Lift off the plate and pull back the rubber boot. It has a lip that fits over the sheetmetal of the tunnel; take care not to tear the boot as you pull it back.

4.3a   Transmission mount (2WD models)

4.3b   Transmission mount (4WD models)

4   If the transmission is a 5-speed, place the shift lever in the first gear position. If it is a 4-speed, place it in the second gear position. Remove the three bolts attaching the shift lever assembly to the transmission and carefully lift out the lever. Plug or cover the hole with a clean rag.

Installation

5   Apply a thin coat of RTV sealant to both sides of the two gaskets (one over and one under the shift lever stopper plate).
6   Apply multi-purpose grease to the shift lever bushing and all shift lever sliding surfaces.
7   The remainder of installation is the reverse of removal. Tighten the fasteners securely.

---

4   Transmission mount – check and replacement

Refer to illustrations 4.3a and 4.3b

Check

1   Insert a large screwdriver or pry bar into the space between the transmission extension housing and the crossmember and try to pry up slightly.
2   The transmission should not move from the crossmember. If there is any cracking or separation of the rubber from the mounting plate, replace the mount.

Replacement

3   Support the transmission with a jack. Place a block of wood on the jack head to serve as a cushion. Remove the fasteners attaching the mount to the crossmember and the transmission **(see illustrations)**.
4   Raise the transmission slightly with the jack and remove the mount.
5   Installation is the reverse of removal. Be sure to tighten the nuts/bolts securely.

---

5   Manual transmission – removal and installation

Removal

1   Disconnect the negative battery cable from the battery.
2   Remove the air cleaner assembly (see Chapter 4), then remove the starter (see Chapter 5).
3   Raise the vehicle and support it securely on jackstands. Place a drain pan under the transmission, remove the drain plug and allow the transmission to lubricant to drain.
4   Remove the driveshaft(s) (see Chapter 8).
5   Remove the shift lever (see Section 3).
6   Disconnect the speedometer cable where it enters the transmission. Bend back the retaining strap that holds the speedometer cable housing to

the frame crossmember and pull the speedometer cable away from the engine and transmission. Lay it on top of the left frame rail to keep it out of the way.
7   Push forward on the parking brake lever and disengage the cable from the lever. Loosen the parking brake cable housing clamp in front of the frame crossmember and slide the cable housing forward to free it from the support bracket on the crossmember. Lay the cable on top of the left frame rail to keep it out of the way. Remove the pin attaching the rear parking brake cable balancer to the parking brake lever.
8   Unplug the electrical connector for the back-up light switch (just behind the steering box). Disconnect the clutch cable from the clutch control lever at the transmission bellhousing. Back off the clutch cable adjuster and put as much freeplay as possible in the cable. Pull the rubber dust cover from the end of the clutch cable and slip the cable through the mounting boss on the transmission bellhousing. Lay the clutch cable on top of the left frame rail to keep it out of the way.
9   Remove the splash shield from the front of the transmission. It is attached to the engine with two bolts and to the transmission with two bolts.
10   Remove the bolt attaching the exhaust pipe bracket to the transmission.
11   Support the engine with a hoist or, if a hoist isn't available, a floor jack placed under the engine oil pan (place a wood block on the jack head to serve as a cushion). Remove the bolts that attach the transmission bellhousing to the engine block.
12   Remove the two nuts that attach the transmission to the transmission support crossmember.
13   Support the transmission with a sturdy jack (preferably one equipped with wheels or casters). Remove the transmission support crossmember.
14   Carefully move the transmission straight back and away from the engine by moving the transmission supporting jack toward the rear of the vehicle. It would be very helpful to have an assistant at this point. You must pull the transmission straight back until it is completely free from the engine or damage to the input shaft may result.
15   Slowly lower the jack and move the transmission out from under the vehicle.

Installation

16   Installation is the reverse of removal. Be sure to check the clutch disc to make sure it is centered (see Chapter 8) before sliding the transmission into place. Also, before installation, apply a coat of lithium-based grease to the end of the transmission input shaft and the splines.
17   With the help of an assistant, line up the clutch with the transmission input shaft. Make sure the engine and transmission are in a straight line, not angled in relation to each other. Carefully slide the transmission forward until the bellhousing contacts the engine block. To properly engage the clutch disc and the transmission input shaft, you may have to rotate the crankshaft slightly (with a wrench on the bolt holding the pulley to the front of the crankshaft). Do not force the input shaft into the clutch. If the trans-

mission does not move forward smoothly, either the clutch disc/input shaft splines are not lined up, or the transmission is cocked at an angle.

18 Once the transmission is in place, support it securely and tighten all of the mounting bolts to the torque listed in this Chapter's Specifications.

19 Don't forget to fill the transmission to the proper level with the recommended lubricant (see Chapter 1).

20 Be sure to adjust the clutch as described in Chapter 8.

---

6   Manual transmission overhaul – general information

Refer to illustrations 6.4a, 6.4b, 6.4c and 6.4d

Overhauling a manual transmission is a difficult job for the do-it-yourselfer. It involves the disassembly and reassembly of many small parts. Numerous clearances must be precisely measured and, if necessary, changed with select fit spacers and snap-rings. As a result, if transmission problems arise, it can be removed and installed by a competent do-it-yourselfer, but overhaul should be left to a transmission repair shop. Rebuilt transmissions may be available – check with your dealer parts department and auto parts stores. At any rate, the time and money involved in an overhaul is almost sure to exceed the cost of a rebuilt unit.

Nevertheless, it's not impossible for an inexperienced mechanic to rebuild a transmission if the special tools are available and the job is done in a deliberate step-by-step manner so nothing is overlooked.

The tools necessary for an overhaul include internal and external snap-ring pliers, a bearing puller, a slide hammer, a set of pin punches, a dial indicator and possibly a hydraulic press. In addition, a large, sturdy workbench and a vise or transmission stand will be required.

During disassembly of the transmission, make careful notes of how each piece comes off, where it fits in relation to other pieces and what holds it in place.

Before taking the transmission apart for repair, it will help if you have some idea what area of the transmission is malfunctioning. Certain problems can be closely tied to specific areas in the transmission, which can make component examination and replacement easier. Refer to the Troubleshooting section at the front of this manual for information regarding possible sources of trouble.

Chapter 7 Part B   Automatic transmission

Contents

Specifications

Band adjustments

Kickdown band adjusting screw
    Through 1986 . . . .   3-1/2 turns backed-off from 52 in-lbs
    1987 through 1989 . . . .   No adjustments necessary
    1990 and later
        Pick-ups . . . .   2-7/8 turns backed-off from 72 in-lbs
        Monteros . . . .   No adjustments necessary
Low/reverse band adjusting screw
    Through 1986 . . . .   7 turns backed-off from 43 in-lbs
    1987 through 1989 . . . .   No adjustments necessary
    1990 and later
        Pick-ups . . . .   6 turns backed-off from 30 in-lbs
        Monteros . . . .   No adjustments necessary

Torque specifications
Ft-lbs (unless otherwise indicated)

Torque converter-to-driveplate bolts   25
Kickdown band adjusting screw locknut
    Through 1986   35
    1990 and later   30
Low/reverse band adjusting screw locknut
    Through 1986   30
    1990 and later   25
Oil pan bolts
    1983 through 1986 . . . .   150 in-lbs
    1987 through 1989 . . . .   42 in-lbs
    1990 on . . . .   156 in-lbs
Transmission-to-engine bolts
    1983 through 1986 . . . .   22 to 30
    1987 on . . . .   31 to 40

---

1   General information

All vehicles covered in this manual come equipped with either a five-speed manual transmission or an automatic transmission. All information on the automatic transmission is included in this, Part B of, Chapter 7. Information on the manual transmission can be found in Part A of this Chapter.

Due to the complexity of the automatic transmissions covered in this manual and the need for specialized equipment to perform most service operations, this Chapter contains only general diagnosis, adjustment and removal and installation procedures.

If the transmission requires major repair work, it should be left to a dealer service department or an automotive or transmission repair shop. You can, however, remove and install the transmission yourself and save the expense, even if the repair work is done by a transmission shop.

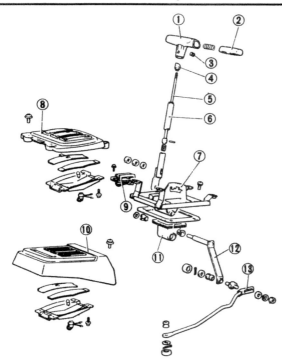

3.1   Exploded view of the shift linkage assembly

---

2   Diagnosis – general

Note: *Automatic transmission malfunctions may be caused by five general conditions: poor engine performance, improper adjustments, hydraulic malfunctions, mechanical malfunctions or malfunctions in the computer or its signal network. Diagnosis of these problems should always begin with a check of the easily repaired items: fluid level and condition (see Chapter 1), shift linkage adjustment and throttle linkage adjustment. Next, perform a road test to determine if the problem has been corrected or if more diagnosis is necessary. If the problem persists after the preliminary tests and corrections are completed, additional diagnosis should be done by a dealer service department or transmission repair shop. Refer to the Troubleshooting Section at the front of this manual for information on symptoms of transmission problems.*

Preliminary checks

1   Drive the vehicle to warm the transmission to normal operating temperature.
2   Check the fluid level as described in Chapter 1:
   a) If the fluid level is unusually low, add enough fluid to bring the level within the designated area of the dipstick, then check for external leaks (see below).
   b) If the fluid level is abnormally high, drain off the excess, then check the drained fluid for contamination by coolant.
   The presence of engine coolant in the automatic transmission fluid indicates that a failure has occurred in the internal radiator walls that separate the coolant from the transmission fluid (see Chapter 3).
   c) If the fluid is foaming, drain it and refill the transmission, then check for coolant in the fluid or a high fluid level.
3   Check the engine idle speed. **Note:** *If the engine is malfunctioning, do not proceed with the preliminary checks until it has been repaired and runs normally.*
4   Check the throttle control cable for freedom of movement. Adjust it if necessary (see Section 4). **Note:** *The throttle cable may function properly when the engine is shut off and cold, but it may malfunction once the engine is hot. Check it cold and at normal engine operating temperature.*
5   Inspect the shift linkage (see Section 3). Make sure that it's properly adjusted and that the linkage operates smoothly.

Fluid leak diagnosis

6   Most fluid leaks are easy to locate visually. Repair usually consists of replacing a seal or gasket. If a leak is difficult to find, the following procedure may help.
7   Identify the fluid. Make sure it's transmission fluid and not engine oil or brake fluid (automatic transmission fluid is a deep red color).
8   Try to pinpoint the source of the leak. Drive the vehicle several miles, then park it over a large sheet of cardboard. After a minute or two, you should be able to locate the leak by determining the source of the fluid dripping onto the cardboard.
9   Make a careful visual inspection of the suspected component and the area immediately around it. Pay particular attention to gasket mating surfaces. A mirror is often helpful for finding leaks in areas that are hard to see.
10   If the leak still cannot be found, clean the suspected area thoroughly with a degreaser or solvent, then dry it.
11   Drive the vehicle for several miles at normal operating temperature and varying speeds. After driving the vehicle, visually inspect the suspected component again.
12   Once the leak has been located, the cause must be determined before it can be properly repaired. If a gasket is replaced but the sealing flange is bent, the new gasket will not stop the leak. The bent flange must be straightened.
13   Before attempting to repair a leak, check to make sure that the following conditions are corrected or they may cause another leak. **Note:** *Some of the following conditions cannot be fixed without highly specialized tools and expertise. Such problems must be referred to a transmission repair shop or a dealer service department.*

Gasket leaks

14   Check the pan periodically. Make sure the bolts are tight, no bolts are missing, the gasket is in good condition and the pan is flat (dents in the pan may indicate damage to the valve body inside).
15   If the pan gasket is leaking, the fluid level or the fluid pressure may be too high, the vent may be plugged, the pan bolts may be too tight, the pan sealing flange may be warped, the sealing surface of the transmission housing may be damaged, the gasket may be damaged or the transmission casting may be cracked or porous. If sealant instead of gasket material has been used to form a seal between the pan and the transmission housing, it may be the wrong sealant.

Seal leaks

16   If a transmission seal is leaking, the fluid level or pressure may be too high, the vent may be plugged, the seal bore may be damaged, the seal itself may be damaged or improperly installed, the surface of the shaft protruding through the seal may be damaged or a loose bearing may be causing excessive shaft movement.
17   Make sure the dipstick tube seal is in good condition and the tube is properly seated. Periodically check the area around the speedometer gear or sensor for leakage. If transmission fluid is evident, check the O-ring for damage.

Case leaks

18   If the case itself appears to be leaking, the casting is porous and will have to be repaired or replaced.
19   Make sure the oil cooler hose fittings are tight and in good condition.

Fluid comes out vent pipe or fill tube

20   If this condition occurs, the transmission is overfilled, there is coolant in the fluid, the case is porous, the dipstick is incorrect, the vent is plugged or the drain-back holes are plugged.

---

3   Shift linkage – check and adjustment

Refer to illustrations 3.1, 3.3, 3.8, 3.9 and 3.10

1983 through 1986 models

1   The control rod is adjusted where it connects to the control arm **(see illustration)**.
2   Raise the front of the vehicle and support it securely on jackstands. Loosen the adjusting locknut on the control rod-to-control arm joint.

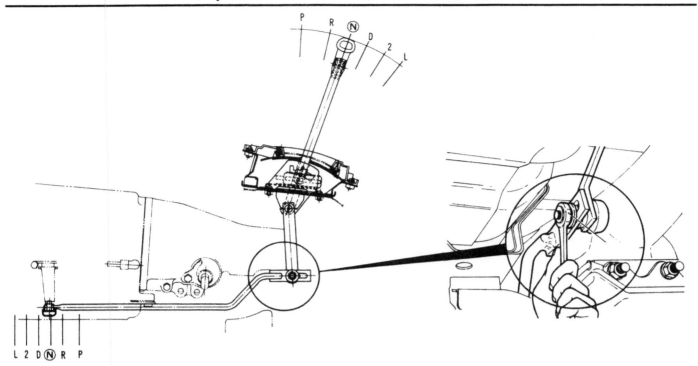

3.3   Loosen the locknut on the shift control rod, place the shift control lever and the selector lever in the "N" positions, then tighten the locknut

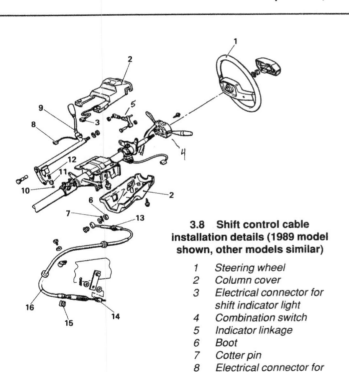

3.8   Shift control cable installation details (1989 model shown, other models similar)

1   Steering wheel
2   Column cover
3   Electrical connector for shift indicator light
4   Combination switch
5   Indicator linkage
6   Boot
7   Cotter pin
8   Electrical connector for overdrive switch
9   Shift lever
10   Steel ball
11   Ball support
12   Spring
13   Locknut
14   Adjuster block
15   Clip
16   Cable

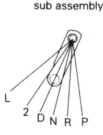
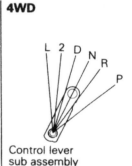

2WD Control lever sub assembly

4WD Control lever sub assembly

3.9a   After the locknut has been loosened and the shifter on the column has been placed in the N range, set the selector lever on the transmission in the N position and tighten the locknut

3   Place the shift control lever (on the left side of the transmission) in the neutral position. Place the selector lever (inside the vehicle) in the neutral position also **(see illustration)**.

4   At this point, the control rod adjustment is made automatically. Tighten the control rod-to-control arm adjusting locknut securely.

5   Set the parking brake, then apply the brakes, then check to make sure the engine does not start while the shift lever is in the "D", "L", "2", or "R" position. At the same time check to be sure that the engine starts in the "N" and "P" positions.

6   Set the shifter lever in the "R" position to check that the backup lights are illuminated, and not illuminated in any other position (make this check with the engine off).

1987 and later models

7   Remove the steering column cover (see Chapter 11).

8   Loosen the adjuster locknut at the shift lever end of the cable **(see illustration)**.

9   Put the shift lever (on the steering column) and the control lever (on the left side of the transmission), in the "N" position **(see illustration)**.

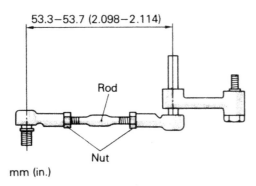

53.3–53.7 (2.098–2.114)

Rod

Nut

mm (in.)

3.10   If necessary, adjust the length of the indicator needle linkage

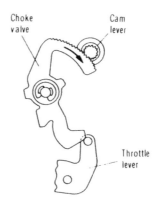

Choke valve

Cam lever

Throttle lever

4.2   Make sure the automatic choke is fully disengaged before making the throttle control linkage adjustment

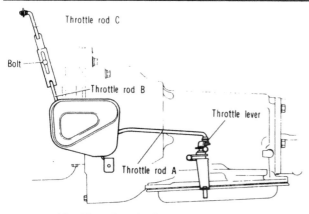

Throttle rod C

Bolt

Throttle rod B

Throttle lever

Throttle rod A

4.3   Throttle rod adjustment details

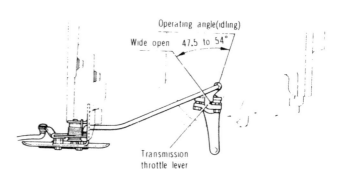

Operating angle(idling)

Wide open   47.5 to 54°

Transmission throttle lever

4.5   The transmission throttle lever should move from idle to wide-open in a 47.5 to 54-degree arc

10   To adjust the link loosen the locknut and rotate the rod to the proper length **(see illustration)**. Check to make sure the pointer on the shift indicator aligns with the proper position.

11   Tighten the locknut.

12   Install the steering column cover (see Chapter 11).

---

4   Throttle control cable/linkage – adjustment

---

1   The throttle control linkage adjustment is very important to proper transmission operation. This adjustment positions a valve which controls shift speed, shift quality and part-throttle downshift sensitivity. If the linkage is adjusted so it is too short, slippage between shifts may occur. If the linkage is adjusted so it is too long, shifts may be delayed and part-throttle downshifts may be very erratic. **Warning:** *When working under the vehicle be sure to support it on sturdy jackstands.*

1983 through 1986 models

Refer to illustrations 4.2, 4.3 and 4.5

2   Start and run the engine until it reaches normal operating temperature. With the carburetor automatic choke disengaged from the fast idle cam **(see illustration)**, adjust the engine idle speed (by turning the speed adjusting screw to the specified rpm (see Chapter 1). Turn the engine off.

3   Loosen the bolt so rods B and C can slide back and forth easily **(see illustration)**.

4   Gently push rod A all the way to the rear. Push rod C up so that the throttle is against the stop, then tighten the bolt so that rods B and C can't move in relation to each other.

5   Open the throttle valve in the carburetor completely and observe the transmission throttle lever. It should move from the idle position to the wide open position in an arc of approximately 47.5-degrees to 54-degrees **(see illustration)**.

6   Make sure that when the throttle linkage is returned to the fully closed position (idle) the throttle lever on the transmission also returns to the idle position by force of its return spring.

1987 through 1989 models

Refer to illustration 4.9

7   Check the engine idle adjustment (see Steps 1 and 2).

8   Make sure that the throttle lever, brackets and rods are not bent.

9   Measure the length between where the cable stops (at full throttle) and the top of the cable cover **(see illustration)**.

10   If it is out of adjustment, adjust the cable bracket by moving it up or down.

1990 and later models

Refer to illustrations 4.12 and 4.15

11   Be sure the control cable is attached to the bellcrank.

12   Pull gently on the control cable and check for proper adjustment at the transmission in the idle position **(see illustration)**.

13   Adjust the engine idle (see Steps 1 and 2).

14   Adjust the cable using the adjusting nuts on the cable bracket, so the space between the cable stop and the cable housing is between 1/32 to 3/64-inch.

15   Now move the throttle to the full-open position and adjust the space between the cable stop and housing to 1-5/16 to 1-3/8 inch **(see illustration)**.

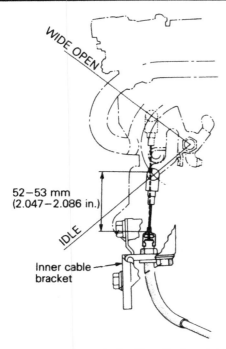

52–53 mm
(2.047–2.086 in.)

Inner cable
bracket

**4.9 Throttle control cable adjustment details
(1987 to 1989 models)**

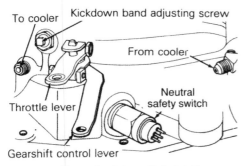

5.1 Neutral safety switch details

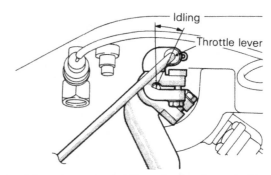

**4.12 When the engine is idling, the throttle control lever on the
transmission should be within the range shown**

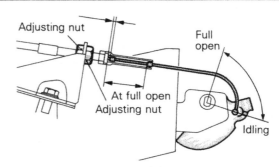

4.15 Throttle control cable adjustment details

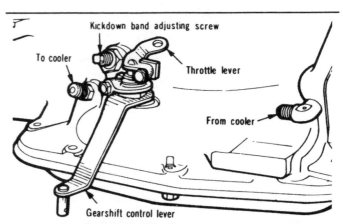

**6.1 The kickdown band adjusting screw is located near
the shift control lever**

5 Neutral safety switch – check and replacement

Refer to illustration 5.1

Check

1   The neutral safety switch is the center pin of the three-pin switch on the side of the transmission. The switch provides a ground for the starter solenoid in the Park and Neutral positions **(see illustration)**.
2   To test the switch, unplug the electrical connector from the switch and test for continuity between the switch and the transmission case (there should be continuity only when the transmission is in Park or Neutral).
3   If the switch fails the test, check the shift linkage adjustment (see Section 3).

Replacement

4   Unplug the electrical connector and unscrew the switch from the transmission. Some transmission fluid will spill out so have a container to catch it.
5   Make sure the shift lever fingers are centered in the switch opening.
6   Wrap the threads of the new switch with Teflon tape or coat the threads with RTV sealant. Install the new switch into the transmission case and tighten it securely.

7   Add the recommended type of automatic transmission fluid to the transmission to bring it up to the proper level (see Chapter 1).

6 Bands – adjustment

Refer to illustrations 6.1, 6.5 and 6.9
Note: *Always support the vehicle with jackstands.*

Kickdown bands

Note: *When the carburetor throttle is opened quickly (90% or more), the kickdown valve opens applying fluid to the shift valves. The transmission then downshifts according to the vehicle speed and throttle pressure from 4 to 3, 3 to 2 or 2 to 1.*

1   The adjusting screw for the kickdown band is located on the left side of the transmission **(see illustration)**.

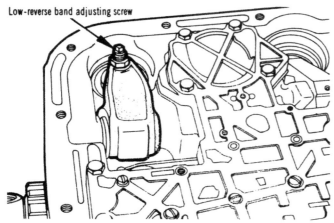

6.5   The rear band adjusting screw is accessible after removing the transmission oil pan

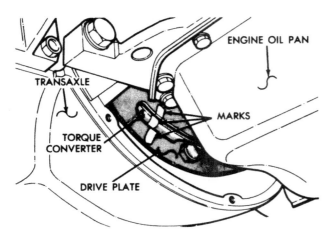

7.6   Mark the relationship of the torque converter to the driveplate

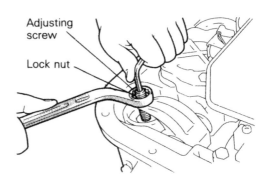

6.9   Hold the adjusting screw still while tightening the locknut

7   Automatic transmission – removal and installation

Refer to illustration 7.6, 7.11a and 7.11b

Removal

1   Disconnect the negative cable from the battery.
2   If you're working on a 4WD model, remove the knob from the transfer case shift lever.
3   Raise the vehicle and support it securely on jackstands.
4   Drain the transmission fluid (see Chapter 1), then reinstall the pan.
5   Remove the torque converter cover.
6   Mark the relationship of the torque converter to one of the studs so they can be installed in the same position **(see illustration)**.
7   Remove the torque converter-to-driveplate nuts. Turn the crankshaft for access to each nut. Turn the crankshaft in a clockwise direction only (as viewed from the front).
8   Remove the starter motor (see Chapter 5).
9   Remove the driveshaft(s) (see Chapter 8).
10   Disconnect the speedometer cable.
11   Detach the electrical connectors from the transmission **(see illustrations)**.
12   Remove any exhaust components which will interfere with transmission removal (see Chapter 4).
13   Disconnect the throttle control linkage rod or cable.
14   Disconnect the shift linkage.
15   Support the engine with a jack. Use a block of wood under the oil pan to spread the load.
16   Support the transmission with a jack – preferably a jack made for this purpose. Safety chains will help steady the transmission on the jack.
17   Remove the rear mount to crossmember bolts and the two crossmember-to-frame bolts.
18   Remove the two engine rear support-to-transmission extension housing bolts.
19   Raise the transmission enough to allow removal of the crossmember.
20   Remove the bolts securing the transmission to the engine.
21   Lower the transmission slightly and disconnect and plug the transmission fluid cooler lines.
22   Remove the transmission dipstick tube.
23   Move the transmission to the rear to disengage it from the engine block dowel pins and make sure the torque converter is detached from the driveplate. Secure the torque converter to the transmission so it won't fall out during removal.

Installation

24   Prior to installation, make sure the torque converter hub is securely engaged in the pump.
25   With the transmission secured to the jack, raise it into position. Be sure to keep it level so the torque converter does not slide forward.

2   Loosen the adjusting screw locknut and back it off five turns. Check the adjusting screw to make sure it turns freely. Lubricate it if necessary.
3   Tighten the adjusting screw to the torque listed in this Chapter's Specifications.
4   Back the adjusting screw off the number of turns listed in this Chapter's Specifications. Hold the adjusting screw at that point and tighten the locknut.

Low/Reverse band

5   The low/reverse band is accessible after removing the transmission oil pan **(see illustrations)**. The band should be adjusted at the same time the transmission fluid and filter is changed (see Chapter 1).
6   After the oil pan has been removed (see Chapter 1), loosen the adjusting screw locknut.
7   Tighten the adjusting screw to the torque listed in this Chapter's Specifications.
8   Back the adjusting screw out the number of turns listed in this Chapter's Specifications.
9   Hold the adjusting screw with a wrench so it can't turn **(see illustration)**, then tighten the locknut to the torque listed in this Chapter's Specifications.
10   Install the transmission oil pan and bring the fluid to the proper level (see Chapter 1).

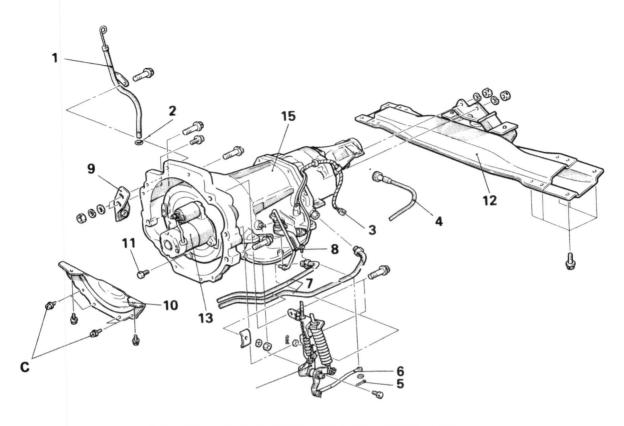

7.11a Transmission installation details (typical 2WD model)

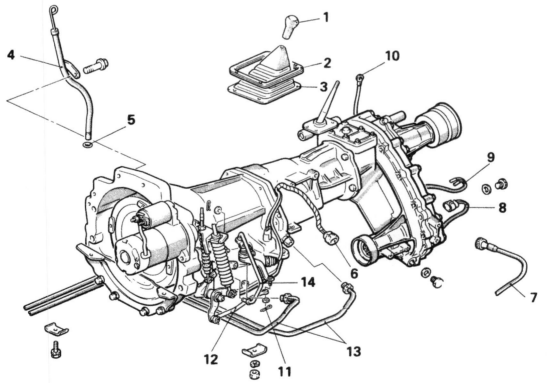

7.11b Transmission installation details (2.4L 4WD model shown, 3.0L 4WD models similar)

26   Turn the torque converter to line up the studs with the holes in the driveplate. The mark on the torque converter and the stud made in Step 5 must line up.

27   Move the transmission forward carefully until the dowel pins and the torque converter are engaged.

28   Install the transmission housing-to-engine bolts. Tighten them securely.

29   Install the torque converter-to-driveplate nuts. Tighten the nuts to the torque listed in this Chapter's Specifications.

30   Connect the transmission fluid cooler lines. Install the transmission mount crossmember and through-bolts. Tighten the bolts and nuts securely.

31   Remove the jacks supporting the transmission and the engine.

32   Install the dipstick tube.

33   Install the starter motor (see Chapter 5).

34   Connect the shift and throttle control cable/linkage.

35   Plug in the transmission electrical connectors.

36   Install the torque converter cover.

37   Install the driveshaft(s).

39   Connect the speedometer cable.

40   Adjust the shift linkage.

41   Install any exhaust system components that were removed or disconnected.

42   Lower the vehicle.

43   Fill the transmission with the proper type and amount of fluid (see Chapter 1), run the engine and check for fluid leaks.

Chapter 7 Part C   Transfer case

Contents

Specifications

Torque specifications   Ft-lbs
4WD indicator light switch 22
Transfer case-to-transmission nuts and bolts 22

---

1   General information

Four-wheel drive models are equipped with a transfer case mounted on the transmission housing. Drive is passed through the transmission and transfer case to the front and rear axles by the driveshafts.

On these models the transfer case is combined with the transmission to form one unit. The transfer case can't be removed without first removing the transmission from the vehicle. Because of the special tools and techniques required, disassembly and overhaul of the transfer case should be left to a dealer service department or properly equipped shop. You can,

however, remove and install the transmission/transfer case yourself and save the expense, even if the repair work is done by a specialist.

---

2   Shift lever – removal and installation

Refer to illustrations 2.1a and 2.1b

The procedure for removing the transfer case shift lever is essentially the same as for removing the manual transmission shift lever **(see illustrations)**. Refer to Chapter 7 Part A, Section 3, and follow the procedure outlined there.

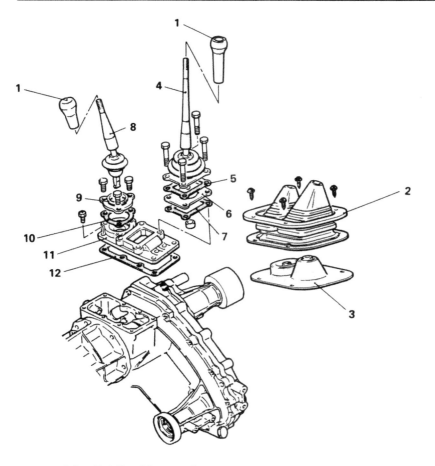

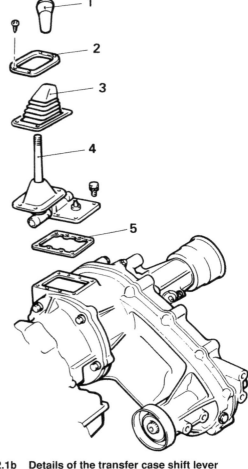

2.1a   Details of the transfer case and transmission shift levers (manual transmission)

1	Shift lever knob	7	Gasket
2	Dust cover retaining plate	8	Transfer case shift lever
3	Shift lever cover	9	Control housing cover
4	Transmission shift lever	10	Gasket
5	Gasket	11	Control housing
6	Stopper plate	12	Gasket

2.1b   Details of the transfer case shift lever (automatic transmission)

1	Shift lever knob
2	Dust cover retaining plate
3	Shift lever cover
4	Transfer case shift lever
5	Control housing gasket

3.2   Location of the 4WD indicator light switches (arrows)

3   4WD indicator light switches – removal and installation

Refer to illustration 3.2

1   Raise the vehicle and support it securely on jackstands.
2   The 4WD indicator light switches are located on the right-hand side of the transfer case housing **(see illustration)**.
3   Unscrew the switch and remove the steel ball.
4   Installation is the reverse of removal. Be sure to apply Teflon tape or a small amount of RTV sealant to the threads. Tighten the switch to the torque listed in this Chapter's Specifications.
7   Lower the vehicle.

4   Transfer case overhaul – general information

On these models the transmission/transfer case assembly is designed to be overhauled as a unit. Consequently, overhaul should be left to a repair shop specializing in both transmission and transfer cases. Rebuilt units may be available – check with your dealer parts department and auto parts stores. At any rate, some cost savings can be realized by removing the transmission/transfer case unit and taking it to the shop (see Part A or B of this Chapter).

Chapter 8   Clutch and driveline

Contents

Specifications

Clutch

Hydraulic system fluid type .... See Chapter 1
Clutch disc minimum lining thickness .... 0.012 inch
Clutch pedal freeplay .... See Chapter 1

Front hub turning force (4WD models) (measured with spring scale)

1983 .... 3.31 lbs
1984 on .... 1 to 4 lbs

Driveline

U-joint journal endplay .... 0.024 inch
Brake contact surface depth .... 0.470 to 0.480 inch
Front hub axial play .... 0.001 inch
Driveaxle axial play .... 0.008 to 0.020 inch

Torque specifications

	Ft-lbs (unless otherwise indicated)
Clutch pressure plate-to-flywheel bolts	12 to 14
Driveline	
U-joint flange bolts (front or rear driveshaft)	36 to 43
Center bearing pinion locknut	116 to 159
Center bearing bracket nuts	20 to 22
Rear axle	
Bearing retainer/brake backing plate-to-axle housing nuts	36 to 43
Differential pinion shaft nut	137 to 180
Front axle (4WD models)	
Differential carrier bolts	58 to 72
Free-wheeling hub body assembly bolts	37 to 43
Manual free-wheeling hub cover bolts	96 to 120 in-lbs
Differential pinion shaft nut	137 to 180
Right front driveaxle flange bolts	37 to 43

---

1   General information

The information in this Chapter deals with the components from the rear of the engine to the rear wheels and to the front wheels on 4WD models, except for the transmission and transfer case (4WD models), which are dealt with in the previous Chapter. For the purposes of this Chapter, these components are grouped into four categories: clutch, driveshaft, front axle and rear axle. Separate Sections within this Chapter offer general descriptions and checking procedures for each of these groups.

Since nearly all the procedures covered in this Chapter involve working under the vehicle, make sure it's securely supported on sturdy jackstands or on a hoist where the vehicle can be easily raised and lowered.

2   Clutch – description and check

Refer to illustration 2.1

1   All models equipped with a manual transmission feature a single dry-plate, diaphragm spring-type clutch **(see illustration)**. The actuation is either through a cable or hydraulic system.

2   When the clutch pedal is depressed on cable-actuated models, the clutch cable moves the release bearing into contact with the pressure plate release fingers, disengaging the clutch disc. On hydraulically actuated models, hydraulic fluid (under pressure from the clutch master cylinder) flows into the release cylinder. Because the release cylinder is connected to the clutch fork, the fork moves the release bearing into contact with the pressure plate release fingers, disengaging the clutch disc.

3   Terminology can be a problem regarding the clutch components because common names have in some cases changed from that used by the manufacturer. For example, the driven plate is also called the clutch plate or disc, the clutch release bearing is sometimes called a throwout bearing, the release cylinder is sometimes called the operating or slave cylinder.

4   Due to the slow wearing qualities of the clutch, it is not easy to decide when to go to the trouble of removing the transmission in order to check the wear on the friction lining. The only positive indication that something should be done is when it starts to slip or when squealing noises during engagement indicate that the friction lining has worn down to the rivets. In such instances it can only be hoped that the friction surfaces on the flywheel and pressure plate have not been badly worn or scored.

5   A clutch will wear according to the way in which it is used. Much intentional slipping of the clutch while driving – rather than the correct selection of gears – will accelerate wear. It is best to assume, however, that the disc will need replacement at about 40,000 miles (64,000 km).

6   Because of the clutch's location between the engine and transmission, it cannot be worked on without removing either the engine or transmission. If repairs which would require removal of the engine are not needed, the quickest way to gain access to the clutch is by removing the transmission as described in Chapter 7.

7   Other than to replace components with obvious damage, some preliminary checks should be performed to diagnose a clutch system failure.

a)   The first check should be of the fluid level in the clutch master cylinder (hydraulically actuated models). If the fluid level is low, add fluid as necessary and re-test. If the master cylinder runs dry, or if any of the hydraulic components are serviced, bleed the hydraulic system as described in Section 9.

b)   To check "clutch spin down time", run the engine at normal idle speed with the transmission in Neutral (clutch pedal up – engaged). Disengage the clutch (pedal down), wait nine seconds and shift the transmission into Reverse. No grinding noise should be heard. A grinding noise would indicate component failure in the pressure plate assembly or the clutch disc.

c)   To check for complete clutch release, run the engine (with the brake on to prevent movement) and hold the clutch pedal approximately 1/2-inch from the floor mat. Shift the transmission between 1st gear and Reverse several times. If the shift is not smooth, component failure is indicated. Measure the hydraulic release cylinder pushrod travel (hydraulically actuated models). With the clutch pedal completely depressed the release cylinder pushrod should extend substantially. If the pushrod will not extend very far or not at all, check the fluid level in the clutch master cylinder. The system may need to be bled (see Section 9).

d)   Visually inspect the clutch pedal bushing at the top of the clutch pedal to make sure there is no sticking or excessive wear.

e)   Under the vehicle, check that the release fork is solidly mounted on the ball stud (hydraulically actuated models).

Note: *Because access to the clutch components is an involved process, any time either the engine or transmission is removed, the clutch disc, pressure plate assembly and release bearing should be carefully inspected and, if necessary, replaced with new parts. Since the clutch disc is normally the item of highest wear, it should be replaced as a matter of course if there is any question about its condition.*

3   Clutch components – removal, inspection and installation

Refer to illustrations 3.10 and 3.12

Warning: *Dust produced by clutch wear and deposited on clutch components contains asbestos, which is hazardous to your health. DO NOT blow it out with compressed air and DO NOT inhale it. DO NOT use gasoline or petroleum-based solvents to remove the dust. Brake system cleaner should be used to flush the dust into a drain pan. After the clutch components are wiped clean with a rag, dispose of the contaminated rags and cleaner in a covered container.*

Removal

1   Access to the clutch components is normally accomplished by removing the transmission, leaving the engine in the vehicle. If, of course, the engine is being removed for major overhaul, then the opportunity should always be taken to check the clutch for wear and replace worn components as necessary. The following procedures assume that the engine will stay in place.

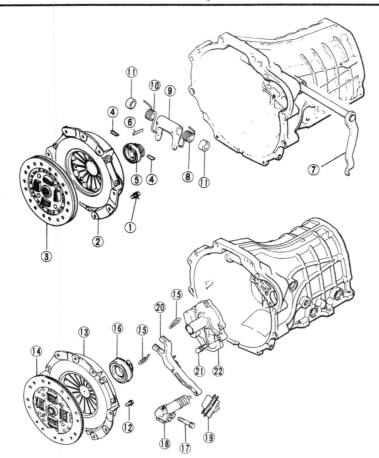

2.1 Exploded views of the clutch components

Cable-actuated models (top)

1 Bolt
2 Clutch pressure plate assembly
3 Clutch disc
4 Spring clip
5 Release bearing
6 Spring pin
7 Clutch control lever
8 Return spring
9 Release fork
10 Return spring
11 Felt packing

Hydraulically actuated models (bottom)

12 Bolt
13 Clutch pressure plate assembly
14 Clutch disc
15 Spring clip
16 Release bearing
17 Bolt
18 Release cylinder
19 Boot
20 Release fork
21 Ballstud
22 Bearing retainer

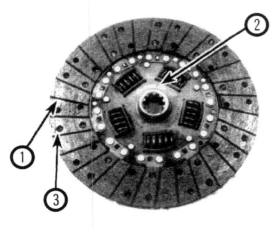

3.10 The clutch disc

1 Lining – this will wear down in use
2 Marks – "Flywheel Side" or something similar
3 Rivets – These secure the lining and will damage the pressure plate if allowed to contact it

2 Remove the release cylinder (hydraulically actuated models) without disconnecting the hydraulic line (see Section 8). Support the cylinder out of the way by a piece of wire from the undercarriage.

3 Referring to Chapter 7 Part A, remove the transmission from the vehicle. Support the engine while the transmission is out. Preferably, an engine hoist should be used to support it from above. However, if a jack is used underneath the engine, make sure a piece of wood is used between the jack and oil pan to spread the load. **Caution:** *The pickup for the oil*

pump is very close to the bottom of the oil pan. If the pan is bent or distorted in any way, engine oil starvation could occur.

4 To support the clutch disc during removal, install a clutch alignment tool through the clutch disc hub.

5 Carefully inspect the flywheel and pressure plate for indexing marks. The marks are usually an X, an O or a white letter. If they cannot be found, apply marks yourself so the pressure plate and the flywheel will be in the same alignment during installation.

6 Turning each bolt only 1/2-turn at a time, slowly loosen the pressure plate-to-flywheel bolts. Work in a diagonal pattern and loosen each bolt a little at a time until all spring pressure is relieved. Then hold the pressure plate securely and completely remove the bolts, followed by the pressure plate and clutch disc.

Inspection

7 Ordinarily, when a problem occurs in the clutch, it can be attributed to wear of the clutch disc assembly. However, all components should be inspected at this time.

8 Inspect the flywheel for cracks, heat checking, grooves or other signs of obvious defects. If the imperfections are slight, a machine shop can machine the surface flat and smooth, which is highly recommended regardless of the surface appearance. Refer to Chapter 2 for the flywheel removal and installation procedure.

9 Inspect the pilot bearing (if equipped) (Section 6).

10 Inspect the lining on the clutch disc. There should be at least 1mm of lining above the rivet heads. Check for loose rivets, warpage, cracks, distorted springs or damper bushings and other obvious damage **(see illustration)**. As mentioned above, ordinarily the clutch disc is replaced as a matter of course, so if in doubt about the condition, replace it with a new one.

11 Ordinarily, the release bearing is also replaced along with the clutch disc (see Section 4).

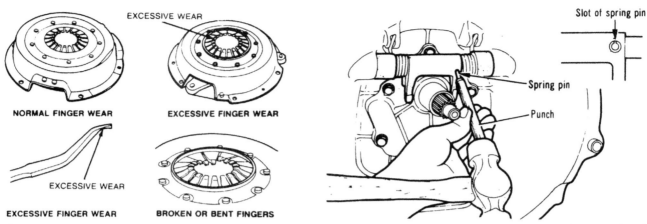

3.12   Replace the pressure plate if the diaphragm spring fingers exhibit these signs of wear

4.4   Drive out the spring pins with a hammer and punch – the pin slots must be at right angles to the shaft when reinstalled

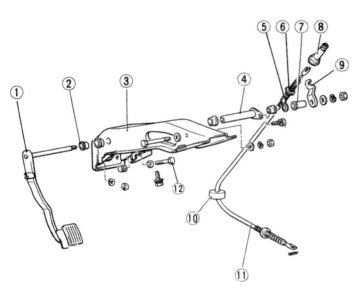

5.1   Typical clutch cable details

1	Clutch pedal	7	Spacer
2	Bushing	8	Insulator
3	Support	9	Pedal lever
4	Pedal rod	10	Pad
5	Spring	11	Clutch cable
6	Adjusting wheel	12	Stop bolt

12   Check the machined surfaces of the pressure plate and the diaphragm spring fingers **(see illustration)**. If the surface is grooved or otherwise damaged, replace the pressure plate. Also check for obvious damage, distortion, cracking, etc. Light glazing can be removed with medium grit emery cloth. If a new pressure plate is indicated, new or factory-rebuilt units are available.

Installation

13   Before installation, carefully wipe the flywheel and pressure plate machined surfaces clean with a rubbing-alcohol dampened rag. It's important that no oil or grease is on these surfaces or the lining of the clutch disc. Handle these parts only with clean hands.
14   Position the clutch disc and pressure plate with the clutch held in place with an alignment tool. Make sure it's installed properly (most replacement clutch discs will be marked "flywheel side" or something similar – if not marked, install the clutch with the damper springs or bushings toward the transmission.

15   Tighten the pressure plate-to-flywheel bolts only finger tight, working around the pressure plate.
16   Center the clutch disc by ensuring the alignment tool is through the splined hub and into the pilot bearing in the crankshaft. Wiggle the tool up, down or side-to-side, as needed, to bottom the tool in the pilot bearing. Tighten the pressure plate-to-flywheel bolts a little at a time, working in a criss-cross pattern to prevent distorting the cover. After all of the bolts are snug, tighten them to the torque listed in this Chapter's Specifications. Remove the alignment tool.
17   Using high temperature grease, lubricate the inner groove of the release bearing (refer to Section 4). Also place grease on the fork fingers.
18   Install the clutch release bearing as described in Section 4.
19   Install the transmission, release cylinder and all components removed previously, tightening all fasteners to the proper torque specifications.

---

4   Clutch release bearing – removal and installation

Refer to illustration 4.4

Removal

1   Disconnect the negative cable from the battery.
2   Remove the transmission (Chapter 7).
3   Detach the spring clip(s), then slide the release bearing off the transmission input shaft **(see illustration 2.1)**.
4   On cable-actuated models, drive out the two spring pins and slide the clutch control lever out of the bellhousing and remove the release fork **(see illustration)**.
5   On hydraulically actuated models, detach the fork from the ballstud by pulling it straight off.
6   Hold the bearing and turn the inner portion. If the bearing doesn't turn smoothly or if it's noisy, replace it with a new one. Wipe the bearing with a clean rag and inspect it for damage, wear and cracks. Don't immerse the bearing in solvent – it's sealed for life and to do so would ruin it.

Installation

Cable-actuated models

7   Wipe the control lever shaft bushings in the bellhousing clean, then apply a thin coat of multi-purpose grease to them. Slide the control lever/shaft assembly into place along with the felt packings, return springs and the clutch arm.
8   Engage the return spring in the clutch arm, install the spring pins with the slots at right angles to the shaft **(see illustration 4.4)**. Apply a few drops of clean engine oil to the felt packings.
9   Slide the release bearing and carrier assembly into position and install the spring clips. Make sure they are properly engaged in the clutch arm and release bearing carriers.

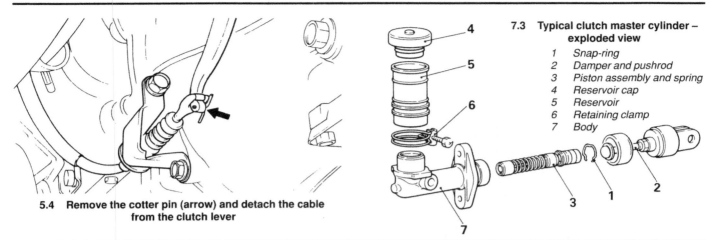

5.4   Remove the cotter pin (arrow) and detach the cable from the clutch lever

7.3   Typical clutch master cylinder – exploded view
1   Snap-ring
2   Damper and pushrod
3   Piston assembly and spring
4   Reservoir cap
5   Reservoir
6   Retaining clamp
7   Body

Hydraulically-actuated models

10   Lubricate the clutch fork ends where they contact the bearing lightly with moly-based grease. Apply a thin coat of the same grease to the inner diameter of the bearing and also to the transmission input shaft bearing retainer.

11   Install the release bearing on the clutch fork so that both of the fork ends fit into the bearing tabs. Make sure the spring clip seats securely.

12   Lubricate the clutch release fork ball socket with moly-based disulphide grease and push the fork onto the ball stud until it's firmly seated. Check to see that the bearing slides back and forth smoothly on the input shaft bearing retainer.

All models

13   The remainder of the installation is the reverse of the removal procedure, tightening all bolts to the specified torques.

5   Clutch cable – removal and installation

Refer to illustrations 5.1 and 5.4

1   Loosen the cable adjusting wheel at the firewall in the engine compartment and the pedal stop bolt to provide enough slack to unhook it from the clutch pedal **(see illustration)**.

2   Raise the vehicle and support it securely on jackstands.

3   Unhook the return spring from the clutch lever.

4   Disconnect the cable from the clutch lever **(see illustration)**, pull it forward through the bracket, detach any retaining clips and remove it from the vehicle.

5   Installation is the reverse of removal, taking care there are no kinks in the cable which will cause it to bind.

6   After installation, adjust the freeplay (see Chapter 1).

6   Pilot bearing – inspection, removal and installation

1   The clutch pilot bearing is a ball-type bearing used on some models which is pressed into the rear of the crankshaft. Its primary purpose is to support the front of the transmission input shaft. The pilot bearing should be inspected whenever the clutch components are removed from the engine. Due to its inaccessibility, if you are in doubt as to its condition, replace it with a new one. **Note:** *If the engine has been removed from the vehicle, disregard the following steps which do not apply.*

2   Remove the transmission (refer to Chapter 7 Part A).

3   Remove the clutch components (Section 3).

4   Using a clean rag, wipe the bearing clean and inspect for any excessive wear, scoring or obvious damage. A flashlight will be helpful to direct light into the recess.

5   Check to make sure the pilot bearing turns smoothly and quietly. If the transmission input shaft contact surface is worn or damaged, replace the bearing with a new one.

6   Removal can be accomplished with a special puller but an alternative method also works very well.

7   Find a solid steel bar which is slightly smaller in diameter than the bearing. Alternatives to a solid bar would be a wood dowel or a socket with a bolt fixed in place to make it solid.

8   Check the bar for fit – it should just slip into the bearing with very little clearance.

9   Pack the bearing and the area behind it (in the crankshaft recess) with heavy grease. Pack it tightly to eliminate as much air as possible.

10   Insert the bar into the bearing bore and lightly hammer on the bar, which will force the grease to the backside of the bearing and push it out. Remove the bearing and clean all grease from the crankshaft recess.

11   To install the new bearing, lubricate the outside surface with oil then drive it into the recess with a hammer and a socket with an outside diameter that matches the bearing outer race.

12   Pack the bearing with lithium base grease (NLGI No.2). Wipe off all excess grease so the clutch lining will not become contaminated.

13   Install the clutch components, transmission and all other components removed to gain access to the pilot bearing.

7   Clutch master cylinder – removal, overhaul and installation

Refer to illustration 7.3
Caution: *Do not allow brake fluid to contact any painted surfaces of the vehicle, as damage to the finish may result.*

Removal

1   Disconnect the hydraulic line from the master cylinder and drain the fluid into a suitable container.

2   Remove the master cylinder flange mounting nuts and withdraw the unit from the engine compartment.

Overhaul

3   Remove the retaining clamp and pull off the reservoir **(see illustration)**.

4   Push the piston down and remove the snap-ring with a pair of snapring pliers or a small screwdriver.

5   Pull out the piston assembly and spring.

6   Examine the inner surface of the cylinder bore. If it is scored or exhibits bright wear areas, the entire master cylinder should be replaced.

7   If the cylinder bore is in good condition, obtain a clutch master cylinder rebuild kit, which will contain all of the necessary replacement parts.

8   Prior to installing any parts, first dip them in brake fluid to lubricate them.

9   Installation of the parts in the cylinder is the reverse of removal.

Installation

10   Position the clutch master cylinder against the firewall, inserting the pedal pushrod into the piston. Install the nuts, tightening them securely.

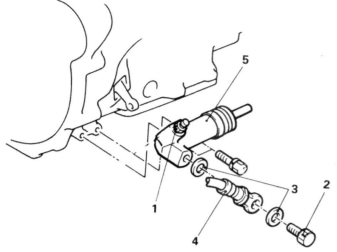

8.3   Clutch release cylinder installation details

1	*Bleeder screw*	4	*Hydraulic line*
2	*Banjo bolt*	5	*Body*
3	*Washers*		

11   Bleed the clutch hydraulic system following the procedure in Section 9, then check the pedal height and freeplay as described in Chapter 1.

8   Clutch release cylinder – removal, overhaul and installation

Refer to illustrations 8.3, 8.6a and 8.6b

Removal

1   The clutch release cylinder is located on the side of the transmission bellhousing.
2   Raise the vehicle and support it securely on jackstands.
3   Disconnect the hydraulic line from the release cylinder. This is done by removing the bolt from the banjo fitting on the cylinder body **(see illustration)**.
4   Remove the bolt(s) and pull off the release cylinder.

Overhaul

5   Pull off the dust boot and pushrod.
6   Mount the release cylinder body in a padded vise and use compressed air to force the piston and spring out of the bore **(see illustrations)**.
7   Unscrew and remove the bleeder screw.
8   Examine the surfaces of the piston and cylinder bore for scoring or bright wear areas. If any are found, discard the cylinder and purchase a new one.
9   If the components are in good condition, wash them in clean brake fluid. Remove the piston cup and discard it, noting carefully which way the cup lips face.
10   Obtain a repair kit which will contain all the necessary new items.
11   Install the new piston cup using your fingers only to manipulate it into position. Be sure the lips face in the proper direction.
12   Dip the piston assembly in clean brake fluid before installing it and the spring into the cylinder.
13   Reinstall the bleeder screw.
14   Complete the reassembly by installing the pushrod and the dust cover. Be sure the dust cover is secure on the cylinder housing.

Installation

15   Installation is the reverse of the removal procedure. Use new sealing washers at the banjo fitting. After the cylinder has been installed, bleed the clutch hydraulic system as described in Section 9.

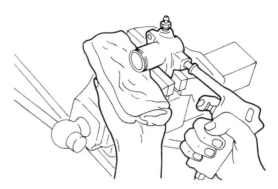

8.6a   With the cylinder padded to catch the piston, use compressed air to force the piston out of the bore – make sure your hands are not in the way of the piston!

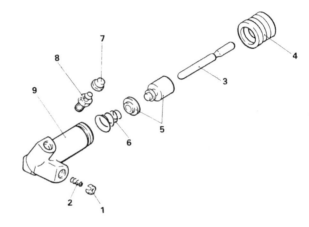

8.6b   An exploded view of the clutch release cylinder

1	*Valve plate*	6	*Conical spring*
2	*Spring*	7	*Cap*
3	*Pushrod*	8	*Bleeder screw*
4	*Boots*	9	*Cylinder body*
5	*Piston and cup assembly*		

9   Clutch hydraulic system – bleeding

Caution: *Do not allow the brake fluid to contact any painted surface of th vehicle, as damage to the finish will result.*

1   Bleeding will be required whenever the hydraulic system has bee dismantled and reassembled and air has entered the system.
2   First fill the fluid reservoir with clean brake fluid which has been store in an airtight container. Never use fluid which has drained from the syster or has bled out previously, as it may contain grit and moisture.
3   Attach a rubber or plastic bleed tube to the bleeder screw on the re lease cylinder and immerse the open end of the tube in a glass jar contair ing an inch or two of fluid.
4   Open the bleeder screw about half a turn and have an assistant quick ly depress the clutch pedal completely. Tighten the screw and then hav the clutch pedal slowly released with the foot completely removed. Repea this sequence of operations until air bubbles are no longer ejected from th open end of the tube beneath the fluid in the jar.
5   After two or three strokes of the pedal, make sure the fluid level in th reservoir has not fallen too low. Keep it full of fresh fluid, otherwise air wi be drawn into the system.
6   Tighten the bleeder screw on a pedal down stroke (do not overtighte

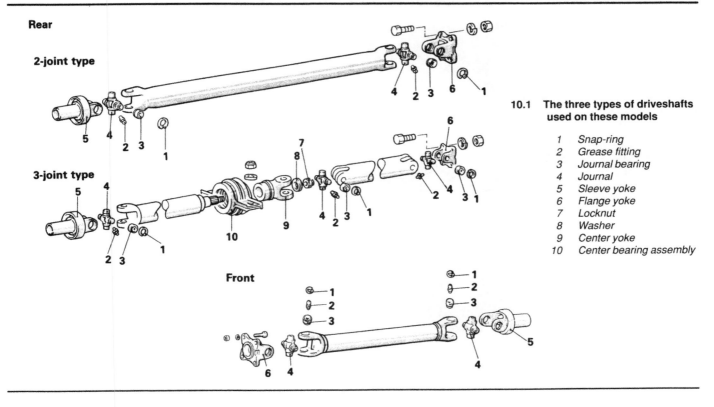

Rear

2-joint type

3-joint type

Front

10.1 The three types of driveshafts used on these models

1 Snap-ring
2 Grease fitting
3 Journal bearing
4 Journal
5 Sleeve yoke
6 Flange yoke
7 Locknut
8 Washer
9 Center yoke
10 Center bearing assembly

it), remove the bleed tube and jar, top-up the reservoir and install the cap.

7   If an assistant is not available, alternative 'one-man' bleeding operations can be carried out using a bleed tube equipped with a one-way valve or a pressure bleed kit, both of which should be used in accordance with the manufacturer's instructions.

pension angles independent from each other.

Because of the complexity and critical nature of the differential adjustments, as well as the special equipment needed to perform the operations, we recommend any disassembly of the differential be done by a dealer service department or other repair shop.

10 Driveshafts, differentials and axles – general information

Refer to illustration 10.1

Three different driveshaft assemblies are used on the vehicles covered in this manual **(see illustration)**. Some use a one-piece driveshaft which incorporates two universal joints, one at either end of the shaft.

Others use a two-piece driveshaft which incorporates a center bearing at the rear of the front shaft. This driveshaft uses three universal joints; one at the transmission end, one behind the center bearing and one at the differential flange.

4WD models use two driveshafts; the primary shaft runs between the transfer case and the front differential and the rear driveshaft runs between the transfer case and the rear differential.

All universal joints are of the solid type and can be replaced separately from the driveshaft. The driveshafts are finely balanced during production and whenever they are removed or disassembled, they must be reassembled and reinstalled in the exact manner and positions they were originally in, to avoid excessive vibration.

The rear axle is of the semi-floating type, having a 'banjo' design axle housing, which is held in proper alignment with the body by the rear suspension.

Mounted in the center of the rear axle is the differential, which transfers the turning force of the driveshaft to the rear axleshafts, on which the rear wheels are mounted.

The axleshafts are splined at their inner ends to fit into the splines in the differential gears; outer support for the shaft is provided by the rear wheel bearing.

The front axle on 4WD vehicles consists of a frame-mounted differential assembly and two driveaxles. The driveaxles incorporate two constant velocity (CV) joints each, enabling them to transmit power at various sus-

11 Driveline inspection

1   Raise the rear of the vehicle and support it securely on jackstands.

2   Slide under the vehicle and visually inspect the condition of the driveshaft. Look for any dents or cracks in the tubing. If any are found, the driveshaft must be replaced.

3   Check for any oil leakage at the front and rear of the driveshaft. Leakage where the driveshaft enters the transmission indicates a defective rear transmission seal. Leakage where the driveshaft enters the differential indicates a defective pinion seal.

4   While still under the vehicle, have an assistant turn the rear wheel so the driveshaft will rotate. As it does, make sure that the universal joints are operating properly without binding, noise or looseness. On long-bed models, listen for any noise from the center bearing, indicating it is worn or damaged. Also check the rubber portion of the center bearing for cracking or separation, which will necessitate replacement.

5   The universal joint can also be checked with the driveshaft motionless, by gripping your hands on either side of the joint and attempting to twist the joint. Any movement at all in the joint is a sign of considerable wear. Lifting up on the shaft will also indicate movement in the universal joints.

6   Finally, check the driveshaft mounting bolts at the ends to make sure they are tight.

7   On 4WD models, the above driveshaft checks should be repeated on all driveshafts. In addition, check for grease leakage around the sleeve yoke, indicating failure of the yoke seal.

8   Check for leakage at each connection of the driveshafts to the transfer case and front differential. Leakage indicates worn oil seals.

9   At the same time, check for looseness in the joints of the front driveaxles.

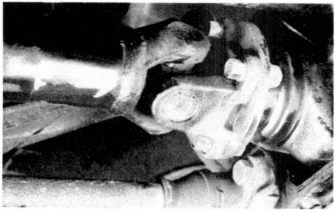

12.1   Mark the direction the driveshaft faces

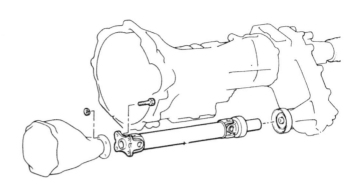

12.3   Typical front driveshaft installation details

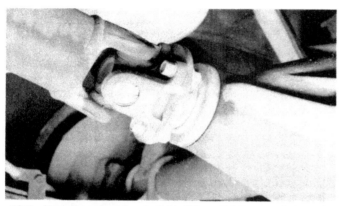

12.7   Mark the rear driveshaft-to-differential flange relationship

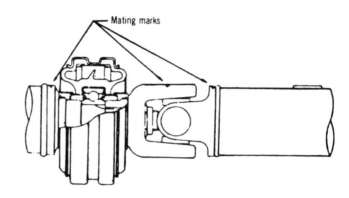

13.1   Make sure to mark the relationship of the universal joints driveshaft and center bearing before beginning disassembly

12   Driveshafts – removal and installation

Front driveshaft (4WD)

Refer to illustrations 12.1 and 12.3

1   Raise the front of the vehicle and place it on jackstands. Mark the relationship of the front driveshaft flange to the front differential companion flange so they can be realigned upon installation. Also mark the direction the driveshaft faces **(see illustration)**.

2   Lock the driveshaft from turning with a large screwdriver or prybar, then remove the four nuts and bolts from the front flange.

3   Detach the flange from the front differential, withdraw the shaft from the transfer case and lower the driveshaft from the vehicle **(see illustration)**.

4   Installation is the reverse of removal. Be sure to align all marks and tighten the flange bolts to the torque listed in this Chapter's Specifications.

Rear driveshaft

Refer to illustration 12.7

5   Raise the rear of the vehicle and support it on jackstands.

6   Remove the nuts holding the center support bearing bracket to the frame (three-joint type).

7   Mark the edges of the driveshaft rear flange and the differential companion flange so they can be realigned upon installation **(see illustration)**.

8   Remove the four nuts and bolts.

9   Push the shaft forward slightly to disconnect the rear flange.

10   Pull the yoke from the transmission/transfer case while supporting the driveshaft (two-joint type) or driveshafts and center bearing assembly as a unit (three-joint type) with your hands.

11   While the driveshafts are removed, insert a plug in the transmission/transfer case to prevent lubricant leakage.

12   Installation is the reverse of the removal procedure. During installation, make sure all flange marks line up. When connecting the center bearing support to the frame, first finger-tighten the two mounting nuts, then make sure that the bearing bracket is at right angles to the driveshaft. Tighten all nuts and bolts to the torques listed in this Chapter's Specifications.

13   Center bearing – replacement

Refer to illustrations 13.1, 13.3, 13.4 and 13.5

1   Remove the driveshaft (see Section 12). Mark the relative positions of the universal joints, driveshafts and center bearing **(see illustration)**.

2   Disassemble the center universal joint so the driveshaft can be separated into two pieces (Section 14).

3   Support the driveshaft in a padded vise and remove the center yoke nut **(see illustration)**.

4   Pull the center yoke off, pry the center bearing bracket loose (be careful not to damage the rubber mount or any dust seals) and remove the center bearing bracket assembly **(see illustration)**. The bearing bracket can be disassembled.

5   Using a puller, remove the bearing from the shaft **(see illustration)**.

6   Prior to installation, lubricate the contact surfaces of the bearing and driveshaft with multi-purpose grease.

7   Slip the bearing onto the shaft and fit the bracket to the bearing. The bracket mounting rubber should fit securely into the bearing groove all the way around it's circumference.

8   Align the mating marks on the shaft and the center yoke and slip the yoke into place on the shaft. Install the washer and a new nut and tighten the nut securely.

9   Assemble the center universal joint as described in Section 14.

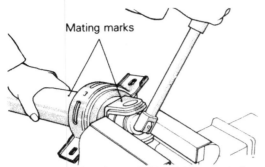

13.3   With the center bearing and driveshaft mounted securely in a vise, remove the center yoke nut

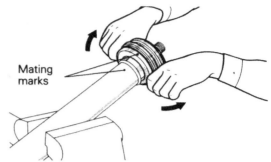

13.4   Work the center bearing bracket assembly back-and-forth while pulling it off the shaft

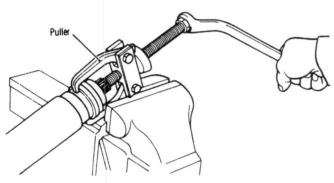

13.5   Pull the bearing off the shaft with a puller

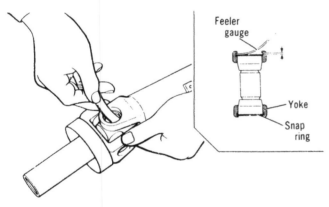

14.12   Use a feeler gauge to check the snap-ring-to-bearing clearance (U-joint journal endplay)

14   Universal joints – replacement

Refer to illustrations 14.5 and 14.12

Note: *Selective fit snap-rings are used to retain the universal joint spiders in the yokes. In order to maintain the driveshaft balance, you must use replacement snap-rings of the same size as originally used.*

1   On three-joint type driveshafts, it's a good idea to dismantle the center universal joint first so that the driveshaft can be broken into two pieces, which makes the job easier.

2   Clean away all dirt from the ends of the bearings on the yokes so the snap-rings can be removed with a pair of snap-ring pliers or long-nose pliers.

3   Support the universal joint in a vise equipped with soft jaws and remove the snap-rings. If they are very tight, tap the end of the bearing with a hammer to relieve the pressure.

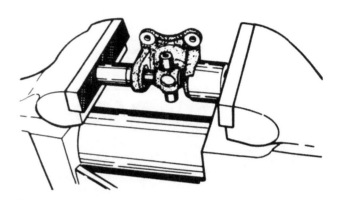

14.5   To press the universal joint out of the driveshaft, set it up in a vise with the small socket (on the left) pushing the joint and bearing cap into the large socket

4   You will need two sockets to remove the bearings from the yokes. One should be large enough to fit into the yoke where the snap-rings were installed and the other should have an inside diameter just large enough for the bearings to fit into when they are forced out of the yoke.

5   Mount the universal joint in the vise with the large socket on one side of the yoke and the small socket on the other side, pushing against the bearing. Carefully tighten the vise until the bearing is pushed out of the yoke and into the large socket **(see illustration)**. If it can't be pushed all the way out, remove the universal joint from the vise and use a pair of pliers to finish removing the bearing.

6   Reverse the sockets and push out the bearing on the other side of the yoke. This time, the small socket will be pushing against the cross-shaped universal joint journal end.

7   Before pressing out the two remaining bearings, mark the universal joint journal (the cross) so it can be installed in the same position during reassembly. Also mark the relationship of the yokes to each other.

8   The two remaining universal joints can be disassembled following the same procedure. Be sure to mark all components for each universal joint so they can be kept together and reassembled in the proper position.

9   When reassembling the universal joints, replace all needle bearings and dust seals with new ones.

10   Before reassembly, pack each grease cavity in the universal joint journals with a small amount of grease. Also, apply a thin coat of grease to the new needle bearing rollers and the roller contact areas on the universal joint journal.

11   Apply a thin coat of grease to the dust seal lips and install the bearings and universal joint journals into the yoke using the vise and sockets that were used to remove the old bearings. Work slowly and be very careful not to damage the bearings as they are being pressed into the yokes.

12   Once the bearings are in place and properly seated, install the snap-rings and check the clearance (U-joint journal endplay) with a feeler gauge **(see illustration)**. This is done with both snap-rings in place and the bear-

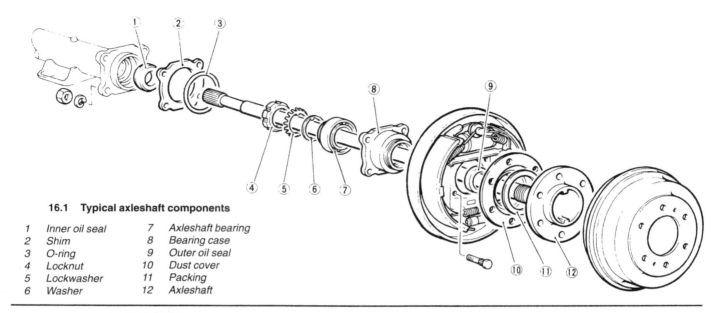

16.1 Typical axleshaft components

1	Inner oil seal	7	Axleshaft bearing
2	Shim	8	Bearing case
3	O-ring	9	Outer oil seal
4	Locknut	10	Dust cover
5	Lockwasher	11	Packing
6	Washer	12	Axleshaft

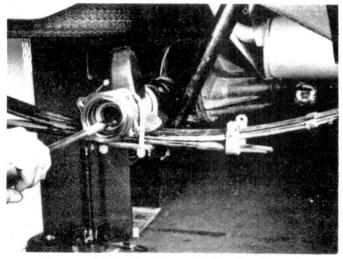

16.9 Use a hooked tool to remove the oil seal from the axle housing

ings and journal pressed toward one side of the yoke. Measure the clearance at the opposite side of the yoke. Compare this measurement with those in the Specifications Section at the beginning of this Chapter. If the measurement is greater than specified, install a snap-ring of a different thickness and recheck the clearance. Repeat the procedure until the correct clearance is obtained. If possible, use snap-rings of the same thickness on each side of the yoke so the driveshaft balance isn't affected.

---

15 Rear axle assembly – removal and installation

---

1   Loosen the rear wheel lug nuts, raise the vehicle and support it securely on jackstands placed underneath the frame. Remove the wheels.
2   Support the rear axle assembly with a floor jack placed underneath the differential.
3   Remove the shock absorber lower mounting nuts, detach the lower part of the shocks from the axle brackets and compress the shocks to get them out of the way (see Chapter 10).
4   Disconnect the driveshaft from the differential companion flange and hang it with a piece of wire from the underbody (see Section 12).
5   Disconnect the parking brake cables from the parking brake lever at

each rear wheel (see Chapter 9).
6   Disconnect the rear flexible brake hose from the brake line above the rear axle housing. Disconnect the rear axle breather hose on top of the axle housing (if equipped). Plug the ends of the line and hose or wrap plastic bags tightly around them to prevent excessive fluid loss and contamination.
7   Support the rear axle assembly with a jack.

Leaf spring models

8   Remove the U-bolt nuts from the leaf spring seats and raise the axle assembly slightly with the jack.
9   Remove the rear spring shackle bolts and lower the rear of each leaf spring to the floor.

Coil spring models

10   Remove the stabilizer bar bolts.
11   Remove the rear suspension lower arms and lateral rod.

All models

12   Carefully lower the axle assembly to the floor with the jack, then remove it from under the vehicle. It would be a good idea to have an assistant on hand, as the assembly is very heavy.
13   Installation is the reverse of the removal procedure. Be sure to tighten the bolts and nuts and the driveshaft companion flange bolts to the torques listed in this Chapter and Chapter 10's Specifications. Bleed the brakes (see Chapter 9).

---

16   Rear axle oil seal – replacement

Refer to illustrations 16.1, 16.9, 16.15 and 16.17
1   The axleshafts can be removed without disturbing the differential assembly. They must be removed in order to replace the oil seals and when removing the differential carrier from the rear axle housing **(see illustration)**. **Note:** *Read this entire procedure before starting work.*
2   Raise the rear of the vehicle and support it securely on jackstands. Block the front wheels to keep the vehicle from rolling.
3   Remove the rear wheels and release the parking brake.
4   Remove the drain plug and drain the differential lubricant into a suitable container. When the draining is complete, finger-tighten the drain plug in place.
5   On drum brake models, remove the brake drum from the end of the axle and the metal brake line from the wheel cylinder by referring to Chapter 9. The brakes do not have to be disassembled to remove the axles. On 1992 and later Monteros with rear disc brakes, refer to Chapter 9 for brake disassembly.

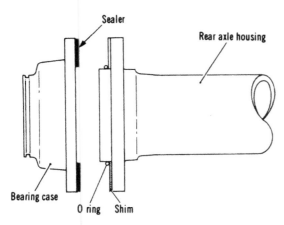

16.15   Apply a thin, even coat of silicone sealer to the area shown on the bearing case

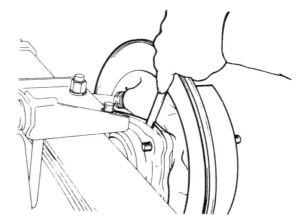

16.17   Use a feeler gauge to measure the gap between the bearing case and the axle housing

6   Remove the parking brake cables from the vehicle as described in Chapter 9. Do not disconnect the cables from the levers in the rear brake assemblies. If only one axle shaft is being removed, remove only the cable on the side of the vehicle that the axle shaft is being removed from. If both axle shafts are being removed, both parking brake cables must also be removed.

7   Remove the four nuts and lock washers attaching the bearing case and brake backing plate to the axle housing and withdraw the axle, the bearing case, the brake backing plate and brake assembly from the axle housing. A slide hammer-type axle puller may be required to dislodge the bearing housing from the axle housing. Do not pry between the two flanges, as damage to the gasket sealing surfaces will result. Support the axle shaft as it is removed from the axle housing to prevent damage to the old seal in the end of the axle housing.

8   Remove the O-ring and shim (or shims) from the rear axle housing flange. Retain the shims for reassembly.

9   Pry or pull the oil seal out of the housing with a screwdriver or a slide hammer-type seal puller **(see illustration)**.

10   Thoroughly clean the seal mounting area, and install a new seal (with the rubber side facing out) using a hammer and a block of wood or other suitable tool. Tap the seal carefully into place around its entire circumference and make sure it is properly seated in the axle housing.

11   At this point, the axleshaft assembly should be taken to a dealer service department or a automotive machine shop if the outer oil seal or wheel bearing has to be replaced.

12   Before beginning the assembly procedure, remove all old gasket sealer and any rust from the mating surfaces of the bearing case and the axle housing. Also, thoroughly pack the bearing case and axle housing end with high-temperature wheel bearing grease and lubricate the lip of the oil seal in the axle housing.

13   If both axle shafts have been removed, the left-side shaft should be installed first during reassembly

14   Install a 0.040-inch (1.0 mm) shim and a new O-ring into place on the left end of the axle housing.

15   Apply a thin, even coat of silicone-type gasket sealer to the mating surface of the bearing case and carefully install the left-side axle/brake assembly into the rear axle housing **(see illustration)**. (Do not damage the oil seal in the process). It may be necessary to turn the axle slightly to engage its inner splines with the differential. You may have to tap gently on the axle hub with a soft-faced hammer to seat the bearing case in the end of the axle housing.

16   Install the four lock washers and nuts attaching the bearing case and brake backing plate to the axle housing. Tighten the nuts to the torque listed in this Chapter's Specifications.

17   Install the right-side axle into the housing without a shim or O-ring in place, and temporarily tighten the attaching nuts to a torque of 5 in-lbs. When the axle is installed in this manner, a gap will exist between the bear-

ing case and the axle housing end flange, which must be measured with a feeler gauge **(see illustration)**.

18   Separate the axle shaft from the housing and select a shim with a thickness equal to the gap measured in the previous step. Also, select a shim with a thickness of from 0.020 to 0.079-inch. A list of available preload adjusting shims is included in the Specifications Section at the beginning of this Chapter.

19   Install the previously selected shims and a new O-ring into place on the end of the axle housing.

20   Apply a thin, even coat of silicone-type gasket sealer to the mating surface of the bearing case and carefully install the axle assembly into the housing. Install the lock washers and nuts and tighten the nuts to the torque listed in this Chapter's Specifications.

21   Using a dial indicator, check the axial play of the axle shaft by pulling out and pushing in on the axle shaft hub. If the play is more or less than specified, remove the right-side axle again and replace the shims with shims that are thicker or thinner, as required.

22   Reinstall the axle and recheck the axial play. If necessary, repeat the procedure until the correct amount of play is obtained.

23   Install the parking brake cables, hook up the brake lines and install the brake drums by referring to Chapter 9. Also, bleed the brakes at the rear wheel cylinder as described in Chapter 9.

24   Tighten the rear axle housing drain plug to the torque specified in Chapter 1 and fill the housing to the proper level with the recommended gear lubricant (see the *Recommended Lubricants and Fluids* Section at the front of Chapter 1). Install the filler plug and tighten it to the specified torque.

25   Install the wheels, lower the vehicle to the ground and test drive it. Check for leaks where the wheel bearing case attaches to the rear axle housing.

---

17   Pinion bearing oil seal – replacement

---

1   It isn't uncommon for front or rear bearing oil seal to fail, resulting in gear lubricant leaking past the the seal and onto the driveshaft flange yoke. The seal can be easily replaced without removing the differential.

2   Raise the vehicle and support it securely on jackstands.

3   Remove the drain and fill plugs and drain the lubricant into a suitable container. After the lubricant has drained, install the plugs finger tight.

4   Separate the driveshaft from the differential and hang it out of the way by a piece of wire from the underbody (see Section 12).

5   Remove the differential pinion nut. On the 4WD model front differential, have an assistant apply the brakes to lock the front wheels from turning. On rear differentials, engage the parking brake to lock the rear wheels.

6   Use a gear puller tool to detach the differential flange yoke.

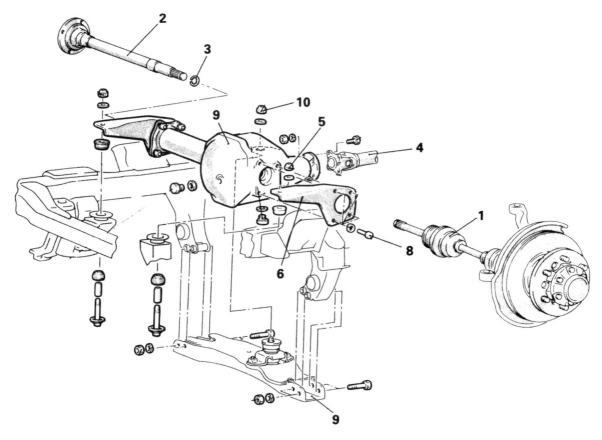

18.6   Front axle differential details

1	Steering knuckle and driveaxle assemblies	5	Self-locking nut	8	Bolts
2	Inner shaft	6	Left differential mounting bracket	9	Front suspension crossmember
3	Circlip	7	Self-locking nut	10	Self-locking nut
4	Front drive shaft				

7   Carefully pry off the dust cover for access to the seal. Note which side of the seal faces out and pry it out of the differential, taking care not to damage the pinion shaft splines.
8   Clean the seal outside diameter and the contact surfaces of the differential and pinion shaft.
9   Lubricate the seal lip with moly-base grease and place it in position in the differential. Working around the circumference, a little at a time, tap the seal evenly into the differential using a hammer and block of wood until it's fully seated.
10   Install the seal dust cover.
11   Clean the contact surface of the differential end yoke and apply a thin coat of moly-base grease. Install the yoke onto the pinion shaft, rotating it as necessary to line up the splines.
12   Tap the yoke fully into place with a soft face hammer, then install the large washer and a new self-locking nut on the pinion shaft.
13   To help seat the pinion shaft bearings properly, release the brakes (front differential) or parking brake (rear differential) and snug up the nut while holding one of the wheels to keep the shaft from turning as it is tightened.
14   Tighten the nut to the torque in the Specifications Section at the beginning of this Chapter. This torque figure is very important because it determines the preload on the pinion shaft bearings.
15   Connect the driveshaft and fill the differential with the specified lubricant (Chapter 1). Tighten the fill and drain plugs securely.

16   Lower the vehicle, test drive it, then check for evidence of leakage around the pinion and yoke.

18   Front differential assembly (4WD models) – removal and installation

Refer to illustration 18.6
1   Loosen the wheel lug nuts, raise the front of the vehicle and support it securely on jackstands. Remove the wheels.
2   Drain the lubricant from the differential (Chapter 1).
3   Remove the driveaxles and pull the inner shaft out of the right side axle tube (a slide hammer-type tool with a flange adapter may be required to remove the inner shaft from the differential).
4   Remove the front driveshaft (see Section 12).
5   Support the differential assembly with a floor jack.
6   Remove the left differential mounting bracket and the bolt holding the right bracket to the frame **(see illustration)**.
7   Remove the front crossmember-to-frame bolts and carefully lower the differential and crossmember as a unit.
8   Installation is the reverse of the removal procedure. Be sure to tighten the bolts/nuts securely and refill the differential with the recommended lubricant (Chapter 1).

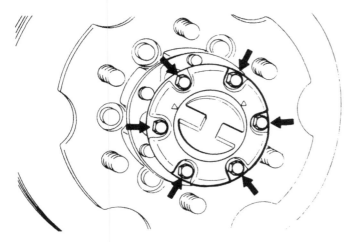

19.3a   On manual locking hubs, the cover is held in place by bolts (arrows)

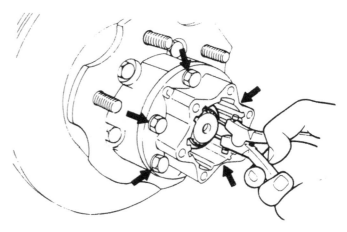

19.3b   On manual locking hubs, remove the snap-ring, then the bolts (arrows)

19.4a   On automatic free-wheeling hubs, the cap can be unscrewed by hand or with a wrench such as this oil filter wrench

19.4b   Lock the hub from turning with a large screwdriver and use a socket with the proper head to remove the bolts

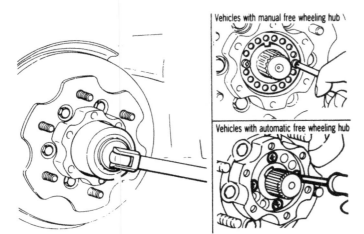

19.6   A special socket is required to remove the locknut and free the hub – lockwashers are held in place by screws

19   Front hub assembly (4WD models) – removal, bearing repack, installation and adjustment

Refer to illustrations 19.3a, 19.3b, 19.4a, 19.4b, 19.6, 19.9, 19.21, 19.23, 19.25 and 19.26

Note: *Special tools and a great deal of care are required to remove and install the hub on 4WD models, so be sure to read through the entire procedure before beginning work. It may be a good idea to leave the job to a dealer service department or repair shop.*

Removal

1   Raise the front of the vehicle and support it securely on jackstands.
2   Refer to Chapter 9 and remove the brake caliper/pad assembly. Do not disconnect the hose from the caliper and do not allow the caliper to hang by the hose – support it with a section of stiff wire so there is no strain on the hose.
3   On manual free-wheeling hub models, turn the control handle to the free position and remove the hub cover (see illustration). Remove the snap-ring from the end of the driveaxle with snap-ring pliers, then remove the bolts and separate the free-wheeling hub assembly from the wheel hub by pulling it straight out (see illustration).
4   On automatic free-wheeling hub models, unscrew the free-wheeling

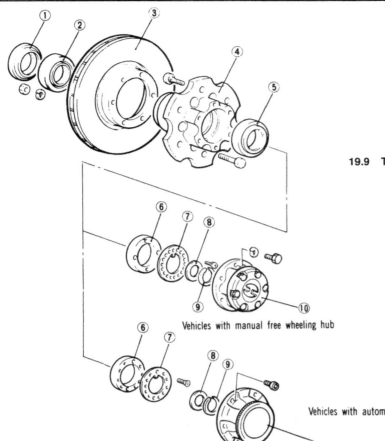

19.9   Typical free-wheeling hub components – exploded view

1   Seal
2   Inner wheel bearing
3   Brake disc
4   Hub
5   Outer wheel bearing
6   Locknut
7   Lockwasher
8   Shim/spacer
9   Snap-ring
10 Manual locking hub
11 Automatic locking hub

Vehicles with manual free wheeling hub

Vehicles with automatic free wheeling hub

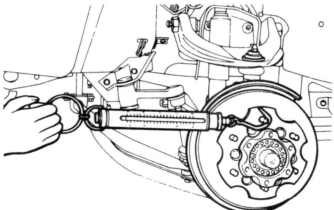

19.21   Check the hub turning force with a spring scale

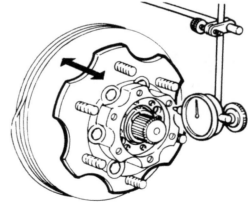

19.23   Use a dial indicator to check the hub axial play

hub cover (if it cannot be done by hand, wrap a rag around it and use an oil filter wrench, large pipe wrench or similar tool to loosen it) **(see illustration)**. Remove the O-ring from the hub cover, then remove the snap-ring and spacer/shim from the end of the driveaxle. Loosen and remove the bolts (a special tool is needed for this), then detach the free-wheeling hub from the wheel hub by pulling straight out on it **(see illustration)**.

5   On all models, remove the screws and detach the lockwasher from the hub.

6   Using the special socket (available from your dealer or most auto parts stores) and a breaker bar, remove the locknut **(see illustration)**.

7   Carefully remove the hub from the spindle (don't drop the outer bearing).

Bearing repack

8   Use a screwdriver to pry the grease seal out of the rear of the hub. As this is done, note how the seal is installed.

9   Remove the inner wheel bearing from the hub **(see illustration)**.

10   Use solvent to remove all traces of the old grease from the bearings, hub and spindle. A small brush may prove helpful; however make sure no bristles from the brush embed themselves inside the bearing rollers. Allow the parts to air dry.

11   Carefully inspect the bearings for cracks, heat discoloration, worn rollers, etc. Check the bearing races inside the hub for wear and damage. If the bearing races are defective, the hubs should be taken to a machine shop with the facilities to remove the old races and press new ones in.

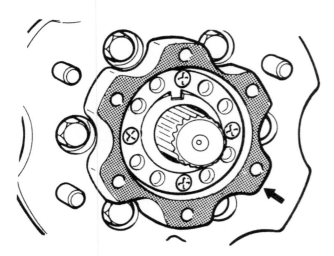

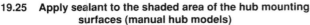

19.25   Apply sealant to the shaded area of the hub mounting surfaces (manual hub models)

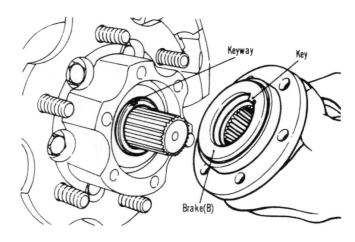

19.26   Make sure the key and keyway are aligned as shown when installing the automatic locking hub

Note that the bearings and races come as matched sets and old bearings should never be installed on new races.

12   Use high-temperature front wheel bearing grease to pack the bearings. Work the grease completely into the bearings, forcing it between the rollers, cone and cage from the back side.

13   Apply a thin coat of grease to the spindle at the outer bearing seat, inner bearing seat, shoulder and seal seat.

14   Put a small quantity of grease behind each bearing race inside the hub. Using your finger, form a dam at these points to provide for extra grease and to keep thinned grease from flowing out of the bearing.

15   Place the grease-packed inner bearing into the rear of the hub and put a little more grease outside of the bearing.

16   Place a new seal over the inner bearing and tap the seal evenly into place with a hammer and block of wood until it's flush with the hub.

17   Apply a thin coat of grease to the seal lip.

Installation and adjustment

18   Slide the hub into place on the wheel spindle (be careful not to damage the seal), then install the outer wheel bearing and adjust the bearing preload as follows:

19   Using the special tool and a torque wrench, tighten the locknut to 94 to 145 ft-lbs while turning the hub by hand.

20   Loosen the locknut to relieve the pressure on the bearing, then retighten it to 18 ft-lbs (25 Nm).

21   On 1983 models (manual free-wheeling hub), back the nut off 30-degrees, then install the lockwasher. If the holes in the lockwasher and locknut do not line up, loosen the locknut (20-degrees maximum). Attach a spring scale to one of the wheel nut studs and pull on the scale to see how much force is required to turn the hub **(see illustration)**. It should take one to four pounds of force. If it doesn't, repeat the locknut tightening procedure. Apply grease to the inner surfaces of the free-wheeling hub assembly and coat the mating surfaces of the hubs with semi-drying gasket sealant, then install the free-wheeling hub and tighten the bolts in a criss-cross pattern. Check the axial play of the driveaxle and make sure it is within the specified range (see the driveaxle installation procedure in Section 20), then install the hub cover assembly with the control handle and clutch in the free position. Tighten the bolts in a criss-cross pattern.

22   On 1984 models, loosen the locknut about 30 to 40 degrees, then check the force required to turn the hub as described in Step 21 (it should be one to four pounds). Install the lockwasher. On models with automatic free-wheeling hubs, adjust the brake contact surface depth by adding or removing shims (see this Chapter's Specifications).

23   On 1985 and later models, loosen the locknut about 30 to 40 degrees, then check the force required to turn the hub as described in Step 21 (it

should be one to four pounds). Check the axial play of the wheel hub as shown in the accompanying illustration (see this Chapter's Specifications), then install the lockwasher. If the holes in the lockwasher and locknut do not line up, loosen the locknut slightly (40-degrees maximum).

24   On 1984 and later models, install the free-wheeling hub assembly.

25   On models with a manual hub, apply grease to the inner surfaces of the free-wheeling hub assembly and coat the mating surfaces of the hubs with semi-drying gasket sealant, then install the free-wheeling hub and tighten the bolts in a criss-cross pattern **(see illustration)**. On 1984 models only, check the axial play of the driveaxle and make sure it is within the specified range (see the driveaxle installation procedure in Section 20). On all models, install the hub cover assembly with the control handle and clutch in the Free position. Tighten the bolts in a criss-cross pattern.

26   On 1984 models with an automatic hub, apply semi-drying gasket sealant to the hub mating surfaces, then align the key of Brake B with the keyway in the spindle as shown in the accompanying illustration and install the hub assembly. Make sure the free-wheeling hub and the wheel hub make contact when light pressure is applied to the free-wheeling hub (if they don't, turn the hub as required). Install the mounting bolts and tighten them in a criss-cross pattern. Install the shim/spacer and snap-ring on the end of the driveaxle. Recheck the hub turning force and compare it to the figure obtained before the free-wheeling hub was installed. The difference should be less than 3.1 pounds – if it isn't, the free-wheeling hub is probably installed incorrectly (remove and reinstall it). Check the driveaxle axial play and compare it to the Specifications at the beginning of this Chapter (see Section 20 for the driveaxle installation procedure).

27   On 1985 and 1986 models with an automatic hub, recheck the hub turning force with a spring scale, then align the key of brake B with the slot in the spindle and install the hub assembly **(see illustration 19.26)**. Make sure the free-wheeling hub and the wheel hub make contact when light pressure is applied to the free-wheeling hub (if they don't, turn the hub as required). Install the mounting bolts and tighten them in a criss-cross pattern, then install the shim and snap-ring on the end of the driveaxle. Recheck the hub turning force and compare it to the figure obtained before the free-wheeling hub was installed. The difference should be less than three pounds – if it isn't, the free-wheeling hub is either assembled or installed incorrectly (remove and reinstall it and/or disassemble and reassemble it). Remove the free-wheeling hub and apply semi-drying gasket sealant to the hub mating surfaces. Then reinstall it and tighten the bolts in a criss-cross pattern.

28   On 1984 through 1986 models with an automatic hub, apply grease to the cover O-ring and attach it to the cover. Install the cover and tighten it securely.

29   On all models, reinstall the brake caliper and wheel and lower the vehicle to the ground.

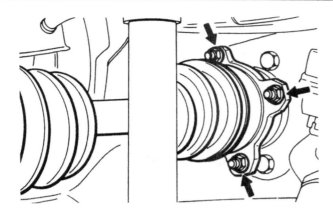

20.6   The right driveaxle is attached to the inner shaft with bolts and nuts (arrows)

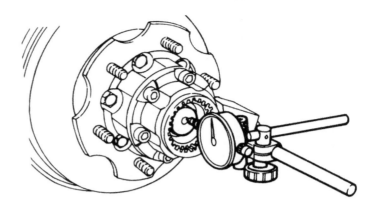

20.12   Check the driveaxle axial (end) play with a dial indicator

21.2   Remove the DOJ outer race circlip with a screwdriver

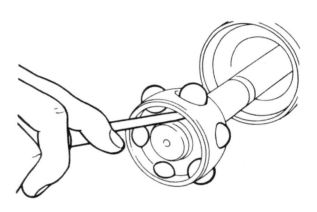

21.4   Raise the balls with a screwdriver to remove them from the cage

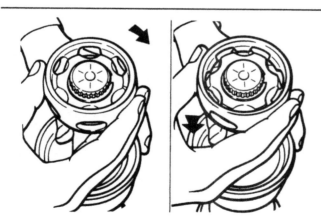

21.5   Turn the cage 30-degrees to disengage it from the inner race, then slide it down the driveaxle shaft

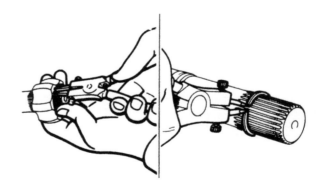

21.6   Remove the snap-ring, the inner race and the circlip from the shaft

20   Front driveaxles (4WD models) – removal and installation

Refer to illustrations 20.6 and 20.12

Removal

1   Raise the front of the vehicle and support it securely with jackstands, then remove the wheels and the brake caliper assemblies (see Chapter 9).

Do not disconnect the hoses from the calipers and do not allow the calipers to hang by the hoses – suspend them with pieces of stiff wire so there is no strain on the hoses.

2   Detach the free-wheeling hub cover assemblies and remove the snap-rings from the end of the driveaxles. Manual hub covers are held in place with several bolts, while automatic hub covers can be unscrewed from the hub (see Section 19).

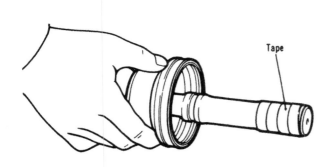

21.7   Wrap the splines with tape to prevent damage to the boot as it is removed

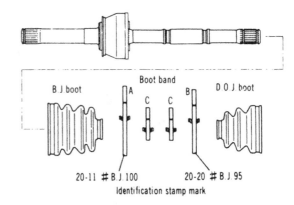

21.14   Boot and band installation details

3   Remove each steering knuckle and front hub assembly as a unit (see Chapter 10).

4   Grasp the inner and outer joints and pull the left driveaxle out of the differential. Be careful not to damage the differential oil seal with the driveaxle inner splines as it is removed.

5   Use a jack to raise the right lower suspension arm, then remove the nuts and detach the shock absorber from the upper mount. **Caution:** *Do not lower the jack until after the shock absorber has been reattached.*

6   Remove the nuts and bolts that attach the right driveaxle flange to the inner shaft **(see illustration)**, then carefully pull out the driveaxle. Remove the circlip from the inner end of the left driveaxle and replace it with a new one.

Installation

7   Attach the right driveaxle to the inner shaft flange, install the bolts and nuts and tighten them to the torque listed in this Chapter's Specifications.

8   Attach the right shock absorber to the upper mount bracket and tighten the nuts.

9   Install the left driveaxle in the differential and seat it by tapping on the outer end with a soft-face hammer.

10   Install each steering knuckle and hub assembly and attach the balljoints, then adjust the driveaxle play as follows:

11   Install the snap-ring on the end of the driveaxle, but do not install the spacer/shim.

12   Mount a dial indicator on the front hub or brake disc and position the stem of the dial indicator against the end of the driveaxle as shown in the accompanying illustration.

13   Move the driveaxle in and out and note the reading on the indicator. This is the axial (end) play. **Note:** *On vehicles with automatic locking hubs, turn the driveaxle in both directions until resistance is felt (this is the center of the turning stroke), then check the driveaxle play with the dial indicator.*

14   If the axial play is not as specified, select a shim/spacer from the sizes available that will produce the correct play.

---

21   Front driveaxle boot replacement and Constant Velocity (CV) joint overhaul (4WD models)

Refer to illustrations 21.2, 21.4, 21.5, 21.6, 21.7, 21.14 and 21.19

Note 1: *If the CV joints exhibit signs of wear indicating need for an overhaul (usually due to torn boots), explore all options before beginning the job. Complete rebuilt driveaxles are available on an exchange basis, which eliminates much time and work. Whichever route you choose to take, check on the cost and availability of parts before disassembling the vehicle.*

Note 2: *Obtain a new rubber boot kit for each joint on the driveaxle before*

beginning disassembly. Do not disassemble the Birfield (outer) joints – if they are worn or damaged, new driveaxles are in order.

1   Remove the boot bands by prying up the ends with a screwdriver or by cutting them off (new bands must be used during reassembly).

2   Use a screwdriver to remove the large circlip from the DOJ outer race **(see illustration)**.

3   Pull the driveaxle out the the DOJ outer race and wipe away as much of the grease as possible.

4   Push the balls in the DOJ cage up with a screwdriver and remove them **(see illustration)**.

5   Separate the cage from the inner race by turning it 30-degrees and sliding it down the driveaxle **(see illustration)**.

6   Remove the snap-ring from the driveaxle with snap-ring pliers, then pull off the inner race and slide the cage off the shaft **(see illustration)**.

7   Remove the circlip and the boots from the driveaxle. Wrap tape around the splines on the DOJ end of the shaft so the boots are not damaged by the splines **(see illustration)**.

8   Remove the dust covers with a large screwdriver.

9   Clean all of the components with solvent, then check the dust covers for damage and wear. Look for water, rust, foreign material and damage in the Birfield joints.

10   Inspect the driveaxle shafts for distortion and worn splines. Check all circlips for distortion and cracks.

11   Check the rubber boots for damage and cracks. **Note:** *Replace the boots with new ones, even if they appear to be in good condition.*

12   Check the cage, inner race, outer race and balls of each DOJ joint for wear and damage.

13   Drive new dust covers onto the joints with a section of pipe and a hammer. For Birfield joints, the pipe must be 2.710-inches in outside diameter with a 0.090-inch wall thickness. For DOJ joints, the pipe must be 2.240-inches in outside diameter with a wall thickness of 0.240-inch.

14   Wrap tape around the driveaxle splines, then install the new boots and bands on the shaft. The Birfield and DOJ boots are different sizes and shapes, so make sure they are correctly positioned on the shaft **(see illustration)**.

15   Slip the DOJ cage onto the shaft, smaller diameter first. Install the circlip and make sure it is seated in the shaft groove, then install the inner race and snap-ring. Make sure the snap-ring is seated in the groove.

16   Apply the specified grease (included with the boot kit) to the DOJ inner race and cage. Slip the cage into place on the inner race and turn it 30-degrees to align the ball races, then install the balls and lubricate them with the grease.

17   Pack the DOJ outer race with 1.8 to 2.8 ounces of the specified grease, then slide it onto the driveaxle while aligning the balls and races.

18   Pack an additional 1.8 to 2.8-ounces of grease into the outer race, behind the inner race and cage, then install the circlip (make sure it is seated in the groove).

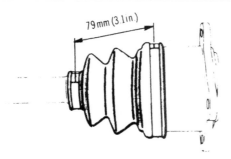

21.19   The DOJ boot dimension must be as shown when the band clamps are installed

19   Slip the boot over the outer race and adjust the joint until the dimension shown in the accompanying illustration is achieved. Slip a screwdriver between the joint and boot to equalize the pressure, then install the band clamps (follow the directions in the boot kit).
20   Pack the grease supplied with the boot kit into the Birfield joint to replace the grease that was wiped off, then install the boot (the clamping instructions are supplied with the boot kit).
21   Repeat the procedure for the remaining driveaxle.

22   Front axle disconnect solenoid and actuator – check and replacemen

Refer to illustration 22.1
1   On some 4WD models, the front axle is engaged into four-wheel drive by a vacuum-operated solenoid valve assembly and actuator which operates a free-wheeling clutch assembly **(see illustration)**.

Check

2   With the engine running, disconnect the hose from the vacuum source and check for strong vacuum.
3   Disconnect the electrical connectors from the solenoid valve assembly and check for 12 volts at the connector's blue-yellow wire. Check for continuity to ground at the yellow-green wire (with four-wheel drive engaged).
4   With the solenoid valves disconnected, check the resistance across the solenoid terminals. The resistance should be 36 to 46 ohms at 60-degrees F. If not within these specifications, replace the solenoid valve assembly.
5   Turn off the engine and check the vacuum hoses and pipes from the solenoid valve assembly to the actuator for kinks, cracks, or other damage.
6   Disconnect the vacuum hoses at the actuator and, with a hand vacuum pump, apply vacuum to one side and then the other of the actuator (be sure to cap the other side when applying vacuum). The actuator should shift the free-wheeling clutch in and out. If it doesn't, replace the actuator.

Replacement

7   To replace the solenoid valve assembly, remove the vacuum hoses and electrical connectors from the solenoid valves.
8   Remove the fasteners and replace the solenoid valve assembly.
9   To replace the actuator, remove the vacuum hoses and pin connecting the shift rod to the actuator.
10   Remove the fasteners and replace the actuator assembly.

22.1 The front axle disconnect solenoid, actuator and free-wheeling clutch assembly used on some later 4WD models

1   Vacuum hoses
2   Check valve
3   Solenoid valve electrical connectors
4   Solenoid valve assembly
5   Vacuum pipe assembly
6   Vacuum tank
7   Pin
8   Actuator assembly
9   Differential mounting bracket
10   Housing tube
11   Free-wheeling engage switch
12   Gasket
13   Free-wheeling clutch assembly
14   Front differential carrier assembly

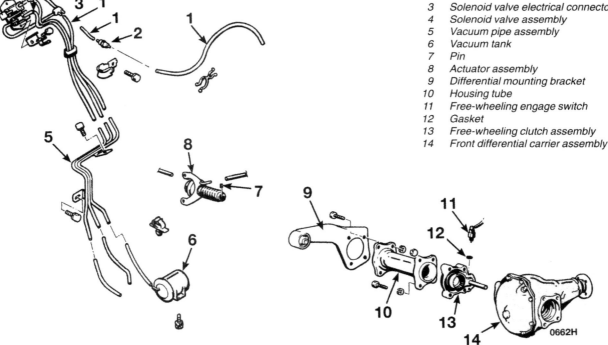

Chapter 9   Brakes

Contents

Specifications

General

Brake fluid type	See Chapter 1
Brake booster pushrod protrusion	
1987 and earlier	0.004 to 0.020 inch
1988 on	0.028 to 0.043 inch

Disc brakes

Minimum brake pad thickness	See Chapter 1
Disc minimum thickness*	
1986 and earlier	0.72 inch
1987 on	0.803 inch
Disc runout	0.006 inch

* Refer to the marks stamped on the disc (they supercede information printed here)

Drum brakes

Minimum brake shoe lining thickness	See Chapter 1
Brake drums	
Standard drum diameter	
2WD models	9.49 inch
4WD models	10.0 inch
Maximum drum diameter*	
2WD models	9.57 inch
4WD models	10.08 inch
Brake shoe return spring free length (duo-servo brakes)	
Primary (green)	4.35 inch
Secondary (grey)	4.23 inch

* Refer to the marks stamped on the drum (they supercede information printed here)

Torque specifications

Ft-lbs (unless otherwise indicated)

Brake caliper mounting bolts
    Sliding caliper . . . .   51 to 65
    Floating caliper
        Upper mounting bolt . . . .   29 to 36
        Lower mounting bolt . . . .   23 to 30
Caliper mounting bracket bolts
    2WD models . . . .   51 to 65
    4WD models . . . .   58 to 72
Caliper inlet fitting . . . .   120 to 144 in-lbs
Disc-to-hub bolts
    2WD   36
    4WD . . . .   36 to 44
Wheel cylinder mounting bolts . . . .   13 to 15
Master cylinder mounting nuts . . . .   72 to 108 in-lbs
Power brake booster mounting nuts . . . .   72 to 108 in-lbs
Wheel lug nuts . . . .   See Chapter 1

1   General information

The vehicles covered by this manual are equipped with hydraulically operated front and rear brake systems. The front brakes are disc-type. Earlier models use a sliding caliper while later models use a floating caliper.

The rear brakes on all models are drum-type. Earlier models use a duo-servo type rear brake while later models are equipped with leading/trailing type.

These models are equipped with a dual master cylinder which allows the operation of half of the system if the other half fails. This system also incorporates a blend proportioning valve which limits pressure to the rear brakes under heavy braking to prevent rear wheel lock-up. Later models have a Load Sensing Proportioning Valve (LSPV) mounted to the frame and connected to the rear axle by a link.

All models are equipped with a power brake booster which utilizes engine vacuum to assist in application of the brakes. The parking brake operates the rear brakes only, through cable actuation.

There are some notes and cautions involving the brake system on this vehicle:

  a) Use only DOT 3 brake fluid in this system.
  b) The brake pads and linings contain asbestos fibers which are hazardous to your health if inhaled. Whenever you work on the brake system components, carefully clean all parts with brake cleaner. Do not allow the fine asbestos dust to become airborne.
  c) Safety should be paramount whenever any servicing of the brake components is performed. Do not use parts or fasteners which are not in perfect condition, and be sure that all clearances and torque specifications are adhered to. If you are at all unsure about a certain procedure, seek professional advice. Upon completion of any brake system work, test the brakes carefully in a controlled area before putting the vehicle into normal service. If a problem is suspected in the brake system, do not drive the vehicle until the fault is corrected.
  d) Tires, load and front end alignment are factors which also affect braking performance.

2   Disc brake pads – replacement

Warning: *Disc brake pads must be replaced on both front wheels at the same time – never replace the pads on only one wheel. Also, the dust created by the brake system may contain asbestos, which is harmful to your health. Never blow it out with compressed air and don't inhale any of it. An approved filtering mask should be worn when working on the brakes. Do not, under any circumstances, use petroleum-based solvents to clean brake parts. Use brake cleaner or denatured alcohol only!*

Note 1: *When servicing the disc brakes, use only high-quality, nationally recognized name brand pads.*

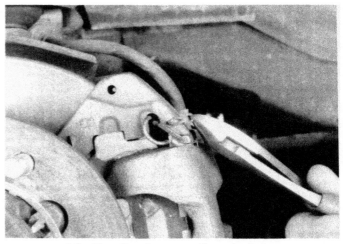

2.3   Use pliers to remove the spigot pins

Note 2: *The vehicles covered by this manual are equipped with either sliding or floating calipers. To determine which type of caliper your vehicle has, look at the caliper with the wheel removed. If there are spigot pins like the one shown in illustration 2.3, you have sliding calipers. If there are no spigot pins, you have floating calipers.*

Note 3: *This procedure applies to both front and rear disc brakes.*

1   Remove the master cylinder reservoir cap and siphon out approximately half of the fluid into a container. Be careful not to spill fluid onto any of the painted surfaces – it will damage the paint.

2   Loosen the front wheel lug nuts, raise the front of the vehicle and support it securely on jackstands. Remove the wheels. Work on one brake assembly at a time, using the assembled brake for reference if necessary.

Sliding caliper

Refer to illustrations 2.3, 2.4a, 2.4b, 2.4c, 2.5a, 2.5b, 2.6 and 2.9

3   Remove the two spigot pins from the stopper plugs **(see illustration)**. Each caliper has two stopper plugs and each plug has two spigot pins.

4   Pull the stopper plugs and pad support plates out from the caliper **(see illustrations)**. Move the caliper assembly up-and-down to separate it from the caliper mounting bracket as you pull it off the bracket **(see illustration)**. If the caliper bracket interferes with the brake line, remove the upper bolt. Hang the caliper out of the way on a piece of wire.

5   Remove the pads from the caliper bracket **(see illustration)**. Separate the shim from the outer pad. Remove the inner and outer pad clips and the pad clips labeled "B" from the caliper mounting bracket **(see illustration)**.

6   With the shim installed on the outer pad, slip the new pads into place **(see illustration)**.

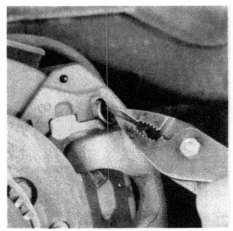

2.4a Pull the stopper plug out with
pliers, followed by . . .

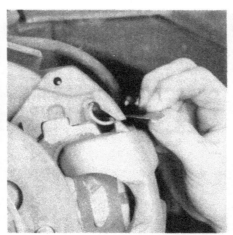

2.4b . . . the pad support plate

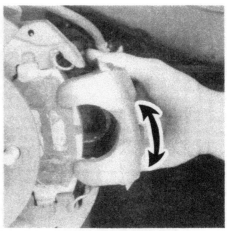

2.4c Work the caliper up-and-down
while pulling it off the brake bracket

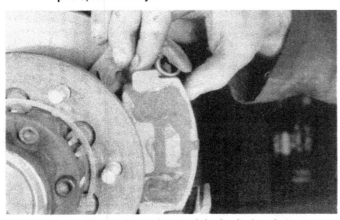

2.5a Rotate the pads out of the brake bracket

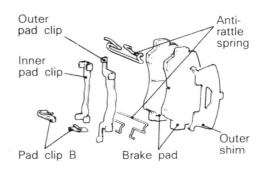

Outer
pad clip
Inner
pad clip
Pad clip B   Brake pad
Anti-
rattle
spring
Outer
shim

2.5b Typical brake pad components

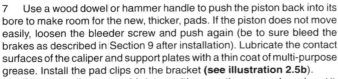

2.6 It's a good idea to apply a coat of brake anti-squeal
compound to the backs of the shims

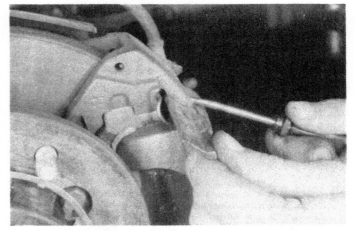

2.9 Pry the caliper up with a screwdriver and then insert the
stopper plate

7   Use a wood dowel or hammer handle to push the piston back into its bore to make room for the new, thicker, pads. If the piston does not move easily, loosen the bleeder screw and push again (be to sure bleed the brakes as described in Section 9 after installation). Lubricate the contact surfaces of the caliper and support plates with a thin coat of multi-purpose grease. Install the pad clips on the bracket (see illustration 2.5b).
8   Slide the caliper assembly into position over the new pads and seat it on the mounting bracket. If removed, install and tighten the upper caliper bracket bolt.

9   Install the pad support plates, stopper plugs and spigot pins (see illustration). Repeat the procedure on the other wheel.

Floating caliper
Refer to illustrations 2.10, 2.11a, 2.11b, 2.12, 2.13a and 2.13b
Note: *Some 1992 and later models are equipped with dual-piston calipers on the front wheels. Although the photographs in this procedure show pad replacement on a single-piston caliper, the procedure is the same for dual-piston calipers.*
10   Using a large C-clamp, bottom the piston back into the caliper bore.

2.10   Use a C-clamp to bottom the piston in the bore

2.11a   Unscrew the caliper bolt with a box-end wrench or socket so the bolt head will not be rounded off

2.11b   Rotate the caliper up for access to the pads

2.12   Slide the pads away from the disc, out of the caliper bracket

2.13a   Remove the lower . . .

2.13b   . . . and upper pad retaining clips from the bracket

The frame end of the C-clamp should be positioned on the backside of the caliper body and the screw should bear on the outer brake pad **(see illustration)**.

11   Remove the caliper lower mounting bolt and rotate the caliper up to allow removal of the pads **(see illustrations)**.

12   Remove the anti-rattle springs (if equipped) and pull the brake pads and shims from the caliper bracket **(see illustration)**.

13   Remove the retaining clips from the bracket **(see illustrations)**.

14   Clean the mounting surfaces of the caliper and bracket, removing any dirt or corrosion. Install new retaining clips in the bracket.

15   Coat the shims with disc brake grease and install the pads and shims into the caliper bracket. Install the anti-rattle springs (if equipped).

16   Install the wear indicator (if equipped), then swing the caliper down over the pads. Install the lower mounting bolt, tightening it to the torque

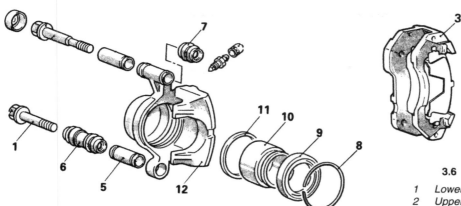

3.6   Floating caliper – exploded view

1	Lower mounting bolt	7	Dust boot
2	Upper mounting bolt	8	Boot ring
3	Caliper support	9	Piston boot
4	Sleeve	10	Piston
5	Sleeve	11	Piston seal
6	Dust boot		

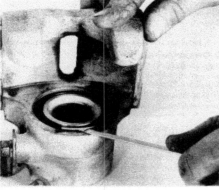
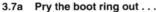

3.7a   Pry the boot ring out . . .

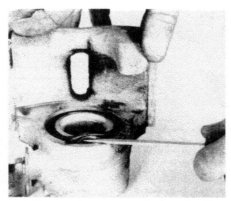

3.7b   . . . then remove the boot itself

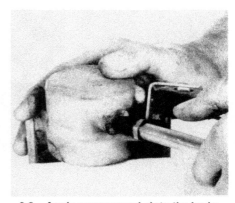

3.8   Apply compressed air to the brake fluid hose connection in the caliper body – position a wood block between the piston and the caliper to prevent damage

listed in this Chapter's Specifications.

17   Repeat the procedure on the other wheel.

All models

18   Install the wheels and lower the vehicle. Firmly depress the brake pedal a few times to bring the pads into contact with the disc. Check the fluid level in the master cylinder, topping it up if necessary.

19   Road test the vehicle carefully before placing it into normal use.

3   Disc brake caliper – removal, overhaul and installation

Warning: *Dust created by the brake system may contain asbestos, which is harmful to your health. Never blow it out with compressed air and don't inhale any of it. An approved filtering mask should be worn when working on the brakes. Do not, under any circumstances, use petroleum-based solvents to clean brake parts. Use brake cleaner or denatured alcohol only!*

Note: *If an overhaul is indicated (usually because of fluid leakage), explore all options before beginning the job. New and factory rebuilt calipers are available on an exchange basis, which makes this job quite easy. If it's decided to rebuild the calipers, make sure that a rebuild kit is available before proceeding. Always rebuild the calipers in pairs – never rebuild just one of them.*

Removal

1   Remove the cap from the brake fluid reservoir, siphon off two-thirds of the fluid into a container and discard it.

2   Loosen the wheel lug nuts, raise the front of the vehicle and support it securely on jackstands. Remove the wheels.

3   Remove the brake hose inlet fitting bolt and detach the hose. Have a rag handy to catch spilled fluid and wrap a plastic bag tightly around the end of the hose to prevent fluid loss and contamination.

4   Remove the caliper (see Section 2). On floating calipers, remove the upper mounting bolt, then detach the caliper from the bracket.

Overhaul

Refer to illustrations 3.6, 3.7a, 3.7b and 3.8

5   Clean the exterior of the caliper with brake cleaner or denatured alcohol. Never use gasoline, kerosene or petroleum-based cleaning solvents. Place the caliper on a clean workbench.

6   On floating calipers, remove the sleeves and dust boots **(see illustration)**. **Note:** *On later models with four-wheel disc brakes, the front disc brakes are floating, dual-piston calipers. The overhaul procedure for the dual-piston caliper is the same as for the single-piston caliper; simply repeat the procedure for each piston. In Step 8, since only one piston will be ejected at a time, block the first-ejected piston loosely back in place while you apply air pressure again to eject the second piston.*

7   Using a small screwdriver, pry the piston boot ring from the caliper. Then pry out the boot **(see illustrations)**.

8   Position a wooden block or several shop rags in the caliper as a cushion, then use compressed air to remove the piston from the caliper **(see illustration)**. Use only enough air pressure to ease the piston out of the

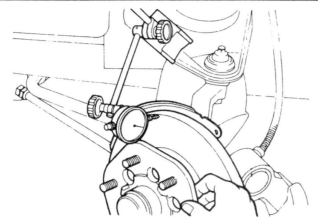

4.4a   Check the disc runout with a dial indicator positioned approximately 1/2-inch form the edge of the disc – if the reading exceeds the maximum allowable runout, the disc will have to be resurfaced or replaced

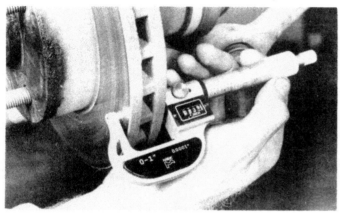

4.5   Use a micrometer to measure the thickness of the disc

bore. If the piston is blown out, even with the cushion in place, it may be damaged. **Warning:** *Never place your fingers in front of the piston in an attempt to catch or protect it when applying compressed air, as serious injury could occur.*

9   Using a wood or plastic tool, remove the piston seal from the groove in the caliper bore. Metal tools may cause bore damage.

10   Clean all components in brake cleaner or clean brake fluid and blow dry with compressed air. Check the cylinder bore and pistons for signs of wear, corrosion or surface defects such as scoring and replace if necessary.

11   The dust seal and piston seal must always be replaced when the caliper is overhauled.

12   To reassemble the caliper, lubricate the piston seal and piston with brake lube (usually supplied with the overhaul kit) or brake fluid, install it in the groove in the caliper bore, then lubricate the seal and the bore.

13   Carefully insert the piston into the caliper using only finger pressure.

14   Apply brake lube to the piston and then install the boot in the piston and caliper. Insert the boot ring into the boot.

15   On floating calipers, apply brake lube into the sleeve and dust boots **(see illustration 3.6)**. Then install the sleeve dust boot to the caliper and insert the sleeve into the dust boot. Apply brake lube into the upper mounting bolt hole and then install the dust boot to the caliper.

Installation

16   On sliding calipers, refer to Steps 8 and 9, Section 2 for the installation procedure.

17   On floating calipers, install the upper mounting bolt, swing the caliper down into position and tighten the upper mounting bolt and lower mounting bolt to the torque listed in the Specifications Section at the beginning of this Chapter.

4.4b   Using a swirling motion, remove the glaze from the disc with emery cloth

18   Install the flexible brake hose to the caliper. Be sure the hose does not interfere with any suspension or steering components.

19   Install the wheel and tire.

20   Bleed the brake system (see Section 9).

21   Lower the vehicle to the ground. Test the brakes carefully before placing the vehicle into normal operation.

---

4   Brake disc – inspection, removal and installation

Refer to illustrations 4.4a, 4.4b, 4.5 and 4.7

Note: *The following procedure applies to both front and rear disc brakes.*

Inspection

1   Loosen the wheel lug nuts, raise the vehicle and support it securely on jackstands. Remove the wheel. On rear disc brakes, reverse and install two wheel lugs nuts to hold the disc securely in place.

2   Remove the brake caliper as outlined in Sections 2 and 3. It's not necessary to disconnect the brake hose. After removing the caliper, suspend the caliper out of the way with a piece of wire from the underbody. Don't let the caliper hang by the hose and don't stretch or twist the hose.

3   Visually check the disc surface for score marks and other damage. Light scratches and shallow grooves are normal after use and may not always be detrimental to brake operation, but deep score marks – over 0.015-inch (0.38 mm) – require disc removal and refinishing by an automotive machine shop. Be sure to check both sides of the disc. If pulsating has been noticed during application of the brakes, suspect excessive disc runout.

4   To check disc runout, place a dial indicator at a point about 1/2-inch from the outer edge of the disc **(see illustration)**. Set the indicator to zero and turn the disc. The indicator reading should not exceed the limit listed in this Chapter's Specifications. If it does, the disc should be refinished by an automotive machine shop. **Note:** *Professionals recommend resurfacing of brake discs regardless of the dial indicator reading (to produce a smooth, flat surface, that will eliminate brake pedal pulsations and other undesirable symptoms related to questionable discs).* At the very least, if you elect not to have the discs resurfaced, deglaze the brake pad surface with medium-grit emery cloth (use a swirling motion to ensure a non-directional finish) **(see illustration)**.

5   The disc must not be machined to a thickness less than the specified minimum thickness. The minimum thickness is cast into the inside of the disc. The disc thickness can be checked with a micrometer **(see illustration)**.

Removal

6   Remove the caliper mounting bracket bolts and lift the bracket off.

7   On front disc brakes, remove the front hub/disc assembly, referring to Chapter 1 for 2WD models or Chapter 8 for 4WD models. Unbolt the disc from the hub **(see illustration)**. On rear disc brakes, remove the retaining screws (if installed) and/or the lug nuts previously installed and lift off the disc.

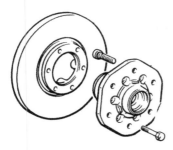

4.7   Remove the bolts from the disc/hub assembly, then separate the two components (it may be necessary to tap the disc off with a hammer and a block of wood)

Installation

8   On front disc brakes, install the disc to the hub, tightening the bolts to the torque listed in this Chapter's Specifications in a criss-cross pattern.

9   On front disc brakes, install the front disc and hub assembly and adjust the wheel bearing (see Chapter 1 [2WD] or Chapter 8 [4WD]).

10   On rear–disc brakes, slide the disc dack back into place. It's not necessary to reinstall the retaining screw.

11   Install the caliper mounting bracket, tightening the mounting bolts to the torques listed in this Chapter's Specifications. Position the pads in the bracket and install the caliper (refer to Section 3 for the caliper installation procedure, if necessary). Tighten the caliper bolts to the torque listed in this Chapter's Specifications.

12   Install the wheel, then lower the vehicle to the ground. Depress the brake pedal a few times to bring the brake pads into contact with the disc. Bleeding of the system will not be necessary unless the brake hose was disconnected from the caliper. Check the operation of the brakes carefully before placing the vehicle into normal service.

---

5   Drum brake shoes – replacement

Refer to illustrations 5.2a and 5.2b

Warning: *Drum brake shoes must be replaced on both rear wheels at the same time – never replace the shoes on only one wheel. Also, the dust created by the brake system may contain asbestos, which is harmful to your health. Never blow it out with compressed air and don't inhale any of it. An approved filtering mask should be worn when working on the brakes. Do not, under any circumstances, use petroleum-based solvents to clean brake parts. Use brake cleaner or denatured alcohol only!*

Caution: *Whenever the brake shoes are replaced, the retractor and hold-down springs should also be replaced. Due to the continuous heating/cooling cycle that the springs are subjected to, they lose their tension over a period of time and may allow the shoes to drag on the drum and wear at a much faster rate than normal. When replacing the brake shoes, use only high-quality nationally recognized brand-name parts.*

Note: *The brakes on your vehicle are either duo-servo or leading/trailing type. If you're not sure which type your vehicle has, study the brake assembly with the drum removed and compare it to illustrations 5.4a and 5.28.*

1   Loosen the wheel lug nuts, raise the vehicle and support it securely on jackstands. Remove the wheel(s).

2   Pull off the brake drum. If you have difficulty removing it, screw an 8 mm bolt into each of the two threaded holes in the drum **(see illustration)**. Tighten each bolt one-half turn at a time to back the drum off the axle flange. It may be necessary to retract the brake shoes away from the inside of the drum. This is accomplished by removing the rubber plug in the backing plate and turning the adjuster star wheel with a screwdriver until the shoes no longer contact the drum **(see illustration)**.

3   Before removing anything, clean the brake assembly with brake cleaner – DO NOT use compressed air to blow the dust from the brake assembly! Take a long, close look at the relationship between the parts before disassembling the brake assembly.

5.2a   Thread two bolts into the brake drum to draw it off the axle flange

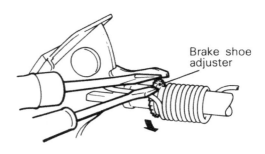

Brake shoe adjuster

5.2b   Use one screwdriver to hold the adjuster lever out of the way and turn the starwheel with a second screwdriver

---

Duo-servo type

Refer to illustrations 5.4a, 5.4b, 5.4c, 5.5a, 5.5b, 5.7, 5.12, 5.15, 5.16, 5.18 and 5.21

4   Disengage the brake return springs from the pivot and remove the forward spring **(see illustrations)**.

5   Disengage the adjuster cable from the pivot **(see illustration)** and remove the rear brake return spring and cable guide **(see illustration)**.

6   Disengage the adjuster cable from the auto-adjuster lever.

7   Spread the parking brake lever pivot retaining clip and remove the clip and wave washer from the pivot **(see illustration)**.

8   Remove the brake shoe hold-down cups, springs and pins by pressing in on the cup and rotating it 90-degrees. A special, inexpensive tool is available at auto parts stores for this purpose, but a pair of pliers will suffice.

9   Remove the front brake shoe by disengaging it from the adjuster spring and adjuster.

10   Separate the parking brake lever from the rear brake shoe and slide out the parking brake strut and spring.

11   Remove the adjuster lever from the rear brake shoe.

12   Check the brake return springs for cracks and other damage. Check adjuster lever and the adjusting latch for wear and damage. Make sure the star wheel can be screwed into and out of the adjuster. Clean the star wheel threads and lubricate them with high-temperature grease if any resistance is felt. Measure the adjusting cable length and compare this measurement to the specifications **(see illustration)**.

13   Check the wheel cylinders for signs of brake fluid leakage, repairing them or replacing them if necessary (see Section 6).

14   Check the drum inside diameter and compare the measurement to the one cast into the drum. Inspect the drum for hard spots, cracks, score marks and grooves. Hard spots will appear as small discolored areas. If they can't be removed with emery cloth or if any of the other conditions

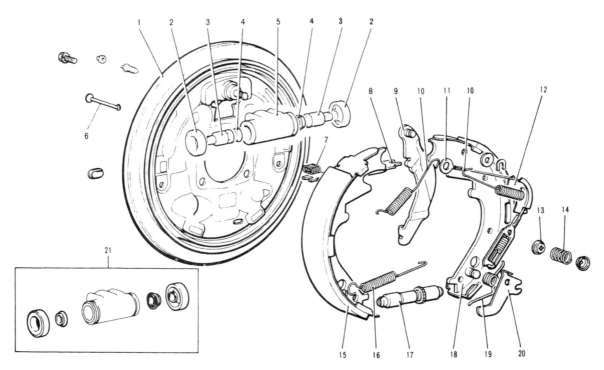

5.4a   Duo-servo type drum brake – exploded view

1	Backing plate	7	Anti-rattle spring	12	Cable guide
2	Wheel cylinder boot	8	Parking brake strut	13	Hold-down cup
3	Wheel cylinder piston	9	Parking brake lever	14	Hold-down spring
4	Wheel cylinder cup	10	Shoe return spring	15	Primary shoe
5	Wheel cylinder	11	Adjuster cable	16	Adjuster spring
6	Hold-down pin				

17	Adjuster assembly
18	Secondary shoe
19	Adjuster spring
20	Auto adjuster lever
21	Wheel cylinder repair kit

5.4b   Use pliers or a special tool to disengage the rear return spring from the pivot

5.4c   Remove the forward spring with adjustable pliers

5.5a   Remove the adjuster cable from the pivot

listed above exist, the drum must be taken to an automotive machine shop to have it turned (machined on a lathe). **Note:** *Professional mechanics recommend resurfacing the drums whenever a brake job is performed. Resurfacing will eliminate the possibility of out-of-round drums.*

15   Inspect the backing plate ledges for grooves **(see illustration)**. If the grooves are not too deep, they can be removed by filing or sanding the backing plate. If the grooves are too deep, the backing plate must be replaced or the brake shoes will hang up in the grooves.

16   Check the free length of the primary (green) and secondary (grey) brake shoe return springs **(see illustration)** and compare this measure-

ment to the one in the Specifications Section at the beginning of this Chapter. Replace any springs that are stretched with new ones.

17   Install the adjuster spring and lever onto the rear brake shoe.

18   Place the parking brake strut into position with the spring on the forward end **(see illustration)**. Note that the parking brake struts will be stamped 'R' for the right side of the vehicle and 'L' for the left side of the vehicle.

19   Install the parking brake lever into the hole at the top of the rear brake shoe. Slip the waved washer and a new retaining clip onto the pivot. Bend the ends of the clip with pliers so the clip fits tightly on the pivot.

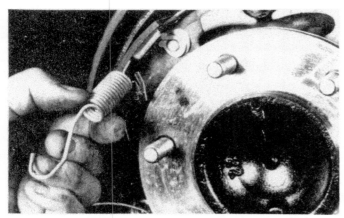

5.5b   Detach the rear return spring and cable guide

5.7   Use pliers to spread the parking brake lever pivot clip, then remove the clip and wave washer

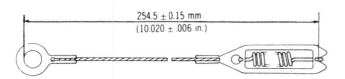

5.12   Measure the adjusting cable to make sure it hasn't stretched

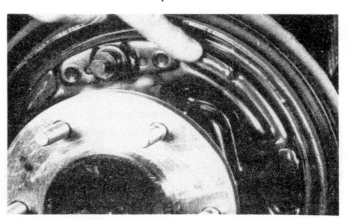

5.15   Check the backing plate for grooves like this – if they're deep, the backing plate will have to be replaced

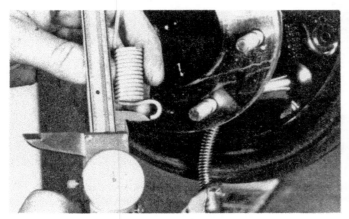

5.16   Measure the return springs to make sure they aren't stretched

5.18   Place the parking brake strut into position with the spring on the forward end (left side struts are stamped 'L' and right side 'R')

20   Install the auto adjuster assembly and spring into position between the lower ends of the brake shoes. Make sure that the auto adjuster mechanism is properly installed or it will not operate.

21   Lubricate the backing plate shoe contact points with multi-purpose grease **(see illustration)** and place the brake shoes into position on the backing plate, making sure they are properly aligned with the wheel cylinder. Do not damage the wheel cylinder boots. Engage the parking brake lever.

22   Install the brake shoe hold-down pins, springs and cups.

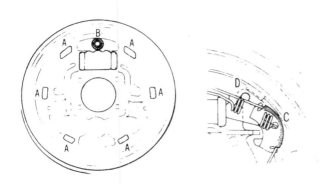

5.21   Lubricate the backing plate and adjuster cable at the points shown

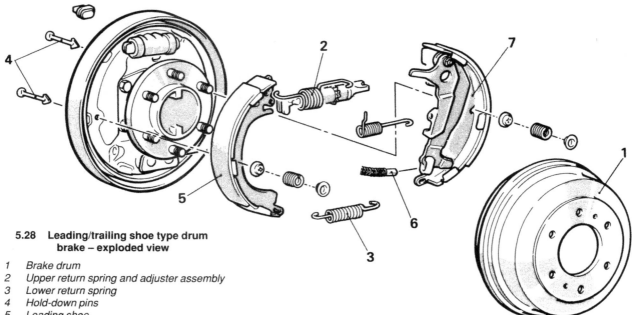

5.28 Leading/trailing shoe type drum brake – exploded view

1   Brake drum
2   Upper return spring and adjuster assembly
3   Lower return spring
4   Hold-down pins
5   Leading shoe
6   Parking brake cable
7   Trailing shoe and adjuster lever assembly

5.29   Use pliers or a special tool like this one to remove the hold-down springs

5.30   Rotate the leading shoe down and unhook the return spring

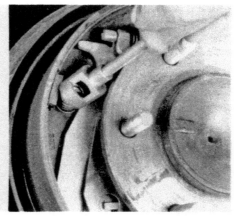

5.31a   Remove the trailing shoe hold-down spring . . .

23   Hook the adjuster cable into the hole on the auto adjuster lever. Place the cable guide into position on the rear brake shoe and insert the shoe end of the return spring into the hole in the shoe.

24   Lift up on the end of the auto adjuster lever and place the adjusting cable eyelet over the brake shoe pivot at the top of the backing plate.

25   Place the end of the rear return spring over the pivot, then install the forward return spring.

26   Double-check to make sure all the springs and cables are properly installed. Operate the adjuster mechanism by pulling the adjusting cable toward the edge of the backing plate. The adjuster lever should ratchet over the adjusting wheel and engage the next tooth when the cable is pulled.

27   Turn the brake adjuster star wheel by hand until the brake drum will just fit over it, then install the drum. Install the wheels and lower the vehicle to the ground.

Leading/trailing type

Refer to illustrations 5.28, 5.29, 5.30, 5.31a, 5.31b, 5.31c, 5.36, 5.38, 5.39, 5.40a and 5.40b

28   Use pliers to detach the upper return spring **(see illustration)**.

29   Remove the leading brake shoe hold-down spring and pin **(see illustration)**. This is accomplished by grasping the spring cup with a special tool or a pair of pliers, pushing down and rotating it 90-degrees, disengaging it from the pin. Place a finger behind the pin to prevent it from being pushed out.

30   Remove the leading brake shoe and disconnect the lower spring **(see illustration)**.

31   Remove the trailing shoe hold-down spring and pin, remove the shoe, disconnect the parking brake cable from the adjuster lever and remove the shoe **(see illustrations)**.

32   Detach the adjuster assembly from the shoe.

33   Check the wheel cylinders for signs of leaking fluid, replacing or rebuilding them if necessary (see Section 6).

34   Check the brake drum for hard spots, cracks, score marks and grooves. Hard spots will appear as small discolored areas. If they can't be removed with emery cloth or if any of the other conditions listed above exist, the drum must be taken to an automotive machine shop to have it turned (machined on a lathe). **Note:** *Professional mechanics recommend resurfacing the drums whenever a brake job is performed. Resurfacing will eliminate the possibility of out-of-round drums.*

5.31b ...rotate the trailing shoe and adjuster assembly down ...

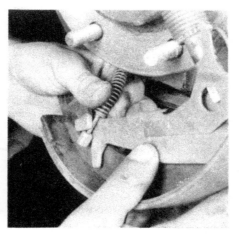

5.31c ...then unhook the parking brake cable

5.36 Lubricate the contact surfaces of the backing plate

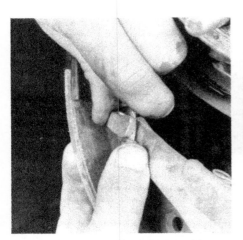

5.38 Hook the parking brake cable to the adjuster lever

5.39 Connect the leading shoe to the lower return spring and rotate the shoe up into position

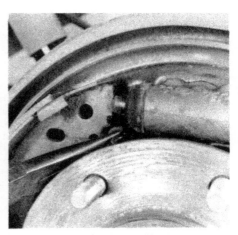

5.40a Use needle-nose pliers to connect the upper return spring

35 Unscrew the brake adjuster, clean it and apply a little high-temperature grease to the adjuster screw threads. Assemble the adjuster screw, turning it in completely.

36 Lubricate the contact surfaces of the backing plate and wheel cylinder clevis with high-temperature grease **(see illustration)**. Be careful not to get any grease on the brake shoe surfaces.

37 Install the adjuster assembly to the trailing shoe.

38 Connect the parking brake cable to the lever and position the shoe against the backing plate **(see illustration)**. Install the hold-down pin and spring.

39 Connect the leading shoe to the lower spring and rotate it up into position **(see illustration)**. Install the hold-down pin and spring.

40 Install the upper return spring **(see illustrations)**.

41 Wiggle the brake shoe assembly to center it on the backing plate. Make sure the tops of the shoes are seated in the slots of the wheel cylinder clevis' and the bottoms of the shoes are resting under the tabs of the anchor plate.

42 Adjust the brakes by turning the star wheel on the adjuster assembly until the drum will just fit over the shoe assembly. Install the drum and wheel. Don't forget to tighten the lug nuts to the torque specified in Chapter 1. Repeat the operation on the other wheel, then road test the vehicle carefully before placing it into normal service.

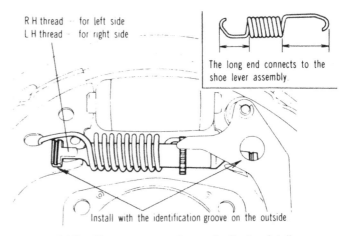

R H thread – for left side
L H thread – for right side

The long end connects to the shoe lever assembly.

Install with the identification groove on the outside

5.40b Upper return spring and adjuster details

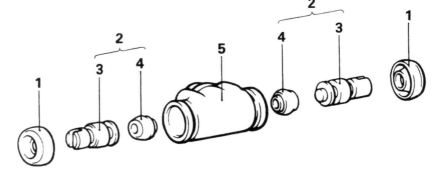

6.7 **Wheel cylinder – exploded view**

1   *Boots*
2   *Piston assemblies*
3   *Pistons*
4   *Piston cups*
5   *Wheel cylinder body*

---

6   Wheel cylinder – removal, overhaul and installation

Refer to illustration 6.7
Note: *If an overhaul is indicated (usually because of fluid leakage or sticky operation), explore all options before beginning the job. New wheel cylinders are available, which make this job quite easy. If it's decided to rebuild the wheel cylinder, make sure that a rebuild kit is available before proceeding. Never overhaul only one wheel cylinder – always rebuild both of them at the same time.*

Removal

1   Raise the rear of the vehicle and support it securely on jackstands. Block the front wheels to keep the vehicle from rolling.
2   Remove the brake shoe assembly (see Section 5).
3   Remove all dirt and foreign material from around the wheel cylinder.
4   Disconnect the brake line using a flare-nut wrench. Don't pull the brake line away from the wheel cylinder.
5   Remove the wheel cylinder mounting bolts.
6   Detach the wheel cylinder from the brake backing plate and place it on a clean workbench. Immediately plug the brake line to prevent fluid loss and contamination.

Overhaul

7   Remove the bleeder screw, piston cups, pistons, boots and piston assemblies from the wheel cylinder body **(see illustration)**.
8   Clean the wheel cylinder with brake fluid, denatured alcohol or brake system cleaner. **Warning:** *Do not, under any circumstances, use petroleum-based solvents to clean brake parts!*
9   Use compressed air to remove excess fluid from the wheel cylinder and to blow out the passages.
10   Check the cylinder bore for corrosion and score marks. Crocus cloth can be used to remove light corrosion and stains, but the cylinder must be replaced with a new one if the defects cannot be removed easily, or if the bore is scored.
11   Lubricate the new piston cups with brake fluid.
12   Assemble the brake cylinder components. Make sure the lips on the piston cups face in.

Installation

13   Place the wheel cylinder in position and install the bolts.
14   Connect the brake line and install the brake shoe assembly.
15   Bleed the brakes (see Section 9).

---

7   Master cylinder – removal, overhaul and installation

Refer to illustrations 7.11a and 7.11b
Note: *Before deciding to overhaul the master cylinder, check on the availability and cost of a new or factory rebuilt unit and also the availability of a rebuild kit.*

Removal

1   The master cylinder is located in the engine compartment, mounted to the power brake booster.
2   Remove as much fluid as you can from the reservoir with a syringe.
3   Place rags under the fluid fittings and prepare caps or plastic bags to cover the ends of the lines once they are disconnected. **Caution:** *Brake fluid will damage paint. Cover all body parts and be careful not to spill fluid during this procedure.*
4   Loosen the tube nuts at the ends of the brake lines where they enter the master cylinder. To prevent rounding off the flats on these nuts, the use of a flare-nut wrench, which wraps around the nut, is preferred.
5   Pull the brake lines slightly away from the master cylinder and plug the ends to prevent contamination. On models with a remotely mounted fluid reservoir, disconnect the fluid hoses from the master cylinder and plug the ends to prevent fluid loss.
6   Remove the mounting nuts and pull the master cylinder off the studs and out of the engine compartment. Again, be careful not to spill the fluid as this is done.

Overhaul

7   Before attempting the overhaul of the master cylinder, obtain the proper rebuild kit, which will contain the necessary replacement parts and also any instructions which may be specific to your model.
8   Inspect the reservoir or inlet grommet(s) for indications of leakage near the base of the reservoir. If the reservoir is attached to the master cylinder, remove the mounting screw(s) and remove the reservoir.
9   Place the cylinder in a vise and use a punch or Phillips screwdriver to fully depress the pistons until they bottom against the other end of the master cylinder. Hold the pistons in this position and remove the stop bolt(s) on the side of the master cylinder. Remove the two check valves or connector block and the copper gaskets.
10   Depress the pistons once again, then carefully remove the snap-ring at the end of the master cylinder. Snap-ring pliers are needed on later models.
11   The internal components can now be removed from the cylinder bore **(see illustrations)**. Make a note of the proper order of the components so they can be returned to their original locations. Also note which direction the lip of each seal faces so the new seals can be installed the same way. **Note:** *The two springs are of different tension, so pay particular attention to their order.*
12   Carefully inspect the bore of the master cylinder. Any deep scoring or other damage will mean a new master cylinder is required.
13   Replace all parts included in the rebuild kit, following any instructions in the kit. Clean all reused parts with clean brake fluid or denatured alcohol. Do not use any petroleum-based cleaners. During assembly, lubricate all parts liberally with clean brake fluid. Be sure to tighten all fittings and connections securely.
14   Push the assembled components into the bore, compressing them with the screwdriver or punch and install the stop bolt(s).
15   Compress the piston assemblies and install the new snap-ring, making sure it is seated properly in the groove.

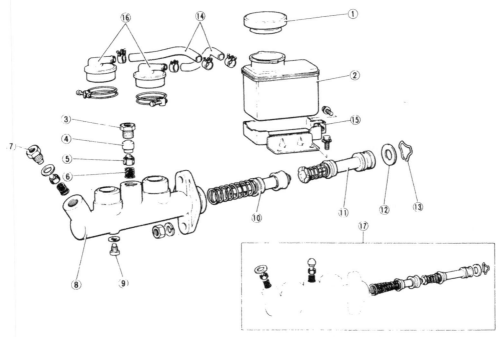

7.11a   Typical earlier model master cylinder – exploded view

1	Reservoir cap	5	Check valve	9	Stop bolt	13	Stopper ring
2	Fluid reservoir	6	Check valve spring	10	Secondary piston assembly	14	Reservoir hose
3	Check valve cap	7	Valve case	11	Primary piston assembly	15	Bracket
4	Rear line seat	8	Master cylinder	12	Piston stopper	16	Chamber covers
						17	Master cylinder rebuild kit

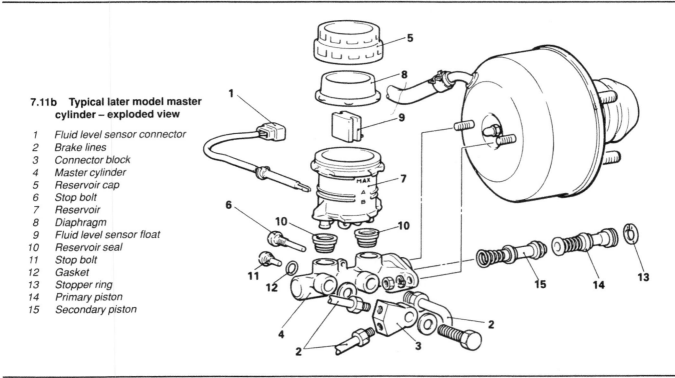

7.11b   Typical later model master cylinder – exploded view

1   Fluid level sensor connector
2   Brake lines
3   Connector block
4   Master cylinder
5   Reservoir cap
6   Stop bolt
7   Reservoir
8   Diaphragm
9   Fluid level sensor float
10   Reservoir seal
11   Stop bolt
12   Gasket
13   Stopper ring
14   Primary piston
15   Secondary piston

16   Before installing the new master cylinder it should be bench bled. Because it will be necessary to apply pressure to the master cylinder piston and, at the same time, control flow from the brake line outlets, it is recommended that the master cylinder be mounted in a vise, with the jaws of the vise clamping on the mounting flange.

17   Insert threaded plugs into the brake line outlet holes and snug them down so that there will be no air leakage past them, but not so tight that they cannot be easily loosened.
18   Fill the reservoir with brake fluid of the recommended type (see Chapter 1).

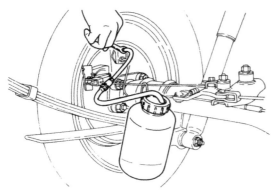

9.8 When bleeding the brakes, a hose is connected to the bleeder valve at the caliper or wheel cylinder and then submerged in brake fluid – air will be seen as bubbles in the hose and container when the valve is opened – all air must be expelled before moving to the next wheel

19 Remove one plug and push the piston assembly into the master cylinder bore to expel the air from the master cylinder. A large Phillips screwdriver can be used to push on the piston assembly.
20 To prevent air from being drawn back into the master cylinder the plug must be replaced and snugged down before releasing the pressure on the piston assembly.
21 Repeat the procedure until only brake fluid is expelled from the brake line outlet hole. When only brake fluid is expelled, repeat the procedure with the other outlet hole and plug. Be sure to keep the master cylinder reservoir filled with brake fluid to prevent the introduction of air into the system.
22 Since high pressure is not involved in the bench bleeding procedure, an alternative to the removal and replacement of the plugs with each stroke of the piston assembly is available. Before pushing in on the piston assembly, remove the plug as described in Step 19. Before releasing the piston, however, instead of replacing the plug, simply put your finger tightly over the hole to keep air from being drawn back into the master cylinder. Wait several seconds for brake fluid to be drawn from the reservoir into the piston bore, then depress the piston again, removing your finger as brake fluid is expelled. Be sure to put your finger back over the hole each time before releasing the piston, and when the bleeding procedure is complete for that outlet, replace the plug and snug it before going on to the other port.

Installation

23 Install the master cylinder over the studs on the power brake booster and tighten the attaching nuts only finger tight at this time.
24 Thread the brake line fittings into the master cylinder. Since the master cylinder is still a bit loose, it can be moved slightly in order for the fittings to thread in easily. Do not strip the threads as the fittings are tightened.
25 Fully tighten the mounting nuts and the brake fittings.
26 Fill the master cylinder reservoir with fluid, then bleed the master cylinder (only if the cylinder has not been bench bled [see Steps 16 through 22]) and the brake system as described in Section 9. To bleed the cylinder on the vehicle, have an assistant pump the brake pedal several times and then hold the pedal to the floor. Loosen the fitting nuts to allow air and fluid to escape. Repeat this procedure on both fittings until the fluid is clear of air bubbles. Test the operation of the brake system carefully before placing the vehicle in normal service.

---

8   Brake lines and hoses – inspection and replacement

---

1   About every six months the flexible hoses which connect the steel brake lines with the front and rear brakes should be inspected for cracks, chafing of the outer cover, leaks, blisters, and other damage (Chapter 1).
2   Replacement steel and flexible brake lines are commonly available from dealer parts departments and auto parts stores. Do not, under any

circumstances, use anything other than genuine steel lines or approved flexible brake hoses as replacement items.
3   When installing the brake line, leave at least 0.75 in (19 mm) clearance between the line and any moving or vibrating parts.
4   When disconnecting a hose and line, first remove the spring clip. Then, using a normal wrench to hold the hose and a flare-nut wrench to hold the tube, make the disconnection. Use the wrenches in the same manner when making a connection, then install a new clip. **Note:** *Make sure the tube passes through the center of its grommet.*
5   When disconnecting two hoses, use normal wrenches on the hose fittings. When connecting two hoses, make sure they are not bent, twisted or strained.
6   Steel brake lines are usually retained along their span with clips. Always remove these clips completely before removing a fixed brake line. Always reinstall these clips, or new ones if the old ones are damaged, when replacing a brake line, as they provide support and keep the lines from vibrating, which can eventually break them.
7   Remember to bleed the hydraulic system after replacing a hose or line.

---

9   Brake system – bleeding

Refer to illustration 9.8
Warning: *Wear eye protection when bleeding the brake system. If the fluid comes in contact with your eyes, immediately rinse them with water and seek medical attention.*
Note: *Bleeding the hydraulic system is necessary to remove any air that manages to find its way into the system when it's been opened during removal and installation of a hose, line, caliper, wheel cylinder or master cylinder.*
1   It will probably be necessary to bleed the system at all four brakes if air has entered the system due to low fluid level, or if the brake lines have been disconnected at the master cylinder.
2   If a brake line was disconnected only at a wheel, then only that caliper or wheel cylinder must be bled.
3   If a brake line is disconnected at a fitting located between the master cylinder and any of the brakes, that part of the system served by the disconnected line must be bled.
4   Remove any residual vacuum from the brake power booster by applying the brake several times with the engine off.
5   Remove the master cylinder reservoir cover and fill the reservoir with brake fluid. Reinstall the cover. **Note:** *Check the fluid level often during the bleeding operation and add fluid as necessary to prevent the fluid level from falling low enough to allow air bubbles into the master cylinder.*
6   Have an assistant on hand, as well as a supply of new brake fluid, a clear container partially filled with clean brake fluid, a length of 3/16-inch plastic, rubber or vinyl tubing to fit over the bleeder valve and a wrench to open and close the bleeder valve.
7   Beginning at the right rear wheel, loosen the bleeder valve slightly, then tighten it to a point where it is snug but can still be loosened quickly and easily.
8   Place one end of the tubing over the bleeder valve and submerge the other end in brake fluid in the container **(see illustration)**.
9   Have the assistant pump the brakes slowly a few times to get pressure in the system, then hold the pedal firmly depressed.
10   While the pedal is held depressed, open the bleeder valve just enough to allow a flow of fluid to leave the valve. Watch for air bubbles to exit the submerged end of the tube. When the fluid flow slows after a couple of seconds, close the valve and have your assistant release the pedal.
11   Repeat Steps 9 and 10 until no more air is seen leaving the tube, then tighten the bleeder valve and proceed to the left rear wheel, the right front wheel and the left front wheel, in that order, and perform the same procedure. Be sure to check the fluid in the master cylinder reservoir frequently.
12   Never use old brake fluid. It contains moisture which will lower the boiling point of the brake fluid and also deteriorate the brake system rubber components.
13   Refill the master cylinder with fluid at the end of the operation.

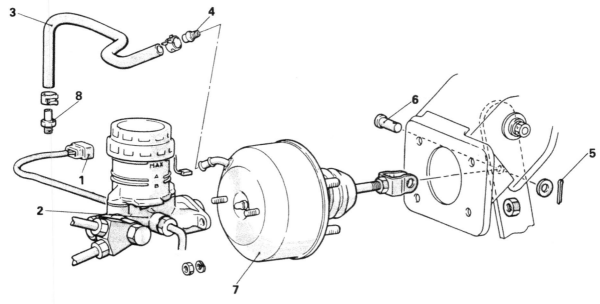

10.7   Typical power booster mounting details

1	Brake fluid level sensor connector	4	Check valve	7	Brake booster
2	Master cylinder	5	Cotter pin	8	Fitting
3	Vacuum hose	6	Clevis pin		

10   Power brake booster – check, removal and installation

Refer to illustrations 10.7 and 10.14

Operating check

1   Depress the brake pedal several times with the engine off and make sure that there is no change in the pedal reserve distance.
2   Depress the pedal and start the engine. If the pedal goes down slightly, operation is normal.

Airtightness check

3   Start the engine and turn it off after one or two minutes. Depress the brake pedal several times slowly. If the pedal goes down farther the first time but gradually rises after the second or third depression, the booster is airtight.
4   Depress the brake pedal while the engine is running, then stop the engine with the pedal depressed. If there is no change in the pedal reserve travel after holding the pedal for 30 seconds, the booster is airtight.

Removal

5   Power brake booster units should not be disassembled. They require special tools not normally found in most service stations or shops. They are fairly complex and, because of their critical relationship to brake performance, it is best to replace a defective booster unit with a new or rebuilt one.
6   To remove the booster, first remove the brake master cylinder as described in Section 7. On some vehicles it is not necessary to disconnect the brake lines from the master cylinder, as there is enough room to reposition the cylinder to allow booster removal.
7   Locate the pushrod clevis connecting the booster to the brake pedal **(see illustration)**. This is accessible from the interior in front of the driver's seat.
8   Remove the clevis pin retaining clip with pliers and pull out the pin.
9   Holding the clevis with pliers, disconnect the clevis locknut with a wrench. The clevis is now loose.
10   Disconnect the hose leading from the engine to the booster. Be careful not to damage the hose when removing it from the booster fitting.

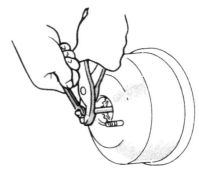

10.14   To adjust the length of the booster pushrod, hold the serrated portion of the rod with a pair of pliers and turn the adjusting nut in or out, as necessary, to achieve the desired setting

11   Remove the four nuts and washers holding the brake booster to the firewall. You may need a light to see these, as they are up under the dash area.
12   Slide the booster straight out from the firewall until the studs clear the holes and pull the booster, brackets and gaskets from the engine compartment area.

Installation

13   Installation procedures are basically the reverse of those for removal. Tighten the booster mounting nuts to the torque listed in this Chapter's Specifications. Tighten the clevis locknut securely.
14   If the power booster unit is being replaced, the pushrod protrusion must be checked and, if necessary, adjusted. Connect a hand-held vacuum pump to the fitting on the booster and apply 20 in-Hg of vacuum. Measure the distance from the master cylinder flange face on the power booster to the end of the pushrod, comparing your measurement with the value listed in this Chapter's Specifications. Turn the end of the pushrod in or out to achieve the desired setting **(see illustration)**.
15   Install the master cylinder.

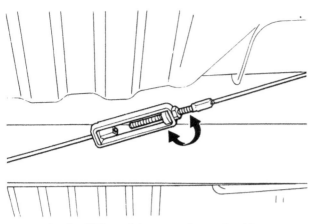

11.3   On 2WD models, rotate the turnbuckle to adjust the parking brake cable

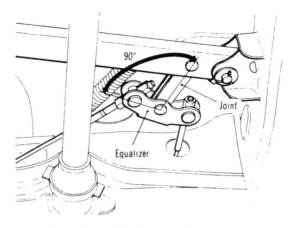

11.4   On 4WD models, the equalizer and joint on the parking brake assembly must be at right angles to the each other as the parking brake adjustment is made

12.3a   Typical lever-type parking brake front cable details

1   Console panel
2   Inner box
3   Floor console
4   Bracket
5   Cable adjuster
6   Cable connection
7   Lever pin
8   Nut holder
9   Cable equalizer
10 Cover
11 Parking lever stay
12 Bushing
13 Parking brake switch connection
14 Parking brake lever
15 Switch
16 Cover
17 Sealer
18 Cotter pin
19 Clevis pin
20 Front parking brake cable

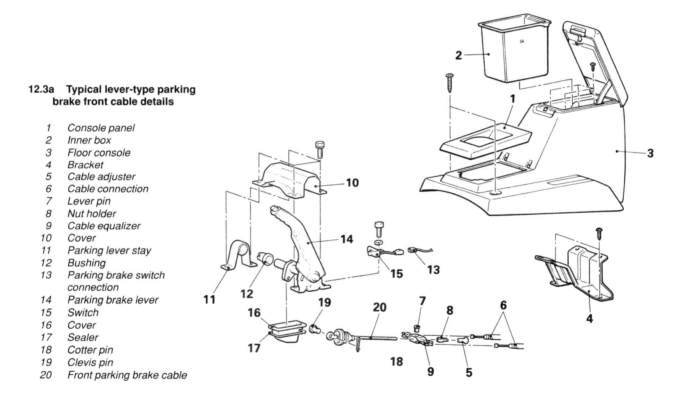

16   After the final installation of the master cylinder and brake hoses and lines, the brake pedal height and freeplay must be adjusted (see Chapter 1) and the system must be bled (see Section 9).

11   Parking brake cables – adjustment

Refer to illustrations 11.3 and 11.4

1   If the parking brake doesn't keep the vehicle from rolling when the handle is applied 4 to 6 clicks on lever-type parking brakes or 16 to 17 clicks on umbrella-type models, adjust the cable.
2   Raise the vehicle and support it securely on jackstands.
3   On 2WD models adjust the parking brake turnbuckle until the stroke

of the pull handle is as specified **(see illustration)**. Make sure that the brake balancer is nearly parallel with the center line of the vehicle.
4   On 4WD models, turn the nuts on the equalizer end of the cables. Make sure the equalizer is maintained at a 90-degree angle to the joint as the nuts are tightened **(see illustration)**.
5   Remove all slack from the parking brake cables. After adjustment apply the parking brake several times and check that handle travel is 4 to 6 clicks on lever-type parking brakes or 16 to 17 clicks on umbrella-type models. Make sure the rear brakes don't drag when the parking brake is released. Check to see that the parking brake light on the dash glows when the handle is applied.
6   Lower the vehicle and verify that the parking brake will hold the vehicle on a moderate incline. If it still won't keep the vehicle from rolling, inspect the rear brakes as described in Chapter 1.

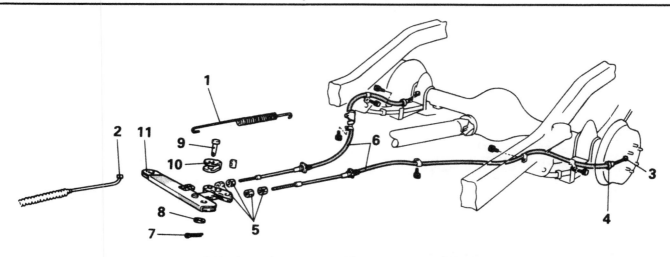

12.3b   Typical lever-type parking brake rear cable details

1	Return spring	4	Cable-to-brake	6	Rear cable	9	Clevis pin
2	Cable end		shoe lever connection	7	Split pin	10	Spacer
3	Stopper	5	Adjusting nuts	8	Washer	11	Lever assembly

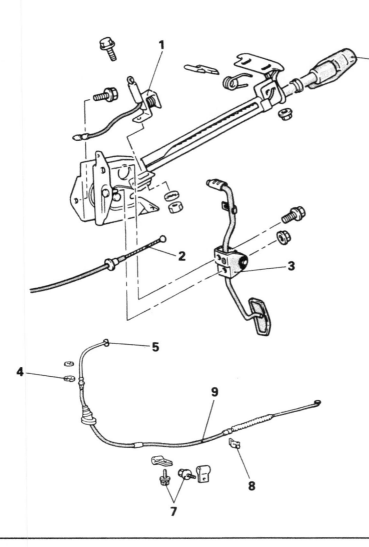

12.3c   Umbrella-type parking brake front cable details

1   Parking brake switch
2   Accelerator cable
3   Pedal bracket
4   Snap-ring
5   Parking brake front cable end
6   Parking brake pull rod
7   Bolts
8   Clip
9   Parking brake front cable

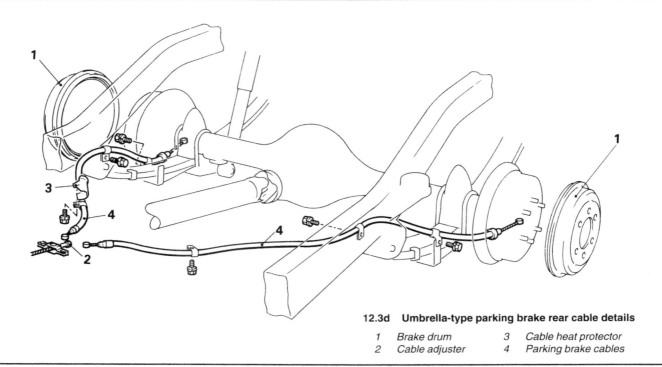

12.3d Umbrella-type parking brake rear cable details

1	Brake drum	3	Cable heat protector
2	Cable adjuster	4	Parking brake cables

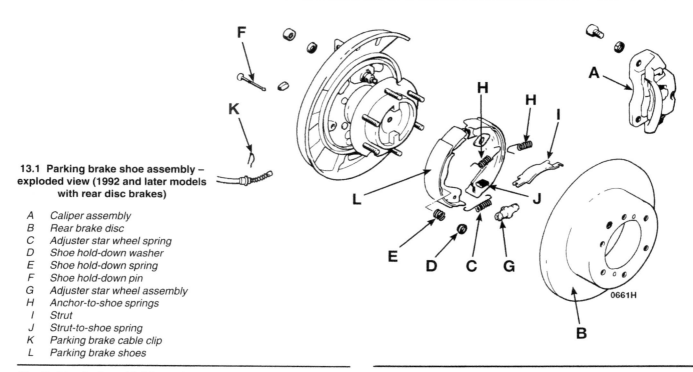

13.1 Parking brake shoe assembly – exploded view (1992 and later models with rear disc brakes)

A   Caliper assembly
B   Rear brake disc
C   Adjuster star wheel spring
D   Shoe hold-down washer
E   Shoe hold-down spring
F   Shoe hold-down pin
G   Adjuster star wheel assembly
H   Anchor-to-shoe springs
I   Strut
J   Strut-to-shoe spring
K   Parking brake cable clip
L   Parking brake shoes

12   Parking brake cable(s) – replacement

Refer to illustrations 12.3a, 12.3b, 12.3c and 12.3d

1   Raise the vehicle and support it securely on jackstands.
2   Disassemble the rear brakes and remove the ends of the parking brake cables from the parking brake levers (Section 5).
3   Remove the return spring (if equipped), separate the parking brake cables at the adjuster, then remove the bolts and the cables **(see illustrations)**.
4   Installation is the reverse of the removal procedure.
5   Following installation, adjust the parking brake (see Section 11).

13   Parking brake shoes (1992 and later models with rear disc brakes) – replacement

Refer to illustration 13.1

1   Loosen rear wheel lug nuts, raise the rear of the vehicle and support it securely on jackstands. Remove the wheels and brake disc (see Section 4). Work on the brake assemblies one side at a time, using the assembled brake for reference, if necessary **(see illustration)**.
2   Remove the brake caliper as described in Section 2.
3   Release the parking brake lever and rotate the brake disc (rotor). If the disc does not turn freely, or will not pull off, remove the adjustment hole

rubber plug (located on the back side of the backing plate). Turn the star-wheel counter clockwise with a flat-bladed screwdriver approximately 3 to 4 clicks to retract the shoes and allow for the disc/drum assembly to slide off. Pull disc/drum assembly off.

4   Remove the adjusting wheel spring.
5   Remove the parking brake shoe hold-down spring, washer and pin.
6   Remove the adjuster and the anchor-to-shoe springs, then remove the strut and strut-to-shoe spring.
7   Remove the brake shoes.
8   Disconnect the parking brake cable.
9   Remove the lever assembly from the rear brake shoe.
10   Installation is the reverse of removal. Repeat the operation on the other wheel. Don't forget to tighten the lug nuts to the torque specified in Chapter 1. Road test the vehicle carefully on a level road, away from traffic, before placing it into normal service again.

14   Anti-lock Brake System (ABS) – general information

A Rear Wheel Anti-lock Brake System (Rear Wheel ABS) is used on some 1990 and later model trucks and 1990 and 1991 Monteros. The Four Wheel Anti-lock Brake System is used on 1992 and later Montero models. The Rear Wheel ABS system consists of a control unit (computer), hydraulic unit (anti-lock brake valve), a speed sensor on the differential, G-sensor, an ABS relay, a pressure differential switch and a check connector for troubleshooting. The Four Wheel ABS system consists of an electronic control unit (ABS computer), a hydraulic unit (anti-lock brake valve), four-wheel speed sensors (located behind each brake rotor), an ABS power relay (located under the dash), a G-sensor (located next to the manual brake lever), a motor relay and valve relay (located on the hydraulic unit) and an ABS warning light.

The ABS control unit prevents the wheels (rear wheels only on Rear Wheel ABS) from locking up by sensing the drop in wheel speed and modulating hydraulic pressure to the brakes accordingly.

Because of the complexity of this system, we don't recommend any attempt to service it at home. If you're experiencing difficulties with the wheels locking up during braking, take the vehicle to a Mitsubishi dealer service department or other qualified repair shop.

Note:

Chapter 10
Suspension and steering systems

Contents

Specifications

General

Strut bar (2WD models)
   Jam nut rear face-to-bar end (1984 and earlier models) . . . .   3.8 inch
   First nut front face-to-bar end (1985 and later models) . . . .   2.8 inch
4WD models
   Torsion bar anchor-to-crossmember measurement (A in Illustration 5.8)
      1983
         Left . . . .   5.73 inch
         Right . . . .   5.35 inch

General (continued)

1984 through 1988	
Left	5.82 inch
Right	5.62 inch
1989 on	
Left	5.63 inch
Right	5.21 inch
Torsion bar anchor bolt projection (B in Illustration 5.8)	
1983	
Left	2.17 inch
Right	2.68 inch
1984 through 1988	
Left	
2.0L engine	2.80 inch
2.6L engine	3.0 inch
Right	2.68 inch
1989 on	
Left	3.94 inch
Right	3.39 inch
Bump stop-to-bracket clearance (A in illustration 5.10)	
1988 and earlier	2.8 inch
1989 and later models	3.0 inch

Torque specifications

Ft-lbs (unless otherwise indicated)

Front suspension

Upper balljoint-to-steering knuckle nut	43 to 65
Upper arm shaft-to-frame bolt	72 to 87
Lower balljoint-to-steering knuckle nut	87 to 130
Lower balljoint-to-lower arm bolt	
2WD	22 to 30
4WD	39 to 54
Lower arm shaft-to-crossmember nut or bolt	84 to 120 in-lbs
Lower arm pivot shaft nuts	
2WD	40 to 54
4WD	101 to 116
Upper shock absorber nut	108 to 156 in-lbs
Lower shock absorber bolts	84 to 120 in-lbs
Torsion bar locknut	29 to 38
Torsion bar anchor arm bolt B	69 to 87
Strut bar-to-lower arm bolts	54 to 61
Strut bar-to-frame outer nut	54 to 61
Stabilizer bar mounting bracket bolts	84 to 120 in-lbs
Stabilizer bar link bolts	84 to 120 in-lbs

Rear suspension

Leaf spring type	
Rear shackle pin nuts	33 to 43
Front shackle pin nut	87 to 116
U-Bolt nuts	72 to 87
Rear shock absorber nuts	13 to 18
Coil spring type	
Trailing arm-to-frame nut	94 to 108
Trailing arm-to-axle bolts	137 to 220
Lateral rod nuts	80 to 94
Stabilizer bar bracket bolts	22 to 29
Lower shock absorber bolt	80 to 94
Upper shock absorber nut	29 to 36

Steering

Steering gear-to-frame bolts	33 to 41
Flexible coupling-to-steering gear pinch bolt	11 to 15
Pitman arm-to-steering gear nut	94 to 108
Pitman arm-to-relay rod nut	26 to 32
Idler arm bracket-to-frame bolts	26 to 28
Idler arm-to-pivot shaft nut	
2WD	29 to 43
4WD	32
Tie-rod end-to-relay rod nut	26 to 32
Tie-rod end-to-steering knuckle nut	26 to 32
Steering wheel nut	26 to 32
Wheel lug nuts	See Chapter 1

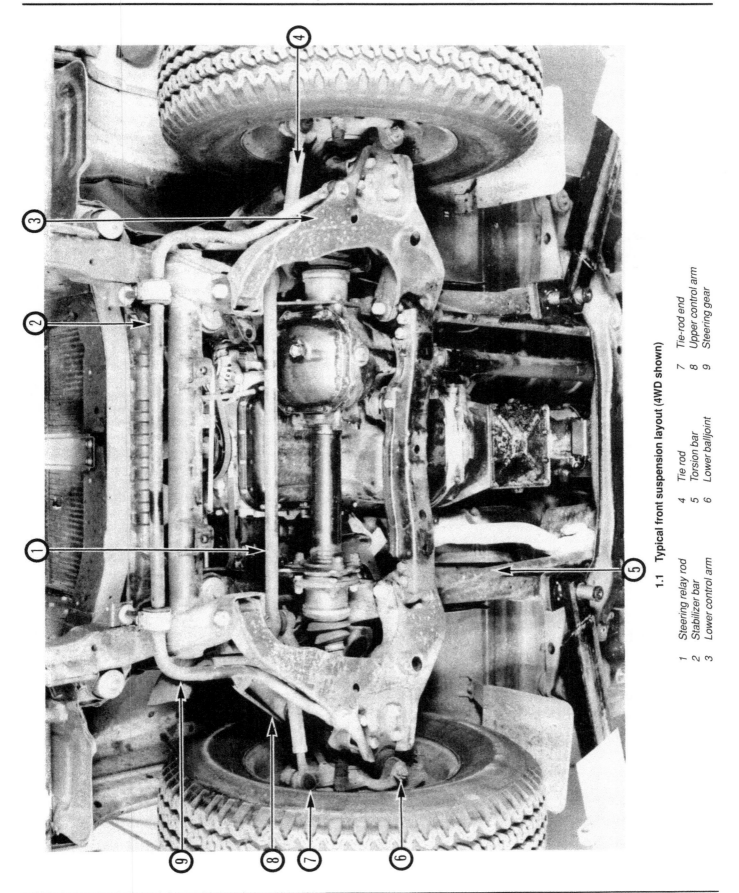

1.1 Typical front suspension layout (4WD shown)

1 Steering relay rod	4 Tie rod	7 Tie-rod end
2 Stabilizer bar	5 Torsion bar	8 Upper control arm
3 Lower control arm	6 Lower balljoint	9 Steering gear

1.2 Typical leaf spring type rear suspension layout

1 Upper shock absorber mount
2 Leaf spring

3 Spring U-bolt
4 Spring through bolt

5 Lower shock absorber bolt

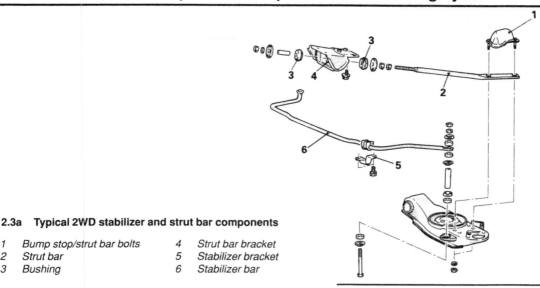

2.3a   Typical 2WD stabilizer and strut bar components

1	Bump stop/strut bar bolts	4	Strut bar bracket
2	Strut bar	5	Stabilizer bracket
3	Bushing	6	Stabilizer bar

1   General information

Refer to illustrations 1.1 and 1.2

The front suspension on the vehicles covered by this manual is an independent type, made up of upper and lower arms, torsion bars (4WD models) or coil springs (2WD models), balljoint-mounted steering knuckles and shock absorbers **(see illustration)**. Some models are equipped with a stabilizer bar to limit body roll during cornering.

The rear suspension consists of the rear axle housing, leaf springs and shock absorbers **(see illustration)**. Some later models use coil springs with a trailing arm and track rod arrangement to locate the axle. Information regarding axles and the rear axle housing can be found in Chapter 8.

The steering system is composed of a steering column, steering gear, Pitman arm, relay rod, two tie-rod assemblies and an idler arm. Some models feature power assisted steering, which includes a belt-driven pump and associated hoses to provide hydraulic pressure to the steering gear.

Frequently, when working on the suspension or steering system components, you may come across fasteners which seem impossible to loosen. These fasteners on the underside of the vehicle are continually subjected to water, road grime, mud, etc., and can become rusted or "frozen," making them extremely difficult to remove. In order to unscrew these stubborn fasteners without damaging them (or other components), be sure to use lots of penetrating oil and allow it to soak in for a while. Using a wire brush to clean exposed threads will also ease removal of the nut or bolt and prevent damage to the threads. Sometimes a sharp blow with a hammer and punch is effective in breaking the bond between a nut and bolt threads, but care must be taken to prevent the punch from slipping off the fastener and ruining the threads. Heating the stuck fastener and surrounding area with a torch sometimes helps too, but isn't recommended because of the obvious dangers associated with fire. Long breaker bars and extension, or "cheater," pipes will increase leverage, but never use an extension pipe on a ratchet – the ratcheting mechanism could be damaged. Sometimes, turning the nut or bolt in the tightening (clockwise) direction first will help to break it loose. Fasteners that require drastic measures to unscrew should always be replaced with new ones.

Since most of the procedures that are dealt with in this Chapter involve jacking up the vehicle and working underneath it, a good pair of jackstands will be needed. A hydraulic floor jack is the preferred type of jack to lift the vehicle, and it can also be used to support certain components during various operations. **Warning:** *Never, under any circumstances, rely on a jack to support the vehicle while working on it. Whenever any of the suspension or steering fasteners are loosened or removed they must be inspected and, if necessary, replaced with new ones of the same part number or of original equipment quality and design. Torque specifications must be fol-*

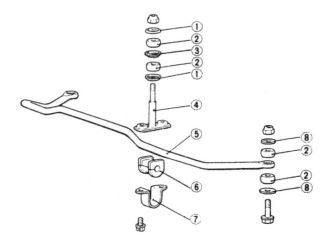

2.3b   Typical 4WD stabilizer bar components

1	Cap	4	Stabilizer bar link	7	Bracket
2	Stabilizer bar bushing	5	Stabilizer bar	8	Washer
3	Cap	6	Bushing		

lowed for proper reassembly and component retention. Never attempt to heat or straighten any suspension or steering component. Always replace them with new ones.

2   Front stabilizer bar – removal and installation

Refer to illustrations 2.3a and 2.3b

Warning: *Whenever any of the suspension or steering fasteners are loosened or removed, they must be inspected and, if necessary, replaced with new ones of the same part number or of original equipment quality and design. Torque specifications must be followed for proper reassembly and component retention.*

Removal

1   Raise the front of the vehicle and support it securely on jackstands. Apply the parking brake.

2   On 2WD models, remove the strut bars (see Section 4).

3   Remove the stabilizer bar-to-lower arm link nuts and bolts, noting how the spacers, washers and bushings are positioned **(see illustrations)**.

3.3   Remove the locking and mounting nuts on the upper end of the shock absorber shaft

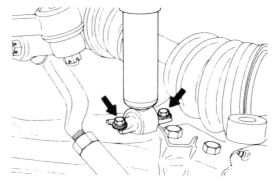

3.6   On 4WD models, the lower shock absorber mounting bolts (arrows) are accessible from the top side of the lower control arm

4   Remove the stabilizer bar bracket bolts and detach the bar from the vehicle.

5   Pull the brackets off the stabilizer bar and inspect the bushings for cracks, hardening and other signs of deterioration. If the bushings are damaged, replace them.

Installation

6   Position the stabilizer bar bushings on the bar. Push the brackets over the bushings and raise the bar up to the frame. Install the bracket bolts but don't tighten them completely at this time.

7   Install the stabilizer bar-to-lower arm bolts, washers, spacers and rubber bushings and tighten the nuts securely.

8   Tighten the bracket, bolts and link nuts securely. Lower the vehicle and release the parking brake.

---

3   Front shock absorber – removal and installation

Refer to illustrations 3.3 and 3.6

Warning: *Whenever any of the suspension or steering fasteners are loosened or removed, they must be inspected and, if necessary, replaced with new ones of the same part number or of original equipment quality and design. Torque specifications must be followed for proper reassembly and component retention.*

1   Jack up the front of the vehicle and place it securely on jackstands.

2   Remove the front wheels.

3   Remove the nuts holding the shock absorber to the upper mount **(see illustration)**. Clamp a pair of locking pliers to the flats at the top of the shock rod to prevent it from turning. **Note:** *If the vehicle has remote-controlled variable shock absorbers, the actuator assembly is bolted to the top of the shock absorber stud end. To remove the actuator, loosen the two bolts that hold the actuator to the mounting bracket, then remove the upper shock absorber hold-down nut and actuator mounting bracket. Remove the lower shock absorber hold-down nut and actuator washer assembly with the stud pin. Be careful not to bend the stud pin on the washer assembly*

4   Remove the upper washer and rubber cushion from the shaft of the shock absorber.

5   On 2WD models, remove the two bolts holding it to the lower arm from below, then lower the shock absorber down through to the lower arm and remove it from the vehicle.

6   On 4WD models, remove the two shock absorber-to-lower control arm bolts (accessible from the upper surface of the arm), then fully compress the shock absorber and lift it up and over the arm to remove it **(see illustration)**.

7   Installation is the reverse of the removal procedure. Make sure the washers and bushings are assembled in the proper order. Tighten the bolts and nuts securely.

---

4   Front strut bar (2WD models) – removal and installation

Refer to illustrations 4.6a, 4.6b and 4.6c

Warning: *Whenever any of the suspension or steering fasteners are loosened or removed, they must be inspected and, if necessary, replaced with new ones of the same part number or of original equipment quality and design. Torque specifications must be followed for proper reassembly and component retention.*

1   Raise the front of the vehicle and support it securely on jackstands. Apply the parking brake.

2   Remove the outer nut from the strut bar **(see illustration 2.2a)**.

3   Remove the nuts holding the strut bar to the lower arm and drive out the two bolts holding the strut bar to the arm. The strut bar may spring back, so be careful when removing the bolts.

4   Push up on the rear of the strut bar to clear the control arm, then move the strut bar to the rear and out of the front frame bracket. As this is done, note how the rubber bushings and large washers are installed in the strut bar.

5   Inspect the strut bar and bushings for wear or damage. Replace parts as necessary with new ones.

6   Installation is the reverse of the removal procedure. Note that the strut bar marked with an 'L' must be installed on the left side of the vehicle **(see illustration)**. When installing the strut bars to the brackets, set the distance 'A' between the end of the strut bar and the face of the nut to the distance listed in this Chapter's Specifications **(see illustrations)**. Connect the strut bars to the lower control arms and tighten the strut bar-to-lower arm bolts to the torque listed in this Chapter's Specifications. Lower the vehicle and tighten the outer nut to the torque listed in this Chapter's Specifications.

7   Have the vehicle's front end alignment checked.

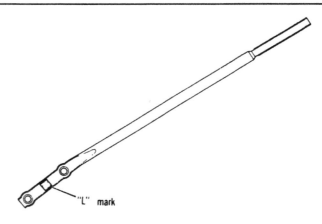

4.6a   Make sure the strut bar with the 'L' mark goes on the left side

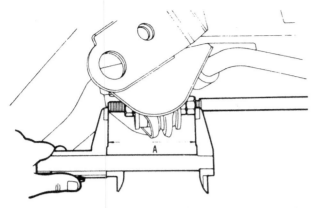

4.6b   On 1984 and earlier models, the strut bar dimension 'A' is measured as shown

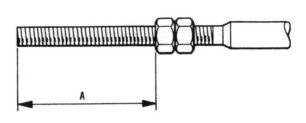

4.6c   Measure the face of the nut to the end of the strut to get dimension 'A' on 1985 and later models

5.2 Torsion bar components

1   Dust cover
2   Anchor arm mounting nut
3   Anchor arm assembly
4   Torsion bar

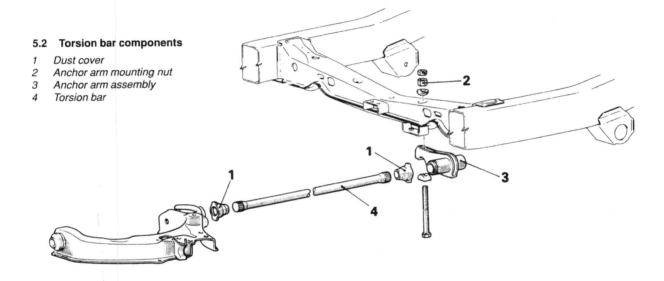

5 Torsion bar (4WD models) – removal, installation and adjustment

Refer to illustrations 5.2, 5.3, 5.8 and 5.10

Warning: *Whenever any of the suspension or steering fasteners are loosened or removed, they must be inspected and, if necessary, replaced with new ones of the same part number or of original equipment quality and design. Torque specifications must be followed for proper reassembly and component retention.*

Removal

1   Loosen the wheel lug nuts, raise the front of the vehicle and support it securely on jackstands, then remove the wheel and the brake caliper assembly (see Chapter 9).
2   Remove the anchor arm dust covers **(see illustration)**.
3   Mark the torsion bar directly opposite the mark on the anchor arm **(see illustration)**. **Caution:** *Do not punch or scratch the torsion bar – use paint to make the mark.*
4   Loosen the jam nut and adjusting nut at the anchor arm assembly until the torsion bar can be slipped out of the anchor arms.

Installation and adjustment

5   When reinstalling the torsion bar, apply grease to the torsion bar and anchor arm splines, the adjusting bolt threads and the inside of the dust boots.

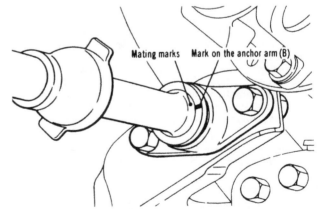

5.3   Mark the torsion bar before removing it, but DO NOT scratch it or make a mark with a centerpunch

6   If both bars have been removed, the right torsion bar can be distinguished from the left by checking the end of the bar. Look for an L or an R stamped into the end of each bar (R is right, L is left).
7   Position the marked end of the bar into the anchor arm with the mating marks aligned (if a new bar is installed, align the white spline with the mark on the anchor arm).

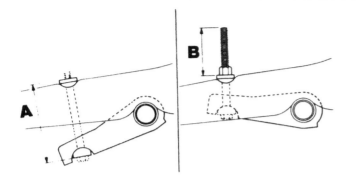

5.8   Make sure the adjusting bolt measurements A and B are as specified as the torsion bar is installed

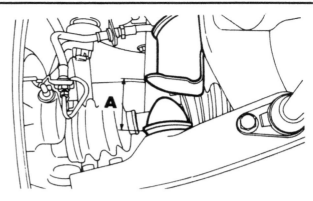

5.10   If the distance A from the bump stop to the bracket is not as specified with the vehicle weight on the suspension, the torsion bars may require further adjustment

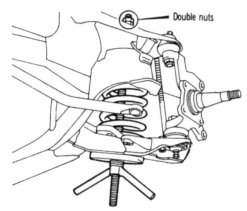

6.2   Use a special compressor tool to compress the spring (the number shown is the manufacturer's special tool number)

7.3   On 4WD models, loosen the torsion bar anchor nuts (arrow)

8   With the rebound stop on the upper arm in contact with the frame, make sure the distance from the underside of the adjusting bolt head to the bottom face of the nut on the left side ('A' in the accompanying illustration) and the right side ('B' in the illustration) is as specified (see this Chapter's Specifications), then assemble the torsion bar and the rear anchor arm.

9   Tighten the adjusting nut until the distance from the adjusting nut bottom face to the top of the bolt is as listed in the Specifications Section at the beginning of this Chapter.

10   Reinstall the hub, wheel and brake caliper, then lower the vehicle and measure the distance from the bump stop to the bracket with the vehicle unloaded (**see illustration**). Compare this measurement to the Specifications Section at the beginning of this Chapter. If necessary, tighten the adjusting nut on the 'anchor arm until the distance is as specified.

6   Front spring (2WD models) – removal and installation

Refer to illustration 6.2

Warning: *Whenever any of the suspension or steering fasteners are loosened or removed, they must be inspected and, if necessary, replaced with new ones of the same part number or of original equipment quality and design. Torque specifications must be followed for proper reassembly and component retention.*

Removal

1   Loosen the wheel lug nuts, raise the front of the vehicle and support it securely on jackstands. Apply the parking brake. Remove the wheel.

2   Use a special spring compressor tool to compress the spring (**see illustration**). **Warning:** *When compressed, the spring is under consider*

able tension and could cause personal injury if it comes loose. Use great care when operating the spring compressor and follow the manufacturer's instructions.

3   Remove the steering knuckle (see Section 10).

4   Once the steering knuckle has been removed, slowly and carefully release the pressure on the spring by loosening the spring compressing tool.

5   While supporting the lower control arm with a jack, withdraw the spring compressing tool. Remove the spring and spring seat from the spring tower.

Installation

6   Place the spring and seat in position in the spring tower and rotate the lower control arm up until the spring is supported by it. **Note:** *The spring must be installed with the closely spaced coils at the bottom.*

7   Install the spring compressing tool and slowly compress the spring, making sure it is properly seated in the spring tower and the lower control arm groove.

8   Install the steering knuckle and remove the spring compressor.

9   Install the wheels and lower the vehicle.

7   Front suspension upper arm – removal and installation

Refer to illustrations 7.3, 7.5a and 7.5b

Warning: *Whenever any of the suspension or steering fasteners are loosened or removed, they must be inspected and, if necessary, replaced with new ones of the same part number or of original equipment quality and design. Torque specifications must be followed for proper reassembly and component retention.*

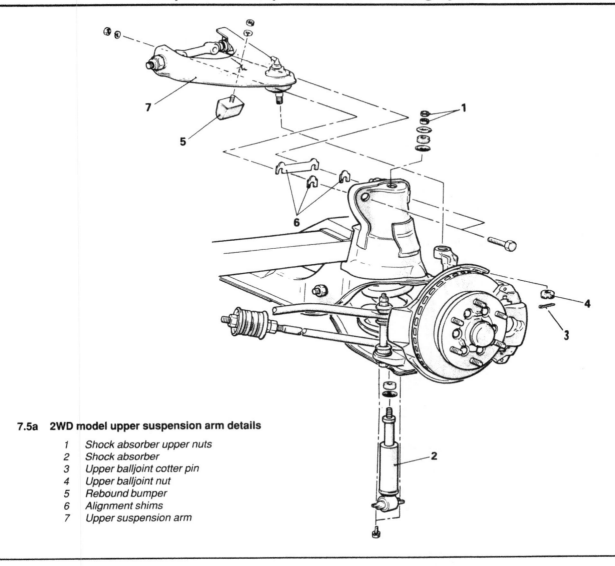

7.5a   2WD model upper suspension arm details

1   Shock absorber upper nuts
2   Shock absorber
3   Upper balljoint cotter pin
4   Upper balljoint nut
5   Rebound bumper
6   Alignment shims
7   Upper suspension arm

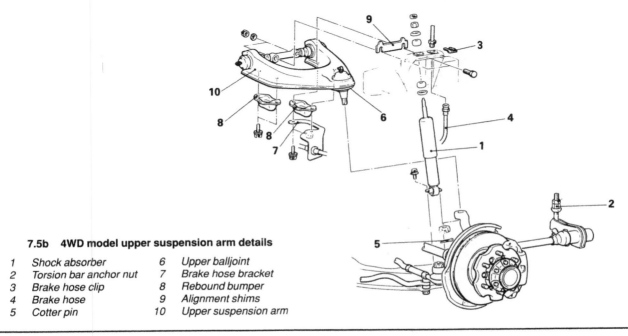

7.5b   4WD model upper suspension arm details

1	Shock absorber	6	Upper balljoint
2	Torsion bar anchor nut	7	Brake hose bracket
3	Brake hose clip	8	Rebound bumper
4	Brake hose	9	Alignment shims
5	Cotter pin	10	Upper suspension arm

Removal

1   Loosen the wheel lug nuts, raise the front of the vehicle and support it securely on jackstands. Apply the parking brake. Remove the wheel.

2   On 2WD models, remove the steering knuckle and front spring (see Section 6).

3   On 4WD models, support the lower arm with a jack. The support point must be as close to the balljoint as possible to give maximum leverage on the lower arm. Release the torsion bar tension by fully loosening the anchor nut(s) **(see illustration)**.

4   On 4WD models remove the cotter pin and nut and separate the upper balljoint from the steering knuckle, but be careful not to let the steering knuckle/brake caliper assembly fall outward, as this may damage the brake hose (see Section 9).

5   On all models, remove the upper arm-to-frame bolts, noting the positions of any alignment shims. They must be reinstalled in the same locations to maintain wheel alignment **(see illustrations)**.

6   Detach the upper arm from the vehicle. Inspect the bushings for deterioration, cracks and other damage, replacing them, if necessary. On later 4WD models, it may be necessary to loosen the body mount nuts and raise the front of the body with a jack to provide sufficient clearance to allow removal of the upper arm.

Installation

7   Position the arm on the frame and install the bolts. Install any alignment shims that were removed. Tighten the bolts to the torque listed in this Chapter's Specifications.

8   On 4WD models, connect the balljoint to the steering knuckle and tighten the nut to the torque listed in this Chapter's Specifications.

9   On 2WD models, install the spring and steering knuckle.

10   On 4WD models, tighten the torsion bar anchor bolt(s) and adjust the bumper stop-to-bracket clearance as described in Section 5, Step 10.

11   Install the wheel and lug nuts and lower the vehicle. Tighten the lug nuts to the torque specified in Chapter 1.

12   Drive the vehicle to an alignment shop to have the front end alignment checked and, if necessary, adjusted.

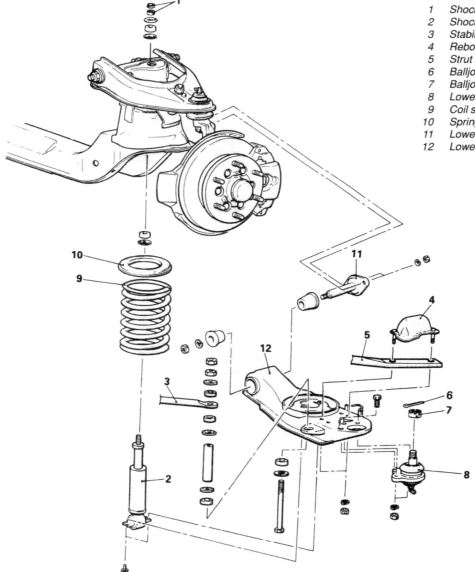

8.2   2WD model lower control arm details

1   Shock absorber nuts
2   Shock absorber
3   Stabilizer bar
4   Rebound bumper
5   Strut bar
6   Balljoint cotter pin
7   Balljoint nut
8   Lower balljoint
9   Coil spring
10   Spring seat
11   Lower arm pivot shaft
12   Lower control arm

8   Front suspension lower arm – removal and installation

Refer to illustrations 8.2 and 8.3

Warning: *Whenever any of the suspension or steering fasteners are loosened or removed, they must be inspected and, if necessary, replaced with new ones of the same part number or of original equipment quality and design. Torque specifications must be followed for proper reassembly and component retention.*

Removal

1   Loosen the wheel lug nuts, raise the front of the vehicle and support it securely on jackstands. Remove the wheel.

2   On 2WD models, remove the spring and steering knuckle (see Section 6). Remove the pivot shaft nuts, then pull the shaft out or drive it out with a hammer and drift punch and detach the lower arm **(see illustration)**.

3   On 4WD models, remove the torsion bar (see Section 5) and unbolt the lower balljoint from the control arm. Remove the lower arm pivot nuts and shafts and lower the arm from the vehicle **(see illustration)**.

Installation

4   Inspect the lower arm bushings for deterioration, cracking and other damage. If the bushing is in need of replacement, take the lower arm to an automotive machine shop to have the old bushing pressed out and a new one pressed in.

5   On 2WD models, slip the pivot shaft into the crossmember and through the control arm and bushing from the rear. Use a soft-face hammer to tap the shaft into place. Install the lock washers and nuts holding the rear of the shaft in place. Install the washer and nut on the front of the pivot shaft. Position the arm at normal ride height with a jack and tighten the nuts to the torques listed in the Specifications Section at the beginning of this Chapter.

6   On 4WD models, connect the balljoint to the lower arm and install the bolts and nuts. Position the arm at normal ride height and tighten the pivot shaft nuts to torque listed in the Specifications Section at the beginning of this Chapter. Install the torsion bar (see Section 5).

7   Install the wheel and lug nuts. Lower the vehicle and tighten the lug nuts to the torque specified in Chapter 1.

8   Drive the vehicle to an alignment shop to have the front end alignment checked and, if necessary, adjusted.

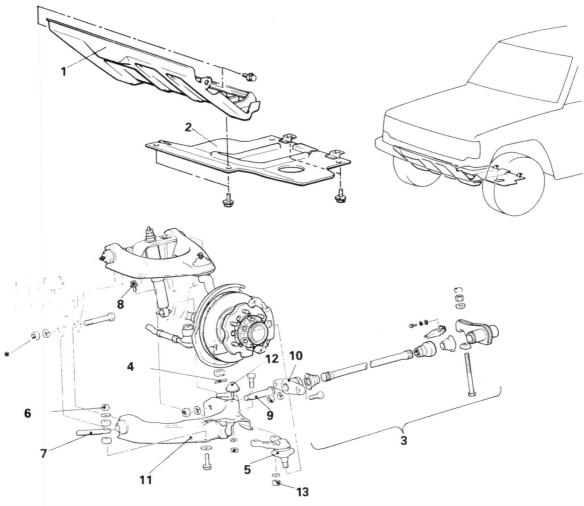

8.3   4WD model lower control arm details

1	Skid plate	5	Lower balljoint	8	Shock absorber nuts	11	Lower control arm
2	Under cover	6	Nut	9	Lower control arm pivot shaft	12	Rebound bumper
3	Torsion bar	7	Stabilizer bar	10	Torsion bar anchor	13	Lower balljoint nuts
4	Cotter pin						

9   Balljoints – check and replacement

Warning: *Whenever any of the suspension or steering fasteners are loosened or removed, they must be inspected and, if necessary, replaced with new ones of the same part number or of original equipment quality and design. Torque specifications must be followed for proper reassembly and component retention.*

Check

1   Raise the vehicle and support it securely on jackstands.

2   Visually inspect the rubber seal for cuts, tears or leaking grease. If any of these conditions are noticed, the balljoint should be replaced.

3   Place a large prybar under the balljoint and attempt to push the balljoint up. Next, position the prybar between the steering knuckle and the arm and apply downward pressure. If any movement is seen or felt during either of these checks, a worn out balljoint is indicated.

4   Have an assistant grasp the tire at the top and bottom and shake the top of the tire in an in-and-out motion. Touch the balljoint stud castellated nut. If any looseness is felt, suspect a worn out balljoint stud or a widened hole in the steering knuckle boss. If the latter problem exists, the steering knuckle should be replaced as well as the balljoint.

Replacement

Upper control arm balljoint

5   The balljoints on upper control arms are pressed into place. Consequently, replacement requires removing the upper arm and taking it to a dealer or other properly equipped shop to have the balljoint pressed out and a new one installed.

Lower control arm balljoint

2WD models

6   Remove the front spring and steering knuckle (see Section 6).

7   Remove the bolts and nuts, then detach the balljoint from the control arm **(see illustration 8.2)**.

8   Place the new balljoints in position and install the bolts and nuts. Tighten the bolts to the torque listed in this Chapter's Specifications.

9   Install the spring and steering knuckle.

4WD models

10   With the vehicle raised and supported, position a floor jack under the lower arm – it must stay there throughout the entire operation. Remove the wheel. Remove the balljoint cotter pin and loosen the castellated nut a couple of turns, but don't remove it (it will prevent the balljoint and steering knuckle from separating violently).

11   Using a balljoint separating tool, separate the balljoint from the steering knuckle. There are several types of balljoint tools available, but the kind that pushes the balljoint stud out of the knuckle boss works the best **(see illustration 10.9)**. The wedge, or "pickle fork" type works fairly well but it tends to damage the balljoint seal. Some two-jaw pullers will do the job, also.

12   Remove the castellated nut and disconnect the balljoint from the steering knuckle.

13   The balljoint is retained to the suspension arm by bolts and nuts. Remove the bolts and nuts, then detach the balljoint from the arm. Take note of how the balljoint is positioned on the arm – the new one must be installed the same way **(see illustration 8.3)**.

14   Position the new balljoint on the arm and install the nut or bolts, tightening them to the torque listed in this Chapter's Specifications.

15   Insert the balljoint stud into the steering knuckle boss, install the castellated nut and tighten it to the specified torque. Install a new cotter pin. If necessary, tighten the nut an additional amount to line up the slots in the nut with the hole in the balljoint stud (never loosen the nut to align the hole).

16   Install the wheel and lug nuts. Lower the vehicle and tighten the lug nuts to the torque specified in Chapter 1.

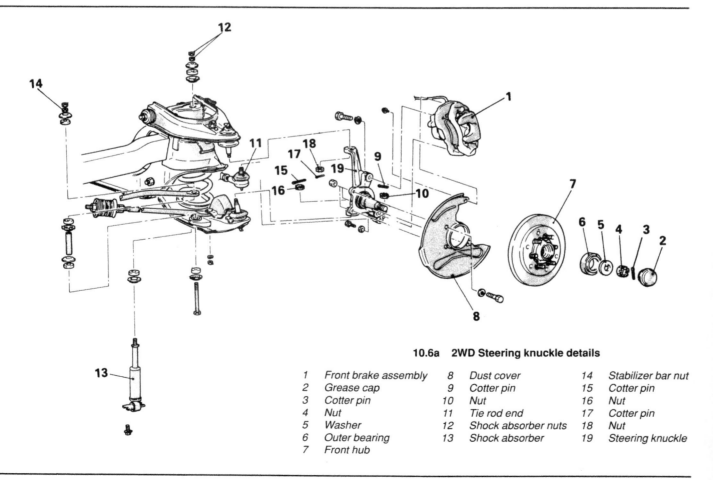

10.6a   2WD Steering knuckle details

1	Front brake assembly	8	Dust cover	14	Stabilizer bar nut
2	Grease cap	9	Cotter pin	15	Cotter pin
3	Cotter pin	10	Nut	16	Nut
4	Nut	11	Tie rod end	17	Cotter pin
5	Washer	12	Shock absorber nuts	18	Nut
6	Outer bearing	13	Shock absorber	19	Steering knuckle
7	Front hub				

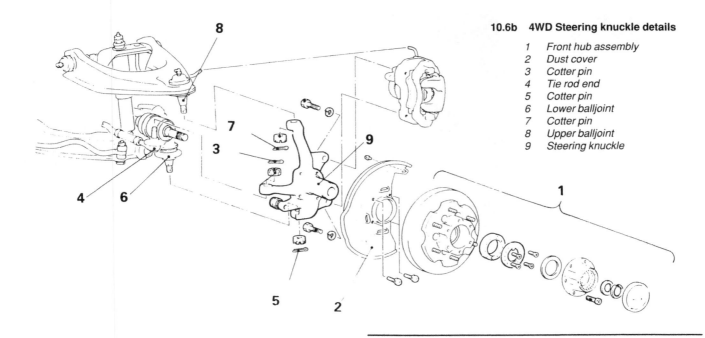

10.6b   4WD Steering knuckle details

1   Front hub assembly
2   Dust cover
3   Cotter pin
4   Tie rod end
5   Cotter pin
6   Lower balljoint
7   Cotter pin
8   Upper balljoint
9   Steering knuckle

10   Steering knuckle – removal and installation

Warning: *Whenever any of the suspension or steering fasteners are loosened or removed, they must be inspected and, if necessary, replaced with new ones of the same part number or of original equipment quality and design. Torque specifications must be followed for proper reassembly and component retention.*

Removal

Refer to illustrations 10.6a, 10.6b and 10.9

1   Loosen the wheel lug nuts, raise the vehicle and support it securely on jackstands placed under the frame. Apply the parking brake. Remove the wheel.
2   Remove the brake caliper and place it on top of the upper arm or wire it up out of the way. Remove the caliper mounting bracket from the steering knuckle (see Chapter 9 if necessary).
3   Remove the front hub assembly and brake disc (see Chapter 9).
4   On 2WD models, separate the stabilizer bar from the lower control arm (see Section 2) and remove the strut bar (see Section 4).
5   Separate the tie-rod end from the knuckle arm (see Section 18).
6   Remove the cotter pins from the upper and lower balljoint studs and back off the nuts one turn each **(see illustrations)**.
7   Remove the shock absorber (see Section 3).
8   On 2WD models, install a spring compressor tool and compress the front spring to the point that the rebound bumper on the upper control arm clears the spring tower by approximately 1/2-inch. **Warning:** *When compressed the spring is under considerable pressure and could cause serious personal injury if it comes loose. Be careful that nothing slips or moves.*
9   Using a special tool, separate the suspension arms from the steering knuckle **(see illustration)**. There are several types of tools available, but the kind that pushes the balljoint stud out of the knuckle boss works the best. The wedge, or "pickle fork" type works fairly well, but it tends to damage the balljoint seal. Some two-jaw pullers will do the job, also. Once the balljoints have been released from the tapered holes in the knuckle, remove the nuts completely and carefully detach the knuckle. On 4WD models, be careful not to damage the CV joint boots when detaching the driveaxle. On some early 2WD models it will be necessary to unbolt the knuckle and detach it from the spindle.

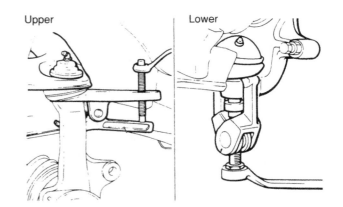

Upper   Lower

10.9   To separate the suspension arms from the steering knuckle, special tools must be used to force the balljoint studs out of the tapered holes in the steering knuckle (the numbers shown are the manufacturer's special tool numbers)

Installation

10   Place the knuckle between the upper and lower suspension arms and insert the balljoint studs into the knuckle, beginning with the lower balljoint. Install the nuts and tighten them to the torque listed in this Chapter's Specifications. Install new cotter pins, tightening the nuts slightly to align the slots in the nuts with the holes in the balljoint studs, if necessary.
11   On 2WD models, make sure the spring is compressed enough so that the spring pressure doesn't interfere with the proper tightening of the balljoint nuts. Remove the compressor tool.
12   Install the shock absorber.
13   Connect the tie-rod end to the knuckle arm and tighten the nut to the torque listed in this Chapter's Specifications. Be sure to use a new cotter pin.
14   Install the strut rod and connect the stabilizer bar.
15   On 2WD models, install the hub and brake disc assembly (see Chapter 9).
16   Install the brake caliper mounting bracket and caliper (see Chapter 9).
17   Install the wheel and lug nuts. Lower the vehicle to the ground and tighten the nuts to the torque specified in Chapter 1.

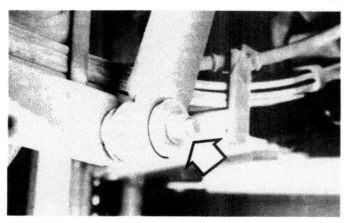

11.3   The lower mounting nut on the rear shock absorber (arrow)

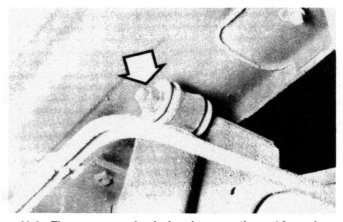

11.4   The upper rear shock absorber mounting nut (arrow)

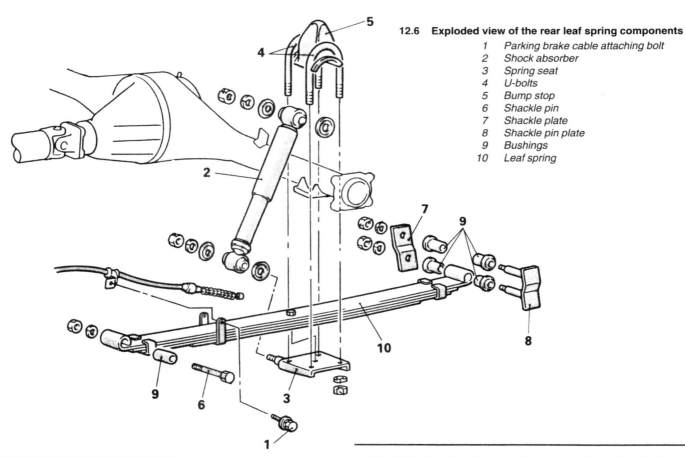

12.6   Exploded view of the rear leaf spring components

    1   *Parking brake cable attaching bolt*
    2   *Shock absorber*
    3   *Spring seat*
    4   *U-bolts*
    5   *Bump stop*
    6   *Shackle pin*
    7   *Shackle plate*
    8   *Shackle pin plate*
    9   *Bushings*
    10   *Leaf spring*

11   Rear shock absorber – removal and installation

Refer to illustrations 11.3 and 11.4

Warning: *Whenever any of the suspension or steering fasteners are loosened or removed, they must be inspected and, if necessary, replaced with new ones of the same part number or of original equipment quality and design. Torque specifications must be followed for proper reassembly and component retention.*

1   If the shock absorber is to be replaced with a new one, it is recommended that both shocks on the rear of the vehicle be replaced at the same time.

2   Raise and support the rear of the vehicle according to the jacking and towing procedures at the front of this manual. Use a jack to raise the differential until the tires clear the ground, then place jackstands under the axle housing. Do not attempt to remove the shock absorbers with the vehicle raised and the axle unsupported.

3   Unscrew and remove the lower shock absorber mounting nut to disconnect it at the spring seat **(see illustration)**.

4   Unscrew and remove the upper mounting nut at the frame and remove the shock absorber **(see illustration)**. **Note:** *If the vehicle is equipped with remote-controlled variable shock absorbers, remove the actuator assembly before removing the shock absorber.*

5   If the unit is defective, it must be replaced with a new one. Replace worn rubber bushings with new ones.

6   Install the shocks in the reverse order of removal, but let the vehicle be free standing on the ground before tightening the mounting nuts.

7   Bounce the rear of the vehicle a couple of times to settle the bushings into place, then tighten the nuts securely.

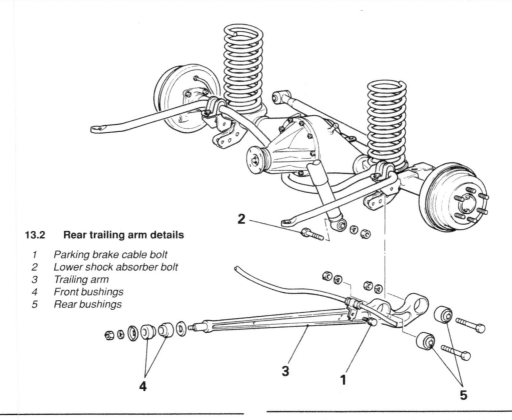

13.2   Rear trailing arm details

1   Parking brake cable bolt
2   Lower shock absorber bolt
3   Trailing arm
4   Front bushings
5   Rear bushings

---

12   Rear leaf spring – removal and installation

Refer to illustration 12.6
Warning: *Whenever any of the suspension or steering fasteners are loosened or removed, they must be inspected and, if necessary, replaced with new ones of the same part number or of original equipment quality and design. Torque specifications must be followed for proper reassembly and component retention.*

1   Jack up the vehicle and support the frame securely on jackstands.
2   Remove the rear wheels and tires.
3   Place a jack under the rear differential housing.
4   Lower the axle housing until the leaf spring tension is relieved, and lock the jack in this position.
5   Disconnect the shock absorber from the spring seat (see Section 11).
6   Remove the U-bolt mounting nuts **(see illustration)**.
7   Remove the U-bolts and spring seat.
8   Remove the bolt and detach the parking brake cable from the spring. Remove the nuts and the shackle pin assemblies, then lower the spring from the vehicle.
9   If the bushings in the spring or frame are deteriorated, replace them. If you need to replace the bushings in the spring, take the spring to an automotive machine shop to have the old bushings pressed out and new ones pressed in.
10   Installation is the reverse of the removal procedure. Lubricate the shackle pins and bushings with lithium-based grease. When installing the U-bolt and shackle pin nuts, tighten them to the specified torque values (see this Chapter's Specifications).

---

13   Rear suspension trailing arms (coil spring models) – removal and installation

Refer to illustration 13.2
Warning: *Whenever any of the suspension or steering fasteners are loosened or removed, they must be inspected and, if necessary, replaced with*

new ones of the same part number or of original equipment quality and design. Torque specifications must be followed for proper reassembly and component retention.
1   Raise the vehicle and support it securely on jackstands
2   Remove the parking brake cable bolt **(see illustration)**.
3   Remove the nuts and bolts and detach the trailing arm from the vehicle.
4   Installation is the reverse of removal. Tighten the nuts and bolts to the torques listed in the Specifications Section at the beginning of this Chapter before lowering the vehicle weight onto the suspension.

---

14   Rear suspension lateral rod (coil spring models) – removal and installation

Refer to illustration 14.2
Warning: *Whenever any of the suspension or steering fasteners are loosened or removed, they must be inspected and, if necessary, replaced with new ones of the same part number or of original equipment quality and design. Torque specifications must be followed for proper reassembly and component retention.*
1   Raise the vehicle and support it securely on jackstands
2   Remove the left side parking brake cable bolt **(see illustration)**.
3   Remove the left side lower shock absorber bolt.
4   Remove the left side trailing arm bolts (see Section 13).
5   Remove the nuts and detach the lateral rod.
6   Installation is the reverse of removal. Tighten the nuts and bolts to the torques listed in the Specifications Section at the beginning of this Chapter before lowering the vehicle weight onto the suspension.

---

15   Rear suspension coil spring – removal and installation

Refer to illustration 15.3
Warning: *Whenever any of the suspension or steering fasteners are loosened or removed, they must be inspected and, if necessary, replaced with new ones of the same part number or of original equipment quality and de*

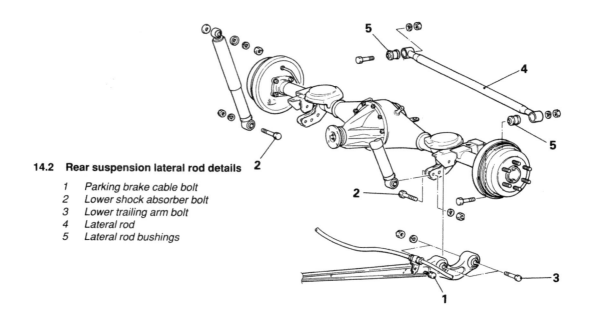

14.2   Rear suspension lateral rod details

1   *Parking brake cable bolt*
2   *Lower shock absorber bolt*
3   *Lower trailing arm bolt*
4   *Lateral rod*
5   *Lateral rod bushings*

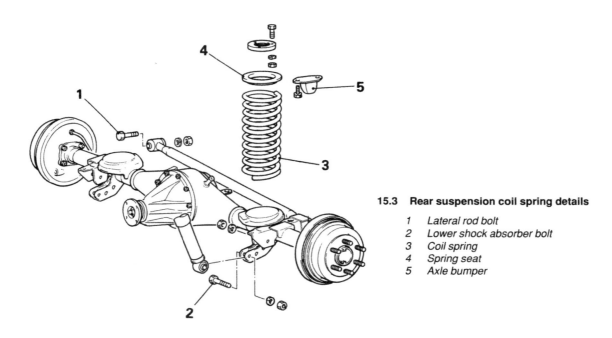

15.3   Rear suspension coil spring details

1   *Lateral rod bolt*
2   *Lower shock absorber bolt*
3   *Coil spring*
4   *Spring seat*
5   *Axle bumper*

sign. Torque specifications must be followed for proper reassembly and component retention.

1   Raise the vehicle and support it securely on jackstands
2   Support the axle with a jack.
3   Remove the right side lateral rod bolt **(see illustration)**.
4   Remove the lower left shock absorber bolt.
5   Lower the axle and remove the springs and seats.
6   Installation is the reverse of removal. Tighten the nuts and bolts to the torques listed in the Specifications Section at the beginning of this Chapter before lowering the vehicle weight onto the suspension.

16   Rear stabilizer bar (coil spring models) – removal and installation

Refer to illustration 16.2
Warning: *Whenever any of the suspension or steering fasteners are loosened or removed, they must be inspected and, if necessary, replaced with new ones of the same part number or of original equipment quality and design. Torque specifications must be followed for proper reassembly and component retention.*

1   Raise the vehicle and support it securely on jackstands

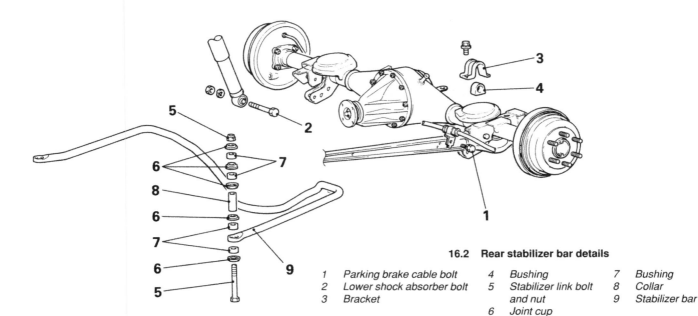

16.2   Rear stabilizer bar details

1	Parking brake cable bolt	4	Bushing	7	Bushing
2	Lower shock absorber bolt	5	Stabilizer link bolt	8	Collar
3	Bracket		and nut	9	Stabilizer bar
		6	Joint cup		

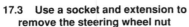

17.3   Use a socket and extension to remove the steering wheel nut

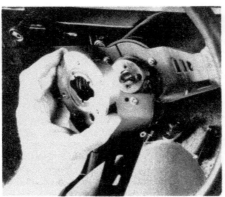

17.4   Remove the screws and lift off the horn plate (if equipped)

17.6   Remove the steering wheel from the shaft with a puller – DO NOT hammer on the shaft!

2   Remove the parking brake cable attaching bolt **(see illustration)**.
3   Remove the lower left shock absorber bolt.
4   Remove the stabilizer bar bracket bolts and detach the brackets and bushing.
5   Remove the stabilizer link bolts and detach the bar from the vehicle.
6   Installation is the reverse of removal. Before lowering the vehicle weight onto the suspension, tighten the bracket bolts to the torque listed in the Specifications Section at the beginning of this Chapter. Tighten the nuts on the stabilizer link bolts securely.

---

17   Steering wheel – removal and installation

Refer to illustrations 17.3, 17.4 and 17.6
Warning: *Whenever any of the suspension or steering fasteners are loosened or removed, they must be inspected and, if necessary, replaced with new ones of the same part number or of original equipment quality and design. Torque specifications must be followed for proper reassembly and component retention.*

Removal

1   Disconnect the cable from the negative battery terminal.

2   Using a small screwdriver, pry off the horn button or center pad and unplug the horn switch connector.
3   Unscrew the steering wheel nut **(see illustration)**
4   Remove the horn plate (if equipped) **(see illustration)**.
5   Mark the steering wheel hub and the column shaft with paint to ensure correct repositioning during reassembly.
6   Remove the wheel using a puller **(see illustration)**. **Caution:** *Do not hammer on the wheel or the shaft to separate them.*

Installation

7   Realign the steering wheel and the column shaft using the paint marks. Install and tighten the retaining nut to the torque listed in this Chapter's Specifications, then attach the horn plate and button or center pad.
8   Hook up the negative battery cable.

---

18   Steering linkage – removal and installation

Warning: *Whenever any of the suspension or steering fasteners are loosened or removed, they must be inspected and, if necessary, replaced with new ones of the same part number or of original equipment quality and design. Torque specifications must be followed for proper reassembly and component retention.*

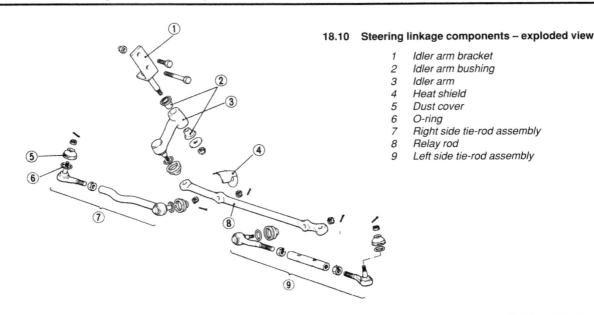

18.10   **Steering linkage components – exploded view**

1   *Idler arm bracket*
2   *Idler arm bushing*
3   *Idler arm*
4   *Heat shield*
5   *Dust cover*
6   *O-ring*
7   *Right side tie-rod assembly*
8   *Relay rod*
9   *Left side tie-rod assembly*

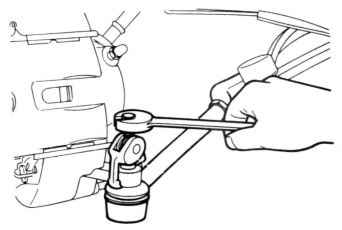

18.11   **Use a puller to separate the tie-rod end from the steering knuckle**

1   All steering linkage removal and installation procedures should be performed with the front end of the vehicle raised and placed securely on jackstands.

2   Before removing any steering linkage components, obtain a balljoint separator. It may be a screw-type puller or a wedge-type (pickle fork) tool, although the wedge-type tool tends to damage the balljoint seals. It is possible to jar a balljoint taper pin free from its eye by striking opposite sides of the eye simultaneously with two large hammers, but the space available to do so is usually very limited.

3   After installing any of the steering linkage components, the front wheel alignment should be checked by a reputable front end alignment shop.

Pitman arm

4   Remove the nut securing the Pitman arm to the steering gear sector shaft.

5   Scribe or paint match marks on the arm and shaft.

6   Using a puller, disconnect the Pitman arm from the shaft splines.

7   Remove the cotter pin and castle nut securing the Pitman arm to the relay rod.

8   Using a puller, disconnect the Pitman arm from the relay rod.

9   Installation is the reverse of the removal procedure. Be sure to tighten the nuts to the torques listed in this Chapter's Specifications and install a new cotter pin.

Tie-rod

Refer to illustrations 18.10 and 18.11

10   Remove the cotter pins and castle nuts securing the tie-rod to the relay rod and knuckle arm **(see illustration)**.

11   Separate the tie-rod from the relay rod and knuckle arm with a puller **(see illustration)**.

12   If a tie-rod end is to be replaced, loosen the jam nut and mark the relationship of the tie-rod end to the tie-rod with white paint. When installing the new rod end, thread it onto the tie-rod until it reaches the mark, then turn the jam nut until it contacts the rod end. Don't tighten it fully at this time.

13   Turn the tie-rod ends so they are at approximately 90-degree angles to each other, then tighten the jam nuts to lock the ends in position.

14   The remaining installation steps are the reverse of those for removal. Make sure to tighten the castle nuts to the torques listed in this Chapter's Specifications.

Idler arm

15   Remove the nut securing the idler arm to the bracket **(see illustration 18.10)**.

16   Remove the cotter pin and castle nut securing the idler arm to the relay rod.

17   Using a puller, disconnect the idler arm from the relay rod.

18   Slide the idler arm off the bracket shaft and remove it from the vehicle.

19   Installation is the reverse of the removal procedure. Be sure to tighten the nuts to the specified torque and install a new cotter pin.

19   Steering gear – removal and installation

Warning: *Whenever any of the suspension or steering fasteners are loosened or removed, they must be inspected and, if necessary, replaced with new ones of the same part number or of original equipment quality and design. Torque specifications must be followed for proper reassembly and component retention.*

Note: *If you find that the steering gear is defective, it is not recommended that you overhaul it. Because of the special tools needed to do the job, it is best to let your dealer service department overhaul it for you (or replace it with a factory rebuilt unit). However, you can remove and install it yourself by following the procedure outlined here. The removal and installation procedures for manual steering and power steering gear housings are identical except that the inlet and outlet lines must be removed from the steering* gear housing on power steering-equipped models before the housing can be removed. The steering system should be filled and power steering systems should be bled after the gear is reinstalled (see Section 22).

1   Raise the front of the vehicle and place it securely on jackstands. Apply the parking brake.
2   Place an alignment mark on the steering shaft flexible coupling and the gear housing worm shaft to assure correct reassembly, then remove the coupling pinch bolt.
3   Disconnect the power steering line connections from the steering gear. Plug the lines so the fluid will not drain.
4   Disconnect the Pitman arm and the left tie-rod from the relay rod (see Section 18).
5   Remove the bolts securing the gear housing to the chassis and lower the gear from the vehicle.
6   Installation is the reverse of the removal procedure. Be sure to tighten all nuts and bolts to the torques listed in this Chapter's Specifications.

20   Steering freeplay – adjustment

Refer to illustration 20.6

1   Raise the vehicle with a jack so that the front wheels are off the ground and place the vehicle securely on jackstands.
2   Point the wheels straight ahead.
3   Using a wrench, loosen the locknut on the steering gear.
4   Turn the adjusting screw clockwise to decrease wheel freeplay and counterclockwise to increase it. **Note:** *Turn the adjusting screw in small increments, checking the steering wheel freeplay between them.*
5   Turn the steering wheel halfway around in both directions, checking that the freeplay is correct and that the steering is smooth.
6   Hold the adjusting screw so that it will not turn and tighten the locknut **(see illustration)**.
7   Remove the jackstands and lower the vehicle.

21   Power steering pump – removal and installation

Warning: *Whenever any of the suspension or steering fasteners are loosened or removed, they must be inspected and, if necessary, replaced with new ones of the same part number or of original equipment quality and design. Torque specifications must be followed for proper reassembly and component retention.*

Note: *If you find that the steering pump is defective, it is not recommended that you overhaul it. Because of the special tools needed to do the job, it is best to let your dealer service department overhaul it for you (or replace it with a factory rebuilt unit). However, you can remove it yourself using the procedure which follows.*

Removal

1   Position a container to catch the pump fluid. Disconnect the hoses from the pump body. As each is disconnected, cap or tape over the hose opening and then secure the end in a raised position to prevent leakage and contamination. Cover or plug the pump openings to so dirt won't enter the unit.
2   Loosen the pump belt adjustment until the drivebelt can be removed from the pump pulley (see Chapter 1, if necessary).
3   Remove the pump mounting bolts and lift the pump out of the engine compartment.

Installation

4   Installation is the reverse of the removal procedure. When installing the pressure line, make sure there is sufficient clearance between the line and the exhaust manifold.
5   To adjust the drivebelt tension, see Chapter 1.
6   Fill the power steering fluid reservoir with the specified fluid and bleed the power steering system (see Section 22).
7   Check for fluid leaks.

20.6   Loosen the locknut with a wrench and use a screwdriver to turn the adjusting screw – when tightening the locknut, be sure to hold the screw to keep it from turning

22   Power steering system – bleeding

1   Check the fluid in the reservoir and add fluid of the specified type if it is low.
2   Jack up the front of the vehicle and place it securely on jackstands.
3   With the engine off, turn the steering wheel fully in both directions two or three times.
4   Recheck the fluid in the reservoir and add more fluid if necessary.
5   Start the engine and turn the steering wheel fully in both directions two or three times. The engine should be running at 1000 rpm or less.
6   Remove the jackstands and lower the vehicle completely.
7   With the engine running at 1000 rpm or less, turn the steering wheel fully in both directions two or three times.
8   Return the steering wheel to the center position.
9   Check that the fluid is not foamy or cloudy.
10   Measure the fluid level with the engine running.
11   Turn off the engine and again measure the fluid level. It should rise no more than 0.20 in (5 mm) when the engine is turned off.
12   If a problem is encountered, repeat Steps 7 through 11.
13   If the problem persists, remove the pump (see Section 22), and have it repaired by a dealer service department.

23   Front end alignment – general information

Refer to illustration 23.1

A front end alignment refers to the adjustments made to the front wheels so they are in proper angular relationship to the suspension and the ground. Front wheels that are out of proper alignment not only affect steering control, but also increase tire wear. The front end adjustments normally required are camber, caster and toe-in **(see illustration)**.

Getting the proper front wheel alignment is a very exacting process, one in which complicated and expensive machines are necessary to perform the job properly. Because of this, you should have a technician with the proper equipment perform these tasks. We will, however, use this space to give you a basic idea of what is involved with front end alignment so you can better understand the process and deal intelligently with the shop that does the work.

Toe-in is the turning in of the front wheels. The purpose of a toe specification is to ensure parallel rolling of the front wheels. In a vehicle with zero toe-in, the distance between the front edges of the wheels will be the same as the distance between the rear edges of the wheels. The actual amount of toe-in is normally only a fraction of an inch. Toe-in adjustment is controlled by the tie-rod end position on the inner tie-rod. Incorrect toe-in will cause the tires to wear improperly by making them scrub against the road surface.

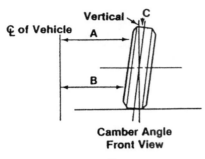

**Camber Angle
Front View**

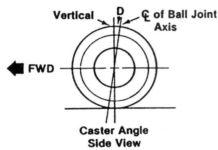

**Caster Angle
Side View**

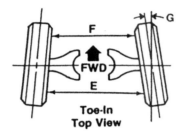

**Toe-In
Top View**

23.1   Front end alignment details

1   A minus B = C (degrees camber)
2   E minus F = toe-in (measured in inches)
3   G = toe-in (expressed in degrees)

Camber is the tilting of the front wheels from the vertical when viewed from the front of the vehicle. When the wheels tilt out at the top, the camber is said to be positive (+). When the wheels tilt in at the top the camber is negative (-). The amount of tilt is measured in degrees from the vertical and this measurement is called the camber angle. This angle affects the amount of tire tread which contacts the road and compensates for changes in the suspension geometry when the vehicle is cornering or travelling over an undulating surface.

Caster is the tilting of the front steering axis from the vertical. A tilt toward the rear is positive caster and a tilt toward the front is negative caster. Caster angle affects the self-centering action of the steering, which governs straight-line stability. Caster is adjusted by moving shims from one end of the upper arm mount to the other.

24   Wheels and tires – general information

Wheels can be damaged by an impact with a curb or other solid object. If the wheels are bent, the result is a hazardous condition which must be corrected. To check the wheels, raise the vehicle and set it on jackstands. Visually inspect the wheels for obvious signs of damage such as cracks and deformation.

Tire and wheel balance is very important to the overall handling, braking and ride performance of the vehicle. Whenever a tire is dismounted for repair or replacement, the tire and wheel assembly should be balanced before being installed on the vehicle.

Wheels should be periodically cleaned, especially on the inside, where mud and road salts accumulate and eventually cause rust and, ultimately, possible wheel failure.

Tires are extremely important from a safety standpoint. The tread should be checked periodically to see that the tires have not worn excessively, a condition which can be dangerous, especially in wet weather.

To equalize wear and add life to a set of tires, it is recommended that they be rotated periodically. When rotating, check for signs of abnormal wear and foreign objects in the tread or sidewalls (refer to Chapter 1, Routine Maintenance).

Proper tire inflation is essential for maximum life of the tread and for proper handling and braking. Tires that are wearing in an abnormal way are an indication that their inflation is incorrect or that the front end components are not adjusted properly. Take the vehicle to a reputable front end alignment and repair shop to correct the situation.

Chapter 11   Body

Contents

1   General information

These models feature a separate boxed steel frame and body. Certain components are particularly vulnerable to accident damage and can be unbolted and repaired or replaced. Among these parts are the body moldings, doors, bumpers, hood, tailgate and all glass.

Only general body maintenance practices and body panel repair procedures within the scope of the do-it-yourselfer are included in this Chapter.

2   Body – maintenance

1   The condition of your vehicle's body is very important, because the resale value depends a great deal on it. It's much more difficult to repair a neglected or damaged body than it is to repair mechanical components. The hidden areas of the body, such as the wheel wells, the frame and the engine compartment, are equally important, although they don't require as frequent attention as the rest of the body.

2   Once a year, or every 12,000 miles, it's a good idea to have the underside of the body steam cleaned. All traces of dirt and oil will be removed and the area can then be inspected carefully for rust, damaged brake lines, frayed electrical wires, damaged cables and other problems. The front suspension components should be greased after completion of this job.

3   At the same time, clean the engine and the engine compartment with a steam cleaner or water soluble degreaser.

4   The wheel wells should be given close attention, since undercoating can peel away and stones and dirt thrown up by the tires can cause the paint to chip and flake, allowing rust to set in. If rust is found, clean down to the bare metal and apply an anti-rust paint.

5   The body should be washed about once a week. Wet the vehicle thoroughly to soften the dirt, then wash it down with a soft sponge and plenty of clean soapy water. If the surplus dirt is not washed off very carefully, it can wear down the paint.

6   Spots of tar or asphalt thrown up from the road should be removed with a cloth soaked in solvent.

7   Once every six months, wax the body and chrome trim. If a chrome cleaner is used to remove rust from any of the vehicle's plated parts, remember that the cleaner also removes part of the chrome, so use it sparingly.

3   Vinyl trim – maintenance

1   Don't clean vinyl trim with detergents, caustic soap or petroleum-based cleaners. Plain soap and water works just fine, with a soft brush to clean dirt that may be ingrained. Wash the vinyl as frequently as the rest of the vehicle.

2   After cleaning, application of a high quality rubber and vinyl protectant will help prevent oxidation and cracks. The protectant can also be applied to weatherstripping, vacuum lines and rubber hoses, which often fail as a result of chemical degradation, and to the tires.

4   Upholstery and carpets – maintenance

1   Every three months remove the carpets or mats and clean the interior of the vehicle (more frequently if necessary). Vacuum the upholstery and carpets to remove loose dirt and dust.

2   Leather upholstery requires special care. Stains should be removed with warm water and a very mild soap solution. Use a clean, damp cloth to remove the soap, then wipe again with a dry cloth. Never use alcohol, gasoline, nail polish remover or thinner to clean leather upholstery.

3   After cleaning, regularly treat leather upholstery with a leather wax. Never use car wax on leather upholstery.

4   In areas where the interior of the vehicle is subject to bright sunlight, cover leather seats with a sheet if the vehicle is to be left out for any length of time.

5   Body repair – minor damage

See photo sequence

Repair of scratches

1   If the scratch is superficial and does not penetrate to the metal of the body, repair is very simple. Lightly rub the scratched area with a fine rubbing compound to remove loose paint and built up wax. Rinse the area with clean water.

2   Apply touch-up paint to the scratch, using a small brush. Continue to apply thin layers of paint until the surface of the paint in the scratch is level with the surrounding paint. Allow the new paint at least two weeks to harden, then blend it into the surrounding paint by rubbing with a very fine rubbing compound. Finally, apply a coat of wax to the scratch area.

3   If the scratch has penetrated the paint and exposed the metal of the body, causing the metal to rust, a different repair technique is required. Remove all loose rust from the bottom of the scratch with a pocket knife, then apply rust inhibiting paint to prevent the formation of rust in the future. Using a rubber or nylon applicator, coat the scratched area with glaze-type filler. If required, the filler can be mixed with thinner to provide a very thin paste, which is ideal for filling narrow scratches. Before the glaze filler in the scratch hardens, wrap a piece of smooth cotton cloth around the tip of a finger. Dip the cloth in thinner and then quickly wipe it along the surface of the scratch. This will ensure that the surface of the filler is slightly hollow. The scratch can now be painted over as described earlier in this section.

Repair of dents

4   When repairing dents, the first job is to pull the dent out until the affected area is as close as possible to its original shape. There is no point in trying to restore the original shape completely as the metal in the damaged area will have stretched on impact and cannot be restored to its original contours. It is better to bring the level of the dent up to a point which is about 1/8-inch below the level of the surrounding metal. In cases where the dent is very shallow, it is not worth trying to pull it out at all.

5   If the back side of the dent is accessible, it can be hammered out gently from behind using a soft-face hammer. While doing this, hold a block of wood firmly against the opposite side of the metal to absorb the hammer blows and prevent the metal from being stretched.

6   If the dent is in a section of the body which has double layers, or some other factor makes it inaccessible from behind, a different technique is re-

quired. Drill several small holes through the metal inside the damaged area, particularly in the deeper sections. Screw long, self tapping screws into the holes just enough for them to get a good grip in the metal. Now the dent can be pulled out by pulling on the protruding heads of the screws with locking pliers.

7   The next stage of repair is the removal of paint from the damaged area and from an inch or so of the surrounding metal. This is easily done with a wire brush or sanding disk in a drill motor, although it can be done just as effectively by hand with sandpaper. To complete the preparation for filling, score the surface of the bare metal with a screwdriver or the tang of a file or drill small holes in the affected area. This will provide a good grip for the filler material. To complete the repair, see the Section on filling and painting.

Repair of rust holes or gashes

8   Remove all paint from the affected area and from an inch or so of the surrounding metal using a sanding disk or wire brush mounted in a drill motor. If these are not available, a few sheets of sandpaper will do the job just as effectively.

9   With the paint removed, you will be able to determine the severity of the corrosion and decide whether to replace the whole panel, if possible, or repair the affected area. New body panels are not as expensive as most people think and it is often quicker to install a new panel than to repair large areas of rust.

10   Remove all trim pieces from the affected area except those which will act as a guide to the original shape of the damaged body, such as headlight shells, etc. Using metal snips or a hacksaw blade, remove all loose metal and any other metal that is badly affected by rust. Hammer the edges of the hole inward to create a slight depression for the filler material.

11   Wire brush the affected area to remove the powdery rust from the surface of the metal. If the back of the rusted area is accessible, treat it with rust inhibiting paint.

12   Before filling is done, block the hole in some way. This can be done with sheet metal riveted or screwed into place, or by stuffing the hole with wire mesh.

13   Once the hole is blocked off, the affected area can be filled and painted. See the following subsection on filling and painting.

Filling and painting

14   Many types of body fillers are available, but generally speaking, body repair kits which contain filler paste and a tube of resin hardener are best for this type of repair work. A wide, flexible plastic or nylon applicator will be necessary for imparting a smooth and contoured finish to the surface of the filler material. Mix up a small amount of filler on a clean piece of wood or cardboard (use the hardener sparingly). Follow the manufacturer's instructions on the package, otherwise the filler will set incorrectly.

15   Using the applicator, apply the filler paste to the prepared area. Draw the applicator across the surface of the filler to achieve the desired contour and to level the filler surface. As soon as a contour that approximates the original one is achieved, stop working the paste. If you continue, the paste will begin to stick to the applicator. Continue to add thin layers of paste at 20-minute intervals until the level of the filler is just above the surrounding metal.

16   Once the filler has hardened, the excess can be removed with a body file. From then on, progressively finer grades of sandpaper should be used, starting with a 180-grit paper and finishing with a 600-grit wet or dry paper. Always wrap the sandpaper around a flat rubber or wooden block, otherwise the surface of the filler will not be completely flat. During the sanding of the filler surface, the wet-or-dry paper should be periodically rinsed in water. This will ensure that a very smooth finish is produced in the final stage.

17   At this point, the repair area should be surrounded by a ring of bare metal, which in turn should be encircled by the finely feathered edge of good paint. Rinse the repair area with clean water until all of the dust produced by the sanding operation is gone.

18   Spray the entire area with a light coat of primer. This will reveal any imperfections in the surface of the filler. Repair the imperfections with fresh filler paste or glaze filler and once more smooth the surface with

sandpaper. Repeat this spray-and-repair procedure until you are satisfied that the surface of the filler and the feathered edge of the paint are perfect. Rinse the area with clean water and allow it to dry completely.

19   The repair area is now ready for painting. Spray painting must be carried out in a warm, dry, windless and dust free atmosphere. These conditions can be created if you have access to a large indoor work area, but if you are forced to work in the open, you will have to pick the day very carefully. If you are working indoors, dousing the floor in the work area with water will help settle the dust which would otherwise be in the air. If the repair area is confined to one body panel, mask off the surrounding panels. This will help minimize the effects of a slight mismatch in paint color. Trim pieces such as chrome strips, door handles, etc., will also need to be masked off or removed. Use masking tape and several thicknesses of newspaper for the masking operations.

20   Before spraying, shake the paint can thoroughly, then spray a test area until the spray painting technique is mastered. Cover the repair area with a thick coat of primer. The thickness should be built up using several thin layers of primer rather than one thick one. Using 600-grit wet-or-dry sandpaper, rub down the surface of the primer until it is very smooth. While doing this, the work area should be thoroughly rinsed with water and the wet-or-dry sandpaper periodically rinsed as well. Allow the primer to dry before spraying additional coats.

21   Spray on the top coat, again building up the thickness by using several thin layers of paint. Begin spraying in the center of the repair area and then, using a circular motion, work out until the whole repair area and about two inches of the surrounding original paint is covered. Remove all masking material 10 to 15 minutes after spraying on the final coat of paint. Allow the new paint at least two weeks to harden, then use a very fine rubbing compound to blend the edges of the new paint into the existing paint. Finally, apply a coat of wax.

6   Body repair – major damage

1   Major damage must be repaired by an auto body shop specifically equipped to perform unibody repairs. These shops have the specialized equipment required to do the job properly.

2   If the damage is extensive, the body must be checked for proper alignment or the vehicle's handling characteristics may be adversely affected and other components may wear at an accelerated rate.

3   Due to the fact that all of the major body components (hood, fenders, etc.) are separate and replaceable units, any seriously damaged components should be replaced rather than repaired. Sometimes the components can be found in a wrecking yard that specializes in used vehicle components, often at considerable savings over the cost of new parts.

7   Hinges and locks – maintenance

Once every 3000 miles, or every three months, the hinges and latch assemblies on the doors, hood and cargo door should be given a few drops of light oil or lock lubricant. The door latch strikers should also be lubricated with a thin coat of grease to reduce wear and ensure free movement. Lubricate the door and cargo door locks with spray-on graphite lubricant.

8   Windshield and fixed glass – replacement

Replacement of the windshield and fixed glass requires the use of special fast-setting adhesive/caulk materials and some specialized tools and techniques. These operations should be left to a dealer service department or a shop specializing in glass work.

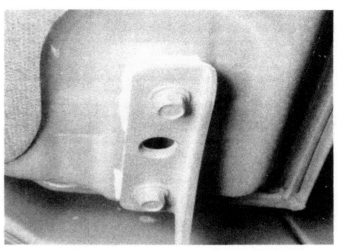

9.2   Use a scribe or marking pen to mark the hinge locations

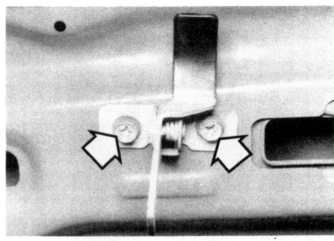

9.7   Loosen the bolts on the catch assembly (arrows) to adjust the position – be sure to mark the edges first so it can be returned to the original location

9   Hood – removal, installation and adjustment

Refer to illustrations 9.2, 9.7, 9.10a, 9.10b and 9.11
Note: *The hood is heavy and somewhat awkward to remove and install – at least two people should perform this procedure.*

Removal and installation

1   Use blankets or pads to cover the cowl area of the body and the fenders. This will protect the body and paint as the hood is lifted off.

2   Scribe or mark alignment marks around the hinge plate to insure proper alignment during installation **(see illustration)**.

3   Disconnect any cables or wire harnesses which will interfere with the removal.

4   Have an assistant support the weight of the hood. Remove the hinge-to-hood nuts or bolts.

5   Lift off the hood.

6   Installation is the reverse of removal.

Adjustment

7   Fore-and-aft and side-to-side adjustment of the hood is done by moving the hood in relation to the hinge plate after loosening the bolts and by loosening the catch adjusting screws and repositioning it (see the accompanying illustration and illustration 9.2).

8   Scribe a line or paint the edges around the entire hinge plate so you can judge the amount of movement.

9.10a   Loosen the mounting bolts (arrows) and adjust the latch assembly

9.10b   Turn the height adjustment screw with a screwdriver (early models)

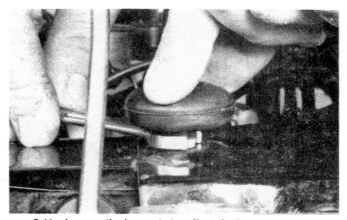

9.11   Loosen the jam nuts to adjust the bumper screws (early models)

9   Loosen the bolts and move the hood into correct alignment. Move it only a little at a time. Tighten the hinge bolts and carefully lower the hood to check the alignment.

10   If necessary after installation, the entire hood latch assembly can be adjusted in-and-out as well as from side-to-side on the hood so the hood closes securely and is flush with the fenders. To do this, scribe a line around the hood latch mounting bolts to provide a reference point for the side-to-side movement. Then loosen the bolts and reposition the latch assembly as necessary to adjust the side-to-side movement and use a screwdriver to turn the height adjustment screw to adjust the hood up-and-down **(see illustrations)**. Following adjustment, retighten the mounting bolts and adjustment screw locknut.

11   Finally, adjust the hood bumpers on the hood so the hood, when closed, is flush with the fenders **(see illustration)**.

12   The hood latch assembly, as well as the hinges, should be periodically lubricated with white lithium-base grease to prevent sticking and wear.

---

10   Radiator grille – removal and installation

Refer to illustrations 10.1a and 10.1b

1   The radiator grille is held in place by clips and, on some models, screws. Remove any screws and disengage the grille retaining clips with a small screwdriver **(see illustrations)**.

2   Once all the retaining clips are disengaged, pull the grille out and remove it.

3   To install the grille, press it in place until the clips lock it in position.

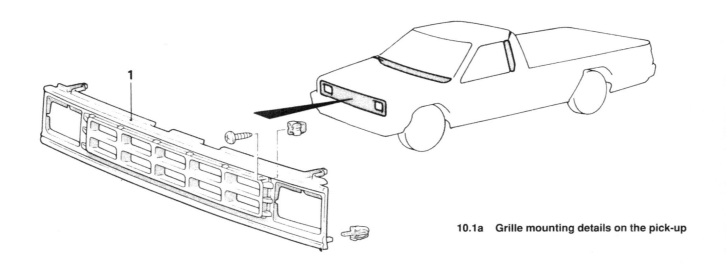

10.1a   Grille mounting details on the pick-up

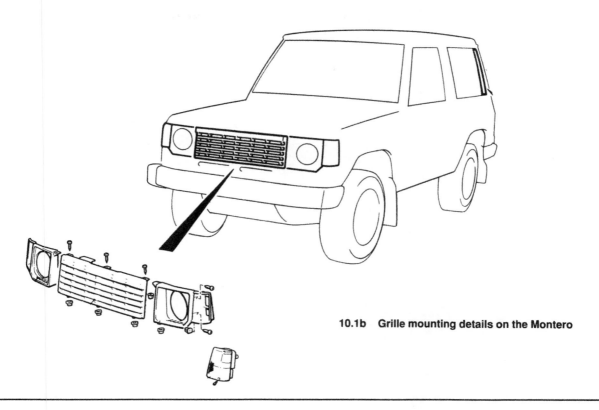

10.1b Grille mounting details on the Montero

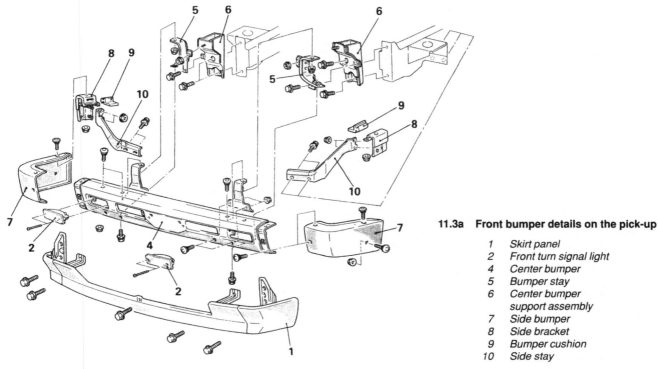

11.3a Front bumper details on the pick-up

1	Skirt panel
2	Front turn signal light
4	Center bumper
5	Bumper stay
6	Center bumper support assembly
7	Side bumper
8	Side bracket
9	Bumper cushion
10	Side stay

11 Bumpers – removal and installation

Refer to illustrations 11.3a and 11.3b

1 Disconnect any wiring or other components that would interfere with bumper removal.

2 Support the bumper with a jack or jackstand. Alternatively, have an assistant support the bumper as the bolts are removed.

3 Remove the retaining bolts and detach the bumper **(see illustrations)**.

4 Installation is the reverse of removal.

5 Tighten the retaining bolts securely.

This photographic sequence shows the steps taken to repair the dent and paintwork damage shown above. In general, the procedure for repairing a hole will be similar; where there are substantial differences, the procedure is clearly described and shown in a separate photograph.

First remove any trim around the dent, then hammer out the dent where access is possible. This will minimise filling. Here, after the large dent has been hammered out, the damaged area is being made slightly concave.

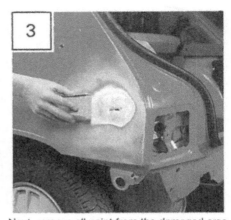

Next, remove all paint from the damaged area by rubbing with course abrasive paper or using a power drill fitted with a wire brush or abrasive pad. 'Feather' the edge of the boundary with good paintwork using a finer grade of abrasive paper.

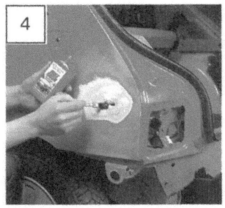

Where there are holes or other damage, the sheet metal should be cut away before proceeding further. The damaged area and any signs of rust should be treated with Turtle Wax Hi-Tech Rust Eater, which will also inhibit further rust formation.

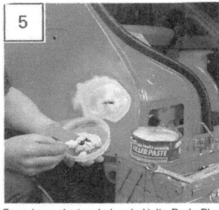

For a large dent or hole mix Holts Body Plus Resin and Hardener according to the manufacturer's instructions and apply around the edge of the repair. Press Glass Fibre Matting over the repair area and leave for 20-30 minutes to harden. Then ...

... brush more Holts Body Plus Resin and Hardener onto the matting and leave to harden. Repeat the sequence with two or three layers of matting, checking that the final layer is lower than the surrounding area. Apply Holts Body Plus Filler Paste as shown in Step 5B.

For a medium dent, mix Holts Body Plus Filler Paste and Hardener according to the manufacturer's instructions and apply it with a flexible applicator. Apply thin layers of filler at 20-minute intervals, until the filler surface is slightly proud of the surrounding bodywork.

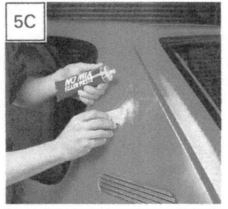

For small dents and scratches use Holts No Mix Filler Paste straight from the tube. Apply it according to the instructions in thin layers, using the spatula provided. It will harden in minutes if applied outdoors and may then be used as its own knifing putting.

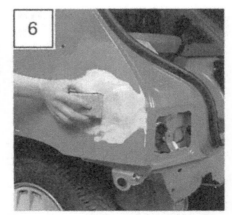

Use a plane or file for initial shaping. Then, using progressively finer grades of wet-and-dry paper, wrapped around a sanding block, and copious amounts of clean water, rub down the filler until glass smooth. 'Feather' the edges of adjoining paintwork.

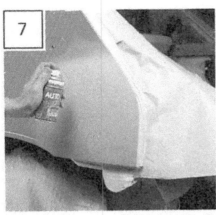

Protect adjoining areas before spraying the whole repair area and at least one inch of the surrounding sound paintwork with Holts Dupli-Color primer.

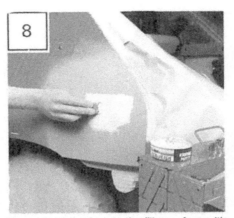

Fill any imperfections in the filler surface with a small amount of Holts Body Plus Knifing Putty. Using plenty of clean water, rub down the surface with a fine grade wet-and-dry paper - 400 grade is recommended - until it is really smooth.

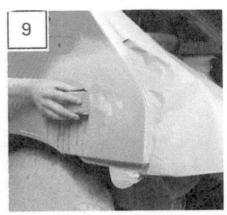

Carefully fill any remaining imperfections with knifing putty before applying the last coat of primer. Then rub down the surface with Holts Body Rubbing Compound to ensure a really smooth surface.

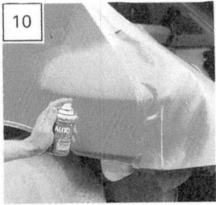

Protect surrounding areas from overspray before applying the topcoat in several thin layers. Agitate Holts Dupli-Color aerosol thoroughly. Start at the repair centre, spraying outwards with a side-to-side motion.

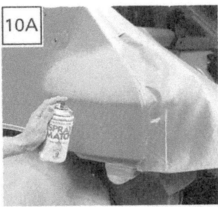

If the exact colour is not available off the shelf, local Holts Professional Spraymatch Centres will custom fill an aerosol to match perfectly.

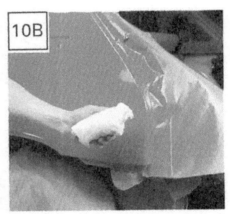

To identify whether a lacquer finish is required, rub a painted unrepaired part of the body with wax and a clean cloth.

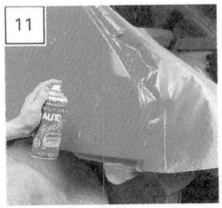

If no traces of paint appear on the cloth, spray Holts Dupli-Color clear lacquer over the repaired area to achieve the correct gloss level.

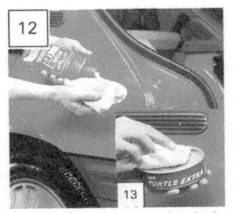

The paint will take about two weeks to harden fully. After this time it can be 'cut' with a mild cutting compound such as Turtle Wax Minute Cut prior to polishing with a final coating of Turtle Wax Extra.

When carrying out bodywork repairs, remember that the quality of the finished job is proportional to the time and effort expended.

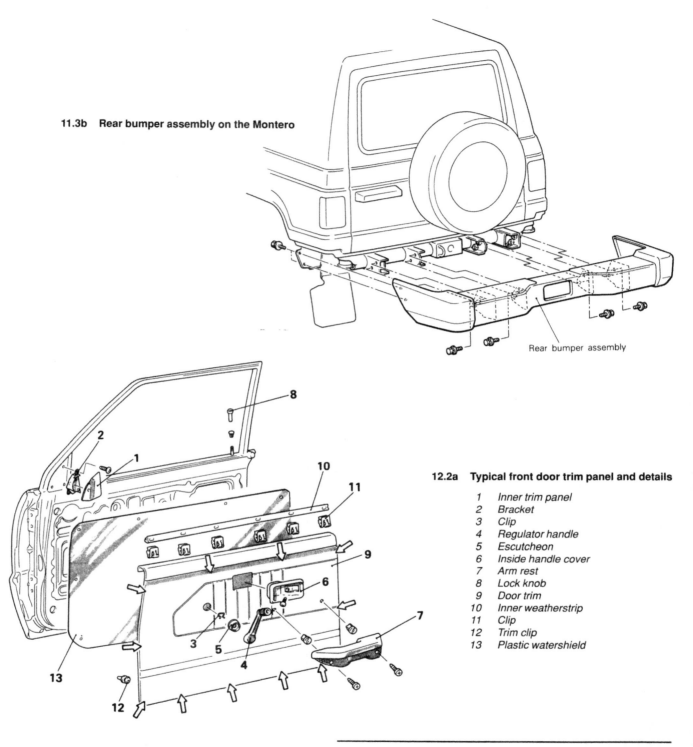

11.3b   Rear bumper assembly on the Montero

Rear bumper assembly

12.2a   Typical front door trim panel and details

1   *Inner trim panel*
2   *Bracket*
3   *Clip*
4   *Regulator handle*
5   *Escutcheon*
6   *Inside handle cover*
7   *Arm rest*
8   *Lock knob*
9   *Door trim*
10   *Inner weatherstrip*
11   *Clip*
12   *Trim clip*
13   *Plastic watershield*

12   Door trim panel – removal and installation

Refer to illustrations 12.2a, 12.2b, 12.2c, 12.3 and 12.4

1   Disconnect the negative cable from the battery.
2   Remove all door trim panel retaining screws and door pull/armrest assemblies **(see illustrations)**.
3   Remove the window crank, using a wire hook or crank removal tool (or a rag) to pull out the retaining clip **(see illustration)**.

4   Insert a putty knife between the trim panel and the door and disengage the retaining clips **(see illustration)**. Work around the outer edge until the panel is free.
5   Once all of the clips are disengaged, detach the trim panel, unplug any wire harness connectors and remove the trim panel from the vehicle.
6   For access to the inner door, carefully peel back the plastic watershield **(see illustration 12.2a)**.
7   Prior to installation of the door panel, be sure to reinstall any clips in the panel which may have come out during the removal procedure and remain in the door itself.

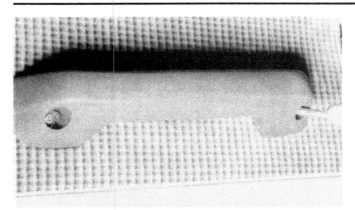

12.2b   Remove the screws from the armrest

12.2c   Remove the screw from the inside handle cover

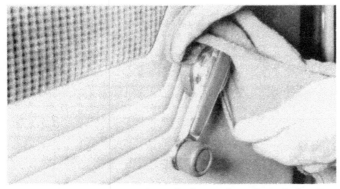

12.3   Use a shop rag to force the horseshoe shaped clip off the shaft

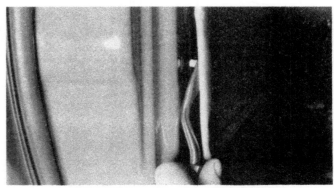

12.4   Carefully pry the door panel off the door

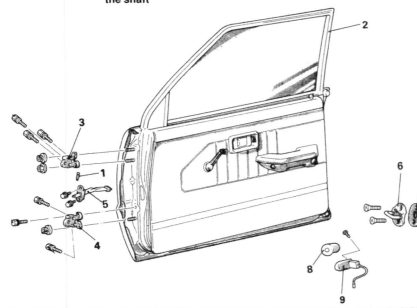

13.4a   Door hinge details on the pick-up

1   *Spring pin*
2   *Door*
3   *Door upper hinge*
4   *Door lower hinge*
5   *Door check*
6   *Striker*
7   *Striker shim*
8   *Door switch cap*
9   *Door switch*

8   Plug in the wire harness connectors and place the panel in position in the door. Press the door panel into place until the clips are seated and install the armrest/door pulls. Reinstall the clip and press the manual regulator window crank onto the shaft until it locks.

13   Door – removal, installation and adjustment

Refer to illustrations 13.4a and 13.4b

1   Remove the door trim panel. Disconnect any wire harness connec-tors and push them through the door opening so they won't interfere with door removal.
2   Place a jack or jackstand under the door or have an assistant on hand to support it when the hinge bolts are removed. **Note:** *If a jack or jackstand is used, place a rag between it and the door to protect the door's painted surfaces.*
3   Scribe around the door hinges.
4   Remove the hinge-to-door bolts and carefully lift off the door **(see il-lustrations)**.
5   Installation is the reverse of removal.

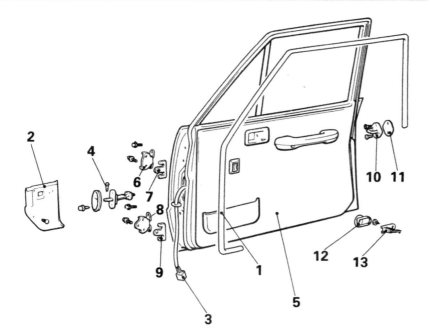

13.4b   Front door hinge details on the Montero

1   Door opening trim
    (power window)
2   Cowl side trim
3   Wiring harness con-
    nector (power window)
4   Spring pin
5   Door
6   Door upper hinge
7   Door upper hinge shim
8   Door lower hinge
9   Door lower hinge shim
10 Striker
11 Striker shim
12 Door switch cap
13 Door switch

14.3   Scribe or use a marker to make marks around the bolts and hinges on the cargo door

6   Following installation of the door, check the alignment and adjust it, if necessary. The door lock striker can be adjusted both up-and-down and sideways to provide positive engagement with the lock mechanism. This is done by loosening the mounting screws and moving the striker as necessary.

---

14   Rear cargo door – removal, installation and adjustment

Montero models

Refer to illustrations 14.3 and 14.4

Removal and installation

1   Disconnect any wire harness connectors and push them through the door opening so they won't interfere with door removal.
2   Place a jack or jackstand under the door or have an assistant on hand to support it when the hinge bolts are removed. **Note:** *If a jack or jackstand is used, place a rag between it and the door to protect the door's painted surfaces.* **Note:** *Remove the spare tire to help lighten the door weight.*
3   Scribe around the door bolts **(see illustration)**.
4   Remove the hinge-to-door bolts and carefully lift off the door **(see illustration)**.
5   Installation is the reverse of removal.

Adjustment

6   Following installation of the door, check the alignment and adjust it if necessary as follows:
   a) Up-and-down and side-to-side adjustments are made by loosening the hinge-to-body bolts and moving the door as necessary.
   b) The door lock striker can also be adjusted both up-and-down and sideways to provide positive engagement with the lock mechanism. This is done by loosening the mounting screws and moving the striker as necessary.

Pick-up models

Refer to illustration 14.7

Removal and installation

7   Remove the wire assembly retaining bolts and the wire assembly from the rear door **(see illustration)**.
8   While an assistant holds the door, remove the bolts from the hinge body.
9   Lift the door from the vehicle.
10   Installation is the reverse of removal.

Adjustment

11   Following installation of the door, check the alignment and adjust it if necessary as follows:
   a) Up-and-down and side-to-side adjustments are made by loosening the hinge-to-body bolts and moving the door as necessary.
   b) The door lock striker can also be adjusted both up-and-down and sideways to provide positive engagement with the lock mechanism. This is done by loosening the mounting screws and moving the striker as necessary.

---

15   Door latch, lock cylinder and handles – removal, installation and adjustment

---

Front door

Refer to illustrations 15.4, 15.7, 15.8, 15.9a and 15.9b

Removal and installation

1   Remove the door trim panel as described in Section 12.
2   Remove the plastic watershield, taking care not to tear it.
3   Remove the inside lever link clip and detach the link from the door lock assembly.

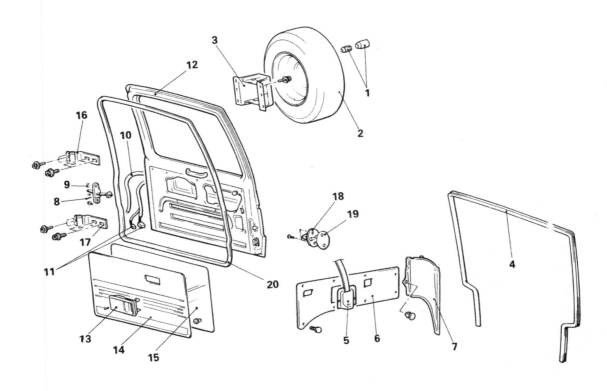

14.4   Rear cargo door details on the Montero

1	Spare tire lock cylinder	6	Quarter trim	11	Wiring harness connectors	16	Door upper hinge
2	Spare tire	7	Rear pillar lower trim	12	Back door	17	Door lower hinge
3	Spare tire carrier	8	Cotter pin	13	Inside handle cover	18	Striker
4	Rear opening trim	9	Clevis pin	14	Back door trim	19	Striker shim
5	Retractor cover	10	Washer tube	15	Watershield	20	Weatherstrip

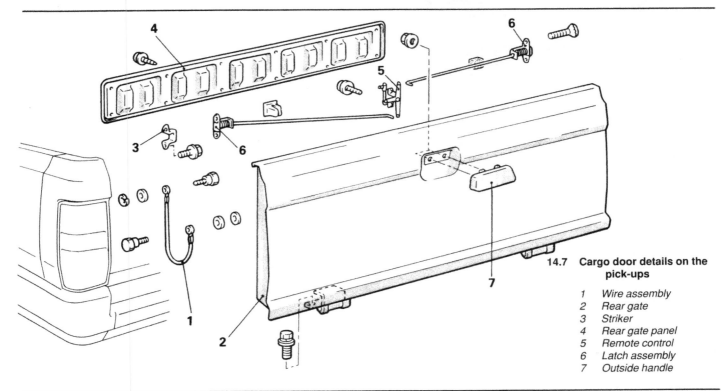

14.7   Cargo door details on the pick-ups

1   Wire assembly
2   Rear gate
3   Striker
4   Rear gate panel
5   Remote control
6   Latch assembly
7   Outside handle

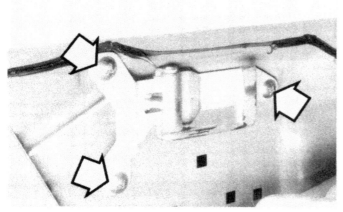

15.4   Remove the interior door handle screws (arrows) from the body

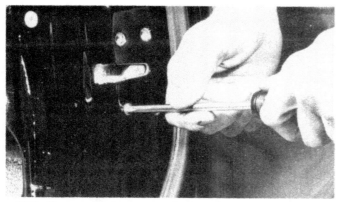

15.7   Remove the four screws holding the latch assembly to the door

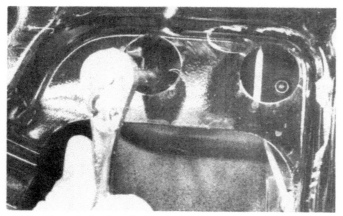

15.8   The exterior handle is attached to the door with two bolts that are accessible from the inside

4   Remove the screws that retain the interior handle assembly and lift it out **(see illustration)**.
5   Remove the glass run channel.
6   Disengage the door lock rod from the door latch assembly.
7   Remove the door latch assembly mounting screws **(see illustration)** and lift out the door latch assembly.
8   If necessary, remove the two nuts retaining the exterior handle and lift it out **(see illustration)**.
9   Remove the door lock cylinder through the outside of the door **(see illustrations)**.
10   Installation is the reverse of removal. **Note:** *During installation, apply grease to the sliding surface of all levers and springs.*

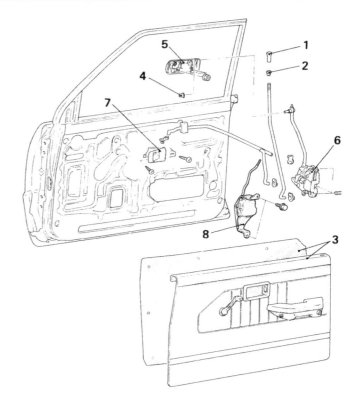

15.9a   Front door lock and handle details on the pick-up

1	Inside lock knob	5	Outside handle
2	Inside lock knob bush	6	Door latch
3	Door trim and watershield	7	Inside handle
4	Link clip	8	Door lock actuator (power door lock)

Adjustment
Refer to illustration 15.11
11   To adjust the outside door handle freeplay, remove the retaining cli from the actuating rod and turn the connector up or down to remove th freeplay **(see illustration)**.

Cargo door
Refer to illustration 15.14
Removal and installation
12   Remove the door trim panel as described in Section 12.
13   Remove the plastic watershield, taking care not to tear it.
14   Remove the inside lever link clip and detach the link from the door loc assembly **(see illustration)**.
15   Remove the screws that retain the interior handle assembly and lift out.
16   Disengage the door lock rod from the door lock assembly.
17   Remove the door lock assembly mounting screws and lift out the doc lock assembly.
18   If necessary, remove the two nuts retaining the exterior handle and li it out.
19   Squeeze the retaining clip with pliers and push the door lock cylinde through to the outside of the door and remove it.
20   Installation is the reverse of removal. **Note:** *During installation, appl grease to the sliding surface of all levers and springs.*

Adjustment
Refer to illustration 15.21
21   To adjust the outside door handle freeplay, remove the retaining cli from the actuating rod and turn the connector up or down to remove th freeplay **(see illustration)**.

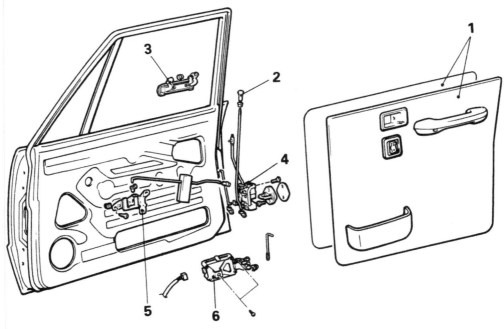

15.9b   Front door lock and handle details on the Montero

1	Door trim and watershield	3	Outside handle	5	Inside handle
2	Inside lock knob	4	Door latch	6	Door lock actuator (power door lock)

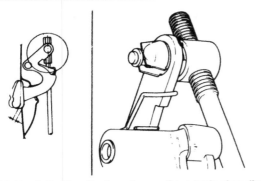

15.11   Adjusting the freeplay on the exterior handle

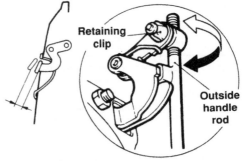

Retaining clip

Outside handle rod

15.21   Adjusting the freeplay on the exterior handle of the rear cargo door – Montero shown, but pick-up similar

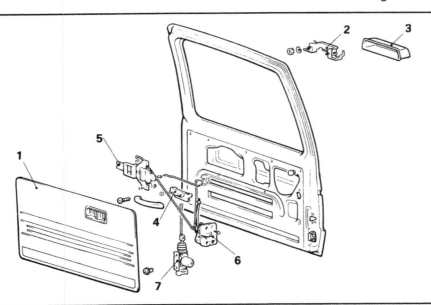

15.14   Cargo door lock and handle details on the Montero

1   Trim and watershield
2   Garnish bracket
3   Garnish
4   Outside handle
5   Inside handle
6   Door lock assembly
7   Door lock actuator (power door lock)

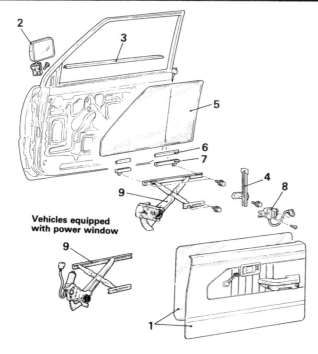

Vehicles equipped
with power window

16.2   Door window and regulator details

1   Door trim and watershield
2   Outside rear view mirror
3   Outer weatherstrip
4   Rear lower sash
5   Door window glass
6   Pad
7   Glass holder
8   Power window switch
9   Window regulator

16   Door window and regulator – removal and installation

Refer to illustrations 16.2

1   Remove the door trim panel and plastic watershield (see Section 12).
2   Remove the screws from the window bottom channel assembiy and lower the window glass **(see illustration)**.
3   Pry the two glass seals from the window opening. Remove the window glass by tilting it to detach the regulator arm from the glass channel

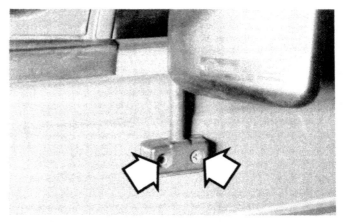

17.2   On low-mount mirrors, remove the screws (arrows) from the outside area of the door

and then sliding the glass up and out of the door.
4   Remove the regulator retaining screws.
5   Detach the regulator and guide it out of the opening in the door.
6   Installation is the reverse of removal.

17   Outside mirror – removal and installation

Refer to illustrations 17.1 and 17.2

1   On some mirrors, use a small screwdriver to pry the screw cover o the mirror base **(see illustration)**.
2   Remove the screws and lift the mirror off the door **(see illustration**
3   Installation is the reverse of removal.

18   Instrument cluster bezel and trim panels – removal and installation

Refer to illustrations 18.1a, 18.1b and 18.1c

1   Remove the hole covers (if equipped) and screws from the bezel o trim panel **(see illustrations)**.
2   Pull the bezel or panel out, detach it from the dashboard and remove it
3   Installation is the reverse of removal.

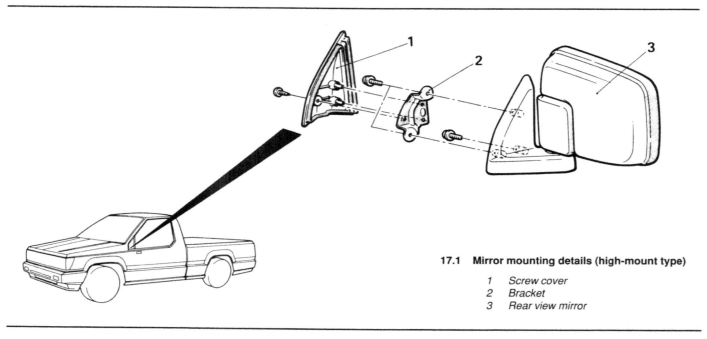

17.1   Mirror mounting details (high-mount type)

1   Screw cover
2   Bracket
3   Rear view mirror

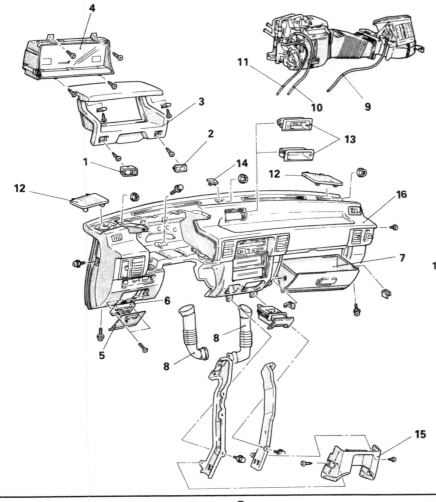

18.1a   **Instrument cluster and trim panel details on the pick-ups**

1   Hazard warning flasher switch
2   Screw hole cover
3   Instrument cluster bezel
4   Instrument cluster
5   Fuse box cover
6   Fuse box assembly
7   Glove box
8   Defroster duct
9   Air selection cable
10 Mode selection cable
11 Temperature control cable
12 Speaker cover
13 Parcel box or clock
14 Screw hole cover
15 Center cover
16 Instrument panel

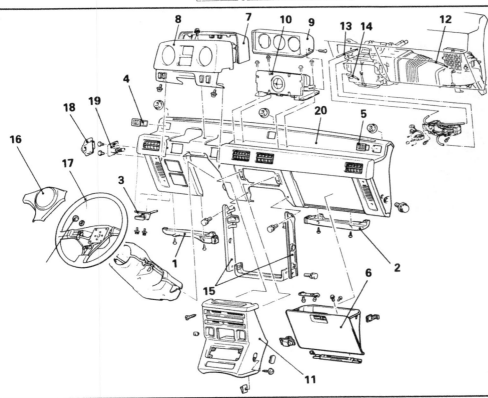

18.1b   **Instrument cluster and trim panel details on the Montero**

1   Lap heater duct A
2   Lap heater duct B
3   Hood release cable bracket
4   Demister grille (left)
5   Demister grille (right)
6   Glove box
7   Instrument cluster
8   Instrument cluster bezel
9   Combination meter pad
10 Combination meter case
11 Center panel
12 Recirculation/fresh air
    changeover cable
13 Mode selection control cable
14 Water valve control cable
15 Center reinforcement
16 Horn pad
17 Steering wheel
18 Fuse box cover
19 Fuse box assembly
20 Instrument panel

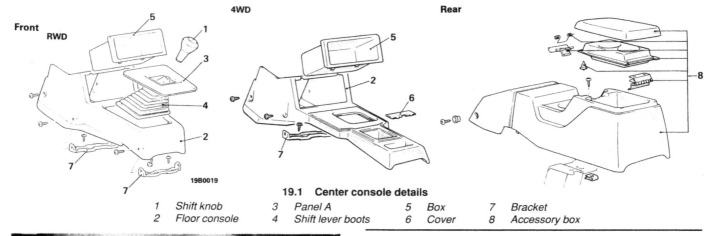

19.1   Center console details

| 1 | Shift knob | 3 | Panel A | 5 | Box | 7 | Bracket |
| 2 | Floor console | 4 | Shift lever boots | 6 | Cover | 8 | Accessory box |

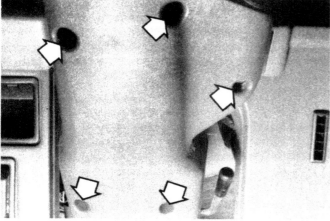

18.1c   Remove the screws (arrows) and separate the steering column trim panel

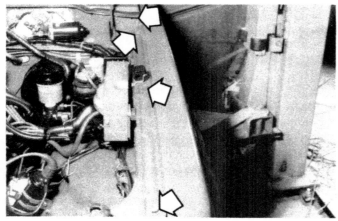

20.3a   Remove the bolts (arrows) from the front fender

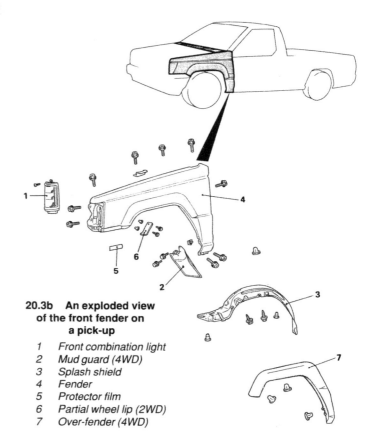

20.3b   An exploded view of the front fender on a pick-up

1   Front combination light
2   Mud guard (4WD)
3   Splash shield
4   Fender
5   Protector film
6   Partial wheel lip (2WD)
7   Over-fender (4WD)

20   Front fender – removal and installation

Refer to illustrations 20.3a and 20.3b

1   Raise the vehicle, support it securely on jackstands and remove the front wheel.
2   Disconnect the antenna and all light bulb wiring harness connectors and other components that would interfere with fender removal.
3   Remove the fender mounting bolts **(see illustrations)**.
4   Detach the fender. It's a good idea to have an assistant support the fender while it's being moved away from the vehicle to prevent damage to the surrounding body panels.
5   Installation is the reverse of removal.
6   Tighten all nuts, bolts and screws securely.

19   Center console – removal and installation

Refer to illustration 19.1

1   On front consoles, remove the shift knob from the shift lever **(see illustration)**.
2   Remove the panel screws from the console base.
3   On front consoles, remove panel A from the console along with the shift lever boot.
4   Lift the console from the passenger compartment.
5   Installation is the reverse of removal.

Chapter 12   Chassis electrical system

Contents

1   General information

The electrical system is a 12-volt, negative ground type. Power for the lights and all electrical accessories is supplied by a lead/acid-type battery which is charged by the alternator.

This Chapter covers repair and service procedures for the various electrical components not associated with the engine. Information on the battery, alternator, distributor and starter motor can be found in Chapter 5.

It should be noted that when portions of the electrical system are serviced, the negative battery cable should be disconnected from the battery to prevent electrical shorts and/or fires.

2   Electrical troubleshooting – general information

A typical electrical circuit consists of an electrical component, any switches, relays, motors, fuses, fusible links or circuit breakers related to that component and the wiring and connectors that link the component to both the battery and the chassis. To help you pinpoint an electrical circuit problem, wiring diagrams are included at the end of this book.

Before tackling any troublesome electrical circuit, first study the appropriate wiring diagrams to get a complete understanding of what makes up that individual circuit. Trouble spots, for instance, can often be narrowed down by noting if other components related to the circuit are operating properly. If several components or circuits fail at one time, chances are the problem is in a fuse or ground connection, because several circuits are often routed through the same fuse and ground connections.

Electrical problems usually stem from simple causes, such as loose or corroded connections, a blown fuse, a melted fusible link or a bad relay. Visually inspect the condition of all fuses, wires and connections in a problem circuit before troubleshooting it.

If testing instruments are going to be utilized, use the diagrams to plan ahead of time where you will make the necessary connections in order to accurately pinpoint the trouble spot.

The basic tools needed for electrical troubleshooting include a circuit tester or voltmeter (a 12-volt bulb with a set of test leads can also be used), a continuity tester, which includes a bulb, battery and set of test leads, and a jumper wire, preferably with a circuit breaker incorporated, which can be used to bypass electrical components. Before attempting to locate a problem with test instruments, use the wiring diagram(s) to decide where to make the connections.

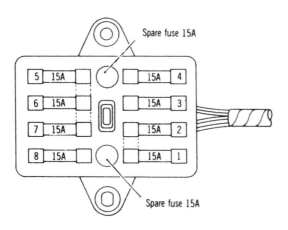

3.1   Fuse block diagram – early models

State of fuse blown due to overcurrent

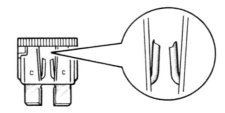

State of fuse blown due to thermal fatigue

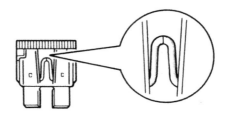

3.3   On later models, miniaturized fuses are used – overcurrent or thermal fatigue can cause them to fail

Voltage checks

Voltage checks should be performed if a circuit is not functioning properly. Connect one lead of a circuit tester to either the negative battery terminal or a known good ground. Connect the other lead to a connector in the circuit being tested, preferably nearest to the battery or fuse. If the bulb of the tester lights, voltage is present, which means that the part of the circuit between the connector and the battery is problem free. Continue checking the rest of the circuit in the same fashion. When you reach a point at which no voltage is present, the problem lies between that point and the last test point with voltage. Most of the time the problem can be traced to a loose connection. **Note:** *Keep in mind that some circuits receive voltage only when the ignition key is in the accessory or run position.*

Finding a short

One method of finding shorts in a circuit is to remove the fuse and connect a test light or voltmeter in its place to the fuse terminals. There should be no voltage present in the circuit. Move the wiring harness from side-to-side while watching the test light. If the bulb goes on, there is a short to ground somewhere in that area, probably where the insulation has rubbed through. The same test can be performed on each component in the circuit, even a switch.

Ground check

Perform a ground test to check whether a component is properly grounded. Disconnect the battery and connect one lead of a self-powered test light, known as a continuity tester, to a known good ground. Connect the other lead to the wire or ground connection being tested. If the bulb goes on, the ground is good. If the bulb does not go on, the ground is not good.

Continuity check

A continuity check is done to determine if there are any breaks in a circuit – if it is passing electricity properly. With the circuit off (no power in the circuit), a self-powered continuity tester can be used to check the circuit. Connect the test leads to both ends of the circuit (or to the "power" end and a good ground), and if the test light comes on the circuit is passing current properly. If the light doesn't come on, there is a break somewhere in the circuit. The same procedure can be used to test a switch, by connecting the continuity tester to the switch terminals. With the switch turned On, the test light should come on.

Finding an open circuit

When diagnosing for possible open circuits, it is often difficult to locate them by sight because oxidation or terminal misalignment are hidden by the connectors. Merely wiggling a connector on a sensor or in the wiring harness may correct the open circuit condition. Remember this when an open circuit is indicated when troubleshooting a circuit. Intermittent problems may also be caused by oxidized or loose connections.

Electrical troubleshooting is simple if you keep in mind that all electrical circuits are basically electricity running from the battery, through the wires, switches, relays, fuses and fusible links to each electrical component (light bulb, motor, etc.) and to ground, from which it is passed back to the battery. Any electrical problem is an interruption in the flow of electricity to and from the battery.

3   Fuses – general information

Refer to illustrations 3.1, and 3.3

1   The electrical circuits of the vehicle are protected by a combination of fuses, circuit breakers and fusible links. The fuse block is located under the instrument panel on the left side of the dashboard **(see illustration)**.

2   Each of the fuses is designed to protect a specific circuit, and the various circuits are identified on the fuse panel itself.

3   On early models, glass cylinder type fuses are used. On later models, miniaturized fuses are employed. These compact fuses, with blade terminal design, allow fingertip removal and replacement. If an electrical component fails, always check the fuse first. A blown fuse is easily identified through the clear plastic body. Visually inspect the element for evidence of damage **(see illustration)**. If a continuity check is called for, the blade terminal tips are exposed in the fuse body.

4   Be sure to replace blown fuses with the correct type. Fuses of different ratings are physically interchangeable, but only fuses of the proper rating should be used. Replacing a fuse with one of a higher or lower value than specified is not recommended. Each electrical circuit needs a specific amount of protection. The amperage value of each fuse is molded into the fuse body.

5   If the replacement fuse immediately fails, don't replace it again until the cause of the problem is isolated and corrected. In most cases, the cause will be a short circuit in the wiring caused by a broken or deteriorated wire.

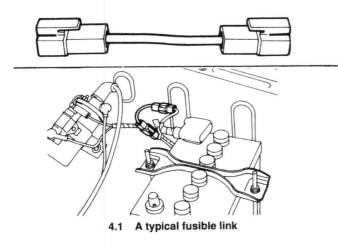

4.1   A typical fusible link

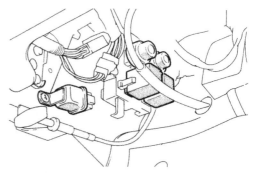

6.2   This group of relays is located under the driver's side of the instrument panel

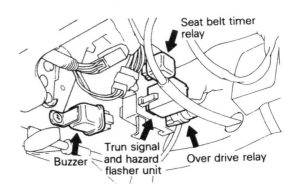

7.1   Turn signal/hazard flasher location

4   Fusible links – general information

Refer to illustration 4.1

Some circuits are protected by fusible links. The links are used in circuits which are not ordinarily fused, such as the ignition circuit **(see illustration).**

Although the fusible links appear to be a heavier gauge than the wire they are protecting, the appearance is due to the thick insulation. All fusible links are four wire gauges smaller than the wire they are designed to protect.

Fusible links cannot be repaired, but a new link of the same size wire can be put in its place. The procedure is as follows:

a) Disconnect the negative cable from the battery.
b) Disconnect the fusible link from the wiring harness.
c) Cut the damaged fusible link out of the wiring just behind the connector.
d) Strip the insulation back approximately 1/2-inch.
e) Position the connector on the new fusible link and crimp it into place.
f) Use rosin core solder at each end of the new link to obtain a good solder joint.
g) Use plenty of electrical tape around the soldered joint. No wires should be exposed.
h) Connect the battery ground cable. Test the circuit for proper operation.

5   Circuit breakers – general information

Circuit breakers protect components such as power windows, power door locks and headlights. Some circuit breakers are located in the fuse box.

On some models the circuit breaker resets itself automatically, so an electrical overload in a circuit breaker protected system will cause the circuit to fail momentarily, then come back on. If the circuit does not come back on, check it immediately. Once the condition is corrected, the circuit breaker will resume its normal function. Some circuit breakers must be reset manually.

6   Relays – general information

Refer to illustration 6.2

1   Several electrical accessories in the vehicle use relays to transmit the electrical signal to the component. If the relay is defective, that component will not operate properly.
2   The various relays are grouped together in several locations **(see illustration).**

3   If a faulty relay is suspected, it can be removed and tested by a dealer service department or a repair shop. Defective relays must be replaced as a unit.

7   Turn signal and hazard flashers – check and replacement

Refer to illustration 7.1

Turn signal flasher

1   The turn signal flasher, a small box or canister-shaped unit located under the driver's side of the instrument panel **(see illustration),** flashes the turn signals.
2   When the flasher unit is functioning properly, an audible click can be heard during its operation. If the turn signals fail on one side or the other and the flasher unit does not make its characteristic clicking sound, a faulty turn signal bulb is indicated.
3   If both turn signals fail to blink, the problem may be due to a blown fuse, a faulty flasher unit, a broken switch or a loose or open connection. If a quick check of the fuse box indicates that the turn signal fuse has blown, check the wiring for a short before installing a new fuse.
4   To replace the flasher, simply pull it out and press in a new one.
5   Make sure that the replacement unit is identical to the original. Compare the old one to the new one before installing it.
6   Installation is the reverse of removal.

Hazard flasher

7   The hazard flasher on most models is integral with the turn signal flasher unit.
8   The hazard flasher is checked in a fashion similar to the turn signal flasher (see Steps 2 and 3).

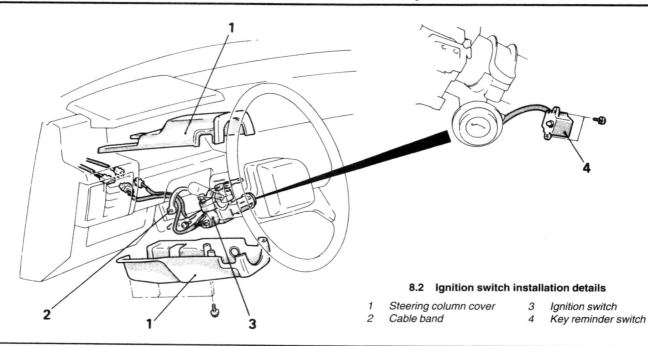

8.2   Ignition switch installation details

1	*Steering column cover*	3	*Ignition switch*
2	*Cable band*	4	*Key reminder switch*

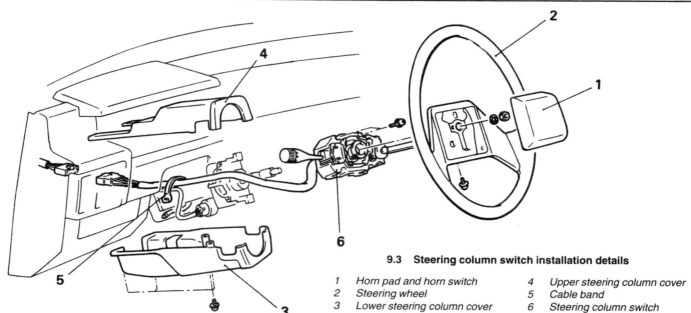

9.3   Steering column switch installation details

1	*Horn pad and horn switch*	4	*Upper steering column cover*
2	*Steering wheel*	5	*Cable band*
3	*Lower steering column cover*	6	*Steering column switch*

9   To replace the hazard flasher, pull it from the back of fuse block.
10   Make sure the replacement unit is identical to the one it replaces. Compare the old one to the new one before installing it.
11   Installation is the reverse of removal.

8   Ignition switch and lock cylinder – removal and installation

Refer to illustration 8.2
1   Disconnect the negative battery cable from the battery.
2   Remove the steering column cover to gain access to the ignition switch/lock cylinder **(see illustration)**.
3   Using wire cutters, remove the cable band.
4   Remove the bolts that hold the ignition switch/lock cylinder to the steering column. **Note:** *On 1988 and later models, the bolts must be cut*

off. Install new bolts on reassembly.
5   Unbolt and remove the key reminder switch and remove the ignition switch/lock cylinder from the steering column.
6   Installation is the reverse of removal.

9   Steering column switch – removal and installation

Refer to illustration 9.3
1   Disconnect the negative battery cable from the battery.
2   Remove the steering wheel (see Chapter 10).
3   Remove the steering column covers **(see illustration)**.
4   Using wire cutters to remove the cable band.
5   Remove the two screws holding the steering column switch.
6   Remove the steering column switch.
7   Installation is the reverse of removal.

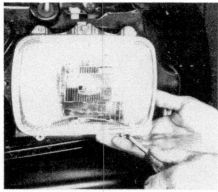

10.3   Remove the four small headlight retainer screws – DO NOT disturb the two larger adjustment screws (sealed-beam type)

10.4   Unplugging the electrical connector (sealed-beam type)

12.1a   Removing the rear light lens

12.1b   To remove a rear light bulb, push it in and rotate it 90-degrees counterclockwise

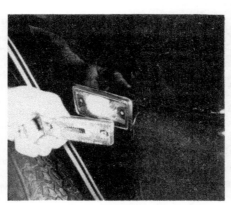

12.1c   Remove the two screws, then pull off the side-marker lens

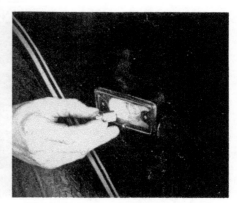

12.1d   To remove a side-marker bulb like the one shown, push it in and rotate it 90-degrees counterclockwise

10   Headlights – replacement

Refer to illustrations 10.3 and 10.4

1   Disconnect the negative cable from the battery.

Sealed-beam type

2   Remove the retaining screws and detach the headlight bezel.
3   Remove the headlight retainer screws, taking care not to disturb the adjustment screws **(see illustration)**.
4   Remove the retainer and pull the headlight out enough to allow the connector to be unplugged **(see illustration)**.
5   Remove the headlight.
6   To install the headlight, plug the connector in, place the headlight in position and install the retainer and screws. Tighten the screws securely.
7   Place the headlight bezel in position and install the retaining screws. Connect the negative battery cable.

Halogen bulb type

8   Disconnect electrical connector at the bulb, then pull out the socket cover and connector.
9   Remove the locking ring by rotating it counterclockwise, then remove the bulb and the locking ring.
10   Insert the new bulb assembly into the locking assembly and reassemble in the reverse order of removal. **Note:** *To replace the left side bulb it's necessary to remove the engine coolant reservoir.* **Caution:** *Never hold a halogen bulb with your bare hands, a dirty rag, etc. The oils on the glass will cause the bulb to create a hot spot and fail prematurely. If any oil or dirt gets on the glass, clean it thoroughly with lacquer thinner or alcohol before installation.*

11   Headlights – adjustment

Note: *The headlights must be aimed correctly. If adjusted incorrectly they could blind the driver of an oncoming vehicle and cause a serious accident or seriously reduce your ability to see the road. The headlights should be checked for proper aim every 12 months and any time a new headlight is installed or front end body work is performed. It should be emphasized that the following procedure is only an interim step which will provide temporary adjustment until the headlights can be adjusted by a properly equipped shop.*

1   Headlights have two spring loaded adjusting screws, one on the top controlling up-and-down movement and one on the side controlling left-and-right movement.
2   There are several methods of adjusting the headlights. The simplest method requires a blank wall 25 feet in front of the vehicle and a level floor.
3   Position masking tape vertically on the wall in reference to the vehicle centerline and the centerlines of both headlights.
4   Position a horizontal tape line in reference to the centerline of all the headlights. **Note:** *It may be easier to position the tape on the wall with the vehicle parked only a few inches away.*
5   Adjustment should be made with the vehicle sitting level, the gas tank half-full and no unusually heavy load in the vehicle.
6   Starting with the low-beam adjustment, position the high-intensity zone so it is two inches below the horizontal line and two inches to the right of the headlight vertical line. Adjustment is made by turning the top adjusting screw clockwise to raise the beam and counterclockwise to lower the beam. The adjusting screw on the side should be used in the same manner to move the beam left or right.

12.1e   To remove the front lens, remove the two screws

14.3a   Removing the radio control stud nuts
(1986 and earlier models)

14.3b   Removing the radio trim plate (1986 and earlier models)

7   With the high beams on, the high-intensity zone should be vertically centered with the exact center just below the horizontal line. **Note:** *It may not be possible to position the headlight aim exactly for both high and low beams. If a compromise must be made, keep in mind that the low beams are the most used and have the greatest effect on driver safety.*
8   Have the headlights adjusted by a dealer service department or service station at the earliest opportunity.

12   Bulb – replacement

Refer to illustrations 12.1a, 12.1b, 12.1c, 12.1d and 12.1e
1   The lenses of many lights are held in place by screws, which makes it a simple procedure to gain access to the bulbs **(see illustrations)**.
2   On some lights the lenses, such as the interior dome light lens, are

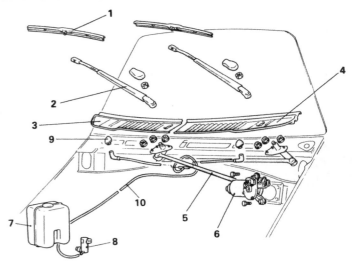

13.3   **Windshield wipers, washer and motor – exploded view**

1	Wiper blade	6	Wiper motor
2	Wiper arm	7	Washer reservoir
3	Right front deck garnish	8	Washer motor
4	Left front deck garnish	9	Washer nozzle
5	Actuator arm	10	Washer hose

held in place by clips. The lenses can be removed either by unsnapping them or by using a small screwdriver to pry them off.
3   Several types of bulbs are used. Some are removed by pushing in and turning them counterclockwise. Others can simply be unclipped from the terminals or pulled straight out of the socket.
4   To gain access to the instrument panel lights, the instrument cluster will have to be removed first (see Section 15).

13   Wiper motor – removal and installation

Refer to illustration 13.3
1   Remove the negative battery cable from the battery.
2   Unplug the electrical connector leading from the wiper motor.
3   Remove the three bolts attaching the motor to the vehicle firewall **(see illustration)**.
4   Pull up on the wiper arm until the actuator arm joint is visible in the access hole, then pry the motor out of the actuator arm joint with a screwdriver.
5   Installation is the reverse of removal.

14   Instrument cluster – removal and installation

Refer to illustrations 14.3a, 14.3b, 14.4, 14.5, 14.6, 14.7 and 14.13

1986 and earlier models

1   If any of the gauges or warning lights need servicing it will be necessary to remove the instrument cluster.
2   Disconnect the negative battery cable from the battery.
3   Remove the control knobs and the nuts on the studs from the radio, **(see illustration)**, then remove the radio trim plate **(see illustration)**.
4   Pull off the heater fan control knob and the heater control lever ends. Remove the nut from the fan control stud **(see illustration)**.
5   Remove the four screws from the cluster trim rim **(see illustration)** and lift it carefully out.
6   Disconnect the wiring harness and the wire lead at the lower right corner of the rim **(see illustration)**.
7   Remove the four screws attaching the instrument cluster to the dash **(see illustration)**.
8   Remove the speedometer cable fitting and remove the cable from the back of the cluster **(see illustration 19.4)**. Disconnect the electrical wire from the buzzer.

14.4   Removing the nut from the fan control stud (1986 and earlier models)

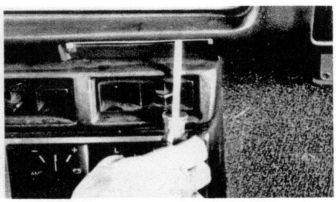

14.5   Removing the cluster trim rim mounting screws (1986 and earlier models)

14.6   Disconnecting the wiring (1986 and earlier models)

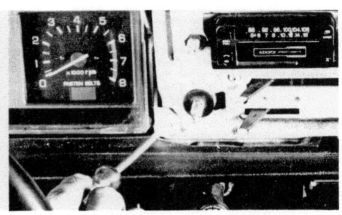

14.7   Removing the instrument cluster mounting screws (1986 and earlier models)

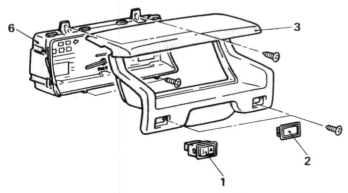

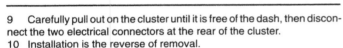

14.13   Instrument cluster mounting details – exploded view (1987 and later models)

1	Hazard switch	3	Hood
2	Hole cover	6	Instrument cluster

15.1   Removing the plastic cover screws (1986 and earlier models)

9   Carefully pull out on the cluster until it is free of the dash, then disconnect the two electrical connectors at the rear of the cluster.
10   Installation is the reverse of removal.

1987 and later models

11   Disconnect the negative cable from the battery. Remove the hazard switch and hole cover.
12   Remove the two lower screws, then lift the instrument cluster hood off.
13   Remove the four screws holding the instrument cluster in place **(see illustration)**.

14   Pull the instrument cluster out, disconnect the speedometer and electrical connectors, then remove the cluster from the vehicle **(see illustration 19.4)**. Installation is the reverse of removal.

---

15   Instrument cluster – disassembly and reassembly

Refer to illustrations 15.1, 15.4 and 15.8

1986 and earlier models

1   Remove the screws holding the clear plastic cover and trim ring in place and lift them off **(see illustration)**.

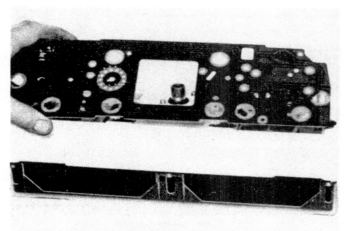

15.4   Lifting off the printed circuit board (1986 and earlier models)

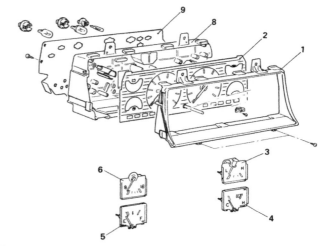

2   Turn the cluster over and remove the nuts from the studs on the right side. Unscrew the buzzer mounting screw and remove the buzzer.
3   Remove the bulb holders from the printed circuit board by turning them counterclockwise.
4   Remove the self-tapping screws and the machine screws. The machine screws have two different size threads, so be sure they are returned to the exact same locations they were removed from. Carefully lift the printed circuit board off the instrument cluster **(see illustration)**.
5   The speedometer is held in position with two screws.
6   Reassembly is the reverse of disassembly.

1987 and later models
7   Remove the two lower screws holding the clear plastic cover.
8   Turn the cluster over and remove the self-tapping screws **(see illustration)**.
9   Remove the bulb holders from the printed circuit board by turning them counterclockwise.
10   Reassembly is the reverse of disassembly.

---

16   Cruise control system – description and check

The cruise control system maintains vehicle speed with a vacuum-actuated servo motor located in the engine compartment, which is connected to the throttle linkage by a cable. The system consists of the servo motor, clutch switch, brake switch, control switches, a relay and associated vacuum hoses.

Because of the complexity of the cruise control system and the special tools and techniques required for diagnosis, repair should be left to a dealer service department or a repair shop. However, it is possible for the home mechanic to make simple checks of the wiring and vacuum connections for minor faults which can be easily repaired. These include:
   a)   Inspect the cruise control actuating switches for broken wires and loose connections.
   b)   Check the cruise control fuse.
   c)   The cruise control system is operated by vacuum so it's critical that all vacuum switches, hoses and connections are secure. Check the hoses in the engine compartment for tight connections, cracks and obvious vacuum leaks.

---

17   Power window system – description and check

The power window system operates the electric motors mounted in the doors which lower and raise the windows. The system consists of the control switches, the motors (regulators), glass mechanisms and associated wiring.

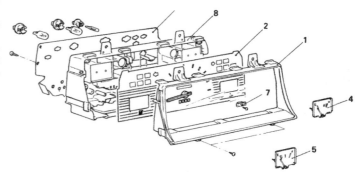

15.8   Instrument cluster – exploded view (1987 and later models)

1   Clear plastic cover
2   Instrument cluster face
3   Oil pressure gauge
4   Engine coolant temperature gauge
5   Fuel gauge
6   Voltmeter
7   Warning indicator reset switch
8   Instrument cluster case
9   Printed circuit board

Because of the complexity of the power window system and the special tools and techniques required for diagnosis, repair should be left to a dealer service department or a repair shop. However, it is possible for the home mechanic to make simple checks of the wiring connections and motors for minor faults which can be easily repaired. These include:
   a)   Inspect the power window actuating switches for broken wires and loose connections.
   b)   Check the power window fuse/and or circuit breaker.
   c)   Remove the door panel(s) and check the power window motor wires to see if they're loose or damaged. Inspect the glass mechanisms for damage which could cause binding.

---

18   Power door lock system – description and check

The power door lock system operates the door lock actuators mounted in each door. The system consists of the switches, actuators and associated wiring. Since special tools and techniques are required to diagnose the system, it should be left to a dealer service department or a repair shop. However, it is possible for the home mechanic to make simple

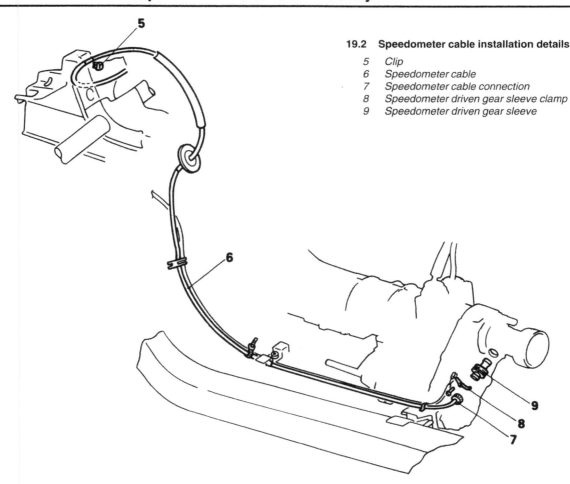

19.2   Speedometer cable installation details

5   Clip
6   Speedometer cable
7   Speedometer cable connection
8   Speedometer driven gear sleeve clamp
9   Speedometer driven gear sleeve

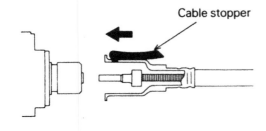

Cable stopper

19.4   On most models, when attaching or detaching the speedometer cable from the speedometer, press down on the end of the cable stopper

checks of the wiring connections and actuators for minor faults which can be easily repaired. These include:

a) Check the system fuse and/or circuit breaker.
b) Check the switch wires for damage and loose connections.

Check the switches for continuity.

c) Remove the door panel(s) and check the actuator wiring connections to see if they're loose or damaged. Inspect the actuator rods (if equipped) to make sure they aren't bent or damaged. Inspect the actuator wiring for damaged or loose connections. The actuator can be checked by applying battery power momentarily. A discernible click indicates that the solenoid is operating properly.

19   Speedometer cable – replacement

Refer to illustrations 19.2 and 19.4

1   Disconnect the negative cable from the battery.
2   Disconnect the speedometer cable from the transmission **(see illustration)**.
3   Detach the cable from the routing clips in the engine compartment and pull it up to provide enough slack to allow disconnection from the speedometer.
4   Remove the instrument cluster screws, pull the cluster out (see Section 14) and disconnect the speedometer cable from the back of the cluster **(see illustration)**. **Note:** *On 1991 and later Montero models with a ratio adapter, after removing the instrument cluster, rotate the adapter to the left or right to release the locks and pull the adapter out.*
5   Remove the cable from the vehicle.
6   Prior to installation, lubricate the speedometer end of the cable with spray-on speedometer cable lubricant (available at auto parts stores).
7   Installation is the reverse of removal.

20   Wiring diagrams – general information

Since it isn't possible to include all wiring diagrams for every year covered by this manual, the following diagrams are those that are typical and most commonly needed.

Prior to troubleshooting any circuits, check the fuse and circuit breakers (if equipped) to make sure they're in good condition. Make sure the battery is properly charged and check the cable connections (see Chapter 1).

When checking a circuit, make sure that all connectors are clean, with no broken or loose terminals. When unplugging a connector, do not pull on the wires. Pull only on the connector housings themselves.

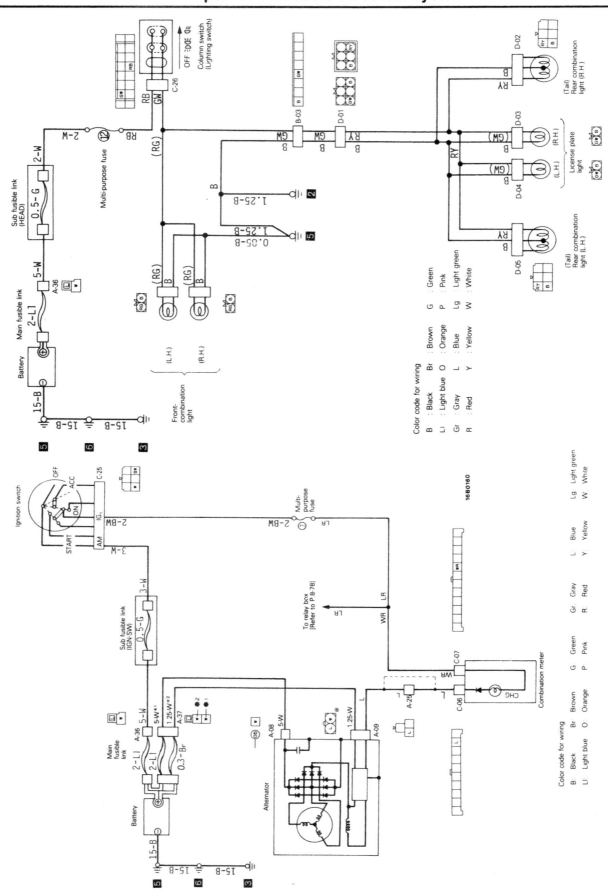

20.2   Tail/position/license plate lights

20.1   Charging circuit

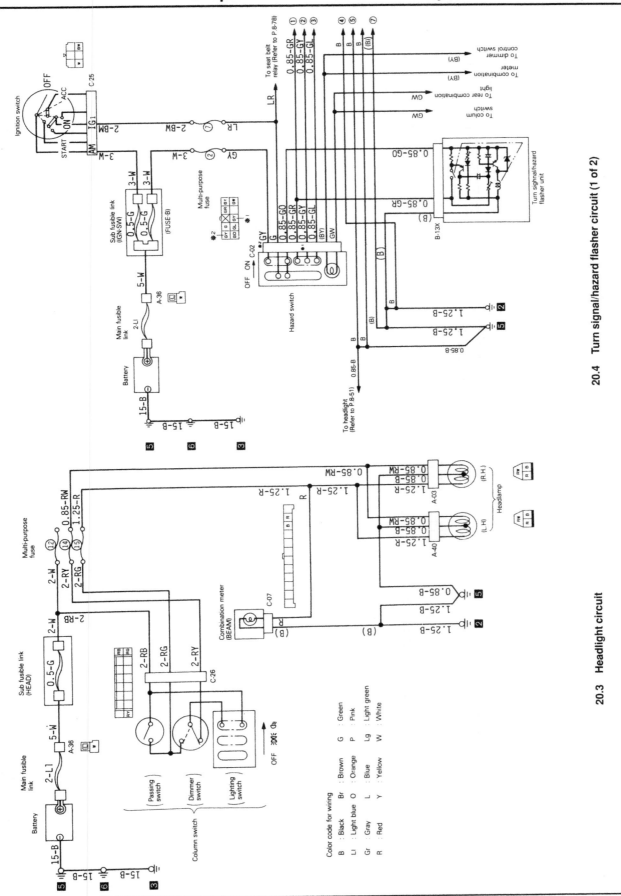

20.4 Turn signal/hazard flasher circuit (1 of 2)

20.3 Headlight circuit

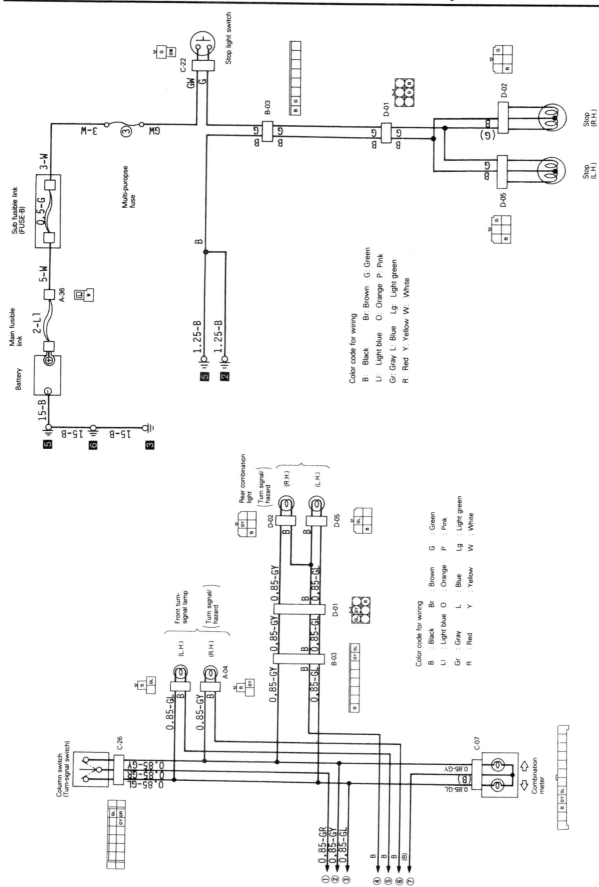

20.6   Stop light circuit

20.5   Turn signal/hazard flasher circuit (2 of 2)

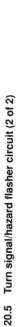

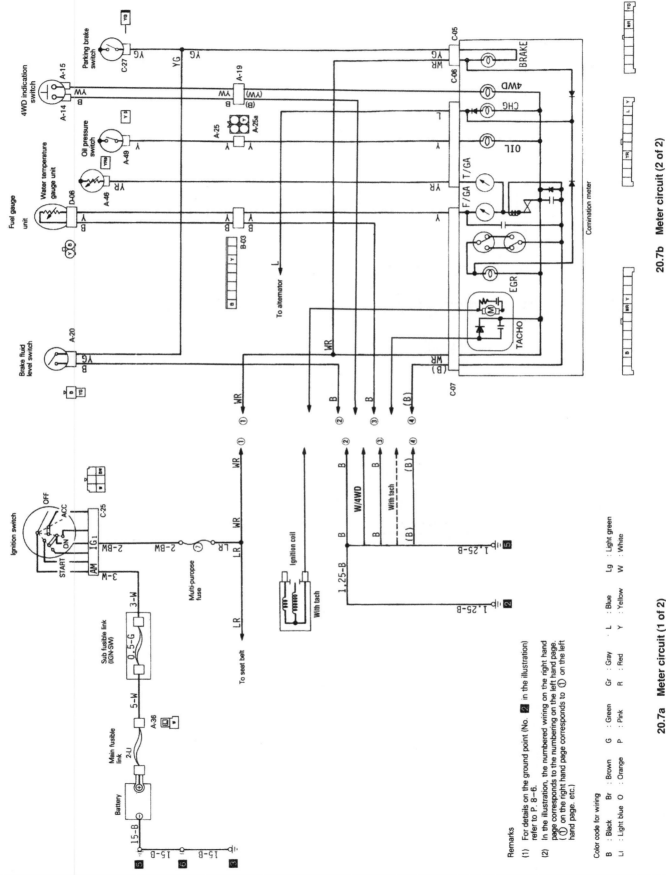

20.7b Meter circuit (2 of 2)

20.7a Meter circuit (1 of 2)

Remarks

(1) For details on the ground point (No. [2] in the illustration) refer to P. 8–6.

(2) In the illustration, the numbered wiring on the right hand page corresponds to the numbering on the left hand page. (① on the right hand page corresponds to ① on the left hand page, etc.)

Color code for wiring

| B | : Black | Br | : Brown | G | : Green | Gr | : Gray | L | : Blue | Lg | : Light green |
| Ll | : Light blue | O | : Orange | P | : Pink | R | : Red | Y | : Yellow | W | : White |

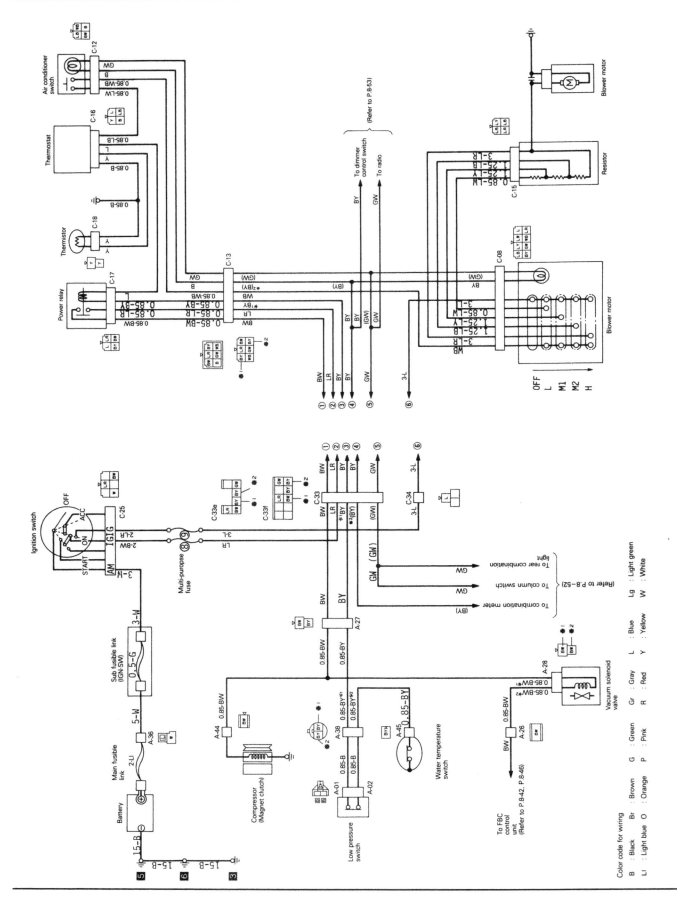

20.8b   Air conditioner circuit (2 of 2)

20.8a   Air conditioner circuit (1 of 2)

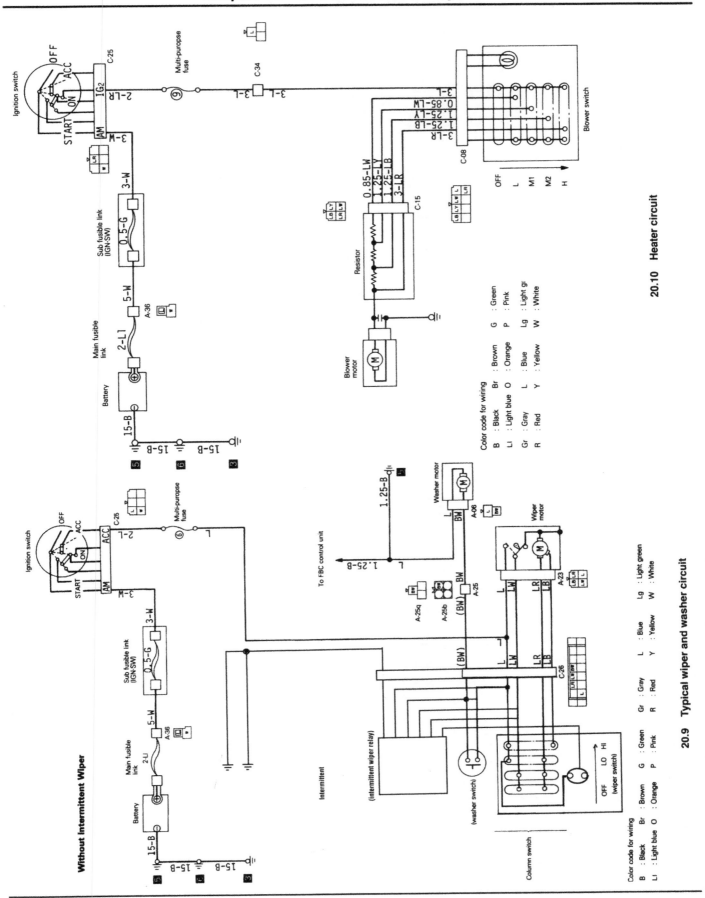

20.10 Heater circuit

20.9 Typical wiper and washer circuit

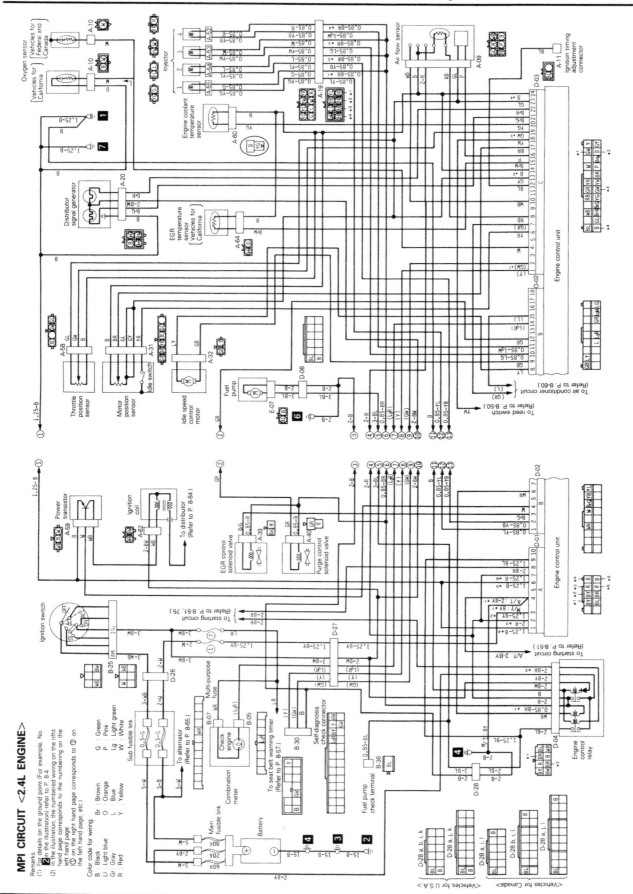

20.11b   Fuel injection circuit (2.4L engine – 2 of 2)

20.11a   Fuel injection circuit (2.4L engine – 1 of 2)

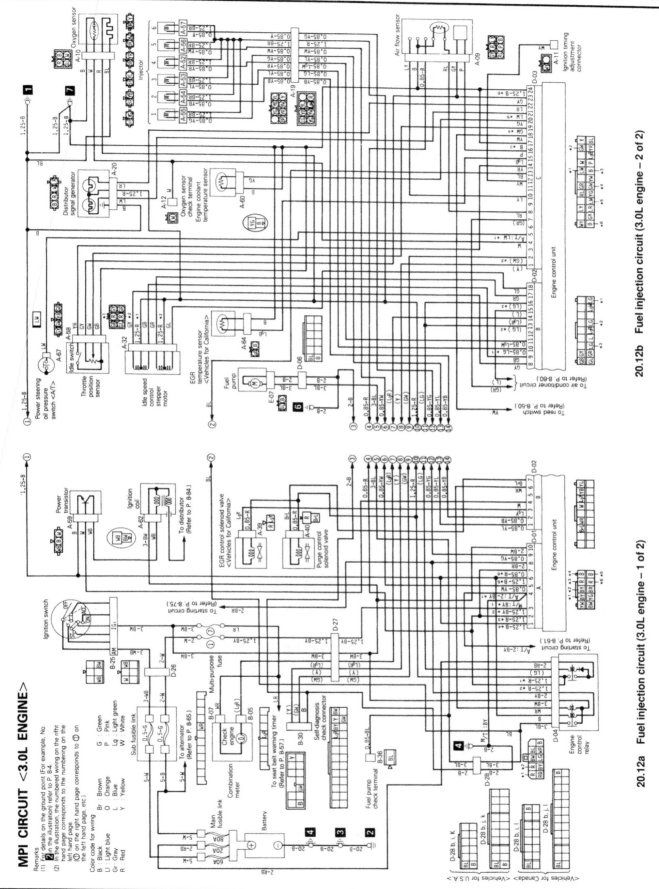

MPI CIRCUIT <3.0L ENGINE>

Remarks
(1) For details on the ground point (For example, No. **2** in the illustration) refer to P. 8-4.
(2) In the illustration, the numbered wiring on the right hand page corresponds to the numbering on the left hand page.
(① on the right hand page corresponds to ① on the left hand page, etc.)

Color code for wiring
B : Black   Br : Brown   G : Green
Lt : Light blue   O : Orange   P : Pink
Gr : Gray   L : Blue   Lg : Light green
R : Red   Y : Yellow   W : White

20.12a Fuel injection circuit (3.0L engine – 1 of 2)

20.12b Fuel injection circuit (3.0L engine – 2 of 2)

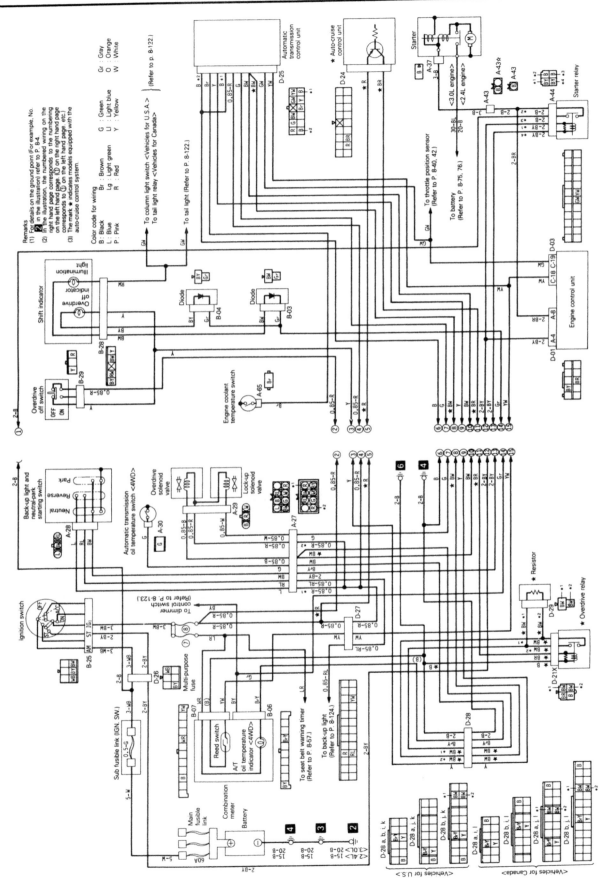

20.14b   Automatic transmission circuit (2 of 2)

20.14a   Automatic transmission circuit (1 of 2)

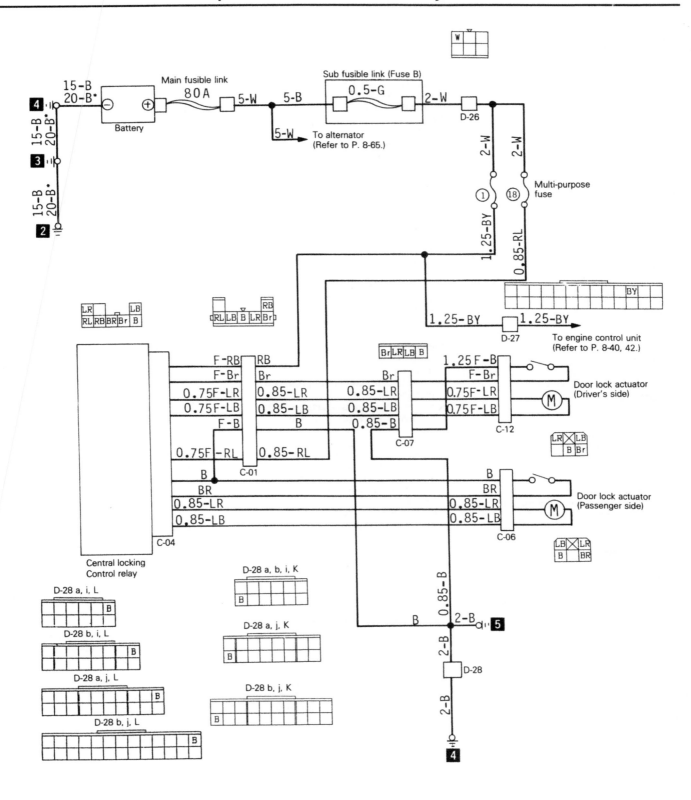

Color code for wiring
B : Black   Br : Brown   G : Green   Gr : Gray
L : Blue   Lg : Light green Ll : Light blue   O : Orange
P : Pink   R : Red   Y : Yellow   W : White

20.15   Power door lock circuit

Index